Shanghai on the Métro

A CENTENNIAL BOOK

One hundred books
published between 1990 and 1995
bear this special imprint of
the University of California Press.
We have chosen each Centennial Book
as an example of the Press's finest
publishing and bookmaking traditions
as we celebrate the beginning of
our second century.

UNIVERSITY OF CALIFORNIA PRESS

Founded in 1893

Shanghai on the Métro

Spies, Intrigue, and the French between the Wars

Michael B. Miller

UNIVERSITY OF CALIFORNIA PRESS

Berkeley / *Los Angeles* / *London*

The publisher gratefully acknowledges the contribution provided by
the General Endowment Fund of the Associates of the University of
California Press.

University of California Press
Berkeley and Los Angeles, California

University of California Press, Ltd.
London, England

© 1994 by
The Regents of the University of California

Library of Congress Cataloging-in-Publication Data
Miller, Michael Barry, 1945–
     Shanghai on the Métro : spies, intrigue, and the French between
the wars / Michael B. Miller.
          p.   cm.
     "A Centennial book."
     Includes bibliographical references and index.
     ISBN 0-520-08519-1
     France—History—1914–1940.   2. France—Foreign relations—
1914–1940.   3. Intelligence Service—France—History—20th century.   4. Espionage—France—History—20th century.   I. Title.
   DC369.M525   1994
944.081—dc20   93-34114
                                                       CIP

Printed in the United States of America
9 8 7 6 5 4 3 2 1

For Mary,
and in memory of Madeleine Louys

Contents

Illustrations

Acknowledgments

Over thirteen years of research and writing I have incurred many personal and intellectual debts. A good number of these I owe to archivists. We all have our horror stories to tell about the archives, but what mattered more was Madame Bonazzi rushing through my F60 *dérogation*, Daniel Farcis guiding me into the Panthéon files, Erik Le Maresquier making me feel as if I had died and gone to heaven at the navy archives, the gentleman with the mustache and gravelly voice who was our lifeline at the Outre-mer archives, the incomparable xeroxer at the Archives nationales, the monsieur at the SNCF archives who mailed me the notes I had forgotten on my desk, the great service at the police archives, the professional camaraderie at the Quai d'Orsay archives, the recurrent welcome at the army archives, Herr Moritz awaiting my arrival at the Militärarchiv, and so on. My thanks therefore go out (in no hierarchical order) to Jean Favier, the Directeur général des archives de France; Chantal Bonazzi of the section contemporaine, Madame Le Moel of the section moderne, and the various staffs of the Archives nationales; Général Delmas and the staff at the Service historique de l'armée de terre; Pierre Chassigneux, Bernard Garnier, Monsieur Poisson, and the staff of the archives of the Préfecture de police; the staff at the Archives du ministère des affaires étrangères; the staff at the Bibliothèque nationale (from the librarians in the front to the unparalleled reference personnel, to the people who brought me my tons of books); the staff at the Bibliothèque nationale annex at Vincennes; the staff at the Outre-mer section of the Archives nationales; Daniel Farcis and his staff at the

Ministère de l'intérieur et de la décentralisation: mission des archives nationales; Jean-Pierre Busson, Erik Le Maresquier, and the staff at the Service historique de la marine; the staff at the Société nationale des chemins de fer français archives; the staff at the Archives contemporaines at Fontainebleau; the staff at the Bibliothèque de documentation internationale contemporaine; the staff at the Fondation nationale des sciences politiques archives who made available the Daladier papers; Georges Weil, Directeur des services d'archives de Paris; the staff at the Centre de documentation juive contemporaine; Dr. Maria Keipert and the staff of the Auswärtiges Amt Politisches Archiv, in particular Claus Wiedey; Dr. Henke, Frau Jacobi, Herr Scharmann, and the staff at the Bundesarchiv; Herr Loos and the staff at the Abteilung Militärgeschichte of the Bundesarchiv, especially Herr Moritz; Ronald Bulatoff and Helen Solanum of the Hoover Institution on War, Revolution, and Peace; John Taylor of the National Archives; and Maja Keech of the Library of Congress.

For sales and printing figures of books, I am indebted to Madame Daudier of Payot, Jean-Pierre Dauphin of Gallimard, Monsieur Grey-Draillart (on Baudinière), Monsieur Henriquez of Tallandier, Monique Jeanin of Fayard, Monsieur de Lignerolles of Berger-Levrault, Brigitte Martin of Plon, Monsieur Mery of Grasset, and Françoise Tallon for the Editions du Masque. Their expense of time and energy on behalf of a stranger, and their goodwill, are deeply appreciated.

I am grateful to Syracuse University for funding two of my summer research trips through senate summer research funds; for subsidizing maps, photographs, and permission fees; for providing me with a semester of research leave in fall 1986; and for permitting me to take a year off at half-pay in 1988–89 to begin writing this book. In this regard, special thanks go to Karen Hiiemae who enabled me to postpone to the following year one of my summer research grants when personal reasons required that I remain in Syracuse. Upon my request David Stam obtained the microfilmed records of the Shanghai Municipal Police files for Syracuse's library collection, and I am grateful to him for support with this and all the other collections he has made available to me. I would like to thank as well Method Milac for his support of history research at Syracuse. Without the help of Dorcas MacDonald and her Interlibrary Loan staff, I would probably still be completing my research. Thanks also to associate librarian Randy Bond for his help on the history of aviators.

My greatest debts are, of course, to friends and historians. John

Cairns was an early supporter of this work, and his advice and encouragement have sustained me throughout. Stephen Blumm read initial drafts, collaborated on the title, and, with Ruth Lowe, has provided me with the friendship we usually only dream of. John and Carolyn Bargeron have been good friends and strong supporters from the project's first days. My former colleagues at Rice University heard an early draft in 1982, tolerated its stupidities, and encouraged me to go on. Trips to Paris were inseparable from lunches and dinners with my close friend Françoise Roignant, the good company of Josianne and Michel Cercus, and the special moments with Madeleine Louys, who unfortunately did not live to see this work completed. With Paris also came the intellectual and personal companionship of Irwin Wall, Joel Blatt, Lenard Berlanstein, Catherine and Bob Young, Joan Scott, Maurice Lévy-Leboyer, Patrick Fridenson, Ken Mouré, Martina Kessel, Gordon Dutter, Vicki Caron, Donna Ryan, Michael Fitzsimmons, David Gordon, Mary Jo and Bob Nye, Dick and Ann Tashjian, Bob and Elborg Forster, and Kim and Anne Munholland who are forever identified with our luncheon expedition to Giverny.

The first two chapters of this book were written in Wolfenbüttel, Germany, the sort of place where one quickly spots a new dog in town. My life there was made immeasurably comfortable because of the presence of Jill and Jochen Bepler, Peter Albrecht, Franklin Kopitzsch, Ursula Stephan, and Paul Casey, without whom no dinner party was ever complete. I would also like to thank the librarians of the Herzog August Bibliothek and Sabine Solf for all the help they gave me. Others who contributed to the completion of this work in one way or another include Fred Marquardt, Robert Wohl, Steve Beaudoin, David Slavin, Gilbert Badia, Theodore Draper, Robert Silvers, Michael Simpson, Jill Harsin, Elizabeth Weston, Martin Wiener, James Friguglietti, George O. Kent, Bernard Lewis, Robert Johnston, Ronald Newton, and Annetta Gattiker-Caratsch. Dan Field and Wendy Goldman assisted me with the transliteration of Russian names and Walter Ullmann assisted with the correct spelling of Romanian, Serb, and Croatian names; any inaccuracies or botch-ups are entirely my own. Jonathan R. Hancock prepared the two maps for this edition. Sheila Levine, Erika Büky, and Edith Gladstone at the University of California Press have been a pleasure to work with and have carefully overseen the production of this book. I would also like to thank my colleagues in the European history seminar at Syracuse for their comments on my presentations over the years. I include here even my friend Joe Levine who lambasted one paper, kept me after in the hallway for half an hour while he continued to list all its deficiencies, and then had the gall to ask for a lift home. (There is, however, justice in this world. It was winter in Syracuse, my car was parked on an incline, and Professor Levine had to get out and push.) Finally, the friendship of Jeanée Sacken, Scott Strickland, Elizabeth Sanders, Richard Bensel, and Michael Dintenfass has meant a great deal over the years.

Mary Lindemann has read (and practically listened to) every word on these pages. I could recount without end how her opinion has mattered. But when I think of her and this book, I prefer to recall the Plaza Athenée, rue de Tournon, the terrasse at Beauvilliers, breakfast at Vézelay, the Frankfurt train station, Hardenbergstrasse, St. Gennys; and what history, writing, and our lives together mean to us both.

Introduction

One could do worse than begin with Battiti. Who he was or what he was about we will perhaps never know, although the very mystery surrounding the man forms part of his story. He first stepped out of the shadows in the late 1920s in French intelligence reports from Tangier, establishing a brief presence in French police dossiers before vanishing as stealthily as he had come, never to reappear in the files that I have seen for the subsequent years. Among the very first reports on the man is one dated 28 April 1928, placing him in the company of the gunrunner Caruana. Several weeks later he turns up again as the recipient of copious mail, a high-stakes gambler, a disburser of substantial sums of money despite no visible means of support, and as an individual with suspicious ties to Djebala tribesmen. The report notes that the Spanish police, as anxious as the French to uncover who "this Battiti" is, have already made one unsuccessful attempt to burglarize his apartment and that a second team of police is on its way from Tetouan "in order to learn once and for all what Battiti is doing in Tangier." By mid-May the French police in Tangier have compiled their own substantial dossier on the man. They identify him as a German national named von Horn (or so they believe; none of this is certain), and they think he might be the Lieutenant-Colonel von Horn who served in German intelligence in Switzerland during the First World War. They trace him three years earlier to Melilla and place him as an agent of Impex, a German import-export firm with its own voluminous documentation in French counter-espionage files. They identify his base in Melilla as Richellane's jewelry shop in the calle Alphonse XIII, and they learn that he uses his position as a watchmaker there to cover his efforts to liaise with a Riffian nationalist leader fighting a colonial war with the French at the time. They follow him to Gibraltar in 1926 where Battiti sets up shop at the Hotel Cecil and gambles heavily at the baccarat tables. There, they remark, he first meets the ubiquitous Caruana, whose business transactions extend to loans *à la petite semaine*. In October 1927 they are with Battiti as he decamps to Tangier where, the report goes on, he has in the successive months assembled a network of agents and dubious associates. On their list are Jacques H., an ex-legionnaire and wireless operator, and a German agent called Rossi, alias Rauss, who worked for German espionage in Spain during the war and now roams from Tangier to Spain to Portugal to the Canaries posing as a traveling photographer. There is also a Russian geometer, L.; an Italian woman, M., on her way to the Canaries, most likely, the police believe, to organize contraband shipments into southern Morocco in liaison with Rossi and Caruana; and a printer named D. charged by Battiti with organizing a union movement along Communist lines. In August 1928 the police report that Battiti has met with the Communist F. and recruited Zoïa K., a Russian dancehall girl, as another of his liaisons and couriers. A report from 10 September registers yet another Battiti agent, Laura U., who is traveling to Ceuta in the company of Caruana. The communiqué adds that Battiti's relations with Italian representatives in Tangier are tight and that every morning he visits the Italian consulate. On the nineteenth of September the police note that Laura U. has left for Casablanca and has met in Tetouan with Adolph Langenheim, a German mining engineer and the most notorious German agent in Morocco between the wars, according to French counterintelligence files. From the sixth of October comes a report placing Battiti with a German army major in Ceuta. On the twenty-fifth the police are identifying the woman M. as the wife of the chief Italian Fascist in Tangier. But then in early November a British police inspector tips off Battiti that he is under surveillance and he goes to ground. A year later, however, the French again unearth Battiti, this time as the linchpin in a gunrunning scheme to dissident tribes in southern Morocco. The traffic is traced to a far-flung organization extending from New York to Buenos Aires where the contraband weapons are loaded on trawlers. From there the "goods" are shipped to the Canaries and unloaded and stored at an old tuna fishery (used by the Germans as a clandestine supply base for submarines during the war) until the time is favorable for transshipment to the Moroccan coast. The security official writing the report places a man named Battiti at the center of these operations, now identifying him as the bearer of an Argentine passport, but of "uncertain nationality." Numbered among his associates are the Casablanca agent of the Oldenburg Portugiesische Dampfschiffs-Reederei—a Hamburg shipping company with yet another impressive file of its own in the Sûreté archives—and the Moroccan head of a troupe of acrobats. There are cryptic allusions to grand German designs behind the gunrunning. The British Intelligence Service is also implicated. Then, as before, the record is silent.[1]

There is nothing exceptional about the case of Battiti. The archives are full of these kinds of stories, so that this book could just as easily begin with an account of the White Russian gunrunner Paul D.; or the Cuban passport affair of the late 1930s that embroiled refugees, spies, and assorted sleazy characters; or a 1926 report out of Shanghai charting the coming and going of Bolshevik agents. If the choice is Battiti then this is because of the typicality of the matter, the odor it carries of interwar files. The ominous pointers to German machinations, globally appointed and colonially focused, the lumping together of German, Italian, and Communist threats, the inevitable glance back to the First World War are all repetitions of countless other dossiers, as is the fragmentary, inconclusive, and shifting nature of the reports. Even the reference to acrobatic troupes recalls a police report of 1937 warning about traveling performers—the troupes Porro, Macadam ("specializing in ports of war"), Chang Tee See ("based in Berlin"), Karry and Pet Pagee, Jonny and Billa ("trained monkey number . . . the trainer . . . speaks French but pretends not to"), and Frilli—all of whom were suspected of spying for a foreign country. Investigations turned up nothing, although this too repeats the archival record from these years.[2] In one other way the Battiti case speaks of the twenties and thirties. German intrigues in Morocco were nothing new. Like much of the official and printed record from these decades, the Battiti affair reached back to earlier episodes, exhibiting a strain of continuity across the divide of war. Yet the cast of characters, the almost storybook quality of the particulars were postwar in flavor. People like Battiti and his entourage, common as they were after 1918, simply do not turn up in the prewar files.

What did end up in the files, as well as what turned up in the stories, novels, reportage, and endless chatter on spies between the two world wars is the subject of this book. My intention is a simple one: to write about interwar espionage and intrigue as a means of writing about interwar France. The conventional concerns of the history of espionage—

strategic planning or the institutionalization of intelligence organizations[3] — may creep occasionally into the narrative, but they are not what this book is about. Rather I am interested in how the milieu and literature of espionage changed with the First World War, how each between the wars was a product of its times, and thus how their history and their stories illuminate the distinctive features of the age. Change and the flavor of change, or what might be called mood and styles, are the true focus of this work. I began this book with the desire to write about the First World War as a divide in modern European history, but to do so in ways that would reach beyond what we already know about the breakup of empires or the rise of new political systems; and that intent has remained with me throughout the project. If I have chosen to write that history by dwelling on spies, it is because spies have struck me, as they often struck contemporaries, as emblematic of the period, and because spies have drawn me toward the softer realms of moods and atmosphere that I wanted to explore without straying very far from the harder realities of security that dominated these years and gave them their identity as lying between one war and another. But it is the age that I am writing about and consequently I have ranged widely, from refugee circles in Paris to motor caravans through the Gobi or travels to Angkor Wat, because the history of interwar espionage was encapsulated within these larger histories of exile, adventure, travel, and globalization that were themselves shaped by the war and expressive of the changes that followed.

Initially I thought that by tracing the origins to fifth-column imagery I could produce the story I wanted to tell. The image seemed to speak reams about the postwar years. Coined in the Spanish civil war it linked espionage symbolically with the ideologies and causes of the thirties and with the drift toward a second European war. Behind the image lurked the methods and strategies identified with fascism and international bolshevism to the point that they appeared to define them. And embedded within fifth-column accusations were the fears and insecurities and internecine bickering we have tended to assign to Third Republic France in the years before its collapse. But the more I dug back into the prewar years for comparisons and contrasts the more difficulties I found in this initial approach.

On the one hand I discovered that the reaction to defeat in 1870 had generated a literature and an official frame of mind that, at the very least, had anticipated the fifth-column idiom of the late 1930s. Nor could I ignore the spy scares that had swept across France with the outbreak of the First World War. On the other hand I came to realize that the fundamental difference between the spy worlds that followed and preceded the war was simply the richness of the postwar milieu and its literature compared to what had come before. That richness was one of character and of stories told, but I also use the word to encompass the varied strains to world history that came with an age of war and revolution, greater globalism, more intense organization, and permanent geopolitical flux, all of which gave definition to the history of espionage between the wars. And by richness I also mean the complexity of styles and moods in these years, nuanced ways of thinking whose tonalities, like the place-name of Shanghai, rang of the great shaping events of the century, crumbling worlds, fear and decline, but also of the untrammeled pursuit of mystery and romance, and of the coming together of politics and adventure. In such richness, broadly defined, could be found the seeds for the specific fifth-column image as it emerged at the end of the thirties but also a range of sentiments and changes that embraced far more than insecurities or alarms and that explained far better than these the fascination that spies held for contemporaries. Humor, romanticism, consumerism, love of ambiance, the love of telling a good story, an enchantment with the memory of the war, twentieth-century adventures, and a facility for making light of events determined as much as dark forebodings how the French thought about spies in the interwar era. These traits too deviated from my original conception because they suggested that the traditional framework with which we regard interwar France and into which fifth-column imagery seemed to fit so snugly was itself in need of revision.

Richness, then, of context and moods, has determined the two themes of this book, first that interwar espionage had a character of its own that it acquired from the complexity of its times and second that the French possessed greater self-assuredness than we have been inclined to see in these years. For most historians 1914 was a dividing line in French history to the extent that it introduced new issues of a social and economic nature and new international pressures, all of which proved intractable problems for a French political system and social order founded a half-century earlier. Thus our perception of these years as a time of troubles.[4] Certainly the espionage and intrigues of the *entre-deux-guerres* lead us back to these difficulties. But because they lead to much else that conflicts with our traditional interpretation or simply wanders beyond it I have come to question whether "crisis" or "scarring" or "the unraveling of the republic" best characterize the French experience after the Great War. This book will incorporate that questioning — not to dismiss earlier interpretations, because to do so would be foolish, but rather to broaden the way we think about France and the French in the postwar period. What I have attempted is to write a history that looks forward from 1914 without feeling the compulsion to read back into the age the termination of the republic in 1940. The France I have come upon was one deeply focused on the present yet not necessarily uneasy with that intrusion.

The events of these years have often led historians to divide the period between the twenties and the thirties, the former a decade that began badly but then rolled smoothly, the latter an unrelenting chronicle of bad times and pressures brought upon by the depression and a deteriorating international situation. Years of research, however, into the Battitis of the world have convinced me that where espionage was concerned, the division lines fall with the war far more than between one decade and another. Indeed what began principally as a study of the thirties was forced by events and characters back into the twenties. The result is a work that concentrates on the 1930s because that was where the action (and sources) was greatest, but that treats the interwar years as a *bloc*.

Although my perspective is that of a French historian, my subjects are not exclusively French. Nor can they possibly be since only an expansive reach out into the world can capture the full dimensions of interwar espionage or display the largest connections between historical change and what compelled the French to write about spies. Accordingly I have brought into my account the experiences of Russians in Mongolia and Germans in Afghanistan and, most of all, the special milieu that was Shanghai between the wars to recreate the historical backdrop to adventures or romantic quests against which so much of the history of espionage was set in the twenties and thirties. Throughout I have utilized mostly French sources, French archives, and the published commentaries of contemporaries, especially those of French travelers, to show how my story pertains to the French. Where I have dwelt on the published adventures of foreigners, the reader should keep in mind that most often these writings were translated and read about in France. Yet I make no claims that what I am writing about is distinctively French; indeed I suspect that British or German scholars could produce a very similar history about their own countries. That commonality, however, does reinforce one of the principal arguments of this study: that the distinctive features we have noted in the French people during these years —

insecurity, defeatism, insularity, and the inadequacies of the late Third Republic — may not best sum up their moods and orientations between the wars. What I have tried in particular to do is to take the French out into the world in ways that have not been attempted before and to merge their experience with world history. Therein too lies a central theme of this work: the pronounced globalism that came with the war and its reflection in the milieus and literature of spies.

In writing this book I have relied heavily at times on the techniques of telling stories. I must confess that in part this comes from a certain atavistic impulse to return to the pleasures history first held for me many years ago. But this is also a book about the stories the French had to tell about spies, and particularly the relish with which they told them. Between the wars the French reveled in telling tales. They created stories out of adventures, politics, and travels, and they regarded intrigue and espionage as inexhaustible sources for spinning great yarns. The unabashed eagerness with which they surrendered to that whimsy is itself part of the history I wish to tell here because it catches wider dispositions and idioms from these years and because the very fancifulness of the telling forces us to rethink how French men and women envisioned their times. Stories, moreover, return us to the ambiguity of interwar spy imagery, and thus to the textured flavor of these years. When the French painted their pictures of spies they did so from a palate that held many colors. Their portraits could be deep and alarmist, but also playful and superficial. Often the same kinds of characters and plot elements appeared in a wide variety of stories where shifts in tone swung meanings from the potentially frightful to the merely laughable. In such shifts these stories echoed the greater complexities to be found in stories of the war or stories retailed by the press where what mattered most was how the tale was told. Telling stories, then, was often the medium through which the interwar French best revealed themselves; to recover moods and tempers, I have used it as well.

If there is a constraint on my desire to retrieve the lives and legends from these years it lies mostly in the ravages of war, the paper shortages,[5] the restrictions on access to files, and the almost compulsive need to embellish and fabricate that have bequeathed an archival record that is fragmentary at best and a printed record that places serious strains on credibility. Someday a book will have to be written about the process of *dérogations* — those special archival dispensations that allow one to peer into officially closed records. I am grateful to the French for opening so much to me, probably far more than is allowed for researchers in Great

Britain. I do wish, however, that the contents of those boxes locked away in the cellars or warehouses were not so tantalizingly displayed in the inventories, and that a certain number of boxes that were made available had not had certain dossiers — always the best — removed in advance. Even with access one must move gingerly through a welter of sensationalism and indeterminacy, a rule to be applied with still greater rigor to practically anything on espionage that worked its way into print. Throughout I have chosen skepticism over credulity and have demanded that the sources convince me of their veracity.

I suspect that introductions are best when they are kept brief, since books should persuade by their execution, not their pronouncements. The reader, therefore, need be detained by only a few more remarks. First, I have defined espionage widely to encompass all sorts of covert operations and have elected to use the words espionage and intrigue interchangeably if for no other reason than stylistic considerations dictate I do so. Second, I have managed to trace printing figures, and some sales figures, for a number of the books I have consulted. I have introduced these into the notes at the place I felt would be of greatest use. There can be no consensus on how to interpret these figures, although one source has suggested that a printing of more than five thousand was *pas mal* (not bad) for the period, and I see no reason to quarrel with that perspective. Third, I have retained in most cases the interwar spelling of Chinese names and place-names because these are more familiar to general readers and because to conform to more contemporary usage would, in the context of this work, be anachronistic. Russian and Eastern European names I have converted from French to English spelling, and I have applied a single-system approach for names taken from English language sources to avoid inconsistencies. I have, however, left the names of authors and fictional characters as they originally appear in the French or the English, and I have elected to do the same for several individuals where changes strike me either as improper or uncertain. Finally, to conform with the rules of *dérogation,* I have concealed the names of many individuals.

Figure 1. *From the cover of Jeanne and Frédéric Régamey's* Hidden Germany.
(Courtesy Bibliothèque nationale — Paris)

CHAPTER ONE

War

Few images are more evocative of the interwar years than that of the secret agent. After the First World War there was no escaping the figure of the spy. Celebrated, notorious, unheard of secret operatives recorded their wartime adventures with a shameless reach for posterity or fortune. For really the first time the French wrote spy novels. Almost all were dreadful — and this assessment is charitable — yet the writers cranked them out for an eager and faithful market. Charles Lucieto wrote nearly a dozen episodes for his series, *La guerre des cerveaux*. Covers proclaimed sales as high as one hundred and twenty thousand, although these figures were about as credible as the stories within. But Charles Robert-Dumas's tales of the French Deuxième Bureau did sell from twenty-four thousand to forty thousand copies, and these were high numbers for the 1930s. The publisher Baudinière edited a series it called "The Secret War," printing some sixty-odd volumes with sales figures estimated at fifteen thousand to twenty thousand copies each. Translations of Fu Manchu novels appeared in the thirties. The French gobbled these up; printings of thirty-five thousand copies apiece almost always sold out by the end of the decade.[1] Alongside the novelists were reporters and spy experts, although it was often difficult to distinguish either from the fiction writers. Newspapers dredged up old spy stories or piled on new ones to promote sales. The publicity was scarcely necessary. The interwar years seemed to glide, with hardly a pause, from one spy sensation to the next: the breaking of spy rings, spy trials, assassinations, kidnappings of White Russian generals, submarine hijackings, terrorist plots. In the twenties, and especially in the thirties, the mysterious spy surfaced as a familiar figure. Secret agents invaded all kinds of literature. They were in travel accounts. They were in playful novels, for example, Maurice Dekobra's immensely successful *Madonna of the Sleeping Cars*. Serious writers like Malraux wrote about spies.[2]

Why this was so and what it represents is largely the story this book has to tell. Certainly the place to begin is the political context or atmosphere of the times, for the era seemed to conspire in favor of the secret agent. The defining attributes of these years — international insecurity, totalitarian politics, refugee floods, civil war, and political polarization — militated toward thinking about spies. The Russian revolution triggered a fetish with internationals, the image of a Europe of international camps that permeated and divided nations from within and whose operatives were identified as spies and saboteurs. There was, to be sure, a Red International, but also a White International, a Green International, a Fascist International, and even something called a Cagoule International, after the group of right-wing French extremists popularly known as the hooded ones (or *cagoulards*). In 1938 one author was writing of *The International of Spies, Assassins, Cagoulards, and Provokers in the Service of Fascism*,[3] a sign of how readily ideological politics induced sightings of enemy combines after the war. With the rise of fascism came an unrestrained disposition to believe in vast and powerful espionage organizations and a Europe swarming with larva-like goons in leather trench coats. The basic text on German espionage in the thirties was a Communist refugee publication called *The Brown Network*. It recounted how the Gestapo, with its 2,450 foreign agents and its 20,000 informants, was prepared to murder, torture, sabotage, blackmail, threaten, and spy throughout the world, and how behind this organization existed a formidable support apparatus that transferred money through travel and steamship bureaus, infiltrated operatives into the Central European train system, ran espionage schools, sent and received coded messages, and maintained vast files on all enemy agents, émigrés, and enemies of the Führer.[4] By the 1930s, therefore, the air crackled with talk of spies. Caught on the wrong side in Spain, George Orwell discovered how easily in these years political differences translated into accusations of espionage.[5] From the Soviet purges came a demonstration of how an era of revolution and counterrevolution redirected politics to behind-the-lines battles and rendered the secret agent a stereotype. After 1917, and certainly after 1933, the word spy became all but an automatic indictment of someone on the other side.

Refugees played no small role in the identification of secret agents with totalitarian threats. Refugees, first from bolshevism, then from fascism, imported stories of terror and conspiracy, while their own murky worlds of politics cum intrigue provided occasion for still more lurid narrations. Consistently one will find, if one pages through the published accounts of spies and terrorists between the wars, that the source is a refugee. "The Gestapo . . . is everywhere. . . . No Frenchman can imagine the power of this organism," a refugee tells a journalist with the first reports of Nazi terrorism in Europe.[6] When White Russian generals are kidnapped off the streets of Paris it is refugees who all but issue the press communiqués. For fabricated accounts there are fabricated refugees, cicerones to unravel the mysteries that no one can solve. And fifth-column imagery, the most celebrated spy vision of the century, is, to a considerable extent, a refugee story.

Properly speaking the fifth-column image came out of the forties as much as the thirties. The term can be traced to 1936 when General Emilio Mola boasted that he had four columns marching on Madrid, but that the decisive blow would be dealt by a fifth from within. But there was no rush to appropriate the phrase, and the few references that appeared over the rest of the decade were nearly always associated with Spain. The image never did infiltrate official language. I have located only a handful of references to "fifth column" in the archives, one in 1937 in regard to Spain, two others in May 1940 after the term was already becoming fashionable in the press.[7]

What turned the image into a commonplace was first the Nazi takeover in Norway and then the German victory in the west. In the miserable days of spring 1940, as the Germans marched or dropped from the air, the fifth column took on its familiar shape: German minorities and ideological fellow travelers forming secret armies from within; fifth-column parachutists descending in Dutch or French uniform, often with wireless sets, perhaps dressed as priests or in other civilian disguise; one hundred thousand Nazi soldiers, camouflaged in Holland, preparing "Hitler's hour"; Weygand secreting the army to his command in Syria — in short, German clandestine operations, systematically readied in advance and supported by treachery in high places, leading to defeat.

Today we know that there was little substance to these rumors, but for those who managed to get out of France it was a message of urgency they carried across the Atlantic, repeating and embellishing the stories until, together, the stories formed a mythology. The myth served many purposes. It provided the Left with a powerful hammer to beat against the Right, and it struck as well a blow for national honor by denying defeat upon the field of battle. At the most basic level it offered a means of exorcising shock, of explaining, as one person has written, the seemingly inexplicable. Then, after war's end, what had worked for national honor could also work for personal reputations, and by 1945 the tarnish here was especially thick. So again one dipped into the fifth-column well. General Maurice Gamelin, who had lost the Battle of France, lowered the bucket several times, reeling up the discovery that German victory had been the result not only of everyone else's mistakes, but of fifth-column intrigues too. Few were willing to let the myth drop because it was such an easy way to write off the last five years.[8]

Yet etymologies do not tell us everything, and in this case they do not reveal much at all. If the articulation of fifth-column imagery came only with the forties, the basic concept borrowed heavily from the twenties and thirties, leaning considerably on the refugee texts *The Brown Network* and its sequel, *The Nazi Conspiracy in Spain*.[9] Nearly everyone who wrote about fifth columns in the forties was to steal copiously from the 1935 edition. In fact nearly all the paraphernalia of the myth — card indexes, spy schools, terrorist camps, radio wars and clandestine radio transmissions — had worked their way into the official reports and printed literature of the interwar years. Imagery of war was also a part of the background, explaining again why the secret agent preyed upon imaginations after 1918.

In the interwar years thoughts about espionage were another means for thinking about war in the twentieth century. No one who has traveled in France and seen the war memorials in every town or village or has studied the interwar years and witnessed the forced memory of the war — the books and memoirs, the pilgrimages to Verdun, the monuments to everything imaginable (even the carrier pigeons, "their wounded and their heroes," got a monument in 1936)[10] — can ignore the powerful hold the First World War held over French minds after 1918. This was a war that everyone would have preferred to forget, but it was also one that the French loved to recall, and in those memories spies played a not inconsiderable role. Stories of famous spies and memoirs of secret agents formed part of the vast literature that issued from the war. Even more, when espionage writers told of "the secret war," "the white war," "the silent war," "the spy war," "an underground war without mercy," "a permanent war, underhanded, secret . . . [a] war in broad peace," they were expressing fundamental thoughts about how war was waged in their century.[11] Secret-war imagery, like fifth-column imagery (and like the steady flow of reports into counterespionage files), spoke to the feeling of living between a war that had passed and a war that was coming, and that espionage was the bridge between the one and the other. The image captured the sense of war as a permanent condition of life in the twentieth century, an experience prolonged in people's minds no less than it was prolonged beyond armistices and treaties on different fronts by different means. Despite official endings the war invaded people's lives, penetrated civilian society, finding the most visible embodiment of that sensation in the behind-the-lines figure of the spy. Lurking, like the Great War, the spy was a projection of the awareness that the presence of war would not go away.

Indeed between the wars French absorption with spies paralleled more haunting ruminations on war in the future. Speculation about a next war invariably dwelt on the role of the bomber, a breakthrough weapon that could visit the horrors of war—conventional, gas, germ; all options were possible—upon civilian populations. Unlike the last war, the next war would avoid stalemate because armies would possess the means for striking behind fronts and breaking both the capacity to supply and the will to persist. There is a rather large literature from the twenties and thirties on the more ghastly side to these visions.[12] It ranges from expert figures on how many planes plus how many gas bombs were required to liquidate a city to novels like Florian-Parmentier's *Abyss,* in which a gas and germ war in 1960 kills two hundred and twenty million people or Victor Méric's *War to End All Wars,* which compellingly catches the central image of all of this writing: that when the slaughter comes again, it will fall not on the troops at the front, but on the civilians back home.[13]

None of this speculation was very far removed from thinking about spies who operated behind lines in wartime to cripple civilian morale and the ability to fight. In their modern guise as terrorists and subversives, spies provoked the same kinds of perceptions as those envisaged by the future-war writers: the vulnerability of civilian populations to mass death and destruction, the realization that through new technology this result could come at the hands of a small number of people, and the expectation that terror, panic, and demoralization were now the key weapons of attack. Consequently secret agents, like gas bombs and germ bombs, came to penetrate future-war writing. Florian-Parmentier's account of mass annihilation in 1960 included the landing of special detachments behind enemy lines, dressed in enemy uniforms and armed with machine guns. Their mission was to disorganize services, to cut communications, and above all to spread confusion and terror among the civilian population. Elsewhere there were discussions of spies who pinpointed targets for bombers or who, as enemy pilots, traveled to Paris on one pretext or another to learn the best places to drop their fire bombs and gas the city's population. "The war of the future," predicted the German Ludwig Bauer, "will be a war of perfected technique, with a manpower reduced and rationalized. A few thousand chemists, engineers, pilots, mechanics, filmmakers, and spies will do for a start."[14]

In turn spy novels and spy reportage were littered with material about biological and chemical warfare. *War and Bacteria,* a 1937 spy novel, related German plans to launch a first strike of microbes. Pierre Yrondy's *From Cocaine . . . to Gas!!!* fantasized about German plans to destroy the French with drugs, bacilli, and gas. In the next war, Yrondy insisted in his preface, "the most important battles will be the work of various espionage agents. They will be — and are already — charged with sowing death in the great centers and thus exterminating civilian populations." Charles Lucieto wrote about gas in *Delivered to the Enemy,* as did Charles Robert-Dumas in *The Lead Idol* and Jean Bommart in *Helen and the Chinese Fish.* Commandant Georges Ladoux, who headed military counterintelligence during the First World War, introduced gas and germ warfare into a spy novel he wrote in the 1930s. Marcel Nadaud and André Fage's 1926 reportage on crime and espionage argued that the Germans were preparing for chemical and bacteriological warfare in the future. Perhaps what made the association instinctual, or irresistible, was the frequency with which the two paraded together in real life, surfacing with the Moscow purge trials, Cagoule revelations, and a host of sensational Parisian affairs.[15]

At base there remained the inevitable exchange: contemplating wars of terror and disorganization in an era that anticipated a next war led to thinking about espionage, sabotage, and subversion. The presumption spread to government authorities who, responsible for forestalling covert action, took their charge seriously. Much of the next chapter will examine their record. Still, an item scooped from the archives illustrates once more the close connections that were drawn between waging modern war and the role of secret agents, particularly because it returns us to the foundations of fifth-column thinking.

Of all the permutations in military tactics after the First World War, none straddled better the parallel tracks to espionage and future war imagery than the formation of paratroop units. In the spring of 1940, the parachutist descended upon the scene as a stock figure in fifth-column mania. Few accounts from these days are complete without the familiar stories of parachute sightings of epidemic proportions or of near lynchings of French pilots who had parachuted from burning planes only to be mistaken for German agents. Civilians readily connected expectations of how the next war would be fought with soldier-operatives who dropped from the sky, behind enemy lines, on missions of disruption and terror. The same connections were drawn by police and military men who throughout the thirties had observed developments in paratroop tactics, especially in the Soviet Union, the recognized pioneer in paratroop deployment. Later the focus would shift to Germany; one cannot help but notice how closely leadership in paratroop tactics conformed to French targeting of espionage threats. The reports from the thirties make for interesting reading with their communications about thousands of trained Soviet parachutists, the prospects for total surprise and disruption of mobilization, the debates on the effectiveness of large airborne units in the densely populated areas of Western Europe, and the damage that could be done by small detachments, scattered by parachute on assigned intelligence or sabotage missions.[16]

Reports out of Poland following the Nazi invasion particularly command one's attention because they represent the official equivalent of the peasants with pitchforks who hunted for parachutists the following May. Their tales of German intelligence agents and sabotage teams dropping behind Polish lines, "setting machines on fire, sowing confusion in the rear, sabotaging telephone and railway lines, and then disappearing into the civilian population," and their conclusions that here were sabotage operations unprecedented in military history, "unquestionably play[ing] a leading role in the German offensive," preview almost to a word the fifth-column stories that would circulate with abandon in the years to come. Later we will see how the Germans had in fact trained and dispatched such sabotage teams, although with substantially more limited intentions and consequences than these communiqués would have one believe. What matters here is less the truth than the reaction to these exceptional findings, especially those of a later, longer report dating from March 1940. It had been drawn up not by French observers or agents but by the Polish high command, who then communicated it to the French government. Admittedly, Polish armed forces officers had been in a position to know about German subversion, yet they also had reasons to fob off their very real military collapse, and this fact should not have escaped the authorities in Paris. Nevertheless, the director general of the Sûreté nationale circulated the report to prefects and police under the label Top Secret, and without comment. As combat in the west drew near, the French were primed for a war of espionage and sabotage as well as a war of the continual front.[17]

So the secret agent was a constant if troubling companion to the French between the two wars. That case, whether one looks at political imagery or thoughts about war, can be made with little difficulty. Still, one needs to probe deeper to discover just what this represented historically. Consider, for example, two episodes, one from the 1930s, the other from the late nineteenth century. In early 1934 the police received a tip that at 4, square Gabriel-Fauré in Paris a number of Germans were telephoning daily to Berlin. The informant suggested these could be Nazi agents, paid by Hitler to spy on the French or to foment revolution. The inevitable investigation followed, with the inevitable conclusion. The Germans were wealthy men with families or businesses in Germany.[18] One can almost sense in the dossier left behind the detective's vexation and lassitude as he made one more senseless trip, climbed the inevitable stairs, interviewed the necessary witnesses, and then wasted more time typing his report with his cold, nubby fingers.

One is reminded of the Schreiber matter from the late 1880s. Hermann Conrad Schreiber was a German national who had lived most of his life in France. In 1889 officials in the Ministry of Interior were trying to expel him. Their case against Schreiber was based upon accusations they had received from his neighbors. According to the townspeople of Villeneuve-la-Guyard, Schreiber had had too much good fortune recently to have come by it honestly. Almost inexplicably, and despite his natural sloth, he had built a prosperous trade in jewelry. His personal expenses were so exaggerated, his shop's range of wares so beyond the needs of his clients, that one could conclude only that the business was a pretext for Schreiber's residence in town. Moreover, Schreiber had acquired a horse and carriage and traveled on what he called commercial trips but what were obviously voyages of a more suspicious nature. He even went to Paris. Then he discontinued his trips, preferring to receive commercial travelers at home. The townspeople were certain these men were spies. The more the citizens of Villeneuve-la-Guyard thought about Schreiber, the more they dredged up suspicious memories of the man and his family. It was said that he had welcomed the German invasion of 1870 and had interpreted for the enemy. He had raised his son to hate France and the boy had once declared in public that when the next war came the Schreibers would go to Germany, only to return soon after in the wake of the German army. It was a known fact that Schreiber's brothers and sisters lived across the border, and that one of the brothers was a German officer. The townspeople took their tale to the authorities who placed Schreiber on the "list of suspects B" and considered him a threat in the event of mobilization. Now they were seeking to deport him, but the Ministry of Foreign Affairs was obstructing their efforts. The Interior Ministry wanted to know why.

The Quai d'Orsay's response was scorching. The Ministry of Interior had no certain proof against Schreiber, only presumptions. Perhaps the Sûreté would discover proof if it bothered to place him under surveillance. Thus far this had not been done. The charges against Schreiber rested on the fact that he had bought a horse and carriage and traveled without telling his neighbors where he was going and on the remarks of a child who had probably been sorely treated by the other children in town. Schreiber's neighbors said he had spied for the Germans in 1870, but nineteen years earlier, when spies were seen everywhere, they had left him alone and had spread no such rumors. Schreiber had lived in France for forty years. If he was going to be expelled, then one should have against him "not suspicions, but *certitudes*." Thus the storm over a matter that, like the telephone calls half a century later, rang of the same spy fright, the same baseless accusations, the same stereotypes and absurdities, and the same wearied disgust from at least part of officialdom.[19]

The problem for the historian of the interwar years is that these kinds of resemblances turn up with an almost rhythmic frequency. There is a set of dossiers in the BB18 series in the archives of the Ministry of Justice reviewing the cases of individuals accused of espionage for foreign powers. Most are mundane affairs—individuals caught outside fortresses or near military installations. From the point of spy literature they do not make for particularly interesting reading, except for the fact that in bulk and detail the pre–World War I dossiers do not appear substantially different from those of the twenties or thirties.

Elsewhere certain motifs are repeated as if spy stories could not exist without them. Take for example the figure of the spy in priest's clothing. Rumors of parachuting priests and nuns in hobnailed boots were a familiar feature of fifth-column rumors sweeping over France in 1940. Even the authorities were on the lookout for secret agents disguised as priests. Throughout the heated days of April and May the Vatican took the precaution of notifying the French Foreign Office of the travels of

German priests, so likely was it that any German passengers, including German missionaries, would be hauled off ships and interned as suspects. The Quai d'Orsay hastened to oblige the Holy See, but it was no less quick to request that names and destinations be submitted at least eight days before departure to run the necessary checks on the individuals in question. Some diplomats thought even this was too obliging. The minister plenipotentiary to Ecuador, Jean Dobler, worried himself into a dither over the pending arrival of the Reverend Father Fisher because Fisher was a secular ecclesiastic and no French missionary to the country was secular clergy. Fisher, moreover, had requested this assignment and had been supported by the directors of Pio Latino College in Rome "who," Dobler added "are German Jesuits." Dobler suggested that since Father Fisher was young, one ought to inquire about his military status. "If Monsieur Fisher is in physical condition to bear arms, we must acknowledge that he is officially or *unofficially* on German military reserve; and in this case I advise against according him favorable treatment and allowing him to pass our blockade." Just what a German priest's contribution in Ecuador would have been to the German war effort was never quite spelled out by the French minister plenipotentiary. But he did urge an immediate investigation of the man.[20]

One wonders, however, how far back the spy-priest image can be traced, especially in anticlerical France. It certainly did not originate in 1939–40. Paul and Suzanne Lanoir, precursors of interwar spy "experts," argued during the First World War that German agents were infiltrating French lines in clerical garb. Colonel Walter Nicolai, who ran German intelligence during the First World War, described how his men had discovered a French officer dressed as a priest. Undoubtedly real-life clergy who served in Allied intelligence networks in occupied territory during the war conferred upon the image a certain verisimilitude. Yet even before the war Captain Raoult Rudeval had included priests' robes in his discussion of secret agent disguises.[21]

One could be tempted to argue that fifth-column imagery was possible only after the experience of the twenties and thirties; yet this will not hold either. British invasion literature from the turn of the century, equally replete with visions of mass infiltration by spies and saboteurs, has been well documented. Germany had a comparable fright before the war and so did France, as we shall soon see.[22] Once war broke out spy mania gripped all countries. Lights at night, wash hung out to dry, accents, any unusual behavior were cause for suspicion. The same stupidities of 1940 pervaded the earlier war. The Lanoirs, whose own contribution to the asininity level of spy-talk was disproportionately high, recalled how an angry Parisian crowd in 1915 nearly cut to pieces "spies" signaling to Zeppelin raiders overhead. Their prey, so it turned out, were a policeman on a counterespionage mission and a representative of an Allied embassy, meeting in an upper-story room and failing to turn out their light immediately after the warning had sounded. Only the intervention of the concierge saved their lives. Jean Tillet, who worked with French security in the First World War, tells an even better story of an old man, sick and living alone near army headquarters during the second battle of the Marne. Every evening, near ten o'clock, the man takes to the nearby bushes and woods, returning to his house a half-hour later. The amateur detectives of the village begin to suspect a spy in their midst. After all they are only six kilometers from the front and most evenings the old man disappears just when enemy planes pass overhead. They try to follow him, but never successfully, so they go to the authorities. The next night counterespionage agents are hidden along the old man's path. The woods are guarded:

Ten o'clock at night. In the woods. The dry rasping sound of leaves, then a human form stops near a thicket. An agent is nearby, well placed to see and hear what happens. After some fumbling about the belt, the man squats. One can guess what wafts the lookout's way. . . . Without hurrying, the "suspect" straightens up, tidies up, and goes home. The performance is repeated over several consecutive nights. At mathematically the same hour, the old newsvendor returns to the woods to satisfy a natural need, without worrying about the planes and their bombs.[23]

Like spy-crazy letters and tips or alarms of spies in priest's clothing, the fifth-column scare often repeated what the French had experienced once before. Not even the theme of espionage, war, and remembrance was without antecedents; indeed espionage literature before World War I was largely a variation on thinking about defeat a quarter century earlier.

It will not do, then, to write about interwar espionage in isolation. One must turn back, first to the years before the war, then to the war experience itself, to consider what changed with the war and what did not, and how the milieu and literature of espionage between the two wars shared the distinctive features of their times.

Spies have probably existed at all times in all places. A recent book on espionage called it the second oldest profession, although many have wondered how it differs from the first. Spies appear in the Bible, and

Homer has told us of the Trojan horse. Walsingham, Mendoza, and Parma had their networks of informants. Richelieu used spies, as did Frederick the Great. Both the revolutionary governments and particularly Napoleon had their improvised contingents of agents. Later in the century, as the French reflected on their failures — the very lack of an intelligence system in the Franco-Prussian War — they liked to recall these earlier successes. Throughout the nineteenth century the spy remained a dubious figure in France, but Napoleon's operative, Charles Schulmeister, was clearly an exception.[24] Espionage may have been dirty work, but victory could serve as a powerful detergent.

Institutionalization of intelligence gathering and prolonged thinking about spies are, however, relatively new and have their roots in remembrance of and preparation for modern warfare. For the French (as for the Germans) that war came in 1870, as did the impression that followed, and lasted, that mass armies fought modern wars, but perhaps secret agents won them. For forty years after the Franco-Prussian War German phantoms would populate French literature on espionage while counterespionage sleuths would stalk covert agents who never existed. Two generations would repeat the weedy legends that flowered out of the ashes of defeat, particularly those told of William Stieber, Bismarck's master spy, who had paved the way for German invasion and flooded eastern France with thirty thousand secret agents. As time wore on there would be new versions or reports of German conspiracies, including accusations against Jews as German spies that reached a crescendo during the debates over Dreyfus, although the image of the Jewish German agent had predated the affair and would continue after the anti-Semitism of the Dreyfus years abated. Léon Daudet's *Avant-guerre,* published in 1913 and asserting that Jews in command of commerce and industry were going to betray France in the next war, would sell eleven thousand copies within the course of the year.[25] Meanwhile French officials would conduct relentless dragnets for spies, and would proceed, haltingly and sketchily, toward the creation of a professional intelligence network. All of this in reaction to a German spy threat that was perceived to have made the difference in the Franco-Prussian War and to have remained a presence in the years that followed.

The reality, as might be supposed, was considerably different. The Prussian army possessed no intelligence service at the time of the Austro-Prussian War and only sought to create one following the poor intelligence it obtained during that campaign. By the Franco-Prussian War some progress had been made. A report from November 1870 identified agents in Lyons, Rouen, Lille, Amiens, Antwerp, Switzerland, Denmark, Italy, and Austria. Moreover valuable information arrived, as it had in 1866, from Baron von Schluga, a renegade Austrian officer living in Paris. (Von Schluga, Agent 17, was transmitting first-rate intelligence out of Paris as late as 1914. One serious historian of espionage calls him the greatest spy in German history.) But even by 1870 the Nachtrichtendienst was but a jerry-built organization, a far cry from the puffery of the Stieber legend. The best source we have on German espionage before 1918 — an official study undertaken by Generalmajor Fritz Gempp in 1927 — concludes that German intelligence in 1870 was a small, primitive, poorly prepared operation that occasionally got lucky. Stieber, who later received much attention, was only a police official, responsible for the security of Bismarck and the king and for counterespionage in the field. There is no reason to believe he made a serious contribution to spying on the French, let alone to German victory.[26]

Well after 1870 German intelligence remained a less than formidable force. Little money and apparently even less status were accorded the service, so that IIIb, as German intelligence came to be known, grew only slowly and rather painfully. Both Gempp and Nicolai have argued that German intelligence in these years was markedly inferior to that of its rivals, especially French espionage and counterespionage which were larger, better coordinated, and repeatedly successful in the operations they mounted against the German empire and her agents. One wonders. Sources from the French side do not confirm this picture, and Christopher Andrew's recent study of the British Secret Service has revealed how amateurish and embryonic British intelligence was down to 1939, despite the assumption of the rest of the world that the English were congenital spy masters. There appears to be a pattern, repeated on all sides and throughout contemporary history, of ascribing to the other side the prowess one would like to claim for one's own. Most likely Gempp and Nicolai were right only in their assessment of their own organizations and that all intelligence services shared in the inadequacies that characterized IIIb in the late nineteenth century.[27]

Later documentation does suggest that as the war approached, a serious effort was made to increase the operational strength and efficiency of German intelligence. When then Major Nicolai assumed command of IIIb in 1913 he found, in Gempp's words, "a well organized and well led team corresponding to modern requirements." The decision to appoint Nicolai, who had directed espionage operations against Russia with some success, was probably a wise one, despite Nicolai's own disclaimer that he was far too junior to run IIIb and that his selection merely demonstrated the army's indifference to intelligence matters. The number of agents abroad substantially increased in the last years before the war. A chart drawn up in spring of 1914 indicates preparation for wartime intelligence stations in thirty cities, including New York, Buenos Aires, and Tokyo, as well as major posts in Geneva, Copenhagen, Antwerp, and Basel. In the last days of July 1914, the Koblenz station was receiving reports from agents in Nancy, Paris, Lille, Sedan, and Laon. The real test came that summer, when the government and high command depended on intelligence reports to determine how far preparations for war were proceeding in France and Russia. In general, the information was good. "The system works!" judged the Koblenz station chief on 28 July. Still, it did not work all that well. Once war was declared and borders sealed, IIIb virtually lost contact with its agents in France. Information dribbled in from other sources, but not enough to prevent serious deficiencies in what was known about French troop deployment following mobilization. Similar breakdowns occurred elsewhere. Despite the dispatch or recruitment of agents in Istanbul, Sofia, and Romania, and the arrangement for money drops, after war was declared information from the Balkans was embarrassingly thin. There had also been plans for sabotage. Projections called for the destruction of bridges in the east along the Russian army's line of advance. As of August 1914, IIIb was still looking for agents to take on this assignment. In the west there were plans to disrupt French rail traffic, and here agents had been found. But there is no evidence that these missions were undertaken, let alone accomplished.[28]

Such was the German record as we know it. Still the French remained haunted by visions of spies in these years, and what is necessary is to trace how widespread their spy mania could be between defeat in 1870 and the First World War, and the forms it could take, before then considering what lay behind it. There is no better place to begin than with the myth of William Stieber because the stories that grew up about this less than extraordinary man effectively captured and contributed to the speculation about espionage. He was, in the literature of the nineteenth century, the premier master spy, the architect of victory in 1866, and then again in 1870. He was said to be a man of a thousand faces who traveled with a suitcase stuffed with wigs, a supply of false beards, a pocketbook full of cash, and carte blanche from Bismarck. On his own he scouted out the land, listened to the people, and then dotted the countryside with his agents, most notably in eastern France, which he inundated with thirty thousand spies camouflaged as farmers, farm workers, serving girls, maids, office employees, and the proverbial commercial travelers. He was shrewd, devious, and ruthless, and because of him German armies overwhelmed their enemies with ease.

The story, as we know, was a grand fabrication, but it circulated through France — probably well before the publication of Stieber's memoirs in the early 1880s — and remained a staple of beliefs throughout the prewar period because like fifth-column mythology some seventy years later it offered a convenient means of writing off a humiliating defeat. Self-anointed spy authorities like the Lanoirs picked the story up and retailed it as God's truth,[29] but more striking is how the legend, or some variation upon it, crept into more serious literature. Perhaps the most respected treatise on intelligence in the late nineteenth century, a two-volume methodical study by General Jules-Louis Lewal on the tactics of intelligence gathering in time of war, noted that German officers had "flooded" into eastern France before 1870, traveling as tourists or as legitimate citizens. Two doctoral theses written by military men echoed this theme. One spun out the whole story — the extraordinary Mr. Stieber; thirty thousand spies — citing the Lanoirs as his source. Not even the *Grande encyclopédie* knew how to define espionage without referring to the large numbers of secret agents that had infiltrated France before 1870.[30]

With the passage of time the myth was embellished and reformulated, especially by the Lanoirs who insisted that tens of thousands of German agents remained in France, observing, charting, living as honest citizens, and ready for the sabotage of French rail lines at the outbreak of war. If all of the Lanoir writings were put together, they would probably run the gamut of indispensable motifs in the repertoire of spydom: agent-priests, bordello stings, and traveling circuses identified as "spy nests." Again what catches the eye is not only the vision but how more respectable types like Captain Fernand Routier, who swallowed a big gulp of Lanoir in his dissertation, went on to regurgitate their "facts" as well.[31]

A very similar picture appeared in the press, most frequently in the eighties and nineties, but with an edgy consistency that continued down to the war. The *Petit Parisien* in 1896 recalled the army of German spies that had swarmed over France in 1870. The *Aurore* the following year wrote of the incalculable number of German spies in Paris. The *Petit Journal* a decade later described a massive and methodical German penetration of Belgium not unlike what a future generation would describe as a German fifth column. These are but a sampling of clippings that still cram dossiers in the archives of the Sûreté and the Prefecture of Police. Their specifics can be readily discounted, but what matters is their number, and the way the stories of the spy peddlers received a public hearing. It cannot be said that the French were less concerned with German espionage before the war than they were after 1918.[32]

There were also some spy novels from these years, although not very many and even more forgettable than those written later. Only one author — Captain Danrit — can be called in any way interesting. Shortly before the war, Danrit wrote a book which he called *The Alert*. It is about the mission of the French engineer, Paul Vigy, and his team of three saboteurs to blow up a railroad bridge in German-held Lorraine immediately upon the outbreak of war. Vigy is told that if he succeeds, he will stall the advance of two German army corps by at least several days and that German morale will suffer a stunning blow. The novel begins with German invasion imminent. For the mission to work, the team must proceed to the bridge immediately and await a prearranged signal that war has begun. The team moves at night to the bridge, receives its signal, and plants its charges. But the blowing up of the bridge will also destroy the house of the semaphore guard along the railway line and one member of the team is in love with his daughter. Thus he warns the daughter who tells her father who alerts the people in the nearest village, and the team is forced to flee before planting all their explosives. They do detonate their charges and damage the bridge, but not enough to prevent the movement of troops for more than a few hours. Vigy perceives, however, that structural damage has been substantial, and that should a locomotive and its tender be driven over the bridge before repairs have been made, the bridge will collapse. So the team works its way to Thionville, steals a locomotive, drives it over the bridge — jumping off at the approach to save themselves — and the bridge collapses. Now begins the getaway. Vigy's goal is to reach Luxembourg. One of the team, however, has suffered a bad sprain in the jump, and they cannot go on foot. They stop a car on the road and discover it belongs to a Dane who fled the Germans forty years earlier and now lives a rich life in Argentina. The Dane hears their story and then tells them incredible news: at the very last moment, under threat of Russian intervention, the Germans held back. There was no invasion. There is no war. The team has committed an international crime. They are outlaws. The Dane is sympathetic, however, drives them to his yacht in Antwerp and takes them to Argentina where they will be safe.[33]

Two things make this book remarkable. First, there is a distinctly twentieth-century quality to it. *The Alert* reads like a spy movie: the reconnaissance of the target, the assembling of the team, the advance at night, the success-failure-success progression of the mission, the getaway, the suspense are all there. Second, there is nothing else like this novel from these years. Danrit was a prolific writer, but the standard Danrit story was a far different animal. It is not easy to type, although the words turgid and racist will do for a start. Most are multivolume affairs that make for laborious days on the hard chairs of the Bibliothèque nationale. The titles are revealing: *War in the Twentieth Century: The Black Invasion,* followed inevitably by *The Yellow Invasion.* They are filled with the worst racist stereotypes, and, as one might expect, the stereotypes extend to Jews. As the black (really Muslim) invasion rolls toward Jerusalem, the Jews hire mercenaries to do their fighting, but are massacred anyway. There are Jewish traitors in the novel, and when it is over, and Europe reapportioned along lines favorable to France, "what remained of Semitism was relegated to Syria." In Danrit's hands the apocalyptic framework becomes less a means of telling a good story than a vehicle for expressing his loathing of all things socialist, capitalist, republican, and English. The black invasion advances relentlessly, using not only its vast numbers but also the weapons of cholera and yellow fever (did Danrit know that the latter was also called "black vomit"?). Its forces place sick troops in the front lines to infect their enemies and drop infected bodies from a stolen European airship. The French counter with a military dictatorship, the end of a money economy, public prayers, theaters that put on only classical plays, a serum against cholera, and poison gas dropped by "aérostats." France saves Europe and England is invaded, demoted to Little Britain, and put under the rule of a Danish prince. But in the sequel a divided, antimilitaristic France has no such luck against the yellow invasion that overruns Europe with bestial ferocity. The British aid the Asians but lose their empire nevertheless in a weak stab at a happy ending. *The Inevitable War,* yet another three-volume work, is Danrit's dream come true. England attacks France, French submarines erase British naval superiority, France invades Britain, parades through the country, and leaves Britain a second-rate power.[34]

None of these books can be called spy novels proper. They are hate books, adventure books, travel books, science fiction books. But Danrit also writes about spies. In *The Inevitable War,* the British fight with a worldwide espionage network. The yellow invasion advances through its sheer force of numbers; but it too utilizes secret agents throughout the world. The books as spy books, however, are difficult to place. They are like British invasion literature from these years, yet they are grounded far more in one man's prejudices and fantasies than in the historical context we associate with the former. In certain ways they share some of the future war imagery of the twenties and thirties that would stir thinking about spies, yet their apocalyptic vision is again idiosyncratic, approximating more the yellow-peril fears roused by Japanese victories in the Russo-Japanese War[35] or later anti-Bolshevik literature than the visceral fears of a war that would strike behind lines and exterminate millions. As a genre they extend well beyond prewar spy concerns, yet they also anticipate little in the format of postwar spy novels; their combination of adventure and espionage differs from the connection between the two that would follow the war.

They are, in effect, largely identifiable for their strands of late-nineteenth-century right-wing imagery about imperial rivals and dangers and enemies at home. Yet it can be said that in this respect they conform in one way to the essentials about prewar spy writing: they situate the spy almost entirely in a context of alarmism and political demonology, particularly that of the nationalist right. The xenophobia of Danrit runs like a thread through the literature on espionage before the war. Daudet's anti-Semitism and novels like *The Yellow Invasion* were its most blatant form, but it appeared as well in the constant references to German agents lurking among German nationals in France. The conjecture of Schreiber's neighbors, the inner demons that eructed a letter on a million spies outside Toulouse, were simply another manifestation of these sentiments.[36]

Foreign revolutionaries, foreign terrorists, and the agents of foreign secret police invited further concerns. Their intrigues resulted in a series of "affairs," including discoveries of German police spies among socialist circles in Geneva and Zurich (the Haupt affair of late 1888); disclosures and arrests of Russian terrorists in Paris following bombing experiments in woods outside the capital (the Russian bomb affair of spring 1890); the assassination of a Russian general in his hotel room in Paris (the Padlevskii-Seliverstov affair of late 1890); the identification of the Russian terrorist and police agent Azef in 1909; and then the unmasking of a high Okhrana (or Russian secret police) official as a former agent provocateur working in Paris (the Landesen-Harting affair of 1909). The Haupt affair produced lists of secret agents in London and Paris, revelations of cases of dynamite to be planted on revolutionaries, and speculation that the Berlin police director, Krüger, had conspired with Russian revolutionaries in Switzerland to assassinate the czar, although there is no hard evidence to confirm this last charge. Out of the Padlevskii and Azef affairs came stories of dramatic escapes and multiple personalities. With the unmasking of Landesen came the startling revelation that the Russian bomb affair of nearly twenty years earlier had been, in part, a Russian secret police sting mounted by the then Okhrana police chief in Paris, Rachkovskii.[37]

Not surprisingly the affairs were turned into Paris press sensations, previewing in certain ways the splashy coverage of refugee intrigues in the 1930s.[38] But they also focused attention on foreign revolutionaries as troublemakers or on the penetration of repressive secret police organizations into France and thus became a subject for attacks from both Right and Left, again elevating discussion of spies and secret agents to the level of foreign threat and political nemesis. They were also troubling matters for the French police to whom the presence of foreign police agents on French soil was neither unknown nor entirely unwelcome. The menace of anarchist attacks, inflated fears of revolution, and the concern that terrorism might jeopardize Franco-Russian relations all provided the authorities with reason enough to keep tabs on militants from abroad. Their tracking was extensive, yet it consistently revealed international liaisons—anarchists and other revolutionaries on the move from one city to another; relations between militants in France and militants in London, Barcelona, Milan, Switzerland—that required international cooperation among police officials and reciprocity for foreign police missions.[39] Moreover the police had no illusions about their ability to penetrate Italian and Spanish anarchist circles or the community of Russian émigrés. Foreign police operating in France with a stable of agents (preferably a small stable) could do things French police simply could not do on their own. An international conference held in Rome in 1898 to address the wave of anarchist terror paved the way for formal international police cooperation, although in reality this conference simply ratified and encouraged expansion of police liaisons already underway.[40]

With these ties came serious liabilities. Relations with the Russian police appear to have been especially close,[41] but required tolerance of the counterterrorism of Rachkovskii and his successors (which included a bombing at an anti-czarist rally in 1905 that French police traced to the Okhrana). The Harting revelations of 1909 were an embarrassment for French and Russians alike. The press follow-up and then a parliamentary inquest forced the government to shut down its quasi-official (if not all unofficial) connections with the Russian police, while the latter in turn was obliged to shift its operation to a private detective agency, albeit one directed by an old Okhrana agent.[42] One wonders just how extensive the Okhrana operation was abroad. A police report from 1901 refers to a "great number of agents," and at the time of the Harting disclosures an ex-agent provided the press with a list of fifteen Paris operatives. These included former French, German, and Scotland Yard policemen. After the revolution, former Okhrana officials reduced to writing their memoirs argued that only a handful of agents had been stationed abroad, occasionally supplemented by flying squads out of Moscow and St. Petersburg. And yet the files of the Paris Okhrana office, which was the hub of Russian police operations in Europe, fill 216 boxes. These currently reside at the Hoover Institution and await their historian.[43]

A still greater liability was espionage. The Italian police were so brazen in this regard that the flabbergasted French turned to words like "bizarre" and "enigma" to describe their persistent and contemptuously open assault on French secrets. Italian commissars came across the border, presented credentials, talked of coordination in the war on anarchism, and then proceeded to travel to Toulon or along the Alpine frontier. They recruited spies from among the Italian community and placed French intelligence agents under surveillance. More often than not the anarchists they claimed to be tracking were their own secret agents. The French kept forcing their recall and the Italians obliged, dispatching replacements who differed only in their skill or their discretion in carrying out the same old assignment. Some were quite good at their work and lasted a long time. Others were imbeciles like the Ventimiglia policeman who began and ended his career with the arrest and twenty-seven-day sequestration of an innocent Frenchman on charges of espionage. Compounding the problem was the presence of irredentist societies working the Italian community in the Alpes-Maritimes. Consular support of these activities was no less flagrant than the intrigues of the Italian police.[44]

These episodes with foreigners and foreign police anticipated the large role refugees and secret police would play in the intrigues of the twenties and thirties, but they also remind one that espionage was occasionally a very real matter for French security officials before the war. The latter point would be superfluous were it not for the fact that French authorities were no less prone than the Lanoirs or Captain Rou-

tier to look for spies under nearly every foreigner's bed. Foreign governments admittedly were running agents in France, and at times the
French found them out. The names that surfaced with the Haupt disclosures were already known to the French police and were linked to a
ring of press correspondents suspected by the French of spying for the
Germans. The ringleader was a man named Beckmann who had had a
long and jaded career in France and whom the police identified as Bismarck's personal operative. In report after report from 1887 to 1890
the police traced lines that led back to Beckmann. They were convinced
that he recruited his agents among indigent Germans in Paris who were
given his name by the German embassy. They also traced agent recruitment to Consul General Beckmann in Geneva, the elder brother of the
Beckmann in Paris. How much truth lay in these reports we can only
guess, but it is likely the French were on the right track.[45]

They may also have had a good hunch about Commandant de Mendigorria, the Spanish military attaché who associated with the von
Schwarzkoppen from the Dreyfus affair and whose fortune was too
small to place him beyond suspicion. The spy rumors that swirled about
his mistress, an Australian adventuress, may have only been rough-
minded conjecture. But there was reason to question a voyage her lover
was making to Switzerland. De Mendigorria said he was going simply
to conduct an official study. The French suspected, however, an errand
for Schwarzkoppen that would take the Spaniard on a tour of their border defenses between Toul and Pontarlier or, as a report on the case
read: "At the Spanish embassy it is said that his absence will last three
months, and none of the military or civilian attachés believe that Commandant de Mendigorria is going to study the Swiss army. They all put
on a sniggering smile when they speak of this mission."[46] The police
were also probably right about a man named Kannengieser who was
constantly seen around French military installations or talking to French
soldiers. His expenses were high, his income was low, and he frequently
was paid in German currency. A number of incriminating photographs
were found in his possession. The French slapped Kannengieser into
prison for a year, fined him a thousand francs, and banned him from
France for ten years.[47]

There are still other cases that the French police cracked. But the tone
of their records lies elsewhere, in the extravagance and spy mania we
have seen in the spy writers. The police too accepted the Stieber myth—
"We are convinced that among the personnel constituting family mes-
sengers, valets, *la haute domesticité* can be found the same German espio-

nage as before the war"—and they accepted its embellishments—"In every tiny village along the Franco-Belgian border, there was [after 1873] on the Belgian side an agent, artisan, rentier, or policeman who received information from similar agents in France."[48] A report from 1882 in this regard is instructive. Information comes in that the German government has recently dispatched a large number of secret agents to Paris to scrutinize public opinion and governmental policy in France. A police report is requested. The official who responds says that he cannot confirm this intelligence and quite sensibly proceeds to elucidate the difficulties in uncovering German agents among the large German population in Paris: there simply are not enough police to put every German in the capital under surveillance. For once the reader of these files appears to have tapped a vein of rationality in the bedrock of hyperbole. But the official continues. There is no need, he reports, for the Germans to dispatch agents. There are already in Paris nearly a hundred thousand Germans, well placed in industry, in commerce, and all devoted to their country and government. Their correspondence home certainly provides the German authorities with all the information they can use on public opinion in France. Moreover, he notes, all these Germans, like their fellow countrymen in eastern France, are in the army reserve and, in the event of war, will serve as scouts for their troops "just as happened in 1870." "Our eastern region," he concludes, "is, in a manner of speaking, occupied by the German army."[49] The vein crumbles, revealing more bedrock underneath.

To the authorities' credit, they did exonerate a good number of suspects. Not everyone shared the fate of Schreiber. Throughout the seventies and eighties and into the nineties, however, a large number of people were placed under surveillance or investigated as accusations rolled in from tipsters or police informants who seemed as disposed to spy hunting as the popular writers were.[50] Practically every German traveling in France fell under suspicion. One wonders how any private messages ever got through, so thick were the telegrams tracking the movements by rail of possible enemy agents. The commissioners on watch in the train stations displayed extraordinary talents for spotting German officers simply by looking at passengers. Thus, for example: "Signal for surveillance four German tourists claiming to be professors coming from Stuttgart via the Alps. . . . Three are thirty years old, the fourth older, wears glasses, bald, expansive forehead, officer's countenance"; or, "Signal the departure by the noon train from Bourg to Paris of a suspicious foreigner named Franz G. . . . He claims to be a commercial traveler, has as baggage a big black trunk with straw hat samples and he carries a suitcase in his hand."[51]

The same mentality that produced all this paper led to the creation of the notorious Carnet B: the lists of suspects or dangerous people who were to be arrested immediately upon a declaration of war. At the time of its inception in the late 1880s, the French authorities had in mind primarily German spies. One historian has shown how spy fright in the late eighties and early nineties was so intense among the officers in the statistical section of the Deuxième Bureau that plans were drawn up for the internment of nearly one hundred thousand foreigners at the outbreak of hostilities.[52]

There is a strange thinning in the documentation on espionage following the turn of the century, surprisingly so since these were the years when German intelligence was funneling more agents into France and when war clouds grew darker and darker. One explanation for this narrowing of the paper trail would be the growing attention devoted to socialism. We know, for example, that the Carnet B underwent a radical transformation in the last years before the war, shifting its focus to antimilitarist French workers who, authorities feared, would sabotage mobilization. Yet the listing of espionage suspects remained heavy in the eastern departments and the total number of "spies" to be arrested in 1914 was 710, certainly far greater than the number of enemy agents operating in France.[53] Military authorities continued to plan for the forced movement and even the internment of foreigners[54] but did not believe they could list every secret agent. Obsession with spies followed from suspicions of who might be out there as well as the identification of known suspects. Spies who could be listed were less dangerous than spies who could not. More likely there are fewer records on espionage from these years because many no longer exist or are hidden away, a straightforward answer to a curious problem, but one that experience in working with espionage files suggests is correct.

Whatever the reason, public and authorities alike were bedeviled by visions of spies in the years after the Franco-Prussian War. No study of espionage in the twentieth century can neglect this fact. Inevitably to understand why this was so one turns back to the war itself, to French defeat but also to the coming of modern warfare fought with mass armies between two nations. It is the latter as much as the former that explains the enduring popularity of the Stieber legend and its permutations over time. Clearly the Franco-Prussian War inflicted deep wounds on French honor and an unabating sense of vulnerability that forced an exorcism through stories of spies. But the Franco-Prussian War, misleading as certain of its signals turned out to be for the character of war in the twentieth century, nevertheless introduced Europeans to a new level of warfare where complex maneuvering of great armies by rail, a collision of nations, and the prospect that defeat would beget revolution became the dominant factors. The war demonstrated the critical importance of mobilization and hence the necessity of unhindered rail traffic in the first days of fighting between two vast military machines. As it evolved into a fight between French and Germans, it ushered in an era of national competitiveness and assured that the next war would again be a war of peoples and nations. And with defeat for the French came revolution and the bloody civil war of the commune.

Harbored within such modern-war verities were multifarious compartments for secret-agent phantoms and all sorts of reasons for conjuring up spies. As warfare became more technologically complex, weak spots multiplied and vulnerability intensified. Secret agents who blew bridges or sabotaged switching stations could have a crippling impact on every stage of the fighting. Moreover national identities and fears of revolution now raised the stakes of war considerably, producing a comparable escalation in the fear that a single turning point—a secret plan stolen, a railroad delayed, an army corps steered through enemy territory—could decide everything. Spies now held in their hands not only the fate of armies, but also of nations and, worse, social classes.

Such fears projected well beyond 1870 primarily for three reasons. First, nationally conscripted armies enlarged the size of fighting forces and the need to coordinate their deployment through sophisticated command of vital rail and communication networks. Second, the Third Republic, for political and economic reasons, created through its schooling and road building programs a more tightly knit national community than ever before and thus, despite the persistence of deep ideological differences, magnified or reinforced national identities. Third, the rise of organized socialist parties, allied to beliefs that war could be the midwife of revolution,[55] focused energies, particularly on the Right, on internal subversive forces with international connections. Fear of spies blended in with fears of revolutionaries who could destroy France from within. Both had transnational loyalties, both were effective in time of war, and both operated behind military lines.

In combination the latter two factors—national identities and preoccupation with subversives—could be especially potent for imagining spies. One consequence was that older strains of conspiratorial thinking, the plot mentality of revolutionary politics or the nightmare of guillotines stashed away in cellars,[56] projected into international conspiracies of the Stieber variety or took the form of German manipulation of the workers' movement.[57] At a more nefarious level it could lead to the conflation of alien identities with potential secret agents. A spy, of course, in the thinking of certain polemical minds, could be anything at all — a sign of republican corruption or Semitic perfidy — because the figure of the spy remained the symbol of treachery. Here too the evolution of warfare into a collision of nations turned people to thinking about spies as a way of expressing their hatred of a people who had defeated them once, against whom they sought vengeance, and yet whom they continued to fear.

This element of hatred cannot be minimized. It seeps through in the images of a France infested and betrayed by a people who fought without honor, or perhaps even more, in the desire to reduce to underhanded advantages the very real strength possessed by the Germans. This hatred took many shapes: the anti-Semitism of Daudet and of many participants in the Dreyfus affair, the omnipresent racism of Danrit, the general public's readiness to espy German agents within the workers' movement; but most often it was simply hatred of the enemy and especially of Germans. In this the French had no monopoly. Hatred and vulnerability could be close companions in the decades leading up to the First World War, spy mania one of their waste products. British jitters produced yet another scare literature in these years as fear of German invasion by sea combined with a hunt for spies from within. What stands out, again, is how closely allied the secret agent had become with the perception of how wars would be fought by the turn of the century.

It is possible to discern something else in the repeated return to 1870 and the fantastic tales of German espionage. The Franco-Prussian War may not, in reality, have been a war of spies, but it was, on the German side, a war of methodical staff work and planning, a lesson lost on few people. After 1870 the French acknowledged that war in the future would be more systematized than before, and this turn to method and organization implied a wider role for intelligence gathering and an institutionalization of intelligence services. The next war, in 1904, continued to drive home both perception and fact. From the Russo-Japanese War have come sources suggesting that the Japanese organized espionage and sabotage rings behind Russian lines in Manchuria and that they opened liaisons with Russian revolutionary parties and nationalist movements, having laid the groundwork for these ties several years in advance.[58] We will probably never know the extent to which espionage figured in the Russo-Japanese War, whether it was widespread or simply insignificant, nor even how much real knowledge of operations filtered through to the European public. But the war served up another full plate of spy stories and another vision of powerful espionage services even if, in the French version, these depicted the Japanese mastery of German spy methods.[59] Again the identification between planning, intelligence, and victory in contemporary war found affirmation.

Such an identification could be one more stimulus for frenzied spy hunting, but it could also, in expert hands, be an argument for building up France's intelligence apparatus, which had been virtually nonexistent in 1870. For some professionals Stieber was undoubtedly a useful symbol, his legend a gift to be worked and kept alive in order to promote methodical development of a French espionage system. The fine line between credulity and manipulation is difficult to draw and perhaps never existed. Both dimensions to spy thinking could inhabit a single psyche. Still the argument for greater French planning, predicated on the mythical German example, exists in prewar literature on espionage, particularly in those works written by military men. Lewal repeated the 1870 mythology, yet his two volumes were a serious manual on intelligence gathering in time of war. If by intelligence he meant principally tactical reconnaissance in the field, he also argued that effective action by a modern army required satisfactory information that derived only from methodical, systematic preparation in peacetime. "To receive information, it is necessary to know in advance how to obtain it, which procedures to use, which agents to resort to, what their training should be. What matters is to have a method, and especially a well organized service." Agents abroad, Lewal insisted, must be implanted well ahead of hostilities. This the Germans had understood before 1870, and it had given them an edge. Writing his own manual some twenty-five years later, a lieutenant colonel who had served in French intelligence returned to the same critical point. Functional espionage networks in wartime were established in peacetime. They could not be improvised in a moment of need, "as one tried to do, on the French side, in July 1870."[60]

After 1870 the French army did take measures to improve military intelligence, which was not a difficult task to carry out since on the eve of the Franco-Prussian War the army maintained not a single agent in Germany.[61] Shortly following the war a statistical and reconnaissance section in the War Ministry was created for espionage purposes, eventually to evolve into the intelligence section (*section de renseignement,* or SR) of the Deuxième Bureau. Meanwhile intelligence work, especially counterespionage, was assigned to the Préfecture de police in Paris and the Sûreté générale, although jurisdictions were never clearly defined. Even the Quai d'Orsay occasionally ran its own agents on an ad hoc or part-time footing.[62] We have already discussed the zeal with which the police discharged their duties. Documentation from the Deuxième Bureau is unfortunately sparser.[63] One historian records that by 1880 the SR was stationing agents in Leipzig, Frankfurt, Cologne, Berlin, Vienna, Dresden, and Mannheim, and obtaining good information from them. Another describes chaos within the SR, a service so encrusted in intrigue and so slovenly in its practice that it could not distinguish real evidence from the false reports it itself was manufacturing. Whichever was true, the Dreyfus affair of the 1890s represented a nadir in French intelligence history, the failures of 1870 notwithstanding. When the dust cleared, the SR was reorganized and counterespionage made the preserve of the Sûreté.[64]

In the decades before the war French intelligence turned in a creditable, if mixed, record. There were substantial French leads in cryptography, although these were squandered in interservice rivalries and political squabbles. There were occasional coups such as the Vengeur documents that outlined the von Schlieffen plan and fell into French hands, although some historians question this story and in any event French intelligence had little to do with obtaining the material. If analysis of German intentions was occasionally cloudy and even contradictory, the SR produced sufficient information to foresee both the use of reserves and the strike through Belgium. Failure to plan accordingly must be allocated to Joseph Joffre and his generals, not to the Deuxième Bureau.[65]

At an operational level the SR displayed occasional sophistication, but its shoestring organization belied the claims of Nicolai and Gempp. Through Danzas and Co., a freight forwarding firm headquartered in Basel with a branch in Mannheim, the SR ran a courier service to its agents in Germany. Later it sent correspondence via a firm located on rue Bréa and through small business clients in Germany. Some of the latter provided cover addresses for information sources in Munich, Cologne, Frankfurt, and Berlin. The German police eventually closed in on each letter network, only to discover among the French correspondents a district commander on the western border, two noncommissioned officers in Stuttgart and Mannheim, and an artillery sergeant in

Koblenz.[66] Just before the First World War French intelligence maintained stations in Belfort, Nancy, and Mézières directed against Germany and stations in Nice and Grenoble directed against Italy.[67] The central office in Paris was manned by four officers assisted by a civilian clerk and a retired Republican guard who doubled as photographer and orderly. When Captain Andlauer was posted to the Belfort station in spring of 1913, his assistants numbered two: a lieutenant and a retired gendarme. There was no secretary. The mission was quartered in a single room so obviously situated that no agent could visit without the risk of exposure (by the following year Andlauer had moved to more favorable accommodations). Special commissioners in the Sûreté were to collaborate with Andlauer, but most concentrated their efforts on political intelligence for their prefects. The local military commander regarded the captain as a thirty-sixth-rate chargé d'affaires. The embassy in Switzerland was no help at all. Andlauer's monthly budget was twenty-five hundred francs. Despite these constraints Andlauer managed to organize a respectable network that could operate in wartime and assure communications. As of July 1914 he had also recruited and equipped several "*destructions*," although it is not clear whether this referred to the blowing up of bridges in case of retreat or the dispatch of saboteurs behind enemy lines.[68] Thus by war's eve French intelligence had come some distance from the sorry days of 1870. Greater method, but also spy fright, nurtured the build-up of an espionage service, as they did elsewhere.[69] But progress was spotty and financial support chintzy, and people like Lewal and Rollin had had reason to push for all they could get.

This, then, was the espionage world for the French before the Great War. Looking back from the interwar years one is struck by the antecedents, the prefiguring of what would come later, and yet the sense of being still a spy world away. Practically everything one stumbles across in the interwar period — sabotage and subversion, refugee intrigues, foreign police operations, espionage in Africa and Asia, an ominous spy presence, even gas and germ warfare[70] — turns up in the files or literature on espionage before 1914. But it is rudimentary and single-dimensional compared to espionage after the war. Thus in 1908 Lieutenant Colonel Rollin writes that espionage techniques of the past are outdated, that railroads, wirelesses, telephones, automobiles, balloons, dirigibles, "perhaps television tomorrow," have revolutionized the way intelligence services will operate in the future.[71] Yet the methods and practices he describes say little about these revolutionary techniques, almost nothing about the real changes to come, and read curiously like espionage in the past. One writes about sabotage but only occasionally, plans sabotage missions but only in the most preliminary way. There are colorful characters, some lively espionage rings, particularly in Eastern Europe where minority populations and disputed frontiers create special opportunities and incentives for intrigue.[72] But there are no Battitis, nothing of the cast that will haunt counterespionage files after the war. Abroad there are flashes of global concerns. Moroccan intrigues produce a fair amount of paper. The Russo-Japanese War gives way to visions of Japanese spies throughout Asia. Just before the First World War the governor general in Indochina reports on an Asian-wide revolutionary movement. A few years earlier, the police report on the terrorist Safranskii and his ties to Hindu nationalists. There is the German chart from 1914 that plans wartime intelligence stations in New York, Buenos Aires, and Tokyo. An undated but post-1914 French colonial report traces German financing of Indochinese nationalists back to 1912. There is also the Great Game on the frontiers of India and indications of comparable stratagems spreading to the Middle East in the years right before the war. But all this activity forms a paltry record when likened to postwar global intrigues. Even the international content is muted alongside the postwar European circuits.[73]

Most of all, in thinking comparatively, one recognizes the hard edge to the earlier literature. It is alarmist and mean spirited and concentrates in the figure of the spy, who before the war was repeatedly characterized as evil and dishonorable. The imagery was inseparable from the wider belief that Germany was the superior spy nation because her people were natural spies, untroubled by the dirty, criminal side to espionage whereas France contained a people of standards and honor. French spies were neither unknown nor uncelebrated, but a character in a novel who was French and a spy owed the combination to reasons that were accidental, temporary, or excused by exigencies. Despite the advocation of peacetime intelligence there remained an ambivalence about spying or the impression of arguing a minority case, facts of life imprinted on the Andlauers from personal experience.[74] That imagery would not disappear after 1918, but it would no longer dominate either. After the war the spy would be a more absorbing, multidimensional figure and the literature of espionage would draw on far more than fear and hatred. Here especially is where the divide can be charted. Before the war there was alarmism aplenty, but, with the exception of a few sensational affairs, practically nothing else to the espionage scene. Following the war this would change, as espionage became a more complex, more sophisticated subject for the French. For spying, as for nearly everything else, the Great War separated one era from another.

Where the prewar years contemplated, projected, the war years created, acted. The result was a very different spy world in the twenties and thirties from what the spy masters and spy writers had known before 1914. Changing context in part explained those differences. The intrigues of Communists, fascists, or refugees like the White Russians introduced an ideological context, a method, and a scale that were absent from espionage before the war. The richness of postwar espionage derived largely from the opportunities for intrigue — war in Spain or in China, for instance, or the transient quality to postwar settlements — and from the assortment of individuals that floated about after the war. Because the postwar actors, organizations, and occasions that defined interwar espionage were themselves largely creations of this war, the war experience could be seen to account for what changed with the twenties and thirties.

Yet it was also the war's power to propel imagination into action and reality that explains the shifts in espionage after 1918. Those shifts toward greater professionalism, greater globalism, and deeper perceptions of a behind-the-lines threat, or toward an interweaving of heroism, romanticism, adventure, and espionage that prevailed in the interwar years, all drew on the experience and facts of wartime intrigue. How the secret war was fought between 1914 and 1918 determined the grounds upon which it would be waged and perceived in the era that followed. It is necessary, therefore, to examine the wartime intelligence record, looking at how wartime espionage was conducted, what it attempted, what it achieved, and what was beyond its reach. Throughout the following account two themes will predominate. First, the scale of the war led to a prodigious broadening of the size and scope of wartime espionage organizations, operations, and methodology. Second, the total and global character of the war generated a covert war that extended beyond intelligence gathering to sabotage and subversion and spread its operations all over the world. Once set in motion, these features would not disappear when the war itself came to a close.

All intelligence services grew substantially with the war. Three dozen officers worked in Austrian intelligence in 1914, several hundred by the war's end. Altogether several thousand men passed through the service in the course of four years.[75] Even these numbers did not encompass the full range of intelligence gathering on the Austrian front. In 1916 an Austrian station operating out of Bucharest with agents in Iasi and Galati and individual observers along the Prut kept a careful watch upon Romanian troop deployments and Russian reinforcements. Their information was good, yet more complete intelligence required radio intercepts and intelligence exchanges with the Germans and Bulgarians. Counterespionage broke cases with comparable coordination, for example, the Jorga-Firmian affair, which involved the Romanian military attaché, a Romanian student (Jorga), a count (Lattenzio Firmian) and his accomplices Benuzzi and Rensi, Benuzzi's mistress, the Spanish ambassador and the Italian admiralty, and which was cracked only with the help of the German IIIb, the Austrian attachés in Madrid and Berne, and the consul general in Zurich.[76]

The size and complexity of Austrian operations were the rule rather than the exception. Thousands of people worked in German intelligence during the war. One IIIb station, Antwerp, was running over a hundred agents in early 1916. MI5, British counterespionage, began the war with a staff of nineteen. By war's end the staff numbered nearly eight hundred fifty. Dozens decoded radio intercepts. The number of British agents on the continent, if one includes Belgians and Dutch, ran into the thousands.[77] There are no statistics for the French, but there is no reason to assume that the numbers varied significantly from those for the Austrians, Germans, or British. Shortly into the war French intelligence subdivided into six sections: the SR, centralization, postal and telegraphic control, economics, an interallied bureau (for coordination among the British, French, and Belgians), and aerial propaganda. The Sûreté continued to conduct counterespionage operations, although now in liaison with the military's own counterespionage service. Intelligence operations were replicated in the field. Everywhere in Europe there was considerable expansion. Even the reports inflated numbers, like the 1917 wire from the attaché in Petrograd that 170 Greek spies had departed Berlin for the Macedonian front.[78]

The SR men on the spot must have felt as if they had rolled through a time warp. Before the war Andlauer had painfully scraped together a network of informants. Slowly, cautiously, as he told it, he would collect a name. Slowly, cautiously, he would negotiate a rendezvous, generally in Switzerland. Once face to face with the informant he would put his cards on the table, receive a sardonic smile along with a refusal, or perhaps a request for several days' reflection, but then no sign of life. Only one out of ten accepted an assignment, a poor success rate for so much trouble and time. With the coming of war, Andlauer had more volunteers — primarily Alsatians — than he could use. His station expanded in functions as well as in numbers. A separate *bureau d'exploitation,* housed in a separate building, sifted through mountains of information about German military movements. When material was verified it was coordinated with the British to compile an enemy order of battle.[79]

To get information the spy masters turned to every human and mechanical means they could think of. The key was to identify how and where the enemy was deploying its divisions. All sides used radio intercepts with varying degrees of effectiveness. The Germans and Austrians planned tactical, even strategical, moves with the information they culled from Russian transmissions. Tannenberg was the classic example of what could be accomplished when an army was stupid enough to broadcast *en clair,* but even when the Russians resorted to code their enemies could determine certain troop movements. The French, who had developed considerable mastery in cryptography before the war, broke German codes with greater success than the Germans experienced in deciphering French ones. Room 40 in the British admiralty was celebrated for its cracking of German naval transmissions, but a large team of military code breakers on the continent made only limited contributions.[80] More directly the spies took to the air to reconnoiter behind enemy lines. Pilots became famous for their gladiatorial combats in a war that crunched human beings in the millions, but the real role of the fighters was to clear the skies for the scouts.[81]

On the ground, methods ranged from mundane to daring. The thousands of interrogations of prisoners of war were tedious, although they could yield valuable information on the positioning of troops. Andlauer's exploitation bureau meticulously scanned official German publications for details on promotions or courts-martial, for example, where a recent court-martial had been held, from what division its officers were drawn, or what unit the accused had belonged to. Jean Tillet, who worked with French intelligence, said there was really nothing difficult about getting information. All a spy had to do was to sit down in a café behind the front and watch and listen to the men who passed by.[82] The problem was how to get agents behind the lines. The best way was to recruit people who were already there, a technique that favored the Allies since the Germans fought the war on occupied territory. Both the French and British organized networks of civilians to watch German train movements. Like most espionage, the work required high levels of discretion and diligence. At one post a family watched trains day and night through a curtain, alternating shifts and keeping count with various kinds of food, for example, beans for soldiers and coffee for guns. The work was monotonous and terribly risky. A French network based in Liège was betrayed to the Germans in 1915, and two years later treachery and chain arrests all but erased a British-run operation. Altogether, several thousand civilians watched trains for the British and the French, the majority of the agents working for the British in occupied Belgium. One British network, the Dame blanche, numbered over nine hundred agents by the end of the war.[83] At Belfort Andlauer had great success recruiting Alsatians. Perhaps his best find was the agent Carlos, who supervised alcohol shipments to German headquarters on the western front. The position ideally situated Carlos for identifying troop emplacements at any given moment. Using his mistress as his courier, Carlos sent messages to a pharmacist named Zugmeyer in Basel who communicated the intelligence to Belfort station.[84]

How many agents were landed by air behind enemy lines remains a mystery. As early as 1915 French intelligence reported on sending in agents by airplane, but there is no way to tell if these were proposals or summaries of landings actually carried out. Colonel Nicolai of IIIb insisted that French agents, including Alsatian deserters, came in by air. The Alsatians wore German uniforms under their clothing, discarded their outer garments upon landing, and blended in among German army formations. The French wore civilian clothes and French uniforms underneath in the event they were threatened with capture. The difficulty in reading Nicolai's memoirs is knowing when he is telling the truth. Some tall tales are easy to spot, some stories are credible. The above seems borderline. The Englishman George Hill claimed to have landed agents behind lines on the Balkan front. His adventures suggest this was not a routine operation. One Serbian agent took him to a landing site covered with boulders. Another, a Greek, was so terrified once they took to the air that he collapsed in the plane upon landing and had to be flown directly back to base. Hill's greatest fear was that his propeller would stop turning as he brought the plane to a halt and that he would have to get out and restart it in a hurry, perhaps slicing himself into human julienne. Once he was forced to perform this maneuver and deftly turned it over to the man he was trying to land. The man, trying and trying to no avail, succeeded in getting the engine going just as a patrol appeared upon the scene. Unfortunately Hill too was known to stretch the truth on occasion.[85]

Another problem surfaces here. Spies were accustomed to lying through their teeth, and heads of intelligence services could bamboozle with the best of them. Colonel Paul Ignatiev, a Russian intelligence liaison stationed in Paris, said he purchased the services of an Italian "commercial" organization that fed him data on troop movements in Austria-Hungary and Germany. Ignatiev's contact was a man called Frantchesko, but the real boss was a little old man in Milan. Once Ignatiev met the old man who said he had people all over the world, none of whom would dare to betray him. "As he said these words a flash of cold cruelty passed over the old man's face, and I avoided his glance so as not to show him that I had understood."[86] Perhaps this was true, but it has the feel of the storytelling that pervaded espionage literature in the interwar years. Very little that these men said could be taken at face value, a difficulty not only for future historians but for the spy masters themselves as they sought to weed out the true from the false. Counts of trains could probably render accurate information if the agents were meticulous, but intelligence from other sources might just as easily be disinformation. The French constantly attempted to plant phony intelligence on the Germans. They fed false reports into Switzerland knowing these would be picked up by Swiss intelligence and probably passed on to the German military attaché who had a close working relationship with the Swiss general staff. They also baited known German operatives with counterfeit intelligence that was carefully coordinated with details the French were feeding in elsewhere. German military attachés appear to have been easy marks. The one in Bucharest recruited an employee in the Russian embassy to identify Russian disinformation, unaware that his man worked for Russian intelligence. Overall none of this activity seems to have made any difference. More often than not Russian efforts to mislead the Germans merely betrayed their real intention. Still all sides kept trying. All used double agents, and all funneled in false information through prisoners of war.[87] The spy world was enshrouded in a mist of half-truths and deception that remained with it once the shooting was over.

To get information out agents concealed data in fountain pens, shoe polish tins, cakes of soap, overcoat buttons, coins, oranges, or behind postage stamps. They corresponded via classifieds in the newspapers or used the spy's old standby, invisible ink. IIIb's agents carried with them a handkerchief or a pair of socks soaked in special liquid. When the time came to send a message they immersed the handkerchief in water (preferably rainwater), let it sit three to four minutes to form the ink, and then squeezed the contents into a receptacle. Then they ran a moistened sponge over glossed paper to remove the glaze and waited for it to dry naturally. Once ready to write, they transcribed their message, using regular ink on the first and third pages, invisible ink on pages two and four. The French, however, were on to this method by the end of 1915. British scientists discovered that the least detectable kind of invisible ink could be made from semen, which, one might assume, would solve the problem of carrying incriminating evidence on one's person, with certain age and gender limitations. Another advantage was that an inexhaustible supply was always at hand. But the technique was not recommended to agents in the field.[88]

There was the other ageless standby, the code, so multifarious in its possibilities that one example will suffice. In 1915 von Krohn, the German naval attaché in Madrid and a man much given to playing at espionage (one cannot credit his projects with a more mature verb), dispatched Carlos de Heredia Bentabol to Marseilles and Toulon to identify targets for German torpedoes. Heredia was to correspond via telegram or the post, identifying destination with letters — for instance, *T* for Turkey, *E* for Egypt — and boats by proper names beginning with vowels — for instance, Edward signified two English ships, Emile two French ships. There were also codes for cargoes, for example, a proper name beginning with a consonant signaled numbers of troops on board. Thus a telegram reading "Otto sick requests Hamilton to join him at Toledo. He will leave the 27th. Heredia" translated into "Four English ships (*Otto*) carrying six thousand men (*Hamilton*), cannons and munitions (*Heredia*) leaves the 27th for the Dardanelles (*Toledo*)." This not terribly ingenious code was known to the French by October 1915.[89]

Perhaps the most widely used means of communication was the carrier pigeon, which performed the same function as the portable radio in the Second World War. Pigeons were used on all fronts because they could return messages ten to twenty times faster than humans stealing across guarded frontiers. It was dangerous to be caught behind lines with pigeons, and even more dangerous to attempt to smuggle them in to train watchers and agents. The Allies overcame the latter difficulty by devising contraptions for infiltrating the birds via parachute. There was always a tinge of the farcical connected with the pigeons. For some reason pigeon folklore tended to degenerate into stories about parrots. It was said that one spy had painted a pigeon in bright colors to resemble a parrot on the premise that troops who fired at carrier pigeons would pay less attention to a parrot flying across Belgium. Christopher Andrew recounts how a British general was informed that carrier pigeons had been crossbred with parrots to produce a super-pigeon capable of delivering oral reports. The French tended toward bathos, bestowing the croix de guerre upon one pigeon and building a monument to other pigeon heroes. There was, however, something universal in that sentiment. General John Pershing awarded a Distinguished Service Cross to a carrier pigeon named Cher Ami who flew through heavy enemy fire and suffered severe wounds yet nonetheless made it home with word of an American battalion cut off by the Germans. In the 1930s the Japanese proclaimed pigeon 4237 "a model soldier" and buried it in a military cemetery with full honors for completing its mission despite a killer attack by a falcon. And from the Gulf War comes this news release:

Brits Cite Parakeets for War Bravery

Gibraltar (AP) — Six parakeets pressed into service aboard a British destroyer during the Gulf War received citations Monday for bravery.

British Forces spokesman Capt. Leo Callow said the six birds were received with honors at Shell Jetty by children from St. Georges School, who had lent them to the navy to detect chemical gas.

The birds, belonging to the Melopsittacus undulatus group, were recruited to serve on board the HMS Manchester as part of the ship's chemical detection system when it headed toward the Persian Gulf last January.

Actually the pigeons were worth the attention. Quick and reliable, they were indispensable to some of the train-watching circuits and saved courier lives in the process.[90]

Still some agents had to cross borders, and this was tricky business with wartime passport controls. Whereas the French had required passports only of Russians before the war, they now introduced strict, formal conditions for all foreigners wishing to enter French territory. Passports with officially stamped visas became mandatory as of August 1914.[91] Throughout Europe border controls tightened as lax procedures gave way to demands for formal papers in order. The spies countered with false papers fabricated by their intelligence services or procured through other means. Turkish agents traveled to Morocco with Greek and Italian passports. German agents posing as Greeks or Romanians acquired papers from the French representative in Buenos Aires. Neutral papers, clearly, were the most desirable. At Rotterdam the Germans purchased passports from a contact in the town hall for the price of one hundred pounds sterling each, and they replicated the stamp and signature of the Dutch consul in Barcelona to manufacture their own sham papers from Holland. In China they organized an operation to supply their agents with the necessary documents. Germans and Austrians stranded in the United States at the outbreak of war bought papers from unemployed seamen or drifters to make it back through the British blockade. Sometimes the Germans simply stole papers from neutrals traveling through their country. In Switzerland a Jewish gang sold bogus identity papers to all comers.[92]

As with codes, invisible ink, and carrier pigeons there was nothing new in the fabrication of false papers. Nonetheless, there was a stepping up of intensity whose tone and feel previewed the intrigues of the interwar years. The scale and technical proficiency with which bogus documents were manufactured in the First World War rang of the traffic in the twenties and thirties and had no precedents before 1914. After the war the controls remained, as did the use of counterfeit passports and visas whose demand was forced up by the appearance of large numbers of stateless people and the descent of still more frontier barriers. In the menacing, sinister quality to border crossings between the two wars ran undercurrents of intrigue not unlike those introduced by the wartime passage of clandestine agents.[93]

Thus one facet to espionage in the First World War was the sheer quantitative vault to a new level of action that all but mass-produced spies and tricks of the trade just as the war churned out men and material in every other theater of fighting. Yet another was the conversion of sabotage and subversion into routine forms of intelligence work. Very quickly the secret war turned into a war of covert operations. Demolition teams swung into action in Galicia, blew up bridges in the Balkans, worked their way up rail lines in the Carpathians, infiltrated behind lines in Belgium and France. Factories were dynamited, ships and depots set on fire. Agents traveled with incendiary bombs in the shape of pencils, or with the more sinister weapons of disease. The French warned against German plans to poison their horses, but they were scarcely lily-white. They too experimented with germ warfare or submitted plans to destroy the harvest in Hungary. Andlauer tells of an SR conference where his chief flourished anthrax and glanders tablets, prepared by the Pasteur Institute, before the assembled officers. A promised conference on typhoid never took place, but Andlauer found uses for the first series of germs. "Without boasting of extraordinary results, I can admit to having on my conscience several hundred piglets in the Frankfurt region and also some cattle that left Switzerland for Germany in perfect health but abruptly departed this life once over the border."[94]

Nothing, however, seems to compare with the sabotage organization—the S-Service—that the Germans operated out of Spain.[95] The direction was confided to the three principal agents in the Iberian peninsula—the ambassador Ratibor, the military attaché von Kalle, and the naval attaché von Krohn (replaced by Steffan in 1918)—but eventually the service was run through the cover of a brokerage firm based in Bilbao with branches in the major Spanish cities. The S-Service's schemes bordered on the fantastic, the products of fertile imaginations running feverish and sick. Von Krohn proposed dumping cholera germs into Portuguese rivers to force a border closing with Spain and to undermine Portuguese ties with the Allies. A Professor Kleine from the Cameroons said the plan could be easily executed with two glass tubes and gelatinized cultures (this same Kleine, incidentally, appears in a report from 1921 referring to a wartime project under his direction at the German hospital in Madrid to manufacture typhus bacilli for export to Salonika, Africa, and southern France; whether the report is true cannot be verified).[96] The scheme sounds typical of von Krohn, whose judgment ranged from poor to plain stupid and who compromised himself badly in a personal affair with a French double agent.[97] Berlin nixed the cholera proposal, but it gave the go-ahead for sabotage missions in France and Portugal including the destruction of ships, factories, and livestock. Cultures for contamination initially arrived from Berlin, but soon the S-Service was cultivating its own. An agent from Switzerland delivered explosive materials camouflaged in pencils and thermos bottles, while other materials traveled from Zurich via Italy hidden in toy chalets. Some factories were blown up in Lisbon, but the results in France were paltry compared to preparations and ambitions. Faulty materials thwarted one agent's efforts. Another reported great successes to Ratibor, but these were all fairy tales; the agent worked for French counterintelligence.

These adventures (and travesties) point to yet another facet of First World War intrigue: the importance of the periphery. The targets, of course, were the warring nations, but for obvious reasons the spies fought their war largely in places like Spain, Holland, Norway, and Switzerland. Spies could not operate with impunity in neutral countries, but they had far more room for maneuver there than behind enemy lines, and the presence of one nation's spies invited the dispatch of another's until intelligence and counterintelligence whorled into an elaborate, incestuous, self-sustaining enterprise. Moreover neutral countries were sources of supply or staging areas for transshipment, and these too drew spies as sugar draws flies. Much of the intrigue in Holland centered on German efforts to circumvent the blockade by importing blacklisted materials via Dutch middlemen operatives. German intelligence in Scandinavia worked behind fronts such as the International Agency (wholesalers) in Sweden and through agents like the industrialist S. and the merchant A., both based in Copenhagen, and Gertrude L., who worked as a typist for North Sea Packing in Stavanger. German saboteurs planted bombs in Narvik and were suspected of setting fires in factories and warehouses, including one in Trondheim that destroyed a considerable quantity of goods destined for Russia. In Spain, Ratibor and Co. worked the embassies and ministries for tidbits of military intelligence, and von Kalle built an espionage network centered on Bordeaux with agents operating in Paris, Le Havre, Cherbourg, Brest, Marseilles, and Toulon. His principal informer brought all sorts of interesting information fed him by French counterintelligence; he too was a French double agent.

As in Holland and Norway, the secret war in Spain focused on shipping. The Germans wanted information on the quantities and kinds of supplies coming in and particularly intelligence on shipping routes and patterns that they could send to their submarine commanders. The German admiralty instructed von Krohn to gather information on maritime traffic and cargoes throughout the Atlantic, and von Krohn responded by establishing a network of informers from Barcelona to Cádiz to Bilbao who reported ship cargoes and itineraries, convoy assembly points, and other data necessary for submarine warfare. In turn the French and British filtered agents into Spain to fight against the spies and to watch the submarines.[98]

The greatest of spy playgrounds was Switzerland. In the 1940s the Swiss liked to refer to themselves as a lifeboat. For the First World War the appropriate analogy would have been a luxury liner on a secret agent cruise. One can imagine how easily the simile could be extended: the public room encounters; nods in the corridors; exchanges at dinner or in the casino; intrigues — petty and grand — in the staterooms; a constant, underhanded flow of news, gossip, innuendo, and assignation; dirty work down below; a crew that steered, serviced, and supervised but intervened only in moments of exception. Such was Switzerland between 1914 and 1918. Shift the analogy slightly to one vast resort — suspects in reports are nearly always identified with the hotel they are staying in — and the picture is practically complete. The Italians called Lugano "Spyopolis," a city of Swiss, Slav, German, Russian, Italian,

Spanish, Dutch, Brazilian, and French spies. Ladoux of French counter-espionage, in one of his few credible passages, told a man he was sending into Switzerland:

There is where people the Allies consider undesirable, outlaw, [or] suspect take refuge. Some have always been traffickers. Others are only spectators at first. Or they are fine fellows with nothing to do. Now, the cost of living is high over there. Room costs are always going up. After several weeks refugees bereft of means are forced to earn money. The spy trade is there, it's tempting, just about the only job they can get except for another obvious one. Moreover the two trades go together. Charming and spying, that's what three out of ten — let's be modest — suspicious neutrals turn to.[99]

The assessment was not far off the mark. Mata Hari was the most celebrated of these kinds of spies (despite the fact that she did almost nothing in the war). But there were plenty of other *femmes galantes* whom French intelligence identified as suspects or prospects and who traveled or worked at some point in Switzerland. A sampling from one file produces Marguerite S., German-born, a singer calling herself Radhjah, a sometime French agent when she worked the Corso Theatre in Zurich; Marie M., who traveled to Switzerland to see her Austrian lover; Frida M., born in Hamburg but a French national, a dancer in several Geneva establishments, "signaled as a spy"; and Juliette T., a Swiss national, an *artiste,* who made suspicious trips across the border into France.[100]

A neutral country bordering on four belligerent states, a haven for exiles and draft dodgers, a spa for the rich and a retreat for the invalided, an exchange point for prisoners of war, a land of business and transshipment, a tryst for international lovers, Switzerland offered an unparalleled setting for wartime intrigue. The country was a contact point for information, a nexus from which spies were dispatched and to which spies returned with reports. It was a locale where nationals from belligerent states had legitimate reasons for congregating, thus making it a round-the-clock rumor mill and an ideal milieu for picking up stray pieces of intelligence. Spies all but tripped over one another in train compartments, in lobbies, or at dinner engagements. The scene has probably been fixed for all time in Somerset Maugham's Ashenden stories about a British spy in Switzerland during the war (Maugham himself worked in Switzerland for British intelligence):

While he waited for his dinner to be served, Ashenden cast his eyes over the company. Most of the persons gathered were old friends by sight. At that time

Geneva was a hot-bed of intrigue and its home was the hotel at which Ashenden was staying. There were Frenchmen there, Italians and Russians, Turks, Rumanians, Greeks, and Egyptians. Some had fled their country, some doubtless represented it. There was a Bulgarian, an agent of Ashenden, whom for greater safety he had never even spoken to in Geneva; he was dining that night with two fellow-countrymen and in a day or so, if he was not killed in the interval, might have a very interesting communication to make. Then there was a little German prostitute, with china-blue eyes and a doll-like face, who made frequent journeys along the lake and up to Berne, and in the exercise of her profession got little tidbits of information over which doubtless they pondered with deliberation in Berlin. She was of course of a different class from the baroness and hunted much easier game. But Ashenden was surprised to catch sight of Count von Holzminden and wondered what on earth he was doing there. This was the German agent in Vevey and he came over to Geneva only on occasion.[101]

The archives bear out the ambiance of the literature. French intelligence in Switzerland turned up people like the Greek Athanassiades who had run guns for the Turks in the Italo-Turk war and then an espionage service between Greece and Egypt for the German military attaché in Athens. Now he was in Geneva where he associated with a shady assortment of individuals. He was not, the SR noted, to be confused with another Athanassiades who resided in Lausanne and was equally suspected of espionage. The French also stumbled onto a German spy in Zurich named Willer and his associate, another German agent named Brigfeld, who had been born in Patras but was now living in Zurich where he was mixed up in Greek affairs. There was Alexandroff, a questionable Bulgarian, and a Colonel Bratsaloff, whose espionage organization sounds suspiciously like a private operation. Another report identified forty-two Turkish agents stationed in Switzerland in 1918.[102]

At a more prosaic level French agents tracked the movement of goods, watching for contraband imports to Germany via Switzerland.[103] Away from the hotels agents like Lacaze ran low-level yet dangerous operations that seeded informers throughout Switzerland and on into Germany. Relying largely on Alsatians like himself, Lacaze was able to set up a listening post in a modest hotel in Basel. Another operative, code-named Hubert, traveled to Germany on business trips. On his journeys Hubert jotted down a meticulous record of his affairs and expenses. Orders totaling 580 marks from Schmidt and Co., or room costs and tips at the Hotel Metropole in Stuttgart, were just that. But numbers regarding stamps, cards, and beer referred to troop units and their movement by train. Lacaze never gave his name or his address to his agents. He told them the time of day and the place for their next meeting and that he would send them a postcard reading simply, "Best wishes, Louise," whose date would be the day of the rendezvous. The agent was to arrive no sooner than five minutes before and no later than five minutes after the prescribed time. If the agent needed to see him in the interim, the agent was to take out an advertisement in a Swiss newspaper, for example, listing a kitchen stove for sale. Either Lacaze would come the next day or he would send his postcard with the date.[104]

As in Spain, the espionage war in Switzerland turned toward a war of covert operations. It was from Switzerland that explosives made their way to the peninsula and it was through Switzerland that Andlauer's agents struck at livestock for Germany. In the last year of the war authorities discovered a cache of munitions, grenades, and propaganda that had been brought in from Germany and transferred via the German consulate in Zurich to an Italian deserter. The conclusion of French counterespionage was that the German general staff was planning terrorist attacks in France and Italy through a secret terrorist operation it was organizing in Switzerland.[105] In the wake of German sabotage adventures in Spain and elsewhere, this was not that farfetched a perception.

In the end almost all the secret war on the periphery turned into a war of sabotage and subversion because that, ultimately, was what all peripheral strategy in the First World War was about: striking where the enemy was weakest, diverting his attention and forces, undermining his cohesion, and undercutting his sources of supply. As the conflict escalated into a global war expeditionary forces sailed to faraway places like Iraq, Egypt, and the Dardanelles, and fought sideshows in East Asia and eastern and southern Africa. However the weapons of choice in global strategy remained sabotage and subversion because these dangled before the eyes of the war makers the hope that a very few hands might yet pluck great ripe fruits from the tree of victory.

All sides fought a covert global war. The Allies produced the most celebrated subversive — T. E. Lawrence — so celebrated that other adventurer-spies would be reduced to the generic Lawrence epithet: the German Lawrence, the Japanese Lawrence.[106] Yet the easiest territory for the Allies to exploit was central and southern Europe, whereas they themselves, as the holders of empire, were most vulnerable to the subversive intrigues of their enemies. It was the Germans who had the greatest field of play and the wildest visions to match, although in the end they had precious little to show for their efforts.

In the Americas, German agents, often fighting competing covert wars with one another, occasionally operating on orders from Berlin (via the intermediary of Madrid station), more often than not marauders on the loose and running amok, hatched an unending series of grandiose schemes. They were going to sabotage American munitions factories and harbor facilities. They would place explosives on ships carrying supplies to Europe. Strikes would be fomented, the Panama Canal Zone would be sabotaged, the Tampico oil wells would be destroyed. They intrigued with Mexican generals to strike north against the Yankees and thus embroil the United States in a Mexican war, or they schemed to overthrow Venustiano Carranza and to replace him with generals or a dictator more compliant with the war needs of Germany. The Zimmermann telegram was merely one variation on a steady stream of German proposals to make use of Mexico in the global strategy of war. Still further south they planned to sabotage mining operations in Chile or to destroy livestock destined for Europe.

Some of these projects were actually executed. In 1916 German agents set fire to the Black Tom shipyard in New York and a factory in New Jersey. Another German agent named Jahnke, who had been a private detective and presumably an arms and drug trafficker in San Francisco before the war and who was one of the few German spies with the wits and skills to match his imagination, claimed to have destroyed several ships and a factory in Tacoma, Washington. Other agents smuggled bacteriological gelatins to a man named Arnold working in Latin America as a spy, propagandist, saboteur, and, apparently, specialist in germ warfare. In early 1918 Arnold reported that mule shipments to Mesopotamia had been "copiously worked," and that his sabotage of Argentine horse shipments to France had met with success. But these were mere drops in the bucket compared with what had been anticipated. Most projects never got off the ground either because the authorities in Berlin refused to send money or scrapped schemes as unfeasible or because most of the German agents were an incredible collection of blockheads who played right into the hands of their enemies. The Allies too, especially the Americans, ran their own covert war in Mexico. Practically all German agents were constantly under surveillance, and there is reason to believe that the British sabotaged a German radio station in Ixtapalapa, although the source, as usual, was anything but credible. Everyone, including Carranza, seems to have been running a network of agents.[107]

Elsewhere the Germans sought to raise North Africa against the French and British, Persia against the British and Russians, India against the British, and Indochina against the French. They and their Turkish allies promulgated a jihad, or Muslim holy war, as money, arms, and agents poured into Morocco. In Libya Turkish and German agents goaded the Senoussi to strike at Egypt's western border. A Turkish expeditionary force marched toward Suez, preceded by Turkish secret service guerrillas and supported by Turkish agents in Cairo, while German agents planned the sabotage of the canal and the raising of Egypt. On Christmas day 1914 the German explorer Leo Frobenius left Damascus for Abyssinia to fan an insurrection in the Sudan. Indian revolutionaries were wooed, promised support. As far away as Madrid von Kalle contemplated the dispatch of agitators to India. Two expeditions, under von Hentig and Niedermayer, set off across Persia to incite the Afghans to rush upon India's northwestern frontier. Another German agent, Wassmus, headed toward southern Persia to organize tribal harassment of the British. Still other agents, including members of the Afghanistan expeditions, prodded Persia toward war against the British and Russians, offering money, munitions, and officers as support for the enterprise. A sabotage team temporarily cut the oil pipeline in Persia and stood ready to seize or destroy the installation at Abadan. Meanwhile agents in Latin America dreamed of covert operations in China and provoking Japan against Britain, some indication of the way the war gulled imaginations into fantasizing strategies of worldwide subversion. More materially German intrigues and money came together with nationalist movements to stir up troubles in French Indochina.

As in the Americas, none of these projects amounted to much. There was to these vast enterprises a whimsical and improvised character that too often outstripped German resources. In the end the Germans had little more to offer than resourceful agents and vague promises of money, arms, and postwar restraint. Personal rivalries and shoddy planning supplanted method and organization. Quarrels rent the Afghanistan expeditions while authorities forwarded Niedermayer's baggage through the Balkans with the label Traveling Circus attached to the cases. They might as well have plastered the boxes with red stickers reading Espionage. The consignment was confiscated in Romania after a customs official opened a case and found a machine gun and bullet packets within. Bribes lubricated the passage of a second baggage shipment. The men on the spot like von Hentig and Niedermayer were capable of extraordinary exploits (and on the level of maneuver, if not that of grand politics, they consistently outwitted their adversaries and then their pursuers).[108] At the very least, however, the subversion of empires required a stronger military presence than either a handful of Germans or their Turkish ally could muster and greater coordination between German and Turkish policy in Asia. French, British, and Russian countermeasures were vigorous, a lesson not lost on the shah of Persia and the emir of Afghanistan who might have had little liking for the English but who understood power and the consequences that come with lost causes. In Indochina the nationalist movement was too weak and divided to be more than an annoyance. Ultimately German global intrigues mattered more for what they signified than for what they accomplished. They were ambitious, even at times ingenious; but they produced practically nothing in the way of concrete results.[109]

This could be the epitaph for all the spies who perished in the First World War. The secret war was fought in great numbers, all over the world, yet it cannot be said to have altered in any way the outcome of the conflict. No doubt the mountains of tactical intelligence—troop and ship movements, orders of battle—helped prevent blunders and save lives. But all sides compiled this kind of intelligence and plenty of lives were wasted nonetheless. It is difficult to see how the basic facts of the war—Allied victory in the west, Russian defeat in the east, a war of stalemate and attrition—were in any way the result of intrigue and espionage or could in any way have been changed by them. Even bold strokes like the interception of the Zimmermann telegram did not have the strategic consequences some have attributed to them. There were no secrets whose discovery would divert the course of the war, and raw intelligence itself was only as good as the staff's evaluation of it and then the decisions the generals made as to whether to use it. There was something insular, almost bubblelike about much of the spy war: spies pitted against other spies, tracking and neutralizing one another. It was a fascinating, dangerous game played by all sides, but one wonders whether the risks were any more vindicable than those for the men who went over the top or whether the successes meant any more than a trench captured here or a freighter sunk there. One is reminded of Paul Allard's 1936 debunking of Basil Thomson, the fabled head of British counterespionage in the First World War, who, summoned by *Paris-Soir* to solve the sensational Prince murder in the mid-1930s, "collapsed in his seat at a famous Dijon restaurant following libations and gastronomic excesses that seem to have been the principal concern of 'the man of a hundred faces.'"[110] A bit cruel and certainly unfair, but also an exposé of the inflation of spy reputations and the role of the spy from a man who made a living passing on every espionage story he heard.

Intrigue, then, did not shape the First World War, but the war did shape intrigue and in this relation the historian can find something significant. More than the bloated accomplishments of spies it was espionage's ability to capture styles and moods that came with the war and to replicate in its symbolic presence the changes introduced by that cataclysm that make it worthy of our attention. Those characteristics of interwar espionage that would bind it to its times — its copiousness, its scale and subversive orientation, its global reach, its methodical proficiency, and its more diverse or sophisticated motifs and imagery — emanated from the far-reaching consequences of the Great War, but also from the war experience itself and the way war made real what previously had been only imagined or conjured. Postwar espionage never lost what it acquired with the dramatic expansion of intelligence operations during the conflict, nor did the French forget the lessons the war taught them about the vital importance of rear lines and imperial security that would feed postwar obsessions with spies. Invariably as this study progresses it will retrace its steps to that conflagration, whether in discussing spy fears of the late 1930s and memories of wartime subversion and sabotage, or in reviewing the interwar spy literature that grew out of the war, or in recounting the ties between espionage and adventure on the one hand and the wartime exploits of a von Hentig on the other. War in 1870 began one era in espionage; but a wider, deeper, far more bountiful one surfaced with the spy wars fought out from 1914 to 1918.

———————

Perhaps it is Impex that tells us best how sharp the break was between one era and another. We are talking about a German import-export firm (hence its name Impex), in reality an intelligence front, based in Barcelona but with branches that the French unearthed in other Spanish cities in the early twenties, or so they believed. The firm traded in a variety of goods — machines, mining equipment, automobiles, dyes, pharmaceuticals — imported from Germany and then reexported to Spanish Morocco. But mostly its exports were guns and munitions and French agents backed these charges up with a litany of others against the house. Impex claimed to be a branch of a central business in Madrid, but there was no foundation to this declaration. Impex's trade was lively, but rarely was it conducted under the firm's own name. A Spanish freight-forwarding company that had collaborated with German espionage in the war and reputedly held to those arrangements shared a ground floor

Map 1. *Spain and the Moroccos.*

and interior staircase with Impex, covering the latter's "shady and sus-pect" traffic to Morocco. Running Impex's warehousing was a water-front tough, Luciano A., who had spied on Allied shipping during the war for the Germans and had attempted to plant time bombs on boats. Across the Mediterranean at Melilla and Ceuta Impex had connections with the B. brothers, importers and exporters suspected of shipping arms to Arabs in both Spanish and French Morocco. The director of Impex was a man who had worked for the Mannesmann brothers (a name we will return to) before the war, and his two associates were German agents. All three took their orders from Pablo S., the German intelligence agent in charge of operations in Morocco or from the Rüg-geberg brothers, who ran German intelligence in Spain after the war (and reports from French files suggest the continued presence of a siz-able German operation in the Iberian peninsula).

Tales about Impex passed onto the French were charged with mysti-fications and dense atmospherics. The house was frequented "by everyone Barcelona numbers among former and current German agents or Spaniards notoriously Germanophile. Impex receives numerous cases that it mysteriously dispatches to southern ports; it sends agents to Melilla who meet there with Moroccan dissidents." There were communiqués on Max W., who appears to have been running Impex by December 1922, describing his voyages to Spanish and French Morocco (*"without papers,* he claims") in the course of which he held long conversations with a Jewish banker and shipper. In August 1922 a secret bulletin to the Ministry of Colonies related the arrival of Karl G. and Friedrich L. from Madrid and Málaga, Impex agents recalled to headquarters for days of close quartering with the bosses before setting out for Andalusia, and who blabbed at the Gambrinus Bar prior to departure that they were on an urgent mission to Ceuta, Melilla, Tetouan, and Tangier. Such reports were heaviest from the fall of 1921 through the course of the following year. Then the reports faded, although Impex died a slow death in French consciousness. Late 1925 produced still more references to Impex, this time recounting the questionable conduct of Walter R., a former German policeman who had lived for some time in Barcelona, traveled frequently to Morocco, had his mail addressed to a Dutch company care of a post-office box in Santander, and whose principal occupation seemed to be recruiting secret agents for Germany. R. was closely associated with Impex, as well as with a man suspected of infiltrating narcotics into France. Several years later the Battiti affair once again (appropriately) resurrected mention of Impex.[111]

For Morocco, where international intrigue was endemic from the end of the century, all but writ into the resonance of the place-name, Impex was a likely phenomenon. Before the war the pattern of resentment, defiance, and outright revolt upon which the French had built their command of the country[112] had set the stage for foreign intrigues against the conquering nation. Pan-Islamic conspiracies, aimed at fomenting tribal risings and launched out of Cairo, had created moments of discomfort before they sputtered out rather ingloriously, the few men who made it to Morocco falling easily into French clutches.[113] Germans had run guns on the freighters of the Atlas, OPDR, and possibly Woermann lines, all three shipping companies out of Hamburg, the latter two operating a scheduled service to Morocco or the west coast of Africa by the turn of the century. Heinrich Ficke, the German vice-consul, had watched benignly as the Atlas's *Zeus* unloaded its contraband cargoes at Tangier and Casablanca, although he was also the company's local representative, and rogue diplomacy and commercial imperatives (both the Atlas and OPDR lines were running more ships than their routes warranted; Atlas went into liquidation shortly after its founding) more than official scheming may well have explained this trafficking in arms.[114]

There were also the Mannesmanns, six brothers in all, who owned a successful seamless pipe company in Germany and who had come to Morocco in pursuit of mining concessions. Mavericks and adventurers, they were German robber barons whose enterprise radiated great force and energy, but they could also be malevolently self-destructive and inclined to plot when they could not get their way. Thwarted at obtaining French government approval for the extensive mining concessions they had won from Moroccans, the Mannesmanns turned to intrigues. They incited separatist movements in the south of the country and worked with gunrunners. They maintained an arms depot on one of their farms, and their geological expeditions into the Atlas distributed guns and anti-French propaganda. During the Agadir crisis in 1911 Mannesmann agents sought, unsuccessfully, to create an incident that would force a German troop landing. Their wide connections with the German community in Morocco, their contingent of engineers, mining assessors, and protected nationals who traveled all over the country, and their success in wrapping themselves in the cloak of German national interests to the point that pan-Germans looked upon the Mannesmanns as the principal tacticians of an imperial strategy, appalled the French, who had every reason to regard the brothers as German secret agents, although it is not certain that German authorities who negotiated Mannesmann claims did not grow to despise the brothers as much as the occupiers did. Nonetheless Mannesmann was a name the French would not forget easily, as report after report from the war, and the Impex file, attest.[115]

But the background to Impex was really the First World War and Germany's effort to raise the tribes against the protectorate. There, overseas, amidst the casbahs and the desert, no less than on the trailways of Europe, the war propelled the French into a world of spies they scarcely knew before the firing began. Wartime in Morocco cultivated the same assortment of ninety-day spooks and inflated support networks, the same grandiose projects and spy-counterspy battles that it produced on the continent. Under the banner of a jihad German agents, money, arms, and propaganda flowed toward the country.[116] First came a German officer named Lang, traveling with an American passport and probably calling himself Francisco Farr, although a number of reports including one as late as 1918 refer to him as Francisco Fart.[117] Then when Lang took ill and died in 1915, German contact with Abd-el-Malek in the north continued through Albert Bartels, a former tradesman who had come to Morocco in 1903, had learned to speak Arabic, had been interned in 1914 but had escaped, and who had, at least for some time before 1914, worked for the Mannesmanns — exactly the sort of connection that the French were apt to seize upon.[118] Later the Germans sent out a Dr. Kuhnel, who took on the identity of José Maury from Colombia and who carried a credit for a considerable sum of money to organize more rebel resistance.[119]

To finance and arm a full-scale war of Moroccan resistance (even if this never came about) required the creation of a considerable infrastructure of support and supply and this the Germans established only after 1914. They operated agent networks in the towns of Spanish Morocco — Ceuta, Tetouan, Melilla — and transit bases on the Canaries. In neutral Spain German intelligence easily recruited agents among the thousands of German nationals who had arrived since the beginning of the war from West Africa, Morocco, Latin America, and Portugal. Ratibor, von Kalle, and von Krohn in Madrid provided central direction for Moroccan affairs, although operations spread throughout the country. In Barcelona the Germans established their propaganda center. Contraband arms shipments passed through Seville and Cádiz. Melilla's staging base was in Málaga. There at a small brasserie in the calle Marques de Larrios the gathering often included a Mannesmann brother, the engineer Langenheim, whose name would reappear in French intelligence reports in the twenties and thirties, and a man named Stalwinger.[120]

None of this made any difference at all, despite the fact that Lyautey's wartime correspondence paints a picture of unrelieved alarm about the danger of pan-Islamic propaganda and "Germano-Islamic" intrigues.[121] Germans and Moroccans could agree on common enemies but on little else. Coordination between rival Moroccan factions was tenuous at best, while relations between Abd-el-Malek and his German liaison, Albert Bartels, were horrid, bordering on the mutually contemptuous and recriminatory. Realizing that their anti-imperialist clothing was full of holes, the Germans sought Turkish cover, but that garb proved tawdry and frayed. Turkish agents dispatched to Madrid in late 1915 squabbled with their ally, demanded more money, and threatened to tell all to the French if the Germans did not pay their way to America. Spanish police arrested another Turkish agent, posing as Manuel Rodriguez from Peru, for sexually abusing a little boy.[122] As for Stalwinger of Málaga, he was little more than a brute, an ex-legionnaire who went under the names Pfeffer, petit doseur, and Fulenkampf, notable mostly as a type of gorilla that would overcrowd the spy worlds in the interwar years. The Germans kept him around because he would do anything. His contribution to the war was probably less than nil: money sent from Madrid was wasted on his private debaucheries, and a mission to Algeria ran aground when in an alcoholic stupor he announced that he was planning to encourage desertions among French legionnaires. By mid-1915 he was confiding in a man who was a French counterespionage agent.[123] Then there was the captured informant Georg Regenratz. Under interrogation he refused on his honor as a German officer to confide a German code, at other times offered if set free to go to Berlin and bring back important documents, spoke of his needy mother and his personal finances, which were a mess, and, in the end, spilled the beans about circuits for infiltrating agents into North Africa.[124] Even without these clowns the French had little to fear. They countered the German offensive with vigorous counterintelligence measures and their own contingents of tribesmen, retained a monopoly of firepower and control of the sea, and introduced smart policies regarding the indigenous population, such as the creation of jobs. These, more than German failures, held Morocco for France.[125]

Yet the Bartels, the Langenheims, the von Krohns, and the Regenratzes, as well as the Mannesmanns, when taken together, represent the distance intrigue had traveled since 1914. Their enterprises produced no results but stirred up plenty of noise and a thorough air of mystery, and that was the kind of clandestine war the Germans brought to Morocco: submarines that surfaced in the night with money and armaments; false passport ateliers in Italian port cities; thugs gone to seed with too much drink and amateur adventurers who took on names like Si Hermann (Bartels) and blew up railway bridges in the back country; a mysterious German woman who appeared in Melilla, called herself English, proclaimed her engagement to a typewriter salesman out of the Transvaal, and promenaded at night with a Spanish captain of police.[126] The postwar years would offer no better, but also no worse.

The memories were themselves a legacy, because what the war left behind was the almost unerring tendency to reproduce the details and imagery of First World War espionage. Nearly every report carried with it something from the wartime experience, although not always in the same way. Occasionally it was conditioning, the inclination to think about subversion following a war of insurrection or the far-flung dimension to interwar reporting after a war that had witnessed German arms shipments to Morocco, sabotage plans at Suez, and expeditions to Afghanistan. At other times it was a sense that the intrigues of wartime were continuing, as in the reports of German/pan-Islamic combines, now with Comintern imagery cooked in, that piled up in the years immediately following the armistice and repeated the basic facts — conspiracy, systematic coordination, global connections — of the First World War in Morocco. Or there was simply the discovery of spy rings and operations strikingly similar to those of the war.[127]

And that is where Impex fits in, because in this shadowy company we can see how nearly all these strands could come together. As a covert operation Impex emerged from the war and the events that had followed. For some of its operatives like Luciano A., the war with its gluttony for agents had been the initiating experience. For others, like the Communist agitator Fernando V., who hung out at the edges of Impex reports, it was postwar milieus that created openings and reasons for action. Still others stepped out of the war, like freight-forwarding accomplices or Friedrich Rüggeberg who had worked for German intelligence in Spain during the fighting.[128] In the references to Mannesmanns as directors behind the scenes there remained the nagging inclination to identify a chameleonlike consistency to German intrigues carried over from earlier times. Yet mostly there was to Impex a subversive, far-reaching quality — reports on the firm extended its operations to the Cameroons or converged with warnings of insurrections throughout the Muslim world — that carried with it the aroma of intrigue since 1914.

Above all else Impex projected the fullness that came with the war. It recalled the German wartime organization assembled in Spain to run arms and money and agents to Morocco, although not any organization that had preceded those years. In that respect even the question of veracity placed Impex squarely within the postwar scene. Whether Impex, as the files reconstruct it for us, was fiction or reality is not at all certain. The reporting was extensive and the details specific. Everything tempts us to believe that the operation, in some form, existed. But if Impex was a fabrication it was of postwar construction, a vision of German espionage in Spain and Morocco concocted out of the wartime experience and the focus of intrigue in the *après-guerre* world: subversion, communism, colonial security, and global surveillance. In its details and its internal coherence, Impex could be imagined only after the war. Such was the case of nearly all interwar intrigues in Morocco. Whether fact or fiction, their building materials were those of the war and of the conditions that followed.

Thus over the years the differences with the past grew more pronounced. By the 1930s espionage in Morocco reflected the organizational and global designs characteristic of the interwar age. Gone were the reports of rogue settler intrigues or the fastidious details on individual arms shipments. In their stead materialized broad schemes of infiltration and espionage launched from European centers with method and operational sophistication and matched by extensive and systematic accounts on the French end.[129] Seditious techniques now included movies, records,[130] or the beaming of subversive radio messages across vast expanses of the world — the radio wars, as they came to be called toward the end of the decade.[131] Characters and networks were those that only the postwar period would know. As before, Germans predominated, but the heady brews of the thirties encompassed all the bogeys: Italian Fascists (who initiated the radio wars and whose infiltration of the Moroccan Italian community was carefully watched), Spanish Nationalists once the civil war began, and in other extensive communiqués, agents of the Comintern.[132]

Spanning nearly all of these was the overarching presence of Shakib Arslan. William Cleveland, in his authoritative biography of this influential yet relatively powerless pan-Islamist, has exposed the mythic dimensions to French and British images of the man as the ultimate string puller in the Arab Middle East. In reality Arslan led a ragged, if heated, existence. He was a mentor and a spokesman, but rarely a conspirator. The mysterious powers bestowed upon him by imperial officials were, however, symptomatic of an era in which nationalist agitation coincided with systematic subversive activity from abroad. Arslan spurred on the myth with his close ties to Germany and his apologies for Mussolini. Essentially he would turn to anyone who he thought would support the Arab cause, and if French documents are to be believed — and on Arslan they are suspect — he was also in league with the Communists. In this he too, like Impex, was a product of his times. He had been won over by the kaiser's proclamation of support for the Arabs at the end of the century, but the truly formative years for the man were those of the German-Ottoman alliance in the First World War and the active pursuit of Islamic independence. Forever after he was a creature of his own personal memories and missions in that war. But then so, too, were the French who never forgot the pan-Islamic experience of 1914–1918, nor the intrigues that followed, and who, caught in crosscurrents of the age, turned him into the formidable force that he almost certainly would have liked to be.[133]

All of which recalls the problems with which this chapter began: exactly what changed with the war? In a sense espionage has always been about war. In the twenties and thirties it was about many wars: the Rif war in the northern mountains of Morocco, the Spanish civil war, the erupting war in the Pacific, the war people expected to come. But above all it was about the war that had been fought between 1914 and 1918. Out of this war came the people and the imagery that made up the espionage worlds of the interwar years. Bolshevism, fascism, and future-war literature channeled interwar espionage down avenues of subversion and sabotage or of covert networks of global dimensions. Yet it was the First World War that turned these into the conventions of espionage just as, in effect, the new ideological systems and next-war speculation were themselves products of that war. After the war, espionage in its themes and motifs was always, in some way, a reflection back on the years of fighting and the world that had followed, whether through secret-war imagery or secret-agent memoirs or the constructs and visions of how espionage was conducted.

In this it drew on the network of materials that had developed from espionage and war in the late nineteenth century. At times the parallels could be striking, particularly when the imagery gravitated toward spy mania or when espionage was incorporated into the literature of military defeat. The Franco-Prussian War set people thinking about spies and protracted the consciousness of espionage deep into peacetime. It led to the creation or expansion of intelligence services on a permanent footing and to intrigues not always dissimilar from those that preoccupied authorities in the interwar years. The institutionalization of espionage operations made possible the spy battles of the First World War, and in certain ways anticipated those battles just as prewar espionage themes often previewed those of the postwar.

But rarely were the themes exactly the same. There was, for example, no equivalent to secret-war imagery before 1914. After 1870 French thinking on espionage often turned back to the Franco-Prussian War, but it did so as a disquisition on defeat, German danger, and German iniquity, or as an argument for constructing an intelligence service before the next conflict. Secret-war imagery after 1918 was different. It issued from sentiments made possible by four years of a war that seemed as if it never would end and by the sense of fluidity and unsettlement unleashed by this war that carried clear through the armistice and the treaties. Secret-war imagery was about extension and permanence. It was an expression of unending war, a description, more than a warning, of a war continuing on clandestine fronts where spy masters were the generals and secret agents the combatants. "'Making war in peacetime,'" wrote Colonel Nicolai in his memoirs in the twenties, "that is the best definition of the present role of the secret service."[134]

Comparable distinctions could be found in fifth-column imagery. There was something timeless, universal to fifth-column projections. No age nor place could call them all their own. The late nineteenth century spawned a genre of literature and reporting about the covert threat from within. Spy panics erupted everywhere with the outbreak of war in 1914. Attached to fifth-column imagery in the thirties and forties was a tradition trailing back into time. Yet fifth-column thinking in these years was also different from any that had preceded it, possessing identifications peculiar to its age. Partly this was a matter of perceptions. When people wrote or spoke of *the* fifth column they had in mind a specific conspiracy without antecedents. Fifth column described a fascist mode of operations first witnessed in the Spanish civil war and then deployed on a grander scale by the Nazis. It connoted modern espionage techniques — propaganda, sabotage, subversion, and terror — practiced by twentieth-century political systems. For contemporaries fifth column was a custom-fitted concept. The very perception of newness, the conferring of a name — fifth column — made it novel, separate, distinct from the past.

Likewise the fifth-column image that crystallized in spring 1940 was a sum greater than its parts, but one whose equations were sturdy and whose calculations faltered only at the end. The power of the First World War to make real what in the past had been primarily imaginary contributed to the subsequent inflation of the role of the spy despite the failure of espionage to alter in any way the course of that conflict. The experience of total war underscored the cardinal importance and hence the vulnerability of centers behind the front lines as well as imperial resources spread across the globe, all of which had been subject to infiltration or attack by espionage networks during the war. Sabotage, subversion, revolutionary tactics, the sheer number of spies and then the number of their memoirs all projected into the interwar years the perception of the secret agent as a potent force in shaping world events. Later, internationals of all stripes and colors, the ideological clashes of the thirties, secret-police tactics carried abroad, colonial shakiness, and future-war imagery gave to fifth-column thinking a specificity and coherence unknown in earlier spy panics.

Moreover, if fifth-column imagery was prone to extraordinary flights of fantasy, its essentials never strayed very far from realities. Refugee politics, with their plague of double agents and their tactics of terror and infiltration, familiarized a generation of French citizens to an espionage style that surfaced elsewhere in the form of Comintern subversion or fascist penetration of national populations abroad. The greater scale of networks after the war, their greater system and method, carried fifth-column overtones, as did the new technological opportunities for behind-the-lines infiltration like the radio wars fought over North African airwaves. Out of the thirties came the fabulous tales of the purge trials and the very real terrorist attacks by the Cagoule or, as we shall see, by fascist agents in France. The very nature of the Spanish conflict — ubiquitous, terrorizing — bestowed credibility on the concept that was born with that struggle. Thus in 1940 authorities and populations could envision as real or reasonable the intrigues ascribed to the German fifth column, because fifth-column imagery evolved out of espionage milieus they had known since the Great War. Indeed after the senseless orgy of spy panic in the first days of August 1914, one might have expected greater skepticism in the future, much as Europeans discounted reports of the Holocaust because they had heard similar stories in the previous conflagration. Only the experience of intrigue in the course of that conflict, and then throughout the twenties and thirties, can explain the persistence of these hysterics as another world war began.

Just as the First World War altered the character of espionage, intrigue in the decades that followed reflected historical change more than it did historical continuity. The remainder of this book will examine those changes and the shared relations of espionage and history between the two wars. Subsequent chapters will explore spy literature and the global dimensions to espionage after 1918. They will show how spy tales reflected a particular kind of interwar writing, how themes and style were those of the twenties and thirties, and how there was a complexity of vision to this literature, one where a danger was present but not necessarily overwhelming. They will also show how the far-flung reach of interwar intrigue borrowed from the war, from adventure and travel and a need for romance, from the present-mindedness of these years, and from the realization of an altered relation between the periphery and the center. First, however, one must turn to milieu, and to the richness and representativeness of intrigue in the *entre-deux-guerres*.

Figure 2. *Taxi of the Don. From W. Chapin Huntington,* The Homesick Million.

CHAPTER TWO

Milieu

Spy fiction between the wars was never as good as fact. No one wrote stories that match the ones in the archives. Looking back from the late twentieth century, one is startled at how authentic the stereotypes are. In mood, setting, action, and stock characters, the period need concede nothing to the spy novels and spy movies. For rendezvous in the 1920s Soviet intelligence agents met at the Closerie des Lilas in Paris, German agents at the Café Gambrinus in Barcelona. There was a Café Central in Tangier where spies and gunrunners gathered and a Hotel Morandi in Cairo frequented by men suspected of working for Italian intelligence. Shortly before the Rif war a German fluent in French, Spanish, and Arabic traveled from Larache to Rabat disguised as a Jew. He called himself Chemnaoun Benzakour, but he also carried on his person a passport made out to Manuel Barrero. At Rabat he visited a Swiss who resided in the city, then he moved on to Casablanca. The man for whom he traveled was Langenheim, a German engineer who had come to North Africa in 1907, was listed in the twenties as "one of the most important German agents in Morocco," and in 1940 was identified as a central figure in a comprehensive German program of espionage, propaganda, insurrection, gunrunning, and sabotage. Langenheim's description in French counterespionage files might have come out of a dime novel: "Settled long ago in Morocco, obliged by his mining explorations to wander on foot throughout the territory, living the life of a native, he knows every stone, every person, every caïd. . . . In native matters it seems that he controls the agents, ensures suspect transports toward the French frontier, sustains liaisons with nationalist Moroccan chiefs." At El Ksar there was another German agent named Heinrich R. who had converted to Islam and taken the name Abdallah, although others knew him as Moumen el Islami and El Alemani. He traded in skins, but he was also an intriguer.[1]

We have created images of this interwar shadow world that are not belied by the facts. Espionage in the twenties and thirties was about spy rings, kidnappings, hijackings, and murders. Its milieu was inhabited by a host of dubious figures who were sucked into intrigues or who swooped down like great filthy carrion eaters when the pickings were ripe. Victims commingled with double agents, informants, gangsters, and professional spies. The aura was that of great battles to be won, of tense, pressing, high stakes affairs. Underneath lay brutality, deceit, and an exceptionally high quotient of slime. But beyond the atmosphere were other dimensions, steeped in historical meaning as well as in ambiance and remindful of how the description of a milieu forces one to think about a particular period in time.

Organization is a place to begin. Espionage in the interwar years was considerably more organized, more elaborate, and more methodically professional than it had been before 1914. Intelligence services had laboratories, they equipped their agents with technologically sophisticated instruments, and they developed international, even worldwide, circuits. The Soviets recalled agents to Moscow for instruction, the French broadened their networks and systematized operations. Organization characterized ways of proceeding, but also ways of perceiving. French counterespionage identified Berlin and Vienna centers, described central pan-Islamic committees pulling strings all over the globe. There were always exceptions. British intelligence could be remarkably dilettantish (although less so than it had been before the war).[2] Proliferation of agencies led to jurisdictional disputes and inefficiencies within national intelligence communities. There remained plenty of amateurs on the loose, and the gaffes were so frequent and occasionally so extravagant that it is possible to write endlessly about the preposterous side to espionage in these years. Still the flow was toward more refined method and professionalism, and the description holds when compared with the past.

The question is why this change came about. One is tempted to turn back to the wartime experience, where method and technological inventiveness became matters of necessity so that the postwar apparatus, even when pared back, was substantially more elaborate and geared for refinement than it had been before the First World War. The war also tightened the world, spread intrigues and counterintelligence across oceans and continents, and this change too demanded more system and control. Such explanations provide credible answers, as would a focus on the rise of new political systems after the war and the creation of international organs like the Comintern that built sophisticated circuits and support networks and forced more sophisticated countermeasures in return.

Yet the history of intrigue also reveals affairs like the case of the Eisenberg-Shilmayer gang. Its members ran a traffic in false passports in the thirties that preyed upon foreigners, especially refugee Jews, desperate for papers. Police called them "a veritable enterprise" and "an international organization," and when the cops cracked the ring, along with two others that may or not have been related, they netted altogether thirty-one people. About a year later the Sûreté broke another gang that extended from Poland to France with ring members active in Belgium and Germany.[3]

Thus all sides to intrigue after the war, even those on the margins and independent of political infrastructures, exhibited a certain measure of organization. Cases like the Eisenberg-Shilmayer affair point to the wider rule of system and method throughout the interwar years of which trends in espionage were only one sampling. Again the same factors — war, technology, revolutionary politics and their combinations — were often at play. In addition there was a sheer, irresistible surrender to organization propelled by the war that spread to all forms of activity. Fordism or government planning were, of course, its most obvious representations. Even in France, where neither was particularly strong, the state, no matter how reluctant, could be a powerful force in the economy, extending its reach to railroads, steamship lines, oil, and eventually the aircraft industry. Business performance, if generally disappointing, witnessed a marked increase in mergers in the 1920s and greater methodization — revision of procedures, introduction of advisory boards, more flexible control structures — in the 1930s. Department stores, for instance, that had rationalized operations before the First World War now self-consciously discussed organization and brought in efficiency experts. Mass production, standardization, and the creation of extensive marketing networks — business techniques pioneered in the nineteenth century — spread to popular culture in the twentieth, particularly through the medium of American cinema. The advent of new, national forms of entertainment, combined with the radical politics of the Left and the Right, led to more orchestration and control of leisure than ever before.

No realm, in fact, seemed exempt from the relentless compulsion to methodize. In France before the war immigration had been largely spontaneous. During and after the war it was characterized by government regulation and organized business recruitment with agencies or representatives operating abroad. The paperwork and preparation preceding the Croisière jaune expedition across central Asia in 1931–1932 predated the caravan by several years, filled files in the Ministry of Foreign Affairs and required advance trips to reconnoiter and set up supply depots. Crime, too, displayed all the signs. Drug traffickers built organizations on an international, even global, scale. A man like Elie Eliopolus got his start as a supplier to the Greek army during the war. By the end of the twenties he had moved into narcotics with his own network of suppliers, couriers, laboratories, and factories. Another trafficker, Louis-Théodore Lyon, reportedly controlled morphine laboratories in Istanbul and Sofia, several heroin labs in France, and a band of intermediaries tying one phase of operations to another. In this respect Eisenberg and Shilmayer, who recall to a degree earlier white slaving traditions, were on a wider level merely symptomatic of the patterns of their day. The world was becoming a tightly knit, highly managed place in which to live, and if business and revolutionary governments led the way, nearly everyone and everything fell into line. So the size and system of espionage after the war not only marked it off from earlier forms. More completely they set spying within the structures and inclinations of the age.[4]

Opportunities for intrigue grew after the war, flourishing in the twenties and thirties with a lushness that prewar espionage had not enjoyed. Interwar intrigues were protean, multidimensional. They occurred everywhere, poured into interstices, flowed in a steady stream as espionage wound beyond the traditional objectives of military intelligence. The postwar presence of communists and fascists introduced an intensity and multifariousness to espionage that was greatly responsible for this luxuriating character and that made spying quite different from what it had been before 1914. Because the war opened the way to revolution and fascism, and because it left behind a fragile international balance, the levels of intrigue experienced in wartime did not diminish significantly after 1918.

Still other reasons for this pervasiveness reached deeper into the legacies of the war in ways that certain personal histories reveal. Richard Sorge, perhaps the most celebrated spy of the thirties and forties, was to remark that "the World War of 1914–1918 had the most profound influence on my entire life. Even if I had never been motivated by other considerations, the World War alone would have been enough to make me a Communist. I was eighteen-and-a-half years old when the war broke out, a high school student living in the Lichterfelde district of Berlin." The son of a well-to-do petroleum engineer, he was an eager volunteer in the summer of 1914. Four years of war, three wounds, disheartening leaves home, and encounters with socialists changed his outlook forever. Invalided out of the war by 1918 he turned toward radical politics while pursuing a doctorate in political science. By 1920 he had deeply immersed himself in Communist party activities in Hamburg. Eventually he was to serve in Comintern and Red Army intelligence, first in Europe, then in Shanghai, and then in Tokyo where he ran a spy ring that was fabulously successful. A complex man of storied proportions — he was a scholar, womanizer, boozer, and mesmerizing raconteur, a secret agent operating in Japan as a Nazi party member and the foreign correspondent of the *Frankfurter Zeitung,* using his cover to gain access to the inner sanctums of the German embassy to the point that he occasionally served as its courier of secret messages abroad — he nevertheless remained a committed Communist. If his life merged with the intrigues of the twentieth century it was a life that had been shaped by the war, caught up in its powerful, transforming whorl. The war, as he acknowledged, metamorphosed him into a conscious agent for change, and the war as well created both the movement and the conspiratorial apparatus through which the new Sorge could carry out these desires. In this he was not unlike the other idealists who flocked to communism following the war, equally committed to changing the world and providing the revolution with its army of activists. Some would become organizers, some would drop out, and others — the Richard Sorges, the Walter Krivitskys, and the Ignace Reisses — would pass from political work to the more clandestine networks of spies. Communist intrigue was their medium, but they were its motor, and it was the trajectory of their lives that in good part contributed to making espionage what it was between the wars.[5]

Different lives on less lofty planes shared as well in the making of that history. The case of Captain Gardiner is instructive here because it shows how easy was the slide from adventure or fortune hunting into international intrigue in the *entre-deux-guerres.* Charles Alfred Percy Gardiner was a British seaman and salvager before the war. Perhaps he also commanded a ship in the Chilean revolution, laid mines in the waters of Port Arthur, and led a unit of Australian Bushmen in the Boer War, as he claimed during his trial for fraud in 1925 (charges on which he was eventually acquitted). In the Great War—and this comes from more credible witnesses—he was called up as a salvage expert and then commissioned by the navy to captain a Q-boat, the deadly submarine hunters camouflaged as tramp steamers that were yet another side to the covert war of demolition and sabotage carried out by special units under civilian cover. By 1918, if not earlier, he had thus stepped across into the realms of the shadow dwellers, although how far so at first is not altogether certain. From reports of his trial it would seem he followed his high sea deceptions with a foray into the shipbuilding business, wooing backers, they would claim, with fraudulent promises. By 1921 the company was out of business, and in 1923, ordered to appear before bankruptcy court, Gardiner skipped the country, returning only in spring of 1925 when he was arrested and brought up on charges.[6]

Yet a French police report emanating from a source who in the past had proven worthy of attention tells a far more interesting story. Gardiner, the source claimed, had shifted gears only slightly after the war, falling in with a Glasgow bootlegger to North America. By 1923 the Glasgow patron had joined a British syndicate holding the rights to Mannesmann mining concessions in the Rif. The concessions were potentially valuable, but, spread across the Spanish Moroccan mountains, they lay within a region engulfed in a war of rebellion. The plan of the syndicate was to ship arms to the rebels, a strategy they believed would win rebel friendship and guarantee their mastery over the area. What the syndicate needed was a man to smuggle the weapons through, someone daring, resourceful, and experienced in covert operations; and for this they turned to Captain Gardiner. Gardiner, in turn, took as his accomplices men like himself, adventurers and former officers in the war with postwar experience in illicit activities. Mostly he recruited among gunrunners to Ireland (it is possible that Gardiner too had been engaged in this contraband), and he utilized the same sources and organization as this traffic had employed, diverting guns and ammunition from war surplus depots in northern France with the collusion of insiders in the firm charged with liquidating the stocks. In 1925 the scheme ran aground as one of Gardiner's confederates, operating on his own and in alliance with German secret agents, encouraged Abd-el-Krim to attack French forces in northern Morocco, a move that initiated war with the French and doomed the rebellion to failure. On this score the French police informant was almost certainly wrong. Still Gardiner was clearly mixed up in the Rif in some way or another. That he, the syndicate, and clan-destine German emissaries should cohabit the same French police report was indicative of how easily adventure and rapacious enterprises shaded into murkier affairs in the twenties and thirties.[7]

Europe ran over with Captain Gardiners after the war. Adventurers and mercenaries there had always been, but wartime buccaneers cut loose by the peace now made such types a dime a dozen. Lured on by easy opportunities like gunrunning to Morocco and China and then to Spain, they drifted in and out of espionage affairs. The Gardiner case had all the ingredients — former Q-boat commander, ex-army officers, war surplus weapons, peripheral war caught up in great power politics, the mix of easy money with spies, adventure turned counterespionage matter — that made the world ripe for intrigue following the armistice.[8] Postwar intrigues were largely a product of this availability of personnel joined to this excess of occasions, this abundance of Gardiners and syn-dicates and adventures swept up in the great swings of history.

Subsequent soldiers of fortune would follow a similar glide path from adventure to espionage, passing through the great international affairs of the moment. H. D. provides yet another good example. Born too late to have fought in the war, he made a certain reputation for himself in the postwar years as a pilot and stunt flier. He flew reconnais-sance and bombing missions for the negus against the Italians and then fought as a fighter pilot in Spain on the side of the Second Republic. Idealism may have inspired him initially, but he was later to remark that both wars had remunerated him handsomely. By the late thirties he was headed east, steering toward the fog of less honorable adventures. In Asia he offered his services to the Chinese air force but received no bids in return. He then — on the rebound? victim to the viperous spells of Shanghai? — fell in with an American named Wagner who ran some-thing called the American Asiatic Trading Company and was suspected by police of working for Japanese intelligence. In 1938 Wagner and H. D. were embarked on highly suspicious travels concerning Chinese air bases and the location of Chinese military aircraft and by spring of that year the Shanghai municipal police were identifying H. D. as a Jap-anese agent. By the end of the decade the man was hopelessly mired in unsavory circles. With the coming of the Second World War he was living in Shanghai with a woman named Evelyn O., herself no slouch when it came to a past. Born of British parents, she married a partner in a firm associated with the Soviet enterprise Exporthleb and financed by Moscow as a conduit into Britain. After her husband's suicide in

1933 she traveled to Manila, where she met and married Paco O. He was listed as "a trusted employee of the Manila branch of Elizalde and Company," but undoubtedly that designation changed when his departure from the firm was followed by the disclosure that bonds worth forty thousand pesos could not be accounted for. A year after her liaison with H. D., she was keeping time with an Italian "commander." H. D., at the time he was living with O., was reportedly without funds and hatching plans to establish a male brothel for rich women on the avenue Joffre with the intention of blackmailing its clientele. In the summer of 1940 he broke into the hotel room of a German captain to steal some papers but was caught in the act (there is no indication who had hired him). Volunteering for the British army, he was, "needless to say" — the language is that of the police — turned away. Thus the personal journey of an adventurer and mercenary between one world war and another.[9]

Like the Captain Gardiners of the world, here too was a type, the pilot soldier of fortune whose call to action and pursuit of lucre sucked him into the great events of the era and then into the intrigues spun off on their margins. After 1918 they were common enough figures. Toughs or glamour seekers, they inhabited an age when adventure was hinged to war and revolution, a volatile mix of inclination and circumstance that pitched them into the vortex of politics and the sinister, more dubious spheres where life stories unraveled with an all too recognizable fatalism. The pull of fliers toward espionage eluded not even the comic-strip writers who captured, ironically for H. D., the ineluctable connection in the tale of Captain Easy who engages as a spy for the Chinese air force.[10]

Still other creatures of the times clogged the spy files, their life histories illustrating no less vividly how intrigue could swell and distend in our period. None of these were more prominent than the refugees of the century, and among them the White Russians who perhaps more than anyone lent intrigue its flourish after the war. Castoffs from the great cataclysm, they introduced yet another type, the adventurer through circumstance or misfortune rather than personal disposition. Take the émigré W., for example. Like Battiti he was one of those persons who surface momentarily in the archives and then slip completely from sight. Extravagant, he followed a life course repeated by hundreds or thousands. Before the Russian revolution he had been a prominent jurist. Following 1917 he was a refugee, arms broker, intriguer, and crook. As a scam artist he swindled investors with flashy connections and promises of quick money. His operations extended to gunrunning and his acquaintances to White Russian revanchists; French agents on the trail of a vast shipment of Mausers tied him to secret arms depots in Germany, Chinese warlords, assorted notorious characters, and wild schemes for a counterrevolutionary march back into Russia.[11] Like others he was thus the refugee-on-the-make, a man cut off from his past and set loose in a world awash with opportunity for those who cared only about the color of money. Berlin, Paris, Istanbul, Shanghai all knew their W.'s after the war. They were familiar figures in the landscape, some operating on a grand scale, others scraping by with any dirty business that might come their way, men and women with international connections, set off on the margins, global scramblers, and available.

If they descended so effortlessly into intrigue it was because their milieu was riddled with secret agents, spies, and private espionage organizations. Much of the spice to interwar intrigue came from these White Russians and their endless (almost always futile) battles in a clandestine war with Soviet security forces. Again circumstances, in the shape of the political collisions of their day, molded their lives, although here too they remained simply a type. To their clandestine labyrinths one could add other intrigues, those, for example, of anti-fascist Italians in the 1920s or Balkan terrorists dissatisfied with postwar border arrangements and abetted by the revisionist powers of Hungary and Italy. Refugees and spies thus went hand in hand during the interwar years. In this there was a whiff of prewar intrigues among refugee circles, but not one that was particularly sharp. In the scope and organization of their groups and cabals, and their secret police nemesis, they far outdistanced those who had preceded them. Moreover refugee circles now were easily swept up, as they had not been before, in international politics and espionage. Indeed to a considerable extent it was the refugees and their politics that made interwar espionage different from what had come before.

The wealth of spies in these years thus leads back to the Sorges, the Gardiners, the H. D.'s, and the W.'s. The history of espionage between the two wars was in large measure their history, a story of people and groups who came out of the war and who gravitated toward intrigue as if this were now their natural habitat. For some it was force of circumstances, for others it was opportunity; but for all it was the consequence of a war and an afterwar that rearranged their lives and cast espionage into an inviting, familiar setting that drove them to conspire or spy. There was an almost inexorable process of fusion between wartime experiences, postwar milieus, and espionage. That made espionage and intrigue not only a series of events or episodes but a medium through which certain characteristics of the interwar years came to be expressed. Availability of personnel was one side to this process. The intrusiveness of history was another. As in the cases of Gardiner, W., and the wider spectrum of émigré politics, crime and the fate of refugees point to what that too could represent.

It is not possible to write about espionage and intrigue without bringing in crime. Sensationalist spy stories and sensationalist crime stories took turns crowding each other off the front pages of the mass Paris dailies, as if the one were interchangeable with the other. Some people, like the authors of *The Army of Crime, Cocaine, Espionage After the War,* saw no difference at all between the milieus.[12] Every intelligence service had its crooks and outer circles of rogues, villains, and sleazy characters. British intelligence worked with Belgian smugglers during the war and counted some dubious figures among a number of its agents.[13] The Gestapo and Sicherheitsdienst (security service, or SD) employed confidence men, sometimes to their later chagrin.

No agency shied away from these kinds of characters, least of all the French secret service (or SR). At Riga in the late thirties and in early 1940 the SR was running a collection of pirates and reprobates as key agents in their Baltic operations. One of these was a man named Paschkowski, who recruited operatives for the French among German nationals returning from Estonia. Since 1937 Paschkowski had owned the Marelu restaurant on the Majorenstrasse in Riga, an establishment with an international clientele. Money to purchase the restaurant came from the wife of a former Russian cavalry officer, whom German counterespionage suspected of working for French and Latvian intelligence. In 1939 the officer was traced to a French casino in Cannes. Paschkowski's wife worked for a business firm in Riga from which she had embezzled money, although no formal complaint had been filed since the firm itself had been keeping false books. As German counterintelligence noted, "The Paschkowski family is not held in high repute in Riga." Among Paschkowski's contacts was Karl Kuschkewicz, who had been dismissed as Latvian consul in Danzig in 1924 for trafficking in false passports. From Danzig Kuschkewicz had traveled to Switzerland, where he offered his services simultaneously to French and German intelligence while Latvian officials demanded his extradition on charges of corruption and cocaine smuggling. Yet another Riga agent was an important Estonian figure known to be trafficking in weapons on the side.[14]

There was also Alexander Wasmus-Swirles, alias Fred Swirles and English Fred, whose origins were obscure — either Scottish or German — and who had led a checkered past living off *Tipstergeschaften* and other shadowy activities. He had emigrated to France, probably to put greater distance between himself and the German police. He was recruited by the SR, traveled to Switzerland and Holland on his English passport (although reportedly he spoke almost no English), and seems to have had special contacts with German émigrés desperate for money and whose services he employed or whose information he bought. He also worked with Rudolph Stallmann, known to various people as Lemoine, von Konig, and Rex. Like Swirles, Stallmann was a man whose past was a mystery. He too had left Germany for Paris where he immersed himself in a number of enterprises best described by the French word *louche*. The SR protected him from the French police, and in return he placed his multiple talents at their disposal, supplying false or authentic passports from practically any country, committing burglaries, infiltrating microphones into hotel rooms, and traveling abroad on special missions. Among his contacts was a man named Bauer-Mengelberg who procured travel papers to Argentina and Paraguay for Jewish refugees (Bauer-Mengelberg was especially well connected with the Paraguay consul in Paris) and whom the Germans equally suspected of working for French intelligence. According to a German list of French spy bureaus compiled during the occupation, Stallmann was running nine different offices in Paris, the two principal ones appearing to have been located at 27 rue de Madrid and 5 rue de Lisbonne. He was arrested by the Germans in 1942 but saved his neck by feeding his captors information, including the names of French agents. After the liberation the SR looked after him a bit — in that strange mélange of honor and moral squalor that comes with the profession — but he died of illness while still under detention.[15]

People like Stallmann or Kuschkewicz had their uses. Others, like W. or Gardiner, the police and professional spies could do without, but these kinds of schemers and confidence men kept cropping up with disturbing frequency in intelligence reports between the wars. Some were sharks out for a killing who found themselves inexorably entangled in espionage nets, and some were simply small fish hauled up with the others, because by the 1930s police either were coming to presume that spies and criminals might be the same thing or found that as they investigated the one they kept turning up the other. That is what happened to Alice L., whom the Prague police arrested in 1935 on charges of circulating counterfeit currency and stolen securities. Asked to investi-

gate from the French end, the Sûreté produced a thick dossier that tied
L. to swindlers and also to men who may have been arms traffickers and
spies; its conclusion was that nearly all of this gang of foreigners, L.
included, were in some way or another agents of a foreign power.[16]

Within the archives are many such tales, in which criminals and spies
cohabited or were seen as the same. The stories are interesting in themselves, and they remind one of the difficulty in reading the files when
often the source of information was habitual tricksters; this is a problem
that will be taken up shortly. The constant overlapping of milieus also
suggests how intrusive international politics could be in the interwar
years. This intrusiveness came from more than the familiar forced
choices of the Popular Front era when people were obliged to declare
their commitments. Rather it entailed the inescapability of the present
after the war, a difficulty of detaching oneself from the events of the
moment. One form of this was a present-mindedness that hung over
the period and intruded endlessly upon people's consciousness. The literature of the twenties and thirties betrays an acute sense of living in a
world shaped by the facts of the century: war, revolution, and global
reordering. This present-mindedness could lead to alarmist thoughts
about the next war or share the immediacy of Popular Front politics,
but it did not have to be only that. There was always a looser, even
amused or self-assured side to present-mindedness that future chapters
will explore, for example, in storytelling or travel.

The present impinged on people's lives as well by catching them up
in contemporary events and international politics. Adventure exhibited
this feature between the wars; so too did intrigue. The fluidity of interwar intrigues, their protean, nearly ubiquitous quality was representative of the intrusive, inescapable character of the period. People
crossed the line into intrigue almost unawares, fell into intrigues, or
were swept up within them through sheer force of circumstances. Like
availability, the opportunities that drove criminals to take advantage of
international crises readily entangled them with spies and secret agents.
Gunrunning was the most obvious example and Spain would be
the consummate moment. Yet this kind of entanglement proceeded at
a varying pace all through the period. It is not incongruous to come
across an adventurer like Gardiner in counterespionage reports on the
Rif war, but he might have wondered what he was doing there, or how
his pursuit of fast money had embroiled him with (presumed) spies and
foreign agents. Alice L. may have been a secret agent, but quite likely
she too was simply an adventuress living on the shady side of the law

and suddenly caught in an affair of espionage that took her unawares. Intrigue kept spreading out after the war, drawing in more and more people. A crook like Israel Meyerowitz, who before the war ran white-slave traffic between Poland and Argentina and employed the services of smugglers to get his women across borders,[17] operated nevertheless within a clearly defined milieu; such types in the twenties and thirties turned up as traffickers in false papers or guns and then found themselves rubbing shoulders with spies. Criminals, therefore, were the easiest catch. But Jewish refugees who sought nothing more than personal security also found themselves sucked into intrigues either because they had nothing else to offer as collateral or because the scramble for passports and visas ensnared them in a sleazy milieu operating on the edges of espionage, or at times deep within it. This is why one cannot write the history of interwar espionage simply as the story of intelligence services. Too many other people found their lives intertwined with spies or spooks. The intersections or crossovers came easily in an era of blurred distinctions between private life and the great events of one's times.

The multidimensionality and pervasiveness of espionage, then, derived largely from the availability of people and the intrusiveness of events in the years after the war. It was also a consequence of flux. There was a certain kaleidoscopic character to interwar intrigues. Combinations were always forming, then changing. Associations tended to run together, producing ultimately an effect of confusion and impermanence. Ustasha terrorists, for example, could be identified with Rome and Berlin, the kidnappers of White Russian generals with Moscow and Germany. White Russian intrigues had feeder lines into practically all camps. At the beginning of the twenties converging tracks led back to Bolsheviks, Germans, and pan-Islamists, at the end of the thirties to Bolsheviks and Nazis. The convergence of intrigues and their shifting quality echoed in the number of double agents who appear in the files. Spies and intriguers shifted quarters as if they were playing musical chairs. Betrayals and sellouts approached epidemic proportions. Nothing was immutable.

In this too espionage shared in the character of its times. Like espionage and intrigue, the interwar years tended toward flux and unsettlement. Their mutability and confusion showed up in French writing about the Soviet Union or the Pacific; the urge to travel and report; the traveling personality of literary characters who drifted, lacked moorings, were always on the move; the fascination with movement in the air or in automobile caravans; as well as the shifting political combinations and the unsettlement of international conditions. These were difficult years to sort out, when the sense of movement was so palpable but when final destinations or outcomes were not at all clear. The very open-endedness of the period contributed to the flourishing of espionage. Flux generated intrigues, a side to the twenties and thirties that secret-war imagery captured so well in its vision of prolonged, unsettled battles fought out in the shadows by clandestine means. And flux shaped intrigues, made their confusions a repetition of wider circumstances. From its era espionage took its combinations and its multiple possibilities. If there were so few fixed points to interwar espionage it was because there were scarcely any at all in the interwar world.

Rarely did espionage cast off this odor of the age. There were the conventional, nearly timeless moments, for instance, the pursuit and arrests of German agents in the military regions of eastern France. Most of those caught were small fry with few credentials other than access to secrets and a willingness to sell these for cash, although occasionally the odd sensational affair erupted from these spy wars.[18] Yet the real history of espionage between the two world wars seemed to lie elsewhere, in the toughness and violence of secret service marauders and in a global subversive reach that arose against a background of war and revolution and the brittleness of empire. Wherever secret agents trod in the twenties and the thirties they left behind the imprint of their century. Their double dealings, their abductions, their networks, and their terror carried with them the smell of politics, civil strife, and the behind-the-lines battles that came with realignments after the war. In that dank air one senses once again the ineffable quality of atmosphere that hung over the spies and intriguers and that sealed their connections with a set moment in time. Atmosphere, availability, intrusiveness, and flux were the defining characteristics of interwar espionage. From the conjunction of the four emerged its milieu.

———————

But what, if anything, can we know for certain of that milieu? Consider, for example, the following case whose documentation can still be found in Archives nationales box 14754.[19] An editor at the time of the Marseilles assassinations of the king of Yugoslavia and the French foreign minister meets a man in Brussels who claims to be an orchestra conductor and a secret agent for Belgian counterintelligence. The spy tells the editor that he has just returned from Cologne where he has learned that an "international mafia" in the pay of the Germans is preparing to knock off the president of the Third French Republic, the commander-in-chief of the French army, and Benito Mussolini. Upon his return to Paris the editor repeats the conversation to a local official and a report works its way to a desk in the Sûreté and eventually into the dossiers of box 14754. The historian who comes across this paper will smile, perhaps shake his head, and then flip to the following pages in the stack. But the fact that the document has made its way there, preserved for posterity, is in itself troubling and raises the question of what to make of everything else in all those boxes on all those shelves that *dérogations* spring loose from the guardians of state secrets. "Truth" in the archives admittedly is at all times elusive, but the historian who sloshes into the files on espionage can wonder whether there is anything solid to grab hold of in those cartons. Before writing the history of espionage in this period, therefore, one does well to begin with the problem of the sources. A review of certain cases or reports will illustrate the bedevilment of these dossiers. It will also show that through the fog of indeterminacy and deceit a certain reality can emerge, and that judgments can be made that are not always a leap into the dark.

The sources are, frankly, perplexing—most clearly so in regard to credibility. Authorities themselves questioned or complained about the information that came in, an indication of how confounding these documents can be. For instance, in 1922 the minister of colonies received a report from the French representative in Riga that detailed the activities of communist agents in French Indochina. The minister forwarded the report to the governor general in Hanoi, but he prefaced it with a note of skepticism. The language of the report, the minister indicated, suggested that the original source was a Russian, probably an individual selling information for profit, and perhaps the man was exaggerating the facts "in order to magnify, simultaneously, the importance of the service rendered and that of the reward."[20] In 1937 an inspector of the Police mobile expressed his exasperation with efforts to get to the bottom of terrorist attacks in the south of France. He said there was no question that the attacks were related to the civil war in Spain. The problem was determining who was responsible:

It is a tricky matter . . . to establish the origins of these bombs and the reasons why they were placed. Our information comes only from partisans, agitators, spies, and traffickers who abound throughout the Midi and who are mostly foreigners, more precisely, Italians, Spaniards, and Germans. The information is often vague, contradictory, or concocted because it is furnished by secret agents serving one or even several causes, themselves immersed in that whole atmosphere, deceiving one another, and gathering intelligence that they accept without any control.[21]

This milieu was always a problem for contemporaries, as it remains one for the historian today. Too many crooks or shady figures inhabited the spy world or hung about its fringes, furnishing tips for money or for protection or working directly for French counterintelligence. Their access to information was often indisputable, but their credibility was not. One wonders how many reports came from people like Kuschkewicz or Paschkowski or the White Russian Zavadskii-Krasnopol'skii who mucked around in sleazy affairs and whom Inspector Faux-Pas-Bidet used as an informant. These were easy targets for suspicion and control. Yet nearly all information carried with it a certain dubious quality. Everyone in this milieu deceived and dissembled, including the professionals whose efficiency or survival depended on their mastering the art of subterfuge. Le Carré was right to make his perfect spy a chameleon-like figure, a compulsive liar, and the son of a confidence man.[22]

Thus even reports with a semblance of accuracy could be the product of prestidigitation or quackery. A case from the years right before the First World War suggests the complexity of the problem. In the early 1900s French intelligence stationed a man in Antwerp, Europe's principal port of arms shipments, to monitor arms smuggling to Morocco. Over the next several years this "correspondent in Antwerp" filed a steady stream of communiqués signaling contraband weapons concealed in crates labeled "locks," "candles," "matches," "cement," or simply "mixed cargo." The shippers, the correspondent argued, were Germans working with the complicity of their government and the captains of lines plying the waters between Europe and Africa. Antwerp, where customs inspections were lax, was the nodal point for charging the cargo.[23]

The reports were short, detailed, and precise. They were also fabricated, according to another informant reporting to the Ministry of the Interior. No identity was given for the second correspondent. One suspects the sort of seasoned detective who would make the weary journey up the stairs in the 1930s, a gumshoe who knew the twenty kilometers of docks at Antwerp, drank coffee with customs officials, occasionally bought dinner for maritime agents, told them good stories, got along, offered last cigarettes, and had a good ear for distinguishing rumor from fact. His report on the matter, written in 1907, merits consideration in detail for what it suggests about the correspondent in Antwerp's reporting techniques.

The report begins with a series of bulletins recently filed by the correspondent in Antwerp. In every instance the SR agent has got the facts wrong. According to the correspondent, the Woermann Line has suspended departures for Morocco because of "Moroccan difficulties (read: the presence of French ships)." But, the second informant reports, the Woermann Line has no regular service to Morocco (the service was in fact suspended four years earlier).[24] The correspondent writes that the German freighter *Ascania* left Antwerp on the twelfth, having embarked eighteen crates of guns labeled as "locks." The second informant reports that the *Ascania* departed Antwerp on the tenth. Its cargo was phosphates and the customs men are certain of this. They saw no crate that looked as if it might contain rifles, not even under the denomination of "locks." Again the correspondent writes that the *Mogodor* of the OPDR loaded two boxes of matches that looked suspicious and that he forced one box open, discovering that the merchandise has been concealed within a second box of zinc sheets. His suspicions aroused, the correspondent gives the freighter's itinerary; the authorities should watch this boat. The second informant reports that matches are always packed in zinc boxes placed within a crate of wood. This protects them from humidity. "There is nothing in all this that would surprise the initiated." And so it goes. The second informant matter-of-factly corrects one error after another, like a man who realizes he is dealing with an idiot but must, for professional reasons, contain his temper.

Continuing, the detective acknowledges that Antwerp is the center of clandestine arms shipments. Nonetheless he doubts that the correspondent in Antwerp is capable of ferreting out the information he has been forwarding to Paris. Step by step the detective reviews the procedure of shipping illegal arms. The customs officials, he notes, are sharp and knowledgeable, but they are instructed not to intervene and limit themselves to verifying markings and numbers of boxes.[25] Once a box has been sealed and labeled no one, not even maritime agents or *douaniers,* know or care what is inside. Consequently it is easy to get suspicious, to go to the quai, for example a quai where a ship is loading cargo for Morocco, to identify boxes that might contain arms, to write down their markings and their numbers, to check the ship's manifesto posted with the central customs office to identify what is officially within, and then to write reports where suspicions become facts, and where a veneer of data passes for insider information. The detective is careful not to say outright that this is what the correspondent in Antwerp is doing. But he admits that such a method of operation is possible and that this correspondent seems better informed than the detective believes any one individual can be. Indeed this correspondent knows everything in Antwerp, except for the facts that he almost never gets straight. The detective ends with a demonstration of how easy it is to fabricate provocative information out of nothing substantial. "All that [ship itineraries] I have read in the *Lloyd Anversois*. You can see how easy it would be to embroider upon it. One has discovered this, one has learned that; one is going to check at Lillo, and so forth, and so forth."[26]

The report is arresting, a virtuoso performance that points to how fraudulent and misleading these files can be. Its follow-up is equally disturbing. Despite the second informant's devastating critique the correspondent in Antwerp continued to forward his reports and the authorities continued to take these seriously, sending them on to various ministries and to appropriate officials in Morocco. Whether there were reasons to dismiss the second informant's reservations, or whether the correspondent was replaced by another, or whether there was a bias in favor of the correspondent's intelligence — these are questions without any answers. Reports in the Ministry of the Navy indicate that not a single bulletin from Antwerp ever led to confiscation of an arms shipment to Morocco — largely for lack of machinery to do anything about them — and that in 1910 the authorities gave thought to ending the SR position in that city.[27] Still the reports continued, illustrating the difficulty of distinguishing fact from fantasy in the espionage files.

Little, then, is certain about the sources, and to the puzzles of professional sharpsters and confounders can be added the familiar problem of working in espionage files: the rumors and innuendoes passed on by suggestible agents; the agents predisposed to find evidence of foreign intrigue under certain villainous beds. Myriads of paper in the archives bear an official stamp yet simply do not ring true, or convey information counter to what other historians have found. Other kinds of reports fall into a middle ground, taxing credibility, but only to a point, and lying beyond the means to confirm. Reliability is at a premium in these files, and the problem is compounded by the fragmentariness or lack of resolution to a large part of the espionage record.

The Second World War has done more than its share to thin out the archives. Whole files and (worse) half files have completely disappeared, and the continued process of secrecy compounds the difficulties. The result is a partial record that stymies the historian's ability to verify or to follow suspicions to their conclusion. War loss, however, only explains part of the problem. Lack of resolution was also a contemporary bugbear, so that the record that remains is often incomplete because authorities themselves frequently never got to the bottom of affairs. At times suspects were tipped off or were exceptionally cautious or reports had no substance in the first place. At other times investigations went nowhere because police ran into roadblocks.

For example, when police missions went abroad in 1934 to learn more about the Ustasha terrorists who had planned and executed the Marseilles assassinations and who had close ties to Hungary and Italy, they met with nothing but frustration. One Sûreté inspector, Charles Chennevier, traveled to Rome and to Janka Puszta (the Hungarian farm where the terrorists had trained) for naught. Italian and Hungarian authorities stalled him and threatened him, and a friend in the Italian police who had promised information sent word by a prostitute that he was leaving Rome immediately. This melodramatic tale, recounted in Chennevier's memoirs,[28] is borne out by the reports of two other detectives dispatched abroad: Inspector Royère who went to Turin to question Ante Pavelic, the leader of the Ustashi, and Eugen Kvaternik, the coordinator for the assassination squad, who had been arrested; and Commissaire Barthelet who stopped in Budapest. Royère's stay in Turin was an exercise in futility. He was not permitted to see the two men and he was told that the address at which Pavelic had been living could not be divulged in order to protect his wife and two children from the vengeance of the Yugoslav government. Royère sat in the office of Questor Stracca and listened to lies, half-lies, and omissions so conspicuously incredible that if they had been true must have testified to the thorough incompetence of the Italian police. On Questor Stracca's desk sat a fat dossier from which a few pieces of information, "only what was difficult to refuse me," floated Royère's way. Stracca told the detective that Pavelic had arrived in Turin in October 1933 under the name of Giovanni Suicbenk, but that he had come to the attention of the Italian police only after the assassinations when officials drew up a list of all foreigners in the city. Once arrested, Stracca boasted, Pavelic had been submitted to a "searching interrogation," words Royère could not resist following with *sic* in his report. Royère's visit was reduced to a formality. He returned home having learned nothing substantially new.[29]

Barthelet's experience in Hungary was similar. In Budapest he ran up against a stone wall of official silence and defiance. The director of the political police, Hetenyi, told him that an independent investigation into the case was out of the question and that only if Barthelet accepted this condition would his stay in Budapest be "without difficulties," a scarcely veiled threat that Barthelet comprehended perfectly. The French detective had no difficulty identifying the two plainclothesmen who tailed him wherever he went. On the evening of 3 December Barthelet met briefly with Hetenyi. They fixed an interview for the following day when Hetenyi would provide an official response to questions concerning Hungarian connections with the Ustashi. Hetenyi failed to show up for the meeting. Barthelet ran into him as he was leaving the building, much to the Hungarian's embarrassment. Hetenyi said to come back at six in the evening of the fifth and then rushed away. The next day Barthelet gained entry to Hetenyi's office, but the Hungarian said he was absorbed with important affairs and could talk only for a moment. Barthelet, who by this time was coming to the end of his tether, made some remarks about the cavalier manner in which the Hungarian police were investigating the affair. Hetenyi handed over some papers in Hungarian and said others would follow right away. Eventually Hetenyi did give Barthelet a written response, but it merely skirted the issues. When Barthelet complained that the answers were insufficient, he received another runaround and another note that was no more satisfactory than the first. Like Royère, he returned to Paris with little to show for his efforts.[30]

In different ways the frustrations that Royère and Barthelet met recurred time and again in the interwar years. The police were not without resources and sometimes cracked big cases, for example, the Switz-Stahl affair that led to the arrest of dozens of people. Other times their investigations turned up no incriminating evidence and petered out into an unsatisfactory conclusion of plausible suspicions and exasperating dead ends. One classic instance was the investigation of the kidnapping of General Kutepov in 1930. The police had every reason, and many indications, to suspect a Soviet secret police operation. But they never could prove their case and there were alternative interpretations as to just what had happened, so in the end they called off the hunt and acknowledged their inability to resolve the affair. The kidnapping of Kutepov's successor, General Miller, seven years later produced nearly identical suspicions and results.

Cases like these represent the archives' dominant side. The record on espionage and intrigue is pitted with doubts, false leads, and unresolved episodes. There is always the question of whether a report is believable or whether authorities who identified suspects and circulated information were caught up in a self-created milieu of fantasy and paranoia.

Still, the historian who travels through this bog will find the occasional terra firma. For example, the authorities vetted reports and evaluated many sources, so that frequently one has some idea where officials stood with the raw material they received. There was no strict rating system, but indications that the informant was a beginner or "an absolutely sure source," or one of a number of designations in between, have left a charting of sorts for the sea of paper that washed across desks in the Sûreté or Deuxième Bureau and then on, after sorting, to ministries all over Paris.

Among the very best sources were agents who had penetrated foreign intelligence services or foreign agents who had gone over to the French or been turned by counterintelligence. One of these was a counterespionage official named Doudot who infiltrated the German Abwehr station in Münster so successfully that he could identify more than thirty German agents working in France. There was also a man named Gessmann who worked for the German intelligence post at Lindau. An Austrian national and an opponent of the Nazis, Gessmann offered his services to the Sûreté. Like Doudot, Gessmann signaled German agents working in France. The French watched him carefully and tested him; they were certain he was not a German plant.[31]

Agents like Doudot and Gessmann were exceptions, but they represent what a good or reliable source could be and consequently the credibility of certain intelligence sent up the ladder. According to one intelligence officer from the thirties, the French possessed "a very thorough knowledge of the German secret services."[32] Agents in the field often duplicated assignments to provide further control over incoming intelligence, and the SR's central bureaus carefully scrutinized raw data.[33] Moreover the evaluation system was complemented by verification or follow-up reports by the police. The archives are filled with these. Many led nowhere, revealing once again the murkiness of information or a frustrating inability to uncover hard evidence. Yet these too attest to the controls the French placed on the intelligence they received and circulated. Nor did an inconclusive follow-up necessarily mean that suspicions were unfounded. In this respect the case of Samuel I. is useful.

In the fall of 1932 a baggage handler who worked the sleeping cars on the Paris-Bucharest express brought the following story to the police. He said that in June he had been approached by a man who he thought was a German. The man had told him that he represented American companies with patent rights in Europe and that he would pay the baggage handler to carry their secret correspondence from Vienna to Paris. If the baggage handler agreed, a woman would board his train in Vienna, hand him the correspondence, and then leave the train at Linz. Once in Paris the baggage handler would go to a meeting place designated in advance and hand over the correspondence to a man carrying a copy of *L'Auto* magazine. The baggage handler agreed and on 19 October he met a man at the Temple métro station in Paris. They took a short walk and the baggage handler slipped him an envelope. The man was the same one who had approached the baggage handler in June. It was apparently at this point that the baggage handler went to the police.

The police identified the man as Samuel I., an Austrian, and they placed him under surveillance. At the time Samuel I. was living at a hotel on the rue de l'Exchiquier. Later he moved into a room on the avenue Mozart where he stayed, departing and then returning periodically, for at least another year. He played his business affairs close to the vest, although he claimed to be a commercial representative selling typewriters. He received little mail and no visitors, and he came and went at regular hours. The police uncovered little more except that Samuel I. was in contact with a man named John T., a naturalized Nicaraguan of Russian origins. John T. ran a photojournalism agency called Globe Photo out of an office on the Champs-Elysées. The police placed this man too under surveillance and turned up nothing but suspicious details. They learned that John T. had come to Paris in 1930, presenting himself as an importer and a forwarding agent for foreign firms that he declined to identify. Then he had traded in cutlery and porcelain before turning to photojournalism. From its inception Globe Photo received considerable mail from abroad, particularly from Vienna and Berlin. Before moving to the Champs-Elysées, John T. had shifted his office to the premises of an Austrian national who sold calendars and calendar books made in Germany. The Austrian's shop was on the boulevard du Temple, and Globe Photo was still located there at the time that the baggage handler made his drop with Samuel I. in the vicinity. John T. frequented the German embassy, the race track, and gambling houses. His acquaintances included a trader in semiprecious stones and the director of a White Russian newspaper. Nothing about John T. seemed ordinary. Yet there were no clear connections to espionage and police could not determine the nature of his relationship with Samuel I. or discover anything incriminating about the initial target of surveillance. By early 1934 both Samuel I. and John T. had left Paris, and the investigation was shelved. Then in December 1935 the Yugoslav police uncovered a Comintern operation in Belgrade, and in January they arrested more people. One of these was Samuel I., whom the Belgrade authorities held on charges of espionage. Under interrogation, Samuel I. admitted that he was a Communist agent and that he had first come to Paris in 1931 as a courier for Soviet intelligence. The Yugoslavs passed this information on to the French.[34]

So suspicions were not always fabricated out of thin air, nor were the character-types that one might pack into the spy novels without real-life counterparts. The case of Samuel I. is illuminating because it shows how often the difference between confirmation or inconclusiveness in reporting was merely a lucky break. Some spies, particularly amateurs who had one particular piece of knowledge to sell and who were small fry in an enemy's operation, could be easy catches for the police. Others, professionals or people with expertise and connections, were slippery characters who slithered in and out of police files. Occasionally they aroused suspicions, set off an alarm, but then they were gone or were so smooth that police could never get a hold on them. Their only trace was the original unauthenticated warning, one of the hundreds or more that came in every year from cranks, meddlers, and suggestible informants as well as from agents with access to knowledge and the occasional poor slob who fell into something that, as the baggage handler did, he took to the authorities. The police learned that many of these were without substance, but they also learned that some accusations eventually proved true. They took their investigations seriously when there was some plausibility to the case, and the matter of Samuel I. suggests a reason for historians to do the same. Occasionally the police were right about the suspects they identified, even if their investigations went down blind alleys.

The question, of course, remains: how many of these cases were true, or, put otherwise, how many Samuel I.'s were there on the loose? The revelations of sensationalist spy affairs provide a few answers here. Some were breathtakingly outlandish, exposing how intrigue-ridden these decades could be. Other answers come from the German archives, although haltingly so because war damage and willful destruction have erased many of the interwar records. The German Foreign Ministry file on agents and espionage in Spain, 1920–1935, gives some indication of what the researcher will find in these papers. A large portion of this dossier concerns the lost baggage of a Frau von Popowitsch, who claimed to have worked once for German intelligence in the Iberian peninsula during the First World War. Perhaps some history lies embedded in this affair — light directed momentarily on the daily life of bureaucracies or on the petty obsessions of one-night-stand agents. Espionage, however, cannot be counted among the tales it has to tell.[35]

At their best, the German archives disclose how easy it was to pass on misleading material since the Germans themselves often had little control over their agents or were beset by impostors posing as *Vertrauensmänner,* confidential agents. Counter to instructions Gestapo branch offices dispatched agents abroad on their own initiative, while interagency competition created its own jumble of intelligence operations, so bad, for instance, in Yugoslavia in October 1939 that the military attaché stationed in Belgrade protested against an SD organization that, he said, was out of control.[36] There was also the unending problem of fraud. Throughout the thirties Foreign Ministry representatives abroad complained of people who dropped in from the blue, without accreditation, claiming to work for the Gestapo or the SD or the Abwehr and asking for money or special assistance. Some turned out to be genuine, others were fake. The problem appears to have been pandemic, sparing no agency. In the Rome office of the Mittel-Europäischen Reisebüro a man named Hermann Krebs approached a travel agent with a request to exchange German currency. Krebs said he was an SS agent and that he never had difficulty converting German credits into foreign exchange. The travel agent was an SD plant whose curiosity was piqued. He asked Krebs what he was doing in Rome. Krebs replied that he was on an intelligence mission. The SD man reported the matter and received the response that Krebs was no SS agent but a con man with a record.[37]

The situation was complicated by the fact that German agencies had a record of employing dubious characters whose talents were better geared to swindling and defrauding than they were to gathering intelligence. The Gestapo was burned by a man named Schneekloth whose police record was as long as his arm. During the war Schneekloth had rented out part of his house in Amsterdam to German intelligence and had worked for the Germans as an agent, but there had also been strong indications that he had been selling them out to the French. Nevertheless, in the thirties Schneekloth was back in German employ, this time as an informant on the activities of German political refugees in the Netherlands. He appears to have conned a Gestapo official mercilessly, dishing up any piece of information that would sell, until another official uncovered the racket. There were other cases of people like this who had cheated the authorities once and were attempting to do so again, given the warnings to beware of such characters that emerged from agencies like the Abwehr or the Foreign Ministry. Indeed, even once the Germans were on to Schneekloth they had reason to fear that he would continue to represent himself as one of their agents.[38] For the Germans, as for the French, the spy world was filled with impostors, and matters were complicated still further because not all of these were crooks. In the fall of 1938 the Gestapo arrested a Czech agent masquerading as a Gestapo official and carrying false identity papers to this effect. The man had infiltrated Sudeten German circles as an agent provocateur and had sought to encourage acts of sabotage or terrorism that could be blamed on German secret agents. During his interrogation he admitted to seeing a whole stack of false German papers in Prague.[39]

For the French this state of affairs could only be confusing. Tramping through Europe were bogus *V.-Männer*, con artists, swindlers, impostors talking up their missions or intimating of operations they knew about, either because they scented profit in the story or sought self-aggrandizement or because once having put on the identity they were content to wear it forever. It is not difficult to imagine the consequences: their inevitable encounters with French counterintelligence agents who would see through some but not through all the practiced bamboozlers nor through the men and women who at one time had worked for German intelligence and had once, perhaps, been known to the French as the genuine article. Add to this the freelancers who *were* secret agents but who were out of control and one can begin to account for some of the wilder reports that strain credibility yet nevertheless were filed and circulated by authorities who had reason to believe them. None of this welter of identities and individuals clarifies the question of which reports were true, and which ones were not. But it does show another side to the coin of deception and credulity. The French could be mistaken not because they deluded themselves or gave way to panic but because, at times, they were simply taken in. Paradoxically, these sets of files can confirm one's faith in the reporting process.

There are, however, better morsels to chew on. The records of the Bremen Abwehr station—only a branch of one Abwehr post—turn up a number of agents working in France and North Africa. One of these was Kurt Wertheim, who was born in Duisburg in 1901, spoke French, Arabic, and Dutch, served in the French Foreign Legion, and was an active agent for Bremen from 1937. Another was Paul Kuehner, a powerfully built man with graying hair and gray-green eyes, who was quick, intelligent, and spoke French, English, Spanish, and a little Arabic. For years he represented Krupp interests in Morocco. From 1936–1939 the Stuttgart station ran him as a secret agent in France. Later he transferred to Bremen operations and worked in occupied France until he was arrested for embezzlement in 1943. German security files contain the biography — irritatingly sketchy — of Marcel Tsunke who worked for party foreign intelligence and traveled to France, Spain, and Spanish Morocco in this capacity in the late thirties. He turns up in another report from March 1940, planning sabotage missions in France and Latin America. The SD agent planted in the Rome travel bureau acknowledged an earlier mission in Morocco. The Foreign Office records disclose a man named Sparwasser who in May 1939 appeared on the doorstep of the German consul in Tetouan proclaiming himself a Saharan scholar and an agent for the Abwehr. Sparwasser said he had come to North Africa to devise ways of interfering with French troop transports through the desert. The consul wrote Berlin for instructions and received a coded telegram that suggests Sparwasser may have been what he claimed. Shortly after war was declared the Tangier police arrested Sparwasser as he was attempting to cross over into Spanish Morocco in Arab clothing. He fed them a story that was not very credible, but several months later he was free and returning to Germany under the auspices of the Madrid Abwehr station. Once home he was to undergo training to determine his fitness for "special work" with Abwehr II (sabotage and subversion). There is also the report of Captain Xylander who traveled officially — evidently at French invitation — to North Africa in the first months of 1939. Xylander supplied what military intelligence he could, discounted subversion possibilities in Algeria and Tunisia, said they were more promising in Morocco, and recommended, among other things, clandestine arms shipments to all three colonies and the preparation of sabotage action that would be carried out in coastal areas once war was at hand. When war did come, German intelligence dispatched sabotage missions abroad to destroy French and British shipping. Traces of these can be found in files concerning covert operations in the Mediterranean. In early spring 1940 an agent named Rühle went to Fiume, Trieste, and Sušak to investigate possibilities for wrecking Allied boats in these ports and to establish the contacts that would enable him, or others, to execute these missions. At the same time codes were developed so that telegrams reading, "Send in x days x kg. mackerel in y crates," would specify quantities of fuses and explosives to be forwarded. Meanwhile security officials were discussing infiltrating radio transmitters and sabotage materials into France via Italy.[40] None of this is surprising but nevertheless helps explain the warnings that came in to the French from spring 1939 on regarding sabotage of their ships and other sensitive targets. Altogether, the German archives, like their French counterparts, possess remarkable powers to exasperate and confound, yet they too offer reason, at times, to believe that French counterintelligence was on the right track.

Finally, there are the reports that panned out. Investigations from 1937 show how even the most dire material forwarded by counterintelligence agents could indeed be fact. In the spring of that year there was a wave of terrorist attacks across Mediterranean France. Among these was a bomb explosion that ripped through the Bordeaux-Marseilles express, killing one person and injuring five others. The first break police had in the case came with the arrest of a man named Cantelli just after he had placed a time bomb above the international tunnel running from Cerbère to Port-Bou. Another lead followed the preliminary interrogation of an Italian named Tamborini living in Perpignan. When the police brought Tamborini in for questioning an Italian vice-consul, Giardini, swooped down on the station and insisted on speaking to Tamborini at once. The police told Giardini that this was not possible, but that they would pass on whatever he had to say to his man. Giardini then said that he had confided a pair of pants to Tamborini for cleaning and that he needed these back right away. Tamborini, upon communication of this rather weird message, replied that he had left the pants at the Bar des Halles, a local hangout known for its Italian Fascist clientele. Not satisfied with this news, Giardini persisted, with visible anger, in his demand to see Tamborini personally to the point that the police had to restrain him. At one moment he managed to get close enough to Tamborini to blurt out before the stunned assembly of police functionaries, "You've gotten yourself caught, you imbecile!" Then Giardini left and picked up his package at the Bar des Halles, although to police it seemed too small to contain a pair of pants. Several months later, further investigations and depositions by Cantelli and Tamborini made clear the reasons for this extraordinary performance.

Tamborini, according to a report put together by Sûreté Inspector Delrieu in October 1937, had known Giardini since the days just after the war and had worked for Italian "political espionage" since 1921. Using the cover of a bicycle racer and mechanic he had traveled throughout Europe, arriving in Spain in late 1935. Following the outbreak of the Spanish civil war, he had worked his way into the FAI (the Federación anarquista ibérica, a militant anarchist movement) in Barcelona. Later he left the FAI and joined the independent Marxist party, the POUM (Partido obrero de unificación marxista). Apparently unmasked as a spy, he moved across the border to Perpignan, where he renewed contact with Giardini and ran a spy ring of Italians and Spaniards. His work seems to have divided evenly between political and military espionage. Of fifty reports he forwarded to Italy, twenty-three concerned the activities of anti-Fascist Italians in France and twenty-seven contained intelligence on military matters. Some military information, including details on Republican formations, he passed on to Franco.

Tamborini told Delrieu that he was not responsible for the bombings, and Delrieu, to a point, was willing to believe him. But he argued in his report that the interrogations of Tamborini and Cantelli and information supplied by a Loyalist double agent who had infiltrated Tamborini's organization pointed toward Fascist Italy as the source of the bombings. Delrieu concluded that the Italians, with the cooperation of Spanish Nationalists, were financing and conducting a major terrorist operation in France "with the intention of destroying supplies destined for Republican Spain . . . and, for political reasons easy to understand, of creating a malaise in France, even troubles to be exploited by anti-French propaganda services working abroad."[41] He was, in fact, not very far off the mark. The arrest and interrogation of former Italian intelligence officials following the Second World War revealed that Italian military intelligence (the Servizio informazioni militari, or SIM) had indeed concocted a broad project of orchestrated terror to disrupt the passage of goods to Republican Spain and to disseminate uncertainty and disarray within France. The schemers had gone so far as to contemplate diffusing the germs of epidemic diseases, although they had never implemented these grotesque proposals. Some of the strikes that were carried out were the work of the right-wing French extremists known as the Cagoule. Others were executed by an Italian squad operating out of Imperia near the French border.[42]

If, then, uncertainty reigns in the archives on spies and skepticism must supersede faith, these files are not the product of a system run amok. The dossiers may tease and frustrate, but it is possible to pick one's way through the minefields and to acquire a sense for what can be discarded and what might be credible. These are not easy archives to work with. But they describe a milieu that reached beyond imagination and fear.

The First World War demanded of intelligence and counterintelligence organizations a scale and method and a professional expertise that they had not known before 1914 and that they would relinquish only reluctantly and partially once the war came to an end and the inevitable pruning occurred. The rise of Soviet networks of considerable magnitude, the unsettled climate in international affairs, the flow of refugees, and the bent toward rationalization, system, and technological innovation in these years assured that neither demobilization nor treaty restrictions would return intelligence battles to their prewar levels. Foreign agents and secret police crisscrossed the world between the wars. They were better equipped, more professional, more obtrusive, and more numerous than they had been before 1914. This difference in size, scope, and method, bequeathed by wartime experience and confirmed by postwar circumstances, marked one distinction between interwar espionage and the intrigues of the past.

Nothing typified the changes more than the international circuits of Soviet espionage. From almost the inception of Soviet rule, French counterintelligence chronicled the exploits of an intelligence system that had no counterpart in the years preceding the First World War. Nothing rational that the French compiled on espionage before 1914 compared with their description of Soviet courier networks, or international transit systems, or Soviet operational centers, or the global scope of Soviet intrigues, or even the details that surfaced when a single case was cracked.

The Switz-Stahl ring, which the French broke in the mid-1930s, provides a good illustration. Ring members ranged across Europe, they utilized cameras or were trained in radio transmission, and they concentrated on military intelligence of a scientific or experimental nature. Operatives included paid agents with access to secrets, but also the kinds of individuals one would encounter in the spy world of the interwar years: party militants, ideological fellow travelers willing to serve the cause and who sometimes were exploited and sucked in over their head; foreigners; agent controllers; and the professional impresario in the background, in this case a man named Boris Rschezki whom the French police never caught. The ring was huge, organizing into a single operation sources, photographers, instructors, runners, and a network of couriers and intermediaries to tie things together. There were thirty-two indictments in the case, indicating the scale that separates this affair from those of the past.[43]

Nearly everything about Soviet espionage bore this hallmark of organization and planning. The same intricacy characterized communist circuits designed to infiltrate agents into France in the 1920s. At higher levels of operations the Soviets worked through regional headquarters or centers. Germany, especially Berlin, whose criminal sweatshops made the city into an entrepôt of forged papers and "special services" after the war, was the most important staging point down to 1933. Another center operated in Vienna, running agents and couriers throughout Eastern Europe and the Balkans. Again, what distinguished this system from prewar ones was not only its structured networks for control, transit, and communications, but also its worldwide extension. Soviet centers were in Berlin and Vienna, but they operated as well in central Asia and Shanghai.[44]

There were several factors militating toward the scale and systematization of Soviet espionage after the war. One was the multiplication of both agencies and functions. Soviet organs of espionage included Red Army intelligence (the Glavnoe razvedyvatel'noe upravlenie, or GRU), the secret police (the Gosudarstvennoe politicheskoe upravlenie, or GPU),[45] the Comintern, and, to a certain extent, Communist parties that the GRU and GPU shied away from as insecure for covert operations but viewed as a reservoir of contacts, couriers, and potential agents.[46] All of these agencies gathered military intelligence, but traditional espionage characterized only a part of their clandestine activities. Surveillance of refugees, dissemination of propaganda, kidnapping, murder, subversion, and ultimately the preparation of world revolution escalated the number of agents and, correspondingly, required the elaboration of support systems that swelled agent ranks still further. Because enterprises were so broad in scope and because they struck at the internal security of nations and empires, evoking considerable vigilance and police repression in response, Soviet agencies were obliged to systematize their methods of operation. The war, in which the scale of intrigue had been comparable, provided certain lessons here, as did failed insurrections like the one in Germany in 1923.[47] The result was the centers, underground circuits, false passport workshops, courier networks, and covers that turned up in police and counterintelligence reports in the twenties and thirties. Moreover, the global expanse of Soviet operations was powered not only by ambitions for world revolution or the perception that the easiest pickings were to be found in the empires, but also by the fear of a capitalist counterrevolutionary onslaught on all geographical fronts and by the dispersion of considerable numbers of White Russian refugees to East Asia, especially Manchuria.

For nearly all nations, however, there was an inexorable drive toward the creation or maintenance of large organized intelligence services after the war, because the war experience or the dangers and opportunities of the interwar years magnified the value of formal intelligence gathering and special operations. For the Germans, defeat and treaty restrictions only temporarily delayed the construction of such networks. Initially German intelligence may have reconstituted itself through quasi-private or loosely assimilated official structures. Nonetheless it was active almost immediately following the war, and although major expansion came only after the Nazi seizure of power, French documentation — for instance the reports on Impex — suggests the possibility of persistently ambitious German operations dating back to the early 1920s.[48] Under the Nazis intelligence capacity spread prodigiously and exorbitantly among a number of agencies. The central organ for espionage was the Abwehr (created under Weimar), but it was quickly rivaled by party operations, especially the SD. In 1939, the RSHA (Reichssicherheitshauptamt), an SS mélange of party and government bureaus that included SD foreign intelligence (now Section VI) and the Gestapo, represented another large (and aggressive) intelligence establishment. Whether any of these branches were running kidnapping specialists or foreign assassination squads (as *The Brown Network* asserted) is doubtful. But the Gestapo did engineer a number of abductions, including the filching and removal of an activist anti-Nazi émigré, Berthold Jacob, across the Swiss-German border in 1935.[49]

Such methods were part of an extensive surveillance net the Gestapo established over émigrés in Europe. The German police infiltrated, tracked, extorted, kidnapped, and apparently even murdered some of their prey, abetted in the less dirty jobs by official cooperation from the German Foreign Office.[50] The methods smacked of earlier police operations dating back to Bismarck's time, yet their scale, organization, and ruthless pursuit paralleled broader strategies of covert activities that fit with Nazi perceptions of the avenues to power and that the war had rendered all but conventional.

Again it is the structured, schematic quality that captures one's attention. From as early as 1934 technicians were working to devise and perfect firebombs for sabotage.[51] The Abwehr devoted one of its departments to sabotage and uprisings, although one should be careful not to exaggerate either its reach or its accomplishments in this area. Nevertheless, in 1936 the Abwehr began recruitment and training of special action units, including paratroopers, to operate behind the lines in

Czechoslovakia, Poland, and the Soviet Union in the event of a conflict. Ukrainians and German minorities from the designated territories provided the manpower.[52] Similar plans had existed before the First World War but only in the most rudimentary form and almost totally lacking in the formal preparation of operational squads. In keeping with Nazi practice other agencies forced their way into the picture. The SD established its own covert liaisons in the east and there were subversive broadcasts over Radio Vienna following the Anschluss in 1938.[53] When the Germans moved into Poland in 1939 Abwehr commando units blew up bridges, train stations, telephone and telegraph lines. Other units, assisted by *Volksdeutsche,* seized key transportation and industrial points to prevent their destruction by Polish dynamiters. Precise, systematic details, including diagrams, laid out methods of procedure and the exact demolition materials to be used. Eight months later similar operations would be employed in the invasion of the Benelux countries and France.[54] Meanwhile the SD was organizing its own sabotage enterprises; the Rühle mission to Yugoslavia in early 1940, for example, was RSHA inspired.

Competition between the Abwehr and SD was replicated at other levels by still other agencies. Further intelligence streamed in through the Foreign Office; the War Economics branch of the OKW (the armed forces' high command, the Oberkommando der Wehrmacht) which was responsible for most, but not all, economic data; the Forschungsamt, a communications intelligence office that intercepted and decoded radio and telephone messages; and other radio intercept agencies attached to the military services. Independent institutes and the information-gathering services of German business firms contributed additional information, although the latter often did so reluctantly and under pressure. Business branch offices abroad occasionally provided cover for agents in the field. The sprawl of intelligence bureaucracies and the irrationality of the political system as a whole meant that German espionage was fragmented and chaotic at the upper levels of intelligence assessment. Historians have not been impressed by its record. At other levels, however, German espionage displayed a tendency toward rationalized structuring and even excessive orderliness. Formal procedures for the exchange of information[55] and the precise definition of jurisdictions and responsibilities within agencies gave an organized complexion to the networks, at least on the surface.

The offensive posture of the new political systems and their obsession with political or ideological enemies abroad conferred a certain edge in the building of large espionage systems. Italian spies, but also OVRA (Opera vigilanza repressione antifascista) agents, terrorist circuits, or the subversive mobilization of Italian nationals abroad, especially in North Africa, clutter French interwar files. Yet even a traditional service like French intelligence ran a considerably larger and more methodical operation than it had before the First World War.[56] The principal conduit of information was the army's SR, which fed raw intelligence to the Deuxième Bureau. Staffing the central SR office were twenty-five army officers, twenty noncommissioned officers and thirty civil servants. The numbers were modest, but they represented more than a fivefold increase over the figures for the prewar years. Because postings shifted over time, it is difficult to establish the full range of SR activity at a single point in the interwar years. In general there appears to have been a rapid increase in stations in the 1920s, then some curtailment — probably with the depression — and then greater expansion as war drew near. The major intelligence posts were located on French soil, and these ran annexes and *antennes* abroad. Three of the main stations focused on Germany, a fourth directed its operations toward Italy, another worked out of Algiers, and a sixth — the Bureau d'études Pyrénéenes — was established at the time of the Spanish civil war. At some point during the interwar years, the SR maintained smaller stations — sometimes only a single central agent — in Prague, Warsaw (1920–1926), Bucharest, the Hague, Riga, Vienna (until 1938), Budapest, Belgrade, Sofia, Copenhagen, Moscow, Berlin (until 1926), Madrid, Rome, Amsterdam, Beirut, Istanbul, Rabat, Tangier, Djibouti (opened in 1933), Tientsin, and Singapore (only temporarily). On the eve of the war and at last with the Quai d'Orsay's acquiescence, the SR rushed agents into a series of consulates including those in Munich, Leipzig, Milan, and Zagreb. Altogether the number of SR agents directed against Germany in the late 1930s totaled fifteen hundred. A slightly smaller number operated against Italy. Most of these were drones, but among them were some exceptional finds that any intelligence service would have sold its soul for (or, more appropriately, taken out a second mortgage on). The SR had come a long way since the days of Captain Andlauer's sad little station in Belfort.

Operations in the Balkans in the late 1930s give some indication of the difference. Beginning in the spring of 1939 German intelligence uncovered several French spy rings in Yugoslavia. One of these seems to have been clumsily conducted, but another, although equally betrayed, appears to have operated with considerable range and dexterity. It ran through a man named George Hartwig, who had served as an officer in Casablanca and Djibouti and since June 1938 was working out of the passport section of the French consulate in Zagreb. The Hartwig of Zagreb took on the airs of a man about town, dispensing money with calculated abandon all the while building a circle of tipsters among hotel doormen, waiters, and demimondaines. Other contacts included an alleged editor with German citizenship; the French director of the Peugeot works in Zagreb ("tall, thin, sporty, salt and pepper hair, travels frequently to Germany"); several White Russians, including one who worked officially for the Zagreb police; a traveling salad oil representative from Vienna; an Albanian medical student; and a Greek jazz band singer whose orchestra appears to have toured Europe (in April 1939 he was playing the Hotel Metropol in Kaunas). Some of these were more agents than informants, assuring Hartwig's liaisons with his contacts in Germany. The organization seems to have worked with a certain success. By spring 1939 Hartwig possessed details on troop movements in the Ostmark, German shell fillings, and other technical matters that he forwarded to Paris via the Orient Express. In January 1940 the RSHA was reporting that French intelligence, driven from Vienna, Prague, and Warsaw, was concentrating a major effort in Yugoslavia and, for this purpose, had sent twelve intelligence officers to Belgrade to liaise with Yugoslav authorities and to expand espionage operations against Germany, Italy, and Hungary. Hartwig's networks were now tied into this wider campaign. The numbers of individuals identified as possible French agents in Yugoslavia by this report totaled thirty-seven, including an operative for sabotage action and a growing contingent of White Russian émigrés.[57]

The SR was only the largest intelligence agency run by the French between the wars. The navy controlled its own, much smaller, SR with stations in Metz, Dunkirk, Nice, and North Africa. This too expanded over time, establishing stations or *antennes* at the Hague, Hendaye, Tangier, Gibraltar, Dakar, and Shanghai, and infiltrating agents into embassies in London, Madrid, Berlin, Warsaw, and Istanbul. All through the period the Colonial Ministry operated a highly effective colonial police that channeled information from disparate parts of the world, particularly in regard to Comintern activities. In 1937 a separate colonial SR emerged. It assumed control of the SR posts in Djibouti and Tientsin and established main stations in Shanghai, Hanoi, Nouméa, Djibouti, Tananarive, Dakar, Brazzaville, and Fort-de-France. Counterintelligence divided between the police (especially the Sûreté nationale), responsible for counterespionage surveillance within France, and the SR, which gathered similar information abroad and stationed counter-intelligence people in all its principal postings. Again in 1937, as the international situation deteriorated, the Ministry of the Interior introduced special counterespionage brigades called the Surveillance du territoire. Meanwhile each service SR maintained a cryptography and tele-communications intercept unit (earlier attached to the general staffs), whose intelligence rivaled that of the best informants abroad. Captain Bertrand, who commanded SR cryptography, was a key participant in the breaking of the Wehrmacht's Enigma code. Additional intelligence came from military attachés, although these reported directly to the Deuxième Bureau.

With expansion came greater method, or a more systematic way of proceeding and assessing. One can see this in the charts and circulars that mapped the range of intelligence operations and defined jurisdictional boundaries or in the monthly reports like the *bulletins de renseignements des questions musulmanes,* or BRQMs, that the overseas section of the army general staff circulated on Muslim affairs or in the sheer amount of paper generated by these services. By the late 1930s the Ministry of Interior was printing annual directories — *menées terroristes* lists — that included mug shots, brief descriptions, and updates on terrorist suspects. When the French evacuated Paris in June 1940, the Préfecture de police loaded the 2,500,000 cards of its general card index, the card indexes of Austrian and Spanish refugees, 692,618 dossiers, and boxes of other documents onto a barge in the Seine and packed the archives of the Fourth Department (concerned with wartime restrictions on foreigners and staffed by over eighty employees) into trucks. All of this represented only a part of police archives. SR stations like the Bureau régional d'études militaires at Metz exhibited in their camou-flaged identification the same compulsion toward self-proclaimed bureaucratic professionalism that typified this organization after the war.[58]

Much of the systematization or professionalization of intelligence work in these years derived from a growing dependency on gadgetry and electronic paraphernalia that rendered all phases of espionage — penetration, communication, eavesdropping, and sabotage — more sophisticated and consequently more effective than they had been before. The French, Germans, and Soviets bugged telephones, intercepted messages, and maintained laboratories or workshops that fabricated what were coming to be the indispensable accoutrements of the well-equipped secret service: false papers, false-bottomed suitcases, miniature cameras, and, for the Germans, poison capsules that could fit within an artificial tooth and be used to escape interrogation. Thus support networks or technical units complemented the work in the field. They analyzed, squeezed down, camouflaged, or counterfeited whatever was necessary to combat the surveillance of counterespionage police. Microdots and two-inch-long cameras were some of their products. So too were scaled-down wireless transmitters, which all three services utilized abroad and which relegated parrot stories to the repertoire of nightclub comedians and historians.[59]

Radio transmissions, whose interception had come to constitute an essential share of counterintelligence operations before the war, now assumed more aggressive functions. They substituted modern technology not only for carrier pigeons but also, as one German expert believed, for the more colorful yet less reliable system of sleeping car attendants and travel agency couriers.[60] Although neither was doomed to extinction — wagon-lit agents remained a fixture in counterespionage files and couriers an indispensable component of any intelligence network — the ability to work a radio or access to someone who could became more and more a professional requirement. Ironically the greater turning toward covert warfare held out at the open level of mass communications even more tantalizing, and explosive, possibilities. By the late thirties all sides were engaging in the *guerre des ondes*. North Africa was an intensely contested battleground, but the subversion wars of the airwaves spread around the globe. The British, Soviets, Italians, Germans, and eventually the French vied for the most powerful and persuasive system of communications. Even the Hungarians built a network of relay stations along their frontiers to broadcast irredentist messages across borders. In the evenings there would be temporary interruptions in programming from Budapest followed by local news bulletins describing disorders between Croats and Serbs, or comparable clashes in Romania and Czechoslovakia. The stories, in their choice of subject and of language — prewar geographic and ethnic identifications — aimed to inflame tension and sow uncertainty, while the medium itself — intrusive, popular, and authoritative in tone — offered propaganda opportunities far in excess of more commonplace methods.[61]

Method, technology, and sophisticated networks in turn produced a more professional agent than those who had worked in earlier times. Only a number truly fit this category. The spy world continued to run over with swashbuckling types who crashed their way through into espionage work and left a mess wherever they went, and with hopeless amateurs whom counterespionage police mopped up right and left with increasing regularity. There were bunglers, dupes, and gushing enthusiasts like the SD plant in the Rome travel bureau who wrote his report as if he had sailed across uncharted oceans and then set foot upon *terra cognita*. Surprisingly the intelligence service that commanded the greatest awe and respect — the British — was often the shoddiest in its preparation of agents.[62] But there were also certain imperatives that drove professionalization forward. One of these was the growing technical cast to intelligence work. Another was the war, whose pumped-up spy scene actuated levels of prowess that had not been necessary before 1914. All through the war years intelligence services improvised and experimented, ruining lives and reputations but leaving behind a fount of experience in building large covert spy rings or working with false papers and covers. After the war there were people who went permanently underground as professional intriguers. A few were refugees and others were communist agents who spent careers living abroad under counterfeit cover and building clandestine networks that could function across borders and elude police nets cast with increasing rigor and adroitness. It was particularly among these Soviet career agents that one finds the professional spy of the era — less an individual trained in espionage technique than an accomplished operator who through experience and skill and commitment to a cause ran sophisticated circuits and survived where others went under.

Take the Soviet agent Ignace Reiss. Through revolutionary service in Germany he was drawn into intelligence work for the GRU, organizing spy networks in Vienna, Prague, and Holland. Later the purges and their ravaging spread to Red Army intelligence drove him into the GPU, but in 1937 he broke formally with Stalin and went on the run. The GPU's mobile assassination squads for liquidating enemies or recalcitrant agents abroad tracked him down and killed him outside Lausanne. Richard Sorge and Walter Krivitsky, Reiss's boyhood friend, fit a similar pattern of spies who honed their skills through years of agitation and revolutionary intrigue.[63]

There was also Leopold Trepper, who may well have been the most professional agent operating for any service in the 1930s and early 1940s. Trepper was born in Galicia in 1904. In the years right after the war he was active in Jewish and communist youth organizations. His militant involvement in Polish workers' politics and subsequent scrapes with police forced his emigration to Palestine in 1924. There he joined the Communist party, became the secretary of its Haifa section, and continued his life as an organizer and agitator. Police repression again forced him to emigrate, this time to France at the end of the decade. In Paris Trepper worked at odd jobs, loading freight trains or scrubbing floors at night at, of all places, the Bon Marché department store. He remained a party militant, already by his midtwenties a veteran of left-wing politics and clandestine activities. In the early 1930s he left Paris in the wake of a Soviet espionage affair, heading for Moscow and, eventually, secret agent work for Red Army intelligence. According to one account, Trepper trained as an intelligence officer and was a seasoned Soviet operative by the outbreak of the Second World War. Trepper, in his memoirs, has debunked this as myth, and has written a withering portrait of Soviet espionage abroad. The problem is that Trepper had good reason to provide an alternative accounting of his life — he has been accused of betraying associates following his capture by the Nazis during the war, and when he returned to the Soviet Union in 1945 Stalin's secret police clapped him in jail. Whichever version is correct, Trepper's activities in Belgium and then in occupied France betrayed all the professionalism of a man who had spent the better part of his life in conspiratorial or covert operations.

In early 1939 Trepper turned up in Brussels as Adam Mikler, a Canadian investor in the Foreign Excellent Raincoat Company. The company was a deep cover for an espionage network that Trepper was assembling for spying on Great Britain. Running the affair was an old Trepper acquaintance from Palestine, Leon Grossvogel. The firm was legally registered and its commercial employees sold raincoats, as far as they knew. Trepper's plan was to let the company build its markets and then to infiltrate it slowly with intelligence personnel in the positions of shareholders, business managers, and department heads. The war caught him short, and by July 1940 he was back in Paris. There he camouflaged himself as Jean Gilbert, manager of another dummy firm called Simex. For the next two years Trepper ran several separate networks and was a leading figure in the Rote Kapelle group spread over Europe. The Germans finally caught up with Trepper in December 1942. He agreed to collaborate as a double agent, although he may well have simply carried through an elaborate scheme prearranged in the case of arrest. Whether he betrayed a number of his agents, Grossvogel among them, we can only conjecture. In September 1943 Trepper escaped and went into hiding. He flew back to Moscow in 1945 and was imprisoned until the death of Stalin.

Trepper was a born conspirator, although, paradoxically, that was why he could be so representative. Before he was twenty he had begun to live under counterfeit identities and devote his life to underground work. Communism gave him his purpose but also the apparatus for assembling his clandestine networks. In this sense Soviet espionage, even if it did not formally train him, did make Trepper the consummate professional. People like Trepper had existed in the past; agents like Trepper were possible only in the political and espionage climate of the postwar years. His expertise fitted the covert worlds within which he moved so that a man who in earlier times might have been a political organizer was in the thirties a secret agent and spy master. No one knew the private Trepper; no one caught him up in conversation. He was a domineering personality who devised his own set of rules for every aspect of intelligence work. Agents were to transmit their reports to couriers only through intermediaries. The intermediary was to wait twenty-four hours before passing the report on to determine if the agent was under surveillance. After a meeting, couriers and intermediaries should keep on the go for at least six to seven hours to cut back the possibility of being shadowed. This kind of deliberation characterized all Trepper's moves. Only through the mistakes of others, and through accident, did the Germans ultimately trap him. Even then, he survived easily. A creature of his times, Leopold Trepper was a model of the emerging twentieth-century spy: committed and daring, yet cold-blooded, methodical, and businesslike in his ways. Personally unfathomable yet historically recognizable, he was a chilling example of what these years could produce. He was, in short, one of those extraordinary individuals you hope you never meet.[64]

For some agents some formal training developed in these years. French counterintelligence repeatedly cited programs for agitators and propagandists in schools in the Soviet Union and, occasionally, in Soviet schools established abroad. A 1926 communiqué from Vienna, for example, reported instruction at Berggasse 26 where twenty-eight students from the Balkans received training in revolutionary tactics.[65] If such a school existed, it was probably a slipshod affair, but Victor Sukolov, a GRU agent, appears to have undergone rigorous training in the late thirties, including instruction in photography, chemistry, and the use of technical equipment, before going abroad on espionage missions (although Trepper in his memoirs says that Sukolov often behaved like an amateur). Marie Josefovna Poliakova, who laid the groundwork for the Soviet intelligence ring operating in Switzerland in World War II, spent nine to ten months at an intelligence school in Moscow at the beginning of the thirties. Red Army intelligence's eastern, political, and code sections all briefed Sorge prior to his departure for China. Other Soviet agents were trained for particular functions, particularly as radio operators at the Moscow Radio School, before assignments abroad. The professional, however, was not entirely a Soviet monopoly. Czech intelligence in the thirties trained certain agents in radio work, secret writing, encoding, and decoding.[66] German intelligence ran its special camps for instruction in sabotage work and guerrilla warfare and one historian has described the specialization and "technocratic professionalism" that marked German espionage at agency level.[67] Other services produced agents capable of running sophisticated networks — Hartwig seems one of these — while the Poles may have mounted some of the most successful intelligence operations of all between the wars.[68]

A turn toward sweep, method, and professionalism thus characterized nearly all intelligence activity in these decades. Behind this trend were developments peculiar to each nation's circumstances. The conspiratorial nature of Soviet espionage, as well as the pool of devoted agents it could draw upon, resulted in spy networks like the Switz-Stahl ring or in the development of talents like Trepper or the equally remarkable Richard Sorge. Nazi politics, revisionism, and fear of refugees abroad explain certain dimensions of the spy agencies that Germans built, as do German technical skill and bureaucratic traditions. A comparable picture could be drawn of Italian espionage between the wars, if, admittedly, certain sectors operated at less sophisticated levels. The French were vulnerable after the war and, for a time, they occupied a forward position in Europe. Their empire was large and in certain places shaky. These, among other things, account for changes in the French SRs.

Yet there were factors common to all. These ranged from the war experience to technological change to the flux in borders and settlements to the sheer compulsion toward organization in the twenties and thirties that reached out and engulfed all walks of life. Under any circumstances intelligence agencies would have grown and become more systematic because that was in the nature of things after the war. Most of all, however, the organizations developed as they did because these were rich years for espionage — full, ripe, intrigue-ridden years — and the various services and their agents responded accordingly.

––––––––

Richness—the incontinent side to clandestine affairs in the twentieth century—distinguished interwar intrigues most from the espionage of the past. Spy wars were real, fought by professional agents in extensive secret networks, but also by combatants who were as likely to be refugees, terrorists, secret police, ideologues, and an infestation of swindlers, hustlers, and traffickers. Beyond institutional history there was the sheer pervasiveness of interwar intrigue that explains in large part why the secret agent was for the French a formidable and evocative figure between the two world wars.

That tangled, verdant side, for example, turns one to gunrunning, a useful place to begin, because it shows the spongelike nature of espionage in these years, the ease with which it absorbed a widening array of individuals into the clandestine enterprises of secret agents. The Gardiners and W.'s were part of a tradition of exploiting regional conflict for personal gain, but their adventures were also symptomatic of the proliferation in arms dealing and the obscuring of the lines between trafficking and espionage that characterized gunrunning in the interwar decades. Well before the First World War traffickers and fortune hunters had shipped arms across frontiers or smuggled contraband weapons into contested areas. The traffic to Morocco and Henri de Monfreid's Red Sea exploits were two examples of this trade.[69] After the war the traffic seems to have broadened as wartime conditions and postwar circumstances expanded the opportunities for illicit arms shipments. How much of this expansion derived from wartime smuggling is difficult to say, but almost certainly there were connections between illicit traffickers in drugs, liquor, and arms following the war and the development of wartime networks in contraband trade to circumvent the Allied blockade. The experience of counterintelligence agents in the Netherlands alone during the war and the creation of Allied control agencies like the Nederlandische Overzee Trust (or NOT) suggest that this traffic was enormous.[70] There was also a vast surplus of weapons available after 1918, some of these dumped legally on the market, others hidden away in clandestine depots. Gardiner made use of the latter as did W. and his White Russian associates. From the war, then, came abundant reserves of arms and munitions and, most likely, the experience and fortunes with which to exploit these. From the postwar years came the adventurers and drifters, men and women on the make and, as important, new markets in contraband weapons. Wars in China and Spain soaked up a huge weapons trade while smaller conflicts like the Rif war in North Africa offered comparable profits.

At the same time trafficking in liquor and especially in narcotics created new infrastructures and knowledge that could be applied to gunrunning when the opportunities were ripe. The pattern of drug dealer or white slaver or both turned arms merchant was a frequent one, particularly in East Asia.[71] The commodity changed with the circumstances, but the technique and contacts remained the same. Indeed the very definition of gunrunning enlarged after the war with article 170 of the Versailles Treaty forbidding the import of arms into Germany or the export of weapons by German manufacturers. Through the early 1930s the French Deuxième Bureau traced a brazen disregard of this provision, identifying imports of arms from Sweden, Holland, and Switzerland and German arms sales to European, East Asian, and Latin American countries.[72]

There is no one phrase to describe the array of arms traffickers in the twenties and thirties. A few were major dealers like Benny Spiro of Hamburg. Spiro built his business shipping arms to Latin America and Africa before the First World War. By the mid-1920s he was closely associated with a large freight forwarding firm in Hamburg, and then a consortium for, as one French agent who was tracking him put it, "the delivery of arms and war materials of all kinds to all possible countries." When war broke out in the Rif, he shipped two thousand rifles (apparently acquired from a hidden depot in Bavaria), a million rounds of ammunition, and medical supplies to the north Moroccan rebels. All of these were World War I surplus and of inferior quality, although the Riffian representatives were permitted a tryout behind Hagenbeck's zoo on the outskirts of Hamburg. Three years later he turned up again in a counterintelligence report as the principal intermediary of two Hamburg houses shipping arms to China via ships flying the Norwegian flag.[73] The French arms firm, Edgar Brandt, did a similar kind of business. Brandt dealt with Ireland, Poland, China, Greece, Latin America, and later with both sides in Spain. In 1935 the firm generated one of its periodic scandals when 310 cases of arms recalled from Argentina were opened and found to be full of stones and sand. There was speculation that the substitution had been arranged in France and the arms diverted to extremist political groups. The mayor of Le Havre announced that the stones resembled the paving blocks of Paris and that the sand came from the Paris region. The truth, in fact, was no less unsavory. Brandt had exported the arms fraudulently to the government of Paraguay, circumventing a French embargo on arms shipments to this nation by listing Argentina as the ultimate destination. A tip to the Quai d'Orsay had forced the recall of the shipment, but Brandt had stalled hoping to find some middle way between reimbursing the Paraguayans or paying a fine that was liable to exceed the value of the cargo. Then the Paraguayans had seized sixty of the crates and someone "by accident" had forwarded the rest. Brandt was left in the dilemma of owning up to these facts or sending back rocks and sand and hoping somehow they would clear their way through customs. For an arms trafficker, the choice was practically foreordained.[74]

With firms like Spiro and Brandt representing the more licit side to the trade, it is not surprising that other, viperlike elements crowded in on gunrunning after the war. Some were adventurers like W., and others were professional traffickers, usually in narcotics, like Mario F., who was also known to police as Joret, Lorenzetti, and Visconti. He was a convicted drug trafficker who in 1938 was running a Franco-Chinese trading agency out of an apartment on the avenue d'Orsay for the purpose of purchasing arms for the Chinese republic. In February 1939, following a police search for narcotics, the affair was shut down, but not before it had "swallowed up" (the words are the Sûreté's) half a million francs of Chinese government funds without delivering one piece of merchandise.[75]

Still others were simply experienced crooks who were lured to the arms trade by the big money to be made in China and Spain. Michael Dennis Corrigan was an example of the kind of confidence man who saw in the political struggles of the period one more scam to be worked for his own venal ends. He was also typical of the way that gunrunning, even on its edges, tended to alloy with secret service matters. Corrigan came to arms trafficking with a lifetime of swindles under his belt. He was Canadian or Irish, depending on which version of his past (and which name) he was handing out. He liked to boast that he had commanded an army of ten thousand rebels in Mexico in the early 1920s and that this adventure had brought him silver mines and oil fields in the Yucatan peninsula. The story fit well with his tendency to pass himself off as a highly placed official with major oil companies, a favorite confidence game that netted substantial amounts of money from a number of victims. One of his marks was a Romanian named Ionescu, whom Corrigan swindled out of half a million francs. When Corrigan later ran into Ionescu by chance in Nice he was forced to hand over money in bank drafts to get him off his back; but the next morning Corrigan, back in high form, conned another fifty thousand francs from Ionescu and then skipped town, leaving behind forty thousand francs in debts to a Cannes luxury hotel.

To a crook like Corrigan the fat pickings to be gleaned from arms deals to China by the late 1930s were all but irresistible, and toward fall 1937 he was developing an elaborate scheme to defraud several arms dealers and, possibly, the Chinese government. The con, however, did not go as smoothly as Corrigan had planned, and in 1938 he was in trouble with British and French authorities, neither of them unfamiliar with Corrigan's practices. The facts of the case were difficult to untangle, largely because all parties involved were equally mired in shadowy activities and no one was prepared to tell the full story. Essentially Corrigan swindled two arms dealers, one British and one French, by posing as an agent of the Chinese embassy in London. The Chinese government, he told them, was having difficulties exporting arms out of Britain but restrictions could be bypassed and profits could be made if the two arms dealers could arrange a series of intermediary sales passing through France. To authenticate his representation, Corrigan was seconded by an embassy official named Mr. Chou, whose receipts and bills of sales were written on official embassy stationery.

The scheme fell apart when several crates broke open on the docks of Marseilles, disclosing not antitank guns or munitions as promised, but plenty of rocks. The French trafficker, who had paid off the British one, immediately created a row, and when the latter, who had paid off Corrigan and Chou, complained to Corrigan, he was told that acting on the counsel of MI5 the real shipment had followed a different routing to Marseilles but that four thousand pounds were still necessary to complete the deal. Meanwhile a police investigation had been triggered by the broken crates and a bill of lading listing "hardware, machine tools, and spare parts." When British detectives questioned Mr. Chou on the matter he told them that he had first met Corrigan at a surprise party and that Corrigan had later approached him with a list of arms that he could supply to the Chinese government. Corrigan, Chou said, had confided at that time that he was working for Colonel Kell, director of MI5, and that Kell was favorably disposed to facilitating arms purchases to China. On these grounds Chou had gone along with Corrigan's representations to the two arms dealers. Police, however, found this story difficult to swallow, particularly once they discovered that Mr. Chou held no official position at the Chinese embassy. More likely, they concluded, Chou was in on the swindle from the beginning. None of the injured parties, however, was planning to sue, and no one was telling all to the authorities for obvious reasons.[76]

People like Corrigan were colorful figures, but they were also indicative of how easily the milieus of criminality and espionage blended during the interwar years. Gunrunning, an undertaking shared by traffickers and secret agents, was one of the nexus points, so that Corrigan's masquerade as an agent of British intelligence, if ludicrous in the circumstances, was scarcely ill-chosen. Alongside the Spiros, Gardiners, and W.'s in files on arms trafficking between the wars, the police and Deuxième Bureau were gathering material on clandestine German arms shipments to the Soviet Union and Italian arms deals with the Ustashi. Later there were reports on the Cagoule as well as on intriguers like Battiti, whose shadowy projects bridged both milieus.[77] This association of gunrunning with espionage was not unusual; it certainly had predated 1914. What was characteristic of the postwar years, however, was how readily the mercenary enterprises of the one spilled over into the intrigues of the other, so that crooks and traffickers and adventurers were increasingly drawn into the world of spies. Gardiner and W., but also Benny Spiro, whose freight forwarding partner, according to a "very good source" for the French SR, was trying to recruit ex–German officers to fight with the Riffians, fit this pattern.[78] By the 1930s crooks like Corrigan took it as a matter of form to pass themselves off as secret service operatives.

War and revolution in China had much to do with encouraging these combinations. The arms traffic to China in the twenties alone was enormous. According to one set of statistics recorded in two French ministerial archives, from summer 1922 to May 1926 various Chinese armies and warlords had clandestinely imported 246,086 rifles, 18,654 pistols, 645 machine guns, 69,117,041 rounds of ammunition, 73 cannons, 69,548 shells, and 72 airplanes. Many of the dealers were career arms merchants, among whom figured a large number of Germans. But the Comintern was also supporting Kuomintang armies in the south, and forwarding military advisers, and thus Soviet or Comintern agents also figured among the middlemen and traffickers, or conspired with the professional traders and contrabanders to ship arms into China. In general the global ideological stakes attached to civil wars in China shrouded all arms deals to that country in the cloak of international intrigue, as would the Pacific war of the thirties when China once again became a mecca for gunrunners who, like it or not, found themselves smack in the middle of great power politics.[79]

Spain sealed the connection. Nowhere did the crossovers come so easily and fully as they did during the Spanish civil war when gunrunning all but blurred the lines between spies, desperadoes, and run-of-the-mill bandits. War in Spain — long, large-scale, on the rim of Europe, and embargoed, in theory, from official arms shipments — was the arms trafficker's paradise, an "El Dorado" as one newspaper put it.[80] Spain had all the virtues to satisfy the greed of the dealers. It was near at hand, it was accessible by land and by sea, and it was voracious in its appetite for arms and munitions. Moreover, the coincidence of war in East Asia inflated the incentives to move into gunrunning while the money flowed freely and indiscriminately. Networks and supply organizations developed for China could easily be shifted to shipments to Spain — exports to the two countries by the same dealers were not uncommon — while the existence of a competitive market on the other side of the world only intensified the bidding by the Spanish combatants.

In these circumstances hustlers and hoodlums of all stripes came running, scrambling to get in on their share of the plunder. Reading through the dossiers on gunrunners to Spain reminds one of certain scenes from literature, the shark feeding by the *Pequod* in *Moby Dick,* for example, or Willa Cather's tale of the wolves and the wedding party in *My Antonia*. Certainly the civil war in Spain was like a bad winter in Russia. The Spanish themselves played into the hands of the traffickers, especially the republic, which was desperate for arms and naive in its business dealings. In one instance the Madrid government paid eight million crowns for Finnish stocks that were totally obsolete. The head of the Finnish volunteer units was heard to remark, "We would have paid someone to take them off our hands."[81] To facilitate purchases the Republicans established, under minimal cover, a central purchasing office in Paris located first on the avenue George V and then transferred to 61 avenue Victor Emmanuel III. Every day a familiar crowd haunted its corridors.[82] Repeatedly the Republicans were cheated, so frequently in fact that one suspects word got around that they were just asking to be taken. Roger Maugras, the French representative to Stockholm and well positioned to observe a certain portion of the trade, wrote that there were so many shady businessmen of all nationalities turning to gunrunning that one could now speak of "a fourth international, that of the traffickers in contraband weapons."[83]

Boats underwent name changes several times, picked up arms cargoes in Europe, transshipped these to French ports, carried invoices assuring the French that the destination was Greece or some distant land, and then proceeded on to Spain in an illegal run for profit. In one hotel in Luxembourg an arms trafficker sold weapons to the Republicans while down the hallway or up the stairs another sold arms to the Nationalists. The police were not certain if the two were acquainted, although it is not difficult to imagine appointments later that evening or the following day with the clients from the opposite side. Among the flotsam and jetsam riding the fast money current to Spain were people like the former bootlegger Jean A. A failure in North America following the war, he returned to France to escape criminal proceedings only to eke out a difficult existence until the generals' revolt offered him new opportunities trafficking in arms. Then, forming a syndicate and cultivating connections with the Spanish embassy, Jean A. scraped together the means to arrange a delivery of one hundred thousand rifles to the republic. The Spanish government agreed and paid out a quarter of a million dollars in advance. But when a government representative was dispatched to oversee the shipment, he discovered that only seven thousand rifles had thus far been purchased and that only four thousand of these had been loaded on board the ship that was to carry them to Spain. The ship's tonnage, moreover, was inadequate for a cargo of the size promised by A. The contract was canceled, but Jean A. kept the advance and sold off his rifles, mostly to Palestine and Morocco, which was one of the reasons the French police were tracking the arms traffickers whenever they could. With the money he had swindled from the Spanish Republicans, Jean A. and his associates thus were launched on a career of trafficking in arms. They used the Spanish advance to purchase a boat called the *Jaron* that in September 1937 was preparing to sail from the Latvian harbor of Liepaja to Bordeaux with a hold full of munitions and several artillery pieces until Latvian officials inspected the cargo. The appearance in their harbor of a ship painted gray on one side, black on the other, and with a hasty name change so shoddily done that the old markings were still observable, had aroused suspicions. Despite these setbacks, police noted in August 1938 that Jean A. was living in a luxury apartment on the Champs-Elysées. His gang controlled a fleet of ships and trafficked in narcotics as well as weapons, fabricating whatever false papers they needed to carry out their affairs. The Spanish civil war wasted hundreds of thousands of lives and crippled a nation, but for some it was a most profitable enterprise.[84]

Pouring into the trade, however, were also secret agents, clandestine organizations, and fellow travelers, driven by the conflict's international dimensions and ideological overtones. By 1937 the Soviet agent Ignace

Reiss was committing the greater part of his efforts to procuring weapons for Loyalist Spain.[85] His boyhood friend and fellow agent, Walter Krivitsky, pulled operatives from England, Sweden, and Switzerland to organize arms smuggling networks to the republic. They established import-export firms in Paris, London, Copenhagen, Amsterdam, Zurich, Warsaw, Prague, and Brussels, and procured forged clearance papers from the GPU passport section. In each agency a GPU agent, masked as a silent partner, oversaw financing and monitored transactions.[86] With ease then, almost irresistibly, the two milieus — private trafficking and international intrigue — slid together. Maugras reported from Stockholm on the Swedish ship *Lola,* which a man named Ericsson had purchased from the Clyde Shipping Company in 1937. The ship had been refitted for speed and equipped with a modern radio system, and was being used to carry munitions to the Republicans in Valence. According to Maugras, whose sources were probably the Swedish police, Ericsson, who was making considerable money from this business, was also the director of the Nafta-Syndicat, a "former Soviet business operation."[87] Two Greeks who were notorious traffickers worked through the Banque commerciale pour l'Europe du nord, a Soviet financial instrument located in Paris.[88] On the other side, agents of the Spanish Nationalists kept a careful watch on Republican purchases. "It should be noted," wrote one police reporter in 1937, "that Franco's supporters abroad have built a complete spy network to prevent the transport of material to the *gouvernementaux,* especially by sea."[89] Some of the agents were right-wing sympathizers whose devotion to the Nationalist cause ineluctably drew them to espionage and to the traffic in contraband weapons.[90] Other agents were the arms traffickers themselves, who played both ends against the middle to squeeze what extra lucre they could from the cash cow in Spain. The *Yorbrook* and *Allegro* affairs were examples of how this was done.

The *Yorbrook* was an Estonian freighter commissioned to carry thirty million francs' worth of armaments from Helsinki to Loyalist Spain. The man arranging the sale was Josef Veltjens, a sinister figure whose full role in the Spanish civil war has yet to be disclosed. An air ace in the First World War and a former freebooter and Nazi party member until Hitler forced him out in 1931 on charges of corruption, Veltjens was an arms trafficker when the Germans turned to him to run weapons and high explosives to the Nationalists in Spain. Veltjens exported arms at the behest of the Naval High Command but he operated on the margins of official channels. By 1937 Hermann Göring, an old comrade

from the war and a personal patron and protector, was using Veltjens
to run guns to the Republican side with the intention of harvesting
some of the free-flowing Spanish gold for the Reich and, at a more
perfidious level, of supplying defective or sabotaged arms to the Loyalists.[91] The *Yorbrook* shipment was one of these shabby, subversive deals.

Because of the size of the shipment, and probably for camouflage,
Veltjens recruited other traffickers to assemble the front money to complete the transaction. He turned in particular to a German émigré
named Goldberg who had quit Germany for Paris in the early 1930s.
Since his arrival in France, Goldberg had amassed a considerable fortune, supposedly through commercial and industrial investments but,
in reality, through trading in weapons. Together with Veltjens Goldberg
brought three other men in on the deal, although one of these was eliminated from the affair (and from his cut of the traffickers' 30 percent
commission) when a crane boom fell on him on the docks in Helsinki.
There was also a sixth confederate, a German named G. G. who was
reported to have worked for German intelligence during the First World
War and who had come to France in 1933 claiming to be a political
refugee. The police, however, suspected that G. G.'s commitment to less
honorable enterprises, especially fraud, had provided the decisive in-
ducement to flee Germany. Goldberg introduced G. G. into the deal "to
appraise the merchandise" and brought him to Stockholm where G. G.
was to await a telegram summoning him to Helsinki. G. G. never made
it. To cut him out of the deal, Veltjens denounced him to the Finnish
authorities and then let it be known to G. G. that he would be arrested
if he tried to cross the border. As a police official noted, the affair from
the beginning was shot through with the maneuvers of adventurers deceiving and duping one another, even though each man knew that he
could not sell out his associates without injuring himself in the process.
Veltjens, of course, had other reasons for keeping G. G. out of Finland,
although these were just as sordid as the desire to appropriate his share
of the commission. Nearly all the arms in this shipment were in some
way unusable, a matter Veltjens had kept not only from the Spanish,
but, at least at the beginning, from his associate Goldberg. His plan was
to complete the deal in Helsinki to collect his money, then to cover his
tracks by seeing that the *Yorbrook* never made it to Spain. He planted a
grenade in the coal stores of the freighter (warning Goldberg, who was
to accompany the ship, not to go on board); when this attempt somehow failed, he informed Franco's secret service of the shipment and
the *Yorbrook*'s course, hoping the Nationalist navy would intercept

the freighter on its passage south. Neither scheme worked, the "vast swindle," as the police called it, coming to the attention of the Republicans who initiated criminal proceedings against Veltjens while informing Goldberg that his presence at 61 avenue Victor Emmanuel III was no longer welcome.[92]

In the *Yorbrook* affair traffickers, one turned quasi secret agent, had colluded with Spanish intelligence. The pattern repeated itself in the *Allegro* affair, although here the connections were drawn even tighter. The *Allegro* was a Swedish ship carrying another of Josef Veltjens's bogus arms cargoes to the republic. In February 1937 Nationalist boats intercepted the steamer five miles west of the cape of Villano and commandeered the shipment. Swedish police investigations into the affair revealed that the *Allegro* had departed Stockholm in mid-January 1937 for the port of Ornsköldsvik, where it was to take on a cargo of paper. Scarcely out of Stockholm, however, the ship had changed course for Warnemünde, where a man named Rosenberg, representing Veltjens's firm, had come on board; then the *Allegro* steamed on to Lübeck, the captain by this point admitting openly that the ship had been "'leased for two months' for special purposes." To mollify the crew for the dangers they would run in Spanish waters, he promised a special cash settlement (which he never paid; it was the crew's complaint they had been cheated that triggered the investigation by the Swedish police). At Lübeck more than thirteen thousand cases of munitions "for Yemen" were loaded on board, although the real destination was the Spanish peninsula. All but one thousand of these crates were filled with bricks. At Lübeck two more of Veltjens's venomous associates came on board, and then the *Allegro* proceeded to Gdynia, where a representative from the Loyalist government embarked to inspect the cargo. Veltjens's men took care that he opened only the cases at the top of the hold, while the captain let slip, once the inspection was concluded, that it really did not matter because the run was a dangerous one and very likely the boat would be captured by the Nationalists. This astounding prophecy proved true, the captain having received instructions to steer a course for cape of Villano where the rebel forces would be waiting. Thanks to Veltjens's swindle and betrayal, Franco's army picked up an easy thousand cases of munitions, while the traffickers pocketed the Republican payment for the full load, interception by the enemy being a risk incurred by the purchaser. Without the grievance of the crew, the true facts of the case might never have surfaced.[93]

Perhaps the only uncertainty in the affair was whether Veltjens (and his protectors) had sold the cargo twice over—the second time to the Nationalists—or whether he was content to cede the shipment to Franco for an out with the Republicans. Both procedures were known to be practiced by a number of traffickers. French police had a list of several arms dealers whom they suspected of contacts with agents of the Nationalist secret service. Indeed Veltjens's collaboration with foreign agents was merely a blatant example of the liaisons that developed between gunrunners and spies in the era of the Spanish civil war. Goldberg was known to be closely connected with a man named B—zkii, who was officially posted to the Soviet commercial mission in France but suspected by French authorities of being a GPU operative. An arms manufacturer and merchant who sold to both sides was suspected of ties to German intelligence. A man named R., who had squandered a fortune in a dissipated life and had then, police believed, trafficked in drugs, was also suspected of running guns over the border to the Spanish Republicans. In late 1937 he turned up in Fez under very dubious circumstances, passing himself off as a French SR agent and carrying a questionnaire pertaining to French defenses in Morocco. French counterintelligence noted a liaison between an English trafficker named H. and "agents of a foreign political police" and had reasons to believe he was also in touch with Franco's secret service. One of his associates, another trafficker named V., was, in the opinion of an untried informant, an agent in the service of an unidentified foreign power.[94]

Gunrunners, intriguers, and spies ran as a pack between the wars, particularly in the thirties when the Spanish civil war all but turned traffickers into the casual agents of intelligence services. To an extent the relation between gunrunners and espionage was representative of the way crime and intrigue fed on each other after the war. It is likely that a history of criminal organization in the interwar years would reveal a strong connection between the opportunities for illegal profit opened by the secret wars of the twenties and thirties—for example, the traffic in arms or in false papers—and the growth of illicit networks in other criminal activities. Criminals had contacts, knowledge, and combines they could place in the service of intrigue and espionage when the profits were tempting and the conditions were right. But the intrigues of the period also funneled money into illegal operations, providing the funds and generating the organizations and experience that could be turned to illicit enterprises like drug trafficking that were equally profitable and no more dangerous. One senses that criminals moved in and out of espionage in these years, dabbling, initiating, and aggrandizing and then shifting strategies and capital back to their more habitual haunts.

Once in, however, they tended to reproduce the attributes of the milieu. The betrayals of gunrunners like Josef Veltjens or Jean A. were not much different from the spy battles that were fought in the Spanish civil war. The use of double agents, sabotage, and behind-the-lines infiltration were standard methods of operation in civil war intrigues. They turn up again and again in the reports on terrorist activities in the south of France in 1937 or on incidents like the attempted hijacking of a Republican submarine, the C-2, in Brest harbor. Nearly all dimensions of espionage related to Spain—the tendency of its intrigues to spread to foreign soil or the involvement of ideological sympathizers—can be found in the files on gunrunners in the late 1930s. Perhaps it was the simple presence of gunrunners in the intrigues of the professionals that was the most telling replication. Gunrunners had little or nothing to do with the ferreting out of military secrets yet were deep into intrigue and thick with the spies because espionage after the war spread well beyond its conventional forms. There was to postwar espionage an imperial quality that reached out and encompassed more and more people and pursuits within the range of its clandestine activity. Much of this was conditioned by general factors, for instance, the lessons and experiences of the First World War or the multifarious role of secret agents in the new political orders like communism. Yet it was tempered also by the nature of the conflicts that drew in the spies. In Spain, the professionals enlarged the scope of their mission. Agents like Reiss or B—zkii arranged money flows, procured weapons and volunteers, assured the shipment of cargoes. Others monitored arms purchases and ship itineraries in order to intercept or interrupt the stream of supplies to the enemy. Just as the military struggles in the peninsula were caught in ideological infighting, so that secret police crawled over the country and into bordering areas like the south of France, so too was gunrunning drawn into the intrigues of the international politics that hung over Spain. The result was a growing ubiquity to espionage, a tendency for spying to intrude itself into the lives of amateurs. Volunteers came to Spain to fight for a cause but found themselves implicated in the spy wars of others. The same consequences confronted the gunrunners. They exploited opportunities in Spain as ruthlessly as they could. However in so doing they too fell into the nets of the intriguers, enmeshing themselves in espionage affairs.

This sprawl of the milieu was one of its defining characteristics after the war. Spy catchers found themselves preoccupied not only with the professionals and their agents but with the adventures of marginal groups like gunrunners who, through the force of circumstances, were coming to occupy a more central place in the reports of counterintelligence agencies. Closer still to the heart of these files were refugee groups whose politics consumed far more police time and paper and whose advance to center stage in the international intrigues of the twentieth century was one measure of the distinction between the espionage of the present and that of the past.

In part the distinction lay in the fact that the refugees came out of the war and the politics that followed. It was the conditions of international life after 1918, the ideological divisions generated by the rise of communism and fascism and the fluidity or lack of finality to postwar settlements, that spawned the refugees and defined their politics. Causes, battles, enemies were, like the refugees, products of their century.

This did not mean that there was no repetition of refugee politics from the prewar years. Each period produced its sensational revelations about foreigners and the secret police who invariably followed. But before the war refugees were a police matter primarily because they were identified with radical political groups. After the war these concerns, if not diminished, were superseded by the tendency of refugee intrigues to get swept up in international politics and espionage affairs, which made the postwar refugees a very different security concern. The transformation conformed to the way nearly everyone after the war lived with the great events of their times, just as the spectacular stories created by the refugees became themselves a vehicle by which international affairs intruded on French consciousness between the wars. What the content of that intrusion turned out to be occupies the subsequent chapter. But here it should be noted that to a degree refugee plights and dramas in the twenties and thirties were simply a mirroring of a wider internationalization of life that followed the First World War.

A similar distinction, up to a point, applies to the secret police who were an inseparable part of refugee politics. How far the GPU differed from the Okhrana will not be determined until the latter's archives are more closely gone over, although Russian collaboration with French police before 1914 did not characterize GPU operations in France, nor was it likely that Okhrana activities were as widespread, subversive, or as closely tied into espionage as those of the Soviet organs following the war. German police operations abroad during Bismark's era appear rather frail by twentieth-century standards,[95] and their monitoring of socialist opponents was not comparable to the pursuit of racial and ideological enemies by the Gestapo in the 1930s. In certain ways it was the Italian police between the wars who seemed most similar to their prewar counterparts, although they possessed an intensity or violence and an ideological component lacking in the earlier period.

Most of all, the refugees gave intrigue a texture it did not own in the past. The history of interwar espionage cannot be written apart from the conspiracies and brouhahas of these people. Some of the most extraordinary tales and certainly the most preposterous characters emanated from their circles. There was almost something novelistic about their affairs, located, to be sure, at the cheaper end of the literature scale. Yet there was also a very serious side to their politics whose consequences were bitterly felt by the last wave of refugees that came in the thirties. Refugees made for good stories, but their intrigues accounted for a good deal of antiforeigner sentiment and for the wariness of authorities who had to decide who was innocuous and who was a threat. Making that decision would not be easy, because of the immersion of the émigrés in the world of the spies and because, like the gunrunners, refugee intrigues reproduced the features that typified espionage between the two world wars.

Among those commanding French attention throughout the thirties were the Ustashi, a collection of Croatian terrorists responsible for the murders of the Yugoslav king and the French foreign minister in Marseilles in 1934. The Ustashi evolved out of the politics of Croatian nationalism and its search for a solution to the southern Slav question that would accord a measure of Croatian autonomy. There had never been unity to this movement. Croatian nationalism before the war divided between a trialist solution within the empire and separation and federation with Serbia into a greater southern Slav state. The creation of a Yugoslav nation dominated by Serbs and without a federalist structure after the war kept the issue alive, but Croatian nationalists continued to divide between federalist and separatist positions. The Ustashi were the extremists, arguing for a policy of terrorism to disaggregate the Yugoslav state. They were never very numerous, and their willingness to collaborate with Italy in exchange for money and weapons precluded the possibility of building a mass following. Their terrorist strategy and their close connections to national enemies made them, however, a serious threat to Yugoslav security.[96] There were, in the Ustashi, echoes of earlier Balkan secret societies, for example their connection with Slavic emigrants overseas, their subjection to secret police surveillance, their choice of terrorism as a method of action, and their goals of national self-determination. To a degree, the Ustashi recalled the nationalist struggles in the Balkans that had preceded and detonated the First World War.[97] Yet their style and their politics, particularly their ties to the revisionist objectives of Italy and Hungary, and later the Nazis, placed them squarely within the postwar scene. In their links with foreign intelligence services or, on a grander scale, in their absorption into the power politics of post–Versailles Europe, the Ustashi were representative of the role that émigrés could play in the secret war of the twenties and thirties.

Thus their terrorism bore the same organized quality that characterized all facets of intrigue after the war. To carry out assassinations or bombings of trains, barracks, and police stations, the Ustashi organized a recruiting service and ran special training camps where they instructed their militants in terrorist tactics and the use of explosives and weapons. The most celebrated camp was Janka Puszta in Hungary, where the assassins of King Alexander had trained. In addition the French and Yugoslavs collected plenty of evidence about other camps in Hungary and Italy, including one near Brescia where the recruits wore gray uniforms and led a soldierly life.[98]

Their assaults could be systematic affairs, like the *attentat* in Marseilles, which was meticulously prepared. The principal actors in the gunning down of the king were Ustasha terrorist soldiers — Pospisil, Rajtic, and Kralj — and the Macedonian triggerman Georgiev delegated by the Macedonian terrorist movement IMRO, which, like the Ustashi, had irredentist claims upon Yugoslav soil and since 1932 had agreed to coordinate terrorist activities with the Croats.[99] Operating behind the scenes was Eugen Kvaternik, who orchestrated the movements of the assassination squad. Kvaternik arranged routings, timetables, aliases, and the necessary false papers that would place the gunmen in the designated locations at the designated times. Initially he traveled separately from the three Ustashi, who began their journey with Hungarian passports, but he and Georgiev joined them in Zurich. The five then proceeded to Lausanne where the three Ustashi purchased new clothing, Kvaternik disposing of their old clothes in a suitcase that he checked at the train station. Leaving Lausanne, the team crossed into France, now using false Czech passports in different names distributed by Kvaternik and taking two separate routes before meeting once again in Paris. In the capital they again took precautions, separating into different hotels.

Several days later, Georgiev and Kralj were dispatched south, receiving from Kvaternik yet another set of false passports in still different names. Before their departure Kvaternik showed Kralj a picture of a man he called Petar and who he said was "our leader." The two men arrived in Marseilles on 6 October, rejoined by Kvaternik on the way, and from here they took a bus to Aix-en-Provence where they checked into a hotel to sit out the three-day interval before the king's arrival in France on the ninth. In Aix Kvaternik took them to a café where Petar and a woman were seated. On the eve of the ninth, Kvaternik told Georgiev and Kralj to go to the Hotel Nègre Coste at 7:00 A.M. and to ask to see Petar, who would give them weapons and grenades. At 1:00 P.M. they were to take the bus to Marseilles and "fire on the king." Then Kvaternik took his leave of the two men. The next day they did as they were told and assassinated the Yugoslav monarch and the French foreign minister. All four terrorists were captured in France, but Kvaternik made it safely back to Italy. According to a garçon who worked in the Nègre Coste restaurant and who was later shown a picture of Ante Pavelic, the Ustasha chieftain and Petar were one and the same.[100]

The Ustashi were able to train with impunity and to act with relative efficiency because they received powerful support from the Hungarians and Italians, who had emerged from the war with equally deep resentments toward treaty arrangements and with avaricious designs on Yugoslav territory. Both saw in the Ustashi a destabilizing element they believed they could exploit to serve their own purposes. Each got burned in the process, so badly after the Marseilles murders that the Italian ambassador to Yugoslavia went so far as to suggest the possibility of buying Pavelic's silence or arranging his "disappearance."[101] The Hungarians, who had ruled over the eastern half of the empire and whose vast territories and populations were dispersed among the successor states, including Yugoslavia, after the war, were the most complicit with Ustasha terrorism. They permitted the Ustashi to train in camps on their soil, which allowed the dispatching of missions across the Yugoslav border, and they provided the Ustashi with necessary papers, including false passports. The Italians supplied the Ustashi with money, arms, and explosives and facilitated Ustasha infiltration into Yugoslavia by way of Zara and Fiume. Ustashi hunted by the Yugoslavs found refuge in Italy. As in Hungary, according to reports following the assassinations, there were Ustasha camps in the peninsula where combat units were readied for terrorist assaults upon Yugoslavia.[102]

Part of the Ustashi's payback was information they traded with all of their patrons. The Croats were up to their necks in espionage work. Gustave Percec, one of Ante Pavelic's closest lieutenants, handed over Yugoslav military secrets to Hungarian officers, including contacts with Hungarian intelligence. Percec had emigrated with Pavelic at the end of the twenties and resided first in Vienna and then in Budapest and at Janka Puszta. When his secretary and mistress reproached him for mixing in dangerous business, he told her, "We work for the Hungarians and do what we are told." What they were not told was, however, another matter. Percec retailed the same information he gave to the Hungarians to other intelligence services, communicating material via the principal Ustasha agent in Vienna, Ivan Pertevic (a former colonel in the Austro-Hungarian army), and via another leading Ustasha in Graz named Duic. According to Percec's secretary who worked for Yugoslav police, Croatian émigrés in Budapest, Italy, and Austria spied for the Hungarians, Italians, and the right-wing Austrian Heimwehr. Other émigrés in Berlin provided the Nazis with intelligence on Austria and Hungary. They received their information from Percec and Pertevic, sending back to Vienna what they knew about conditions in Germany.[103]

Ustasha relations with their enemies were no less tangled or intricate. There was, for example, the controversy that arose over the role of Simonovic, the Yugoslav liaison with the French investigation into the Marseilles murders. Pospisil, one of the terrorists awaiting trial in Marseilles, complained about visits Simonovic had made to his cell. Simonovic said he had merely acted as an interpreter for French police investigators, and French police confirmed that Simonovic had seen the defendants only in their presence. A Ministry of Foreign Affairs note acknowledged that Simonovic had authorization to attend interrogations. But Georges Desbons, the lawyer for Pospisil, Rajtic, and Kralj, persisted in the protests against Simonovic. He said that Simonovic and one of his assistants, a man named Militchevic, had made earlier visits to the three Ustashi at Annemasse, where they had been held before their transfer to the prison in Marseilles. According to Desbons, Militchevic had gained entry to Pospisil's cell on 12 October, three days after the assassination. There he sought to extort from Pospisil a signed confession admitting that he was a communist and that the Ustashi were a communist front. He also proposed that Pospisil assassinate Ante Pavelic, in exchange for which Militchevic would guarantee his freedom. Pospisil refused, Militchevic slugged him, and Pospisil kicked Militchevic in the gut. The next day, Desbons continued, Militchevic returned with Simonovic, who spoke soothingly to Pospisil and urged him to sign the confession. Militchevic played the bad cop in the routine, speaking roughly to Pospisil, saying he was a bandit, and threatening to beat him until he bled all over. Then he made a number of remarks regarding the private parts of Pospisil's mother, told him that he would "stick it up Pavelic's ass *sans* Vaseline," and boasted that he had killed Duic. When Simonovic left the cell, he told Pospisil, "Go ahead to prison. We will come back when you are more supple." This, insisted Desbons, explained the later visits in Marseilles.[104]

Desbons does not come across in these files as a man of substantial credibility, and one is tempted to dismiss this story as a stab at bolstering a sorry defense. But the incident was typical of the conspiratorial labyrinths that developed when police closed in on their quarry. Double agents working for the Yugoslavs riddled the Ustasha organization. The most celebrated of these was Jelka Pogorelec, a bar dancer of considerable beauty who became the secretary and confidante of Gustave Percec. For eighteen months she communicated what she knew to the Yugoslav police until, sensing that her position was becoming untenable, she fled back to Yugoslavia where she wrote her memoirs of her adventures. Another police spy was the man named Kralj, or Malny, who had worked as a chauffeur for the director of the Sûreté générale in Belgrade and who was later to turn up as a member of the assassination squad. Kralj had been ordered to infiltrate the Ustashi as an agent provocateur, a task he carried off successfully until he recanted and went over entirely to the Croats.[105]

With agents like these one wonders just how far Yugoslav penetration went with the Ustashi and whether police motives ended with the monitoring, deception, and containment of the terrorists. There is no answer to this question, just as the issue of Italian complicity in the assassinations remains a mystery. There was plenty of evidence that rolled in after the murders to implicate Mussolini and his government, but most was circumstantial, none was conclusive, and the largest bundle of documents came from the Yugoslavs who had reason to be tendentious under the circumstances. No incontrovertible evidence of Italian guilt will be found in the French archives. The presence of Ustashi in Berlin and past contacts with Nazi officials led to similar charges regarding the Germans, but these accusations were more easily discounted.[106]

After 1934 the French continued to compile data on fascist intrigues and Balkan terrorism. In early 1935 the Yugoslav general staff passed on to the French military attaché in Belgrade information detailing the persistence of Ustasha training camps on Italian soil. Croatian émigrés in uniform, according to the Yugoslavs, were still carrying out military exercises in camps in the Abruzzi, on the Lipari Islands, and elsewhere in the peninsula. Periodically over the next several years the French received warnings about Ustasha terrorism. Balkan nationals of all kinds — Ustasha, IMRO, communist — comprised a substantial portion of the people who turned up on the *menées terroristes* mug sheets that the Sûreté printed after 1937. Their number included people like Stephan J., who was reported to have left an Ustasha camp in Italy with the intention of entering France, or N., who was of Croat or Slovene origins and was "identified as a terrorist and is a member of the 'Special Soviet Service' created within the Italian police; his present address is unknown." At the very end of the decade there was a flurry of reports about Nazi and OVRA connections with the terrorists, particularly the tightening relations between Germans and the IMRO.[107] The subsequent bloody role of Pavelic during the war is well known and does not need repeating.

Closer to home than the Ustashi, and considerably more numerous, were the thousands of Italian refugees who had fled Mussolini's regime and whose presence in France created difficulties for the police since the beginning of their emigration in the early 1920s. With the refugees came the Italian secret police. They infiltrated the *fuorusciti* with spies and informants, planted agents provocateurs who augmented the potential for violence on French soil, and, in the Italian police tradition reaching back before the First World War, joined the Italian SR in the pursuit of French military secrets.[108]

From the clandestine battles of Italian refugee politics came a series of revelations, including some extraordinary ones, about émigrés in the service of the secret police. The most celebrated affair concerned Ricciotti Garibaldi (whose name echoes that of his illustrious grandfather), a leading figure in the émigré community who was also a paid agent of the Fascists. Sûreté investigations into the intrigues of Garibaldi led as well to Guido M., a police spy and agent provocateur who had penetrated Italian refugee circles in France. Like Garibaldi, M. was entangled with a Catalan revolutionary conspiracy that sought Italian refugee collaboration, indeed so thoroughly entangled that he was murdered by Fascist agents ignorant of his role as one of their colleagues. There was also the case of Claudio B., who had come to France in 1926 for his "anti-Fascist beliefs" and who spied on refugees living in Marseilles.[109] Cases like these, and the more general identification of the OVRA with military intelligence, represented an unfortunate legacy for refugees as police attention shifted, by the late 1930s, to a new wave of émigrés from the Third Reich.

But Italians and Croats were next to nothing in the secret worlds they created alongside those omnipresent conspirators, the White Russians. The debris of one era they were a model of another with their armies, their "defense center[s]," their foreign agents, and their spy networks. It was White Russian intrigues that in large part accounted for the persistently high levels of espionage after 1918 as well as for much of the tone that separates interwar intrigues from those that preceded the First World War. A note from the time of the Kutepov kidnapping (1930) remarks that Madame Pepita Reilly, widow of the notorious British agent Sidney, has entertained the general on the eve of his disappearance and that she is prepared to reveal the true facts of the case. The note goes on to state that Kutepov has organized a White Russian army in Yugoslavia to march against Italy should the occasion arise, and that the Italians have engineered his removal and murder. Kutepov's cadaver, it is added, can be produced.[110] This was the sort of extravagance that enveloped the White Russians wherever they went, and it was typical of associations easily drawn between refugee intrigues and international politics following the war. As with the Ustashi, White Russians hitched their wagons to larger political stars so that reports on the Whites were sprinkled with references to the Nazis, the Japanese, Franco, and the Soviets.

With the latter, the connections were all but symbiotic. The revolution of the one had produced the exile of the other, and so intertwined were the two with each other's affairs that one could scarcely distinguish where White intrigues ended and GPU machinations began. Indeed the refugee milieu was so riddled with double agents and agents provocateurs that one might be tempted to believe that the White Russians were nothing more than a hoax perpetrated by the Reds. Again in such matters there were overtones of earlier battles when the tables had been turned and the revolutionaries were refugees, the Okhrana the hunters. Yet the difference lay not only in the episodes but in the milieus that produced them. In their execution and planning, Soviet sting operations and kidnappings bore all the markings of the well-oiled espionage organization for which there was no precedent before 1914. The Whites themselves had little in common with prewar revolutionaries aside from their exile and their conspiratorial politics. The revolutionaries lacked the organized, military, and global character of the Whites, and they did not possess the international political connections that came with the postwar upheavals and territorial settlements. Prewar refugees conspired with one another, but that was not the same as espionage on an international scale. The antibolshevik emigration, however, was mired in espionage and international intrigues. From gunrunning to descriptions of intelligence services, the White Russian presence marks nearly every archival run. Out of this human wreckage, whose very existence symbolized the ending of one age and the coming of another, flowed nearly all aspects of international espionage after the war: its global dispersion; its confusion of perpetrators; its ideological content; its organizational tendencies; its fifth-column associations; and its storylike richness. White Russians alone did not make up the interwar spy world. But one cannot imagine it without them.

At its peak the Russian emigration numbered about one million worldwide. From southern Russia the battered remains of Wrangel's army, and anyone who could join them, evacuated by ship as Red armies broke through the gates of Sebastopol, Batum, and Odessa. Over one hundred and fifty thousand exiles fled in this way, their first port of call Istanbul or islands in the Sea of Marmara or the Gallipoli peninsula, although later most moved on to southeastern Europe, or Berlin, or Paris. Others crossed west into Poland or Germany, or were already there at war's end as prisoners of war, and elected to remain. To the east large numbers of refugees poured into Manchuria or straggled south to Shanghai, particularly after the collapse of the Far Eastern Autonomous Republic in 1922, while others, often small military detachments, fought their way out, living fabulous adventures but enduring unbelievable hardships as they descended south into Mongolia and the Gobi Desert and as far as Chinese Turkestan. Thus White Russians scattered throughout the world and could be found in any remote outpost of the globe in the twenties or thirties. Mostly, however, they concentrated in several well-defined colonies. Istanbul was the first such collection point, but for many the city was merely a way station until passage could be arranged west into Europe. Germany, especially Berlin, was a center early on, because it was close to home, because many prisoners of war simply crossed over from barbed wire encampments to German residence, because visas came easily, and — most of all — because life was cheaper there than practically anywhere else in Europe until the restructuring of the mark after 1923 changed all that and forced the steady decline of the Berlin and German White Russian communities. The great rival to Berlin was Paris, but other major Russian colonies gathered in Prague and Yugoslavia, or in Harbin in the Far East.

Like all refugees the Russians regarded their exile as a temporary state of affairs. That is why few went on to the western hemisphere until the deterioration of conditions in the 1930s, especially in China, forced migration beyond the oceans in any significant numbers. United States immigration restrictions kept many out, and those who proceeded to Latin America in the twenties returned with such horror tales that other would-be adventurers remained put and endured life as it was. Russian reluctance to migrate to distant continents stemmed even more from a desire to remain close to the motherland and from a denial that *this* emigration had anything in common with the mass emigrations out of Europe in the previous century. Conscious of their role as Russia-in-exile, they awaited their day of triumphant return and, in the interim, set about preserving what they could of their worlds from the past. They founded relief organizations, churches, newspapers, and schools, including a university in Prague funded by monies provided by the Czech government. There were Russian restaurants, hairdressers, shops, and bookstores. Between 1918 and 1928 over 180 Russian publishers established themselves abroad, about half of these in Berlin alone during the heyday of the emigration settled in Schöneberg, Friedenau, Wilmersdorf, and Charlottenburg and gathered in literary cafés, especially the Café Léon on the Nollendorfplatz. With the passage of time, however, came the sad dawning upon many that exile was a condition from which there was no escape other than surrender, assimilation, or death, and, steeped in memories, bitterness, and old age, they fought rearguard actions in the thirties to retain their sense of identity and to hold onto their young. Their story, therefore, was far from a happy one. Marring the emigration were all the political divisions and squabbles and the flights from reality that had brought on revolution and defeat in civil war and had flung them into exile by the beginning of the twenties. The one inescapable reality of their lives was their ruin and their struggle for survival. Amidst the samovars and icons was a terrible penury and the insecurities that came with a juridicial condition of statelessness. Many crawled their way out, but many others did not, the basic fact that, along with their craving to go back the winners, made their milieu such a breeding ground of intrigue and every clandestine activity imaginable.[111]

Approximately one hundred and twenty thousand of these refugees eventually found their way to France, which became the undisputed capital of the White Russian exile by the mid-1920s. Some went to work in the mines in the north and others settled along the Riviera, but the largest number congregated in Paris, in the suburbs of Boulogne-Billancourt and Vincennes, in the fifteenth arrondissement along the rue de Vaugirard, or in the seventeenth around the St. Alexander Nevsky Cathedral on the rue Daru.[112] Most White Russians were poor and hardworking, finding employment in automobile factories or other semiskilled work. But there were also the taxicab generals and men's room attendants or practically every other stereotype that titillated French imaginations between the wars.

The Russians were birds of paradise, as one observer has called them,[113] exotic and mysterious figures in a nation seeking color and release after four years of gloom. Ballets, restaurants, and tzigane music played to these needs, although for police the mysteries verged on the sinister side of things and the colors turned to raucous, discordant shades. Their White world was people like Eugène P., who was born in Russia in 1902 and emigrated to France in 1923. He sold bananas and shellfish on the street, then worked as an artiste at a place called La Bohème in the impasse Blanche. Later he found employment as a maître d'hôtel at a series of nightclubs: the Caveau Caucasien, Eros, La Roulotte, the Enfants de la Chance (whose director had pioneered car solicitation by prostitutes and was known as an individual of *basse moralité*), and finally El Monico on the rue Pigalle. At the last club he swindled the owner, suppliers, employees, and customers until the owner found him out and gave him the boot. Without resources he moved in with his mistress, a woman from Rhodes who worked as a bar girl at Chez les Nudistes. By 1938 Eugène P. was nearly back where he had started, the subject of expulsion requests by the Paris police.[114]

There were worse types still, like the gunrunner W. or Eugène H., who came to France in 1924, living for a time an existence *très mouvementée*. He was, in many ways, the flip side to the balalaikas, a frequenter of the pleasure haunts of the capital and, in police words, one of those "foreigners of questionable morality capable of any job bringing in money." He was suspected of trafficking in narcotics and of selling arms to both sides in the Spanish civil war. His brother, who lived in Germany but remained in close touch with Eugène H., reportedly worked for the Gestapo. Or there was Paul D., another of those buccaneers cut loose by the war who pirated whatever profits came floating their way until, eventually, they drifted into espionage. His life followed a certain epic pattern of the times, from civil war veteran to high roller to bust in the depression years of the thirties as a number of his enterprises went belly-up, not always under the most reputable circumstances. By the mid-1930s he was living off frauds, bad checks, and arms sales to Spain. As early as 1925 there were reports tying him to German intelligence. A decade later he was turning up in the reports on Jean A., Goldberg, and Veltjens, and there were suspicions he might be a GPU agent.[115]

Indeed whenever police poked their heads into these clammy caverns they found no end to subterranean creatures. Few caught their gaze more than Zavadskii-Krasnopol'skii, or ZK., as he was known to contemporaries. A former czarist captain, he appears to have kept afloat in the postrevolutionary exile by playing the information markets for whatever they were worth. Within White Russian circles his reputation was appalling. One of the few complimentary remarks I have seen on him was Marina Grey's conclusion that he was probably not a Soviet agent.[116] A police report from 1934 said he had tried to sell information on Russian exiles to the Soviet embassy and to unidentified Frenchmen. A later report, culled mostly from the muddy waters of White Russian correspondence, called him a *louche individu* and said he was "one of the GPU's most energetic, crafty, and dangerous agents." His White Russian accusers claimed he had been expelled from Yugoslavia because of his collusion with the Soviet center in Vienna. Someone, possibly Kutepov, who headed the White Russian veterans organizations in Paris, wrote that "Captain ZK. constitutes the leading figure in the 'mafia' . . . which has succeeded in embedding itself within the Russian emigration." For the French he was dangerous enough to figure on the *menées terroristes* list from 1937. Yet everyone who disparaged ZK. was willing to use him. With the support of Kutepov he set up an independent intelligence service that he called the RIS. Some of the money for this came as well from Commissaire Faux-Pas-Bidet, for whom ZK. worked as a police spy. Another backer was a man named Bogomoletz, who police believed was a former British intelligence agent and an operative for the Romanian secret police. The RIS itself was clouded in mystery. Kutepov's intention was to use it against Soviet secret agents masquerading as refugees, although some said it functioned mostly as a Soviet disinformation agency. Others said it was primarily a private intelligence bureau selling what it knew to the highest bidder, a description that probably came closest to the mark. For the police it was a "shady business."[117]

Nothing about ZK. was beyond suspicion and controversy. His role during the investigations of the Kutepov and Miller kidnappings was questionable at best. Moreover he was closely connected with an official but secret White Russian intelligence network that was run by General Skoblin, himself a Red agent and complicit in the disappearance of General Miller in 1937. ZK. and Skoblin met frequently at night in the small cafés that bordered the Gare Saint-Lazare. Whether ZK. was actively involved in the kidnappings was never disclosed, but few would have been surprised if this had been so. His associations did nothing to dispel the unrelieved distrust that clung to him wherever he went. One RIS collaborator was linked to suspects in the Ignace Reiss murder. Another RIS parasite was a man named Koltypin, who was described in these unforgettable terms:

Koltypin is essentially a contemptible individual, but he should not be taken for an important GPU agent. He's simply barefaced trash, openly selling all information and news that falls into his hands. He sells the Bolsheviks and the émigrés to the prefecture, the émigrés and the prefecture to the Bolsheviks, the Bolsheviks to Burtsev, Burtsev to the Bolsheviks, and so on. In a word, everyone and everything to whoever pays him. He has no hesitation even to sell his own overworked fabrications. Provocation is his life, his element, his sickness, and his sensual pleasure. When he is drunk (and he drinks a lot) he says that he dreams only of outstripping Azef . . . and revealing "the true art of provocation." In a word, Koltypin represents a despicable human type.[118]

Such are the samples to be scraped from the muck of police files on the White Russians. What they all held in common was their insatiable appetite for scheming and the way survival after the war so often steered one into world politics, albeit its seamier side. The war was the starting point, the source of their miseries as it drove them through the maelstrom of history. Then came the opportunities of the twenties and thirties, growth years for intelligence agencies whose never-ending scrounging for information and agents created postings and payoffs for men on the margins. Or there were the vast markets in contraband weapons that offered lucrative returns for people with little or nothing to lose and that led them, if somewhat circuitously, to the camps of the professional conspirers and back into the historical storms from whence they had come. Most of all it was their Russian origins, and hence their clanlike ties to the forces of world revolution, that made spies of the schemers between the wars.

The focus of White Russian intrigues was the Soviet Union. The counterrevolutionaries among the exiles kept their forces in order as best they could, grouping civil war veterans in associations based on former military units. These associations then combined into national unions, for example, the General Union of Associations of Veterans in France or Bulgaria and these national unions in turn affiliated with an umbrella federation in Paris known as the ROVS (Rossiiskii obshchev-oennyi soiuz). Most unions were in Europe, but others were established in Asia and America. The French union in the 1930s claimed ten thousand members. The veterans represented only a part of the postrevolutionary emigration and for most ex-officers or soldiers these organizations functioned as friendly societies. Their leaders, however, had more grandiose intentions. They saw in the federation and the unions a means of retaining an army in readiness by preserving contacts among former officers and soldiers, even when these had dispersed to the four corners of the world. The leaders maintained an air of ranks and discipline in the unions, and they offered courses in military strategy.[119] Their plan was to march back into Russia and overturn the revolution, but in the eternal wait for that day they engaged in a clandestine war of terrorism and sedition, sending sabotage squads into the Soviet Union and seeking contact with counterrevolutionary groups behind Soviet lines. In this they plotted and schemed as if they were masters at the game, but they were in over their heads and the Soviets played them for fools. The GPU struck back with sting operations and double agents that it infiltrated into every White Russian organization. In the 1920s the GPU mounted an undertaking known as "the trust," which lured a number of people to their deaths—including Boris Savinkov and Sidney Reilly—and badly compromised White intrigues from abroad.[120] In the 1930s the GPU hit more deeply at the heart of their opposition by kidnapping and murdering Generals Kutepov and Miller, the successive leaders of the ROVS.

Kutepov disappeared on a Sunday morning in 1930. He was forced into an automobile at the corner of the rues Rousselet and Oudinot in Paris, and that was one of the few certain facts that police ever learned about the affair. Their best guess was that the car had driven to the Normandy coast where Kutepov or his corpse had been loaded onto a Soviet freighter; but neither weather conditions nor coastal terrain seemed to justify this conclusion and conflicting information disturbingly continued to filter in. Eventually the pursuit of Kutepov's kidnappers was abandoned, the full facts of the case remaining shrouded in mystery. Few people at the time doubted that Kutepov had been the victim of the Soviets, but no one could prove it. In 1965 a Red Army publication acknowledged that Soviet agents had eliminated the general, an admission that was probably true.[121]

Kutepov's successor, General Miller, met the same fate seven years later when he went alone to a meeting and vanished forever. Miller, remembering what had happened to Kutepov, had not been so foolish as to set out without leaving others the means to trace his whereabouts. He left behind a note, in which he confided to his aide, Kusonskii, where he had gone and that the rendezvous had been arranged through General Skoblin, another White Russian émigré. Kusonskii was to open the letter if Miller did not return by a predetermined time, but Kusonskii forgot and only when Miller's family reported his absence did Kusonskii remember the note written by the general. Kusonskii and another refugee officer summoned Skoblin to explain what had happened, a summons Skoblin complied with since he was unaware that Miller had identified his role in the fatal rendezvous. But once he discovered the cause of his summons, Skoblin managed to escape from Kusonskii and also disappeared into oblivion.

As the story broke, it was learned that on the day of the kidnapping a Soviet embassy van had made a hurried journey to Le Havre and had unloaded a box that was carried aboard a Soviet freighter, the ship then departing abruptly under irregular circumstances. French authorities disputed this version of events, but the matter was never completely cleared up. Because there were divisions in the émigré camp over Miller's style of leadership some people believed that he had been carried away by militant Whites with pro-Nazi leanings who doubted Miller's capacity for vigorous action and resented his caution over open support for the antibolshevik Nationalists in the Spanish civil war. Others suspected that Skoblin had removed Miller in order to secure command of the ROVS. Since Skoblin had lines out to the Soviets and the Nazis, any interpretation seemed possible. The truth was that the GPU, abetted by Skoblin, had abducted the general, an explanation that carried the greatest authority at the time. No one ever saw Skoblin again, but his wife, a celebrated Russian folksinger known as La Plevitzkaïa, was equally implicated and in 1938 the French brought her to trial. Convicted, she was sentenced to twenty years' hard labor, a punishment that stunned people by its severity.[122]

These affairs were the most sensational ones produced by any refugee milieu, and they emerged from a cabalistic world both risible and lurid. Undeniably an element of burlesque adhered to these exiles. No one expressed it better than the pathetic figure of Kusonskii. Miller left behind a note but Kusonskii forgot it. Later, when Skoblin was taken into custody, Kusonskii and his colleague retired to a room to discuss matters in private, allowing the culprit to slip through their fingers. When asked at Plevitzkaïa's trial to account for his actions, Kusonskii answered, "We thought he [Skoblin] had only stepped out for a moment (laughter)." According to one police witness, Kusonskii was a drunkard who during the war had been nicknamed Zakusonskii, a play on the Russian word *zakuski* for cocktail snacks. Some thought his actions suspicious and he was later deported. But police commissaire Roches, who had investigated the case, discounted these charges, saying Kusonskii was simply "victim to his incompetency."[123] So were most other White Russian intriguers. Their ambitions were preposterous, their enterprises bizarre, their execution inept. They oscillated from supreme naïveté to supreme distrust, all the time accomplishing nothing except embarrassing themselves.

Some of their closest collaborators were Soviet agents, and their headquarters on the rue du Colisée were bugged with GPU microphones.[124] Just how many GPU moles dug their way into the White movements in France was anyone's guess, especially since the urge to conspire was exceeded only by the compulsion to denounce. At some point in the interwar years probably every person who had once lived in Russia or whose name ended in certain three letter combinations had likely been denounced as a GPU spy by another person with the same attributes. The milieu was constantly disgorging weird, extravagant figures like ZK. and Koltypin or like Paul Gorgulov, who in 1932 assassinated the president of France. His fascist tendencies led some to suspect a Nazi connection in the murder, while the White Russian community insisted he was a Soviet agent sent to bring discredit on them. The man gave every impression of mental disturbance, and this was the authorities' conclusion, although the court judged Gorgulov sane enough to hang. Double agents, endless denunciation, grotesque characters, and the hopeless amateurism of people who sent secret messages about "traveling salesmen" through the mails was the White face of intrigue in the twenties and thirties. Even the police were provoked to contempt. There was no reason, noted one official, to believe that restless subordinates had done away with Miller:

given the complexity of events, the Machiavellian polish to the execution, the kidnapping of General Miller can only be the work of an occult group perfectly disciplined and organized and possessing powerful financial means. This is not the case with the Russian émigrés, lacking cohesion, self-devouring, scraping by from day to day, and ethnically incapable, unless they have leaders, of conceiving and especially of executing a plot of this scope.[125]

If nothing else, the White Russians in exile explained Red victory in the Russian civil war.

Yet one cannot dismiss the cold, hard, conspiratorial side to the milieu. Both the Miller and Kutepov affairs exposed one suspicious character after another, a horde of potential GPU spies, and the technical proficiency with which Communist covert operations were carried out abroad. Moreover, papers seized in the wake of the later kidnapping revealed how steeped the Whites were in conspiracy and intrigue. These papers were full of the workings of ZK. and his assorted camp followers. They also disclosed that Miller and Skoblin had been running agents into Russia largely via a conduit through Finland and in 1932 had made additional plans to send twenty agents by boat into the south of Russia. The agents were to stir up a peasant uprising, but the scheme never came off, money for the boat failing to materialize and Miller growing suspicious of his representative in Romania. Those emissaries who did make it through were almost always betrayed, costing the Whites dearly in dedicated personnel and in cash. The financial cost of infiltrating one agent ran to 5,200 francs in expenses. These included 1,000 francs for a guide, 1,000 for two weeks' preparation, 300 for shooting lessons, 150 for a passport, 850 for transportation, and so on.[126]

Bridging GPU successes and White Russian failures was the figure of Skoblin. To this day he remains a controversial character. Everyone who has written on the Tukhachevskii purge has advanced a theory on the role of Skoblin as a liaison between the Soviets and the Germans in this affair, and there is no need to add one more unsubstantiated scenario to those currently floating about.[127] No one knows the full truth about Nicholas Skoblin, although there is good reason to believe that he was a triple agent working for the Whites, Reds, and the Nazis and that he was ultimately loyal only to himself. Before the Miller disappearance he was already suspect in White Russian circles. In the early 1930s a refugee colonel named Fedosenko claimed that he had gone underground as a GPU agent and that he had consequently learned that Skoblin was a traitor. These charges had prompted an inquest by a White Russian court of honor (the preposterous side to these people always finds its way through), but the court had found Skoblin innocent of all accusations. Yet even for some time after this matter Skoblin was entrusted with the direction of a White counterintelligence network known as the inner line. Kutepov had established the network in the late twenties to root out GPU police spies camouflaged as exiles. Its first director was a White officer in Bulgaria. Later Skoblin came to run it, apparently using the organization and its agents to spy on White Russians in France and abroad for his own nefarious purposes.

Since Skoblin was also working with Miller to infiltrate counterrevolutionary agents into Russia, it is not clear whether the inner line doubled as an espionage and sabotage organization or whether these were separate operations; police files on the line are often confusing in this regard. Nor is it clear where the inner line broke off and agencies like the RIS began. Obviously Skoblin and ZK. were using each other, but just how remains open to conjecture. Equally tantalizing are Skoblin's connections with what may have been a special murder squad made up of renegade White officers and utilized by the Soviets for special missions abroad. Elizabeth Poretsky, Ignace Reiss's widow, has argued that such a squad existed and was known to certain GPU agents in Europe. Skoblin was of course tied to Miller's disappearance. He also was in relations with Kudratiev, another White Russian who was among those identified as Reiss's executioners. Whether Skoblin was an organizer or merely an intermediary in these operations is one more unresolved matter. He was not, however, the only White Russian who worked both the Soviet and German sides of the fence. Another was a man named Von Petrov who served in Red Army intelligence but also spied for the Nazis.[128]

Similarly the inner line was only one of a number of covert organizations run by the Whites. Wherever the French turned they seemed to unearth one more White Russian secret agent network. Grand Duke Kirill, they noted, had representatives spread all over the world and a "tightly knit network in Russia of connections and spies with codes, go-betweens, etc." This was almost certainly an enlargement upon the truth, but it was illustrative of the image Russian refugee circles tended to convey. Semenov in the Far East reportedly disposed "of agents not only in Asia but also in Europe." A general Monkevits, who had worked in Russian counterintelligence during the war, was placed by Wrangel and Kutepov "at the head of a network of secret antibolshevik agents." Later he defected to the Soviets. Some suspected him of complicity in Kutepov's kidnapping, particularly because he was "an excellent 'technical' organizer of the most difficult enterprises." Police were constantly struck by the resemblance between White Russian operations and the workings of intelligence agencies. Reviewing Miller's covert activities, especially in the Baltic, one reporter remarked that the general "had established an entire espionage network in different countries in Europe." Another wrote:

In effect, if in appearance Russian veterans' groups, formed into friendly associations, pursue honorable goals of mutual assistance, their leaders are playing out a mysterious part, displaying all the characteristics of a Deuxième Bureau with its intelligence and surveillance services and operating in agreement with certain foreign powers.[129]

The White Russians were the ubiquitous intriguers. Nearly every intelligence agency had its White Russian spies. They worked for the Germans, the British, and the Nationalists in Spain. The French used them in the Balkans in the early 1920s and then again in the late 1930s. The GPU employed them by the handful and, if French police suspicions were correct, so did Red Army intelligence.[130] Nearly every battleground between the wars, clandestine or overt, turned up its White Russians. The Whites fought with warlords in China. At the time of the Rif rebellion in Morocco Wrangel proposed a White Russian expeditionary force at the service of Spain, an overture declined by the Spanish (perhaps they wanted to win). There were reports that Abd-el-Krim was recruiting White Russian mercenaries — typical of what one had come to expect of these people — but the reports were never confirmed and probably were without foundation.[131]

In the 1930s White volunteers headed to Spain to fight with the Nationalists in the civil war. Just how many made it through has never been clear. Most likely the number of émigré ideological warriors was far from substantial. The Nationalists seem to have been reluctant to commission White refugees in their regular forces, in part because they knew that the White emigration was perforated with GPU spies. But Franco also placed agents among the Russian exiles to recruit still more volunteers. Among these was Elisbar V., who went to fight against Bolsheviks in Spain in 1936 and returned several months later when he failed promotion to the rank of second lieutenant. A former taxi cab driver, by 1938 he was living off subsidies provided by the rebels in Spain. There was also Dmitri D., who had come to France in 1927, plying his dancing skills in the tea salons of fashionable establishments and living as a gigolo through the extravagances of well-heeled women. In the thirties he too was identified by the police as a Franco agent, primarily recruiting volunteers to fight against the republic. At more exalted levels Miller, despite charges of caution, negotiated with Franco for the admission of Russian volunteers in the Nationalist armies and sent an envoy, General Shatilov, to Spain to work out the details. Miller's disappearance in the fall of 1937 appears to have cut these liaisons short.[132]

White intrigues thus spread across the political landscape, embroiling the exiles in every contestation or force of the day. The dispersal of the émigrés and postwar power politics made such connections inevitable. For the French, White Russian conspirators were most of all a plague because they brought Soviet agents onto French soil, but no less menacing was the fact that the two foreign powers with whom the Whites were most closely associated were, by the 1930s, Germany and Japan. From the early years of the emigration Germanophile elements among the refugees gravitated toward the most reactionary and radical counter-revolutionary circles in Germany, particularly those based in Bavaria. They penetrated the Ludendorff-Max Bauer group and through a prewar Baltic émigré — Max Erwin von Scheubner-Richter — they developed early ties to the Nazis. The central figure in their intrigues was General Biskupskii, an adventurer and inveterate schemer. Throughout the twenties Biskupskii plotted to launch counterrevolutionary attacks into Russia. His contacts reached back to Bauer and the Nazis and later, in the thirties, the latter elevated him to the leadership of the Russian colony in Germany. He was a man distrusted by his own kind and held in contempt by the Germans, but in the 1930s his appointment to head of the émigré *Vertrauensstelle,* powerless though he was, reflected the coming to power in Germany of militant antibolsheviks.[133] This change in German leadership and politics, combined with émigré fears after 1935 that the French were moving too close to the Soviets, led increasing numbers of White Russians scattered over the continent to look to Germany for direction, an inclination the Nazis were not loath to exploit.

At the same time prospects of war in East Asia and Japanese overtures to refugees who had crossed into China exerted a comparable pull on the far side of the globe. In 1936 French naval intelligence estimated the Russian population in Manchuria to number at least one hundred thousand. Yet that was roughly the estimate Gabrielle Bertrand gave for the Harbin colony alone in 1932, and several years later when she visited the city she found it preserved the *inimitable grouillement slave.* And in 1938 French military intelligence placed the number of Russians in China at approximately a million and a half, although that figure encompassed practically the entire East Asian emigration from northern China to Shanghai and Hong Kong and included Russians long settled in the region as well as those who had fled bolshevism since 1917. Whatever the actual numbers, the White Russians of the Far East were a sizable, motley, and potentially mobilizable mass. They were notorious for their fallen women and for their legions of soldiers and officers who fought for warlords from the Pacific to Turkestan or rode guard on the railroads that rolled through bandit-infested territory. Their ranks extended from rich industrialists and merchants to men and women who had rebuilt ruined lives after years of hardship and struggle to weary survivors — these last making up a vast reservoir of the wretched and poor whom military intelligence summed up as follows:

These have lost everything: country, fortune, dignity, hope in the future. They constitute a pitiful herd, one part of which, living off charity or the poorest of trades, is ruled by the sole question of where its next day's bread will come from, while the other shows no hesitation to resort to the most shameful expedients — even prostituting the women of their family — to hold onto at any price the poor remnants of comfort they are unwilling to lose. The youth of these outcast milieus must furnish, to whoever wishes to buy them, a recruiting base of agitators, tough guys, or secret agents ready for any shady job that one hesitates to entrust to regular organizations.

With Japanese penetration into Manchuria, purchase of the Chinese Eastern Railway in 1935 from the USSR, and then invasion of China proper in 1937, came efforts to enroll these exiles into a Japanese allied (and manipulated) anti-Soviet force. Many of the refugees despised the Japanese, especially those who fell under their overlordship in the north, but there were also dreamy hints of carving out a White Russian province in the Far East, prospects of revanche against the Reds, and, as the French were quick to observe, the sheer lure of giving the White Russians what they had not: "To this people of proscripts they offer recognition of civic rights and property, to powerless chieftains they offer subsidies and armaments, to former officers commissions, to their sons uniforms and military prestige, to the starving bread, and to the ambitious unhoped for positions." The Japanese, moreover, were not without collaborators among the military cadres or leaders of the émigrés. At Tientsin they worked through Pastuchin, attaching to him a major on the general staff of the Japanese SR. Most of all they resurrected the controversial figure of Semenov. Of Cossack-Buriat origins he had made his fortune in the Russian civil war in the east, rising mercurially through the ranks, fighting alongside Baron Ungern-Sternberg, and organizing a renegade White force in Siberia that had slaughtered countless victims from their armored trains aptly named the *Merciless,* the *Terrible,* the *Master,* the *Horrible,* the *Ataman,* and the *Destroyer.* His reputation among many Russians was of the worst, as a crook, a brute, and a man completely sold to Japan. By the 1930s, however, he loomed once again as a White military presence in the Far East, headquartered in Dairen and thoroughly backed by the Japanese, a fact obscure to no one. He too had his watchdog, a certain Colonel Onda.[134]

In fact neither the Nazis nor the Japanese took the White Russians seriously. Neither gave a whit about a White counterrevolution and each had its designs on Russian national territory. For both, the Whites were a card to play, either to expand influence in areas where there was a considerable White presence or, ultimately, as a force to deploy against the Soviet Union. Each proved a difficult partner for the Russians. The Nazis played with Ukrainian separatists the same game as they did with White exiles, and their relations with the latter could blow hot and cold. Japanese rule in Manchuria could be brutal and merciless. The Russian refugees were not oblivious to these problems and especially in France they displayed reservations. But for militants there were no better alternatives, and, in each case, leaders had come forth as advocates of the German or Japanese option.

Particularly from 1935 on (1935 being the year of a Franco-Soviet pact), the French observed the drift of White Russian communities into the German and Japanese orbits. In the most garish reports there were rumors of White Russian brigades forming in Germany or of White Russian sabotage and subversion units operating in Russia in the event of a Japanese-Soviet conflict. The mission for each would be to cut communication and rail lines and to incite a general anti-Communist uprising.[135] At a more down-to-earth level, the French tracked White generals who had thrown in their lot with the Germans or who demonstrated pro-German sympathies — Biskupskii, Turkul, and Glazenap among the former, Miller's successor Abramov (in Sofia) among the latter — and they watched for signs that the alignment with anti-Comintern powers, discernible among Russian exiles elsewhere, was working its effect among émigrés in France. There were times when they sensed that their own exile community was impervious to the emissaries coming from Berlin.[136] But there was also a string of reports running throughout the thirties that pointed to dangers.[137] Thus whatever the conclusion of informants or analyzers, the White Russians were people to watch. They might be sympathetic to the nation that had given them refuge, but they were also connivers and plotters and among these were elements that were thick as thieves with the fascists. Altogether, the French did not know what to expect of Russian exiles in the event of war. However the impression left by the documents, and by practically everything else they discovered about these refugees, is that they looked upon that prospect with neither comfort nor complacency.

What is to be remarked, ultimately, about this milieu, is how cleanly it fit the patterns of espionage after the war and how thoroughly postwar conditions shaped it and gave it its tone. The Russian emigration was a seedbed of conspiracies and clandestine figures, a vast shadowland of grand ambitions and shabby realities. All this was so because of postwar unsettlement, because of the circumstances of the exile and an unrelenting commitment to counterrevolution, and because in a world awash with opportunities from gunrunning to selling information to tracking down spies, ex-czarist officers on-the-make were available and were most often the people to turn to. Their political adventurism fit into the wider pattern of intrusiveness by which the great events of the period pressed in on people and became an inescapable presence or fact in their lives. For White Russians who emerged out of war and revolution this intrusiveness was simply a norm; but it showed up as well in the way their politics were absorbed into the politics of others — Soviet politics, German politics, Spanish politics, Japanese politics — that is, into the greater power struggles of their day. Likewise White Russians revealed the flux of the period in their desire to reverse historical change but also in the range of possibilities open to individuals within their milieu. Before the war the riddle was, who worked for the Okhrana and who did not. A similar question plagued exile circles after the war, although now the riddle was compounded by combinations that took one to Sofia, Burgos, Tokyo, and Berlin. Skoblin's multiple connections, the varied speculation regarding Miller's disappearance, as well as the confusion over Gorgulov, issued from the mutability and interconnectedness of things after the war. As spies and conspirators, White Russians were forever building networks of secret agents and endowing their intrigues with an organized character that mimicked the postwar intelligence agencies. Their intrigues spread over the world, assuming like the international affairs of the period a truly global dimension. Their ideological politics ranged them alongside the Nazis and Falangists, just as their tactics of terror, disruption, and sedition reflected the turn to covert strategies during and after the war. They were, in certain ways, quintessential representatives of the civil war climate in which secret wars were fought in the twenties and thirties, and the suggestion that they might form an organized strike force within the Soviet Union to wreck transportation and incite insurrection placed them squarely within fifth-column projections. For the authorities they were a possible danger at home, one more reason to regard all refugees with suspicion. Yet they were also a source of unending carnival and this too, as we will see, made them representative of moods and attractions and of the fascination espionage could hold for the French. They were, in short, anything and everything intrigue had to offer in the interwar years, typifying a wider milieu that in turn encouraged and explained them.

———

There were still other refugees without whose story no account of espionage between the wars would be complete. These were the Jewish and political refugees who fled Hitler's Reich in the 1930s. They came to France, and wherever else they could get in, under the worst of conditions, a decade of economic depression and intense politicization, that made them unwelcome at best and at worst the objects of hatred and fear. Few exiles would be victimized more by the century, not even the White Russians, whose stories of degradation and the profoundest of miseries must have run into the tens of thousands. Their worst fate would be reserved for the forties, but in the thirties these refugees were battered about, increasingly excluded from jobs and then from the most basic requisite of exile in contemporary times: access to papers and assurance of refuge. They were often the target of charges of espionage, and in fact the very conditions of their emigration drove them inadvertently to cohabit with spies. That in itself forces their entry into this history. Yet like White Russians, Italians, Ustashi, and gunrunners, they belonged to an age whose intrigues — real or imagined — direct us to larger historical matters. Thus far we have dwelt on the broadest of connections, the relation between the character of the intriguers and the character of Europe after the war. But there is also the history of interwar France, and how it is revealed through the history of spies. The German refugees provide answers to that question, and nowhere is that clearer than in the fact of their internments at the outbreak of war and what this says about the late Third Republic.

All the great democracies, it should be noted right away, interned individuals during the Second World War. The French interned enemy nationals; the British interned Germans, Austrians, and Italians; and when the war spread to North America, the United States government rounded up Japanese residents and citizens. Yet the patterns were not quite the same. Unlike in France, internments in Britain did not come en masse until the 1940 spring offensives. Less than two hundred foreigners (out of a total of more than sixty thousand enemy aliens) were interned in Britain with the outbreak of war in the fall of 1939. Only after the first rash of German victories in the west and the circulation of fifth-column stories, now collected into a systematic explanation of Nazi success, did the British (and later the Americans) proceed to large-scale confinements.[138]

The French did otherwise. In September 1939 French authorities rounded up and interned some fifteen thousand German and Austrian nationals, many of whom were refugees. These are the official figures although some historians have suggested that the numbers ran closer to twenty thousand. By mid-November the French had released twenty-five hundred internees, and thereafter the numbers declined still further as internees were liberated, organized into work battalions, or recruited into the Foreign Legion. Nevertheless the following May, when the German invasion began, many who had been set free were reinterned, now joined by large numbers of German and Austrian women.[139] Thus between French internments and the others lay a critical difference in timing, a difference accentuated by the fact that French internments seemed to bridge harsh policies mounted against foreigners in the thirties and the persecutions of the forties when the Vichy government rounded up, interned, and then at German behest deported Jews to the Nazi killing camps in Poland. It is for these reasons that the initial internments in France have borne a heavier historical freight than their counterparts in Britain and North America. Set as they can be within a wider picture of crisis and retreat in the last years before the coming of war, they force the question of the extent to which the republic was sliding toward Vichy even before the first Panzer units broke across the Meuse.[140] But the internments, even if influenced by anti-Semitism and a growing will to impose tough, exclusionary measures upon the foreign-born, were also conditioned by thoughts about security; indeed it is not irrational to argue that security is what they were mostly about, and as such they throw us back on spies and milieus and in turn on official reactions to each. Buried within the security records compiled out of the history of espionage since the First World War are reasons aplenty to explain the decision to intern. What these tell us, moreover, is that internments under the republic, if terribly, tragically wrong, were grounded in experience and the administrative difficulties of police work as much as in prejudice and panic, and that they proceeded from ways of perceiving that were neither those of decay nor of Vichy.

The internments culminated nearly a decade of restrictive measures taken against immigrants. Unlike earlier emigrations, this one was greeted with reluctance, uncertainty, and even hostility almost from the beginning. The French record on taking in refugees was as good as that of nearly any other country, yet even in this land that prided itself on its traditions of refuge, the welcome extended in the very first months progressively ceded to grudging admissions and then restrictive measures taken against those allowed in. The Popular Front of the mid-1930s relaxed certain controls imposed by earlier governments. But the right-leaning Daladier government that followed in 1938 introduced new stringent measures (usually in the form of decree laws) that tightened border surveillance, subjected illegal entry to harsh penalties followed by expulsion, intensified the hunt for clandestine aliens, and provided for forced residence (and later the prospect of camps) for those illegal refugees who had no place to go.[141] In early 1939 the collapse of the Spanish republic and the flood of hundreds of thousands of Spanish refugees across the Pyrenees resulted in the creation of concentration camps; although the numbers were so great and the concentration in a particular area so focused that the internments of the Spanish can only in a limited sense be seen as a prelude to the internments of Germans and Austrians half a year later. Indeed at times French authorities found it convenient to separate Spanish refugee issues into a case all their own.[142]

Whatever the political variations over the course of the thirties, the collision of Nazi repression with closed borders elsewhere (and joining the French in this measure were all customary havens of refuge) had a devastating effect upon refugees. Those who could get across came anyway, only to find that their fate in republican France was no less precarious under the severe restrictions and penalties imposed by successive regimes, especially the tough decree laws of the last Daladier government. Suicides were one measure of the sense of entrapment that haunted anti-Nazi refugees. Already in the first year of the emigration, police noted a sad progression of suicides among prominent German émigrés. In 1933 suicides carried with them the note of despair. By 1938 they rang of fear and the impact of French official policy. There was the case of Emile Schwaetzer, an Austrian doctor who had fled to France in the latter year. Upon his entry Schwaetzer had received an identity card good for thirty days and an exit and reentry visa valid for the same duration. He had then gone on to London hoping to arrange a right to residence and medical practice there (the latter would have been almost certainly unattainable in France). In England Schwaetzer encountered delays and could not obtain an extension of his visa. Terrified by the prospect of imprisonment in France should he return after the expiration of his visa, and learning that two relatives had been denied residence permits in France, he took his own life. Left behind in France were two young children and his wife, who entered a clinic for nervous disorders. One day after Schwaetzer committed suicide, another refugee, sentenced to six months' imprisonment for failure to leave the country, slit his wrists.[143] These were only some of the suicides, and suicides were only the most extreme response to conditions of refuge in France. There are hundreds, probably thousands, of depressing stories to be found in the archives and memoirs from these times.

How far espionage and security concerns shaped the refugee policies of the thirties is difficult to measure. Certainly the overriding factor throughout the decade was the depression and the fear that refugees would compete for a scarce and shrinking allotment of jobs. Moreover, French authorities were beset by all sorts of anxieties regarding refugees from Central and Eastern Europe. They worried that anti-Nazi refugees could endanger Franco-German relations. They feared that the Germans and Poles were dumping their "undesirables" upon them, a term that ranged in its shadings of meanings from criminal elements to communists and Jews.[144] And tormenting French imaginations in the late 1930s was the specter of millions of Jews in Poland, Hungary, and Romania who were under jeopardy of forcible expulsion should liberal nations like the French display a willingness to take in all of the oppressed.[145] The problem is how to separate one factor from another. There were always deep reservoirs of anti-Semitism and xenophobia in France, rising or dropping roughly in concordance with the country's economic fortunes. Certain of the security provisions that came with the decree laws — for example, forced residence and surveillance — were introduced to compensate for the fact that not all refugees could be deported. The 2 May decree law sought to root out clandestines, yet it can also be read as a series of tough measures to keep new refugees out by demonstrating that illegal entries would be prosecuted. Any of the above anxieties can explain its motivations.

But it is also clear that the discussion of what to do about refugees never strayed very far from the issue of spies. Spy novelists, spy "experts," mass dailies and weeklies all played up the theme of the fake refugee spy.[146] There is no reason to assume that state policy was swayed by these allegations, nor is it necessary—even if the means were available—to show a cause and effect relation between public opinion and administrative practice. From the first months of the anti-Nazi emigration, security officials raised on their own the possibility that secret agents disguised as refugees figured among the genuine émigrés. Jean Belin, a commissioner with the Sûreté, later wrote:

We had to look on every German in the country as a potential spy or at least agent of the Nazi party. It did not matter how insistent he was in his anti-Hitler sentiments. We soon found out that some of the seemingly innocent refugees were the most dangerous. There was the additional complication that even those who did not wish to work with the Nazi warlords at home were forced to do so through fear of retaliation on their relatives if they persisted in refusal to collaborate.

These sentiments appear to have been fairly widespread within the police and security ministries. They can be plotted from a memo as early as June 1933 through official reasons given for refugee internments. So ingrained was the fear that refugees could be foreign agents that even those internees permitted to depart for North America in the late fall of 1939 were kept under military guard until their embarkation and were allowed to sail only on French or English ships "to prevent . . . these foreigners, once they have left our territory, from making their way to another continent from where they will more easily be able to return to Germany."[147]

It is not difficult, therefore, to trace throughout government records persistent fears of refugee or fake refugee spies, nor even to show that refugees were interned for security reasons. The more puzzling matter is why officials of the Third Republic came to identify men and women who had fled persecution as potential or real security threats and why thousands were corralled on the presumption that some might be enemy agents.[148] The answers surrendered by the security files are wide ranging and surprisingly complex.

For one thing the police were not decidedly unsympathetic to the plight of refugees, nor was there an unambiguous determination that German refugees constituted a threat to the state. There were people within the police who accepted at face value the anti-Nazi sentiments of the émigrés and who placed these thoughts in written notes in the early stages of the emigration in 1933 and toward its close in February

1939.[149] The police could side with émigrés when describing incidents of provocation and violence, and they could pierce beyond their mission of control to the personal tragedies of people cast adrift in an inhospitable world. There is, for example, the following report, written in March 1939 by an unidentified official with the Paris police, describing the predatory circles descending upon helpless refugees. Touts and canvassers, he notes, sweep through train stations and cafés and hang about consulates looking for émigrés with no place to go. When they hit upon a mark they direct him to their contacts who, for a fee, promise papers and transit visas for foreign lands. In cahoots with both are tourist and emigration agencies, some of these legitimate businesses, that can arrange transportation for the émigrés the touts and contact men steer their way. All three collaborate in this veritable industry of emigration and each extracts what money they can from the hapless refugees. None loses a moment of sleep over whether they will ever deliver the goods. It is, for the writer of the report, a sad and almost scandalous story where refugees figure as innocent victims. "The serious political and religious persecutions to which nationals of several neighboring countries have been subjected, has enabled numerous intermediaries of a sorry morality to reap a profit." That is the note on which the report begins. Organizations, the official goes on, have appeared for the express purpose of exploiting the refugees. As for the latter, "one can only with difficulty blame the refugees for accepting the services of these unscrupulous intermediaries, because for them the only thing that counts is the possibility of flight and life. And it is well-known that these shady contacts succeed where individuals and international conferences fail."[150]

There are, of course, other reports with very different sentiments, but what matters is the mix of reporting, or the mitigating edge, that turns up in these files. The French police in the thirties demonstrated no clear-cut, unqualified prejudice against refugees. What they did express clearly was a frustration with the inconsistency and confusion that accompanied administrative edicts and impromptu decisions. From an executive point of view, French refugee policy in the thirties was a mess. Under the regime of the decree laws, police resources were taxed to the limit. Worse, every new measure handed down from above created gray areas or unenforceable conditions that placed police in exasperating and, at times, ridiculous positions. Aggravating the situation were the frequent interventions in individual cases that provided short-term reprieves from prosecution or expulsion or that requested counterenquiries before imposing penalties, all of which, incidentally, were an indication that republican legal protections, if bruised, were not withered or dead. Compounding matters further were the deep stalls that certain Eastern European consulates went into when asked to process passport renewals for their Jewish nationals, the intervening delay in turn triggering still more reprieves. Thus police found that they were operating in a welter of incoherence and that they were arresting the same people over and over again, a misery for refugee and police alike. Some refugees were arrested by police as many as half a dozen times, all on the same infraction, and still had their cases pending in the spring of 1939.[151]

Even when authorities toed a rigorous line and insisted upon the expulsion of clandestine émigrés, they could be asking the impossible. The Sûreté's special commissioner at Pontarlier near the Swiss border, fed up with escorting expellees out of French territory only to have the Swiss drive them back on his doorstep—the Swiss would accept only their nationals—told the following story of an expelled Hungarian. Try as he might the commissioner could not push the man across into Switzerland. Three or four times he and his Swiss opposite batted the Hungarian back and forth across the frontier. The only way he was able at last to get the Hungarian off French soil was to get him a job with a wild animal act that was passing through Pontarlier on a special train headed for Sweden. The lion tamer agreed to hire the Hungarian to clean up after the animals. They placed the man in a cage with eight lion cubs as the train rolled over the border and dared the Swiss gendarmes to inspect his papers. The Swiss this time looked the other way. Pouring out his frustrations with a policy so muddled that he was forced to resort to this kind of charade, the commissioner noted that such an improvisation could scarcely constitute a general rule of action and, in any case, was, in that trenchantly dismissive French phrase, *inadmissible*. In the future, he advised, if the authorities were earnest about expelling foreigners not in possession of Swiss citizenship, they would do well to direct them to some frontier post other than Pontarlier.[152]

But then what commissioner would want them? This was a tone of exasperation that rang through police reports on refugee policies. Faced with discharging unpleasant and unenforceable duties, the police pleaded for clarity and simplicity in their administrative instructions. Reading through these reports one senses that there was always an element of the Gordian knot about the internments, combined with an Alexandrian desire to slice through the tangle of confusion and hypocrisy and create clear, easy solutions to the refugee issue. Treating people as categories and giving absolute priority to national security was one way out, especially in times of emergency. For the refugees this was scarcely an improvement in their lot, but if it gave the police what they wanted, it did so on grounds of administrative expediency and not those of bias and hateful revenge.

Nor were internments or crackdowns against foreigners new. The search for clandestines, the descents into hotels, the verification of papers, and the push back across borders that characterized immigration policy in the thirties had all occurred in the presumably more tolerant twenties. On the night of 24 April 1925 the Paris police checked five hundred foreigners in various hotels and cafés in the nineteenth arrondissement. Over several nights in late April and mid-May of that year they returned to the same quarter, sweeping through thirty-five hotels and six bars and verifying the papers of two thousand foreigners and five hundred Algerians. On 10 February 1927 they descended upon the hotels of the rue des Rosiers, the rue Quincampoix, and the rue Simon-le-Franc. Dragnet operations like these appear to have been fairly common in the mid-to-late 1920s. Between 1 January 1927 and 28 February 1928 the Paris police initiated *expulsion* and *refoulement* proceedings against 1,808 individuals. During the years 1920–1933 deportation cases averaged 566 per month.[153] In the following decade the numbers would grow, and the personal tragedies would magnify, particularly as refugees who would have formerly been welcome were now among those hiding without papers. But police actions against immigrants and the vigorous pursuit of clandestines preceded the restrictive policies of the thirties.

Moreover, projects for the internment of foreigners in the event of war were nearly as old as the republic. In the late 1880s officers on the general staff and in the Ministry of War contemplated concentrating tens of thousands of enemy nationals in camps in the first days of wartime. Over the next twenty-five years a series of blueprints, drafts, and instructions refined and revised these proposals, primarily in two ways. First more thought was devoted to the logistical difficulties of moving and controlling large numbers of civilians in a period of general mobilization. Pragmatism and methodical planning forced modifications in the perception of what could be done. Second, a ruling by the Ministry of Foreign Affairs in 1906, contested unsuccessfully by the Ministry of War, accorded enemy nationals the option of leaving French territory following the outbreak of war. Those who could make it across the border in the first day of mobilization were free to go. Others who wished to leave would be concentrated in grouping centers and then evacuated to the interior until sufficient transport could be spared to take them abroad. In certain parts of France, enemy nationals who did not wish to leave would be permitted to remain where they lived. Others in the east and in Paris and Lyons were to be evacuated to designated areas, although not interned. The trend therefore was toward more practical, less Draconian measures. The assumption, nevertheless, that foreign nationals would be "excellent enemy intelligence agents" and that "over the entire compass of France it is essential to prevent foreigners from causing harm, provoking disorders, or hindering mobilization" remained the basic impulse behind the drafts and directions, and even within a more tolerant framework the French were still contemplating on the eve of the First World War the movement, surveillance, and control of large numbers of foreigners resident in France.[154]

With the reality of war came the end of restraints. Nearly all the machinery that was to be set in motion in the fall of 1939 — internments, concentration camps, sorting commissions — was pioneered in the First World War. By mid-September 1914 the government ordered the incarceration in concentration camps of all German and Austrian civilians in France. Temporizing measures followed as the authorities worked their way through the exceptions. Among those liberated were enemy nationals with a son or husband in the French army and Austrian subjects of Czech, Serb, Croat, or Bosnian origin. Alsatians posed a special problem. There were Alsatians who had resided in France before 1914, others who had crossed over from Germany following the declaration of war, and others living in territory the French reoccupied in the first days of fighting. The French evacuated all three groups in the summer of 1914. Some — those of longstanding Francophile sentiments or with a family member under arms — went free, but many ended up in special depots and not infrequently were interned with the Austrians and Germans. In November the government appointed a commission to visit the depots and camps and to sort out those Alsatians loyal to France.[155]

Later, reviews of foreigners excluded from general internment orders and a 1915 law authorizing denaturalizations of citizens of Austrian and German origins led to further internments. The records of a commission on foreigners that deliberated throughout 1916 on who was entitled to a *permis de séjour* (or residence permit) and who should be interned extend for nearly two hundred pages, usually with several cases to a page. Among the cases the commission heard were those of Charles E. and a man named Lerche. Charles E. had been born in Hamburg of a German father and a French mother. For thirty-six years he had lived in France. He had married a Frenchwoman, had renounced his German citizenship, and shortly before the war had applied for naturalization. Nevertheless, on the basis of a letter written by the mayor of his town, he had been interned in a concentration camp. Lerche, of Austrian origins, had lived in France since 1887. He had become a naturalized citizen on 30 August 1914 but was then denaturalized the following year and sent to a camp. With two sons serving in the French army he had managed to gain his release; the question for the commission was whether he was entitled to retain his *permis de séjour*. In another case a seventy-two-year-old German, born in France, married to a French-woman and with a nephew in the army, was the subject of an evacuation order (it is not clear whether it had yet been carried out). The Ministry of Justice was not even certain that the man was not a French citizen.

The commission, whose members included representatives of the Ministry of War and the police, as well as prominent individuals like Emile Durkheim, found this case regrettable, as it did those of Charles E. and Lerche. In general it made a sincere effort to winnow out from the list of suspects individuals who had demonstrated their fidelity to France. Even a person like Marie K., a German by origin but the common-law wife of a French soldier, was, in its eyes, entitled to a *permis de séjour*. But for all its judiciousness the commission could not prevent internments nor did it question their legitimacy. Its deliberations reflected the basic contradiction of mass confinements under any republican regime: the inability to mediate between democratic traditions and emergency security measures whose very adoption generated a momentum all their own and yet the persistent effort to do so with reviews and exclusions predicated on standards of rationality and fairness.[156] In 1939 the Third Republic would fail just as miserably in its attempts to find a way between exaggerated security needs and respect for individual liberties. To a large extent it would follow the same pattern it applied in the First World War, rounding up categories of people and then processing the exceptions and exclusions.[157]

Thus the internments of 1939–1940 had a long history behind them. When the Great War came to a close, republican governments picked up where they had left off in 1914, turning out contingency plans for the surveillance, repatriation, and internment of foreigners in the event of a war. By 1926 the blueprints called for the internment of male enemy nationals between the ages of seventeen and fifty upon the outbreak of hostilities, and the evacuation of the remaining men, women, and children to concentration camps pending repatriation (this latter measure was later revised to residence under surveillance). Thirteen years later officials produced an elaborate chart outlining measures to be taken against enemy nationals, political refugees, and stateless persons in "a period of tension or mobilization," most of the first two categories destined for some form of incarceration or surveillance.[158] On the one hand it was a chilling foreshadowing of the persecutions that would come in the succeeding five years. On the other, it was only the most up-to-date version of a long line of projects that extended back to the late 1880s and whose instructions had been executed twenty-five years earlier. Under these circumstances perhaps what mattered most about the internments was the purpose for which they were intended and used. In the Third Republic they represented a more fragile side to civil liberties in France, but their design and application in the late 1930s was no more a step into Vichy than they had been in the First World War or at any time since republican authorities had begun toying with the prospect of mass confinements.

To police frustrations and the history of internments must be added the security climate on the eve of the war. Not astonishingly the roundups occurred amidst a mounting disposition to ferret out spies. Visions of the ubiquitous spy gripped officials throughout civil and military service. Jean Dobler's frantic appeals to keep German priests out of Ecuador[159] were only the extreme version of the Quai d'Orsay's more diplomatic requests that the Vatican clear missionary expeditions in advance. Elsewhere the Quai was obliged to clean up the mess left behind by navy commanders who were grabbing people right and left off passenger ships. Any German on the high seas — refugee, priest, negotiated repatriate — was a target of naval vigilance. In February 1940 the colonial authorities in Oran arrested and interned eleven Germans who had arrived on the *Duchessa d'Aostia* bound for Genoa. Eight came from Tanganyika, three from Nigeria, and all traveled with a British safe passage as part of an exchange agreement with the Germans. Again the Ministry of Foreign Affairs had to intervene to set the men free.

In France civil authorities were obsessed with defeatists and subversives. There is a fat dossier in the F60 series of the Archives nationales filled with cases of people investigated or imprisoned for running off at the mouth. Some were communists and some made truly inflammatory remarks. Others simply let loose after too much to drink (the *débit de boissons* or public house figures frequently in this file), denouncing the war and calling Daladier a *salop,* an *enculé,* a *con,* or other choice phrases.

The penalty for this kind of talk could be eighteen months in prison and several thousand francs in fines. Foreigners not subject to internment were wise to keep their mouths shut, no matter what the provocation. Jacques R., an Italian traveling between two factories on 26 May, learned this the hard way. Forced off the road after his bike had a flat, he blew his top at a French passerby who loaned him his pump but then, intrigued by R.'s accent, asked for his name and country of origin. "I've descended by parachute," R. shouted back. "We are very numerous. We are going to blow up the arms factory and destroy Châtellerault. . . . Long live Hitler! Germany over all." God only knows what the Italian had endured down to that point before going off the deep end, but such talk was idiotic under the circumstances. The Frenchman alerted the authorities, who arrested Jacques R. What sentence he received — and almost certainly he received one — is not recorded.[160]

It is perhaps in this light that one must contemplate the run of bulletins that began to pour in as war tensions heated up in 1939 and then carried over into the following spring: terrorist agents sent into France with explosive and incendiary devices concealed within thermos bottles, gas cans, fountain pens, Faber brand pencils, or false briquettes; two men and a Hungarian dancer traveling under false papers from Argentina to Europe for the purpose of sabotaging French ships; thirty Czech nationals recruited by the Gestapo for missions abroad, especially in France; Italian spies and saboteurs carrying small Gillette shaving kits fitted with coding instructions hidden among razor blades (this from the arrest and interrogation of several Italian agents); terrorist attacks to demoralize and cripple mobilization (accompanied with details on timetables); army counterintelligence assertions that the Gestapo and OVRA "have organized in our country and in French possessions a network of agents of unparalleled breadth"; a man named Lambert recruited by the Comintern in conjunction with the Gestapo to sabotage Allied shipping; Romanian Iron Guard agents trained in Germany for missions of sabotage and terror (this forwarded with accompanying pictures by the Romanian Sûreté in December and again with detailed reports on nineteen Romanian terrorists the following April); enemy sabotage plans targeting French gasoline depots; communist saboteurs, "motivated by ideology and unaware that Germany controls the stakes," run by German spy masters working out of Trier, Aachen, and Freiburg; and then in March 1940 the Polish high command report on "sabotage and parachutist descents."[161]

How many of these bulletins can be taken on face value is difficult to say. Almost certainly many were fabrications or rumors, the product of the same impulses that later drove peasants with pitchforks to surround French airmen who descended from the sky or incited a series of sightings of priests and nuns in hobnailed boots. Some were unsubstantiated by subsequent police checks and some were probably the result of confusion; for example, the reports on Iron Guard saboteurs may have simply scrambled intelligence on Volksdeutsch Romanians whom the Abwehr had recruited for special operations along the Danube.[162] Still, given what we know about French penetration of German intelligence or French rating procedures of their informants, there is no reason to assume that French counterintelligence had gone completely haywire or that all of these alerts were false alarms. Some of the reporting was highly detailed and in at least one case was based on intelligence from captured agents. The one thing that does seem clear is that the French authorities on the eve of the war were primed for a new secret service offensive, although interpretation of even that perspective is clouded by uncertainty as to whether this reflected a surrender to spy mania or a coolheaded retrospective on what had accumulated in the files over the past twenty-five years.

Under any circumstances a spy alert would have placed refugees in a difficult position, and it is here that the history of espionage since the First World War is most revealing about why men and women who had fled from the Nazis were identified nevertheless as a security threat. A hunt for secret agents would, by its very nature, bode ill for people whose foreignness was all too apparent. But counterespionage officials had other reasons beyond atavistic instincts for dwelling on refugees as potential suspects. It has been noted by one historian that foreigners represented the overwhelming majority of persons listed on the Carnet B by 1936.[163] Following the record that police had been collecting on foreigners and refugees since the First World War, one finds nothing surprising in this statistic.

Foreigners, for instance, constituted the principal subjects of the *menées terroristes* mug sheets first printed in 1937.[164] The genesis of these lists is not known, but there is no indication of a general administrative call for the naming of suspects. Most of those who appeared on the sheets seem to have been identified by foreign police or to have crossed over from earlier files on individual cases. State visits elicited some lists and others were general annual musters, but there was also a list on Ukrainian émigrés to be watched, particularly those with German connections.[165] The multiplication of lists and sheets typified the problem that the interwar spy milieu posed for refugees from Hitler's Third Reich: more than its organizational expansiveness or even its turn toward covert operations, the milieu's uncontained sprawl directed suspicions toward German refugees. For twenty years the police and SR had compiled dossiers on refugees tainted by espionage or by dubious liaisons with foreign powers. Sensational events like the Marseilles assassinations or the Kutepov-Miller kidnappings had led them to refugee milieus so mired in intrigue that at times it was difficult to tell who was a secret agent and who was not. Refugees had plotted and conspired and built secret networks. They had raised the specter of cooperation with national enemies and they had joined their enterprises to those of foreign secret services.

Two decades of refugee affairs like these had the power to cast suspicion over all émigrés. The most prominent intriguers, the White Russians, were under close surveillance throughout the thirties. The French expelled some White Russians in the late 1930s and in 1939 they interned others in Le Vernet, the concentration camp reserved for the most dangerous cases.[166] If, however, they refrained from mass roundups of Russians, it was likely to have been for the same reasons that they did not touch the Italians: France was not at war with their homelands, their numbers were too great, and their communities had been well established in France for many years.[167] To a certain extent the misfortune of Jewish and German political refugees was that they suffered not only from their association with other refugees but from their vulnerability. Few had developed roots in France, they were too many to sort out before hostilities but not too many to intern, and they came from the wrong country.

Milieu and vulnerability combined in still other ways. The recurring fear of the French throughout the 1930s was that the Germans were exploiting the anti-Nazi emigration as a means of infiltrating secret agents into France. There were, in fact, German operatives among the refugees. Some were fake refugees, others were bona fide émigrés who offered information in exchange for papers, money, or the right to return. Others the Germans pressed into service through blackmail or comparable forms of persuasion. At least one refugee sold the Germans information on the French intelligence agent known as Fred Swirles or English Fred. Most refugee agents, however, spied on other refugees for the Gestapo and the Auswärtiges Amt.[168] In general they represented a small portion of the Jewish and political émigrés who fled abroad, and it is not clear how actively the Germans recruited them. German Foreign Office records suggest that refugees themselves often took the first steps and that they encountered, initially, a wall of suspicion. An SD official in July 1937 was enthusiastic about the prospect of recruiting émigré agents, but his memo suggests how little had been done by this late date.[169] Altogether the refugee agent, if a reality and a plague to other refugees, was not a serious menace to French security. Yet the French refused to let the matter drop.

One reason for this was the stunning revelations of refugees playing a double, even a triple, game. The unmasking of Ricciotti Garibaldi in the twenties and Skoblin in the thirties clouded the presumed innocence of all other refugees. Berthold Jacob had been lured to his kidnapping by a man who had left Germany in 1933 and had then offered his services to the Gestapo. Less dramatic, but no less unsettling, were the files on Guido M. and Claudio B., both Italian agents who had penetrated anti-Fascist circles. Police traced the Ignace Reiss murder in part to White Russians in Paris; they deported an Italian named Lorenzi who had tried to infiltrate anti-Fascist organizations and was suspected by the SR of working for Italian intelligence; and they learned through captured agents that Italian saboteurs and spies, if stopped by the French, were to claim to be anti-Fascist refugees.[170] Refugee double agents, they knew, were not a fabrication nor was there a neat distinction between those who informed and those who spied. Occasionally police turned up suspected intelligence agents among the German refugees, for example, the dubious figures in the Alice L. affair or a gang of German émigré gunrunners in Antwerp whom the Sûreté suspected of working for the Gestapo.[171] Moreover, the French themselves were recruiting German refugees for intelligence work. Swirles ran Jewish émigré agents and so did Hartwig in Yugoslavia. All of this was to the refugees' credit, but the more deeply they immersed themselves in intrigue, the more they reinforced the tendency to associate their world with that of the spies. There was, as well, the nagging question of why certain refugees had returned to Germany during the early years of the emigration. Some officials saw no reason for Jewish refugees to help the Nazis, but not all were unsure that émigrés could shed their German identity so easily. A colonial SR report from December 1939 remarked that German Jews in Siam had offered their services to the "Nazi community, which treats them with less distrust than they do in Germany."[172]

All of these things undercut refugee credibility, but perhaps the most insidious force at work was simply the intrusive, spongelike character of interwar espionage, as it spread out and absorbed more and more people until lines blurred between one shadowy activity and another. So many crooks, con-men, charlatans, arms dealers, traffickers glided into espionage in the interwar years that in the twenties and thirties, it can be argued, clear divisions between criminal and secret agent underworlds dissolved, giving way to a single, amorphous milieu in which people moved easily among clandestine activities. Those who were drawn into that milieu, even only to its edges and by the force of circumstance, thus risked absorption into the world of the spies, or at least, identification with them. This, in effect, is what happened to refugees.

In no respect was this predicament more gripping than in regard to false papers.[173] Papers — passports, visas, identity cards, residence permits — were the refugees' lifeline, and around that vital need grew a vast, grasping, plunderous underground market in counterfeit documents. Even in the liberal climate of the twenties there were people without the essential documentation and others who stepped forward to sell what they needed. Records on the traffic in false papers extend well back into the years right after the war.[174] The thirties, with its economic crisis, its political and racial persecutions, its mass production of stateless people, and its immigration barriers, occasioned a boom in the trade. Jews in Germany, Austria after 1938, and Poland were determined to get out however they could. They took their papers where they could get them. Black markets ballooned, fed by desperation and greed.

Those who trafficked in papers shared two traits. They were generally, if not exclusively, foreigners. And they gouged their clients for whatever they could get. Prices for false passports ranged from one thousand francs upward, with most generally going for somewhere between five thousand and ten thousand francs. But there was no outer limit. Some passports commanded a thirty-thousand-franc fee. A Hungarian named Steiner, who sat at the Café de la Paix every Wednesday, charged seventy thousand francs for naturalization papers and the same for a Canadian passport, although he also sold Hungarian passports for three thousand francs each. Passport merchants in Vienna, to sweeten their deals, told Jews who were frantic to leave that 25 percent of their costs went to state taxes and that they gave another 10 percent to the poor Jews of the city. Others struck directly at the raw nerves of terror. An Austrian refugee who had made it to France but needed a certificate of refugee status for himself and papers for his wife still in Vienna, was directed to a trafficker named Reich. Reich said he could do it for 150 dollars but the refugee balked at the price. Reich then told the man he ought to think things over but on no account to announce his arrival to the police (the alternative to going the false-paper route) because if word leaked back to the Germans they would lock his wife away in a concentration camp.

Traffickers varied in their scope and their method. Some built international organizations with a clear division of labor between counterfeiters, touts who scoured refugee hangouts — usually cafés — or canvassed in home countries, and middlemen who cut the deals and distributed the papers. Others had special contact men in consulates, and spread out from there. In general anyone desperate with money to spend could always find someone with false papers for sale. The doorman at the Palace Hotel in Zagreb was one go-between. A Viennese Nazi, Dr. P., operated through an insider in the French consulate in Cologne and through a front man in Vienna, an old Persian tout named Goldstein available *en permanence* at the Café Atlashoff. Word of the Cologne connection became an open secret in Vienna, to the point that Jews traveled there on their own to secure a visa firsthand. A Jewish woman named Stein made a scouting expedition in September 1938, then returned in October, grabbing a taxi at the train station and heading straight for the consulate at Woringerstrasse 11. Going directly to a ground-floor office she presented her passport and her husband's, asking for the precious, life-giving stamp. She was told that she would first need a change of residence for Cologne, but that this was no problem and that all she need do was to go to a particular office at the police station and say that she had come from the French consulate (the police bureaucrat was in on the scam). Following these instructions, she then proceeded to a meeting with the consulate employee at the coffee room of the Hotel Marienhoff, where she handed over the passports and four hundred marks. Three hours later she returned to the café and picked up the visaed documents.

There were traffickers who specialized in visas and passports of Latin American countries. Some of these documents were outright fabrications, others were for sale by the consular officials. In a more ingenious scheme, some consuls on the take sold certificates attesting to birth in their country, which the buyers could use to obtain legitimate papers. Alfred U., whom the police arrested and threw into the Santé in 1939, peddled Bolivian visas and Costa Rican passports, procuring the latter from the Costa Rican consul at Palma (Majorca) for four thousand francs each. He also ran a traffic with fake visas from the French consulate in Bari, but his Italian contacts kept the German passports he had forwarded and he had to send a special emissary to get the passports back. No one in this business was clean except for the refugees.

This fact, however, was not so easily discernible to police and army counterintelligence. Refugees on the run carried false passports, but so too did spies, saboteurs, and terrorists. The Ustasha hitmen had journeyed on two sets of counterfeit papers in their passage from Janka Puszta to France. The Imperia gang responsible for the 1937 bombings in the Midi had utilized false papers, as had the men Miller and Skoblin sought to infiltrate into the Soviet Union. The 1939 *menées terroristes* sheets carried an alert for a man named K., alias Peter Von Medem of St. Petersburg, alias Franz Landgraf of Vienna, alias Peter Bertens of Prague, alias Arthur Denier of Lausanne and so on — the list of phony identities ran on for ten lines and included twenty names (K. was fluent in Russian, German, French, Italian, several Balkan languages, and spoke some Polish). He was wanted for espionage and the counterfeiting of documents, and police suspected him of collusion with terrorist groups.[175]

For secret services, false papers were an indispensable tool of the trade. The Germans photographed and systematically studied border crossing stamps of different countries, manufactured special paper, and established a special laboratory for the fabrication of their counterfeit documents.[176] Until 1934 the Soviets ran an unparalleled series of underground counterfeiting shops in Berlin. With thirty thousand rubber stamps on file, a stash of several thousand passports at any one time, and a core of a half-dozen expert photographers, printers, and typesetters supported by an international staff of nearly one hundred and seventy, this Pass-Zentrale literally mass-produced bogus documents for Soviet agents passing to the West or western Communists heading East. Following the Nazi takeover it exported its operations to the Saar and then, after 1935, divided its personnel and goods between Paris and Moscow. When possible the Soviets preferred to use authentic documents, which they altered to fit the secret agents who used them. Volunteers in the International Brigades who surrendered their passports for "safekeeping" — an apparently obligatory procedure — were a fabulous source of supply. Occasionally expert forgers were assigned to Soviet intelligence units, or intelligence officers recruited their own. Often Soviet agents traveled on more than one set of documents, picking up new papers in special rendezvous or drops along the way. Richard Sorge's radioman, Clausen, left Russia on an Austrian passport, flushed it down a toilet in

Paris, and proceeded on to the United States with a Canadian passport he had carried in the false bottom of his suitcase. Once in North America he managed with a hard-luck story to update at a German consulate his own, genuine passport, which a colleague had passed back to him in a Viennese movie theater detour between Paris and New York. When Leopold Trepper traveled to Paris in 1936 and then back to Moscow the following year, he used three passports, each in a different name. Throughout his career he had about twenty aliases bolstered by bogus Austrian, Polish, French, Luxembourg, and Canadian papers.[177]

The French SR seems to have had a predilection for fake Luxembourg and Scandinavian passports, although their agents traveled on those of other nationalities as well. Among their sources of documents was the shadow man Stallmann. Swirles procured papers for his agents from a Pole named Ochwed.[178] Meanwhile French counterintelligence learned quite a bit of the techniques of others through the arrest of foreign agents carrying bogus papers or through police busts of counterfeiting operations. In 1931 the Viennese police broke into a secret Communist workshop on the Wasserburgerstrasse. There they found a modern printing works and a cache of passport forms, licenses, and baptismal certificates. In another apartment they hit on a large file cabinet containing all sorts of identity papers, facsimiles of stamps and signatures used by foreign consular services, and letterheads of business firms. This was not the first bust of its kind, and throughout the period reports kept coming in on counterfeit operations. In 1927 there was a warning about Soviet fabrication of false papers in a trading office in Berlin. A report from 1933 said that the Soviets were shopping for Persian passports for their agents in the Orient. In December 1939 there was an alert on a German shop in Zurich that was buying up Swiss passports and doctoring them for intelligence use.[179]

Set against this background, refugees, many of whom had fake stamps in their passports or fraudulent papers altogether, were obvious targets for lurid suspicions. The very pattern of the market in sham papers, for example, the wide trade in Latin American passports, merely accentuated the problem. False papers from Costa Rica, Guatemala, Bolivia, and the like were among the best sources of personal documents for refugees, but they also served spies. As far back as the First World War there were warnings of German agents traveling on fake Costa Rican papers. GRU intelligence officers crossed borders with Uruguayan passports. The suspicious John T. of the Samuel I. affair carried Nicaraguan papers. Japanese agents operating in France used dummy Nicaraguan passports. Bauer-Mengelberg in Paris, who fostered German Jewish refugee emigration to Latin America, maintained close ties with the Paraguayan consulate but also with Stallmann of the French SR; the Germans suspected him of working for French intelligence. In the first days of 1940 the Sûreté issued a bulletin warning of Chilean and Argentine diplomats in the Netherlands working for German intelligence and capable of issuing fake passports for German secret agents.[180] At the most direct level, therefore, French authorities by 1939 were faced with the problem, very much of their own making, of having to distinguish between clandestines of one sort — refugees — and clandestines of another — spies, each of whom possessed false papers, very often of a similar kind.

Making that distinction was not eased by reports that German "Aryans" were carrying passports "just like those established for Jews (J) so as not to arouse suspicions" and that bearers of these passports had recently turned up in Barcelona.[181] Nor was it eased by the kinds of people the refugees turned to for their credentials. Traffickers, police knew, were a rapacious, shadowy lot who slunk about in the company of ominous figures. The Cuban passport affair of the late 1930s was one example of the unsavory and sinister lower strata that police unearthed when they investigated this corner of the milieu.

The affair began in 1937 with the arrival of a new representative to the Cuban legation in Brussels and his decision to set aside the blank passports left behind by his predecessor. He should have destroyed them, but he did not, and an enterprising employee within the legation sold fifty of the blank forms to another Cuban, a man named Valdès. Valdès paid five hundred francs each for the passports and then unloaded them at triple and quadruple that price to foreigners in need of papers. The profit was too great for Valdès to retire once he had exhausted his original stock. He expanded his operations, bought up expired passports, apparently of Latin American and Spanish origin, doctored them, and then sold these too on the black market. Many of the people who worked for Valdès had FAI (Spanish Anarchist) connections, and a certain portion of Valdès's passports found their way to people belonging to Spanish left-wing extremist groups.

To run his traffic Valdès built a sizable ring of associates and touts, recruiting among those petty hustlers who cluttered then, as they still do today, the underworld's fringes much like the dingy outskirts thrown up about a fathomless and profoundly corrupt great city. There was El Chiléno, a flamenco dancer and Sûreté stool pigeon, a suspected arms trafficker named Ricardo D., and a Spaniard called Delgado who, according to Spanish rumor mills in the capital, had committed the most heinous crimes in FAI-dominated parts of Catalonia. Ricardo D.'s mistress, Gertrude V., was the sister of Dolores V., known also as Lolita V., a woman with close links to Spanish anarchist circles. Delgado was closely linked to Maria B., a dancer at the Lido on the Champs-Elysées and at the Cabaret Eve in the place Pigalle. She was suspected of working for the OVRA. In the inner circle were two Spaniards, Luis F. and Joseph P., who took over the organization when Valdès saw the writing on the wall and fled to Cuba to evade arrest in spring 1938. Several months later police picked up both men and cracked the ring.[182]

Another of Valdès's touts was a Spaniard named Flores, an impostor and thief. Flores passed himself off as a former intelligence officer for the Spanish republic, which was a lie, but both he and Luis F. were operating as spies and informants for an Italian named Giacoma, and unlike any of the petty hoods involved in the affair, Giacoma was a very big fish. On the surface a legitimate and highly successful businessman, Giacoma was in fact running a major OVRA network in France, and from what can be reconstructed out of police files, he was also engaged in military intelligence. For a secret agent like Giacoma, the Cuban affair was obviously only a side venture, but police suspected that he was using Luis F. and Flores as a source of false passports for political refugees he ran to spy on anti-Fascist émigré activities.[183]

These, then, were the kinds of people who sold "to foreigners in search of papers."[184] Few of the traffickers, in fact, were beyond wider suspicions. Some, like Alfred U., had been accused of espionage. Others had clear Nazi connections, like the Nazi dealer Dr. P. in Vienna or a man Winter who trafficked in passports and reportedly had traveled to Paris in the company of German intelligence officers.[185] For the police the traffickers were the scum that floats on the surface of all people's misfortunes, but in a world where criminality, intrigue, and espionage blended so readily into one and another, they were also potentially much more. What the police were coming to think of them all by the end of the thirties can be seen in a cross-referenced dossier the prefecture compiled in 1938 on a hundred foreigners to be expelled from France. The dossier was occasioned by the British state visit that summer, although one can only suspect that the police used their security preparations as an argument to get rid of people they wanted as far away from France as possible. Among those who figured on the list were the White Russians Eugène P., Elisbar V., and Dmitri D., which gives some idea of the kinds of people the police wanted out. Also on the list was the Italian C., a former Comintern militant until the late 1920s, when he had turned one hundred and eighty degrees right and announced his adherence to the Fascist regime. A lawyer with a practice in Paris and Cannes and an apartment on the Champs-Elysées, C. had been abandoned by his wife because of his loose living, his brutish behavior, and, as the report read, because of obscene gestures he had forced his stepson to make in front of his mother. In 1935 this paragon of virtue had offered his services as a Fascist propagandist in exchange for five thousand francs' compensation per month and, according to an informant within his entourage, the Italian secret service had sounded him out about a special assignment to stir up trouble in North Africa. Mostly the people in the dossier divided into several look-alike categories: agents for Franco, agents for the Italian secret services, GPU agents, anarchists, left-wing and right-wing Yugoslav terrorists (including some who had rallied to Italy and Nazi Germany), or generally dangerous figures like the Czech Joseph B., a racketeer locked away in the Santé who had taken up with the ex-mistress of the international crook and counterfeiter Radu Dragulinescu and whose close associates included an automatic weapons specialist (and notorious gun trafficker) who had sold arms to the Spanish Nationalists. Lumped in as well were a half-dozen individuals who trafficked in false papers or in some other way facilitated clandestine immigration into France and who apparently, in police eyes, were indistinguishable from the terrorists, intriguers, revolutionaries, and secret agents who composed the bulk of the file.[186] One senses that by this date the cops were not far off from adding in their clientele too.

In the end there existed multiple reasons for the internment of refugees in 1939–1940. There were precedents for the concentration of foreigners in wartime, and a government leaning toward the right was likely to cede more readily to exaggerated exigencies of national security, especially with official and public moods running in favor of getting tough with "aliens." There was also something of the better-safe-than-sorry approach to the internments, rationalized or tempered by the expectation that sorting-out commissions would correct injustices as they had (theoretically) done so in the First World War. By spring 1939 the French had drafted plans for rounding up refugees along with other enemy nationals, but the blueprints also specified exclusions for certain categories (important people; those with a son in the French army) and set up screening commissions that would liberate others after an initial assemblage.[187] To pressures for a clear-cut and decisive policy toward refugees, internments offered one solution. But the milieu of espionage between the two wars — extensive, multiform, overlapping, and intrusive — itself prompted the decision to intern. Twenty years of reports and experience provided reason enough to be on the lookout for spies, saboteurs, or some vague fifth-column-like threat in the opening days of a war and to wonder whether refugees might serve these purposes. Neither spy fear nor suspicion of foreigners was plucked solely out of thin air or out of a miasma of xenophobia and panic.

In particular, those who fled Hitler appear to have been trapped and condemned by the broad, inclusive nature of that milieu. To the police it was a milieu without edges or regular borders, one that seeped and absorbed like a vast spill of oil, spreading, encompassing, and dirtying everything it touched with the same blackening, indelible stain. Police were familiar with its run-on, drifting patterns and consequently with the mélange of people tarred by its reach. Gunrunning accustomed authorities to its encroaching and congealing properties, particularly the ties between traffickers and spies or the convergence of criminality and international intrigue. Refugees who tumbled into that milieu either because of their clandestinity or their pursuit of the vital passport to safety thus, in a manner of speaking, fell all the way in. Through their use of false papers, or merely through their identification with traffickers, they too crossed unwittingly into the lands of the spies. Increasingly one has the feeling that the authorities decided to intern because they witnessed the descent of the refugees into the nether realms and because they had lost the means of distinguishing between one subworld and another.

That decision bestowed no credit upon the republic. It was scarcely humane or politically intelligent, and it was arguably ineffectual as an emergency security measure. In blunt terms it was crude, stupid, and condemnable. Still it had more to do with ways of perceiving built out of a seemingly rational view of the times than with any presumed republican death rattle or the persecutions of the regime to come. Perhaps its comprehensibility and *republican* fallibility were articulated best in an exchange between the Ministry of the Interior and the Ministry of Foreign Affairs regarding two protected Austrian refugees. Each, a man named B. and his lover M., worked for an officially sanctioned Austrian émigré organization and for this reason had been exempted from previous internment. In late May 1940 the police arrested the pair and placed them into a concentration camp. Did the Quai wish to object? For the

Foreign Ministry's information, the Sûreté was forwarding police reports on the suspects.

B., according to the reports, had belonged to the Austrian Communist party since its inception. He had worked with a section that had come under GPU control and in 1925 had traveled to Moscow, where he remained for some time before leaving on Soviet missions abroad. He had entered France in March 1938 claiming refugee status. Despite his official connections, his behavior had attracted suspicion. At the outbreak of the war he had received a large number of registered letters from Austria and frequent morning telephone calls. At M.'s, where he went every night, he had often been visited by foreigners who, the concierge had reported, "concealed themselves as much as possible and sometimes carried suitcases and all sorts of bundles." Each night he typed letters until early in the morning. Some Austrian émigré officials believed they were under surveillance by Gestapo and GPU agents. Investigations had led them to suspect that B. was the spy. The police noted that B. was a "notorious Communist and was moreover suspected of being a secret GPU agent."

M.'s record was largely the same. She had Communist sympathies and had lived for some time in Moscow, where she had met B. She had worked for the Soviet Film Institute and then for the Café Métropole, which the Soviet government had established to spy on foreigners suspected of anti-Communist tendencies. During this period several foreign specialists in the state metallurgical industry, none of them Communists, had accused her of being a secret agent for the GPU and the Comintern. In France as a refugee she too indulged in fishy behavior. She went out in the mornings, never returning until late in the evenings and then accompanied by B. and carrying suitcases that, word had it, belonged to foreigners interned at Colombes. Other foreigners visited her at her apartment, most of them arousing suspicions because "they returned to her place without announcing themselves." Like B., M. typed into the night, much to the distress of her neighbors. The concierge reported that M. always used German when she spoke on the phone, which was frequent. She too was suspected of spying on other Austrian refugees in Paris. On these grounds the two had been locked away.

The affair revealed some of the worst sides to the police sweeps. The authorities showed no sensitivity, nor even understanding, of internal Communist politics in the thirties, never asking why B. and M. had sought refuge in France instead of returning to the Soviet Union. The police evidence was wholly circumstantial, the better part of it innuendo and gossip of the most disreputable sort. Yet the affair also illustrated how the very conditions of refugee status could arouse police suspicion, particularly under a restrictive immigration regime. Many refugees did meet late at night, carried suitcases or papers for others, received mail from Axis countries, spoke German, and dissembled to avoid calling attention to themselves. Such was the behavior of foreigners abroad, many of whom were without regular papers or were helping others who had entered clandestinely. Often, through the force of circumstances, much that refugees did could give the appearance of questionable activity. Moreover there was a good deal in the background of B. and M. that warranted suspicion. Indeed what is most striking about the affair is not their internment but that they had eluded incarceration so long. If these were the protected ones, the refugees who had been identified as loyal and beyond uncertainty, then what were police to think of the rest for whom no official was personally intervening? People like B. and M. were a danger for the entire emigration because they had the power to jade police sensibilities and to confirm other, far-reaching suspicions. The refugees who streamed out of Nazi Germany and Austria should never have been put behind barbed wire, but it is possible to comprehend why the authorities thought otherwise. The Ministry of Foreign Affairs, incidentally, which was inclined to advocate the liberation of others, wrote back that it did not believe this was a case that merited *une mesure exceptionelle de bienveillance.*[188]

In their decision to intern, the French brought together experience and perception to form a particular vision of their world between the two wars. In similar ways, all of the espionage files from the period may be said to represent a certain way of perceiving or a mental construct of things after the war. Within that construct was always considerable room for imagination and fantasy. The story of the Belgian conductor–secret agent pops immediately to mind, as does a bulletin on a false Daladier traveling through military zones during the "phony war"[189] (or a dozen or so other examples one can dredge from the files, undoubtedly stuffed there by routine-minded bureaucrats or by individuals with a keen sense of humor and an appreciation of the bizarre). Yet one should also point out that the wildest alerts rarely received official accreditation; nothing in the archives suggests that these records constitute a mere conjuring of imagery. Even the most fantastic reporting retained a certain connection with its times. Sources who pointed at German terrorist conspiracies to explain the Marseilles murders revealed through their language and their vision—"the psychology of the afterwar"; methods "inspired by the actions of the Communist International"—a clear fixation with the peculiarities of the age.[190] Certain obsessions might become fixed over time. Those officials who feared that White Russian forces would subvert from within while German armies struck from without were, whether they realized it or not, merely replaying scenarios from the First World War, when the conviction had held that the Germans were employing the Bolsheviks toward the very same ends.[191] Yet here too was a mentality behind such reports that sprang directly from the war and the events that had followed. No matter how warped the reporting process became, certain simple truths were always embedded within.

At a saner level, officials too brought to their reporting a certain way of viewing their moment in history, although this represented less a creating of material than a way of selecting, ordering, categorizing, and patterning. The expectations and priorities are revealing. It is interesting that only rarely did these men look back beyond the war. A prewar construct had also existed: that spies were an ever-present force to reckon with and that every German in France was potentially a spy. That perspective never disappeared entirely, but superseding it was a more protean one anchored to contemporary experiences and realities and thus more aligned to its times. The postwar vision constructed its reports from what the World War and postwar intrigues had taught it to expect. It dwelt on international circuits, agent centers, training schools, organization and method. It presumed a global dimension to espionage threats. It forwarded material on Impex because that did not seem chimerical when set against German intelligence during the war, and it came to write about White Russians as intriguers and double agents because that is what it found when it investigated their milieu.

In particular it incorporated the belief that totalitarian secret services had distinctive features in common and that all operated in peculiar ways consistent with their ideologies. Points of reference became forcibly contemporary. Hence Mussolini's secret police became "a sort of Fascist Cheka," while in fall 1933 army counterintelligence reported that the Nazis were planning to set up operations in Europe "analogous to those that the GPU has organized."[192] Likewise there was an inclination to anticipate subversion and confusion—whether Moscow or Berlin or Rome was the source of specific acts of terror. Ideological methodology now became a distinguishing factor. Gone was the born German spy, espionage a national characteristic transmitted by birth. In his stead was the Nazi, Fascist, or Comintern agent, a professional and ideologically committed operative building networks among sympathizers abroad or among fellow nationals susceptible to blandishments or threats.[193] All of this, to an extent, came out of casework, but it also reflected a manner of interpretation, an implicit set of expectations, and an isolation of the present from the past.

At times the French carried matters to extremes, assigning to the Comintern or to fascists a methodology and design that neither possessed. In this there remained a certain surrender to alarmism or to an innate compulsion to embellish. Yet alarmist tendencies in these years should not be exaggerated. German counterintelligence records are instructive here. The Gestapo worried about French penetration in the same ways French police or the SR fretted about the Germans. From the other side of the Rhine the picture was that of a powerful and aggressive French intelligence offensive infiltrating agents, building networks, stealing secrets, and identifying targets for sabotage. The Germans were just as keen to believe in a refugee spy threat as were the French. They feared (correctly) that the French were deploying refugees against them and in December 1939 the RSHA warned that returning Germans who claimed to have escaped from internment might be turned foreign agents or foreign spies in disguise, using papers lifted from nationals still held in camps.[194] It is difficult to set the two groups of files side by side and to see anything exclusively French in the alerts or alarms issued by the Deuxième Bureau or by the Sûreté. The perception and identification of threats in an unending stream was probably a characteristic of all intelligence services. Each had something to be edgy about or simply gathered material from an intrigue-ridden world in the day-to-day practice of their trade. Placed in comparative perspective these records say little about French vulnerability as a national trait in the interwar years.

What is arresting about the documents on espionage is less the instances of alarm than those of mastery and control. Perhaps these were largely a function of bureaucratic forms of expression. Anonymity and the summary nature of reporting, particularly in long reports like those on Muslim affairs, encouraged an orderly and dispassionate presentation of material. Certainly the greater professionalism and familiarity with milieus, alongside the absence of any further need to explain away defeat, account for differences in the tone of reporting from what had preceded the war. The inventions of the eighties and nineties would have seemed embarrassingly amateurish to the agents of the thirties who had seen plenty in their day to set storytellers afire but who also had years of experience and broken cases behind them and thus operated with a better grasp of the dimensions of the forces and networks arrayed against them. Still, the structure and regularity that characterized counterintelligence files seems also to have reflected a perception that situations were in hand or that the alerts of today would become the cracked or shelved cases of tomorrow. It is not difficult to find moments of alarm or outright spy panic in the interwar period. Yet they cannot be said to have represented a pervasive feeling in these years. For every instance of concern or paranoia there was an affirmation of command or simply the processing of material that was the bureaucratic equivalent of detective journeys up and down the stairs and that suggested an official cast of mind convinced that it would always muddle through.[195] Compared to prewar documentation there was almost a settled quality to reporting between the wars.

Radio wars in North Africa provide a good illustration of this mood. The French knew that they were losing this war. Side by side with the files on Italy's Radio Bari, Germany's Radio Zeesen, and Franco's Radio-Seville were lengthy dossiers on the inadequacy of their own broadcasting in Arabic. Officials noted that their signals were weak and that scheduling was poor. They pointed to difficulties in finding announcers with the proper accents for targeted areas. Compared to Radio Bari in particular their own programming, they argued, was too short and too dull. One person drew up an elaborate chart that showed France trailing its competitors in all forms of propaganda directed at Muslims. Even the Spanish received better marks than the French who were berated in every category and whose ultimate rating was a lowly "deficient."[196] At first glance the radio war files appear to confirm many of the images we hold of the French in these years: their lack of energy; their failure to adapt and compete where new technology and new methods were involved; and their own perception of relative decline.

Yet the authorities, if acknowledging the seriousness of the matter, never worried themselves overly about their Arabic programming. Like the tortoise of the fable they set their own pace, strengthening their signals and lengthening their broadcasts, assured that over time distances would be narrowed and that eventually they would overtake their adversaries. Perhaps they merely played the bureaucratic game of dismissing failure by claiming success (and along the way, of course, they were squashed by a tank). Still, if it was attitudes or outlooks that mattered, then the French expressed no abiding sense of disarray or alarm. Instead they were proud of the progress they were making and of their Italian and German broadcasts that they beamed into Mussolini's and Hitler's backyard. Moreover their ultimate conclusion was that Radios Bari and Zeesen had failed in their mission. In the end, for all their paper "noise" about radio wars, French records exuded a quiet confidence that the situation was under control.[197]

One of the themes of this book is that French moods and perceptions between the wars were more complex and more assured than those painted by a picture of vulnerability, division, and decline. The following chapters will develop this argument further. For the moment it is appropriate to conclude with one of those documents we occasionally stumble upon in the archives and that force us to rethink our presumptions about the subjects we study. I am referring to a note sent by the Radical party of Algiers to the premier of France. It was dated 2 June 1940, approximately at the moment when the last British troops were evacuating from Dunkirk. The note called for a vigorous offensive that would throw the Germans out of the French lands they had "sullied." It requested that the French air force bomb Munich and reduce the city to ashes (as a symbolic gesture), and that it also target other German cities, far from the border, to drive home to the Germans "that their Führer is not the God that he would like to seem." The Radicals of Algiers went on to request measures to forestall a surprise attack by Italy and that in the event of Italian strikes at North African cities the French air force retaliate with bombing runs over the peninsula. They ended their proposals with the reminder that "the best defense remains a good offense" and the assertion that they trusted the army would retake the initiative.[198]

Apparently not all Frenchmen and Frenchwomen had entered the war without the spunk to fight the battle through to the finish.

Figure 3. *Renate Steiner. (Courtesy National Archives)*

CHAPTER THREE

Stories

"No my dear fellow, I can't help you. It's too dangerous. You're risking your skin if you do this, and I won't take on the responsibility with your people. In the French zone I could easily get you out of a bad fix. In the Spanish zone I am powerless, and our neighbors don't trifle with arms smugglers. The firing squad follows hard upon arrest. If you're caught red-handed transporting illicit war material you'll be shot straightaway. You understand why, to my great regret, I won't be able to satisfy your request."

With those cheerless words an old Moroccan friend greets me. However, let's face it, I came to Morocco to connect with arms traffickers . . .

I insist some more. I appeal to our old friendship, to war memories that bind us together, to anything that can crack my companion's unyielding obstinacy. Nothing in his hard face betrays the least susceptibility to my entreaties. So I play my big card.

"I'll try to make do without you."

He pales a bit. His eyelids flutter rapidly. I know I've stung him and now he, in turn, implores me.

"Don't do it. Forget your scheme while there's still time!"

"I tell you again, I have to live with these people. Don't worry, you'll have a letter for my director and another for the consul. In case of a ruckus, if the affair goes badly, you'll know it right away. Then it's up to you to move heaven and earth to get me out of their clutches. Come on. Give a little. I won't rest until you say yes!"

Through the pergola I glimpse the immutable blue sea. A light wind from the east skims softly along its surface. A light mist, raised by the heat, hides the horizon and joins ocean to sky. My listener rises, gaz[es] out. . . . I too leave my seat and draw near.

"Come on, you're not going to let me go back to France empty-handed? What would people say about this wretched *chasseur d'aventures?*"

He shakes his head slowly and before my mulish look murmurs rather than speaks:

"All right, I'm going to try to arrange a meeting for you with a man who knows everything about these sordid transactions. He's made his fortune out of them. Now he's a tidy bourgeois, well off and worth several millions. . . . He knows the men and was one of their chiefs. Although he doesn't do business with them any more, he sees them often. He knows all about their shipments. Needless to say you must give him every assurance of your discretion. However I doubt he'll accept. He's suspicious by habit and by profession."[1]

So begins Hubert Bouchet's front-page exposé in the *Journal* on weapons trafficking to Morocco. Running for a week in the summer of 1931 under the title "En expédition avec les contrebandiers d'armes de guerre au Maroc: Une grande enquête du *Journal*," the series spun a dazzling if predictable tale.[2] There was a meeting with the ex-contraband chieftain — "the bourgeois adventurer" — and then, five days later, a Café X rendezvous with Ahmed, Bouchet's cicerone into the world of the smugglers. "You'll be a gunrunner for a week," Bouchet was told. "You'll live with your companions and share their fears, their dangers, and also their desires." And then there was the promised journey with arms smugglers, by sea from Barcelona to Morocco and then inland by caravan over mountains to the lair of Berber tribesmen. At the end of the series Bouchet recounted the machinations of spies and subversives — Shakib Arslan, Adolphe Langenheim (whom he labeled the German spy master in Morocco), and "certain heads of espionage for a foreign power, fishers in troubled waters and fomenters of riots." These, he argued, were responsible for the upsurge in gunrunning to the Rif. France, Bouchet concluded, must either take forceful measures or face the risk of serious consequences in the protectorate.

Stories, it may be said, are projections of their times, but then what is the historian to make of these articles? They are about gunrunners and spies, but they are also personal adventures, and if their conclusion is often alarmist, that word scarcely describes their tone or their style. One reading could emphasize their investigative probing into subversion in Morocco, yet another could just as easily concentrate on the author's delight in telling a story and the formulaic nature of the series with its trumped-up ambiance and recognizable motifs of reconstituted conversations or mysterious guides into the underworld. Bouchet perhaps was writing an exposé, but he was also selling a story to a mass circulating daily. Once the series ran its course, another followed on contemporary China and then another on the contemporary American Far West.

This combination of danger and storytelling pervaded the literature on espionage between the wars. The genre, even when crafted from pure imagination as most frequently it was, bordered on the hard world of security that we are accustomed to regarding as the central concern of these decades. Still, interwar spy stories were never simply about security, or vulnerability, or any of the other qualities we might attribute to an era suspended between one war and another.

War memoirs are a good case in point. Probably no medium contributed to the escalation in spy stories as did the published reminiscences of secret agents from the war. There were accounts by French spies like Joseph Crozier and Marthe Richard or the spy master Ladoux, but the French publisher Payot also brought out translations of the wartime memoirs of foreign secret agents and spy trackers: Max Wild's *Adventures in the Secret Service, 1914–1918,* Max Ronge's *Espionage,* J. C. Silber's *Secret Weapons: Memoirs of a German Spy in the War Office from 1914 to 1919,* George Aston's *Secret Service: English Espionage and Counterespionage during the War,* and H. C. Hoy's *40 O.B., or How the War was Won* figured among these. The genre added to the sheer bulk of literature on intrigue between the two world wars, and it created a model for telling tales to be picked up by the spy novelists whose numbers and output multiplied dramatically.

Yet at times the influence ran in the reverse. War memoirs were a complex literature with many voices and hence many meanings. They were, at the basic level, about memories of war and thus about living with the war well after its ending. Fastened to the compulsion to write memoirs and the desire to buy them was that indelible, haunting quality of the war that clung to the French in the twenties and thirties and found its complement in the ubiquitous war monuments or in secret-war literature. War memoirs, however, were also about telling stories, admittedly stories about the war but nevertheless stories whose accent was on atmosphere, drama, suspense, and heroics. They were constructed, forced, designed to be fun, and were above all written for a market that craved tales of this kind. In this we can perceive a host of intentions or revelations, all of which lead us far astray from the war as a traumatic, oppressive event. Spy memoirs conveyed a fascination with the war, a desire to tell its story and then tell it again. There was a hankering in this literature to hold onto the war, to sustain its ambiance and its drama for the years to follow. This suggestion may come as a surprise for a period we regard as intense and crisis-ridden; but the willed ambiance of these memoirs, like that of most interwar spy literature, is inescapable. The mood and atmospherics that seem to us a natural product of these years were, to a large extent, a fabrication of writers and their public who often saw in the war less a scar than a source of excitement to prolong and mine for the more mundane times ahead. Such mining, or exploiting, in fact, provided not infrequently the prevalent tone. Focusing on the impact of the war, one is liable to miss the ease with which it was turned into entertainment once the shooting was over. Memoirs were intended to sell, and they demonstrated an endless capacity of the age to transform great events into mass-consumption commodities.[3]

Memoirs were also a way of writing about personal exploits in a world run riot with bureaucracies and technology. Spy accounts especially suited this mode because they suggested that in a war of vast military machines the individual could still make a difference. They were a literature of adventure as well as of war, and they made the spy an intrepid figure like the long-distance fliers whose heroics peppered the front pages through the twenties and thirties. Moreover, war memoirs took on a certain literary cast illustrating how ways of remembering were shaped by postwar values and fashions. The spy as hero was itself a postwar invention that fit the new model of the hard man or woman of action and abandon. In the tales of Crozier, Richard, and Ladoux could be found the characters and styles of Joseph Kessel, Paul Morand, and Maurice Dekobra.

There were, then, a multiplicity of moods embedded in the spy literature of these years, and the historian of interwar France must be sensitive to all of them. Running through the spy tales of the twenties and thirties are the nastiness and fear we might expect of these decades, but also humor, embellishment, and sheer pleasure in spinning a yarn. If the stories people tell are projections of their times, then these stories steer us beyond yearnings for peace and security or the unhinging of the Third Republic toward calmer, less troubled waters. After 1918 the French lived in the shadow of the war and with the press of events in a highly charged time, but they did so in complex, highly nuanced ways. There were perceptions of danger but also tremendous powers to absorb or deflect what might otherwise have been threatening. Spy literature could be both a symptom and cause of the present-mindedness of the period, reflecting and affecting the imprint of current affairs upon the consciousness of people. Yet the shape that intrusiveness took varied widely according to the style and devices of reporting. It could play upon hatreds and anxieties and ideological commitments but also upon more universal desires to read a good story. Under such circumstances, familiar words for the period like *choice* or *vulnerability* capture only a partial reality. Certainly, to the extent that spy tales measured the age, there was no greater exhibition of alarmism after the war than there had been before and what there was shared the stage with effects of a far different kind.

Thus we encounter a character like Mâh le Sinistre in Charles Robert-Dumas's 1935 spy novel *The Lead Idol*.[4] He is Mongolian, a Bolshevik secret agent, a brute and fanatic who slices open the bellies of his enemies in seedy hotel rooms. By day he operates as an exporter in Paris. As a spy he steals French military secrets and sells them to the Germans. A master chemist, he concocts a vapor — his "Ecstasy 136" — that acts as an aphrodisiac on women he desires, but he also fabricates a gas that can annihilate every man, woman, and child in Paris in a matter of hours. Only his weakness for French undercover agent Muguette, who blows his brains out, prevents the release of the lethal gas trigger. Obviously Robert-Dumas piled into Mâh the images and stereotypes of the thirties — the conflation of bolshevism with Asiatic barbarity and of gas wars with spies are two that come readily to mind — and I suppose it is possible to write ad nauseam about the historically conditioned creation of this storyline. But there is also something of Mâh that lurks in the deeper recesses of the mind that people will always pay money to read about and that probably explains why this poorly constructed novel sold more than twenty-seven thousand copies in the midst of the depression. So in the end, like milieu, it is the rich coloration of the literature — the jazzed-up journalism, the tales of spy heroes, the Mâh le Sinistres — that commands our attention. It does so not because there were no more menacing images to spy writing, but because the cheap thrills and storytelling instincts predominated and because they resurrect a side to the *entre-deux-guerres* that we have lost sight of.

Pierre Yrondy's *From Cocaine . . . to Gas!!!* gives some idea of the darker side of spy literature that was nevertheless extensive in these years and should not be forgotten. It tells the tale of a German plot to destroy the French nation through drugs, deadly bacteria, and ultimately gas bombs flown in by drones. Its cast includes an army of touts, pimps, commercial travelers, financiers, worldly salon women, but also Jewish refugees, all of them Nazi operatives or traffickers in narcotics. Spies, the author tells us, will be the determining force in the next war, delivering their lethal blows from behind the French lines. The novel, of course, is nothing more than a contrived piece of nonsense, excruciatingly bad as an art form. Yet it translates a complex of interwar moods into projections of the secret agent as the purveyor of doom and destruction.[5]

The theme of gas wars and spies, for instance, was common to the period, as was the image of the spy as drug dealer. Marcel Nadaud and André Fage's *Postwar Army of Crime, Cocaine, and Espionage* associated the one with the other as did Marcel Montarron's account of narcotics trafficking in *White Poison,* which argued that prodigious narcotics rings could be compared only to espionage agencies. Drug kingpins, Montarron wrote, were neither manufacturers nor gangsters but men "whose vision extends well beyond frontiers . . . they are mysterious masters of the world, people for whom drugs are—who knows?—a means of domination stealthier than a cartridge belt." Drug trafficking appeared in spy novels like Charles Robert-Dumas's *Triangle Brand* and Pierre Darlix's *Last Stop, Smyrna,* in which British intelligence runs guns to counterrevolutionaries in Odessa behind the cover of a floating White Russian opium den. In Charles Lucieto's *Delivered to the Enemy,* published in 1928, a British agent uncovers evidence of massive German rearmament, gets wind of German plans to wage chemical warfare, and learns that the Germans are trafficking in heroin and cocaine to corrupt the elites of their enemies.[6] The equation of spies with drug dealers, in a sense, played on clear connections between drug trafficking and espionage after the war. The volume of each grew substantially in the twenties and thirties. Each employed clandestine organizations that were international in scope and whose methods—for example, codes for communicating intelligence or advising of shipments—seemed indistinguishable. Moreover, the line between them was easy to cross, especially in gunrunning, so that the narcotics trade in general resonated with the close ties that emerged between criminality and interwar espionage; indeed even a drug lord like Louis-Théodore Lyon had reputedly once worked for the Deuxième Bureau.[7] Drugs, like spies, were also silent forces, working behind lines and undermining national strengths from within, and this too explains the compression of the spy and drug trafficker into a single, malevolent presence.

The conspiratorial dimensions to Yrondy's tale were no less representative. The obsession with conspiracy was a convention in France, reaching back to the French revolution and beyond; but it acquired new meanings and greater coherence from the events of war and revolution in the twentieth century. Creating, disclosing, and unraveling conspiracies, particularly through the medium of the spy story, might almost be viewed as a national pastime of the French in the interwar period. Out of the rich dank soil of these decades, fertilized with real tales of kidnappings, spy rings, GPUs, and Gestapos, sprung all kinds of phantoms. There were stories of Lawrence's occult presence in the Middle East and charges of Abd-el-Krim's and Shakib Arslan's role as agents of London, Berlin, or Moscow. There were visions of an international of criminals hired out for subversion to fascists and communists, the cold dread details exposed by *The Brown Network,* and the vogue in Fu Manchu novels whose translations in the thirties were publishing successes; printings of thirty-five thousand copies almost always sold out by the end of the decade. Henry Champly's *Road to Shanghai: White Slave Traffic in Asia,* which touched all bases — conspiracy, sexual depravity, subversion, anti-Semitism, and the Yellow Peril — was no less successful. Its estimated sales topped one hundred thousand.[8] Particularly notable was the *Protocols of the Wise Men of Zion,* which laid out a Jewish plot to dominate the world and whose relation to spy stories was a curious one. Predating the war but diffused widely thereafter, its fantastic charges were accepted with more credence than we would like to believe once Russia had fallen into the hands of radical revolutionaries, not a few of Jewish origins. Even as respectable a publisher as Grasset brought out an edition that sold twenty thousand copies by 1940. Other variations on the theme appeared in D. Petrovsky's *Russia Under the Jews,* Lucien Pemjean's *Toward Invasion,* Céline's *Bagatelles for a Massacre,* Léon de Poncins's *Mysterious Jewish International* (published in 1936 as part of his series, *The Dictatorship of Hidden Forces*), or in Poncins's *Secret History of the Spanish War,* which Ilya Ehrenburg found for sale at a French train station in 1938.[9]

What is to be remarked is how closely other conspiracies paralleled these tales of a Jewish International, and very possibly were modeled upon them. Consider, for example, Robert Boucard's *Intelligence Service Revealed.* According to Boucard, the British intelligence service was the clandestine maker of British foreign policy. Its hand could be found behind the French revolution, the Panama Canal scandal, the murder of Warren G. Harding, the Versailles treaties, and the civil war in Spain. The book, in fact, read as if Boucard were constructing his story from a Jewish conspiracy kit. Everything was there, "occult supergovernment," omnipresent agents, financial stranglehold, source of all troubles, maker of the peace, and a bid for universal domination. On the cover a giant hand gripped the globe. Other editions featured a spider. Comparable parallels turned up elsewhere. Even as earnest a publication as *The Brown*

Network, the émigré description of the Nazi conspiracy including its international associations, its foreign newspaper and radio stations, its travel bureaus, as well as its terror squads, sounded suspiciously like Protocols-talk of the Jewish Telegraphic Agency, the Jewish Bureau of Correspondence, the B'nai B'rith universal order, ad infinitum.[10] Perhaps all visions of international conspiracies will always turn out roughly the same. If they are to be truly frightening, they must all possess secret armies, bottomless resources, worldwide tentacles, and megalomaniacal designs. Yet there was also a Jewish formula, widely disseminated between the wars, whose similarity to others was likely to have been more than coincidental, and whatever the case the correspondence between Jews and spies—yet another of Yrondy's images—was never an accident in these years. Baudinière, publisher of the Secret War series, also put out anti-Semitic tracts. The French edition of Stéphane Richter's *Secret Service* carried advertising for *The Jew or the Parasite International.*[11] Jews were vilified as spies, as they had been at the time of the Dreyfus affair. The Russian revolution and then a wider debate on the danger of foreigners in a decade of depression and deteriorating international conditions guaranteed a renewed fixation with the image.[12] Indeed the refugee spy or fake refugee agent emerged as all but a stock character in the spy literature of the thirties.[13]

Finally there was the sheer demonic force of the spy threat that Yrondy insisted upon and that recurred throughout interwar spy tales. As before the war German spies remained in the foreground, typically methodical, dishonorable, and a threat to the very lifeblood of the nation. They were the habitual villains in the spy novels and, to be sure, of most of the war memoirs. Journalistic accounts dwelt on German military and political espionage. They tracked Gestapo networks in Europe and German secret agents in Morocco. A familiar nemesis like Langenheim or even Nicolai (who, in reality, appears to have had little to do with German intelligence after the war) remained a haunting, lurking figure in the literature. Meticulous portrayals of the technical proficiency of enemy operations and their extensive support systems built to a certain extent upon real phenomena but then blew up the picture beyond all proportion. Fifth-column images, we have seen, would not come with a fury until the forties, yet their direct source was visions from the twenties and especially from the thirties of the danger and methods of German espionage.

There was also a diabolical dimension to the threat that surfaced in Yrondy's drug traffickers and gas bombers, in Lucieto's complement of the same, and in Jean Bardanne's portrait of a mad German scientist in *War and Bacteria*. The Communist menace unleashed comparable visions that can be seen in the nightmarish uses to which the spy as Red agent was put. As to be expected there were elaborate descriptions of Soviet intelligence and subversion networks. But woven into anti-Communist writing between the wars were deeper, darker forebodings that saw in Red Russia the very emanation of anticivilization, a relapse to despotic Asiatic origins welling up from the black holes of centuries past. In this near psychopathological abomination of bolshevism, the authors' fear, hatred, and a reflexive anti-Semitism combined to produce terrifying portraits of Russia as a land of darkness and depravity. There was a gratuitous repetition of stories of GPU terror and bestiality, a quickness to pile up awesome statistics or to detail torture in all its graphic perversity;[14] and this strain too passed to the spy writers.

One need look no further than Charles Lucieto's abysmal spy novels of the late 1920s and early 1930s, whose claims to vast sales, though undoubtedly grossly exaggerated, indicated nonetheless a certain readership. Devoid of suspense, irony, character development, or even logic, these stories relied on ideological imagery alone to drive the plot forward. In *The Red Virgin of the Kremlin*, British superspy James Nobody (!) operates undercover in the Soviet Union as "the virgin's" chauffeur and is told he is expected to perform "night services" for his mistress. Captured, he is subjected to an array of sadistic Bolshevik torturers. Later we learn that the Communists have massacred millions of Russians because party leaders are mostly Jews. In the sequel, *Delivered to the Enemy*, German rearmament proceeds with Russian connivance. In *The Mystery of Monte Carlo* Lucieto presents us with Véra Roudine, a vice-ridden Russian secret police terrorist with erogenous zones most sensitive to the criminal touch: "I have never seen her except in the company of the worst scoundrels the world can produce, and her sadism is such that she had no hesitation to choose as her lover in Moscow that infamous, bloody, ferocious beast Soumkoff, the head executioner of the Cheka."[15]

Nothing in this writing can be called idiosyncratic. Robert-Dumas's *Vitriolic Mask*, which sold over twenty-five thousand copies in the 1930s, featured the Soviet terrorist Doumkine, whose real name was David Saloman Wunschelburg. In *The GPU Spy* (published as part of the Secret War series, whose volumes are estimated to have sold fifteen to twenty thousand copies each), Jean Bardanne created the Jewish sadist Marzoff, master of GPU affairs at Kiev and a man who boasted of shooting a half-million victims. *Goldman-Meyer of Barcelona* (also in the Secret

War series) transported the theme to the Spanish civil war with tales of Jewish-Red terror by the revolutionary FAI (despite this total ignorance of Spanish leftist politics — the FAI was anarchist — the preface assured readers that "the account about to be read is not made up. The facts are authentic: the characters alone have different names for reasons one can guess"). Maurice Laporte's *Red Spies: The Underside to Soviet Espionage in France,* published in 1929, included a horrific depiction of Béla Kun as the "Red butcher": "His moral ugliness, his blemishes, his lack of the most elementary scruples, his proverbial cruelty . . . his frightfully carnal instincts make him, morally speaking, a monster whose characteristics repeat themselves among many foreign and French Communists." No less excessive was Roman Gul's gallery of early Cheka sadists: Remover, the female Hungarian, executing eighty-four victims with probably just as many orgasms; Braude, stripping bare her victims, the better to frisk them before pulling the trigger; Menzhinskii, the chief, the aesthete, the scribbler of erotic stories, conducting GPU terror from his divan.[16]

Such stories recall how the defining attributes of these years — international insecurity, totalitarian politics, refugee floods, civil war, and political polarization — could militate toward thinking about spies. Through images of the spy as conspirator, infiltrator, and malevolent force (driven home by the resort to the sexually destructive female), it is possible to chart the history of interwar anxieties and to see further evidence of an age scarred by vulnerability and a sense that things were spinning out of control. Certainly the rifts in the postwar fabric of the nation led each side to settle on its own brand of enemies and to slander these with the epithet of spy. The Left clamored for harder measures against White Russian and fascist secret agents. The Right fired up its anticommunism or bore down upon the German Jewish spy. To a certain extent the telling of stories about spies was obsessive because it reflected an ideologically divided people preoccupied with determining who was on one's own side and who was with the enemy's. Nor did what was known of the real world of spies impose great strains upon the imagination.

Still one must wonder what to think of the following vignette by a certain French journalist who was one of the most inveterate purveyors of spy alarms in these years. It occurs in 1932 in Berlin in the bureau of a trafficker of stolen or fabricated documents. The trafficker is a man of nebulous origins known only as P. The journalist comes to the office and says he needs important documentation on German armaments, slyly adding that he knows P. can procure these for him. P.'s eyes disappear beneath his heavy eyelids. He reflects for ten seconds — not a short period of silence — and then replies indignantly that the Monsieur is mistaken. The journalist is not fazed. He says he knows that P. served with German intelligence in Egypt in the First World War and that he sold out the Germans to the English. He adds that in 1917 at Geneva "in the affair of the Russian revolution," P. deceived the French and English, betrayed the Italians for the sake of the Austrians, and betrayed the Germans for the sake of the Italians. He knows, moreover, that P.'s clients include Colonel Nicolai and the Soviet government, and that the P. of Berlin is none other than the V. of Moscow and the H. of Belgrade. If P. will not cooperate then the journalist is prepared to go to any lengths, even blackmail, to get what he wants.

P. turns green, his accent becomes sharper. He tells the journalist that one telephone call to the Reich authorities will take care of his visitor. The journalist parries, announcing that he has enclosed everything he knows about P. in a letter that will be handed over to a certain Major Marcks in an hour if the journalist fails to show for a rendezvous. P. tries to riposte but to little avail. He uses his German, English, and French, all heavily accented, on the reporter, trying to determine the intruder's nationality. Failing at this he then turns over a dossier to the newsman, but the latter waves it away. The journalist says that he knows this file was sold to an Englishman in Cologne for one thousand marks, and later to a Frenchman for one thousand francs, and that copies are circulating at a still lower price in Geneva, Madrid, and Rome. The document, moreover, comes directly from the Reichswehr which has released it for purposes of disinformation.

P. tries to pass another worthless document off on the journalist who dismisses it out of hand. Defeated, P. goes to his cupboard and returns with a yellow envelope that he says he is sending off to Moscow. The journalist can copy it in the office or take it with him against a ten thousand mark guarantee. The journalist drops two thousand-franc bills on the table, adding contemptuously that he does not need to furnish Sieur P. with a guarantee. Then he walks out with the papers, telling P. that he will telephone in an hour with the location for fetching the documents. This ends the vignette, but not the account. The journalist, who is the author of a book on secret papers and false passports, tells his readers that only upon descending to the street could he remember that this was Berlin. At P.'s he had the sense that he was in one of those Mediterranean dives in Athens or Galata or Salonika or Alexandria where one hustles cards, sells women, robs Americans, and traffics in arms, secret papers, and false documents. "And these spy dens," he insists, "have been set up in every country since the war."[17]

This preposterous tale was the concoction of Jean Bardanne, who also wrote *The GPU Spy* and *War and Bacteria,* suggested that one-fifth of all Jewish refugees were Nazi spies, and with *Stavisky, German Spy* proclaimed the Stavisky affair the work of international criminals in the pay of Berlin and Moscow. He wrote under a pseudonym, a common characteristic of spy novelists but in this case an indication of a history of flights from reality. His personal life was no less unsavory than his writings, consisting of swindles, fraudulent bankruptcies, and persistent efforts to pass himself off as a Deuxième Bureau agent — which almost certainly he was not. Perhaps the vicious, sinister overtones to his insider books and spy novels that he published with the Secret War series in the thirties were no more than projections of his own sense of failure or of the cynical way in which he conducted his private affairs.[18]

The vignette of P., however, crosses over into other realms of spy writing. It bears the telltale imprint of the age less for its alarms than for its storytelling atmospherics and for the protean backdrop of spies against which the story takes place. Its milieu of traffickers, foreigners of undetermined origins, and secret agents from the First World War carrying on as if nothing had changed recalls the emblematic side to spy literature that arose with the war and did not exist before it. In certain ways that side manifested itself through the correlation of the secret agent with the distinctive new politics of fascism and communism. In the literature Hitler became Gestapo agent number one and the GPU ruled over Russia.[19] The Gestapo, the GPU, and the OVRA kept the card files, launched radio wars, employed terrorists, and maintained armies of secret agents among professionals and criminals.

But the spy as a sign of the times was also a far more diffuse figure. If after 1870 the spy in French literature had been most often a German, the interwar limelight revealed a wide cast of characters. There were Germans but also Soviet spies and assorted refugee internationals, White Russian, Croatian, Macedonian, Ukrainian, Italian, and anti-Nazi émigrés whose intrigues were inseparable from interwar espionage and the checkerboard moves of global politics. There were also Spanish, Italian, Hungarian, Polish, Romanian, English, Japanese, Chinese, and, to be sure, French secret agents who occasionally pushed their way onto center stage. And creeping through the interstices or hanging about in the shadows were those inevitable camp followers of the interwar milieu: private spy rings, rogue agents, gunrunners, and the forgers of papers.

This diffuseness worked into the meaning of the spy. It spoke of menace and danger but also to a sense of living in an age of internationalism and impermanence and to the prolonged presence of the war. Its kaleidoscopic character brought together a multiplicity of spies in a multiplicity of combinations that carried with it moods of uncertainty, though not necessarily those of anxiety. Spies signaled movement and open-endedness, and their very range a world of infinite possibilities. To a degree the diffuseness of the literature, or its many spotlights, softened the blow of living in an era of indeterminacy.

More basic than fear was the gratuitous presence of the spy or of international intrigue to authenticate what the French called the *après-guerre*. Spies lent a feel for living between one age and another or, as P. did, for the carryover of the war. The routine portrait of Comintern agents, Gestapo goons, and refugee conspirators provided a contextualized present for storylines. Thus, as we have noted, spies appeared everywhere after the war as if certain scenarios, settings, or characters could not do without them. They made cameo entrées or functioned as props. Joseph Kessel used them as backdrop or ambiance in his potboilers and the adventurer Perken, in Malraux's *Royal Way*, "[made] me think of the great officials of the Intelligence Service that England employs and disavows at the same time."[20]

Or Maurice Dekobra, whose wildly successful *Madonna of the Sleeping Cars* dabbled in international intrigue, returned more explicitly to the theme of secret agents in the sequel, *The Gondola of Illusions*, but again in the diffusely offhanded manner of these years. Here the beautiful but restless Lady Diana falls in love with Ruzzini, formerly the éminence grise of Italian intelligence during the First World War. There is also Leslie Warren, British intelligence ace who has worked alongside Lawrence, speaks Arabic like a Bedouin, and, as Ruzzini confides to his lover, "is as much at home in the Great Mosque of Mecca as you are in a Park Lane salon." Ruzzini is now running guns to Egyptian nationalists and waging a war of personal revenge against Warren, who had raped his sister. Diana follows Ruzzini to Egypt, unwittingly leads Warren to his hideout, and promises to sleep with Warren (no new adventure for Diana; Warren is one of her past conquests) if he will stay Ruzzini's execution. As Warren begins his advances, he is fatally bitten by a cobra Lady Diana has hidden in her clothes. The novel ends with Warren dead, Ruzzini executed, and Lady Diana contemplating entering a convent, a far cry from Yrondy's horror tale. The real point to the book was titillation and a fast buck turned on a previous winner, but it is noteworthy that between the wars the French were inclined to find that the formula worked best when combined with spies and contemporary politics.[21]

Spies, then, were creatures emblematic of their day, but mostly of life at a specific moment in time. They were, like their array of characters, evocatively diffuse and never reducible to mere paranoia. Admittedly there was much in their literature that spoke to vulnerability, insecurity, and xenophobia. And no one who doted on spies ever wrote of French tentacles. In the spy tales the French came out nearly always as flies, only rarely as the spiders spinning the web. Indeed if this had been all there was to the interwar spy, then it would be easy to see in the imagery a reaffirmation of a sad, dreary finale to the republic. There was, however, a good deal more.

Much of what the French read about espionage they read in the memoirs of wartime spies. Typical of those published in France after the war was George Hill's *Go Spy The Land,* translated into *Ma vie d'espion.* The title was well chosen. Hill had grown up in Russia, the son of an English merchant whose business interests ranged from Siberia to Turkestan. As a boy Hill learned to speak half a dozen languages fluently, and he experienced firsthand the 1905 revolution in which intrigue was a norm. Once, traveling down the Volga with his father, he met a British secret agent who disguised himself first as a German trader and then as an Afghan. Later, as a businessman in Russia, Hill helped smuggle a young revolutionary out of the country. Adventure, intrigue, and false identities were thus familiar elements in his life before the war made them his vocation.

With the coming of the war Hill was a natural for British intelligence. Recruited into the service, he was sent through a special secret agent course run by Scotland Yard specialists. They taught him how to shadow a suspect and how to tell in turn when he was being followed. He learned how to use codes and write in secret ink and was instructed in "all the ruses useful to spies." He also learned Bulgarian, and once he could speak the language British intelligence infiltrated him among Bulgarian internees suspected of harboring a secret agent. Masquerading as a Bulgarian born in America, Hill ferreted out the man he was seeking, who revealed that he was on a mission to organize an espionage center in Scandinavia. Hill's next assignment was Salonika, where he ran agents and occasionally personally reconnoitered the Bulgarian front. He learned to fly and took advantage of this skill to land his agents behind enemy lines. Hill moved on to Alexandria, a city that along with Cairo he described as "hotbeds of intrigue and international espionage. I was associated with a man called Theorides who was a spy in the service of the Greek government. He controlled a band of cutthroats who hovered round the bazaars and were used for all sorts of illegal work. It was Theorides who first told me of the marvellous work that was being done by an Englishman who was disguised and lived as an Arab, Colonel Lawrence of Arabia." Later, at Cairo, Hill met Lawrence, whom he described as calm and reserved.

In July 1917 the British sent Hill to Russia. On the way he passed through Stockholm, "a town . . . full of spies watching the train stations, the hotels, the restaurants, and the night clubs." In Russia he had several adventures and then, after Brest-Litovsk, took charge of gathering intelligence on German troops and German agents remaining in Russia. Occasionally he worked with Sidney Reilly, but Reilly's mission was directed against the Bolsheviks, so the two men largely went their separate ways. Hill claimed that at first he helped the Bolsheviks organize an intelligence division to observe German troop movements and a counterespionage operation to combat German spies. Then he established his own secret network of spies, couriers, and saboteurs who derailed German trains and harassed German units in the Ukraine. Hill arranged arms, money, and passports for his men. When the Bolsheviks ordered his arrest he went underground, growing a beard and assuming a false identity. Disguised as a Russian of German descent, he continued his intelligence and sabotage efforts. Finally he left Russia with Bruce Lockhart. Even after the armistice, Hill was again off on an intelligence mission, this time spying in the Black Sea region with Sidney Reilly. Or so he said. As Christopher Andrew has shown, much that Hill wrote was puffery, but the record was impressive nonetheless. As memoirs went, these were full of intrigue and danger, exactly the sort of thing the French were publishing in droves after the war.[22]

There were many reasons for the wealth of spy literature in the interwar years. One was the gaudy reality of the milieu and another was the usefulness of the spy or of secret-war imagery for expressing international conditions and dangers following the war. Adventure and romanticism, which the following chapter will take up, were significant factors as well in the surge of spy writing. It might also be argued that the rise of the spy novel represented an internationalization of the detective story in a century when international affairs intruded more intensely on the lives and consciousness of individual Europeans. A well-developed tradition of police stories existed in France before 1914 and the genre grew in popularity between the wars. Undoubtedly the spy novel built in certain ways upon the *roman policier,* just as an earlier fascination with master criminals translated into evil, nightmarish visions of enemy spies following the Russian revolution and the rise of the Nazis.[23]

The flood of spy tales also expressed a hunger for war stories once the slaughter had ceased. The war was a horror, but it was no less a story of epic proportions and undoubtedly the greatest adventure of modern times. People who had wondered if they would ever see a life beyond the war now found that they could not live without it. Monuments were a reminder of the carnage the war had left in its wake but they were also a way of holding onto the war, of capturing for the present the great drama of the past. War literature, in more explicit fashion, served much the same purpose. The publishing of war books was an industry, and it really did not matter if the author was French, British, German, or Austrian so long as the book was about the battles or the strategy or the campaigns or the experiences of the First World War. I have found, for instance, a sheet of paper folded into eighths and inserted in a war memoir that lists two hundred and thirty other titles on the war by the same publisher, including advertising for forthcoming editions. Among its listings: Sir George Arthur's *Kitchener and the War (1914–1916);* Baron von Buttlar's *Zeppelins in Combat;* Jules Poirier's *The Bombardments of Paris (1914–1918);* General Youri Danilov's *Russia in the World War;* Antoine Grillet's *Foot Soldier: Memoirs of War, 1914–1919;* Captain Ganzin's *French Cavalry in the World War;* Commandant Delmas's *My Men Under Fire;* Lawrence's *Revolt in the Desert;* General von Kluck's *March on Paris;* Andreas Michelsen's *Submarine War, 1914–1918;* and Filson Young's *On Board the Battle Cruisers.*[24] This thirst for war books and the recounting of exploits led naturally to the writing of memoirs by secret agents and intelligence officers from the First World War. Again there was no discrimination by nationality so long as the author had a story to tell. Many of the spy memoirs published in France were translations of foreign editions. There were also memoirs written by the French. Among the best were the tales of Joseph Crozier and Marthe Richard.

Joseph Crozier was a First World War spy in every meaning of the term. His story would be a familiar one in the next world war, but there was no precedent for it before 1914. The war caught him in Brussels, where he says he was looking into business prospects in aviation, although his interest was also that of the sportsman. He was recruited by the Deuxième Bureau and sent to Barcelona to conclude an arms deal. Then Crozier went to Holland where his real work as a secret agent began. Holland in 1915 was a weak link in the blockade that the Allies had established to starve the Central Powers into submission. Officially all foodstuffs and raw materials imported into the Netherlands passed through the blockade with the stipulation that the Dutch would not reexport them to Germany or to a third country from which they could be forwarded to the enemy. The organization charged with carrying out this regulation was the Nederlandsche Overzee Trust (or NOT), a government clearing house to which all imports were consigned. The task was an impossible one and the country crawled with bootleggers, secret agents, and bottom-line businessmen who found ways to smuggle goods across into Germany. Crozier's mission was to uncover the business houses that were violating the blockade and to forward any other useful intelligence that might come his way.

Arriving in Rotterdam in 1915, Crozier established himself in two locations under two separate identities. On the Mathenesserlaan he set himself up as Pierre Desgranges, an official representative on an obscure French military mission. On the Nieuwe Binnenweg he went under his own name and posed as an importer and exporter of oils and fats, joining the ranks of other unscrupulous businessmen who were prepared to do business with the Germans. To maintain his cover the Allies placed him on their blacklist while liberally keeping open his channels of supply. Crozier became known as a man who could deliver the goods and who was prepared to do so for anyone capable of paying the price. He opened a branch office in Düsseldorf and made a number of business trips into Germany. Through these excursions and through his business contacts in Rotterdam he was able to gather considerable intelligence on how the Germans and their agents were running the blockade. Crozier also operated a furniture business in Heerlen, a soap factory at Schiedam on the outskirts of Rotterdam, and an opium den in Amsterdam. The latter attracted an elegant clientele and served as an additional listening post. Crozier kept his role in the den purposely obscure, and he left the management to a Belgian who was prepared to work against the Germans and who was married to a Creole from the Dutch East Indies.

The personnel in the two houses on the Mathenesserlaan and the Nieuwe Binnenweg were kept distinctly apart. Joseph Crozier the merchant surrounded himself with Belgian business employees. At his military mission Pierre Desgranges collected a diverse group of associates to assist in his intelligence work. These included an old friend, Dr. De Blauw; a Belgian military captain; a fervently Catholic and Francophile farmer from Limburg; a Belgian officer whose family, we are told, had been the victims of terrible German atrocities; and a fanatical monk who, Crozier says, would have done the Spanish Inquisition proud. The French agent also maintained a stable of informants and passers, again rigorously divided between the two cover operations. The informants worked for Desgranges and were drawn from the ranks of crooks, common spies, and deserters who hung about Rotterdam. The passers were mostly smugglers and poachers who operated perpetually outside the law and for whom wartime meant simply outmaneuvering Germans instead of gamekeepers and *douanes*. Recruited by Crozier the merchant, they saw in their *patron* a kindred spirit, a renegade businessman and ringleader who was prepared to take his profits wherever he found them. To help couriers across the border with Belgium the one day and to smuggle contraband into Germany the next posed neither moral nor intellectual dilemmas to these men as long as the money kept flowing, which it did. Under these conditions, Crozier established a successful intelligence network, including one that was able to bring information and men across from Belgium into Holland.

Crozier was playing a dangerous game and he knew it. One false step in Rotterdam and his cover was blown; one mistake in Düsseldorf and a worse fate awaited him. Perhaps his saving grace was that he was prepared to be as ruthless and as dirty as spying in wartime required. Murder pervaded Crozier's account. In his preface he noted that at one point in the war British intelligence warned him to steer clear of the Swiss border so as not to interfere with certain British arrangements. Crozier stated laconically: "I obeyed." Other agents who did not, he added, had long since disappeared. Deeper into his account he described the attempt of a German agent to infiltrate his organization. Crozier and his men chloroformed the German and dumped him into the Meuse. He described his friend, Dr. De Blauw, as a man fascinated with clandestine methods of killing. Once De Blauw waxed lyrical about the qualities of the Indian poison curare. Inject a person with the drug, he noted, and the victim would begin to die within two minutes. First the voice would go, then the limbs would be paralyzed, and then the face. It would be a horrible death, because the victim's mind would remain intact throughout, registering the gradual destruction of the body. But the drug would be as silent as the victim, leaving no trace of the cause of death. Moreover, one could produce the poison artificially out of products available in Rotterdam. Working himself up, the doctor progressed to deadly microbes and the possibility of wiping out millions before anyone suspected a thing. In fact, De Blauw insisted, if the Desgranges gang wanted, it could annihilate all of the Dutch in a matter of weeks. "That is so," Crozier replied to quiet him down, "but in my opinion that would be a shame. It takes all kinds to make a world. There are already too few neutrals and pirates are on the verge of disappearing. The planet, I think, would be a rather boring place if we had only heroes. And then, if Holland perished we'd have to resuscitate her: life is so pleasant here this evening in this peaceful country where everyone feels a little like a king."

The remark brought the discussion to a close, but not the killing. When Crozier's secretary became addicted to opium and betrayed several members of the organization, Crozier had her eliminated. None, not even innocent bystanders, were safe from this crew should they venture into the wrong place at the wrong time. A raid on a German courier way station to America made this chillingly clear. Deployed as lookouts on the Boompjes quai while two men slipped inside the spy house to rifle through papers, Crozier and his gang began to converge upon a lone man walking their way. Then the man veered off, breaking the tension of the false alert. But Crozier left no doubt that if the stranger had made one false move, even by accident, he would have been chloroformed, dumped in the car, and deposited somewhere in the Meuse.

In the second half of the memoirs Crozier shifted his tales of the remorseless world of wartime intrigue to the high seas, recounting his adventures as a wartime privateer. He purchased a Norwegian freighter, the *Hélios,* once shipping became tight in the wake of German submarine warfare, to assure that his contraband supplies could get through. The idea to convert the ship into an armed pirate vessel raiding German supply ships came from his captain, a Dutchman named Scheffer, an old merchant marine officer who was audacious, tough as nails, and interested only in gold. Redesigned as a deadly surface raider, the *Hélios* provided Crozier and his men more occasions to stalk danger and dispatch anyone who got in their way. A ship broker named Hagelen operating out of Rotterdam and smuggling contraband to the Germans caught on to Crozier but was soon to regret it. Joining Hagelen was a German deserter named Lang, who had worked in the past as an informant for Desgranges. The two went to the Norwegian port of Stavanger, where the *Hélios* was charging a cargo. Their plan was to win Scheffer over to their side and then to seize the boat and turn it over to the Germans. Scheffer pretended to go along and invited the two conspirators to dinner aboard the *Hélios*. As they dined, the freighter slipped out to sea. Later that night two sacks containing Hagelen and Lang slid down a plank into the ocean.

Crozier apparently never had any hesitation about doing away with his enemies the moment they posed an immediate threat to him. Murder seemed almost his automatic defense. Julius Becker was another victim. He was a secret messenger carrying special papers to German representatives in New York. The German consul general in Rotterdam asked Crozier (the importer-exporter) to transport Becker on the *Hélios,* confiding Becker's mission and offering to pay Crozier twenty thousand florins for his trouble. The proposition placed Crozier in a ticklish position. En route to America the *Hélios* was to intercept several small ships carrying contraband for Germany, and Becker's presence would create a complication. And yet to refuse would compromise the trust and reputation Crozier had built up among the Germans; so he agreed. Once out to sea, however, Crozier's agents on board the *Hélios* killed Becker. Afterward, an agent went through Becker's papers, read the secret messages, and then impersonated Becker when the ship arrived in New York, delivering the papers as if nothing had happened.

Crozier's maverick style was bound to run afoul of the French authorities. By November 1916, he tells us, he was in such hot water for operating out of channels that he was recalled from Holland, and in February he was assigned to an infantry unit stationed at Besançon. Nine months later, however, resurrected by Clemenceau, Crozier, in the persona of Desgranges, was back in the Netherlands gathering economic intelligence on the Germans. As the war wound down, Crozier's assignment was to keep watch over German and Russian revolutionary circles. March 1919 brought an end to his mission and also to his memoirs, which revealed a sophistication of method and also of milieu that one had not seen before the First World War.[25]

The motifs of Crozier's narrative—the undercover agent, the ruthlessness of the contemporary spy war, the rich milieu of wartime espionage—all turned up in the memoirs of Marthe Richard, perhaps France's most celebrated spy in the First World War. Born Marthe Betenfeld in Lorraine in 1889, the daughter of a worker, Richard spent her early life in a series of revolts against family and the drudgery of sewing-shop work. She tried to run away to Paris, was caught and placed in a religious home, escaped and ran away again, and made it to the capital, where she met Henri Richer, a well-to-do businessman. After a fling with an Italian lover, she settled in with Richer at his Mans estate. There she took up flying, performed at air shows, and survived a crash landing. She and Richer married as he went off to war. He was to die at the front in 1915. She served in French intelligence as a spy, after being rebuffed in her attempts to enlist as an aviator. After the war she married Thomas Crompton, an English businessman, but he died in 1928 of uremia. Between the wars she returned to her earlier love of flying and performed in promotions sponsored by the Ministry of Air in a Potez-43 provided by the government. During the Second World War she joined the resistance (or so she claimed), and afterward she emerged as a cause célèbre because of her campaign to shut down the brothels of France.[26] But long before this grand controversy she had grown accustomed to the spotlight.

Georges Ladoux, the head of French counterespionage in the First World War, made her famous with a book published in 1932 about her adventures as a secret agent in Spain.[27] Three years later, Richard produced her own (and often different) version under the title *My Life as a Spy: In the Service of France,* a tale no less gripping than Crozier's. Invited by Ladoux to join the secret service (the story is now Richard's as she tells it in her memoirs), she demurred until her husband's death at the front.[28] Ladoux sent her first to Sweden on a botched mission and then to Spain where she infiltrated German intelligence and lived her greatest adventures. She posed as a Frenchwoman in search of a fortune and prepared to trade on what she knew or could ferret out about French aviation. Using her own name and her past as a flyer, she appeared a credible source. Von Krohn himself recruited her, giving her a special pen and invisible ink and providing her with the code name S-32. He also told her, in the same tough-guy style that turns up in Crozier, that if she betrayed him her life wouldn't be worth a plug nickel (or three thousand pesetas, as he put it), no matter if she fled to Paris or New York. Eventually she became von Krohn's lover, living the life of a double agent with all the dangers and suspicions that came with that territory. The von Krohns invited her to dinner where they spoke in German to test her avowal that she knew nothing of the language, centering their conversation on the theme that all Frenchwomen were whores and dropping allusions to poisoned dishes for their guest. Richard never batted an eye, a performance that will surprise no one who has ever read anything about her. However she subsequently asked Ladoux to have one of his Madrid agents follow her to give the impression that the French regarded her as a questionable character.

She did not escape suspicion altogether. Either von Kalle or Ratibor, the German ambassador to Spain, tried to have her killed in a boating incident, but she jumped overboard in time and escaped with only a bullet through the shoulder. Von Krohn, however, she played for a fool. Through her intimacy with the man she learned the details of enemy intrigues in Morocco and the location of a secret passageway through the Pyrenees that the Germans were using to infiltrate spies and sabotage materials into France. When von Krohn sent her to Argentina with a packet of weevils destined for Allied food supplies, she contacted a French agent on board ship and destroyed the weevils in ways that would not blow her cover. Her ultimate goal was to drug von Krohn and then steal the contents of his safe. She requested help from French intelligence — narcotics in particular — but they stalled on that matter and demurred again when she requested a visa so she could return once and for all to France. Exasperated and sensing herself abandoned, she finally took matters into her own hands. Inviting von Krohn to a tea salon — a very public place where he could take no immediate action — she told him to his face that she was a French secret agent. Then she went to Ratibor and told him she was von Krohn's lover and that he had given her money out of his secret service funds. To plunge the knife in as deeply as she could, she revealed that von Krohn had confided to her the combination to his safe. Then handing Ratibor a packet of love letters from von Krohn, she walked out of the embassy and returned to Paris. So ended her wartime adventures as a spy. The book had a modern, gritty feel to it with its aura of toughness and of bureaucratic betrayal and it closed on a note of disillusionment that added to the image of the singular, honorable spy forced to maneuver on her own in an inhospitable world.[29]

These were not, however, memoirs to take completely seriously, any more than Crozier's tales or the accounts of Ladoux who was initially responsible for Richard's celebrity and who wrote two additional memoirs of his own, *Spy Chasers: How I Arrested Mata Hari* and *Recollections (Counterespionage)*, which was published posthumously.[30] None of these books could be read as God's truth without a serious dose of credulity. All were written by practiced dissemblers and characters of dubious repute. Crozier was a rogue operator who was already engaging in running battles with officialdom by the end of 1915. He was accused of forwarding imprecise or questionable information and of seeking to avoid any level of control. He shot back that the French representatives in Holland were jeopardizing his cover, and that his intelligence was better than theirs.[31] Most likely Crozier was closer to the truth than were those who attacked him and resented his unorthodox methods and very possibly his superior sources. Whether his removal in November 1916 was a matter of jealousy and bureaucratic revenge remains, however, an uncertain proposition. By the thirties when he wrote up his memoirs he appears to have been dealing in arms, and one is tempted to wonder whether his connections with traffickers preceded his wartime service as a spy. Such activity would explain his initial mission to Spain and perhaps even his success as a smuggler in the war. Ladoux was a man who not only operated in the shadows but cast shadows upon his own incorruptibility. Before 1914 he had been a career officer but also a financier with attachments to questionable speculators. During the war he badly compromised himself in the suspicious affairs that surrounded the sale of one of the great Paris dailies, the *Journal,* to men with German financial backing, among these Paul Bolo Pasha, who was later arrested and executed for trafficking with the enemy. In March 1918 Ladoux was indicted for commerce with the enemy and the following January he entered the Santé prison. Sûreté reports from the time of his indictment do not reveal much confidence in the man. Eventually he was acquitted of all charges, but one of his former associates was found guilty and executed, and the judgment on Ladoux was not without its dissenters.[32] As for Marthe Richard, the facts of her life are buried beneath layers of legend and calumny.[33] Credibility was not a strong suit of these memoirists, whose own lives were a mélange of fact and fable. Joseph Davrichevii, a Russian émigré who was Richard's friend, fellow agent in Spain, and probably her lover, most likely came closest to the mark when he wrote in his own memoirs that to know the whole story of Marthe Richard in the First World War one would have to seat Ladoux, Ignatiev, von Krohn, and the head of British intelligence at the same table and force them to "speak frankly; and even then one wouldn't learn everything. They would lie, all four of them."[34]

Truth, however, was not what these memoirs were about. Nor did they have much or perhaps even anything to do with the war as a traumatic experience. Bearing witness to the war, unburdening oneself of the war, laying claims to the war ("our war"; the *poilu*'s war), and condemning the war were all part of memoir literature,[35] but only a part.

The more familiar memoirs of this sort shared the war market with that other vast literature that sought to return to the great adventures of the war — *On Board the Cruiser 'Gaulois'; Memoirs of Marshal Galliéni; The Marne Campaign in 1914;* or *My Adventures in the Secret Service, 1914–1918* — some memoirs and some not, but all responding to the needs not only of the authors who wrote them but of the editors who published them and the public who bought them. Invited by victory and skirting the great horrors in the West — it is interesting how many of these books were about war on the edges: in the air, at sea, in campaigns to the East — these tales from the war pitched their appeal toward more universal desires. Memoirists like Crozier and Richard, whose war had also been on the periphery and yet about winning, wrote for this market and were part of this literature and consequently of the postwar culture that produced it. They used that literature to justify themselves and to line their own pockets. They did so, moreover, in ways that accorded with the demand for certain types of stories. The result was a new kind of spy and spy literature that has remained with us ever since.

One facet of that change was the shift from the image of the spy as a figure of menace and betrayal to a figure of heroic proportions.[36] The shift was largely a constructed one sprung from the confluence of ego and capitalism. From the pens of Crozier, Ladoux, and Richard came legend and myth, a manufactured mystique that others would also exploit. Richard was clearly the first among equals. Ladoux launched her on the course of fame, and her memoirs that followed were largely designed to cash in on the celebrity and to amend the record as she saw fit. Davrichevii's memoirs added a third version, implicitly acknowledging with his discussion of Marthe that she was a person of public import. By the mid-1930s, Richard figured in three stories of her life or of espionage in Spain that attributed to her a major role in defeating the Germans. She had stolen the secrets of von Krohn, sent German submarines to the bottom of the sea, thwarted sabotage attempts in France and Latin America, and made the world safe for democracy. She was a heroine who had incurred incredible risks and looked danger and death squarely in the face — all in the service of her country. It was a wonderful story that Richard (or Ladoux) sold to the mass Paris weekly, *Paris-Soir,* and to the moviemakers who produced yet another version of her life, starring Edwige Feuillère and Erich von Stroheim. Spy writers like the journalist Paul Allard and Robert Boucard wrote about Richard.[37] To keep the bandwagon rolling, Richard concocted two new accounts of her life as a woman of adventure in the 1930s, *Spies in War and Peace (1920–1938)* and *My Latest Secret Missions: Spain 1936–1938*.[38]

Neither Ladoux nor Crozier could keep up with this pace, but as best he could each touted his own role in winning the war. Counting his book on Richard, who was simply the most celebrated agent he had run, Ladoux produced three sets of memoirs or recollections of his accomplishments as the head of French counterespionage. Crozier wrote three different versions of his own exploits as an undercover agent in the Netherlands, on the high seas, or among German revolutionaries, rivaling the best that Richard had to offer.[39] He too found his way into the mass press — in his case the *Matin* — and he too turned up in Allard as the cold-blooded man of action he had set as his self-image in his memoirs. They had met, Allard said, on the Ile St-Louis, where Crozier had asked, "Do you know how to assassinate? . . . I can give you lessons. I have thirty-eight murders on my conscience." Crozier had then, as Allard recounted, pulled out of his pocket a small metallic tube not unlike a woman's lipstick and released a spring, forcing the sudden emergence of ten deadly needles. "That," he told Allard, "is clean, it's sure, it's humane! Watch how it works. One press of the thumb! The needle shoots out and the poison — a good deal more potent and cunning than curare because it leaves no trace in the blood — penetrates the flesh. Death comes with terrifying quickness. Nothing remains to be done except to throw the body into the water."[40] These were the kinds of stories one could tell about spies or spies could tell about themselves after the war. Their extraordinary adventures, merged with a larger public desire to read about the thrills of the war, vaulted the secret agent to intrepid, heroic status. The status transferred, moreover, to the perhaps only slightly more fictional characters who emerged as the heroes of a new kind of spy writing, Lucieto's James Nobody, for example, or Robert-Dumas's Commandant Benoît of the Deuxième Bureau. The telling of their adventures in a series of books was not much different, either, from the sequels that real spooks like Richard, Ladoux, and Crozier retailed about themselves.

Facilitating the construction of legends was the need to relocate heroism following the war. There was nothing exceptionally heroic about espionage in that conflagration. Infantry charges in the face of machine guns or the retrieval of the wounded demanded as much or more courage and personal sacrifice. They were in fact routine in the war, although that was the problem. In an age of mass organizations and death tolls in the millions, heroics needed more than the reflexive daring of soldiers up and down the line to seize and hold the imagination. Valor required a personal, extraordinary element lost in a war of great grinding military machines. Secret agents offered a return to the personal adventure and thus to the individual as the focus of heroism. Cast alone in a pitiless, dangerous world, spies were thrown back on their own resources of daring and cunning. Only to the extent that they summoned up these qualities could they hope to survive and carry out their mission.

Even more, in a war of stalemate and wasted endeavors, spies created the illusion that an individual could still make a difference. Bureaucratic agencies designed to intercept, decrypt, and analyze telecommunications increasingly encroached on intelligence work, but the literary focus remained on the indispensability of the individual spy. A Crozier in the Netherlands or a Richard in Spain might just tip the balance in the favor of France. Failure of these missions meant the Germans might win. If not, then why bother to send them at all, a question the memoirists were careful not to ask. Heroism without consequence was the reality of the war, but this was not the heroism of public acclamation. Thus the combination of isolation, personal bravery, and exploits with the possibility of singlehandedly turning the tide gave secret agents an edge in asserting a claim to legendary stature. It was the same formula that worked for Lawrence of Arabia or the German Wassmuss whose adventures had truly been extraordinary, even if by and large meaningless. Pilots shared in the same glory often for the same reasons. The principal contribution of aviators in the First World War was reconnaissance for the troops on the ground. At best they were adjuncts to the greater battles on land and sea, and it was only toward the end of the war when they flew in large formations that fighters played more than a negligible role. The air ace was completely peripheral to the outcome of the war yet not in the public's perception. The ace who seemed to return warfare to chivalric encounters garnered the adulation of the masses below.

One cannot but remark upon the correspondence between pilots and spies. Between the two world wars flyers were without doubt the greatest of heroes. Their long-distance flights, often designed to set records, wiped other stories off the front pages. Many of their exploits were unassailably legendary. They flew in all conditions and, in the 1920s, in single-engine planes with open cockpits, no radios, and no weather reports. For those pilots who flew on the Latécoère line over the western Sahara, accidents were frequent and forced landings risked death by dehydration or capture and enslavement by Moors under the most savage conditions.[41] Yet like the reputation of spies, the heroism of pilots was constructed, first by the pilots themselves and then by their publicists who hitched a ride on their fame. The pilots created an ethos of their own, founded on camaraderie, discipline, and duty but also by asserting that flying was purer, nobler, more gallant than practically anything else that humans could accomplish, all the time enslaving themselves to absurd rituals in the service of the business enterprises they worked for, such as the insistence that the mail must go through without a moment's delay no matter what the cost in human lives or machinery. Their honor codes were designed to affirm through a minimum of words the exalted, superior nature of flying.[42] Because most people on the ground shared in the mundane definition of their own lives that fliers assigned to them, they accorded to pilots the status these appropriated. The blaring headlines themselves were a tribute to the rule.

Genuine heroes like Jean Mermoz were destined for idolatry. Mermoz flew on the "line" (the Latécoère route), enduring crash landings and capture and ransom. Later he pioneered mail routes across the Andes. He demonstrated that pilots could fly under the most adverse circumstances, including night flights without instruments or lights from below. Bold, muscular, supremely confident in his command of an aircraft, and absolutely fearless, he never turned away from a challenge. He believed in the sacredness of flying, but he also loved climbing behind the controls of a plane because it allowed him to test the extreme limits of his human powers of skill and endurance. Once, seeking a passage through the Andes where the mountains soared in a solid block nearly three miles high and unable to find an opening for his Laté-25 (whose maximum altitude was a thousand feet less), he looked for an air current that could lift him over the barrier, a perilous maneuver even above far less rugged terrain. He found one, but it carried so forcefully into a down current that he was forced to crash-land on the side of the mountain. Marooned several miles high on a remote tip of the world, he and his mechanic, Collenot, were doomed to a freezing death and snowy entombment. But Mermoz refused to give up. They set off on foot, with three condors circling overhead. After an hour, however, and only five hundred meters' progress, Mermoz realized that they would never make it out alive at this pace. "Collenot," he told his mechanic, "We're going to have to repair the taxi."

Returning to the plane, both men worked through the night, and then another day and night, until Collenot had repaired the plane sufficiently to fly. Then they pushed the aircraft up the side of the incline to gain what starting power they could. Once down the cliff Mermoz was forced to bounce the plane off the edges of ravines to get clear of the mountain. The slightest misjudgment would have meant total failure, but Mermoz carried it off with such improbable success that at first no one would believe his story. (To the trained pilot today it still sounds apocryphal, although Mermoz's biographer insisted the story was true and verified by an expedition sent into the Andes.) When Mermoz disappeared over the southern Atlantic in 1936, he was probably France's greatest flyer. So great was his fame that when a false report of his rescue was released, theater shows stopped to announce the news, strangers embraced in the streets, and people sang in the métro.[43] After his death his friend Joseph Kessel, who had flown in the war and written several hymns to flying, recorded Mermoz's life story in a book that fell nothing short of hagiography. A serialized version ran for several weeks in France's largest daily, *Paris-Soir.* The bound volume sold over seventy-five thousand copies.[44]

Like secret agents, although surpassing them, long-distance flyers offered the interwar imagination something it was seeking in the realm of human action. They demonstrated that feats of daring and adventure and service were still possible in a century that belonged to the masses. There was in flying an inherent fascination with energy and speed or simply with soaring to great heights, but the element of forcing an opening or a space for heroic assertion cannot be discounted. Spies like Marthe Richard could attain similar celebrity because they tapped into the same sentiments of heroism in the life stories they created about themselves. Moreover, neither the pilot nor the spy was a paladin in opposition to the age. Each represented a reformulation of the hero fit for a culture of organization and machinery. Modern spies armed themselves with an arsenal of radio transmitters, miniature cameras, and other high-tech devices for stealing secrets or blowing up factories. They operated often in lonely, perilous isolation — and therein was their appeal — yet behind them lay a network or support system of laboratories, analysts, master spies, safe houses, and couriers. Pilots were people who mastered their machines, used them to affirm their prowess and to exercise control over their self-created destiny. With the technology of aviation they challenged nature to her limits, gambled all, and often came back the winner. At times the machine was the enemy, fragile, ill-equipped, lacking the staying power of its pilot. But there was also a fascination and pride in the machinery, and a constant effort to work it to perfection.[45] Launched into a hostile world on their own, aviators too were tethered to a systematic lifeline just as they coupled their heroics to an ethic of teamwork and interdependence. Even in the pioneering days of the line, pilots flew in teams, touched down at prearranged bases, depended on fast-working ground crews to speed them on their way, and accepted without question the hierarchy of the Latécoère organization. Later, radio signals and bigger planes made flying a coordinated effort. A typical transatlantic flight in the mid-1930s required two pilots, a navigator, a radio operator, and a mechanic. Here is takeoff as Mermoz described it:

> Everyone is already at his post.
> The pilots light up the instrument panel and regulate its intensity. The controls are tested, the engine levers are set in their position for takeoff. . . .
> The mechanic is at his post, alone. . . .
> The navigator has already readied his maps, checked his compasses and drift indicators, taken out his books, placed his sextant within reach and gazed at his slide rule.
> The wireless operator has warmed up his radio, turned it off, turned it back on, adjusted the dials on their circuit with the touch of a watchmaker. Everything is ready. . . .
> The machine, weighted down, little by little gains speed in the deafening noise of the full throttled engines, then . . . the seaplane slides along the surface.
> After some fifty seconds under the stress of the controls, it tears loose from the water.
> The adventure has begun.[46]

Once aloft radio contact with the ground was constant and regular. Within the aircraft speed, position, and fuel consumption were logged for company files. The thrill of flying joined with routinization, because the ultimate aim of aviators and secret agents alike was security and control. Pilots flew to dare the elements but also to demonstrate the regularity of air communication. Even over the Sahara and the Andes this prosaic resolution was the goal. Danger, however, remained the basic element, as it did for spies. For all his expertise and support systems, Mermoz still ended up at the bottom of the ocean. That was why the man, along with his comrades, was so capable of capturing the nation's imagination.

There were other similarities between secret agents and flyers. One flew above ground, one went "underground," but each broke free of the terrestrial humdrum. The drab uniforms of modern warfare had made heroics less dashing. Pilots, in turn, adopted a uniform style all their own, rugged and glamorous, while spies, in imagery if not in fact, dressed in trench coats or the clothing of the enemy, itself unexceptional yet a constant source of peril. Most noticeably the two came together in the same person. The mercenary pilot of fortune tacking toward intrigue was a common enough figure between the wars.[47] H. D. the flyer turned into H. D. the spy. George Hill took up flying on the Balkan front and used planes for secret agent drops behind lines. Both Richard and Davrichevii were pilots before they entered French intelligence. Each was caught up in the mystique of flying. Davrichevii chanted the standard refrain about the aviator's state of grace. Richard spoke to Ladoux about "the baptism of the air" and then, mixing her metaphors, said that one's first flight was like a first love — you never forgot the novelty of the sensation. Crozier had connections to aviation before the war. Sensing the appropriateness of the image, he wrote that intelligence operatives should possess the same qualities as aviators, the same reflexes and economy of movement and the same "impenetrable mask." They must "know and never forget that at their post they risk neither wounds nor captivity but only death. A pilot's crash leaves little hope of another outcome; the spy's no other epilogue than the firing squad."[48] Self-lionizing spies were right to join forces with the flyers, but the effort was not all that necessary. Each provided the culture with sensations and exploits befitting the age. The same impulse that made a Mermoz a darling of the crowds cast the limelight upon a Richard; and from it emerged the spy novel and the secret agent as a hero.

But what heroes these spies! A man who dumped bodies into the Meuse and bragged about thirty-eight murders to his credit. A woman whose exploits began with the surrender of her body to a Prussian. It is difficult to imagine such people as the stuff of heroism or honor before 1914. After the war that was not the case. One thinks, for example, of the fabulously popular *Madonna of the Sleeping Cars,* a breezy pulp novel from the twenties starring Lady Diana Wyndham. She is beautiful, carefree, open to adventure. A French humorist has dubbed her the Madonna of the sleeping cars for the thousands of miles she has traveled on continental railroads. "A consummate bit of irony," she admits, "because although I may look like one, I have none of the other attributes. As a matter of fact, I have been in every European watering-place; I've lost more billet-doux than you could shake a stick at, between the pages of timetables and illustrated magazines."[49] She dances nude at a charity fund-raiser to flout convention and shock society. When she fears her fortune is lost, she goes "slumming" to temper herself for harder times ahead. Plans to recoup her investments by exploiting an oil concession in Russia lead her to Varichkine, a Bolshevik agent with the power to help her. He offers his services in exchange for one night with the celebrated Madonna, yet she proposes marriage, not out of desire for respectability but because she cannot forgo the supreme opportunity to scandalize her peers by marrying a Red. When the novel is over and all castles in the air have come crashing to the ground, she is off again on the Orient Express:

I have a ticket for Constantinople. But I may stop off at Vienna or Budapest. That depends absolutely on chance or on the colour of the eyes of my neighbour in the compartment. I have reserved rooms at the Imperial, on the Ring, and at the Hungaria, on the quay at Budapest: but I am just as likely to sleep in some horrible hotel in Josephstadt or in a palace on the hillside at Budapest. . . . I am, even more than usually, open to suggestion. My life has been monotonous, these last six months. Don't you agree with me, Gérard? It is high time that I changed the menu and dug my spurs into my beloved adventure. A migrating bird, weary of capitals and watering places, I shall make my nest at the will of my desire, I shall sing in the moonlight when the spirit moves me and I shall seek illusions far from the lying world I know so well. I proudly withdraw the pessimistic avowals I made at Glensloy, my dear. . . . Life is always beautiful after all. Men will never be any less stupid. And I'm giving myself exactly six weeks to discover the imbecile who will cater to my whims and ripen in my safe deposit box some golden apples from the garden of the Hesperides.[50]

Other stories like Paul Morand's *Flèche d'Orient* with its celebration of pilot sangfroid and its portrait of the *homme moderne*,[51] or Joseph Kessel's *Siberian Nights* come readily to mind. In the latter the pilot Estienne recounts his adventures at Vladivostok right after the war. It is the time of the Russian civil war and Estienne is in charge of assuring freight shipments to French troops in the hinterland. The train station swarms with refugees; ragged, diseased, they camp out on the floor; one literally has to climb over them to walk across the great hall. On the tracks in the yard a trainload of Semenovtsy has arrived. These are the Cossack troops of the Ataman Semenov, a law unto themselves in the far reaches of civil war Siberia. The tales of the Semenovtsy are chilling. Armed to the teeth, their weapon of preference is the *nagaika,* a whip that can rip a man's skin off with one flick of the wrist. The road to their headquarters in Chita is marked in the winter by human signposts — the naked cadavers of mutilated Red Guards or peasants — their frozen arms pointing in the direction of Semenov. Nevertheless Estienne says that he was curious to meet them "because they inspired in me not only disgust but that sort of morbid attraction that elementary, instinctual violence and a life given over to its commands has always held for me."

Sooner than Estienne anticipated his wish is granted. One of Semenov's men has whipped an employee in the train station because he has run out of candles. A colonel in Kolchak's army comes out to protest. With another flick of the wrist the cossack rips open the colonel's cheek. Instinctively Estienne's hand moves toward his revolver but he has been told not to intervene in *les querelles russes*. A cossack lieutenant arrives and the scene comes to an end. The lieutenant, Artemieff, sees Estienne, takes a liking to him, and invites him to their train out in the yard. Drawn to their violence and barbarism, Estienne immediately accepts. The Semenovtsy train is made of old luxury cars that outdo anything Estienne has ever seen. Booty from their raids and their pillage render them even more dazzling. The Semenovtsy Estienne sees within are everything he could possibly imagine: savage, ferocious, indifferent to human suffering, thoroughly unrestrained in their willingness to resort to violence. At first they are in a subdued mood — "One would have thought beasts of prey at their rest." Then the drinking begins. In the midst of the drinking Grichka, the cossack with the whip in the train station, reappears. He says that he and two companions were ambushed in town and that the other two were killed. The mood in the car suddenly turns ugly, terrifyingly so. The captain complains that because of the foreign troops he is unable to set the port afire. Tartzoff, one of the men in the car, suggests to Estienne that they leave: "Now they are going to get dead drunk and that will end in a shooting."

Tartzoff takes Estienne to The Aquarium, a late-night bar frequented by officers of the Allied forces in the harbor. Another wild, drunken scene ensues. At their table is Major Robinson who, Tartzoff confides, is an officer in British intelligence. The major tosses back one glass of vodka and cognac after another. Then he asks Estienne if he has a revolver. Estienne asks why. Robinson says that he wants to shoot a fat speculator sitting nearby. Then the major collapses in a drunken stupor.

Later Estienne follows Tartzoff to a ramshackle building where an old woman pimps for her daughter. Tartzoff is a client, but this trip he has vengeance in mind; it is the daughter — Aglaé — who has set up the ambush. Grichka and a dozen other cossacks break in. Aglaé spits in Grichka's face. With his *nagaika* he lashes her naked body. Then the cossacks gang-rape her. This time Estienne does try to intervene, but they throw him out a window. As the book closes, he reawakens to find the shanty in flames. It was a story that could be written only after the war and one that Kessel would tell and retell in his construction of the myth of *homo kesselianus*. He himself had lived through most of it, experiencing the same unreserved fascination that had led Estienne into the railway car. "I realized," he later admitted, "that a part of me, in my most troubled inner self, was like them."[52]

Or there was Roger Vercel's tale of Captain Conan that captured the Prix Goncourt in 1934. It too occurs just after the war, on the Balkan front in Romania and Bulgaria. Conan is a brute, a tough guy, a scrapper, and a conqueror, for whom the war has been the grandest adventure. Ripped out of a life so dull he can scarcely summon the will to recall it, he finds his readjustment to peacetime all but unbearable. When Norbert, the narrator, asks Conan what he had done before:

There was a long pause, he seemed to be searching, painfully, unable to tear himself away from the black trench he was staring at. Finally, in a completely different voice, a colorless, bleak, poignant voice, he answered:
"I was in notions, like my father . . ."
Then the voice grew more assured, retrieving the memory of some ancient pride:
"But we also dealt in shirts . . . and some ready-to-wear."
He looked at me:
"And then, you know, once a month, there was the fair, and lots of people . . ."

During the war Conan has discovered for the first time in his life his extraordinary gifts as a hunter and killer of men. The *petit commerçant* is metamorphosed into a warrior, a magnificent one, and placed in command of roughnecks like himself, he fashions them into a crack commando force. De Scève, another officer, tells Norbert that he should have seen them in the war. "One day I came upon them during their training exercises. It was ferocious and soundless: hand-to-hand combat, strikes to the throat, terrific swings with their rifle butts, throws of their hunting knives that quivered wildly as they struck into the planks of their targets. 'All that,' [Conan] explained to me, 'is fantastic because it makes no noise. Only, if you're after prisoners, you've got to do it all over again. They all come in damaged goods! . . . What we need are the Roman gladiator nets I once saw in the movies: with that you'll have your Bul, alive and kicking!'"

What is left for these buccaneers when the war is over is largely the story Vercel has to tell. Conan rebels, swaggers, and crashes through Bucharest as if the war had never come to an end, makes his men and himself into a law of their own. Norbert senses that an explosion is coming:

I perceived in him neither insensitivity nor bravado, but a tenacious desire for combat, combat against the narrow military formalities, the odious routine, the barracks where they intended to break him. If he took as personal offenses the most general of measures, it was because they stung him to the quick, in his deep instincts as a war chief, the instinct of mercenaries who, the fight over, disband and rediscover at least liberty in the absence of battle! He was a man to grab for it, to desert, if the sordid bureaucrats drove him to the edge. I discovered beneath his buffooneries an obstinate revolt that terrified me. They would cage him up, perhaps, but at the cost of several trainers. Unfortunately, people never allow a wild beast to digest its trainer in peace!

Finally the commandos run completely amok, knocking off the Palais de Glace, a popular Romanian nightclub. They shoot the place up, kill the cashier, and kick in a woman's abdomen as they stomp down the stairway; she dies of peritonitis. Norbert, now military prosecutor, clashes with Conan who was not in on the caper but regards it all as a matter of course. What did you expect, he asks Norbert, of men who are good only for fighting and have come to know this of themselves. Norbert responds "with one of those convenient words one always keeps on one's person: adapt." But Conan replies that he might as well tell a dog bred to hunt to make do with salad because the hunting grounds are closed. "Is he supposed to drop his instinct like a turd?" Conan cannot give up the war. Thrown into the jungle he has discovered his paradise, and like a cornered beast he lashes out at the living death closing in on him. A war hero, he is in peacetime a man out of control, a rogue soldier, a *petit bonhomme terrifiant*. Still Norbert and the others are irresistibly drawn to him, and he towers above everyone else in the novel. It is a disquieting yet magnetic portrait of the violence uncorked by the war and of the insurgency of those who would not see it squeezed back into the bottle.[53]

The point is not that the public visage of celebrated spies was a composite of such books nor even of detective stories or movies, although clearly there were certain resemblances (Crozier's little speech to De Blauw, for example, could have come straight from Dekobra). Rather war and revolution had interjected into European culture a willed flirtation with roughness, abandon, and violence that diffused throughout interwar literature and found expression in the spy story. Respect for toughness, for men who wore leather jackets, for women who scorned convention and tempted danger, or for people who carried Brownings was part of the interwar idiom, and it encouraged the writing of tales about spies who inhabited a rough-and-tumble world and fired pistol shots in the dark. A *costaud* like Crozier or an unbridled character like Richard, who once said, "I like to play with fire, with danger, with suspicion," could write proudly of their adventures, indeed play up the rough spots, because life was venturesome after the war and in such a world fame and honor fell to the hardy and to the wild.[54] Postwar culture created space for the spy story, abetted its construction, pushed along the action, and made it respectable.

Ultimately, however, cultural affinity led back to the enormous market in war stories. There was no desire in France to forget about the war. It was an epic to rival the *Iliad,* and people were prepared to read about it over and over again. That insatiable appetite turned the war into a commodity, an experience to be consumed for pleasure and exploited for profit. People wrote about the war to cash in on the market, and when the war stories ran out they concocted new ones to feed the unending demand. Spy stories especially benefited from this hunger not only because secret agents were encouraged to publish their memoirs but because espionage was the perfect medium for keeping the trade in war books alive. It was difficult to create a new version of the Battle of the Marne, but wartime intrigue was infinitely reinventable. Ladoux sensed this when he turned his memoirs into a series of episodic tales strung out over several volumes. It did not matter, for example, that the Swiss hotel intrigues he described read suspiciously like one of the Ashenden stories or that French undercover agents who passed themselves off as Irish nationalists, and chose the name Lord O'Connell as their cover, were not likely to survive the war.[55] War stories sold.

Richard's sequels — *Spies in War and Peace; My Latest Secret Missions* — demonstrated still greater possibilities. These too were an episodic mishmash with Richard floating through life as the Jessica Fletcher of her day, incessantly running into old acquaintances and relatives who draw her back into the spy world. Nearly all the characters in these books are former spies like herself, people whose wartime experiences continue into the postwar years. One is Jeanne, a dancer friend who works for Soviet intelligence. Jeanne tells Richard about her missions in Istanbul right after the war, then in Moscow during the NEP (new economic policy), and then in Berlin. On the verge of a breakdown, Jeanne is desperately trying to break free of the Soviets, who have no intention of letting her go. She hides for three months in a convent, but on the train taking the community to a religious retreat two GPU agents

kidnap her and take her to Paris. There "in the rue Notre-Dame de Lo-
rette, she moves dazed through the crowd that drifts in with the night:
Negroes, prostitutes, pimps, pederasts. They seat her beside a Swedish
industrialist who must be gotten drunk and made to talk."[56] Later Richard learns that Jeanne was seen gambling like a madwoman in Monte
Carlo, then sliding slowly off her chair, dead from poisoning.

Before Jeanne's disappearance, the dancer tells Richard about Jim
Rodwell, a former British agent Richard had encountered in Spain during the war and then again in Romania in 1920. Breaking with the British and horribly disfigured in an explosion, Rodwell has become a Soviet operative and a pyromaniac, using his intelligence work as a pretext
to set fire to boats, trains, and factories. In Berlin Richard meets up with
Nicolas Yorman, a man of mysterious origins who holds at least three
passports and directs a private espionage bureau. Yorman attempts to
recruit her for a mission, and although she refuses he briefs her on two
German spies from the war who are currently running a German spy
ring in France. Richard returns home to track down the network. Soon
she meets her relative Sacha, a Trotskyite who tries to embroil her in his
intrigues. He disappears in the purges. Through an old colleague from
the Deuxième Bureau she is drawn into the spy battles of civil war Spain.
At Hendaye she meets von S., a German spy who operated as a double
agent in Manchuria in 1927, has turned up since on missions in Europe
and Ethiopia, and is now thick in intrigues in Spain. Richard has a partner photograph his papers. Later, with the help of her nephew who
has joined the International Brigades, she unmasks a British intelligence
agent. And so on.

The formula was open-ended, and one suspects that only the intervention of the Second World War prevented yet another spinoff, or
what today would be called *Marthe IV*.[57] In her sequels Richard demonstrated how war stories could be manufactured over and over and over
again simply by translating them into the continued adventures of wartime spies. Essentially all spy literature traded on the same formula,
churning out stories of a war in peacetime with all the adventures and
exploits and intrigues that consumers expected of the war book market.
The secret-war image, with all its attendant suggestiveness of an unending war, was itself little more than a marketing device. It tapped into the
desire to hold on to the war, not simply to commemorate it but to tell
and retell that extraordinary event. Secret-war literature kept the mood
of wartime alive, allowing its purveyors to exploit those urges by recon-
structing war stories out of interwar materials. At its best the formula

was all but seamless. Richard, propelled down an endless stream of adventures set in motion since 1914, found no release from her wartime life as a spy. "In the midst of peace," Allard wrote, "Joseph Crozier has not disarmed."[58]

Perhaps what Richard and her kind understood best was the enormous entertainment potential of espionage. We are so accustomed to seeing the interwar years as a time of scarring and tumult that we tend to neglect the routine and boredom ruling most people's lives, for which the antidote was fabricated escapism. Movies, radio, and long-distance flights answered that need, as did espionage when packaged properly. Impresarios like Ladoux and Richard stuffed their stories with theatrics and ambiance. They invented, inflated, and embellished, giving the public the atmospheric spy world it obviously craved. Richard gave them sex, violence, White Russians, and the *pègre internationale*. For good measure she threw in the Spanish civil war and the purges but only as a backdrop for spinning out her stories, exhibiting how the present-mindedness of the period could be converted into thrills and entertainment and hence into one more commodity for sale. "Yorman and Rodwell," she wrote, "still live off espionage. But espionage that eats away at them, secretly, day and night, in their sleep, in their travels, in their amours, the endless obsession for combat that will kill them just like the others."[59] This was the language of the Saturday matinee. Ladoux went one better in his version of Richard's first meeting with von Krohn. Whisked away by an unknown spy chieftain, she finds herself trapped in a hillside hotel. She tries to break free but the man—von Krohn—bars her way. "You'll leave here only over my dead body," he tells her. "Then I'll leave dead," replies Richard who pulls out a dagger:

Two steps scarcely separate the adversaries. The man seems to stiffen in order to clear them in a bound. But the *aviatrice*'s limpid eyes once again focus on his and paralyze his spirit. An unbelievable struggle takes place within the stranger's inner depths, and by turns he grows pale and then crimson.

A more fearsome battle rages behind the immobile features of the young woman.

And, all at once, the dagger falls from her hands, while a strange luminescence colors her gaze as if it had just filled with all the clearness of the sunset, with all the light of a past that, like the sun, hesitates on the edge of a boundless horizon before sinking beneath the waves.

But the stranger has thrown himself upon her and already his face is up against Marthe's.

"Coward," she has just time enough to cry before walling up her lips, her slight but last refuge menaced by the greedy mouth of the conqueror who envelops her but cannot see, because the Lark's eyelids close along with her lips, the flash of a look, mingling sorrow and contempt, that has taken flight beyond the gilded peaks of the Pyrenees, to the calvary of Menancourt, the tragic Hill 180 where the dead man [Marthe's husband], torn to pieces by German bullets, can now rest in peace.

He is about to be avenged![60]

We are back at the *Journal* article with which this chapter began, and the storytelling that permeated interwar spy writing.

———————

Storytelling—forcing the ambiance or embellishing the reporting or simply the love of spinning out a story—was ingrained in the writing on intrigue between the wars. Memoirists engaged in it shamelessly. Spy novelists, by their sheer presence and proliferation, made telling tales a part of the literature. A spy novel like *The Seven Heads of the Green Dragon* packed in current events, real personages, and the sense of a world gliding toward chaos and destruction.[61] Yet it was also playful, silly, and escapist, blurring reality and make-believe so that a historical present was recreated as fantasy. For the press the temptation to embellish could be irresistible. When the White Russian Kutepov disappeared in 1930, *Détective* magazine put five reporters—*les cinq*—on the trail of the general. To break the case they set off after "the conspirators of destiny," the men and women "who mount their armies, their police, their spies, their faithful, and their traitors" behind locked doors "where no light penetrates." The five went to a "conspirators' tavern." They traveled to an informant's apartment, and then to the Black Cat cabaret in Antwerp. They listened to a blond woman who was a favorite of Russian sailors tell them that she had received no visitors from two Soviet freighters anchored in the harbor ten days earlier. "Something," she divulged to the sleuths from Paris, "must have happened on board." Then the five returned to Paris and a villa in Neuilly where they watched a famous Russian clairvoyant run his fingers over Kutepov's clothing, tremble and grow pale, and finally murmur: "I see him alive carried away on a road. I see him in a dark port. I see him on a ship . . ."[62]

In the hunt for Kutepov, the five and their informants described the extraordinary powers of the Soviet secret police, yet that too was part of the game of making the story as exciting as possible. Seven years later, when the Cagoule story broke, the magazine wrote of "civil-war arsenals," a "putsch in the manner of Hitler or Franco," and how "foreign agents, clerks of the great international sharks — arms merchants, speculators, civil-war organizers — incited and subsidized the Cagoule." But it also said:

A new secret threw out roots in Clermont, city of secrets, a secret more thrilling than adulteries, Friday afternoon teas, [or] Saturday evening secret debauches. One awakened honest bourgeois at ten in the evening, one got them to their cars, one ordered them to Chambéry or Paris to pick up wonderful submachine guns that cooled automatically. They met mysterious emissaries in the deep of the night, at deserted intersections. One had to know passwords.
"Republic!" said the emissary.
"France," repeated the conspirator.
It was stranger than in the detective novels.[63]

This style, with variations, was pandemic. Even at their soberest the mass dailies covered the great intrigues as mysteries to be solved. They followed the *piste* — "The Normandy *piste* holds"; "The place de la Convention *piste* leads nowhere"[64] — until the case could be cracked or the quarry cornered. Instinctively they descended on the *romanesque* or storylike quality of affairs, conflating reality with the artifices of mass entertainment: "The saga continues"; "one has the impression of reading a thrilling and extraordinary detective story"; "the perfect spy from a movie repertoire"; "unfolding like a novel." Headlines introduced "The Characters in the Drama" or "The Day of the Drama."[65]

No story — terror, civil war, espionage — was beyond ornamentation. Paul Schulz, a former Free Corps gangster turned Nazi was "the world-class killer, the killer for pleasure, the beautiful, the formidable, the terrifying beast of prey." *Paris-Soir* ran the story in October 1938 as the sort of spy filler the paper dragged out periodically when it was looking for something eye-catching to round out an edition.[66] *Police Magazine* reported on secret agents in civil war Spain as if they were short story material, replete with narrative, dialogue, melodrama, and sex.[67]

The appetite for jacked-up spy stories or for insider information of the "true tales from the spy world" genre appears to have been boundless in these years. Newspapers pulled them out of the files (or thin air) with abandon, and a new kind of journalist, the professional spy watcher or spy gossip columnist, appeared on the scene. Paul Lanoir had represented a prewar exemplar, but it was really only after the war that this sort of writing moved easily from alarmism to sheer fascination with spies. Although its practitioners could sound clarion calls, they were just as likely to dabble in the espionage "non-story" or in warmed-over exposés, absorbing "the shadow world" into the machinery of consumerism. Bardanne and Xavier de Hautecloque, who wrote a series on the shadow powers of the world—"Les puissances des ténèbres"—for the *Petit Journal* in 1931, were two such traffickers, although a still more prolific scribbler was Paul Allard. Among his many books were *The Truth about the Merchants of Arms; The Quai d'Orsay; Police Anarchy;* and *The Secrets of the Elysées.* He also wrote several works and innumerable articles on espionage posing as an authority. Louis de Jong cited his *When Hitler Spies on France* (completed in September 1939) as an example of French fifth-column writing at the beginning of the Second World War. The typical Allard production, however, was the neatly packaged vignette or atmospheric exposé that merely strung together odds and ends and had no coherence or even purpose except its price on the market. He was, perhaps, an environmentalist ahead of his time in the sense that he recycled everything he wrote. As late as 1939 he was churning out articles for *Paris-Soir* and *Match* on "the code war" ("Yes, a war . . . a permanent war, underhanded, secret. A war smack in the middle of peace that knows neither friends nor enemies. A war of brains, mathematicians . . . of sorcerers") or on "beautiful spies" ("The year 1938 was the year of the beautiful spies. . . . All of them placed their sex appeal at the service of their country . . . and their own interests").[68]

Not all stories followed this pattern. Between the wars intrigue presented two faces to the French. One was the intrusive face through which international events and forces bore in upon readers and made present-mindedness an intense and inescapable fact of the age. This face could be cruelly menacing, reminding one of enemies at home or of vast foreign organizations designed to wreak havoc in France. At its worst it could exploit sensational stories of hijackings and kidnappings as a springboard to ideological attacks or xenophobic excoriations. Or it could simply focus on the international affairs of the moment. The interest in spy stories reflected a desire to read about the present. Espionage and intrigue captured what was new or different about postwar Europe, how the new dictatorships worked, or why a sense of flux persisted beyond the peace. Indeed after the war foreign news more and more dominated the press.[69] Intrigue, especially the great sensationalist stories that broke with nearly uninterrupted regularity and came to supersede crime stories, gave that news a palpable presence. The unraveling of the Kutepov or Miller mysteries riveted readers' attention on the world at large, driving the forces and tensions of that world into the daily consciousness of a mass audience. However, embedded in sensationalism were also tremendous possibilities for embellishment and storytelling and here was intrigue's other face in these years. It is impossible to read through the interwar coverage of intrigue without sensing the sheer pleasure of going with a story that could sell. From intrusiveness to entertainment was a very short step, and few who were in the business of reporting news hesitated to take it. That visage merits a closer look, because like scare stories and memoirs it winds us back deeper into the moods of the thirties.

A story from the margins — that of Matuska the dynamiter — is one striking example because the directions it took and the coverage it evoked were illustrative of contemporary attitudes and styles of reporting. Matuska was an Austrian citizen of Hungarian origins. In 1931 he attempted to wreck two trains, failed, blew up a third train in Germany, and dynamited a fourth — the night express from Budapest to Vienna — at Bia-Torbagy, seventeen kilometers outside of Budapest.[70] The bombings, of which the Bia-Torbagy smash-up was by far the bloodiest, killed twenty-two people and seriously injured another hundred and fifty. In 1934 Matuska went on trial in Budapest and in it the outlines of the affair become telling.[71] The historical dimensions to the case, if one chose to concentrate on them, were conspicuous. Certain evidence, for example, suggested a potential Red lead to follow, and even by 1934, when it was clear that Matuska was a severely disturbed individual, there were some like the presiding judge at his trial who continued to believe in a communist connection. Moreover, Matuska himself was in a way a victim of his times. The Austrian army had trained him in the war to blow up bridges and viaducts, and a relative said that the war had deeply affected his mental condition. There was also the coincidence in timing between the trial and the investigation into the Marseilles murders by Ustasha terrorists. The Ustashi, too, had dynamited trains, and at times the two stories shared the same pages in the mass dailies.

Yet the trial of Matuska had little to do with any of these things. Communism and the war received only a passing mention and parallels with the Ustashi not even that. Instead attention focused on the more bizarre and sensational side to the defendant's character, especially Matuska's revelation that he was under the power of a man named Léo. Matuska said that Léo had first appeared in the form of a classmate who had taught him the meaning of Satan. Then at the age of thirteen he had watched spellbound as a traveling magician put on a show at his school. This person too was Léo who reappeared in the war in the guise of his captain and then later in Vienna as the source of inspiration for his train-smashing feats. A journalist, Baranyi, testified that there had been a real Léo, a man named Jean Kiss, who was well known for his skills as a conjurer and hypnotist. It was Kiss who had so impressed Matuska at the age of thirteen. In his testimony Baranyi said that he had met Léo/Kiss in the company of Matuska at the Café New York in Budapest in the late 1920s and that Kiss had boasted that Matuska was a medium with whom he could do anything. Other witnesses testified that Léo/Kiss was incapable of performing the feats attributed to him. Issues of hypnotism and insanity dominated the trial, quickly pushing the themes of communism or terrorism into the background.[72]

Matuska's tribunal found him guilty of a capital crime, which brought a sad ending to a tragic story. Yet tragedy scarcely characterized the tone of the trial. Speculation about Léo raised it to a strange, even grotesque, level that fell back to earth in moments of base, flat-out fatuity. At one point Matuska threw the courtroom into dead silence by announcing that Léo was present in the hall. Asked to indicate the mesmerist, Matuska pointed directly to one of the judges. The presiding judge gave him three days' special punishment for this tomfoolery, but the defendant's apologies won him temporary mercy and a waiver of the sentence. At another moment an eighty-three-year-old doctor fainted on the witness stand from the heat in the courtroom. A glass of cognac brought him around, but then it was discovered that the witness was the head of the Hungarian antialcohol league and had not taken a drink for sixty-seven years. There was also an incident toward the end of the trial when an attractive young woman sat down as a spectator in the courtroom. Matuska's inclination to sexual excess was well known to the court — in a nine-day period following the dynamiting at Bia-Torbagy he had gone on a twelve-woman binge in the red light district of Budapest — and he began to stare at her intently, ogling the woman to the point that he was oblivious to questions from the presiding judge. Nearly choking with indignation, the jurist sentenced Matuska to five days special punishment. Matuska lashed back at the judge that he was, after all, only a man and that the woman was a good deal more pleasant to look at than *he* was. Later the woman asked the judge not to punish Matuska and once again the sentence was waived.

All this was grist for the media mills. *Détective* magazine labeled Matuska "the Sadist of the Rails," and *Paris-Soir* called him a "monster" and "the greatest criminal of the century." The latter tabloid, well on its way to becoming the most widely read daily in France, pounced on everything that was sensational or amusing about the case. It fastened

on the episodes of fainting and ogling, and when its correspondent recounted that Matuska had earlier promised to tell all in exchange for a
quarter-hour speech in Hungarian, German, English, and French (acknowledging that he knew only the first two languages and would need
time to study the latter), the journalist could not refrain from remarking
that this was equivalent to the condemned man, asked to state his last
wish, replying: "I want to learn Chinese." The newspaper proclaimed
Matuska a man in the grip of a sexual obsession. Only the bloody consequences of his dynamitings, it wrote, could appease that all-powerful
spell. Playing the sexual angle for all it was worth, it sent its correspondent to interview the women Matuska had picked up on his famous
nine-day spree. One said Matuska had taken her to a church and made
her kneel down and repeat a prayer he had written. Another said he had
taken her to a restaurant and told her "The world will have known three
geniuses: Attila, Napolcon, Matuska." Such were *les étranges amours de
Matuska*. When the trial lagged or filler was needed, an article was
dragged out on voodoo in Paris. When it was necessary to set the scene
as the trial was about to begin, the Hungarian capital was draped in
purple:

Not the least contrast to this adventure is to see Budapest, the city of laughter,
the homeland of waltzes . . . Pest where red, gypsy violins sing, Buda where
poets and Magyar saints dream, serve as the setting for this drama of blood,
eroticism, and madness.

In short, what is striking about the Matuska affair is that a case one
might have expected in 1934 to have followed the leads to the Red
specter or to international terrorism could run so readily in other directions. By following the pattern of conventional sensationalism and rendering horrific crimes into public spectacle, the Matuska trial showed
how story lines, commercial pressures, and untrammeled humor could
combine, even in the thirties, to reduce events to a source of mass
pleasure.[73]
    One reason for this kind of coverage was that tales of intrigue and
terror could throw up wildly contrasting moods. There was, of course,
the crueler side to affairs. When Ignace Reiss was murdered by Soviet
agents on a road outside Lausanne in 1937, the story caught the gray,
dispirited tones we associate with the thirties. His life, *Paris-Soir* noted,
was "a document on our times."[74] He was among that generation swept
up in the Russian revolution and devoted totally to its cause. Polish
Communist party worker, Comintern agent, Red Army intelligence

agent, and then, to continue working abroad, GPU agent, marked the stages of his revolutionary career. He had organized spy networks throughout Europe and arranged arms sales to Spain. By 1937 he was disillusioned, sickened by the purges, and determined not to return to a Lubianka bullet in the back of his neck. Aware that he was signing his own death sentence, he nevertheless defected from the party and wrote a letter denouncing Stalin. Then he went into hiding in Switzerland. He made the mistake, however, of retaining contact with an old German socialist friend, Gertrude Schildbach, who under pressure betrayed his whereabouts to the Soviet secret police. To liquidate Reiss the GPU organized an assassination squad among their White Russian operatives in Paris, including Dmitry Smirenskii (known as Marcel Rollin) and Vladimir Kudratiev, who was closely connected with General Skoblin. Others on the hit team were François Rossi (his real name was Roland) and Charles Martignat. As their lookout the squad recruited a young Swiss woman, Renate Steiner, who was seeking a Soviet visa and had been advised to go to the Union for Repatriation of Russians Abroad at 12, rue de Buci in Paris. The union was the cover organization through which Kudratiev and Smirenskii operated. Steiner was unknown to Reiss and would be able to track him without tipping him off. Most likely she had no idea she was marking a man for murder. Afterwards the Swiss police had little difficulty rounding her up and learning everything she knew about the assassination. When the team was ready to move, Schildbach was brought in to set up the target. On September 4 she dined with Reiss in Lausanne and then they went for a drive. That night the Swiss police found Reiss's bullet-riddled body outside town on the Chamblandes road.[75] Today one can follow the story through the newspaper runs in the Bibliothèque nationale. On the front page of the 3 October edition of *Le Journal* are photos of four of the figures involved: Kudratiev sly, diffident, opaque; Smirenskii wearing a peaked worker's cap of the times, tough and brash; Schildbach bespectacled and severe; Steiner aloofly elegant beneath her fashionable hat set at an angle over one eye. A movie seeking to reconstruct the cold, real flavor of the thirties could do worse than model its characters after these pictures.

Yet the decade was itself irrepressibly conscious of the cinematic overtones to its own history, and this too must be taken into account. "As thrilling as the most extraordinary adventure film" was how the same *Paris-Soir* article described Reiss's document on his times. Headlines — "The Life and Death of Ignace Reiss, Secret Agent" — underscored the setting.[76] Even a chilling affair like the Reiss murder could receive such treatment because not everything about intrigue was coolly efficient or menacing, nor was it inexorably fraught with the tragic wreckage of the age. There was also a frivolous and farcical side that could provoke a good guffaw or two and that made espionage a ripe commodity for public amusement.

The microbe affair, occurring as it did at approximately the same time as the liquidation of Reiss, provides a good counterpoint. Gas and bacteria warfare were two of the most dreaded possibilities of the era. The microbe affair fell considerably shy of these fears. Its outlines and cast of characters were, in fact, so deliciously ridiculous that it is difficult to believe that it was not the concoction of some slapstick writer slipped into police archives for comic relief. The heart of the affair was a plan to infiltrate two human guinea pigs, injected with an "anemia" virus, behind Nationalist lines in Spain. The two men would have immunity but would infect Franco's forces and enable the Loyalists to slice through to victory. The masterminds of this harebrained scheme, as best the police could piece it together, were three ne'er-do-wells, Jean P., Jacques M. (also known as Captain Jack), and a mysterious figure called Ivan Ivanovitch, who was possibly the same person as Jean P. or just as likely the figment of someone's imagination. Jean P. came from a well-to-do family (his father was a lawyer and chevalier of the Legion of Honor) and must have been an albatross around the necks of his parents. He passed himself off as a test pilot (a lie), bought and sold cars and films, and generally seems to have led the useless life of a rich boy. According to one police report he also trafficked in weapons. Captain Jack's pedigree was of another sort. He was born in Warsaw in 1911 of Polish parents who probably emigrated soon after to France. He had fought with the Republican militia in the Spanish civil war and seems to have known Maurice Thorez. He had also been charged with swindling money from the Amsterdam-Pleyel committee and was wanted for burglary in the French provinces. As for the guinea pigs, one was an undistinguished journalist named Bouguenec, who was unemployed and living off "expedients" by 1937. The other, Chabrat, had had run-ins with the police, mostly for theft, since the age of eighteen.

For wastrels and desperadoes like these the microbe affair was never anything more than an elaborate scam. It is highly questionable whether the Spanish Republicans or the Nationalists, who were very quickly put on to the plot, were ever so gullible as to take its terms seriously, but somehow it evolved from wild talk to action in ways that the police could never quite determine. Especially uncertain was who was bank-rolling the affair. One police report suggested that the schemers had swindled considerable sums from the Republican government and then to cover their risks sold what they knew to the Nationalist side. A slightly later report concluded that the Loyalists had never swallowed the bait and that financing early on had come from a Nationalist banker and associate of Juan March who realized the propaganda value of cap-turing human germ bombs supposedly unleashed by the republic.

Whatever the intentions, or the backing, the scheme quickly degener-ated into burlesque. A week of preparation before heading south was primarily consecrated to boozing in various Parisian night spots. On the eve of their departure Bouguenec dropped several thousand francs on drinks for himself and five friends at the Chapeau Rouge and then an-other fifty-five hundred francs at the Romance bar on the rue Pigalle (both he and Chabrat had been given a large advance by Jean P.). The next day the two guinea pigs left Paris in a large touring car driven by the chauffeur of Jean P.'s mistress. They reached Bayonne on 11 March and gave themselves over to another week of drinking. Both seem to have shot their mouths off about their "mission," very possibly to assure immediate and easy arrest once they crossed over to the other side. On 19 March they went to a room at the Grand Hotel where a man de-scribed as a French intellectual administered their injections. Then the men got into their car and drove over the international bridge where the Spanish authorities immediately turned them back into France. Bouguenec and Chabrat then holed up at the Hotel Regina in Hendaye where they returned to their habits of easy living until the last of their money was spent and they sent out an SOS to Jean P. He hustled down to Hendaye, chewed the two out, and had them injected once again. According to one source the injections this time were administered by an Englishman named Teddy Graham. According to another they were given by a Spanish doctor in the presence of an officer in Franco's army. Once shot up with the evidence the two men were taken by Jean P. to a path leading across the border and told to follow it. The two obeyed orders and were immediately arrested by the waiting agents of Franco. Several months later press releases out of Spain announced that a Na-tionalist military court had found Bouguenec and Chabrat guilty of spreading infectious diseases behind military lines and that the two had been executed. However, when Bouguenec's father brought charges in court to determine who was responsible for sending his son to his death, Bouguenec *fils* immediately let it be known that he was alive and well in sunny Spain and that he would be returning to France shortly. Through-out the press campaign that followed there was, interestingly enough, speculation that an Englishman named Kerrignan or Karrigan or Céri-gan was mixed up in the affair. The name sounds tantalizing close to that of the flimflam man Corrigan. We will probably never know whether or not he was involved in these shenanigans, but certainly he would have felt at home with these people.[77]

For all its deadliness, a touch of the ridiculous or the absurd clung to intrigue throughout the interwar years. There was Tamborini and his pants in the Perpignan police station and there were the vaudevillian antics of Kusonskii and his comrades. There was also the preposterous but very real story of Karbec, a medium hired at the time of the Kutepov affair to follow the trail of the general.[78] Comparable monkey business can be found in the memoirs of the Soviet defector Besedovskii who had been chargé d'affaires at the Paris legation and who took time from his tales of Red terror and depravity to recall a few priceless stories about the Soviet secret police. One concerned Jean Sosnovskii, the Comintern liaison with party leaders in Warsaw in the early 1920s. Sosnovskii prided himself on his skills as a conspirator, even though he was nearly illiterate and memorized his instructions every night without any under-standing of what they were about. His ridiculous getups — Besedovskii said they had the look of a *carbonaro* in the Opéra-Comique — provided the Polish Sûreté with a direct lead to secret party headquarters. Bese-dovskii also recounted the botch-ups of Petro Dekhtiarenko who had murdered and raped his way through the Russian civil war. Assigned to the Ukrainian mission in Warsaw, he committed gaffe upon gaffe. He hung a sign on his office door — Regional Section of the Warsaw Cheka — until the ambassador, Schumskii, begged him to remove it. Ig-norant of even one word of Polish, Dekhtiarenko plunged nevertheless into the Warsaw black market in state secrets and confidential docu-ments. His greatest coup was procuring a copy of a secret treaty be-tween Poland and Luxembourg. By the agreement, Luxembourg pledged to send an army of two hundred thousand men by sea to its ally in the event of a war between Poland and Russia; in exchange Po-land would cede Poznan to Luxembourg. Schumskii laughed so hard every time he told this story that he broke down in tears.[79]

Such laughter or easy humor amidst more sinister revelations was a reflexive posture in these years, although not one that has been given its due. Like the charlatans and screwups who populated the milieu it too contributed to the disposition to play up the lighter side of a story.

It surfaced in the compulsive urge to pass on a good tale or in a certain style of reporting that never refused a good witticism. Book writers like Besedovskii surrendered to the urge, and so did government officials or influential commentators. The French representative in Stockholm dutifully reported to the foreign minister on a secret session in the Soviet legation where the embassy counselor, Dimitrievskii, had read a confidential circular calling for tougher measures against the opposition in exile. Then, and one can imagine the mischievous grin and the countless other times he buttonholed friends with the story, he appended at the bottom:

Although the following has no relation to the information in this letter, I cannot resist the pleasure of passing it on.

Having been named minister to Mexico, M. Dimitrievskii has refused the assignment because, as he told one of my associates, "there really have been too many revolutions in Mexico."[80]

Albert Londres, one of France's most celebrated foreign correspondents, was a master of the style. His coverage of the war catapulted him to public recognition and over the next fourteen years he filed reports and exposés from all over the world until his untimely death in the *Georges-Philippar* fire off the Somaliland coast in 1932. He could be trenchantly critical but his trademark was droll irony and sarcasm that had the result of making a joke out of a number of the stories he covered. Writing about the white slave trade to Latin America he delighted in parodying the pimps' bourgeois self-delusions, their pleasure in Raymond Poincaré's return to power because solid, secure governments were good for trade, or their images of themselves as modern-day Samuel Smiles:

"The profession of pimp, Monsieur Albert, is nothing for an ordinary man to undertake. We must be administrators, instructors, comforters, and experts in hygiene. We need self-possession, a knowledge of character, insight, kindness, firmness and self-denial; and above all things, perseverance. . . .

"Our profession, unfortunately, is not what it was. The war has done its demoralizing work among us just as it has elsewhere. . . . The world of today seems entirely without decency or self-respect.

"The men of the 'center' [i.e., the white slaver milieu] . . . keep women free from vice. What do they do without us? They smoke, drink, dance, take snow, flirt, and even have affairs with each other."

At these last words the three others displayed the deepest indignation.

"Yes," said Cicero, "they're that depraved."[81]

When Londres traveled to the Balkans to report on terrorism he brought with him the same tongue-in-cheek style. The Macedonian irredentists who dynamited and murdered their way through Bulgaria and Yugoslavia were, in his reportage, *The Comitadjis,* transformed into jokesters and setups for the inevitable punch line. Only the book's conclusion, as Londres turned serious, brought the one-liners to an end. The style was personal but scarcely inimitable. The same ironic penchant for laughing off terror turned up in Jacques Deval's description of train travel in the Far East and in Jean Bommart's Chinese fish stories, the best of the interwar spy novels.[82] Even more, as a model of reporting it set a standard that blended well with other imperatives toward storytelling.

One of these was the thin veil dividing news and consumerism in modern mass media. It would be a mistake to miss in interwar culture, despite the highly charged events of the times, the degree to which mass marketing of news converted information and entertainment into one another. The great dailies of the day — *Paris-Soir, Le Petit Parisien, Le Journal, Le Matin* — all had their point of view (particularly the latter), but their principal purpose was to sell papers, and as many as possible. Anything that might capture public attention was given its day until its run was exhausted and a new story pushed it to the back pages or off the paper altogether. The consequence was that all news could be interchangeable, either sharing its "newsworthiness" with adjacent stories or its successor when its impact was spent. Mass culture had the effect of reducing information to "self-contained miscellaneous items to be consumed or disregarded" by the people who purchased them.[83] Whatever individuals made of what they read is probably forever beyond our comprehension, and not even a Karbec nor a Léo could likely provide a clear answer. Yet the style of presentation, both in layout and coverage, reflected the perception that news was a commodity, particularly if one packaged it properly. Thus simply to pick one of a boundless number of examples, the *Petit Parisien* edition from 23 September 1937 headlined front-page stories on (1) international negotiations at Geneva, (2) Japanese bombings of Canton and Nanking, (3) the 1938 national budget, (4) the arrest of burglars at châteaux and villas, (5) the C-2 affair (the aborted hijacking of a Spanish submarine laid up at a French port), (6) the middleweight boxing match between Marcel Thil and Fred Apostoli, (7) Charles Boyer, (8) Gabriele d'Annunzio being named to the Italian Academy, and (9) a colonial luncheon in Paris. In short there was something for everyone and which story captured the greatest attention is difficult to say, although the very next day's edition gave the biggest headline to Marcel Thil's defeat in the tenth round, while the disappearance of General Miller took over the two right-hand columns. One could point just as well to the juxtaposition of hard news, trumped up news, and advertisements for Lux soap or Carol Lombard's endorsement of Lucky Strike cigarettes on the advice of her voice professor. A five-column article in *Le Journal* on the Miller kidnapping, spread over page three, shared space with a small story headlined "The Gorilla of Villette has been Arrested," an apparent news item about a gorilla who had escaped from his cage because of a corn on his foot that was nothing more than an advertisement for Devil corn removal, available at all pharmacies.[84] This masking of commercialism as news was symptomatic of a market where anything that would sell was given its due and where the most salable side was often presented. Intrigue stories were fascinating and that was how they were played; their spot in the paper was generally one reserved for crime stories or anything else with sensationalizing potential. A run of the mass dailies from this period reveals extensive coverage of Munich or the Stavisky riots; but Hollywood or boxers or pilots — or anything else that could carry people beyond the ordinary — also commanded readers' attention.

In an opening passage from his *Chinese Fish* novel, Jean Bommart captured the feel of the mechanics of this press and its driving appetite for a daily diet of news it could sell. The narrator, René Bordier, is acting copy editor for the Parisian daily *La Nouvelle* and desperately in need of material for the front page. He is counting on the death of a major political figure but the individual in question ungallantly clings to life and with forty-five minutes to go Bordier refiles the obituary in a drawer where it has sat for ten years, periodically updated with a new photo. Feverishly Bordier runs through the agency dispatches. A sex maniac crime offers some filler, but even after cutting and pasting, *le père* Rousseau, the compositor, announces that they are still seventy-seven lines short. The situation for Bordier is bordering on the tragic. He puts in a rush call to Bouquet at the prefecture. Bouquet is the head of the press bureau and a former journalist. He has a prodigious imagination and can recite a sensational story in three lines or a hundred depending on need. Like a produce vendor, Bouquet rattles off the inventory of the day. There is a fire in the rue des Rosiers, but the structure aflame is only a rabbit hutch. Plaintively Bordier reminds him that he needs sixty lines of copy. "Seventy-seven," whispers Rousseau with an eye on the clock. Bouquet then dishes up the death of Rafiquet. "Who's that, a deputy? Oh, the painter Rafiquet. That might be of some use." Then Bouquet really delivers. The car of the marquise de Chaussac has collided with an auto driven by the comedienne Marguita. The marquise's Pekinese is dead. Marguita has a cut on her little finger. "Perfect, magnificent . . . thank you," breathes Bordier as he hangs up the phone. His problems are over. The accident will get a large headline, Rafiquet's death one slightly smaller: "The entire French painting world is in mourning." The man was lucky to have died on a day with a big hole to fill, mutters Bordier to himself; he has never heard of Rafiquet.[85]

The formula had been pioneered in the latter half of the nineteenth century. In the 1860s the *Petit Journal* achieved a daily edition of several hundred thousand issues out of serial novels, cheap murder thrills, low prices, and the exploitation of railroads to build a national distribution network. Prominent coverage of a murder of a family with six children in the Parisian suburbs in 1869 — the Troppmann affair — demonstrated the extraordinary effect sensationalized news could have upon sales. When the Troppmann affair began, the *Petit Journal* was printing roughly three hundred and fifty thousand copies a day; at its end the printing had climbed to six hundred thousand. Other newspapers, most notably the *Petit Parisien* and then *Le Journal* and *Le Matin,* expropriated the formula and developed it further, adding contests, manufactured news, sports, and more attractive layouts to capture a mass clientele. A constant fare of crime or murder stories, occasionally inflated into elaborate dramas as in the case of the Gouffé or Steinheil affairs, remained a major motor of sales. So effective were these *faits divers* in drawing readership that their reporting techniques carried over to coverage of the rest of the news, assuring still wider audiences and circulations. By the eve of the war the *Petit Parisien* alone was printing a million and a half copies a day and altogether the big four flooded the country with four and a half million issues daily.[86]

Not surprisingly the search for salable news extended to fast-breaking stories of intrigue. The demonstrated mass appeal of murders and manhunts destined exposés of the Russian secret police for the front pages, while the tendency of the mass press to report all of its news in the style that it reported street crimes guaranteed dramatic handling of any revelation where politics and the police blotter converged. The murder of General Seliverstov by the Russian émigré Padlevskii in 1890 captured headlines for several days, as did the sensational unmaskings nearly twenty years later of Okhrana agents provocateurs Landesen-Harting and Azef (although curiously the latter affair was not quite the sensation in the *Petit Parisien* or the *Petit Journal* that one might have expected, perhaps because of Franco-Russian relations or Russian subsidies under the table).[87] Immediately after shooting Seliverstov, Padlevskii had gone into hiding, and first the search for his whereabouts and then the revelation that he had been smuggled out of France with the help of a reporter gave the story a life of its own.[88] In 1909 *Le Matin* accompanied its coverage of Azef with the serialization of the memoirs of Michael Bakai, a former official of the Russian police who had quit the force and joined the revolutionaries. "He is going to tell us of the spectacular scenes that he witnessed, the conspiracies he saw fomented, the attacks provoked and organized by secret agents." The material was in fact pretty heady stuff, including a graphic description of an Okhrana torture chamber in Warsaw.[89]

This kind of treatment was expanded and elaborated after the war. Why is not certain, although both the history of the press and of espionage suggest some answers. Clearly one factor was the greater competitive environment for dailies in the interwar years. Particularly in the thirties mounting costs and the loss of readers to a regionally based press led Parisian newspapers to more aggressive marketing and the search for big stories. A more fickle public flitting from one paper to the next accentuated the need to create attractions and capture attention.[90] Another factor was simply technological advance in paper quality and reproduction techniques that permitted a more expansive use of photography in daily printings.[91] Photographs, splashed across the front pages or in ensembles at the back made newspapers more visually alluring. The power of pictures to captivate an audience implied that imagery was everything and that content was synonymous with a story's impressionistic or evocative side. In this regard one must wonder what impact motion pictures had upon reporting styles, obliging or encouraging the latter to charge up the atmospherics that went into articles.

Out of the new competitiveness and new techniques emerged a new press. The great success stories of the interwar years were not the old dailies who sought to adapt as best as they could but the splashy new tabloid *Paris-Soir* or the new illustrated magazines whose rise has been equated in significance with the earlier emergence of a penny press.[92] No one comprehended better than the managing team behind *Paris-Soir* the essentially apolitical desires of a mass readership that craved style over content and devoured any story as long as it was sufficiently interesting or short. What these editors particularly understood was that people bought newspapers less to be informed than to be entertained.

They did not fear big news; they lusted after it. They wanted to experience big events, but without too much effort or anxiety, and hence they preferred the eyewitness feel or the anecdotal, human-interest approach to too much concentration on hard information. They wanted blaring headlines to assure them that a story was important, lots of pictures, and a sense of excitement reined in with a reminder that nothing really mattered. Such conclusions may appear cynical, but there is no other way of explaining the phenomenal success of *Paris-Soir,* which gave its readers exactly these things.

Paris-Soir greeted stories like the Stavisky scandal as a gift from the gods, plastered them all over the front pages, and accompanied them with serials like Georges Simenon's insider tales of the crime milieu — "On the Edges of the Stavisky Affair" — for those who could always read more of the same. For those seeking comparable but different sensations the paper offered Jean Lasserre's "Port of Call Women" (which ran simultaneously with the Stavisky coverage). Foreign affairs always captured attention but same-size headlines trumpeted news about Saint Bernard dogs going to the Himalayas or the gangster Kid Tiger's identity change ("An unbelievable true adventure"). Other non-stories like the stream of anecdotes flowing from the Hitler-Mussolini Rome meeting in 1938 or the front-page article "Madame Scholtz-Klink the '100% Nazi' Rules Over 30,000,000 German Women and Has Just Founded Schools for Fiancés in Every District"[93] dished up the digestible side of the Nazis. Sports had a page of their own, except when they carried over to the front headlines. Layouts were eye-catching. At the end of each issue was a full page of photos, in random order and without hierarchy, like the rest of the news. All of this worked with exceptional results. *Paris-Soir* was the modern paper of its day, housed in a nine-story modern building. Where other papers' profits and readership fell in the thirties, *Paris-Soir*'s soared. Average printings of sixty thousand at the start of the thirties climbed to half a million in early 1932, a million in 1934, more than a million and a half in 1937 and nearly a million and three-quarters in 1939. Daily runs of two million or more were common after 1936.[94] No other paper could claim such a public.

Rivaling the success of *Paris-Soir* were the new photo magazines that exploded upon the market in the twenties and thirties. Designed to cultivate and exploit every mass taste through a jaunty, snapshot view of the world, weeklies like *Ciné Magazine* and *Ciné-Miroir* (for women), *Détective* (for crime fans), or *Vu, Lu,* the later *Vu et Lu,* and *Match* (for the all-purpose news fan) captured an ever-widening readership. Their entrepreneurs came from nearly every corner of the press world. Jean Prouvost, the flashy proprietor of *Paris-Soir,* carried his magical touch over to the hugely successful *Marie-Claire* that sustained an initial printing of half a million and doubled it by the eve of the war. Prouvost was also responsible for the new *Match* that first appeared in July 1938 and whose printings also rose to a million by 1939. Even Gaston Gallimard, who was the publisher for some of the most prestigious authors in France, invaded the market with magazines like the casual quasi-erotic *Voilà* (begun 1931) and *Détective* (begun 1928). Collaborating on each were the Kessel brothers who brought a good feel for the cultivation of mood and ambiance and no restraint whatever in exploiting the flamboyant, sensational side to a story. Joining them on *Détective* were Marcel Montarron, Paul Bringuier, and Louis Roubaud; contributing correspondents included Paul Morand, Albert Londres, and Pierre MacOrlan. *Détective* in particular was a merchandising triumph, making Gallimard a fortune and inspiring a number of imitations. Readers snapped up its sleazy descents into the underworld and its bombastic investigative exposés of crimes, scandals, and intrigue. Its tone was dramatic and often accusatory, but in *Détective* the story was everything and its success built on little more than the promise to titillate, fascinate, and provide a good read. Like Mâh le Sinistre of Robert-Dumas's *Leaden Idol, Détective* appealed to certain universal desires beyond politics or history. Because its editors understood how to package these with a contemporary veneer, they kept the journal afloat for more than a decade. There are no established figures for *Détective,* but printings probably averaged in the hundreds of thousands, especially in the early years with perhaps some dropoff toward the end of the thirties.[95]

Together *Paris-Soir* and *Détective* were powerful media for drawing out the storytelling potential to intrigue. Typically, the spy writer Allard contributed to both. Their significance, however, lay less in their power as a mechanism in place for exploiting possibilities than in their representation of a public desire for reading such tales. There was a side to interwar culture that was fascinated with big news but in ways that extended beyond concerns of the day and that fostered the creation of mass dailies and weeklies like *Paris-Soir, Voilà, Police Magazine,* and *Détective.* The hunger for entertainment, amusement, ambiance, or simply a good laugh competed with the portrayal of France in the grip of events and, judging by circulation figures, was often the winner.

What drove the storytelling capacity forward was the fabulous quality to the stories that broke, particularly in the thirties. The great revelations of the interwar years may have intruded context and events forever upon interwar consciousness. But they were also, quite simply, delicious tales that few imaginations could have invented on their own. Fascist spies, communist secret agents, traffickers and gunrunners, the Spanish civil war, and the incomparable madhouse of White Russian intrigues all but conspired to provide the French with a series of sensations that begged for the telling. Especially the White Russians.

The Kutepov kidnapping was a reporter's dream. First, there was the mystery of why he had disappeared—vanished!—from the streets of Paris on a late Sunday morning in January 1930. Then once it was clear that Kutepov had been snatched, there was *le guet-apens* or the trap and how it had been sprung. Rumors circulated of an extensive surveillance network encompassing nearly all of Kutepov's neighborhood. He had been watched from the shop opposite his building, from the laundry nearby, from the neighborhood café where a spy was permanently on station. There was the trip Kutepov had made to Berlin earlier in January when he had met with two Red Army officers. Had they warned Kutepov that he was in danger or was the meeting part of the setup? There were the circumstances of the snatch: two cars—a gray limousine and a red taxi—a fake policeman who had stationed himself on the rue Rousselet for a number of Sundays, and a mysterious blond woman in a beige coat who may have drawn Kutepov out alone on that fatal morning in January. An ex-officer and taxicab driver denounced Ludmilla Choban as *la dame au manteau beige*. Then he went mad and was confined in a mental home where he screamed to be rescued, believing the Red Army had taken him prisoner. Weeks later, however, there were still rumors of the Lady in the Beige Coat. Ordinarily a brigade of taxicab drivers watched over Kutepov. On the eve of the kidnapping the general had informed his guardian angel for the morrow, a man named Fortunato, that his services would not be required. A different decision might have saved his life, except for the fact that Fortunato overslept the following morning. The former White Russian lieutenant told reporters he was certain someone had tampered with his alarm clock.

After the *guet-apens* came the *piste* or the trail of the kidnappers once they had sped away from the intersection of rues Rousselet and Oudinot. Sightings of the "phantom auto" or gray cars and red taxis poured into police headquarters. At one point there were ninety-eight *pistes*. A police digging crew went to the woods of Meudon but unearthed only a mountain of dirt. A hotel keeper in the Loiret reported that on the day after the kidnapping a gray car covered with mud—indicating a hurried, long journey—had pulled up outside his inn. He said that the curtains were drawn in the car but that he could see three men sleeping in the back. On the front passenger seat was a big sack of meat that could have contained a human body. The driver of the car came in for a glass of rum. He was young, tired, had a two-days' growth of beard, and spoke with a Polish or Russian accent. About thirty seconds after the gray car pulled out a dirty red taxi had also passed by. On the ninth of February there was a report of an earlier sighting of the phantom auto in the region of Mons. On the eleventh it was reported that on the evening following the kidnapping a gray car covered with mud had been spotted in Brussels taking the Antwerp road. On the same day there was a report out of Hamburg; local police had signaled the presence of GPU agents coming from Paris. By the third week of the case there was the Normandy *piste* (based on more sightings) and the possibility that Kutepov or his corpse had been embarked on a Soviet freighter waiting at sea. Meanwhile in Paris there was the recourse to mediums to determine Kutepov's fate. The affair faded out of the newspapers toward the end of February with the best ending imaginable—the only thing certain was that on the morning of 26 January 1930, three men had forced Kutepov into a gray car.

The 1932 murder of the president of France by Paul Gorgulov, a bigamist, rapist, prospective moon traveler, and head of a "Green" Russian Fascist party whose membership numbered only himself, was no less fantastic a story; although the disappearance of General Miller five years later was the best White Russian extravaganza of them all. So luxuriant was this general's story in plot turns and characters that one might almost suspect *Paris-Soir* of commissioning the crime to step up its sales. Even the ideological ax grinder *Le Matin* found the affair and its spinoffs an incredible circus: "Some Russians are plaintiffs! Some Russians are victims! Some Russians are arrested! Some Russians have fled!"[96] The affair had everything: intrigue, mystery, melancholy, sweep, and the inimitable touch of White Russian farce.

There were once again the circumstances of the kidnapping—*la journée du drame*—compounded this time by Kusonskii's unbelievable gaffe and then Skoblin's disappearance from the grasp of his interrogators. There was Plevitzkaïa's alibi for herself and her husband, the passage of time at Caroline's dress shop, which the press studied meticulously to show with elaborate descriptions and charts the holes in the story. There was the mysterious embassy van that had sped from Paris to Le Havre on the day of the kidnapping and then the abrupt departure of the *Maria Ulianova* that seemed to contravene all customs of shipping. Again there was elaborate dissection of the time of the journey, the speed of the van, the size of the crate loaded aboard, and the reasons for the *Maria Ulianova*'s unscheduled sailing. There were the searches of premises, the confiscation of papers, and then the revelations of an émigré international possessing "defense centers," foreign agents, spy networks, and an "inner line" run by a renegade general. There were Fedosenko's accusations. There was Colonel Chimerin the taxi driver whose body was fished out of the Seine in February 1938 ("a 'Russian drama' with all that is vague, troubling, elusive entailed in that term").[97] The police wrote him off as a *déséquilibré* and a suicide, but in letters left behind he claimed to have penetrated to the heart of the affair and to be pursued by invisible enemies. There was Skoblin the double and perhaps triple agent. There were the ubiquitous taxicab generals. Above all there was La Plevitzkaïa.

Her life was a fable, an adventure, the summation of an era. She had been born a peasant girl in the province of Koursk. She had entered a cloister, had begun her novitiate, had run away with the circus, and then with a traveling musical troupe. She had sung in the streets and in the restaurants of Russia. She had met a dancer named Plevitzkii and had married him, hence La Plevitzkaïa. She had sung at the Nizhni Novgorod fair, in the grand concert halls, in St. Petersburg before the czar. She had sung at the front in the war for the Imperial army. She had sung in the revolution for soldiers at the Red Army front, but had then passed into White Russian hands. She had met Skoblin in one of their camps, had fallen in love, and divorced now twice over, had married him. When the White cause was lost she had followed the emigration, continuing her career all over the world. In Bulgaria, Turkey, throughout Europe and America she had sung her haunting melodies. Her home was in Paris, where alongside her husband she had become a fixture of White émigré circles.[98]

When Skoblin vanished she quickly moved to center stage in the case. She was rumored to have attended all her husband's meetings, to have received all her mail in code, and to have run "her agents" throughout France and abroad. In prison she pleaded for her "green bible," fostering suspicions that this held the key to a secret and underhanded correspondence. Her trial in December 1938 was one of the great spectacles of the decade. Taxis of the Don streamed into the courtroom, parading their titles and medals, throwing their squabbles into the public arena, accusing La Plevitzkaïa (and Skoblin) of everything under the sun. Shatilov, who had served as chief of staff under Wrangel and had then driven a cab, said Plevitzkaïa was the éminence grise of her husband, she shot back that he was a detestable man, and he replied that she was a ham. Besedovskii recounted a distant evening of poker at the Soviet embassy with the GPU head of station, recalling how the latter had confided that he had an agent among Kutepov's entourage: a general married to a singer. A taxicab driver with the unfortunate name of Trotsky testified that the Soviets had murdered Miller in a villa on the boulevard de Montmorency and had then packed his corpse into a crate. This caused a considerable stir until it was remarked that Trotsky had been trepanned and that there were earlier contradictory and incoherent depositions from the man. A Madame Gody, who had known Colonel Chimerin and whose own lover was another Russian cabbie who had died under "mysterious" circumstances, came forward with the promise of cracking the case open; but her testimony was a dud and so exasperated the presiding judge that he waved the poor woman away, commenting that there had been much ado about nothing and that the court's time had been wasted. That may have been so, but few others, whether they believed Gody or not, would have come to this judgment. Just one year earlier, when the French correspondent Titaÿna had asked a German official for the lowdown on Hitler's relationship with Leni Riefenstahl, the indignant authority had responded, "How can you even suspect such a thing? Obviously you must come from Paris with ideas like that!"[99] But in 1938 even stick-in-the-mud Germans were hanging on every word of the trial. "The Plevitzkaïa Case . . . ," an embassy official reported back to the Auswärtiges Amt in Berlin, "is so gripping that it can be ranked among the great political show trials and is probably destined for movies, the stage, or novels."[100]

The White Russian affairs were the cream of the decade, but nearly every case that broke in the thirties frothed with the materials for storytelling. Guides, conspiracies, bunglers, strutters, cheap theatrics, the Mata-Hari trope of the mysterious, seductive, or exotic female — Plevitzkaïa, the woman in the beige coat, the blond courier of the Marseilles assassinations, *"la belle* Mingua" of the C-2 affair, Paul Allard's year of the beautiful spies — reappeared with almost premeditated consistency. Stimuli for promotions were all but inexhaustible. The milieu provided stories that amused or boggled the imagination and hence contributed to the growth in a spy writing market. Its richness was itself an imperative toward storytelling because the buffoonery, the circuses, or the sheer dazzling quality of these cases prompted no less an abandon in their narration. Like the microbe affair, the great sensationalist cases of the thirties soared past deep ideological issues or sinister, deadly forces threatening to France. They brimmed with humor, chicanery, extravagance, mystery, curiosity, or outright fascination that made them the showstoppers they became in the press. Moreover from all sides came collusion in storytelling. The mass dailies or weeklies hungered for stories that would sell. The public clamored for the fluff, cheap thrills, and entertainment on which a *Paris-Soir* or a *Détective* thrived. Spy stories that played to the crowd implied a sizable readership hooked on the politics and news of the present so long as these were rendered consumable. In the growing market for spy novels, spy memoirs, or spy sensations to read about one discerns an insatiable appetite for sensation: pure, present-minded, sensation itself. Perhaps it represented a certain wishing away of the threats or dangers by making them digestible, dehorned so to speak. Yet just as likely it reflected active, aggressive urges to play with and enjoy contemporary events until all pleasure was squeezed out and consumed and the story was discarded to make room for a successor.

In between press lords and public were reporters with few scruples about bending the rules. In his memoirs Marcel Montarron tells the story of Georges London, a celebrated court reporter, covering a parricide trial in the provinces. Faced with a first-edition deadline that fell before the opening of the session, and aware that it was the custom of the town to bring the accused on foot from the prison to the courthouse, London phoned in an account of what he was sure would take place: an enraged crowd gathering on the sidewalks and shouting vengeful threats at the defendant. Then he settled back to enjoy his lunch. At one o'clock, glancing through the restaurant window, he saw the gendarmes approaching with their prisoner. Alone. Through deserted streets. Surrounded by absolute silence. "Not even the shadow of a gawker." Taking matters into his own hands, London ran to the door, threw it open, and bawled at the top of his voice: "Kill him." Then satisfied that his professional integrity was intact, he returned to his meal, "his soul at peace with itself."[101] Stories, it appears, were whatever reporters decided to make of them.

Even more, reporters used the *enquête* or the *grand reportage* series as it emerged and developed in these years as a vehicle for their own self-aggrandizing ambitions. Most *reportages* paraded as exposés or fabulous adventures but in essence they were created stories designed to establish for their authors a certain standing and independence and perhaps financial success in the press world. For Albert Londres the *grand reportage* was an opportunity for reforms, but also a compulsive search for raw, unclaimed territory that would be a sensation (why else go to Cayenne or the white slave bordellos of Argentina?) and an object of amusement as well as concern. For Joseph Kessel the *grand reportage* was a title to appropriate and a means to fund adventures. The result, paralleling earlier trends in the cloning of crime stories, was a reporting style that spread throughout the profession and that encouraged the conversion of great contemporary issues or hard pressing news into yet more vehicles for personal triumphs and trumped-up storytelling.

Just to take one example one might consider Edmond Demaitre's series, "Je suis un sans-patrie" (I am a man without a country), that ran in the *Petit Parisien* at the end of 1938.[102] To get his story about the fate of stateless people in the inhospitable climate of the thirties, Demaitre went to ground as a Czech refugee, a veteran of the International Brigades without papers and afraid to return home. He traveled to Nansen headquarters in Geneva. He holed up in a Swiss refugee flophouse where he was told that he was staring at a jail cell at the end of the line. He crossed clandestinely into France. He crossed back into Switzerland. He crossed once again back into France, this time stopped by border guards who chucked him back and forth across the frontier. In Paris he met with a trafficker who explained the range of prices of passports, visas, and identity cards, and the pressures that drove up their costs. Then he wrote up his account, getting his facts right yet scarcely scratching the surface of his subject. Nor does it appear that he ever intended to. Altogether Demaitre spent approximately three days as a refugee. His trips back and forth across the Franco-Swiss border were nonsensical. Every cliché in the trade — forced situations, reconstructed conversations, guides or interlocutors who carried forward the action, conjured ambiance ("with the merchants of sleep"; "the dregs of the milieu"; "the mysteries of the nomad world of the *heimatlos*"), and one-liners — were crammed into the series. In the final article there was an analysis of the situation and a call for a remedy (in this case New Guinea as a Jewish homeland), but no one who has read through the interwar press will be deceived by this obligatory lip-service to serious thinking. The refugee crisis of the late 1930s was real and pressing; for Demaitre it was merely a story. What he produced was an *enquête* with everything this had come to mean by 1938: a packaged, readable vignette of the "I was there" genre that filled the gap between yesterday's exposé and tomorrow's adventure. When more sensational news broke it is hardly surprising that it, too, could be swept up in a style of storytelling.

The lighter, more playful touch to these years was, then, a product of a number of things. There was a market for spy stories that looked to espionage for more than condemnation or self-flagellation and there was also a lively humor to the age that incorporated its way into reporting styles. There were the burlesque or fabulous qualities to affairs that all but forced an accommodating style and there was the confluence of entrepreneurship and demand in a mass media that saw in all news little more than a commodity to sell. To these may be added a conscious romanticizing or pursuit of ambiance whose full dimensions carry over to the following chapter. Perhaps most important was a certain mood in the period that despite its ability to lash out at enemies or to sound alarms was curiously at ease with itself and thoroughly capable of absorbing the present into an object of contemplation and amusement. Writing about intrigue between the wars could, in the end, be anything its authors chose it to be. Some preferred conspiracy, hatred, and fear. More often than not, however, the French chose to write up a good story and to cash in on the pleasures that came with that choice.

So we return to the question of what to make of this literature. Certainly lurking behind the great wealth of spy stories that followed the war were the insecurities and divisions of the interwar period. There was no short supply of the harder side to spy writing. Conspiracy, xenophobia, hate-mongering, vulnerability, ideological divisiveness, antirepublicanism, and anxiety were all present in the literature on espionage between the wars. Both the abundance and the kind of spy tales that surfaced — from the treatment of international communism, refugee politics, the Spanish civil war, or the Moscow purge trials to the Brown Net portraits and future-war literature — make it easy to understand why once war had broken out the French gave themselves over to fifth-column mania.

To a degree the spy became in an era of international tensions the repository for fears that before 1914 had resided elsewhere. Fears over criminality or the social and racial health of the nation were, so to speak, internationalized after the war in the figure of the spy. Thus the merger of criminals and secret agents in the writings of Bardanne and Yrondy (far exceeding the real overlap of milieus) or the projection of social threats onto Bolshevik agents and the conflation of refugee dangers with refugee spies. More broadly, spy literature thrived in an age where international insecurities predominated. Fascination with spies, whatever its form, was prompted by the geopolitical realities of the times. Even Marthe Richard or *Détective* exploited those realities to sell their stories. The spy novel itself represented a certain internationalization of the older *roman noir* tradition. Not surprisingly a greater flow of spy stories gushed forth in the thirties when international events had pushed to the forefront of national attention.

Yet it was also a complex, even, at times, sophisticated literature that represented more than alarmism or spy mania. Part of that complexity was simply the diffuseness to postwar spy writing, for instance, the matter-of-factness in the later "memoirs" of Richard, where spies were the props for setting a scene. One encountered spies everywhere, in all sizes and colors, not as the coordinated elements of a single conspiracy but as the ubiquitous products of international politics in an age of perpetual unsettlement and flux. Much like Major Robinson in Kessel's *Siberian Nights,* the spy became an interwar fixture. No contemporary account was complete without at least one or two secret agents. Common, anticipated, multiform as well as multitudinous, the interwar spy faded into the background noise of the era, a far cry from the Stieber myth that had emerged half a century earlier. Paradoxically routine omnipresence made the spy a less menacing presence and opened avenues for more wide-ranging treatment. Diffuseness of tone or of approach followed accordingly.

The result was that spies in the literature became many things. They were a vehicle for reflecting and writing about contemporary times. They were contemporary adventurers who like pilots satisfied certain universal desires in a century where traditional sources of heroism seemed blocked. They were a source of unending war stories for a nation that consciously and willingly refused to let the war go. And they were a source of ceaseless entertainment in an age that loved a good story and possessed the mechanisms and milieus to produce one. In each respect they were representations of an interwar culture that encompassed a wide range of sentiments and that was given to more than expressions of anxiety, bitterness, or loss of control.

Thus the complexity of spy writing reflected a complexity of moods and that is the lesson this literature leaves with us. Crisis, decline, vulnerability, or whatever words we customarily apply to these years scarcely fit a large body of tales that touched closely on security issues and yet flaunted the inclination to laugh them away. Beneath the tumult and mass demonstrations interwar France displayed a curious ability to stand back and write about the world in detached, playful ways all the while exuding a sense of living with great events in a historical epoch. It would of course be preposterous to suggest that these were happy-go-lucky times but no more so than to suggest that this was a period when the French wrung their hands or each other's throats and lost all sense of humor and control. The truth it seems lay somewhere in between, a commonsensical notion that nevertheless has infrequently seen its day.[103] We cannot escape the fact that in the supposedly darkest days of the thirties spies and intriguers were absorbed easily into the stuff of storytelling. It leaves the impression of a people who could keep on an even keel and who sensed they would somehow muddle through.

Figure 4. *The Croisière jaune leaving Herat.* (L'Illustration/Courtesy Agence Sygma)

CHAPTER FOUR

Shanghai

Inevitably milieu and stories force one to Shanghai. For mystery alone there were Trieste, Tangier, and Istanbul. But nowhere else did traffickers, adventurers, intriguers, and spies come together quite as they did in interwar Shanghai. No other city collected the epithets — "Babylon, Alexandria, Nineveh must have been like Shanghai"; "the greatest prostitution market in the world . . . *le Wall Street de la traite*"; "if Lenin saw Shanghai then he is excusable" — that were flung upon Shanghai. No city deserved them more.[1]

There were in fact several Shanghais. There was the Shanghai of the Chinese, a city with roots extending back as far as five thousand years and already an important trading center by the twelfth century.[2] There was the Shanghai of the Anglo-Americans — the international settlement — a prize of the opium wars and the business center along whose Bund stretched the great trading houses that made Shanghai the commercial capital of the East. And there was the Shanghai of the French — something of a misnomer because the French were a European minority in their own concession — that was the preferred place of residence for the rich but also the lair of the infamous Green Gang who ran the Shanghai underworld between the wars.

Together the three made Shanghai unlike any other city in China. The city was fabulously cosmopolitan. Its population was overwhelmingly Chinese, including many who lived within the two European settlements, but there were also thousands of Westerners — British, Americans, Portuguese, French, Germans, Italians, Spanish, Danes, Swiss,

Belgians, Austrians, Swedes, Czechs, Greeks — whose numbers swelled further as Russian émigrés poured in during the twenties and thirties. From other parts of Asia came Koreans, Indians (especially Sikhs imported as policemen), and Japanese, who, by 1915, had surpassed the British as the largest foreign contingent in the town. In 1910 there were more than a million people in the Shanghai metropolitan area, in 1920 nearly as many as two and a half million. By the mid-1930s more than three million souls crowded into the metropolis, making Shanghai the fifth largest city in the world. Of these over one million, including forty thousand foreigners, crammed into the international settlement, nearly another half million, including sixteen thousand foreigners, into the French concession.[3]

Like other colonialists, the foreigners brought with them their clubs, their mores, their institutions, and their womenfolk, all of which turned portions of Shanghai into a little Britain, a little France, or a little Japan. But these foreigners also brought an extraordinary lust for power and money that, combined with Shanghai's proximity to the mouth of the Yangtze and the security that came with sovereign European settlements, turned Shanghai into an economic dynamo. Something clicked here between Chinese and foreigners — "a human cocktail," as Marc Chadourne was later to describe it[4] — that generated an unbounded scramble for profit in which all nationalities participated. The result was China's most modern city and, in this sense, its most Western as well. First came the great merchant houses: Jardine Matheson, Butterfield and Swire, Russell and Co., and the trading empire of the Sassoons. Then followed the banks whose presence underscored Shanghai's internationalism and its sheer materialist rapacity. The Hongkong and Shanghai Banking Corporation arrived in 1865, the Deutsch-Asiatische Bank in 1889, the Japanese Yokohama Species Bank in 1892, the Russo-Chinese Bank in 1895, the Banque de l'Indochine in 1899, and the International Banking Corporation (First National Bank of New York City) in 1902. As the century wore on factories sprang up, particularly in textiles, making Shanghai a manufacturing hub of the Orient. In all these enterprises — trade, banking, industry — Chinese were active. Chinese invested in European commercial ventures, they built cotton mills, flour mills, machine shops; even compradors could be powerful independent businessmen carving out their own merchant kingdoms. Where older Chinese balked, a new generation caught Shanghai fever and plunged headfirst into the open entrepreneurial waters.[5]

By the interwar years Shanghai was an international metropolis in every meaning of the word. Visitors were absorbed by the power, the activity, and the raw energy that struck them from the first moments of arrival. They saw in Shanghai another New York—"the New York of the Pacific," "the New York of the Far East," "Billion Dollar Row"[6]— because only the New York analogy seemed to capture the unbridled vitality and modernity of this otherwise undefinable concoction. Shanghai itself took pride in this identity. It boasted of its skyscrapers and of possessing the longest bar in the world. There were modern department stores, fifty thousand telephones, sixteen thousand automobiles, well-paved streets (in the settlements), a splendid water filtration system, and a state-of-the-art gas company with the most modern facility anywhere.[7] The same positive note, if more sedately sounded, could be found in the annual reports of the French consul general who all but ruled over the French concession in Shanghai. The concession shared in "a remarkable state of prosperity." It was more and more the residential quarter for the well-off of Shanghai. Rich Chinese in search of security built their opulent villas in the French quarter. The concession was "a very modern city." There were schools, hospitals, and a volunteer fire department equipped with the most modern fire trucks available. The French electricity, water, and tramway company of Shanghai was "one of the most beautiful French operations in the Far East."[8]

But there was also the other Shanghai, the Shanghai of fifty-seven hundred bodies that were left in the streets or vacant lots every year, or the Shanghai notorious for the magnetic effect it exerted upon the low-life of the world. Again there was an almost chemical response between the city and its inhabitants, a catalytic reaction that tended to stimulate the demonic or simply the seamy side to human character. "Shanghai is not a town at all," barks one of the characters in Vicki Baum's novel *Shanghai '37*. "Shanghai is a poison. Man eaters live here, naked cannibalism rules here. This town is the world's refuse heap. Whoever comes here, white or Chinese, has cracked up somewhere before and Shanghai does the rest." That destiny seems to have been Shanghai's from its first days as a European settlement. Mid-nineteenth-century sweeps of hotel rooms flushed out adventurers and outlaws, men who "maintained a prudent silence about their past" and who found a refuge or home among the pirate gangs of Ningpo. By the twentieth century adventure, crime, or any illicit traffic seems to have been synonymous with the very mention of the city.[9]

Paul Crawley was representative of the sort of flotsam that washed up in Shanghai in the twenties and thirties and that gave it its reputation for wickedness and degeneracy: "Shanghai the modern Babylon"; "city saturated in riches and crimes, in vanities and vices, in miseries and poisons"; Shanghai "the city of all luxuries, of all horrors, of all surrenders."[10] Crawley was an American citizen who spoke Japanese, Russian, and Mandarin. In 1922 he was in Shanghai, involved with a man named Goldenberg in a scheme to pirate the film rights to a movie, *Way Down East,* which the two had stolen and copied. They sold their print to a Japanese named Takamura for forty or fifty thousand dollars. Goldenberg cashed the check and the next day his body was discovered — by Crawley — in his home above the Victoria Cinema. Both the money and a diamond ring of unusual cut that Goldenberg always wore were missing.

Crawley skipped town and next surfaced in Harbin. There he met his future wife, a Russian woman who responded to his advertisement for a lady business assistant (few women who came near Crawley were ever to escape his grasp). At the time they met Crawley was rolling in money and wore a flashy diamond ring. He was also running a gambling den, trafficking in guns and narcotics, and managing a film agency of sorts. Among his associates or acquaintances was another Russian named Rybakov who had been born in Petrograd and had attained the rank of captain in the Imperial Russian air corps. In Harbin Rybakov managed the Chinese Eastern Railway Club and then an establishment called the Hotel Modern. In 1925 Rybakov had moved on to Shanghai where he managed the Palais de Danse on Bubbling Well Road.

By the mid-to-late twenties Crawley was back in Shanghai where he and Rybakov renewed their acquaintance and took up with a third person named Wilder. In 1931 the three were engaged in a confidence scheme to peddle "liquid fire" to Chinese generals in the north. Meanwhile Crawley continued to run guns and drugs between Dairen, Soochow, Shanghai, and Canton. In Shanghai he had an array of verminous contacts and accomplices: a Mr. Pan listed by police as a notorious dealer in arms; a man named Bisbierg who was also suspected of running guns; a Mr. (or Mrs.) Gaida who trafficked in heroin; and a Chinese named Ah Lee who, with Crawley, ran the Velvet Sweet Shop in Szechuen Road, a front operation for exporting opium into the United States. Crawley himself appears to have fallen prey to opium, writing one message to his wife on the back of a religious print that the Shanghai police intercepted and described as "the vaporing of one mentally afflicted." By the beginning of the thirties Crawley was smuggling firearms hidden in slot machines into Shanghai and shipping back opium to the United States through a contact aboard an American ship. He packed a pistol wherever he went and he conducted his personal life with all the restraint of a cocker spaniel. He beat his wife, allegedly sexually abused his eleven-year-old daughter, and chased after his servants, who must have quit his employment in droves. In late 1931 the police reported that he had dismissed his housekeeper because she interfered with his attempts to seduce his seventeen-year-old secretary. At roughly the same time it was noted that his chauffeur was in a panic over Mrs. Crawley's threats to tell her husband all about their "relations" if he (the chauffeur) did not buy her a new dress. The chauffeur was terrified that Crawley would bite him, and maybe even kill him. Such was the petty and slimy world of Paul Crawley, whose file reads like a train station detective novel and whom the American authorities picked up on drug charges in early 1932.[11]

The Crawleys of Shanghai were legion between the wars, the city a sink of covers and hangouts. The Buisson brothers worked out of the Fantasio, a dance hall where opium traffickers congregated. The two were small-time crooks on the lam who sailed from Genoa to Shanghai in 1934, set themselves up in the arms trade, and purchased an airplane for drops to their customers. After several years they had the police on their backs and returned to Europe. Later, in the 1940s, Emile Buisson, better known as Mimile, would enjoy a stretch as French public enemy number one. The Italia Hotel in the international settlement was the cover for a Corsican arms merchant who trafficked as well in cocaine and women. The Tsounias gang hung out at the Astoria Café on Broadway and ran their illicit operations behind Boo Kee and Co. on the Bund. Police suspected them of smuggling heroin and morphine into China in cases of cream of rice and cream of barley. The groceries were shipped on Messageries Maritimes liners (a contact aboard one ship was a Russian dining room steward). The Shanghai municipal police (SMP) file on Tsounias revealed connections to the Eliopoulos brothers and to Emmanuel Y., another Greek trafficker in arms and narcotics who was the subject of correspondence between U.S. drug agents and the Sûreté. His cover was an import-export firm on Jinkee Road in Shanghai.[12]

Trafficking was the lifeblood of the city. It always had been. The august houses of Jardine Matheson, Russell, and Dent had all made fortunes importing opium into China in the nineteenth century. Only when speculation by the Sassoons drove down opium profits did Jardine branch out into more respectable enterprises.[13] Where they left off others wormed in. After the war traffickers flocked to the city, first because the China of warlords and then of war made the town a mecca for gunrunners, second because the trade in narcotics was enormous and because efforts to stamp it out simply drove it underground, and third because Shanghai was Shanghai, a wide-open city that served as a last haven for the wasted of the world.

To these can be added a fourth explanation, the fact that Shanghai was in the grip of a vast criminal gang that had infiltrated the political life of the city and had the French police on the take. The most famous man in interwar Shanghai was neither Chiang Kai-shek nor T. V. Soong but a crime lord named Tu Yueh-sheng.[14] Born in 1887 into the kind of poverty that was endemic in China, he had made a long ascent through the Chinese criminal underworld until he and his associates commanded the Green Gang and ruled over perhaps as many as one hundred thousand gangsters. The gang and its subsidiaries ran protection schemes, brothels, gambling dens, and opium shops. It had its hand in kidnappings and armed robberies, and by 1925 it controlled the city's opium trade. Its reach was so great that inevitably it extended to the foreign police forces. In the 1910s and 1920s the chief of the SMP's detective squad was a mobster. Worse still were conditions in the French concession where Consul General Wilden had to acknowledge the shadows that darkened the sweet glow of French accomplishments in the Orient. In 1922 the consul general dismissed the personnel of an entire police post on the payroll of the gang (the sergeant of the post returned to France six hundred thousand francs to the better and set himself up as a major industrialist). In 1924 Wilden dismissed the chief of the Sûreté on similar charges and in the following year he was obliged still again to dismiss the man's successor.[15]

From at least the end of the war, however, the French pursued a modus vivendi with the gangsters, aware that the latter, if indulged — and coopted — could enforce a measure of order on the masses. The key figure in this arrangement was initially Huang Chin-jung, a Chinese detective with the French concession police and a man with close ties to the mob; later the connection was Tu, who began his ascent as Huang's protégé and then edged Huang off to the sidelines. In 1925 the authorities and Tu completed an official agreement that provided de facto recognition of Green Gang activities in exchange for regular payoffs. In 1927 the French extended the agreement as the Green Gang provided additional security forces during the Nationalist march north and the Communist strikes in the city. At the same time Tu struck his own bargain with Chiang, supplying Green Gang hoods to strong-arm the

Reds. Over the next five years the Green Gang all but ran the French concession, tightening their hold through labor racketeering. Eventually the French were forced to strike back, reducing but not eradicating Tu Yueh-sheng's position in the settlement. He remained an extraordinarily powerful man but even more an established figure. In 1935 *Who's Who in Shanghai* identified Tu as "the most influential Chinese resident of the French concession." He was president of two banks, founder and chairman of the board of the Cheng Shih Middle School, president of the Shanghai Emergency Hospital, a director of the Commercial Bank of China, a director of Great China University, a member of the supervising committee of the General Chamber of Commerce, and a member of the Conseil municipal.[16] As such he set the tone for the rest of the city. Tu Yueh-sheng's respectability and the Green Gang's penetration of the power structure virtually guaranteed Shanghai's place as an international harbor of vice.

The binge and scandal of the city took in the White Russians; interwar Shanghai would have been unimaginable without them. Few travelers to Shanghai failed to remark on their presence. To do so would be to visit Paris and miss the Eiffel Tower or to tour Hollywood and ignore the studios. Twenty-five thousand of these refugees descended on the city by the late thirties.[17] They were renowned as the best bodyguards in Shanghai, a profession with a future in a town where kidnapping was a habit. Former Russian officers dressed up as British colonels with revolvers at the ready were said to give "much face" to their masters.[18] Through the streets rolled automobiles with armed Russians on the running boards. Large numbers of the émigrés crowded into the French concession, where businesses were fewer and rents consequently lower.[19] Their cramped quarters reflected their financial condition, which in most cases bordered on the desperate. For many Shanghai was what it was for any immigrant—a place without a past and a chance to start anew. Nadezha Nikiforov's was a typical story. Born in Irkutsk in 1913, she left Russia for China with her parents in 1920, going first to Harbin—until 1933—and then to Dairen. In 1934 they arrived in Shanghai. Her father established himself as a superintendent of the Russian White Flower Society's Home for Tuberculosis and was able to house the family on the premises. Nadezha found work at a local library and then as a cashier at D.D.'s Café-Restaurant in the avenue Joffre. At some point she met a Dutch employee of the Netherlands Trading Society at Medan who was living in Shanghai in the mid-1930s. On 23 July 1937 she sailed on the SS *Potsdam* to Sumatra to rejoin and marry him.[20]

For many others, however, Shanghai was the last, wretched stop on the line. Shipwrecked and destitute, they drifted into every dirty business the city had to offer. In Shanghai that meant a plenitude of possibilities — gunrunning, drug trafficking, petty crime, touting, espionage — but most of all it meant prostitution. More renowned than the bodyguards were the White Russian women who worked the streets and brothels and slept with men of color. Their fall indelibly stamped itself upon the image of the city, making it a symbol of ill repute and a stimulus for sensation. Around *les femmes russes de Shanghaï* grew up a certain literature — pornographic, cheaply sentimental, and laden with the specter of white decline in the Orient. Racism and race fear were deeply embedded in thoughts about the city, the mood that O.-P. Gilbert expressed when he wrote that Shanghai coolies were as "innumerable as flies on a cake" and that through city streets the "Chinese crowd flowed like pus," or when he wrote that "the Europeans live with the mentality of 'packed bags' . . . that mentality of the defeat of the white man."[21] What White Russian women offered was a palpable image that tied these fears to the damage of the war and to realignments in power, although the very choice of the image meant that it was bound to entangle with other moods that the city could evoke. Henry Champly's *Road to Shanghai: White Slave Traffic in Asia,* which may have run through as many as thirty-eight editions, showed how seamy tales and steamy prose, the degradation of Russian women, and intimations of Japanese conspiracies invariably brought together race fear with global speculation and an ambiance that was unmistakably Shanghai's between the wars.[22]

The mystique of writing about White Russians derived in no little part from their immersion in the intrigues of the city. White Russians conspired in Shanghai, built revanchist organizations there, recruited among the Shanghai Russian population for wild schemes of collaboration with Japanese liberators, and funneled intelligence back to the rat nests in Paris.[23] For many, intrigue was built into personal experience, a consequence of being caught up in the sweep of war and revolution. By the force of history these men and women had been turned into adventurers, the adventures themselves locked into the power politics of the age. Born in St. Petersburg in 1895, C. I. Znamenskii had studied mathematics and physics at the university and metallurgy at the Polytechnic Institute, a beginning with all the earmarks of normalcy, except that Znamenskii lived in abnormal times. In 1915 he entered the military and was sent to a school for officers in Irkutsk. Graduated in 1916, he served with the army until April 1917, departed for Harbin, but returned to Siberia in 1918. When the civil war came to Siberia he sided with the Whites and was assigned to military intelligence in Omsk. From 1919 to 1920 he served with Semenov's army at Chita and then with the White forces in Vladivostok, where again his assignment was military intelligence and counterespionage. By 1922 the former student and would-be-engineer was a hardened campaigner and a seasoned spy. As the Whites were forced out of the maritime province Znamenskii emigrated to Harbin and took up a new life as a mathematics teacher. But espionage was now either in the blood or an additional means for the hard-up to scrape by, and Znamenskii, so he claimed, remained "connected with various organs of White Russian military intelligence." In 1934 he emigrated again, along with his wife and three children, this time to Shanghai. There he found work as a drawing teacher in the Ste Jeanne d'Arc College on the Route Doumer, but in 1937 he was filing an application with the Shanghai municipal police for employment in their political section.[24]

Nikolai Vladimirovich Dolzhikov was another of these victims of circumstance who fell just as precipitously into the spy world. A mining engineer, he fled the Soviet Union in 1924, heading first to Manchuria and then to China. If he was looking for security, comfort, or fortune his life was to be a stream of disappointments. There is no indication that the man was an adventurer, yet world politics and choice sent him on a wild ride of adventures that eventually landed him among the intriguers. For two years after leaving Russia he fought with the Russian refugee forces in the warlord army of Marshal Chang Tsung-chang. Chang was the military scourge of Shantung. He was nearly seven feet tall and said to possess "the physique of an elephant, the brain of a pig, and the temperament of a tiger." His Russian cavalry wore dark green uniforms and yellow leather boots and were armed with lances, Mauser pistols, and Chinese beheading swords. Joseph Stilwell called them "the toughest eggs I ever laid eyes on."[25] Dolzhikov served as artillery officer with the crew of one of the marshal's four armored trains. Later he moved on to work in the Japanese coal mines at Fushun, and then he came to Shanghai in 1931. He opened the German Trading Company on the avenue Joffre but the business went bust within the year. That was probably the last permanent employment he enjoyed in the thirties. For the next six years he found casual work, mostly as a mechanic.

When war broke out between China and Japan, Dolzhikov once again took a stab at adventure. Running into a Chinese officer he had known in Shantung, Dolzhikov accepted an offer to join the man's unit as an artillery instructor. His first missions, however, were in intelligence work and after completing these he was told to report to a man known only as Colonel Charlie. The two met in a hotel room on the avenue Joffre where Colonel Charlie introduced Dolzhikov to a Russian named Pertsovskii who would give Dolzhikov his future assignments. His first job for Pertsovskii was a sabotage mission against a Japanese airfield hangar. One man died in this attack (an unknown Russian) and three men including Dolzhikov were wounded. After Dolzhikov recovered, Pertsovskii sent him on another intelligence assignment of a reconnoitering nature and then ordered him once again to lead a team of saboteurs in civilian dress to destroy Japanese pontoons near the Point Island. This time Dolzhikov refused and set up a meeting of his own with a Russian named Soivshkin, another old Shantung campaigner and currently a Japanese agent. From Dolzhikov's later testimony it would appear that he intended simply to discuss options at this meeting. But Soivshkin and another Russian whisked him off in a car to the Japanese consulate, where Dolzhikov was arrested. Two days later he was taken to a safe house on the Woosung Road where he was interrogated by a sergeant in Japanese intelligence and tortured with bamboo sticks, burning cigarettes, and, worst of all, water poured copiously down his nostrils. The Japanese insisted he work for them as a double agent, Dolzhikov refused, but after more water treatment he was forced to relent. Once set free he met with Pertsovskii several times and then, at last, went to the police and appealed for protection. The SMP — perhaps because an earlier French police report contained allegations that Dolzhikov had in fact taken the initiative in betraying information to the Japanese — said they could do nothing for him. This is where the Dolzhikov story leaves off, and one can only guess at what became of the man — alone, defenseless, up to his neck in danger, and probably wondering why he ever left Russia.[26]

Other Russians like A. L. Rubanovich, who changed his name to A. L. Dick and who may have been both a Soviet and British agent, fit more conventional spy patterns, yet he too appears to have gotten his start in the course of the war or in the Russian civil war that followed. During the thirties Dick was in and out of Shanghai, associating with a host of dubious individuals and at one time managing a cabaret in the city's Blood Alley. Such facts, if true, would have made Dick an almost banal figure. Shanghai was to professional spies in the twenties and thirties much what Berlin would become in the fifties and sixties. So prevalent were spies that the city's name became a code word for espionage as it did for criminality and debauchery. Paule Herfort, who visited the city in the late 1930s, called Shanghai "the international homeland of vice, spies, and vultures." *Vu et Lu* suggested the city was overrun with spies, "quintuple agents at the very least." People who wrote about Shanghai invariably brought spies and intrigues into their stories. Even serious writers like Malraux or Charles Plisnier whose Alessandro Cassini dreams of going to Shanghai (instead he is sent on an undercover mission to Italy) identified revolutionary Shanghai as a city of intrigues. The image was scarcely off the mark.[27]

How far back this identity ran is uncertain, although just before the war Shanghai was already becoming a gathering ground for revolutionaries and nationalist agitators.[28] After the war the numbers seem to have exploded as spies and secret agents tramped through the city and set up shop practically at will. In the heady revolutionary years of the twenties Comintern and GPU operatives passed in and out of Shanghai, while the Soviets built up a spy network in China that has been described as extensive.[29] The Kuomintang purge of the Communists in 1927–1928 dealt a stunning blow to Communist expectations in the Orient and to the Comintern organization in Shanghai. Yet even as the Russians withdrew (or were hunted down),[30] they left behind a skeleton organization that was able to rebuild into a serious operation over the next several years.

Throughout the late twenties and the beginning of the thirties, foreign police tracked the comings and goings of Soviet agents. They were forever vigilant regarding Russians like a Madame Bulgakova-Belskii who arrived in Shanghai in December 1928 from Tientsin, where she was believed to have worked as a GPU courier to Peking, Mukden, and Harbin and to have recruited dancing partners to spread Communist propaganda among foreign troops. Following their experience in 1927, the Comintern increasingly relied upon non-Russian agents—Poles, Finns, Estonians, and especially Germans and Hungarians—to carry out their missions in China. Shanghai was the center, the location of the Orient bureau that served as the intermediary between the Comintern in Moscow and Communist parties in the Pacific and that dispatched agents throughout the region. In 1931 came another crackdown: a vast French and British sweep snared Nguyen Ai Quoc (later known as Ho Chi Minh) in Hong Kong and major Comintern figures in Singapore and Shanghai. Even then Shanghai remained a focal point of Soviet intrigues in the East. By 1937 there was once again an Orient bureau based in Shanghai and filtering instructions through to Communists elsewhere. Meanwhile Red Army intelligence (GRU) was running major operations out of Shanghai. Richard Sorge arrived in early 1930 under the cover name of Johnson and built his first extensive spy network there. Later, when he had moved on to Japan, he used Shanghai as a drop point for his courier traffic and as a meeting place for instructions and finances. Sorge's radio operator in Tokyo, Max Clausen, began his life as a GRU agent in Shanghai. It was there that he and Sorge first met, even though the two were working different circuits. Just how many operations Soviet military intelligence had going in Shanghai in the thirties is anyone's guess, but Ursula Hamburger, who was later to carry out spy missions in Switzerland and was the agent Sonia in the Rote Kapelle network, was also in Shanghai on assignment for the Red Army from 1930 to 1935.[31]

During these years it was probably impossible to walk up and down the Bund or to lounge in hotels without jostling up against some secret agent. A man named Pearson, who claimed Uruguayan citizenship and who arrived in Shanghai with the intention of gathering information concerning Japanese and Soviet defenses, had no trouble contacting the agents of several secret services; indeed the report on Pearson read as if the presence of such people was open knowledge in Shanghai, needing only a glance through the yellow pages to find them.[32] Suspicious characters were always passing through, arriving in Shanghai from some other distant port, departing, and then returning like the woman S., who had been born in Riga in 1894 but called herself Czechoslovak by 1940. She spoke eight languages and had traveled widely in Europe and the Orient. In Singapore she ran a shop, but police there listed her as a drug addict, a suspected drug smuggler, and "a sly prostitute." At the time of the Munich crisis she was also identified as a Nazi sympathizer and a person unusually well informed about British and American fleet movements in the Pacific. She appears to have first come to Shanghai in 1928 where she consorted with an Austrian engineer and narcotics trafficker. She may have been back in 1938, and was known to be in contact with another Austrian, this one a doctor and suspected spy living in the city. Ordered to leave Malaya at the end of 1940, she was expected in Shanghai once again the following month.[33]

By the thirties Shanghai was a thicket of spy agencies. Police in the settlements were constantly turning up Japanese agents. In 1935 the Abwehr was running a station in China and by fall of 1937 clearly one in Shanghai, although German operatives in the city can be traced back to the twenties, and other agents from other German postings were filing reports out of Shanghai as well.[34] French naval intelligence maintained a post in Shanghai from as early as 1927, formalizing it into the Shanghai Transit Service in October 1929. The Colonial Ministry opened its own intelligence station in the city in 1937–1938 and by that date there was also coverage from military attachés and an intelligence branch of the French occupation corps not to mention the French concession police, who were deeply engaged in counterespionage and were in liaison with the Sûreté in Indochina and British police in Hong Kong and Singapore. Nevertheless there could never be too many spies in Shanghai, and in July 1938 the Colonial Ministry decided to send Marc Chadourne there on a separate intelligence mission. Despite the protests of the Quai d'Orsay, Chadourne arrived in the city in early 1939 under the cover of writing yet another book on China.[35]

Still if Shanghai was crawling with professionals and was a center for secret service networks, the more typical intriguer in the city was someone like Eckelman, alias Sanders, alias Sanderoff, alias Northquist, alias Marquist, alias Lund, alias Captain Knutsen. He appears to have been born in 1899 of a German father and a Swedish mother, but so little else in his life was verifiable (or believable) that even these facts are open to suspicion. By the latter half of the thirties he was passing in and out of Shanghai and telling these stories about himself: He had been living in Hoboken, New Jersey, when the First World War had broken out and had attempted to return to Germany only to be intercepted by the Russians and imprisoned in a concentration camp somewhere in Siberia. He had escaped from the camp by clinging to the undercarriage of a railroad car and, with the help of a Swedish nurse, had made it back to Germany. He had enlisted in the German navy, become a whiz at coding and decoding, and, discovering a flaw in the codes he was sending, had been summoned back to headquarters in Berlin to devise an unbreakable code, which he had managed to produce. He had finished the war as a commander of a German U-boat (in 1918 he would have been nineteen years old). He had gone on to devise codes for a number of individual and national clients, including China, Japan, Russia, Poland, Yugoslavia, Czechoslovakia, Spain, Basil Zaharoff, and a maharajah of India (Eckelman did seem to have certain skills as a coder and during one of his sojourns in Shanghai opened an office to sell what he called his "Cosmos trading code," but the venture failed miserably). He had flown in the Chinese air force. He was a personal friend and confidant of Chiang Kai-shek. He had traveled to Lhasa disguised as a deaf and dumb barber on a special mission for the Generalissimo. His titles included Doctor of Law, Doctor of Philosophy (with degrees from both Berlin and Leipzig), Doctor of Political Science (from Bonn), Lieutenant Commander in the German Naval Reserve, Rear Admiral in the Chinese Navy, Brigadier General in the Chinese Army, and Commander in the Royal Swedish Navy. An undercover police agent who tracked Eckelman down in the Blue Paradise nightclub and watched him toss down several hot rums was treated to still more tales, among these the revelation that he had helped prepare the attack on a Japanese cruiser in the Whangpoo River in 1937. He was, as the undercover agent concluded, a fabulous raconteur or, as one other person summed him up, "a monumental fakir and liar."

By the late thirties Eckelman was also an accomplished con man who kept dangerous company and was suspected of spying. In 1938–1939 he swindled twenty-nine thousand dollars from an art gallery in New York on the promise of using his Chinese connections to deliver a shipment of Chinese imperial treasures. (The series of letters and telegrams he sent, of transport by camel caravan where no caravan routes existed, of being bombed by the Japanese, shot at by the French, of losing sixteen men and so on are another story all its own.) In Shanghai in the fall of 1939 he took over the flat of a man named Kolacek, a former secretary in the Czechoslovakian consulate who had gone over to the Germans (following the takeover of Prague) and who had reportedly sold secret documents to an unidentified foreign intelligence service. At the same time Eckelman was associating with a known arms dealer reputed to be tied to the Japanese, and in his conversation at the Blue Paradise he let drop that he was in touch with H. D., the aviator turned suspected Japanese agent. Eckelman was known to go armed, and although some suggested he might be simply deranged, both the French and the British suspected he was working for Japanese intelligence.[36]

Like so many others we have met from these years—the Gardiners, the D.'s, the Goldbergs, the Corrigans—Eckelman appears to have been an adventurer who inexorably drifted into espionage or intrigue. All of them illustrate how readily lives were caught up in world events after the war and how, consequently, adventures and intrigues tended to run together. That is what made Eckelman representative of the spies who turned up in Shanghai in the twenties and thirties. Many were professionals but probably many more were men and women who simply chose to lead adventurous if shady existences or people like Znamenskii and Dolzhikov who found their lives transformed by great events that set them coursing down the conduits of history. In either case circumstances and opportunities edged them closer and closer to the intriguers until the two became inseparable. Shanghai, as a city of adventurers, human wreckage, and spies, lubricated the passages that brought them together.

Easing that convergence was the fact that Shanghai itself was increasingly drawn into global history and the cataclysms of the age. The great Western outpost in China was also a conglomeration of workers and a generator of cultural ferment that made it an epicenter of revolution and war. Three historical currents swept over China in the first half of the twentieth century—nationalism, bolshevism, and Japanese expansionism. All three forced dramatic action in Shanghai and all three carried the city into the vortex of world affairs. Perhaps as much as the First World War, the Russo-Japanese War sparked anti-imperial sentiment and the rise of nationalist movements throughout the non-Western world. Almost immediately in China it led to the creation of the Chinese revolutionary alliance. Shanghai became a headquarters of alliance activity and, as one person has described it, a "hotbed of radicalism" that made the city an important center during the revolution of 1911. By 1914 there was, therefore, already in place a tradition of militant agitation in the city.[37]

The consequences of the First World War were to be equally far-reaching. The Japanese conquest of German bases in the Far East and Japanese expansion into Shantung had two immediately provocative results. First, German defeat, like Russian defeat earlier, implied the vulnerability of all colonial powers in China and the prospect that ultimately they might all be evacuated. Second, the series of events that followed—the replacement of the Germans in Shantung by Japanese troops, the imposition of Japan's twenty-one demands, the failure of the Western Allies to support Chinese interests despite China's entry in the war against the Central Powers, and the subsequent humiliation at Versailles, where Japanese advances were upheld—struck the Chinese as a betrayal and as a goad to further action. Together the two ignited a new wave of nationalist demands. The long-term effects were still more imposing. Despite victory the war undermined the foundations of Western power abroad and left the imperialist nations seriously overextended. The Westerners who would increasingly have to seek accommodation knew it, the Chinese knew it, and most of all the Japanese who saw China as a vast economic asset knew it. By war's end the Japanese had supplanted the British as China's principal trading partner and in

Shanghai British cotton spinning mills had ceded first rank to Japanese enterprises.[38] The war with its vast shift in global power had conferred upon Japan precedence in the Pacific. From the 1920s on the Japanese had no intention of relinquishing or even failing to expand that position. They were determined to assert their presence in the region and to secure, at any cost, their economic interests as they defined them. That pursuit, in the context of rising Chinese nationalism and Western imperial investments, would make China a site of clashes and international tensions and eventually the battleground of war.

And there was the Russian revolution. From its inception its leaders intended to lead a world revolution. These ambitions assumed new meanings as, thwarted in the West, the Bolsheviks turned East, seeing in imperial lands or in a country like China the promise of victories and the soft underbelly of capitalism. At its second congress in 1920 the Comintern adopted the strategy of challenging colonialism on a worldwide scale and then reaffirmed that decision at a congress of subject peoples convoked in Baku. There before a mostly Muslim audience, Zinoviev proclaimed a holy war on Western imperialism. Within the Comintern there was division over the proper role of Communists in this assault on the imperialists. Lenin favored an alliance with movements of national liberation. M. N. Roy argued for independent revolutionary organization from below. A slight compromise was worked out, but essentially Lenin's position prevailed, thus setting the stage for the Communist alliance with the Chinese nationalists of the Kuomintang. Initially of marginal significance to the Comintern, China in the twenties was to loom larger and larger until it became the first great testing ground — and failure — to spread bolshevism in the East. In 1920 the Comintern sent its first emissaries to China. In 1923 the Chinese Communist Party joined the Kuomintang, and in January of the same year an agreement between Adolph Joffe and Sun Yat-sen provided for Russian financial and organizing assistance, including the dispatch of Russian military advisers. Both the Russian presence and the cooperation of the Communists were to play a crucial role in the success of the Kuomintang's northern expedition in 1926–1927 that led to the nationalists' command over China. But the centrifugal forces within the alliance were as great as their common objectives, and in early 1927 Chiang Kai-shek turned dramatically and ferociously upon his former allies, driving them out of the Kuomintang and forcing them underground in areas the Kuomintang controlled.[39]

Shanghai was at the center of all these storms. A cauldron of some several hundred thousand workers[40] and the manufacturing capital of China, it would become, with Canton, the country's revolutionary city in the twenties. In 1921 it was the site of the founding of the Chinese Communist Party and in 1923 Sun Yat-sen's home in the French concession was the meeting place for the Kuomintang leader and the Russian Joffe, who hammered out the agreement committing the Bolsheviks to their adventure in China.[41] In 1925 Shanghai was the scene of mass demonstrations, strikes, and boycotts that set off the May Thirtieth Movement, one of the greatest nationalist episodes of the decade and an event that left Shanghai a stronghold of militant radical action. Two years later the Communist-led workers seized control of the city as the northern expedition was marching on its gates. The following month Chiang's troops and the Green Gang smashed the mass movement in a bloody purge repeated throughout Kuomintang China but forever identified with Shanghai because of the extent of revolutionary organization in the city and because Malraux immortalized the event in what many consider his greatest novel.[42]

In the thirties Shanghai remained a historical focal point as the city lived in uneasy peace with Japanese expansionism. Progressively international tensions bore down upon the Whangpoo. In 1931 the Japanese overran Manchuria. In 1932 full-scale fighting erupted between Chinese and Japanese units in Chapei just north of the international settlement. After that the atmosphere grew permanently ominous: 1937 brought war and the fall of Chinese Shanghai; 1941 the overrunning of the international settlement. The Shanghai of the late thirties that Jean Raynaud saw was still the modern Babylon but was also a city of barbed wire and foot patrols and one teeming with refugees. In the river junks and sampans flew French, British, German, and Portuguese flags in the hope of attaining a measure of protection. From half a million residents the French concession swelled to one million three hundred thousand occupants, again reflecting the scramble for security. On the Bund a French light armored car was stationed *en permanence.*[43]

Thus the parade that was Shanghai took place against a backdrop of Comintern intrigues, warships in the Whangpoo, and Japanese bayonets. For the Green Gang, for example, international events were decisive. Huang made his move to chief superintendent of detectives when the war called his superiors back to France. The aftershocks of the war — nationalism, revolution, Japanese power, and a stretching of colonial resources — encouraged the French to accommodate with the mobsters. The gang consolidated its stranglehold in 1927 as Shanghai took center stage in the civil war within the Kuomintang. Japanese aggression in 1932 forced the French to react with vigor and to scale down Tu's influence in the concession.[44] No one — not Crawley, no White Russian — was independent of the context about them. For secret agents it was a perfect milieu.

In a globally closing world Shanghai was a nexus, a place where events were internationally determined and determining. Travelers came to witness and report as well as to enjoy, and they came between the wars in considerable numbers. The town was five thousand miles from San Francisco, nearly nine thousand from Paris, ten thousand from London if one went entirely by sea, but getting there was not very difficult. A premier port of the world, Shanghai was readily accessible. On the Messageries Maritimes Line one could travel fortnightly from Marseilles via Djibouti, Colombo, Singapore, and Saigon, reaching Shanghai in thirty to thirty-two days. On the P & O liners one could make Shanghai in thirty days from London if one took the special express train to Marseilles and then sailed via Malta, Aden, Bombay, and Hong Kong. Hamburg Amerika liners sailed to Shanghai from Hamburg and Genoa, Lloyd Triestino liners monthly from Venice, and if one chose to go overland there was the Trans-Siberian/Chinese Eastern railroad to Harbin with connection on to Shanghai.[45]

Yet if passage was easy and the city compellingly modern, travelers never lost their sense of distance, nor their desire to journey across some invisible line into mystery, exotica, and sensation. They came seeking a Shanghai that was romantic and adventurous, and almost always the city complied with their wishes. "I could have gone to Shanghai and become the French chief of police," says Estienne at the beginning of his tale in Joseph Kessel's *Wagon-lit,* "and you can imagine what a field for adventure that would have been with the traffic in opium, arms, and kidnappings." "What resources here for adventure!" wrote Marc Chadourne in 1931. "Where to begin?" (a question admittedly not easy to answer).

For imaginations in the twenties and thirties Shanghai was the city of evocations and moods, its very name conjuring up a world of bandits, coolies, sampans, forbidden pleasures, traffickers, and spies. Francis de Croisset was disappointed to discover that the train to Peking was filthy and covered in spit and that there was no such thing as a Shanghai Express: "It's only called that in the movies and, alas, we're a long ways from the train that Marlene Dietrich rode." The city was like a vast Hollywood set, real, without props, yet playing to the same spellbinding desires. Few who wrote about Shanghai failed to satisfy those needs, themselves captive to the same hunger for sensation or most skilled at exploiting them. Champly wrote about the white slave traffic to the Far East and called his book *The Road to Shanghai*. Jean Fontenoy wrote a series of lightweight tales about the city and called his book *Secret Shanghai*. *Vu et Lu* described Shanghai as the "incontestable capital of the international underworld," said that "all the clandestine commerce in drugs, from opium to heroin, is centered on Shanghai," called the city "the greatest market in contraband weapons" and the junction point for spies, and entitled its article "Shanghaï: sa grandeur et ses mystères." G. E. Miller wrote of *Shanghai, The Paradise of Adventurers*. Paule Herfort wrote of "shady men and tainted women," of opium, gambling dens, and the criminal class that crept out from its nests at the coming of night. O.-P. Gilbert, who has been quoted copiously in these pages, summoned up five pages of unrelenting atmospherics to describe Shanghai in the late 1930s. Vicki Baum's portrait of the city — "the gigantic town, the vicious town, the industrious, dangerous and endangered town" — continued for nearly three pages to create the same viscous ambiance. Even when it was all over and Shanghai a grim city of the Reds, the code demanded a florid, highly charged style. Thirty years after the fact Edgar Snow took thirty-two lines and more than three hundred words to describe in one sentence the Shanghai he first encountered in 1928 (in a chapter called "Shanghai!").[46]

That is how we like to remember the Shanghai that existed between the wars, victims of our imaginations and a need to foist romantic visions upon the past, although far less so than we might initially believe. It was contemporaries who first imposed that extravagant image, turning Shanghai into everything they and their readers wanted it to be. They asked much of Shanghai and the city gave much in return.

This, then, was Shanghai. Vast, scandalous, "legendary" as Gilbert called it, a special place in the twenties and thirties, and one we are not likely to see again. Intrigue flourished here, perhaps more so than anywhere else, so that the city itself became identified as the lair or the gathering ground of the spies of the world. In a town that collected the sharks and human debris of the universe matters could hardly be otherwise. But that identity was itself caught up in all that Shanghai represented in these years: sweep, globalization, crumbling worlds yet colonial pride, adventure joined to contemporary power struggles, and the pursuit of ambiance. These were themes of the age, defining Shanghai as Shanghai in turn defined its intrigues. Shanghai, the hyperbolic

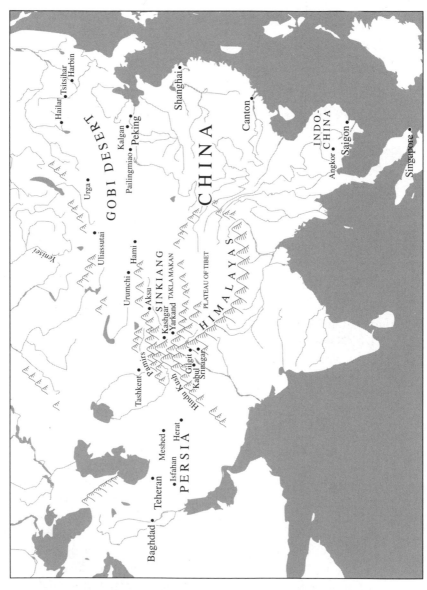

Map 2. *The Adventurer's Asia.*

city, magnified how closely the histories of global compression, adventure, and travel converged with the history of espionage between the wars. Spies and secret agents, as the city suggested, possessed no special realms and moved in larger, more complex worlds. The city brought out their representativeness and their evocative qualities and revealed how again their history joined with that of their times.

From Shanghai it is about twelve hundred miles to the Khingan Mountains in what is now Inner Mongolia. The Chinese Eastern Railway, joining the Trans-Siberian to Vladivostok via the direct Harbin route, runs through these mountains on the Hailar-Tsitsihar stretch; and there in 1915 the German military attaché to China, Major von Pappenheim, planned to blow up a tunnel and interrupt the flow of supplies west to the front. With nine Germans, three Chinese, twenty camels, five horses, and two dogs and traveling as Russian soldiers, von Pappenheim crossed into Mongolia in late January. The expedition passed through Noganou-ta[47] on 31 January, camped at Dabasin-Soume for several days, and then on 5 February set off for Hakhaï-aïl to win the Mongol chieftain Baboutchab over to their side. At Hakhaï-aïl von Pappenheim revealed his intentions and his true identity. He showed Baboutchab bombs he had brought along, detonated a few to demonstrate what they could do, and offered the Mongol leader fifty thousand roubles, arms, and munitions if he would provide three hundred soldiers to escort the raiding party as far as Tsitsihar (or Hailar, according to another account). Baboutchab stalled while he awaited instructions from Urga, not a good sign for the Germans. But von Pappenheim's scheme was doomed from the start. Shortly after the attaché had set out from Peking on the pretense of a hunting trip, the Japanese secret service got wind that something was up and alerted the Russian legation in Peking. At roughly the same time word filtered through to the Russian consul general in Urga from Mongolian detachments on the southeastern frontier that a party of Chinese and Germans had been spotted heading toward Tsitsihar with the intention of destroying a section of the Trans-Siberian. Several days later the consul general was in possession of more precise intelligence reported by Baboutchab. Meanwhile a Russian commercial traveler named Chadrin crossed paths with von Pappenheim's party as they were progressing toward Hakhaï-aïl. Intrigued by their clothing — certainly not Russian-issue — and unable to understand what they were saying, he attempted to approach but backed off when one of the Germans took aim at him. Proceeding on to Hakhaï-aïl Chadrin camped near to

Baboutchab and learned firsthand all about the Germans' conspiracy. On 9 February two of the Germans visited Chadrin in his tent to sound him out and put him off the scent with the story that they had come to Mongolia to prospect for gold. By 9 March Chadrin was reporting what he knew in person to the Russian vice-consul at Hailar, his arrival coinciding with yet another Mongolian report on the would-be saboteurs. Von Pappenheim had set off on a daring expedition but he had failed to reckon with the Russophilia of the Mongols who listened to him, robbed him, and then denounced him to their protectors. For their part the Russians were convinced that they would get their hands on von Pappenheim. But the last sighting of the caravan was on 2 April about three hundred kilometers east of Dolonnur. Several weeks later there were contradictory reports, one that von Pappenheim's party had met a horrendous fate, attacked, pillaged, murdered, the cadavers set on fire, another that the caravan had been seen heading toward Turkestan. That was the last the French captain, de Lapomarède, knew as he filed his report on 30 April to the Deuxième Bureau in Paris. The report sits in the archives of the French army, a reminder of how the war carried intrigues and spy missions to the farthest reaches of the earth, where they remained even after the fighting had stopped.[48]

There is no denying the global expanse of intrigue after the war. Before 1914 there had been a trickle of reports from around the world; after 1918 there was a flood. The credibility of these reports, as always, remains questionable. Certainly some were improbable, even risible. Yet the measured tone of many — a sense of the situation in hand — suggests that spy mania alone cannot account for the sheer growth in the files. If the French saw spies all over the world it was because espionage had assumed global proportions and because after the war one was accustomed to thinking globally.

German intrigues, previously contained to Europe and North Africa, now sprawled across the face of the map. In Africa the German threat spread south, "from Morocco to the Congo . . . with the purpose of controlling the west coast of Africa."[49] French intelligence followed German activities in the Canaries, in the Bissagos Islands (off Portuguese Guinea), in Fernando Poo, and in the Cameroons, watching particularly for globally strategic installations or bases. In the Canaries the French were concerned about Germans "at the crossroads of the routes to Africa and America" and astride the sea lanes via the Cape on to India. German movements were scanned, including those of the German Consul Jacob Ahlers whose farms, it was reported, were a cover for clandestine arms depots.[50] From further south came comparable warnings: night landings of arms and munitions in Spanish Guinea; covert arms shipments to the Cameroons; reports of six thousand Nazi agents spread throughout the former German colonies; communiqués on an Africanwide spy network dividing the continent by sectors.[51] German businesses like the Afrikanische Frucht Compagnie, whose boats were capable of speeds in excess of commercial needs, or Woermann, which had rebuilt its trading outposts with West Africa after the war, were especial targets of French surveillance.[52]

Beyond Africa German intrigues were reported in Syria, India, Java, and Indochina. According to Julius Mader, the Abwehr was in fact operating in such lands as Turkey, Persia, Afghanistan, China, and Japan by 1935 and its agent network, obviously well in place earlier, was achieving its first successes in Latin America in 1936. Two years later an Abwehr-backed putsch in Brazil came to nothing, but in the following year the Germans were again laying plans for extensive subversion in Latin America. At roughly the same time a steward on a Norddeutscher Lloyd steamer was filing reports on Singapore, Hong Kong, and Shanghai, while another confidential agent was traveling through the Dutch East Indies. The French picked up only a bit of this activity, although there are traces in their files such as the report on Karl K., a Gestapo agent who had just completed a mission in Abyssinia and was headed for the Far East, or a report of increasing German infiltration in Egypt and Palestine by 1938.[53]

Japanese intrigues fit a similar pattern. After the Russo-Japanese War there had been some reporting on Japanese intrigues in Southeast Asia, but now the French tracked Japanese spies and covert operations clear across the globe. They followed Japanese conspiracies with White Russian circles and the recruitment of refugee spies, saboteurs, and potential fighting forces.[54] According to French intelligence reports, Japanese agents were spreading over the Dutch East Indies. They were active in China where they trafficked in drugs, weapons, and disorder to unhinge the Chinese and prevent their consolidation as a powerful competitor. Japanese ships sailed through Indochinese waters surveying and photographing places of anchorage. At Port Said the Japanese consul kept tabs on French and British boats passing through Suez, watching particularly for arms cargoes to China. The same man scattered propaganda throughout the Red Sea basin proclaiming friendly Japanese intentions toward the Muslims of Asia. Japanese agents in Europe included a man named Schaeffer who operated in Geneva and a Japanese engineer who gathered intelligence in Belgium. Among Japanese agents in France were a Russian, a German, an Austrian, a Norwegian, a Turk, a Japanese businessman working out of Marseilles, and a Frenchman. Recruitment in Paris for missions abroad was reputed to be common among Russian émigrés and Armenians, like the Armenian A. who held a Turkish passport and was being deployed in Singapore. Alongside the files on Germans and communists the dossiers were comparatively slim and secondary in significance; yet they too attest to a routine global consciousness after the war. Even the process of recording begot a reflexive global response as in the case of the Port Said dispatch that was circulated to London, Rome, Barcelona, Berlin, Moscow, Teheran, Bangkok, Shanghai, Algiers, Tokyo, Jerusalem, and Baghdad (among other places).[55]

Nothing promoted the routine of global thinking, however, quite like the Russian revolution and the Third International's decision to quicken the forces of world revolution. After 1920 the Comintern's agents were everywhere: in North Africa, in Persia, in Afghanistan, in India, in Singapore, in the East Indies, in Indochina, in China. They fomented insurrection, disseminated propaganda, built communist parties, joined nationalist movements, and recruited local revolutionaries who were shipped to Russia, trained in revolutionary doctrine and methods, and then infiltrated back to their homelands. Regional centrals—the Orient bureau in Shanghai, the southern bureau in Hong Kong, the Tashkent section for central Asia—directed operations across international borders and several empires. When one was lopped off, another appeared, making the Comintern the hydra-headed monster French authorities believed it to be. Strategic decisions in Moscow moved men and resources across a worldwide playing board. Against such an assault the French could mount nothing short of a worldwide response. They filed reports on Comintern activities over whole hemispheres of the globe. They noted the coming and going of trained recruits, how many Indochinese, for instance, had been trained at the Stalin School, how many had returned, how many had been caught, how many still were at large.

Counterintelligence agents scanned the routing of resources and the shifts in activities, as in 1925 when they observed cutbacks at the Vienna central and the reassignment of operatives to Morocco and East Asia. Other agents in port cities watched over the worldwide circuits. They followed the peregrinations of sailors whom the Comintern enlisted as couriers or the use of the mails where revolutionary tracts were secreted in newspapers or between the covers of Bon Marché catalogues (which must have sent the Boucicauts spinning in their graves). To combat the Comintern French police and secret agents went on the offensive, developing surveillance networks as multinational as those of the Bolsheviks. The Indochinese Sûreté stationed men in Canton, Hong Kong, Peking, Bangkok, Batavia, and Tokyo. They developed liaisons with the British and Dutch imperial police, forwarding, for example, the Annamese agent "Typhoon" to Singapore in 1933. Their joint operations were often extremely effective, as in the famous roundup of Comintern figures in 1931 and even more so in the progressive breaking of communist organization in Indochina. They were perhaps the most successful European police force operating in the Orient, and their success, combined with the continued revolutionary threat, no doubt encouraged the Colonial Ministry to create in 1937 its own intelligence section that extended to Shanghai, Hanoi, Nouméa, Djibouti, Tananarive, Dakar, Brazzaville, and Fort de France, each station covering a sector served by ten posts and thirteen annexes.[56]

The French authorities, therefore, had concrete reasons to escalate their watch over vast geographical areas. One was German defeat in the war and the dispossession of German colonies by the French and the British. Successive German regimes were bound to see in the empires a source of grievance or a soft target to strike against and just as likely to see in their former colonies a logical place to concentrate this action. Moreover the previous war had demonstrated the willingness of the Germans to wage insurrectionary warfare throughout the empires and the more critical ability of the French and the British to marshal the resources of the world and to bring those resources to the battlefronts in Europe. German bases astride vital sea lanes or German interference at the source of supply could be strategically decisive in a future conflict. Hence the French were wary of German intrigues abroad and determined to maintain surveillance over them, just as the Germans themselves had reason to expand covert operations far beyond Europe.

Another reason was the global realignment that had followed the war. Even before 1914, as a consequence of Japanese victories in 1904, colonial empires like the Dutch or the French had begun to sense a Japanese shadow extending over their possessions in Asia. After 1918 the Japanese clearly established their power in the Pacific as a consequence of Russian defeat and then revolutionary implosion, Japanese gains in the war, and the curious effects of that conflict on European imperialism. On the surface the great empires were larger, more glamorous than ever before. Underneath they rested on rotting foundations eaten away by the war's encouragement to nationalist sentiment and just as much by its depletion of national treasuries. The combination of wartime promises to colonial subjects, mobilization of colonial manpower, exposure of their workers and troops to radical political ideologies, and the mutually destructive nature of the conflict that was not lost on leaders of national liberation movements all corroded the ramparts of imperial fortresses at a time when a new challenger appeared increasingly expansionist. In this respect the climate was ripe for defensive postures and a monitoring of Japanese intentions. Such a monitoring, in addition, required a close look at large expanses of territory — China, all of southern and southeastern Asia — rather than simply a focus on the concessions or on French Indochina.

A third reason was the Bolshevik revolution and the international dimensions it almost immediately assumed. The French had fought battles against national revolutionaries before the war and there had been premonitions of international liaisons among revolutionary conspirators. But, as their own agents acknowledged, the Russian revolution represented something radically different: "the joining into the fray of new men, young, tramplers of all tradition, contemptuous of the older émigrés and their out-of-date ideas, and educated in revolution by the agents of Moscow. That is why one can say that Nguyen Ai Quoc's return to Canton from Russia in 1925 marked a new era in the contemporary political history of the Annamese territories."[57] Comintern infiltration of empires was global in nature, eliciting in return an unalloyed global response. Again the very nature of the threat — its regional centrals and international circuits — required tracking across boundaries and even across continents.

Yet beyond specific causes it seems to have been simply the sheer experience of world war — campaigns in distant lands; troops shipped across hemispheres; intercontinental intrigues; decisive extra-European intervention — that habituated Europeans to thinking and acting more globally than before. The change was admittedly a matter of degree. By the late nineteenth century Europeans were accustomed to reaping the fruits of the world, literally serving them up on their breakfast trays in the morning. Cables and steamship lines tied capital cities to peripheral outposts on outlying continents. Imperialism, the construction of the Trans-Siberian railroad, and the Russo-Japanese War led to grand geopolitical predictions.[58] But the First World War introduced a qualitative difference because it showed how inextricably the fate of Europeans was bound up in worldwide affairs. Whereas European globalism before the war had been predicated on European hegemony, and hence almost a matter to take for granted, globalism after the war reflected shrinking European mastery and consequently a world where events in distant places were more likely to affect European destinies. The postwar world would absorb European history as much as be absorbed by it. Following the war, therefore, there was no scaling back to European dimensions. Travelers rushed over the globe and reported on events in faraway places. Newspapers filled with news of the world. Geopolitical writers speculated on the changes, worldwide in scope, that the war had effected. Europeans sickened by the bloodletting sought alternatives in Eastern cultures and religions.[59] Technology, and long-distance flights in particular, riveted contemporaries' attention over whole oceans and continents while demonstrating dramatically how much tighter or more joined the world was becoming. Radio, too, by the thirties, was a world-binding medium. The *guerre des ondes* that followed — airwave propaganda battles in North Africa, South Africa, Latin America, and the Orient[60] — was symptomatic of how inevitably or routinely intrigues escalated to global stakes between the wars. Thus French authorities remained vigilant because such was their special responsibility; yet their focus on worldwide intrigue shared the same heightened global consciousness that large numbers of the general public carried after the war and that encompassed a sense of interconnectedness as much as a mood of menace or danger.[61]

Interwar spy writing appropriated a comparable global vision, for example, in the ease with which it now took the world as a setting for secret agent action.[62] It did so, however, with a many-sidedness that can be seen in the legend surrounding that bizarre figure, Trebitsch Lincoln. In his day Trebitsch Lincoln was a man of mystery, indulgences, and fairy tales. He was born Ignace Trebitsch, a Jew, in Hungary in the 1870s, he converted to Protestantism and preached in Canada, he served briefly in the British Parliament before World War I, but that was about all contemporaries knew about him. There were rumors of intelligence service work in the Balkans in the early years of the century, and practically everyone agreed that he had been a double agent during the war, although no one was sure just how closely he had worked with the Germans. After the war he was traced to right-wing conspiracies on the continent; rumored to have murdered the Italian socialist Matteoti on orders from London; said to have served the Chinese war-lord Wu Pei-Fu; identified as the Buddhist monk Chao Kung; reported to have joined with brigands, warlords, and Bolsheviks in a holy war to drive the whites out of Asia (to this end fomenting attacks, strikes, riots, and insurrections in Shanghai, Hong Kong, India, and the East Indies); later rumored to have collided with Lawrence in Afghanistan; placed again in the Bolshevik camp in China; and finally tied to the Japanese in Manchukuo with intimations of personally triggering the Sino-Japanese War.

Thanks to Bernard Wasserstein we now have a clear idea about the true life of this man. Trebitsch Lincoln was an adventurer, a con man, and an incessant mythmaker. He advanced financial schemes in the Balkans before the First World War but there is no evidence of embroilment in Balkan intrigues. In the war he briefly contacted German intelligence, although the extent of his role as a spy was practically nil. Later, toward the end of his life, he would reopen relations with German intelligence during the Second World War. Otherwise his exploits as a secret agent were mere fabrication. After the war he was indeed a central figure in the Kapp putsch and among right-wing conspirators. He did go to China and he did worm his way into the entourage of several warlords, perhaps even that of Wu Pei-fu, but his influence on these men was probably slight. He did become a Buddhist monk, but the stories of raising revolts in Asia or manipulating Japanese expansionism were, again, pure fabrication. For much of his later life he was in and out of Shanghai, the proper setting for this sort of misfit. He died there in 1943, during the Japanese occupation.[63]

If the life fell considerably short of the legend, it was, nevertheless, an extraordinary one. Yet it is the legend, far more than the reality, that is the significant feature about Trebitsch Lincoln. As adventurers went he was one of a crowd in the interwar years. Scattered through the archives are dossiers on a host of intriguers and bounders whose lives were as fantastic as his. Yet it was Trebitsch who stood out from the crowd and captivated imaginations between the wars. He was the subject of two full-length biographies published in France in his lifetime, one under the outlandish title *Buddha Against the Intelligence Service* and a second, equally inflated, called *Trebitsch Lincoln, the Greatest Adventurer of the Century*. Robert Boucard wrote about him in his "revelations" of British intelligence and Victor Meulenijzer introduced him into his fanciful account of Lawrence's intrigues. Xavier de Hautecloque devoted two articles to Trebitsch in his series on "The Powers of Darkness" in the *Petit Journal*. In 1934 *Paris-Soir* printed an article on him and then again in June 1938. *Vu* called him "the greatest adventurer of the twentieth century" in two articles in 1932. He turned up in Charles Lucieto's 1928 spy novel, *Delivered to the Enemy,* as a Comintern agent battling imperialism, in Teddy Legrand's 1933 spy novel, *The Seven Heads of the Green Dragon,* and yet again in Jean Bommart's 1940 *Lady from Valparaiso.* He was, in these years, a ubiquitous personality, and the question for the historian is why this was so and what it all meant.[64]

A part of the answer lies in the recurrent theme in the Trebitsch legend of the revolt of Asia. Much of this was a product of Lincoln's own compulsion toward bombastic self-promotion.[65] But Asia as a continent of danger was also a French preoccupation in the twentieth century. The Russo-Japanese War had set minds ablaze, although even more striking from the European perspective was the fratricidal nature of World War I, its incomparable bloodletting, its massive material destruction and fiscal corrosion, and its collapse of a civilization's pretensions to moral supremacy.[66] From the war issued a more assured and challenging Japanese presence in the Orient and a worldwide revolutionary movement set on the subversion of empires. The result was a spate of writing on a new global age, of which three things must be remarked.

First there was the judgment of European eclipse, and of a shift of world centrality to the Pacific.[67] Second there was the strong racial tinge to a considerable part of this literature. It can be discerned most readily in such self-evident works as Maurice Muret's *Twilight of the White Races* or Lothrop Stoddard's *Rising Tide of Color* (translated into French in 1925 with approximately 3,000 sales), but the yellow-peril coin circulated freely in these years and extended as far as traditional targets — Jews — who as Bolsheviks or "Asiatics" were subsumed into the revolt of Asia.[68]

Third there was the way Red Russia was absorbed into this imagery. Anyone who has read the interwar accounts of travel to the Soviet Union and to China will have noticed their similarity. For a whole generation of French the two were lands of filth, barbarism, smells, and swarms. From each came descriptions of dreadful stench, thick odors, and scenes of squatting defecators on open view from train windows.[69] Words like *pulluler, essaimer, grouiller* referred equally to the East and to the Russians. Returning from a visit to Russia in 1932 Marc Chadourne, who seems to have been everywhere in these years, recalled "a memory very precise of a scene . . . that dominates the others; that of a major restaurant in Tiflis whose doorways were guarded by beggars and young boys in rags ready to swoop down whenever a customer got up.

Each time, poor thieving birds, they threw themselves by twos and threes onto the empty table, voraciously swallowing up the remains. . . . Neither the street militia nor the waiters, nor the clients appeared shocked by their presence nor surprised by this evidently daily spectacle. . . . I have seen this sort of thing before. In China . . ." Roland Dorgelès wrote of his trip to Russia, "No one well dressed. No pretty smiles. Cleanliness is an exception. Elegance would be a challenge. Never, except in the Far East, have I experienced anything similar." Or, as Paul Morand put it, "When you reach Asia via Russia the transition is imperceptible."[70]

Such comparisons carried over into more forceful and hence more racist efforts to see in bolshevized Russia a return to Asiatic origins. *Asiatic* in this sense meant despotic, chaotic, barbaric, and brutal, anything that could express the horror that came with communist revolution and placed bolshevism beyond the pale of Western civilization. The argument was a powerful one and it explains much of the appeal of fascism and its call for a recharging of European energies. Yet it also had the effect of displacing ideological debates onto racial ground, offering a fundamentally racist interpretation of Soviet Russia that fused with yellow-peril obsessions. It placed the Red threat in Asia on the plane of an eternal conflict between East and West, endowing it with all the nightmarish characteristics of one more oriental assault upon Europe, one more race invasion, and one more race war. Thus Serge de Chessin's portrait of Russia as a despiritualized and depraved land, "a thick night, an integral darkness, a renewal of the Mongol invasion on a spiritual plane awaiting an apocalyptic raid from bolshevized Asia." Of bolshevism's Asiatic origins, de Chessin made it clear, there could be no doubt:

By their birth as by their education, the leaders of the Third International are not European. If Lenin's Tartar origins were not officially established, his Kalmuck features, the Mongolian projection of the cheekbones, the slanted cut of the eyes, the thick animality of the lips and nostrils would suffice, in the absence of all genealogical research, to reveal a perfect affiliation with the Turanian type. Among the spiritual descendants from the master, virulent Semites, halfbreeds who smack of the Golden Horde's invasion, Scythians got up as Slavs. The world revolution was in the hands of Zinoviev, a formidable Jew; it is now in the hands of Stalin, an oriental mongrel.[71]

In the story of Trebitsch Lincoln, that great patchwork of truth and fantasy that in the end was little more than a mythic projection of its times, we can recognize all of these themes. Woven into the legend of "the Jew Trebitsch Lincoln,"[72] the Westerner turned Easterner, the secret agent who would lead a revolt of Asia much like Zinoviev of Baku, upon whom the image was so clearly modeled, was the new sense of globalism after the war and the fears and maledictions that came with that vision.

Still, one detects something else in the allure of Trebitsch Lincoln and in the life he and others continually reinvented: a fabulous yarn cast against the sweep of the century and a great tale of danger and mystique set in faraway places. Like the war, his was a story that commanded retelling and invited embellishment, and that too is why storytellers found him so tempting a creature to write about. Trebitsch brought globalism together with phobias, but also with the romance of espionage and travel. His life was a profusion of campaigns and adventures spun from the great events of the day. These too made him a myth of his times, capturing softer histories and moods that, no less than alarums, explained the power of intrigue for the French in these years. Those softer histories suggest other connections between global visions and spies; and so they too force themselves upon our attention and lead us back to the voyages and adventures of wartime and after.

———

Werner Otto von Hentig's experience in the Great War was anything but typical, but it did represent what the event was to do for the meaning of adventure in the twentieth century. Born in 1886, the son of a Coburg-Gotha bureaucrat, von Hentig was already fashioning himself into a man of the world by the outbreak of war. After studying at Grenoble, Berlin, Paris, Bonn, and Königsberg, and taking a doctorate, von Hentig continued to travel in England and Belgium before entering the German Foreign Service in 1911. His first posting was Peking, where he witnessed the Chinese revolution. Transferred to Istanbul, he seized the opportunity to travel through Japan and southern China before heading west by way of Java and Sumatra and the eastern coast of Africa. The war caught him in Teheran from whence he hurried home to join his regiment. He took to the field and earned an Iron Cross, first class, in the first year of battle. Then in March 1915 he was recalled to Berlin to take charge of a special mission to Afghanistan. He was twenty-nine years old at this point, much traveled and tested; but only now were his real adventures to begin.

Von Hentig's was the third German expedition dispatched to the emir of Afghanistan with the intent of opening a front on the northwestern frontier of India. A first group had left Berlin in September of the previous year, hastily and clumsily patched together among men practically all ignorant of the lands they were to travel through. Almost immediately the Foreign Office had sought to remedy the situation by sending a second mission of Near Eastern specialists to overtake the first. This was the expedition led by Oskar Niedermayer, who had spent two years in Persia and India before the outbreak of the war. By early 1915 the Foreign Office was planning a third expedition to escort two Indian revolutionaries to Kabul. Looking for an expert to lead the mission, the Auswärtiges Amt fastened on von Hentig. On 14 April von Hentig set out from Berlin accompanied by two Germans — Dr. Becker and Walter Röhr — each previous sojourners in Persia, and by six Indian and Afridi volunteers rounded up in German prisoner of war camps.

The first leg of the journey, to Teheran, was uneventful. Once in the Persian capital, however, von Hentig began to comprehend what dangers lay ahead. To proceed east along the regular caravan routes across northern Persia would mean interception and capture by enemy patrols. Only by traveling across the great salt desert, an unthinkable route in normal times, could he hope to break through to Afghanistan. Even here the constant threat of attack by desert robber tribes would offset the absence of the British or Russians. He would have to mount a caravan of guides and camels, including mules and horses that were impractical for desert travel but essential for the continuation of the expedition once it had crossed to the other side. The travelers would have to proceed quickly, in daytime, through ghastly temperatures in the middle of summer. And even if they survived the tortuous journey they would still have to slip by enemy spies and patrols to cross the border into Afghanistan. The prospects were daunting but in the first days of July, his caravan organized, von Hentig set out for a slow, arduous, and almost deadly passage through the unforgiving wasteland of the Persian desert.

Along the way the caravan experienced every horror the desert could offer: terrible heat, terrible thirst, desolation, men who fell by the wayside, attacks by desert robbers, long stretches completely devoid of water holes, skeletons as the sole indication they had not lost their way. Dr. Becker, who proceeded deeper into the desert to hide their baggage, was set upon by Russians, fought his way loose only to be attacked by desert brigands who wounded him severely in the lung (miraculously he survived through the care of local tribesmen and went on to fight for a year in Baluchistan and Persia until he was betrayed to the English and handed over to the Russians; but that is another adventure to be recounted some other time). At one point, learning that two Russian columns were bearing down on them, the expedition left a water hole and plunged into an unexplored region of the desert, wandering for eight days through this hell hole. At last, nearly three weeks after they had begun, von Hentig and the other survivors emerged on the other side of the *Salzwüste*. There they were joined by Niedermayer, whose expedition also made the desert crossing, the two missions proceeding as one to Kabul following a dangerous break through Russian lines.

At Kabul they accomplished nothing. They had endured tremendous hardships to reach the city, but by spring 1916 they were prepared to endure many more to leave it and return home. On 21 May, close to eight months after their arrival in the capital, von Hentig, Niedermayer, Röhr, and other members of the expedition left Kabul and proceeded northward. After four days, knowing that the British and Russians would attempt to hunt them down, they split into separate parties to throw their pursuers off balance. Niedermayer headed west, back through Russian Turkestan and Persia. Von Hentig headed east, for the Hindu Kush and the Pamirs and then Chinese Turkestan. Ahead of him was a journey that would make the great salt desert crossing seem a trial run. "Above were nameless mountains and deserts, scarcely seen by the eyes of Afghans or Kirghiz, much less trod by human feet." Nevertheless, into that "never seen land" he charged.

His party edged along steep mountain paths no wider than a foot. They plunged into snow drifts that reached their horses' bellies. They forded icy rivers that swept over their animals' ears. They climbed over passes more than thirteen thousand feet high, stopping every twenty to thirty steps to regain their breath. They dodged Russian patrols and then, taking a bad turn, found themselves smack before a Russian encampment. They found a way out and pushed forward into the mountains. As more Russian riders came toward them von Hentig reached for his carbine, telling himself "at least they're not going to get us alive." Again they escaped and ascended still higher. "The following four days," he later noted, "with its tortuous climbing through the mountains I don't like to remember." At last, in the final days of June, they crossed over into Chinese Turkestan and what von Hentig believed to be neutral territory. Very quickly he was disabused of this notion.

In Kashgar Allied representatives intrigued against him and sought his arrest and execution by the Chinese military governor. Only the intervention of a Swedish missionary got him out of the city alive. From Kashgar he struck out across the Gobi, again evading enemy efforts to stop him. By November the desert was behind him. Now traveling was easy and he made his way to Hankow where he found refuge in the German consulate. He remained there until March, when the Chinese broke off diplomatic relations with Germany and von Hentig once again found himself on the run. He headed for Shanghai, made it, and then stowed away on a ship bound for neutral America. By the time he reached Hawaii the United States was in the war, so he jumped ship in the harbor and swam ashore. But that was the end. Realizing the game was over, von Hentig turned himself in to the American authorities. It proved a smart move. They repatriated him and he arrived back in Berlin in June 1917, 788 days and twenty-five thousand miles after he had left. Within months he was writing up his story, revealing little about his mission but telling nearly all about his travels and exploits. His publisher, in a preface, said that in the history of exploration and adventure von Hentig's experiences had rarely been equaled and scarcely surpassed.[73]

If an exaggeration, the boast was not altogether off the mark. A great adventure story, von Hentig's account had also been set against the backdrop of history; and that made a difference. In the past there had been truly remarkable adventure stories. One thinks, for example, of Ross, Nansen, and Peary in the Arctic or of Burton, Speke, and Baker in the tropics or of Caillié in the desert or of Przhevalskii in the mountains. To a degree Von Hentig's ordeals and his triumphs were a twentieth-century continuation of the extraordinary feats of the nineteenth-century explorers. The same motifs obtained: the great, almost superhuman challenge; the passage through faraway lands that practically no white man had seen; and the celebration of indomitable endurance over an inhospitable environment that sought to overwhelm and conquer at every turning. But for von Hentig it was the political factor — in this case the war — that propelled his journey forward, and that was to be the distinguishing feature of adventure in the new century. Again it is possible to recall nineteenth-century precedents. Oskar Lenz, in 1880, disguised as a Turk, penetrated as far as Timbuktu and Senegal, laying the way for a more methodical German penetration of Morocco. Stanley's march to retrieve Emin Bey had clear imperial motives in mind. Przhevalskii's exploratory raids into central Asia received the backing of the Russian government. Marchand's trek from Brazzaville to Fashoda was intended to preempt British command of the Sudan and the result was to bring France and England close to the brink of war. British reconnaissance rides through Turkestan deserts and high

Pamir passes were common enough stuff in the Great Game competition Peter Hopkirk has chronicled.[74]

Here too, however, there were clear differences, two in particular. First, political adventure in the nineteenth century was less pervasive than it would be in the twentieth. The quest for scientific knowledge, the obsession with mapping the unknown, the lure of fame or of leaving one's mark in history, or simply a yearning to reach out beyond security and comforts and to live the life of boys' tales were more likely than not to be the driving force behind earlier adventures. After 1914, as great historical developments penetrated even remote locales, the political adventure story became the rule. Second, the politicized adventures of the nineteenth century, for all their potential repercussions, lacked the envelopment in history that so frequently characterized the great adventures of the war years and after. In Indochina and the Sahara military men could live great adventure stories of conquest, but largely because they were historical sideshows, alone on the margins where nobody cared. Where a man like Marchand, with a decade of explorations behind him, might make history, von Hentig was situated in it. Larger world affairs spun out his adventures and forced perils upon him. Only to avoid enemy detection did von Hentig plunge into the desert and then throw himself into the mountains. Only because he was an enemy in unfriendly lands did he nearly lose his head in Kashgar or was he forced to steal away on a boat to America. For him politics was context, not simply pretense. Outside contemporary history his adventures had no meaning nor were even conceivable.

Thus the Great War introduced a new era in adventure because in that war and after, adventure tended to fuse with the great events of the age. There were still the odd gestures of defiance, Alain Gerbault's solo voyage across the Atlantic[75] or Lindbergh's above it, sheer expressions of human will pitted against the implacable odds. But the voyage to Mecca or Lhasa or to the source of the Nile for the sake of the challenge was becoming distinctly old-fashioned by the twentieth century. Far more often it was war and revolution that set adventures in motion or against which the great adventure tales of the world played themselves out. It could not be otherwise in a century as unsettled as the twentieth and where history was global in its proportions. In the new global age the expedition, the trek, or the descent into serial life-threatening circumstances, was caught up in history, or simply was unlikely to escape it.

In this respect von Hentig's experiences were indeed unparalleled, although only in comparison to earlier conditions. The war produced many such stories, most obviously Lawrence's in the Hejaz, but also that of Albert Bartels, the former trader who found himself leading a revolt of mountain tribesmen in Morocco or the exploits of Marthe Richard who, for whatever the embellishments, lived a life of danger in Spain and on board ship in the south Atlantic. Oskar Niedermayer, von Hentig's onetime companion, shared a no less fabulous adventure on his return from Afghanistan (or for that matter in his efforts to get there). Accompanied by a Persian and an Afghan, he crossed the Kara-Kum desert by night, one step ahead of a pursuing Turcoman party. At Mesched he found the city occupied by a detachment of six hundred Russians. Warned by a friend that the caravansaries swarmed with Russian informants, he set out for Teheran and then joined a caravan for Turkish-occupied Hamadan and safety. On the way they were ambushed and plundered by desert robber bands who cracked Niedermayer over the head and knocked him unconscious. Later he was picked up by Russians, but they failed to recognize who he was and he managed to elude them. Finally, at the end of August, he straggled into Hamadan and eventually made his way back to Berlin. The contrast with the earlier adventures of Burton could not have been greater. A half-century before, the Englishman had assumed a Muslim identity and made an unforgettable but completely contrived pilgrimage to Mecca to accomplish what practically no European had succeeded in doing before him. Niedermayer too disguised himself as a Muslim. He shaved his head, dyed his beard black, dressed as a Turcoman, and even removed a gold crown from a tooth. But he did so as a matter of survival to slip through enemy lines in the midst of a war that was absorbing all of the world.[76]

The war, because it was global, had that ability to turn what had formerly been adventure for the sake of adventure into the accomplishment of a military or political mission. Less than in the succeeding world war, but more than in the past, it swept people up, transported them over vast spaces, and then set them down in exotic lands where they could play out swashbuckling roles on the banks of the Nile or in armed caravans driving through the Caucasus[77] or where they simply found themselves face to face with strange and extraordinary encounters a world removed from their habitual surroundings. "Who could have dreamed," wrote Vera Brittain of her brother after the war, she herself having served in the eastern Mediterranean, "that the little boy born in such uneventful security to an ordinary provincial family would end his brief days in a battle among the high pine-woods of an unknown Italian plateau?" How much more fantastic then the lives of Emile Pagès and his companions who — out of boredom or love of adventure or simply a desire to get away from the trenches or a love affair turned sour — volunteered to operate a radio post in the middle of Siberia? Or the lives of those Czech soldiers who had gone over to the Russians and then traveled the breadth of Eurasia only to be sucked into the Russian civil war? In 1918 Joseph Kessel was beginning his travels across North America and the Pacific to Vladivostok, where he would spend his days stepping over bodies in the train station, a pistol strapped to his waist, a fortune on his person, spend his nights in the make-believe atmosphere of the Aquarium, and where he would pass a never-to-be-forgotten evening of drink among the *nagaika*-wielding Semenovtsy marauders that he would write up over and over again because he could not get it out of his mind and because it was so incredible that there was always a market for its telling. War adventures, in that sense, intimated of the intrusiveness that would so mark the interwar years. When the war was over, people continued to live with the great events of their day as the background noise to their lives, adventure more and more becoming a medium through which individuals were swallowed up in a direct or more immediate confrontation with that reality.[78]

"What distinguished us from our mentors, at twenty," Malraux told Jean Lacouture many years later, "was the presence of history."[79] The line could have been written for practically any of his creations, although the character it fit best was Michael Borodin, who appeared in *The Conquerors* as the cool, methodical professional, which he was. In real life Borodin was no less an adventurer, a river boatman turned revolutionary organizer, Chicago schoolteacher, and then Comintern agent. It was the last role, harnessed to the worldwide Russian revolution, that provided the scope for his prodigious talents and energies and that, by sending him to China, launched him on an enterprise that, despite its utter failure, would be the adventure of a lifetime. Already before his departure for Canton a Borodin legend had grown up around his clandestine work in Mexico, Spain, Germany, and England. In China the legend would burst beyond all proportion, set against the sweep of war and revolution in an ancient, faraway land.

Nearly everything about Borodin's time in China was romantic and oversized. He was sent as political adviser to the Kuomintang and for a while he all but directed affairs in southern China, but he reached Canton via cattleboat to avoid the British and the cloak of secrecy never entirely lifted from the mission. Upon his arrival he found everything in chaos and his own position precarious. Throughout he would be embattled on all sides — by warlords, by dissident communists, by anti-communist Kuomintang leaders, by the suspicions and ambitions of Chiang Kai-shek, by foreign imperialists, by the immense depths between European revolutionary aspirations and Chinese realities and traditions, and by the slipperiness of his own assignment that for all its potential remained a gamble and a somewhat preposterous proposition. But he maneuvered skillfully and won Sun Yat-sen's confidence, and thereby he pushed the Kuomintang forward and gave it direction. During the heyday he was there as the Kuomintang consolidated its hold over Canton, conducted the Canton–Hong Kong blockade, and prepared for the momentous northern expedition. For nearly four years he lived at the very center of the flow of events. He was a European halfway around the world in a ragged, war-torn land, but he was also making history and that made the undertaking all the more spellbinding. As Chiang rose in power and turned against him, he sought to salvage what he could from a disintegrating situation. At revolutionary Wuhan, as the whole enterprise was tottering, he remained a larger-than-life figure to those who still believed he was the one person who could hold things together. Borodin consented to act out that role, but he could see that the end was nearing. Even when it came the adventure continued. He left China by overland caravan across the Gobi desert — a difficult and dangerous journey but the only safe route out for a man with a thirty-thousand-dollar price on his head.[80]

Few forces shaped adventure more in the twentieth century than the Russian revolution. By allying with nationalist or anticolonial movements in the non-Western world it turned remote landscapes into breeding grounds for violent, dramatic episodes. Commissars in central Asia, a Borodin in China, or, to an only somewhat diminished degree, the dozens of Soviet volunteers who also came to China and whose lives for several years were filled with revolution, agitation, war, and considerable peril were all beneficiaries and victims of the revolution's displacement of adventure onto a political plane.[81] The clandestine nature of the enterprise and its international circuits that often wound through distant inhospitable lands were likewise forcing grounds for suspenseful and dangerous experiences. Nearly everything about a Comintern mission — getting to one's base of operations, avoiding capture, living double lives, setting events into motion, moving through the badlands of the world, and then ultimately finding one's way back again — contained the stuff out of which adventure stories were made.

But it was also the stormy effects of revolution, tossing individuals into a maze of life threatening circumstances and casting them into the outer regions of the world, that made the revolution, like the war, a powerful device for coupling adventure to history. What happened to Ferdinand Ossendowski, who found himself on the wrong side of the revolution in Siberia in 1919, is a formidable example; there are indeed few tales more remarkable than his in the annals of adventure in modern times.[82] Proscribed by the Reds, he flees into the forest in the region of Krasnoyarsk. He meets Ivan, a Siberian peasant, who kills two Bolsheviks hunting counterrevolutionaries and shows him how to build a log hearth to keep warm through the Siberian nights. He moves deeper into the forest and hunts to keep himself alive. He is attacked by a bear but finally brings it down with three bullets. In the spring, as the ice of the Yenisei river breaks up, he watches the flow of hundreds of mutilated cadavers, a reminder of his own fate if he is captured by the Reds. That motif never leaves his story. The Bolshevik menace hovers over this tale, a ubiquitous and omnipresent danger that gives his journey meaning and determines its action.

Ossendowski by now is constantly on the run. He goes to a deserted gold mine where he stays for a while with the guardian and his family. He meets an agronomist, a giant of a man who will be his companion for the remainder of his travels. Together they decide to flee Russia, descending into Mongolia and then breaking through to the Pacific and freedom. From this point the adventure assumes the countenance of the great treks for survival, a march through desolate and treacherous lands, buffeted always, however, by the gales of history. They travel through territory infested with Red detachments hunting down White officers. Ossendowski vows never to be taken alive and carries with him cyanide crystals. They travel over rivers and steppes. They pass by villages inhabited by Red spies. As they approach the border between Russia proper and Urianhai (in the north of Mongolia), tension mounts: "three days of constant contact with a lawless population, of continuous danger and of the ever present possibility of fortuitous death." They cross over into Urianhai, where they journey down valleys, over mountains, through burned woods, and across the Yenisei at night to avoid partisans. They have a firefight with Reds. They wrap their horses' hooves in shirts to muffle the sound as they pass close by more of the enemy. By this time Ossendowski and his friend have been joined by a number of former White officers. After a while they divide into two groups. One moves west, where it will run into Red cavalry and be practically wiped out.

Ossendowski, his friend, and sixteen others continue with their plan to reach Lake Kosogol and then strike east for the Pacific.

They ride on, crossing swamps, rivers, and mountains over steep cliff trails. They endure icy winds and freezing rains that soak through their clothing. At a Soyot village they are told that entry into the principality is forbidden. But Ossendowski cures the headman's son of a nosebleed and then the prince's daughter of "blindness" (conjunctivitis). Grateful, the prince provides a guide to Lake Kosogol. In the mountains they are again attacked by Reds, a bad sign that Bolshevik detachments have spread into Mongolia. They force the Reds back and make their way through the mountains down to the Mongolian plains where the going is easier. "But we were not gay, because again before us lay the dread uncertainty that threatened us with new and possibly destructive dangers." They come upon yurts and are again fired on by Reds. They forge ahead, only to learn that Chinese troops bar the way to the Pacific. They alter their plans and strike south through the Gobi and into Tibet. As they enter Tibet all the signs are ominous. At a monastery they encounter brigands who are armed to the teeth. Lone horsemen shadow them, galloping off as they approach. Then they are ambushed and two Russians are killed. They push on and again they are ambushed and lose another man. There is nothing to do but retreat and return to Mongolia. They fight their way out of Tibet at the cost of three more men and several wounded, including Ossendowski, who is hit in the leg. Once out of Tibet the party splits up. The officers leave to join White detachments continuing the civil war in Mongolia. Ossendowski and his companion head for the Mongolian town of Uliassautai.

It is now 1921 and Uliassautai is a center of intrigues between Reds, Whites, Chinese, and Mongols all fighting over control of the land. The question for the refugees in the town—and it is a terrifying one—is how close are the Reds to taking the city. Ossendowski rides out on reconnaissance missions through what he now describes as a magical landscape: "Mysterious Mongolia"; "The Land of Demons." He meets the Tushegoun lama, who possesses strange hypnotic powers. He comes upon Mongol medicine men. And yet he is never far removed from the twentieth century whose politics have invaded this remote and exotic country. At a telegraph post he encounters Red assassins. At the tiny settlement of Khathyl he rides into a panic of White troops who fear an imminent attack by a large Bolshevik contingent and he is forced to flee for his life. Back in Uliassautai there are constant intrigues between Chinese, Mongols, Soviet agents, White Russian troops, renegade White Russians who are little more than bandits, the balance of forces shifting with every rumor of the fortunes of one side or the other. "Once more we found ourselves in the whirl of events."

As the situation deteriorates they leave Uliassautai for Urga (now Ulan Bator). On the way he is summoned by Colonel Kazagrandi who is fighting with Baron Ungern-Sternberg, a murderous White general seeking to carve out a vast central Asian empire independent of the Bolsheviks. To get to the colonel he travels past monasteries and ruins of cities dating back to the time of Genghis Khan. He is stopped by Mongol soldiers led by White Russians — a thoroughly vicious and murderous crew who will gun down anyone they suspect of being a Red, and that is just about everyone they meet. Ossendowski, having made it through the forests, the mountains, the deserts, the firefights, now faces the extravagantly ironical prospect of being killed by his own side. But he manages to convince them he is not a Bolshevik and they let him go. Meanwhile his leg is getting worse, he develops a fever, and he is attacked by dogs in the night. At the final relay post before Van Kure, where Kazagrandi's headquarters are located, he has his fortune told by an old Mongol who prophesies danger from a man with a head in the shape of a saddle. At Van Kure he meets Ungern-Sternberg himself, who greets him before a pool of blood. Ossendowski senses his life hangs by a thread, but he wins the baron's confidence and is free to proceed on to Urga. In Urga he is struck by the fabulous atmosphere of the place where ancient cultures and contemporary conflicts coexist and entangle. In the streets he sees lamas, Tartars, Buriats, but also Ungern-Sternberg's soldiers in blue, Mongols and Tibetans in red and yellow clothing bearing swastika insignias and those of the Living Buddha, and Chinese troops who have gone over to the Mongol armies and wear silver dragons on their uniforms. He is introduced to Colonel Sepailov, a sadistic butcher and a nut case who is Ungern-Sternberg's commandant at Urga. The colonel's head is bald and takes the shape of a saddle. Ossendowski senses once again his life is threatened, but he is now under the protection of the baron, who takes a liking to him and tells him his life story. Life in Urga becomes surrealistic. The baron drives him around in his automobile and then presents him to the Living Buddha. Sepailov tries to kill him but fails. At last Ungern-Sternberg clears the way for a journey to Manchuria and the Pacific and Ossendowski leaves accompanied by the Mongol minister of war. Sepailov tries to waylay them but fails once again. And finally, sometime in 1921, Ossendowski makes it to Peking and out of the rabbit hole of history into which he has tumbled.[83]

So fantastic was the story that Lewis Stanton Palen in the introduction to the French edition (it sold, perhaps, forty thousand copies within a year) went to pains to remind readers that the author was a distinguished scientist. Ossendowski was in fact no novice to Russian politics: he had been active in a Siberian separatist movement in 1905 and then again in the Kolchak government during the Russian civil war. It was the collapse of that government that had precipitated his flight into the forest. Much of his earlier life, prospecting for mineral deposits in Siberia, had been fairly exciting and a preparation for the trials he was to face after 1919. Still Stanton caught the essential difference between earlier encounters with tigers and tarantulas and the tale told in *Beasts, Men and Gods* when he called Ossendowski a twentieth-century Robinson Crusoe and said that "only the extraordinary events of the extraordinary period we live in" could have produced such a memoir.[84]

That time-bounded quality to adventure in these years cannot be denied. The war set it in motion and the Russian revolution kept it going, but nearly everything about the period — its flux or unsettlement, its global connectedness, its political intrusiveness into peoples' lives, and its abundance of opportunities for getting rich out of major historical confrontations — worked to tie adventure and contemporary history together. The pattern pervaded all kinds of adventures. Ella Maillart, setting out on a trek from Peking to Kashmir through Chinese Turkestan in 1935 for the love of adventure and a subject to write about, noted soldiers and troop movements and sensed herself caught in a swirl of clashes of a continental magnitude.[85] Soldiers of fortune or adventurers (in the more pejorative meaning of the word) gravitated toward wars and revolutions of world historical consequence because increasingly these were the sources of action and money. Mercenary pilots who had barnstormed or had fought over Paraguayan jungles were, by the thirties, heading for Ethiopia, Spain, and China.[86] Swindlers like Corrigan and Eckelman, gunrunners like Goldberg, or dubious types like Gardiner drifted inevitably at some point into the main political currents. Those who fell into history and lived adventurous lives as its victims must have been countless. The Russian revolution produced more than its share, but a little over a decade later anti-Nazi refugees who were scrambling for false papers, infiltrating closed borders, and staying one jump ahead of the police were creating their own dismal tales to hand down to future generations.

Thus adventure, like politics or society, has its own history. For the French there were many great adventure stories in these years, but probably none quite so striking as the Croisière jaune. The Expédition Citroën Centre-Asie, or Croisière jaune as it was more popularly known (the term translates roughly as the yellow cruise, but certainly not a leisurely journey), was a motor caravan across the entire breadth of the Asian continent. Its main group left Beirut in April 1931 and rolled into Peking on 12 February 1932. It crossed the central Asian plateaus, attacked the Pamirs, and then, joining with a second group arriving from the east, forced its way through the Gobi and Chinese Turkestan. It was a celebrated moment for the French—a great national epic of sorts—that spawned magazine articles, books by its participants (the official history was printed in nearly forty thousand copies during the depression), and a documentary film shot as the caravan rumbled forward. In a variety of ways it was the quintessential interwar expedition, a series of exploits fabricated from the times that caught the spirit of how adventures were changing.

How this was so can be seen in the story of its voyage, and also in the developments that preceded and enveloped it. The Croisière jaune was not the first Asiatic crossing by car. As early as 1907 the French daily *Le Matin* sponsored a Peking-to-Paris motor race. The race grew out of commercial considerations but also out of what would be a growing tendency in the twentieth century for the expedition proper to mutate into the *raid* or long-distance run. Both the automobile and the airplane opened new possibilities for adventurous dashes across vast stretches of territory. They offered a speed and a mobility hitherto unknown, but the very conquering force of their technology created its own daunting muster of challenges. For nearly every challenge there was a taker, who was quick to dress up the enterprise in talk of colonial missions and extending communication lines or the other clichés of the period, although mostly these cloaked a naked love of adventure. The result was flights and motor trips over inhospitable regions to prove that one could take a plane or a car or truck anywhere in the world and that one could do it the fastest of all. The challengers who entered the Peking-to-Paris race were of this breed. Of the five entries who showed in China—three French, one Dutch, and one Italian car—the Italian team won handily, making the run of nearly eight thousand miles in two months.

The Italians traveled in a specially constructed Itala of thirty-five to forty horsepower through the Gobi and Mongolia into Russian Siberia, skirting the southern reaches of Lake Baikal to Irkutsk, and then westward to Omsk and across into Europe. Not until Nizhni Novgorod did they reach a paved roadbed. Before then they had driven over desert, mud, terrain akin to quicksand, and railway ties, occasionally hauled across rivers by oxen or horses.

Luigi Barzini, a foreign correspondent for the *Corriere della Sera*, accompanied the winners and wrote up the journey in a memorable book that was something of a classic in middle-class Italian households after the war, "one of the traditional gifts bestowed on diligent school boys who passed their examination" and that attested to the resonance of the race to the subsequent postwar generation. The endearing tales of the trip like that of the Chinese clerks at the Gobi telegraph station who dutifully transmitted Barzini's dispatch after writing "No. 1" on the top of the form or of the German *Hausfrau* who shook her fists at the car and shouted out her window, "I know you *canaille!* It was you who ran over my hen last Thursday. Pay up!" as the car drove through her village no doubt contributed to the popularity of the volume. Yet Barzini also captured the true adventure of crossing Asia on wheels in the very first years of automobiles, and his account remains compelling reading today.[87]

The Croisière jaune, however, was something else again. It was a motor caravan of half-tracks, fourteen vehicles and forty-three men in all, methodically planned and organized, and attempting a crossing over mountains where the Itala could not have dared to go. Its adventures emerged from the obstacles and hazards of the landscape, but also from the political turmoils into which it rode. Unquestionably its style built upon prewar developments, for example, the turning toward professionalism of nineteenth-century explorers like Amundsen, who fashioned himself from childhood into the consummate explorer or Peary, who worked out a methodology to make it to the top.[88] In its advance positioning of supplies it repeated, if more systematically, what the Itala team had done over twenty years earlier. But its precedents came elsewhere, from the war years and after.

Of these there were several. One was the Expédition Citroën Centre-Afrique or Croisière noire, a motorized caravan through Africa in 1924–1925 led by the same men who were to sally into the Asian continent seven years later. Devised for its own purposes, the Croisière noire demonstrated that the *autochenilles* or half-tracks the Citroën factories had been developing since the beginning of the decade were capable of all-terrain travel in the most unfamiliar parts of the world. It too, moreover, was a carefully organized operation that had required more than a year of methodical planning and had been preceded or accompanied by five auxiliary missions to arrange supply depots between Algeria and the Indian Ocean. This also would establish a working pattern for the later preparation of the Croisière jaune.[89]

Roy Chapman Andrews's American Asiatic expeditions into the Gobi throughout the 1920s were another antecedent. These were purely scientific missions rather than long-distance runs. Yet their drawing board meticulousness and fascination for technological prowess as well as their military look would also anticipate the Croisière jaune, and their adventures in central Asia would reveal the politicized encounters that awaited any truck caravan through this region in the interwar years. Andrews's goal was to study "the geologic history of central Asia; to find whether it had been the nursery of many of the dominant groups of animals, including the human race; and to reconstruct its past climate, vegetation and general physical conditions, particularly in relation to the evolution of man." Today the expeditions are best known for their discovery of dinosaur eggs, but in the twenties they represented the forced conquest by machines over terrain, through a combination of planning, technology, and militarylike organization. Realizing that "the fenceless rolling grasslands and the gravel desert [of Mongolia] made it possible to run off the trail at will," Andrews took his men by car into a land where there was not a single mile of railroad, where camel caravans traveled at a rate of ten miles a day, and where winter temperatures could drop to fifty degrees below zero. They traveled in Dodges because Andrews had determined that the Fords occasionally in service for caravan runs from Kalgan to Urga were inadequate for the task and that Dodges, when modified, made it "almost impossible to break a spring when traveling on rough ground." Fastidiously, with the heart of a conqueror but the mind of a quartermaster, Andrews planned out the remainder of his options. "We found that the 33 × 4.5 Royal cord tire made by the United States Rubber Company, gave the best service. . . . We carried hundreds of nuts and bolts, almost every conceivable spare part, and the very best tools; our motor experts were highly trained men." He reconnoitered — "it was obvious that the first season must be strictly a reconnaissance"; divided the main force into separate, self-contained units; and arranged for support columns — "the supporting caravan, carrying gasoline, food and other supplies, was dispatched several weeks in advance of the motor party. Its objective was a well-known place in the desert."[90]

Andrews said he did not believe in adventures. "Most of them can be eliminated by foresight and organization." But his expeditions were packed full of them. They encountered bandits as law and order collapsed in the region and consequently discovered themselves caught as well in the aftershocks of the Russian revolution and in the bloody throes of China's civil wars and her passage into the Nationalist era. In 1922 they arrived in Urga just after Ungern-Sternberg's defeat and the shift from a White to Red terror. "Murder and sudden death stalked ahead upon the streets. It was an exceedingly good place to leave." In 1925 they were obliged to take Buriat secret service agents with them into the desert and narrowly escaped arrest. In Peking in 1926 Andrews was caught in a bombing run that came perilously close to blowing him up and the following month he was caught again in a machine gun attack on the road to Tientsin. He rode through a "gauntlet of firing" for three miles, claiming the only reason he was "not riddled with bullets . . . [was] because the Chinese soldier is the world's worst shot." Conditions became so bad that both the 1926 and 1927 expeditions were canceled. By 1928 they were rolling back into the desert, bribing brigands, dodging ambushes, and engaging in a gun battle with bandits, shooting one man's ear off in the fight.[91]

Such adventures were an indication that any motorized convoy through the region in the twenties and thirties would find itself inextricably wound into world politics. Explanations extended from intrigues surrounding air routes and explorers to military prospects for the future but began, as almost always, with the geopolitical effects of the First World War. The war was critical because it disclosed the degree to which European confrontations could distend into global warfare with strategic consequences to action in faraway, exotic, and desolate places. Central Asia in that conflict, for example, had seen subversive expeditions across Persia and Afghanistan, campaigns into the Caucasus, and a tangle of revolutionary politics that fused with world war and spread from Persia to Mongolia. There had been horse patrols through Turkestan and the Pamirs into Mongolia to gather intelligence and prevent tons of supplies from falling into the hands of the enemy (Captain Blacker's adventures, written up after the war, would be recommended reading for the Citroën planners). An armored car convoy — the Dunsterforce — had been introduced into the western reaches of the region to gather intelligence, stymie the Bolsheviks, counter German agents, secure the oilfields of Baku or perhaps destroy them, and build new lines of resistance to the Turks among the Russian, Armenian, and Georgian troops in the area (only the maelstrom of the final act to the First World War could have produced such an idiotic concoction; the expedition failed miserably).[92]

The war had therefore brought disruption, revolution, the precedent of motorized caravans for military-political purposes, and a new history of global intrigue to the region. Even more, it had demonstrated the need to assure communication lines and to move rapidly across large and inhospitable landmasses. A German plan to buy up Mongolian cattle and herd them westward to war-depleted Turkey was instructive here. Reading about it today, one sees it as a fantastic notion, a cattle drive across a continent and through enemy lines in the midst of a global battle that would make the American trails of the west seem trifling by comparison. The French captain who warned of the plan suggested its most likely route would proceed from Chinese Turkestan through the Kilik pass in the Pamirs. But he also added that "there must exist in this southern corridor of the Pamirs . . . unmapped passes with tracks that can be followed by a herd that, having penetrated into the Amou Daria valley, will find in Afghanistan and Persia easy means to reach Baghdad rapidly and from there Asia Minor." He recommended maintaining a close watch over the mountain gorges and passes. Whether the Germans ever mounted such a drive seems highly improbable. Still the prospect pointed to the military significance of pioneering a motorized land corridor across the central Asian highlands. Fourteen years later the Citroën expedition would seek to do precisely that, following almost the exact itinerary in reverse as it moved east from Persia and Afghanistan over Gilgit and Kilik into Chinese Turkestan.[93]

After the war the geopolitical implications to establishing regular and rapid means of communication across vast stretches of the world could be seen in the intrigues spun out of international air routes. Intercontinental routes aroused a host of suspicions. To the French, German air corridors over Asia or Africa were a medium for extending German influence and power around the globe. They recalled the Berlin-to-Baghdad railroad but also more recent associations. The Teheran-Bouchir route flew into "where Wassmuss distinguished himself," the Teheran-Herat line with connections to Tashkent and Kabul penetrated "[the] region agitated by Niedermayer in 1917."[94] Along the west coast of Africa French agents thought they had located secret air bases or straw commercial installations to be converted to military purposes in the event of war.[95]

No attempt to establish communication lines over distant parts of the world could fully escape such political assumptions in the twenties and thirties. It was a way of thinking that bore certain universal traits, but also the mark of the global uncertainty that followed the war and that would easily transfer to any attempt to forge a land route through comparable areas. The connections, however, between a *raid* like the Citroën expedition and the suspicions attached to commercial air routings could also wind deeper. The very concept of a *raid,* for instance, smacked of the earlier long-distance air flights that had pioneered prospects for more routinized air service across oceans or mountains, deserts, and jungles. Moreover, the establishment of regular air transport would require weather stations, radio transmitters, landing strips, and fuel depots in remote corners of the world—Gobi outposts or mountainside air bases that were fabulous stuff for conjuring up great geopolitical intrigues or designs and that, besides, could come into being only with exploration and transport by land.

The career of Sven Hedin shows how these connections could happen. By the interwar years Hedin was one of the most celebrated explorers in the world and a man whose name was inseparable from adventure and expeditions through central Asia. As a boy in Sweden he had immersed himself in the accounts of great, contemporary exploration and had fallen under the spell of someday leading an expedition of his own to the mysterious heartland of the Asian continent. The urge to follow "the clangour of caravan-bells" never left him; at the age of eighty-five he still noted "that in my dreams I hear the melancholy sound of the caravans' bronze bells, that song of the deserts, unchanged through thousands of years." He was headstrong and courageous, thoroughly restless and incurably romantic; but he was also a professionally trained geographer, a skilled mapmaker, a gifted linguist, and an irrepressible self-publicist who understood the connection between public attention and private financing. Most of his life he traveled by horse and by camel, across deserts and into mountains. Practically nothing discouraged him. He crossed the Pamirs in midwinter, tried to penetrate Tibet disguised as a pilgrim, and when this attempt failed, he returned again and pushed his way through, despite British objections. At times he was foolhardy, once leading a caravan across the murderous Takla Makan Desert, losing two men, all but one of his camels, and nearly his own life in the process. Yet nothing held Hedin back. "I longed," he once noted, "for the open air, and for great adventures on lonely roads." His expeditions were long-term affairs, always for scientific purposes, that resulted in a mapping of the Transhimalayas, the location of the precise sources of the Indus and Brahmaputra, and a detailed physical geography of much of central Asia. No one who traveled through Kashgar or Mongolia in the twentieth century did so without sensing his formidable presence.[96]

But to Western circles in the twenties and thirties he was also a suspicious character. British intelligence maintained a file on him and to the Shanghai municipal police he was "notorious for his adventures in international espionage" (he turned up, in all places, in the dossier on Eckelman/Lund).[97] No doubt these suspicions emanated in part from the rumors that inevitably circulated about scientific missions to faraway places and that built upon the tradition of "intelligence rides" along border regions in Asia and Africa.[98] Before 1914 tales of espionage had hung over expeditions to the Near East or treks into the mountains of the Asian subcontinent. After the war the suspicions escalated as French agents tracked German ethnological and sociological enterprises to western Africa or apprehensively watched geological missions traveling from China and Mongolia into Turkestan. Bernard Vernier, who mapped German Middle East intrigues and whose writing caught official notice, warned that German archaeologists, ethnographers, and geologists working from Syria to Iraq might be preparing another "'revolt in the desert' with sabotage of airfields, rail lines, and pipe lines." In fact, there were reasons to be suspicious. The First World War had seen German explorers undertake secret missions and in the thirties German archaeologists were doubling as Nazi propaganda agents in Mesopotamia. Later, in 1940 during the first full year of a second world war, the Abwehr would dispatch a *Sonderkommando* composed of scientists, geographers, geologists, meteorologists, and mineralogists to prepare for military operations in North Africa and the middle band stretching across the continent.[99]

More damning for Hedin, however, were his German connections. All his life he was a Germanophile. He worshipped German culture and, fearing Russian designs on Sweden, regarded the Reich as the principal barrier to a Russian drive westwards. In 1914 he had encouraged the Germans to embark on their Afghanistan adventure, counseling that the emir "burned to break loose against British rule in India." Later in the war he would write favorably of the German war effort, including a nine-hundred-page tome entitled *War Against Russia* that the Germans translated as *Nach Osten!* Neither German defeat nor the rise of the Nazis shook his unwavering belief in the value of things German. He openly acknowledged descent from a Jewish grandparent, yet his relations with Hitler were cordial and he allowed himself, with some reservations, to be used for German propaganda.[100]

By the twenties, moreover, those connections were defining Hedin's work as an explorer and geographer. His last great central Asian adventure — the Sino-Swedish expedition — was an amalgam of conventional scientific missions and grand German schemes to lay out an air route from Berlin to Peking. It originated in a proposal from Hugo Junkers in 1925 to pay all of Hedin's expenses to western China and Turkestan (Sinkiang province) if he would collaborate in preparing the way for regular air service, and when Junkers ran into financial difficulties the following year, Deutsche Lufthansa picked up the project. Thus Hedin was off once again for inner Asia accompanied this time by Swedish scientists and field managers but also by a German meteorologist and German pilots, most of whom had flown in the war. The expedition gathered an enormous cache of information on the geography, geology, archaeology, and paleontology of the region — by 1980 over fifty scientific monographs had issued from its findings — but its principal purpose was to prepare an aerial infrastructure of landing strips, weather stations, and fuel depots in some of the most remote parts of the world. It headed into a country racked by tension between Muslim and Chinese, a zone vulnerable to Comintern propaganda and slowly wound into the Soviet orbit, a land contested between the central Chinese government and independent-minded Turkestan warlords, a territory that by the early thirties was breaking out into open rebellion and warfare, amidst great power maneuvers and foreign intrigues by agents like Colonel Schomberg who roamed the land for British intelligence. The German Foreign Office displayed considerable reluctance to promote a venture clearly diving into a political rat nest and likely to be perceived as more than an innocent commercial enterprise. It insisted on a Swedish identity to the mission — hence the name Sino-Swedish — to avoid visible entanglement in Chinese affairs: a sign of the geopolitical complications that would consume such an expedition in the postwar years.[101]

Hedin's group did, in fact, encounter obstacle after obstacle, running into staunch opposition not only from the Chinese but the British and the Russians who spread rumors of larger, more diabolical intentions to discredit Hedin and his men. Nor were these completely inaccurate. The expedition became a spearhead of German influence in Sinkiang until Russian interference put an end to further German penetration into the area. Meanwhile through the late 1920s Hedin and the Germans proceeded to map prospective weather stations and landing sites for Lufthansa. As the company's exasperation with Chinese stalls progressed with the years, Hedin was obliged to seek additional sources of funding. Yet the Lufthansa identity and the suspicions this aroused stuck to the expedition. When at last in 1933 the surveying, scooping, drawing, collecting, negotiating, cajoling, and managing of a multiheaded, thoroughly modern team exploration came to an end the sixty-eight-year-old Hedin plunged deeper into political waters. With civil war raging in Sinkiang and Soviet influence inexorably gaining, the Nationalist Chinese engaged Hedin to survey motor routes into the territory in a bid to reassert their authority over the province. In late 1933 Hedin, several Swedes, and three Chinese set out in a caravan of two cars and three trucks. Over the next fourteen months they bounced from adventure to adventure, enduring house arrest, confiscation of their vehicles, and at one point an imminent threat of execution. By early 1935 Hedin was back, reporting his recommendations to the Chinese government. He returned to Stockholm in April, nine years after he had initially embarked and at the end of his most prolonged, most fruitful, yet most controversial expedition.[102]

Hedin, then, was a figure who would cast a long shadow over any expedition rolling through central Asia. Few men had lived a life as exciting as his, but he had also dabbled in politics and lent his skills as an explorer and geographer to enterprises that extended beyond science or fame. By the interwar years he brought together in his person adventure, exploration, and the surveying of land and air passages with motorized caravans, but also the geopolitical intrigues and suspicions that could surround all of these undertakings. One contemporary summed it up when he wrote that the opening of corridors for rapid movement across Asia was part of a larger preparation for war that would engulf all of the world and in which geographers and explorers would play as important a role as the diplomats and politicians. Hedin, he suggested, was doing just that, intruding in wider international affairs.[103] For Hedin the Sino-Swedish expedition was the end of the line. It capped a remarkable career that had seen fabulous journeys, worthy discoveries, and immersion in the forces and events that were reshaping Asia. That too made him a forerunner of the Croisière jaune and a creation of his times, because in his own personal voyage from explorer to political adventurer he fell under an essential influence of the age.

Organization, the mania to apply new technology to move human beings and equipment across distant lands, and postwar geopolitics thus formed the background to the Croisière jaune. All three were built into the expedition from the beginning, particularly the last; indeed so politically charged in its design and destination was the Croisière jaune that from start to conclusion it was nearly as much a government venture as it was a Citroën expedition. Just when the moment of conception for a central Asian crossing occurred is a question mark, although most likely it began to germinate the instant the Croisière noire was over. Louis Audoin-Dubreuil, who was second in command to Georges-Marie Haardt on both expeditions, said that Haardt first speculated about leading a caravan to the South Pole and that only when a study proved this infeasible did he turn to the idea of driving across Asia.[104] But after Africa, Asia was the logical terrain for a larger, more challenging, and more sensational enterprise; and both Haardt and Citroën were looking for a sequel, the one because he could not rid himself of the bug of adventure and the other because he knew the extraordinary publicity that would surround a company convoy over the silk route.

Yet as early as 1924 French official thinking was beginning to travel along the same lines. In that year a member of the French legation in Peking, a man named Garreau who spoke Russian and six Asiatic languages, was proposing a personal journey through Hami, Urumchi, and Kashgar in Sinkiang, continuing over the Pamirs to Kabul. He noted the growing political significance of the region, the contest between Soviets and British, the vast oil deposits to be tapped, and the prospect that air service from Europe to the Orient would seek the most direct route across central Asia. His voyage, he argued, would provide an opportunity to investigate the political and economic conditions of Turkestan and the future role that France might play in the area. Garreau's letter to his superiors in Paris now forms the first document in the Quai d'Orsay's dossier on the Croisière jaune, an introduction to the tight collaboration between the state and the adventurers that would include negotiations with foreign powers, reconnaissance missions, the loan of military personnel, and the monitoring of the expedition from its beginning through its end.[105]

The Deuxième Bureau (intelligence section, no less) was brought into the planning, filing in 1927 a detailed report on routing, climate, timing, liaisons, maps, necessary equipment, reconnaissance, and the location of supply bases as if they had been ordered to prepare for a military invasion.[106] Four military attachés were attached to the mission: Captain Bertrand in Teheran, who was to prepare the way for the journey through western Asia and accompany the mission; Waddington, a lieutenant, who was charged with reconnoitering a return route through southern Asia; Lieutenant Commander Pecqueur, a geodesist (or so he was listed), who replaced Bertrand as the Quai d'Orsay began to anticipate Persian opposition if the latter came along; and Victor Point, another lieutenant commander and the nephew of Philippe Berthelot, the Quai d'Orsay's secretary general.[107]

Of the four, Point was to play the most important role. In the mid-1920s he had commanded a gunboat on the upper Yangtze. He was young, less than thirty at the time he joined the expedition, but he was committed, coolheaded, decisive, and a bit of a political animal, all talents he would have to draw on for the next several years. As the planning firmed up he was dispatched to Peking to negotiate rights of passage and to organize supply bases on Chinese territory. There he managed to obtain the necessary authorizations and to secure the services of a French civil engineer named Petropavlovsky,[108] who was an old China hand and possessed the contacts and know-how to oversee routing and provisioning from the China end. Point returned to Paris in spring of 1930, but several months later he was off again for China to position supplies in Mongolia and Turkestan. His orders read that he was on a "reconnaissance expedition," which meant that he was expected to gather political and military intelligence as well as geographical and scientific data. He was to be accompanied by Pierre Teilhard de Chardin and by a radio operator who the Quai d'Orsay insisted should be a military man.[109]

Meanwhile, Haardt and Citroën were lining up sponsors, soliciting authorizations, firming up itineraries, and dispatching reconnaissance missions of their own. They named André Goerger secretary general of the expedition and sent him to Persia and Russia up to the Sinkiang frontier to reconnoiter the land; "the point of attack," according to original plans, would be through Soviet Turkestan. For two years Goerger traveled, met with Sven Hedin, and charted conditions that would hinder or facilitate a passage.[110] At the same time Haardt and the Citroën technical personnel threw themselves into assembling the team and designing the vehicles for the run. All told, nearly forty men would go. Haardt and Audoin-Dubreuil would head up the general staff. They would be accompanied by Pecqueur, Point, Teilhard de Chardin, and Charles Brull, director of Citroën laboratories. A representative of the National Geographic Society of Washington, D.C. (a cosponsor),[111] would go along, as would the archaeologist Jean Hackin and the naturalist André Reymond. There would be a four-man film crew from Pathé Nathan, three radio operators, two doctors, an official historian (Georges Le Fèvre), an artist, an interpreter, a cook, and eighteen mechanics including two chief mechanics, Ferracci and Penaud.

They would travel in seven half-tracks constructed of duraluminum, with six-cylinder forty-horsepower engines that could obtain a maximum speed of thirty-three kilometers per hour. Each vehicle would contain a front section or cabin for ferrying the men, a rear section designed according to the specific function of the truck, and each would tow a trailer containing water tanks, personal baggage, dressing cases, tents, beds, tables, and seats. The lead vehicle would be "the command car," conveying Haardt and his *état-major*. It would carry the maps, documents, weapons, typewriters, "archives," and art supplies. Next would come the scientists and their instruments. The following two trucks would transport the film crew and their equipment, much of it built into special panels on the sides of the vehicle. The radio men and machinery capable of transmitting and receiving over an eight-thousand-kilometer range would constitute half-track number five, to be followed by the mess wagon and finally a combination pharmacy/surgery/workshop truck with drawers and special compartments constructed into the sides behind hinged panels. All of the caterpillar trucks would have lifting panels of some sort, behind which would be fixed a mirror, electric light, and sink to facilitate washing up in the morning. Even today, on the verge of the twenty-first century, one is struck by the sophistication of these vehicles. Equally stunning was the degree of comfort built into an expedition heading out to conquer some of the most forlorn and rugged territory in the world.[112]

Haardt, centralizing operations from an office in the Place de l'Opéra, clearly intended to prepare for any eventuality. Six reconnaissance voyages and five supply missions preceded the Croisière jaune. But nothing came easily. Negotiations with the Soviets went up and down like a yo-yo. First the French could traverse the Soviet Union but on a route north of Soviet Turkestan. Then they were accorded passage through Turkestan. Then in late 1930 the authorization for passage was withdrawn altogether, only several months before the journey was scheduled to begin. Haardt was left with two options, either to cancel or to reroute through the Hindu Kush and the Pamirs. The first, by this point, was no choice at all, but the second required a major reworking of the expedition. Crossing mountains demanded design revisions in the vehicles, and there was no guarantee that even then the half-tracks could make it across. In the face of these difficulties Haardt, determined to plunge on, made the only sensible decision he could: to divide the expedition in two. A main group under his command would proceed eastbound as planned, driving seven lighter vehicles modified for a mountain crossing. At the same time a second group commanded by Point would set out from China in the seven originally built caterpillars and rendezvous with Haardt somewhere in western Chinese Turkestan. If the first vehicles made it over the mountains they would continue as a convoy of fourteen to the Pacific. If not, Haardt and a large body of his men would complete the mountain passage however they could until they joined with Point and motored on westwards. The decision must have cost Haardt dearly, representing as it did the prospect of a cruel diminution of his original goals. Yet nearly all the exploits that followed, making the Croisière jaune the great adventure it became, would be a consequence of these alterations. In the meantime, the pace of preparation quickened considerably. In the Citroën workshops mechanics labored feverishly to produce the new trucks and gear to get over the mountains. Pecqueur, who was now on board the team, was dispatched to Afghanistan to scout out the terrain and negotiate safe conduct through the country. A second Afghanistan reconnaissance was confided to Elie de Vassoigne, who flew to Teheran to inspect the routing between Mazar-i-Sharif and Faizabad in the north.[113]

As the April 1931 jumping-off date approached, the different units of the expedition took up positions. In China Petropavlovsky (whom everyone called Petro) negotiated with Gobi merchants, arranged prices and insurance, bought off the Association for the Protection of Convoys (a collection of brigands and extortionists), filled 11 caravans with petrol, oil, food, tools, and spare parts, and progressively sent into the desert 622 camels loaded with 50 tons of merchandise. The seven *auto-chenilles* destined for Point's group were packed into crates and shipped off to China. Point left for Tientsin to await their arrival. A month later Brull and the mechanics followed via Moscow and the Trans-Siberian. When Pecqueur telegrammed from Afghanistan that a revolt had broken out and that a northern Afghanistan crossing was impossible, Haardt and the Quai d'Orsay won British sanction for yet another re-routing through northern India. The passage through Gilgit would be still less accessible, but by now there was no thought of turning back. On the third of April a British liaison, Colonel Gabriel, left Marseilles for Bombay accompanying several hundred thousand francs' worth of materials and prepared to reconnoiter mountain routes north of Srinagar in Kashmir. In Kabul the French chargé d'affaires forwarded 472 gallons of gas, 42 gallons of oil, 48 pounds of grease, and 13 crates of provisions to Kandahar. Further north, again on the Trans-Siberian, Abel Berger, a Citroën mechanic, was bringing 15 cases of wheel parts for the trucks. On the twenty-fourth of April the Quai d'Orsay was alerting its agents in Germany, Poland, Russia, and China to do what was necessary to facilitate his journey. By then, however, one was beyond preparations; both the Haardt and Point groups were already on their way.[114]

The main column struck out from Beirut on the fourth of April, "veritable tanks [*chars*] launched . . . on the conquest of unknown regions." Traveling at twenty kilometers an hour, perhaps one hundred and fifty kilometers a day, they crossed into Iraq on the twelfth, "cleared" the Tigris by the twentieth, "bivouacked" in Persia, and arrived in Teheran on the twenty-eighth to the welcome of enthusiastic crowds. As they proceeded to the Afghan frontier their Persian escort, Colonel Esfandiary, warned of difficulties ahead. "The country has no roads, trails are not secure, the nomads are turbulent. There is fighting in the north." But they encountered no problems, rejoined Hackin and Pecqueur at Girishk, and arrived in Kabul by the ninth of June. Two weeks later they had reached Srinagar at the base of the Himalayas. The first leg of the trip was culturally impressionable but physically uneventful, the column slicing forward at every stage:

It was a fine squadron, a perfected material, responsive, obedient in the service of its men. This group — soul, flesh, and steel — was a body unto itself, mobile, self-sufficient, capable of living and acting alone in the wilderness. . . .

In all that there was something compact, resolute, expressive, like an affirmation. But for the moment Asia offered no opposition to this concentrated force. She seemed to recede, to defend herself against this intrusion from the West with sand, wind, space, faint distances, and low flat mountains that flared out to reappear and reappeared to vanish.[115]

Before them now, however, rose a massive mountain barrier. No roads led through the mountains, only footpaths and horse trails, and of these only three that afforded passage into China. The first, through Chitral, was closed to all but strategic troop movements. The second, via Leh, climbed to an altitude of nearly twenty thousand feet. They must pass by the third, through Gilgit, insisted Gabriel who had reconnoitered in advance. "With my cars," Haardt replied. Gabriel shook his head. The Gilgit route was only a mule trail, cut out of a mountainside, jutting out over emptiness, winding through glacial valleys before climbing toward high mountain passes. It was closed eight months out of the year, it had just reopened, and no one was sure at the moment that even men on horseback could make it through. There were hairpin turns and gradients of more than forty degrees. Bridges, suspended over gorges and raging torrents below, were unsturdy and had never been tested by the weight of motor vehicles. Between Srinagar and Kashgar was a forty-five-day trek through a land devoid of supplies. The maximum amount of material that a porter could bear was thirty kilos, sixty for a pack horse. An expedition the size of the Croisière jaune, would require at least eight hundred men or four hundred horses, a virtual army that would make a nonsense of logistics.

Still the French tried. They broke down into three groups, leaving at intervals, and they took only two trucks, stripped to essentials, as a symbolic gesture to see how far they could go. At the first bridge, uncertain it would hold, they used steel cables to maneuver the vehicle across. The first car caught to one side and Ferracci had to go out and straighten it, a risky operation for him but one that succeeded. Ahead, however, lay forty-five more bridges before the Kilik pass. As they moved deeper into the mountains the snow on the sides of the trail piled four to five meters thick. Climbing to nearly fourteen thousand feet, the engines lost over 50 percent of their power; but they continued to chug along. Two kilometers past Burzil, on a steep overhang, Cecillon, driving one of the caterpillars, suddenly felt the earth disappear beneath his outer track. Suspended over nothingness, the blood drained from his face, he remained glued to his seat, sweating it out for five hours until a winch worked the *autochenille* onto firm ground. Beyond Astor their march slowed to a crawl behind a meter-by-meter clearing of the path. Seven miles further on there was a complete washout, requiring a dismantling of the cars over a hundred-meter portage, and then a reassemblage on the other side. Throughout the painstaking acrobatics Ferracci pushed the crew along. They lowered the machines by cable down banks, they forded rushing waters, they maneuvered through zigzag turns, and they passed over frail ledges that at one point they rebuilt by hand. At last, twenty-three days out and some several hundred miles into the mountains, they drove into Gilgit. They were the first people in motor vehicles ever to appear there.

This was as far as they were to go in the half-tracks. Ahead lay a struggle at least as commanding as anything they had known up to Gilgit, and Haardt no longer felt he had the time to experiment. From the other side of the Pamirs had come a radio message that Point was in trouble, and Haardt was now pressed to cross over and come to the rescue. He left one car in Gilgit — a monument to what they had done — and consigned the other to Ferracci and his team to dismantle and take back to France. The remainder of the expedition forged on, covering the next thousand miles with horses, yaks, and camels. They climbed to nearly sixteen thousand feet, passed through the Kilik pass, descended into Sinkiang between walls of rose colored granite, quartered in Kashgar, and then set off for Aksu and a rendezvous with Point.

For the China group all the voyage was an adventure. Where Haardt and his men had departed in triumph, Point and his team all but stole out in the middle of the night. They left amidst lurid press charges that eight hundred armed men — including a crack pistol corps — were going to descend from the west to prospect for minerals or that the Croisière jaune was the spearhead of an imperial landgrab for Sinkiang. The very name of the expedition grated on Chinese sensibilities, a fact not lost on the French, who did what they could to cover it over with the more palatable inscription of Croisière trans-asiatique.[116] The Nationalist government imposed a Chinese delegation on Point, which was to intrigue against the mission at nearly every turn and to cause it all sorts of troubles in the Gobi and in Turkestan. As they left for the Great Wall, Kalgan, and the desert, Point learned that a rebellion had broken out in Sinkiang and that it would be wise to postpone the crossing: advice that Point chose to ignore, although not without subsequent peril. If this were not enough, they ground up nearly all their treads shortly out of Peking because of a faulty design and had to return for repairs.

Not until the twenty-fourth of April (by this date Haardt was nearing Teheran) did they make it to Kalgan, only two hundred kilometers away. There they camped at the Pioneer's Inn, famous in the years immediately after the war as a gathering place of European toughs and adventurers. While they awaited the arrival of an emergency shipment of spare treads to replace those they had mounted in Peking — this was the consignment Berger was shepherding on the Trans-Siberian — Point was recalled to Peking to answer new charges. Back in the former capital, Point negotiated, apologized, cajoled, and won the right for the expedition to continue. On 11 May Berger arrived with the track-bands and on the sixteenth they were out of Kalgan, now moving at a fair speed toward inner Mongolia and a new junction with the Chinese delegation. At Pailing-miao the Chinese appeared, mostly scientists, but also a journalist, a general, and a Colonel Tiao who had studied at the Soviet war college and had specialized in espionage.

The Gobi crossing was a race against the elements and dwindling gas supplies. The caravan set out with eight thousand liters, but there were detours around sand dunes and gorges, dead ends in ravines, a retracing to find a way out, and slow running over rocky plateaus and then over every kind of sand. Winds blew sand into everything and at one point the French encountered a full desert sandstorm. Fierce heat burst several *bidons* of petrol, forcing Point in the end to go ahead to Soochow, where their caravans had deposited a reserve, and to return with sufficient supplies for the rest of the vehicles to make it to the town. At Soochow they were nearly trapped by intrigues against them, but Petro used an old connection to get authorization to continue westward. On the twenty-sixth of June they entered Sinkiang province, passing a sign planted at the border upon which someone had scribbled in Chinese: "Don't go west. Danger. Hide your camels in the mountains and wait," a reminder once again that they were heading into a war zone.

The rebellion raging in Sinkiang was a complex matter. It pitted Muslim populations against Chinese overlords, but the balance of forces encompassed the spread of pan-Turanian and Islamic revivalist influence (spurred on by the First World War), Stalin's collectivization policies (which drove a Kirghiz resistance movement across the border), and the impact of the Japanese expansion upon Soviet willingness to intervene in central Asia. Ma Chung-ying, a Kansu warlord whose intrusions on the side of the rebels propelled the revolt into full scale civil war, had suspicious ties to both the Japanese and Soviets that are still debated today. He may even have been manipulated as a Soviet agent provocateur by his Turkish chief of staff, Kemal Kaya, who has been identified as a likely Soviet agent and was perhaps GPU trained. To complete the picture a critical part of the fighting was done by White Russian troops loyal to Chin Shu-jen, the Chinese governor and warlord of Sinkiang (provincial chairman in Kuomintang terminology; but the Kuomintang exercised little authority over the province) until they mutinied against him in April 1933 and drove him from power.[117] It was into this ensemble of regional hostilities, great power politics, and spillovers from the Great War that the Point group now found itself venturing.

Their arrival coincided with the first great phase of the rebellion, the fighting concentrated around the city of Hami. Meeting up with troops along a road littered with the cadavers of humans and animals, they watched as Chinese soldiers fell upon a Muslim cavalryman, hacked off his arms, sliced open his belly, and ripped out his heart as a trophy. Continuing into Hami, they witnessed a town feverishly preparing to defend itself against a Muslim onslaught. By July first they were out of Hami, leaving Petro behind to arrange security for an approaching supply caravan. His intention was to rejoin the column four days later at Turfan, but he was to be overtaken by the attack and then siege of Ma's troops and would not break out of the town until 109 days later.

Moving west, the expedition descended into a depression below sea level where the temperature reached above 120 degrees. By now, however, their minds were on the ravages of war and the question of whether they could make it to Kashgar and the rendezvous with Haardt. At Turfan they were summoned by Chin to Urumchi. Point, smelling a trap, went alone with one truck, leaving Brull in charge of the convoy and with instructions to stay put. Once in Urumchi, Point was held prisoner amidst new intrigues and Chin's urgent desire to confiscate the half-tracks and radios for his war needs. Pressured to call Brull and the convoy to the capital, Point at last ceded but managed to warn them to camp on the outskirts and to dismantle the tracks and the running gear to prevent Chin from seizing the vehicles. There they remained for fifty-two days of negotiations, suspense, threats, clandestine radio messages to the French fleet, and promises of vehicles and radios for Chin sent expressly from the Citroën factories.[118] At last a deal was struck: Point, a radio operator, and a mechanic would go east with Chin's men to establish radio contact between Urumchi and the Hami front in exchange for the freeing of four vehicles to proceed west to rendezvous with Haardt. It was these four trucks that converged at Aksu with the men coming from the mountains on the eighth of October.

At the junction there was an emotional greeting and a meal of roast chicken, pommes frites, salad, crème renversée, coffee, and cognac prepared by the Urumchi group who had arrived first: a reminder that the French will out in a Frenchman even in an outpost in Chinese Turkestan. But the time for celebrating was still a long way off. Back at Urumchi they waited and waited for authorization to leave, sensing themselves imprisoned and watching the last of the good weather fly by. Their plans had prescribed an eastward crossing in fall, but as winter approached they began to prepare for the worst, adapting the trucks with special heating mechanisms and procuring sheepskins, boots, gloves, and fur hats. On the twentieth of November they were stunned by the appearance of a Frenchman named Jacques Salesse who had traveled via Paris-Berlin-Moscow-Novosibirsk-Chuguchak and then nine hundred kilometers over miserable roads with the three cars and radio sets promised to Chin. Eight days later the expedition had its permission to go.[119]

The return promised to be as dangerous as the voyage outbound. At

Hami they discovered their supplies had been pillaged and that Ma Chung-ying, a man they wished to avoid at all costs, was lurking along the road to Soochow. They would have to make it to Soochow and then drive through Kansu, because that was where their reserves had been stashed. But an alternate routing around Ma through the desert would require more gas than they had on hand. Petro remembered that months earlier one of his men had hidden supplies east of Hami, and so they decided to gamble on retrieving these and not encountering the warlord's troops on the way. With no assurance they could make it through, but no alternative except to try, they proceeded out of Hami through a countryside gutted by war. In a daring run Audoin-Dubreuil and Petro went ahead to the secret cache, found the petrol, and returned with enough to get to Soochow. Then they headed into the desert in winter, a line of half-tracks winding through a bleak lunarlike landscape.

As the temperature dropped below zero (Fahrenheit) they ran the engines without stop to keep them from freezing, rolling day and night over several hundred-mile stretches at a time. They pulled into Soochow on the eighteenth of December and had to bribe their way out. Now the weather and the lack of spare parts began to wear down the vehicles. With the temperature nearly ten degrees below zero an engine broke down, requiring eight hours of repairs in the open and the touching of metal with bare hands. Several days later, with the temperature dropping to eighteen below, they had to do more engine repairs and then replace one of the caterpillar tracks. Still a hundred and ten miles from a Catholic mission at Liangchow where shelter and supplies awaited, Haardt exhorted his men to drive through the night, even though they had not slept for three days and the mechanics were running on empty. At last at two in the morning they limped in, greeted by the German fathers although too dead tired to acknowledge their hosts. There they rested through the New Year, celebrating New Year's Day with the missionaries. The Germans toasted international friendship and the end to old enmities, the naturalist Reymond, "Reymond the skeptic," responding by standing and singing *"Ich hatt' einen Kamerad"* in a voice completely off-key, which made the scene all the more haunting.

East of Liangchow they headed into a country swarming with bandits. At a small village they were attacked by independent soldiers (the equivalent of bandits and a scourge of the land) who fired eleven shots into one of the trucks. Audoin-Dubreuil jumped out with his rifle in his hand, the other French followed. More shots were fired at them from soldiers advancing from the fields, a situation running out of control until Balourdet, one of the mechanics, pulled up with a machine gun and fired forty rapid bursts over the heads of the Chinese. A parley of sorts then followed, the Chinese complaining of the French counterattack, the French asking why they had been fired upon, the Chinese replying, "We thought you were brigands," the French cynically responding, "Have you ever seen brigands traveling in cars flying the French flag?" With things smoothed over and the Chinese sufficiently impressed by the French show of force, the convoy was again on its way. The remainder of the journey was now easy riding into Peking, the Croisière jaune arriving on the twelfth of February 1932, 315 days out from the start and 7,528 miles down the road. After much fêting, interviewing, and too little rest, the body of the expedition shipped out to Haiphong for a return southern run through Siam, Burma, India, and Persia. It was a voyage, however, that they would never make. Proceeding south by stages, Haardt arrived in Shanghai on the third of March, just after the clash in Chapei between Chinese and Japanese. He saw a city racked by fighting, in a virtual state of siege, its outer streets strewn with cadavers, while offshore in the Whangpoo warships hovered with their big guns unmuzzled. Continuing on to Hong Kong he took to bed with influenza. On the morning of the sixteenth his men learned the news: he had died of double pneumonia in the night. The expedition finally, prematurely, had come to an end.[120]

That was the Croisière jaune. It was an unforgettable adventure of the sort that only the interwar years could produce. The look was that of the twenties and thirties: the hardened glamour of Haardt in trench coat, broad-brimmed hat on his head, very aware of posing as the modern-day adventurer; the relaxed toughness of the men in leather jackets leaning against their fearsome machines.[121] About them was the air of the late imperial age, a plunge into exotica beyond the intrusions of the past but before the homogenizing erasures of the future. They rumbled through ancient city gates, posed by ruins, passed over lands a time dimension removed from the West, yet in ways that recall standard scenes from the period, lorries edging through crowded bazaar streets, a peasant crouched on a wheelbarrow beneath the wing of an airplane as a soldier in contemporary uniform looks on, the caption reading "Ancient and Modern China Side by Side."[122] In Srinagar Audoin-Dubreuil, who climbed mountains and crossed deserts, dined in evening dress on houseboats. Goerger at the same locale watched a population float by, sensed he had stepped across a cultural time zone; but he gazed as well upon the fashionable rites of an international fast set, a gathering place for round-the-world travelers. There were merchants of precious stones from the East, embroidered silks from Kashmir, carpets from Bukhara, yet also sports shops with equipment for tennis, golf, and polo.[123] The contrasts were those of the expedition, a rough and tumble crew in high-tech gear, conquistadors on wheels, adventurers in a world where their kind ruled as lords. It caught, like its age, a suspended moment in time before the great tidal wave of change, but only just barely. Already a generation beyond the quest for the source of the Nile or the race to the Pole, it was a machine-age demonstration of prowess and a presentiment of the routinized travel to follow. For Haardt and his men there was danger and a tinge of romance, but that came from their historical circumstances and would disappear after them. Their voyage was conquest and travelogue, they were buccaneers and tourists.

The expedition's hero — Haardt — was of the sort that came with the times, a team leader and organizer, a man of enterprise, authority, and technical skill. Unlike a Burton or a Peary he was strangely lacking in a persona, and when he died there was little to be said except for the adventures he had mounted. No one seemed to know very much about Georges-Marie Haardt except that he was an engineer, a naturalized Frenchman born of Belgian parents, and a Citroën company man who sat on the firm's administrative council (he was, in fact, an early associate of André Citroën).[124] Otherwise the facts of his life seemed to fade into unimportance. The *New York Times* said he was forty-six when he died, the *London Times* said he was forty-seven, and the *Petit Parisien* put him at forty-eight. Not even his closest collaborators could come up with more than formulaic expressions for a man who had lived since the first Sahara crossing in the twenties almost solely for adventure but had made these grand, organized affairs, swashbuckling projects designed like a blueprint. André Citroën praised his coolness under pressure, his "spirit of decision," his ability to command, and his "penetrating sense of control necessary for a real leader of men." Audoin-Dubreuil described him as a "chief," a man of adventurous but practical spirit and a planner. Citroën was "the animator, the creator," Haardt "the organizer and *réalisateur*." Blandly these summed up a man who had done such extraordinary things.[125] Yet the heroic quality was clear nonetheless. He had prepared, negotiated, organized, and designed, but then he had led forty men and fourteen half-tracks on a relentless drive across Asia. Among his men he was a presence, and with his death the expedition expired as well. It was a tragic but almost screenplaylike conclusion, lending an air of epic proportions to all of the mission. In this respect he defined the limitations but also the possibilities for heroism in a technological age, a man of complex managerial skills who had guided his team successfully in a great venture across half the landmass of the globe.

It was too an expedition that seemed to come out of one war and to head into another. Its language was military to the core, "clearing" barriers, commanded by a "general staff," identifying its "point of attack," "an assault column out to force its way through the Pamir passes."[126] Military men accompanied the mission, commanded its units, reconnoitered, assumed charge of security. Rolling through the barren wasteland toward Soochow the convoy of half-tracks had a menacing air about it, like a futuristic column of conquerors or of desperate armed men making a run for it through hostile territory. Vulnerable to large enemy contingents it blasted its way through bandit zones. There was a martial toughness to the dress of the crew, and they donned uniforms on the morrow of the death of their chief. Afterwards, when the adventure was over, there remained the memories of a campaign in the field and a mood of male camaraderie that repeated the bonding of the trenches.[127]

In these carryovers of language and styles the expedition showed the effects of the First World War, "the essential condition of consciousness in the twentieth century," as Paul Fussell has called it.[128] But there was also something of the coming war in the Croisière jaune, as if in its forced march through Asia it were the harbinger of future armored columns that would storm across the great landmasses of the world. It recalled Vernier's speculations in the late 1930s of what the Germans might have accomplished if von Hentig, Niedermayer, and Wassmuss had disposed of armored vehicles and airplanes in their theater of operations and his vision that in the next war fleets of tanks would sweep across Asia and North Africa. "The adventures of yesterday," he wrote, "will become the operations of tomorrow." Or it recalled Hauptmann Xylander's report in 1939 on the prospects for motorized fighting in the desert: "The possibility of using motor vehicles and radios has *decisively altered* the usability and significance of the *Sahara Desert for warfare*. Today motor vehicles can conquer in a single day's march distances between water holes that formerly required camel caravans two weeks of danger and troubles to cover." Perhaps what the Croisière jaune projected most was simply the militarized look that tended to pervade large-scale expeditions between the wars. The Andrews missions had displayed it as brazenly as had the Citroën group. And probably no crossing in these years so reminded one of the Croisière jaune as Italo Balbo's

1933 aerial cruise across the north Atlantic: one hundred men in twenty-five seaplanes flying from Orbatello to Chicago via the North Sea, Iceland, and Canada. Each was an adventure, globally cast, carried out by a team of rigorously trained professionals. Each required years of planning, methodical organization, and logistical support services orchestrated in advance. Fundamentally the only difference, aside from the aerial voyage, was that Balbo was a military man leading a military squadron flown in military formation by military pilots. Yet that too was not unlike the Croisière jaune.[129]

From those warlike intonations it was but a step back to the essential signature of the age, an adventure wrapped in world politics and the great events of the day. In a multiplicity of ways — from the Quai d'Orsay's participation to the geopolitical significance of pioneering a land route across postwar central Asia to the legacies of Hedin to the undertow of war and revolution in the East — contemporary affairs intersected with the Croisière jaune. Its great exploit was to be its crossing of Asia on wheels, but the sense of riding into history never left it. "In this country in disorder . . . what has become of the Citroën central Asia expedition?" wrote Goerger in a book about his travels for the expedition in which he set both against the unfolding of deep historical change.[130] Under any circumstances the expedition would have been an adventure, but it became a fabulous one because it collided with rebellion and civil war in Sinkiang. Yet even here, in this remote land where geography blurred into flashes of sensation and names conjured up centuries long past, the clash of global politics made itself felt. Like von Hentig or Borodin or Ossendowski or all the poor souls who fell through the cracks when the foundations split apart in the First World War, the men of the Croisière jaune were swept along by the currents of their century.

If their stories bear retelling in a book about spies it is because between these adventures and espionage there existed an undeniable bond. Many of the great tales of the period — those of Lawrence, von Hentig, Borodin, Trebitsch Lincoln — were, of course, tales of intrigue that solidified ties between the two. They were a testimony to the far-flung global character of espionage in the contemporary world and an impulsion to focus attention on spies and secret agents. But to a greater extent it was what happened to adventure that explains what happened to the genre of espionage. For the former, like the latter, the war was a dividing line, politicizing the exploits of men and women in remote corners of the world as it escalated the globalism of international affairs. The backdrop to adventure in the Himalayas or the Gobi or in exotic lands like Turkestan or China became war and revolution, Japanese expansionism, the waning days of imperialism, and the global stakes and commitments that constituted the sweep of political life in the twentieth century. Like so many other aspects of the age, adventure shared in its present-mindedness and contributed to it. With adventure came reminders of the war and the events that had followed, a sense of living with contingency, with history, in effect intensely with the present. There was as well the intrusiveness — the possibility for that history to impinge upon the lives of individuals — that seems to have clung to the interwar years. The experiences of Ossendowski and his kind caught this intrusion best, but not even the Croisière jaune was exempt from it.

With these changes in adventures came changes in the stories of spies. Out of politicized exploits evolved the modern spy novel, a story of adventure with the politics added in. Such novels had existed in the past, but their proliferation following the war can only be understood in a climate that set adventures against the great events of their times. As the content of adventures underwent change so did their fictions, politicizing into spy stories that adapted the very form modern-day adventures were likely to take. There was, for example, the motif of the innocent bystander swept up in a vortex of intrigue and extraordinary trials that replicated the lives of countless individuals who had been swept up by the war and the Russian revolution. Or there was, particularly in French novels, the motif of the man of daring yet organization that repeated the heroic features of Haardt or of Borodin or the novels of Malraux where contemporary heroism required a setting of grand-scale politics — revolution, civil war — and an organization with a cause to give meaning to action.

Through the metamorphosis of adventures, the postwar spy story therefore became an evocation, an entertainment, and a source for heroics. It was a vehicle for writing about war, revolution, all the overarching events that hung over the present, although as an adventure for its times it reproduced the storytelling qualities of its origins. If politics were added in, the mix was for verisimilitude. Like adventures, what mattered most was the thrill of the story, and where real adventures merged with intrigue — as was often the case — these begged for a continual retelling, yet another reason why the life of Trebitsch Lincoln assumed such compelling proportions. Perhaps in its intrusiveness the spy story suggested a dangerous world. But where networks, support systems, and technology served as a departure point for adventures, it caught the possibility for combining individual heroism with the high-tech imperatives of the bureaucratizing moment. Like Haardt or Borodin or von Hentig and Niedermayer, the spy was the organization man cast in the role of adventurer.

Thus the century's adventures were another provocation to write about spies, imparting to that literature a tone sounding well beyond accusation and fear. They pointed to how closely bound up espionage was with its times; and they demonstrated the multiplicity of connections embedded in the globalism that followed the war, as did the history of travel whose own evolution takes us back again to the history of these years and to the magnetism and moods that spy stories took from them.

————————

Travel and intrigue made good bedfellows after the war. Take, for example, Jean Bommart's Chinese fish stories. One occurs during the First World War in Chile, a hemisphere away from France. Another is set on a ship. The original in the series — *Le poisson chinois* — takes place on the Orient Express. On board are assassins, terrorists, arms merchants, and Georges Sauvin, the title's Chinese fish and Deuxième Bureau secret agent. Ernst, the wagon-lit conductor, works informally for Sauvin. A passenger disguised as an Englishwoman is another Deuxième Bureau operative. Monseigneur Bachou, an Albanian bishop riding the train, is a secret agent working with Sauvin. Douchanovitch, a porter at a Belgrade hotel, is in the pay of Sauvin. False passports, border crossings, the various themes of international travel in the twenties and thirties form a major part of this story, as they did in so many other interwar spy novels. For the spy writer between the wars, travel was nearly an indispensable ingredient. Tales were set in foreign locales. Movement was often the mechanism that forced the plot forward. The milieus of travel — cosmopolitan populations, hotels, trains, especially trains — were recurrent motifs in spy literature. *The Seven Heads of the Green Dragon*, shifting from one capital to another, set a scene on the Orient Express. There was a train scene in Jean Joffroy's *Espionage in Asia*. Robert Métais's *Cell Number Twenty* described how the trains between Belgrade and Hungary were infested with spies. Pierre Yrondy's massive German plot in *From Cocaine . . . To Gas!!!* included "all those travelers, habitués of casinos, international luxury trains, and worldly haunts: auxiliaries of the secret army!" Trains, boats, and hotels were the settings around which Pierre Darlix spun his tales of intrigue. No less common was the creeping of spies into the narratives of travel books, whether these were travel novels like *The Madonna of the Sleeping Cars,* or travelogues dressed up as journalistic exposés like *The Road to Shanghai,* or tales of travel in exotic places like Titaÿna's *Hot Nights,* or stories set in faraway lands like Gilbert's *Dispatches from Asia.* Affinities were unending. Travel and intrigue not only crawled into bed together but embraced, coupled, and formed the beast with two backs, as with Marc Chadourne, who seems to have made a career of writing about his travels in these years but who arrived in Shanghai as a Colonial Office spy at the very end of the 1930s.[131]

None of this coupling should have been surprising in a world crisscrossed by spies shuttling from one destination or continent to another, and where the paraphernalia of travel — border crossings, papers in order — came to assume sinister or life-threatening meanings. Revelations of global spy networks, or memories of Swiss hotel scenes in the First World War, or adventures that devolved into journeys through the gauntlet of history invariably associated travel with espionage. If life imitated art in the shape of Chadourne, art imitated life, borrowing its motifs and its themes from the very real spy world about it.

Ship travel, for instance, intertwined with espionage between the wars. The most notorious boat story from these years was the botched hijacking of the C-2 at Brest in 1937. But there were also tales of phantom ships hanging off the coasts and an incessant outpouring of reports on gunrunners. The burning of two passenger liners, the *Georges-Philippar* off the Somali coast in 1932 (in which Albert Londres perished) and the *Paris* at its home berth in France in April 1939, aroused inevitable charges of sabotage and terrorism. Sailors on ships plying Far Eastern waters formed the backbone in the Third International's courier traffic between Asia and Europe and between communist parties in the Orient. The port cities of Marseilles and Singapore were nodal points where police followed seamen, noting whom they met and what they said. At Shanghai police tracked foreign agents by the ships they took: "The undermentioned member of the GPU arrived in Shanghai from Hankow on January 20, 1930 in the SS *Loongwo*"; "The undermentioned Soviet agent arrived in Shanghai on January 9, 1930 from Tsinanfu via Tsingtao in the SS *Hoten Maru.*" Abwehr agents working out of Bremen included Otto Benecke, a steward on the NDL (North German Lloyd) steamer *Gneisenau* that sailed to Shanghai, Hong Kong, and Singapore; Karl Schulze, a steward on the NDL's passenger liner *Europa;* Herbert Jaenichen, a waiter on the *Europa*'s sister ship *Bremen* who spoke English and French and was in touch with German agents in the United States; and Julius Hundt, who was the chief engineer on the same ship. There were also the confessions of Irene Z., a Latvian woman picked up east of Fez, who acknowledged under interrogation that a German ship captain with the OPDR had engaged her to spy on French military installations.[132]

Spies luxuriated in trains. They stalked their prey in corridors and compartments. They infiltrated the corps of conductors and waiters. They deployed agents at train stations. They had rendezvous on trains. And, if they were terrorists, they occasionally dynamited trains. It was especially the international trains, the *grands rapides,* the luxury expresses, that were haunted by the thieves, con men, drug smugglers, gigolos, secret agents, and terrorists who seem to have constituted a substantial clientele between the wars. In the newspapers of the twenties and thirties can be found a chronicle of murders and thefts aboard the intercities. In 1932 thieves on the Côte d'Azur run lifted five hundred thousand francs' worth of pearls from Lady Howard de Walden and twenty-seven hundred francs in cash from Colonel Jacques Balsam. In 1937 the French police finally broke the Katz gang, which specialized in picking pockets on the French *rapides.* Nicolai Kudrachov, who robbed his way through the Polish express trains, was also a Soviet spy who used his false papers to worm his way into the confidence of his victims.[133] That was the milieu into which professional secret agents integrated easily, particularly among the personnel of the wagon-lits who traversed frontiers as a matter of course and detained the passports of their passengers for border crossings in the night. The Italians developed an extensive network of sleeping car agents to spy upon the opposition to the Fascist regime. The German secret service recruited sleeping car conductors, like Eduard Lieberman, who worked a run into Paris and operated under the cover number of U-2415. Hartwig ran an agent on the sleeping cars of the Sudfranzösische Line and couriers on the Orient Express, and the Deuxième Bureau deployed operatives on the wagon-lits, suggesting that Bommart's *Chinese Fish* was not entirely a work of imagination. Not surprisingly it was a sleeping car baggage handler on the Paris-Bucharest run that the Comintern agent Samuel I. tried to recruit and who put the Sûreté onto his trail.[134]

Interwar train travel attracted spies, couriers, liaisons, and informants, but also hit men — Suvliki, the head of the GPU Berlin station was found murdered on the Moscow-Berlin express in 1932[135] — and especially terrorists. Matuska blew up trains because he was mad, but in China trains were subject to attack by bandits or nationalists opposed to the Japanese invasion of Manchuria and in the Balkans both the IMRO and Ustashi conducted an orchestrated campaign against the expresses zooming down the peninsula. Ilya Ehrenburg recalled a trip from Romania in 1934 where armed guards rode the trains to prevent terrorist attacks. Jelka Pogorelec, Percec's secretary and a Yugoslav Sûreté plant, told how the Croatian terrorists maintained an apartment in Vienna where they manufactured bombs timed to explode on Yugoslav territory. "Dr. Morreale repeated constantly that they had to frighten off tourists from vacationing in Yugoslavia."[136] Closer to home saboteurs targeted trains in the south of France in an orchestrated campaign of terror. It would be trite and grammatically incorrect to say that intrigue rode the trains in the twenties and thirties, but certainly spy writers fabricated little beyond what they could read in the news or pick up from the real spy wars in these years.

Clearly, the milieu provided context for interwar spy writing. But in the almost irresistible attraction to travel as a motif or a setting lay something deeper. There was, of course, travel's suspended character, its compactness within the confines of steamships or trains, as well as the inevitable border crossings that made it an ideal locus for a story of intrigue. Yet, even more, there was the very quality to travel in these years, its style, its themes, and the moods it evoked, all of which spilled over into writing about spies, providing inspiration, cause, but also shape and definition. Between intrigue and travel the same relation obtained as between intrigue and adventure. The one flowed from the other, and behind each lay the force of the age.

No era has been so associated with travel as the interwar years. It was a time when more people traveled than ever before and when more people wrote about their travels or traveled to write, the travel book becoming all but a literary rite of passage between the wars. It was a period that toward its end saw a dawning age of mass tourism. Yet it was also an era when travel could be adventurous, luxurious, and elegant, qualities that have largely disappeared since the Second World War. Leisurely travel was not only possible but often the rule. The Messageries Maritimes offered a seventy-four-day cruise from Marseilles to Port Said, Djibouti, Colombo, Singapore, Saigon, Hong Kong, Shanghai, Kobe, Osaka, Tokyo, Yokohama and back beginning at the cost of seventeen thousand five hundred francs. Or one could sail on the Canadian Pacific's *Empress of Britain* for India, Ceylon, Siam, Hong Kong, Saint Helena, Rio, and other ports over a period of four months. Even regular passage by ship from Europe to the Pacific could take from five to six weeks with a host of stopovers along the way.[137]

The leisurely pace of travel came with wealth or with desire to see and observe rather than to cram one's journey into a time slot. Yet it was also a function of the availability of means of travel between one point and another, particularly if an ocean lay in the middle. Europeans, in fact, cherished speed between the wars, craved it, and gave their custom to it whenever they could. Luxury liners raced across the north Atlantic in quest of the prestigious Blue Ribband. North German Lloyd's *Bremen* and *Europa* took it on their maiden voyages in 1929 and 1930. Five years later the *Normandie,* benefiting from a revolutionary hull design, captured the prize for France on its initial crossing from Le Havre to New York amidst German grumbling and bombastic coverage in the French press ("*Normandie* takes the Blue Ribband"; "*Normandie,* beating the world speed record, approaches New York"). Cunard's *Queen Mary* failed to take the Blue Ribband on its maiden crossing the following year but grabbed it in August before her initial season was over. The most famous trains were the *rapides* and expresses. Travelers could proceed by wagon-lit from Paris to Cairo in six and one-half days, eight if they were going to Teheran, agonizingly slow for today's passengers but fast enough to merit large print advertising in 1938.[138]

Even these speeds, however, were becoming woefully insufficient with the advent of airplanes, which seemed to eradicate distance:

"The Holy Roman Empire. In high school that still left a certain impression.
   "And today:
   "Paris, 4:00 in the morning;
   "Strasbourg, 6:00
   "Prague, 10:00
   "Vienna, 11:00[139]

Into the thirties flying remained an adventure. Ernst Klaar won the hero worship of his son when he flew from Prague to Vienna in 1936 and became "the Lindbergh of Pichlergasse." Yet more and more air travel was becoming routine. In 1937 Air France's network extended over forty thousand kilometers. The airline flew ninety thousand passengers in that year. In 1938 it had two departures weekly from Marseilles to Beirut by seaplane, flying the route in two days and beating the train by sixty hours. The midthirties guidebook *All About Shanghai* carried a full-page ad for Eurasia airlines:

> SEE THE GLORIES OF
> CHINA FROM THE AIR
> Travel by the
> Planes of
> "EURASIA"
> Safe   Speedy   Comfortable

Pioneering the development of air travel and transport in Central and Western China with a vast program outlined and being carried into execution for the linking of Eastern Asia and Western Europe by air.

The advertisement did not mention, as the guidebook did further on, that the line from Lanchow just south of Mongolia to Chuguchak where European train connections could be made, had been discontinued "due to political disturbances"; nor was there any mention of the adventures and intrigues on the ground that went into the building of the air routes. Security, speed, and comfort, especially the comfort that came from the luxurious outfittings that were the mark of travel during these years and retained, for those who could afford it, the clear sense of a class experience, was what the passenger airlines strived for. The *Hindenburg* dirigible was designed for speed, but its accommodations were spacious, there was a dining room, a smoking room, and a sundeck, and on its maiden voyage a crew of sixty attended to the needs of forty passengers whose only discomforts were likely to come from air currents or the German kitchen. France's luxury seaplane the *Lieutenant-de-vaisseau* was designed to carry only sixteen passengers on its transatlantic run. Decorated for the effect of a "flying palace," it contained eight cabins with sixteen beds, and a *grand salon*. The style has disappeared forever from traveling, but then so too did the *Hindenburg,* which burned over New Jersey. For all the appointments, flying remained a new and adventurous means of travel between the wars.[140]

Mostly it is the ocean liners, hotels, and trains that we think of when we think about travel in the twenties and thirties. Trains are embedded in our images of the period. One of the most celebrated photographs that has come down from these years is that of the Spanish Republican army on the way to the front, a row of men in a railway carriage leaning out windows, smiling determinedly, raising their arms in the clenched-fist antifascist salute. Perhaps it is the contrast between their exuberance and the funereal quality of another famous photo from the civil war, the huddled, defeated army straggling across the French border, that makes the earlier picture so striking. But it is also the political overlay to a standard representation from the period, the railroad passenger peering out a half-opened train window in the station, that adds context and expression to the photograph, as if it were impossible to grasp the texture of these years without the intermediary agency of the train. Only the liners were a rival symbol in this last great age of ocean travel. Everyone who traveled between the wars did so at some point by train and by boat. Overseas travel still meant sailing by ship. Overland travel meant riding the rails, and even foreign ministers conducted their diplomatic journeys by train. Each form bespoke a style and an elegance that has pretty well vanished from the face of the earth. Trains had their gatherings in evening dress to welcome in the international expresses. Ships had their lavish sendoffs and their festive arrivals. Trains had luxury cars, private compartments with lime-wood luggage racks and mahogany paneling, corridors done up in mahogany with inlaid leather, and wagon-lits and dining cars as standard first class features. Expresses like the Twentieth Century Limited or the Blue Train were assumed to be institutions. Ocean liners were designed to be the ultimate in travel opulence. With the *Rex* and the *Conte di Savoia,* Germany's *Bremen,* or Britain's *Queen Mary* sailed national prestige. The French Line's *Ile de France,* launched in 1926, was a trend setter in interior decor. The *Normandie,* launched six years later, was probably the greatest ship ever built. As long as three football fields and displacing eighty thousand tons, it was nearly twice as large as the giant liners of the previous generation (the *Titanic* displaced forty-five thousand tons, although only for a few days). On board were lounges, smoking rooms, a movie theater, a huge swimming pool, a tennis court, a library with forty thousand volumes bound in leather, a winter garden, a dining room three decks high, longer than Louis XIV's hall of mirrors, air conditioned, and serviced by seventy chefs. There were two deluxe apartments with four bedrooms each and more than four hundred first-class cabins, each with its own decoration scheme. The crew of thirteen hundred was the pick of the company, which by 1936 employed fifty thousand people and transported seventy-one thousand passengers on the north Atlantic run alone. Nothing captured ship travel better in these years than the *Normandie,* unless it was a *New Yorker* cartoon printed in the early thirties showing a magnificent lobby, a sweeping staircase leading heavenward, palm trees, elegant chairs and stylish people, mammoth columns, and a mother telling her crying little boy in a sailor suit, "But darling, this *is* a ship."[141]

The elegance and opulence is what we recall most, perhaps because we miss it most of all; but there was a wide range of travel conditions in these years, and interwar travelers, who were compulsive narrators and who ventured into every pocket of the globe, left behind them a diverse record of their experiences with the trains and ships and hotels of the world. André Goerger, on his round-the-world travels in conjunction with the Croisière jaune, described nearly every train he took. He moaned about the acrobatics required to undress without banging his head on the couchette above in the curtained sleepers in the overnight from Montreal to New York. He found the Trans-Siberian a boring but comfortable run in the oversized cars preserved from imperial days. Riding a "hard" car from Siberia to Russian Turkestan turned into "a veritable torture." His train to Bombay was pleasant and comfortable, enjoying the inventions that English gentlemen had imported to fight the heat and the insects. In China, after a rough time with students, he remembered most of all the spit, which he described in graphic, drawn out detail. Asian train travel invited wild contrast, often depending upon the nationality of the railway. Jacques Deval admired his first-class car through Japan with its plush arm chairs, its lacquer tables, its library, and its observation platform. But Paul Morand noticed most of all on the Chinese Blue Train out of Peking the flies, the Yangtze red mud in the sinks, and the soldiers armed to the teeth who escorted the conductor down the aisle. Crowds, smells, soldiers, and bandits were common images associated with Chinese train rides between the wars.[142]

Steamship voyages in distant waters threw one back upon national stereotypes. For Paul Morand American ships were powerful, merry, and vulgar, entering ports with a din and leaving with a fanfare, playing jazz twenty-four hours a day, and liberally equipped with telephone lines. On English ships the service was excellent, the food was ghastly, one dressed strictly by the codes, and on Sunday everyone attended services. German and Dutch ships were as polished as beautiful furniture, their meals were too heavy, and their passengers were deadly dull. French boats were "the image of our political Eden: a cozy little Southern gathering of pals disturbed by a few swinish paying passengers." Everything, *en principe,* was either "forbidden" or "impossible." No descents at stopovers because that was expensive, no change of linens, no movies, no music. But the wine cellar was excellent, no expense was spared for decorations featuring the three musketeers, and life in the cabins at night was never boring.[143]

As for hotel accommodations the range was unending. In Europe the grand hotels like the Carleton, the Ritz, and Kempinski's worked their way into the literature as synonymous with international travel. At Giza there was Menna House, several hundred yards from the Pyramids and laid out with splendid gardens and oriental salons. Visitors to the Manila Hotel were uniformly impressed (as they will be today). Otherwise the French found little to praise in Asian hotels. Marc Chadourne complained of the "sinister palaces" of Singapore and Calcutta and found Tokyo's Imperial Hotel hideous. Francis de Croisset recalled the mosquitoes that infested his Saigon hotel room. Morand remarked that the English hotels of Singapore and Hong Kong were hopelessly outdated in their standard of comfort and that their food was inedible. In the evenings, he noted, British clients dressed for dinner "in order to douse bottled sauces on the putrid dishes they swallow without wincing." From there one could descend as low as the imagination would go. Traveling through Persia the journalist Titaÿna stayed at a hotel as good, she thought, as the country had to offer. But the sheets had not been changed in six months and bugs and fleas were everywhere. A traveler more experienced in Persian ways consoled her with the saying that filth was like hunger: only the first eight days mattered. At Samara Goerger found all the hotels filled and was taken by night to a seedy, parasite-ridden dump with only partitions separating one sleeper from another. Recoiling, he insisted that there must be something better than this. In a calm, deeply philosophical voice came the response. "Better, no; worse, yes." The sentence, Goerger remarked, was beyond appeal; he resigned himself to the partitions.[144]

Still the French traveled, all over the world. We know more about the literary travelers, because they left a written record of their journeys. But there were many other voyagers, among these businessmen, colonial administrators, adventurers, or simply ordinary middle-class French men and women who may have traveled a good deal more than we have assumed. Sailing in a Messageries Maritimes mailboat to Indochina in 1937, Henriette Celarié noted that all of her small group of fellow passengers were French: a family from the provinces, an elderly spinster and a fair number of widows, a former seedsman, and a retired cheese merchant. "The average retired French businessman," she noted, "is no longer satisfied with his slippers, his scarf, his skull cap, and his pipe. Advertising, movies, books have awakened in him a taste for traveling. Willingly he sets sail for distant lands."[145] French insularity, an almost hermitlike turning in on self, has been seen as a theme of these years.[146] Yet neither press coverage, which was extensively global, nor administrative concerns (for example, the files on espionage), nor the amount of travel writing, nor what travelers revealed about other travelers, seems to confirm this presumption.[147] Robert Wohl has suggested that Europeans in general were prodigious travelers after the war because they believed themselves "wanderers between two worlds" and because they sought in travel spiritual nourishment and a source of renewal.[148] That is a highly sensible point of view although it might equally be said that the war awakened a desire for travel because it accustomed large numbers of people to moving to distant points around the world and because it accustomed Europeans to thinking more globally about their affairs.

Whatever the urge, the moods that accompanied and enveloped interwar travel to foreign lands could be as varied as the means of getting there. Consider, for example, the voyage by automobile that Guy Larigaudie and Roger Drapier made between Paris and Saigon over a seven-month stretch in 1937–1938. They traveled the twelve thousand kilometers in a used Ford with nearly seventy thousand kilometers already on the odometer. More strictly speaking it was another adventure in the vein of the *raids* across Africa in the twenties, and almost certainly the idea was in part inspired by the Croisière jaune that had made the more difficult central Asian crossing five years earlier. The voyage entailed a certain lust for action, for flirtation with danger or a testing of oneself that in the interwar years tended to combine with travel to faraway places. Linked to travel was a need to affirm oneself, to "taste of risk joined to the poetry of accomplishing a pure and difficult act."[149] Undoubtedly that mood reached back to the war's association of self-assertion with great deeds and toughness, although it could also gather a momentum of its own in a time when the focus was global and travel to distant lands common and accessible; and it explained in part why Larigaudie and Drapier set out on such an arduous journey.

However, they also traveled to play at adventure and to live out the fantasies of a boy's own adventure book. That at least is the tone that pervades Larigaudie's account of their trip. Driving through Afghanistan the young men come across a turbaned horseman with a rifle across the saddle: he seems, Larigaudie tells us, "to have stepped out of a pirate's tale." "Which one should I shoot, the horse or the rider," Guy the Fearless tosses off at Roger. "Let them both live," Roger the Gallant shoots back to Guy. In India a mishap crossing the mouth of the Ganges leaves them "resembling . . . the shipwrecked on the illustration page of a book of adventures." Further on, stuck on a sandbar in the middle of a river, Larigaudie demands two hundred men from the chief of a Bengali village. The chief refuses and sneers back derisively. "We take out our revolvers and, with the barrel of the Smith and Wesson two inches from his face, I threaten the chief in the purest American gangster accent: 'If the car isn't out of the water in half an hour I'll blow your brains out.'" Dangers and risks there were aplenty, but also a deliberate storybook romanticizing, as if the purpose of the voyage had been from the start to step back into the pages of the tales from their childhood.

Yet what is most striking from this narrative is neither the adventure nor the play making but the introduction by General La Font, "Chief Scout de France." The general tells us that of all the wondrous events we are about to read, what he found most rewarding was that no matter how muddied or dirtied the two young men were, they never entered a person's house, or any dwelling, without first washing off in a river and dressing as properly as possible. No matter that their car could only carry essentials, room was found to pack dinner jackets, white suits, and "adequate" linen. "How comforting," the general finds, "this care for correctness in an epoch where, in reputedly elegant places, people with all the leisure in the world to look after themselves impose on others the proximity of their *extra-shorts* and their Lacoste shirts." And waxing on about the virtues of these young men, the general tells of how Guy and Roger, driving down train tracks where no other road existed, spent hours digging up an iron picket that impeded their way but then, despite their fatigue and the long trip ahead, took care to put it back "correctly" into its place. This is not, the general insists, a mere detail. "For me *c'est magnifique* because it is symptomatic of an education, a spirit, because *c'est très scout.*" (The general does not say whether waving a Smith and Wesson in the face of a Bengali chief and threatening to blow his head off is also *très scout.*) This fatuous introduction is from 1939, only months before Europe was to break out in a second world war, and reminds us how varied or idiosyncratic individuals' preoccupations and priorities could be despite the tragic course that lay ahead.[150]

One is obliged to wonder, however, why the general need ever have fretted, for the travel accounts demonstrate that style, elegance, a sense of class rules and the codes of imperialism still obtained in these years, perhaps nowhere so transparently as in the assumption that no matter the climate or the culture, white men dressed in dinner jackets in the evening. Larigaudie took his along, but so too did Audoin-Dubreuil on the Croisière jaune. On his way to Arabia the foreign correspondent Claude Blanchard packed a dinner jacket "haunted by the idea that I might someday run into those celebrated English who dress for dinner even around the bivouac fire." André Goerger noted the terraces filled with men in *smokings* in Saigon, and Andrée Viollis commented on men in *smokings* during a tour of Cochin China with Paul Reynaud and his entourage. In Peking Francis de Croisset rode a rickshaw in his dinner jacket to a dinner at the Bolivian legation. Even Vera Vishniakova-Akimova, one of the Soviet volunteers for revolutionary work in China, commented on how one of her comrades with a limited grasp of English had spoken enthusiastically of the democratic spirit in Shanghai where movie theaters posted No Smoking signs in the lobbies.[151]

Alongside the persistence of the rules of the game, a stylized refusal to accept that worlds were dissolving or had already vanished, and alongside the nonchalance or indifference or however one might choose to describe General La Font's concerns in the face of the imminent storm, there was also the inclination toward humor. That indulgent surrender to making light of events marks the French all through these decades. Morand found sarcasm and Londres made wisecracks, and Jacques Deval joked about the "inconvenience" of traveling through China in the 1930s, where trains were derailed and passengers kidnapped or murdered.[152] Behind such accounts was a considerable element of truth, but most of all a mischievous delight in blowup and dismissal, and a wry reminder of the irrepressible amusement with which the French could be prepared to take on the world between the wars.

To humor can be added still another motif of interwar travel: the urge toward national self-assessment that runs like a thread through the travel literature, although the French who wrote up their voyages conformed to no clearcut point of view. For many the signs of decline were marked in bright letters. In Russia Gide, Schreiber, and Delbos remarked on how rarely they heard anyone speak French. André Goerger told the following story of a stop at a farm in Soviet Turkestan. The local GPU official explained to the farmers that Goerger and his companions were foreigners on a special assignment. "Ingliz" the Kirghiz replied. "Niet, Franzouski" the GPU man told them. The farmers stared wide-eyed, showing no comprehension of what he had said. Then the GPU man had an idea. "Parije" he announced; they come from Paris. That did it. The farmers had never heard of a country called France, but mention of the city of light elicited a gleam of recognition. In the Orient the refrain was the same. Marc Chadourne went through three secretaries in China trying to find one individual who could translate his work. Maurice Dekobra said that the modern Chinese woman spoke English but almost never French. Schreiber reported that nine out of ten Japanese with whom he conversed spoke to him in English and Deval noted that the menus on his Japanese train were printed in English because of the foreign traffic on that line. For René Jouglet France was an absent figure in the Orient. Pierre Billotey expressed practically the same emotion upon arriving in Saigon after a sea crossing had taught him "that the world is an English kingdom."[153]

Yet the confrontation with the world was often far from a negative one. Andrée Viollis spoke to army officers in Japan who expressed their admiration of French military traditions. The Croisière jaune, which regarded itself as a powerful affirmation of French prestige in Asia, witnessed strong indications of French influence as it rolled across Persia. Schreiber spoke mostly English in Japan, but he found French could hold its own with any other foreign language in the country and in Egypt nearly everyone he met seemed to speak French. Both Jean Raynaud and Claude Farrère described how only the French had shown any backbone when the Japanese moved into Shanghai in 1937. Most of all, French travelers abroad retained a deep pride and faith in their empire. Those who came to Indochina, for instance, found more than a haven from an Anglo-Saxon world. They saw a land where the French had built roads, dikes, canals, bridges, schools, and hospitals, investing the best of their civilization. Even the critics who exposed the stupidities and cruelties of settler culture adhered to this point of view.[154] Travel eastward, as too in voyages to the USSR, tapped into deep veins of contentment and affirmation as much as it triggered self-criticism or proffered signs of vulnerability and decline.

Attentiveness to French global significance or French prestige was baggage the French nearly always carried with them; and they did so in ways that draw us closer to the connections between interwar travel and espionage. Travel in the twenties and thirties was a journey into a world dramatically changed by the war and by a series of events of world importance or of such regional significance that in a globally tightened age they threatened to assume larger dimensions. Travel to Palestine or the Middle East was marked by the conflict between Arabs and Jews and by the general prospects for strife across North Africa. Travel to Indochina recalled the inroads of communism, anti-imperialism, and, after the early 1930s, the Yen-Bay massacre. China was the China of revolution, of the great events of Shanghai, of national awakening and colonial crack-up, and then of war in the Pacific that threatened to spread across oceans and continents. The United States was the rising power of international culture and finance, the land of Fordism and, despite the depression, overbearing dynamism. The Soviet Union, the great magnet of travel, was the land of world revolution and the great interwar experiment. Everywhere one went there were signs of an unstable world order and, by the 1930s, of a world depression. Travel had, through the sheer force of events, become a passage into history, recently made or in the making.

Indeed, so interwoven were travel and a feel for living with history that the very mechanisms of travel imprinted themselves upon European perceptions of twentieth-century upheaval, revolution, civil war, and war. Take trains, for example. For those who lived through the Russian revolution nothing seemed to capture better the uprootedness and unraveling of an entire nation than the jammed trains and stations, the trains that barely made it through or never at all, or the train journeys that put life and limb at risk. To the American Oliver Sayler, who witnessed the revolution and who found it "incredible when a train pulled out of a station and utterly beyond belief when it arrived at its destination," the mass scenes of trains seemed to cram into a single image a whole country in flux. Victor Voska, taking a train from Petrograd to Kiev with a Russian lieutenant to escort him, was told:

"You have a choice of accommodations . . . a car reserved for officers or the common coaches. I must tell you that the officers' car is not safe. Often the inhabitants shoot into it." After one look at the common coaches, and one smell of them, I determined to take the risk. . . . We got to Kiev without once having to lie down on the floor, an unusual record for a train journey in Russia at that period.

Later the pervasive image of civil war became the armored train and once again stations choked with people, this time the end-of-the-line refugees bereft of hope. Emigré memoirs told of maddening flights by train before the Bolshevik onslaught, of crowding into freight cars (a premonition of the century's later horrific images), and ultimately complete despair at the final stop with a station or freight car as the sole source of shelter. Joseph Kessel repeatedly described his Vladivostok adventure centered on the train station and the frightening scene of refugees piled so tightly and so deeply that one had literally to step over them to move from one end to another. And when the tide had run its course in the twenties, Ilya Ehrenburg summed up the NEP with the following story of a train near Kiev:

At one of the stations a peasant woman carrying a sack got into the "soft coach" by mistake. The conductor yelled: "Where d'you think you're going? Get out! This isn't nineteen seventeen."[155]

For travelers who followed, to the Soviet Union but also throughout the world, trains and train voyages remained emblematic of the era and its history. Crossing the Polish-Lithuanian border Yvon Delbos watched a railroad employee cover over a part of the corridor map showing Vilna in Poland, a reminder, he recorded, of "the recent scars left by the surgical operations of the peace treaties."[156] In Russia visitors wrote about the *bezprizorniki* (homeless orphans) who clambered over train cars or about prisoner cars shunted onto side rails, the one a reminder of the utter devastation of six years of war and civil war, the other of a revolution that had turned on its own by the mid-1930s.[157] In Italy the cliché was that Mussolini had made the trains travel on time, although trains were also ingrained in the images that memories called forth to explain what Fascism had been largely about. Roland Dorgelès described an Italian innkeeper whose love of order under the Duce was contrasted to the bitter experience of disorder immediately following the war that the man recalled in part this way:

One didn't even dare to travel. Certain days the line was cut: they had blown up the rails. . . . Other times the engineer abandoned his locomotive to go to a meeting. I could tell you about how at Civitavecchia the engineer and the fireman refused to leave because officers had climbed into a car. They didn't want to drive to Rome. So we stood still two hours at the station waiting for them to finish arguing, while employees threw pebbles at the first class [cars], and we were only able to get going again when the officers, very vexed, got off the train. Of course that kind of nonsense couldn't continue.

In China the endless scenes of troop trains came to symbolize a nation heaving and jerking its way through revolution, incessant civil war, national unification, and then war with Japan. Travelers to the Far East wrote about filth, bandits, the pervasive presence of soldiers, and the swarming masses that characterized train journeys in China because that also evoked the fragmentation, anarchy, and historical route from one era to another that seemed China's fate in the twentieth century. Even in the graphic descriptions of spit there was an attempt to grapple with the waning respect for Westerners just as in the obsession with numbers there was a grappling with the immensity of China, its significance, and its atmosphere of movement or flow across time and space.[158]

The envelopment of travel with history made this, perhaps, the first real age of the foreign correspondent. As individual reporters they were scarcely new. Luigi Barzini, who traveled on the Peking-to-Paris race, built a reputation covering foreign wars. Pierre Giffard of the *Figaro*, the *Petit Journal*, and later the *Matin*, accompanied the French army to Tunisia in the early 1880s, witnessed the British occupation of Egypt, and reported on the Russo-Japanese War. But four years of world war and then the unrelenting flow of world news propelled a tendency into a vocation. After the war foreign correspondents became a fixture of news reporting. They fanned out to China, the Soviet Union, Morocco, Palestine and Syria, China again, Ethiopia, Spain, and then once again China. Major presses built far more extensive foreign services than ever before, maintaining bureaus or correspondents abroad. Reporters like Jules Sauerwein, Ludovic Naudeau (who had covered the Russo-Japanese War), Geneviève Tabouis, or Claude Blanchard made careers of traveling and writing about international news. Their presence, their stature, and the growth of their profession signaled the unending appetite for news of foreign provenance and the ease with which the postwar world could satisfy that need. Their numbers and their stories also contributed to a wider disposition between the wars to equate travel with reportage and to set travel, like adventure, within the context of the great events of the day.[159]

In the interwar years their tone was infectious. Travel literature metamorphosed into the investigative report or the assessment of political conditions in the world in books like Andrée Viollis's *Japan and Her Empire* and later *Indochina SOS,* Louis Roubaud's *Vietnam: The Indochina Tragedy,* Jean Dorsenne's *Must We Evacuate Indochina?,* Pierre Lyautey's *China or Japan (1932–1933),* or Jean Raynaud's searing account of *War in Asia.* These authors appropriated the correspondent style — "Slowly we proceed up this river 5,200 kilometers long"; "An hour later I wander through the devastated streets of Wuchang" — or blended travel with the fact-finding mission and dispatches from the front. These were books of inquiry, many written by professional reporters who shared an urge to observe on the spot and a belief in the global interconnectedness of things.[160]

But there was something of the foreign correspondent in nearly everyone who wrote about travels after the war. The grand tour gave way to a pervasive desire to see, to experience, and to report on the century. The borders travelers crossed were now self-conscious ones, drawn as much by the war as by national cultures. The French voyaged to see the China they identified with Borodin and Shanghai or the China torn between nationalism, communism, and Japanese land grabs. They journeyed to the United States and Japan to see the looming new powers in a truly global era.[161] Most of all they traveled to the Soviet Union to report on "the most prodigious experiment ever attempted in human history,"[162] the laboratory of the century, the site of the future, the homeland of revolution, the source of all evil, or simply a land where the consequences of the Great War were on permanent display.

The literature was nearly as prodigious as the experiment. One person has tabulated a list of 125 books written by Frenchmen and Frenchwomen who visited the Soviet Union between 1918 and 1939. The greatest number came in the mid-to-late 1930s, but production was steady throughout.[163] To attempt to describe them all would be merely to catalogue a predictable range of prejudices and political predispositions. The common thread was the motivation to travel to see history in action, and after that the repetitiousness and boredom that is characteristic of most travel writing. Reading through about fifteen of these books readily produces a sensation of déjà vu of the sort that would have driven Marcel to refrain from mixing tea and cookies for the remainder of his days. The authors visit factories, old age homes, collective farms, and the various institutions of a socialized society. They observe the clothing people wear in the streets, the quality of their homes, and whether they exhibit the same human affections as people in the West. There are voyages down the Volga and encounters with the *bezprizorniki*. There are the common reference points; Nizhni Novgorod, for example, is a "future Detroit" or *un Détroit russe*. There are comments about freedom and about obsessions with the five-year plan.[164]

What stands out most, perhaps, are the scenes of return to the West. There was decompression, but also release, liberation, and the affirmation of things French. Emile Schreiber described an explosion of joy among all the foreign passengers in his train, the exchange of congratulations in the corridor as they rolled over the border, and the sight of Germans shouting "Long live Poland." Marc Chadourne described a long, lyrical descent back to France. In Poland everything was softer, more colorful. "No more Sovkhoses; no more 'giants' . . . no more busts of Lenin." Rolling through Germany he admired the flower boxes in the windows. Then rapidly across Belgium and home to farms without elevators, woods without sawmills, rivers without rafts, but bateaux-mouches, the Seine, Paris, rabbit stew, Beaujolais, and a country of harmony, measure, and liberty. Roland Dorgelès, after four months of travel in 1936 through Russia, Germany, Italy, Austria, and Hungary, remarked that from the North Sea to the Adriatic, from the Volga to the Rhine, he had seen nothing but soldiers and one immense barracks flapping with banners. To those of his compatriots who looked elsewhere for models he admonished that abroad he had seen nothing but regimentation and dictatorship. "What can they teach us? A revolution? We made one and it was more fruitful. A dictator? We had one and he was more powerful." Life in France was better, sweeter, and freer. For Georges Le Fèvre it was straightforward simplicity. No one was shot in the streets in Russia, there were no microphones in radiators, one was not followed wherever one went; but "we live well *chez nous*."[165] Again, the French carried with them a satisfaction with their country that accords poorly with the discomposure others have insisted permeated these years.

Whatever the response, what mattered most was that it issued from the present-mindedness of the era. For these travelers as for those who scattered throughout Asia and the Americas (and they were often the same), the rush to evaluate sprang from a deeper urge to travel into the world made by the war. Sailing abroad was to sail into history, sample it, taste of it, and as frequently as not, report on what it had wrought. Even those who traveled with other agendas found that international politics had a way of intruding upon their journeys.

Here is one reason why travel and intrigue could blend so readily between the wars: the intense present-mindedness that nurtured spy writing and caused it to flourish worked the same effect on travel writing as well. A common mental climate infused the genres. Both spy writing and travel writing reflected a desire to report on the forces that had changed the world and were changing it still, and both offered a medium for doing just that. Both grew as the intensity of living with history quickened after 1914. Both expressed the greater global consciousness that came from the war and both profited by it. Consequently it was natural that spy stories and travel stories should run together and that trains and passenger liners where history was experienced and imprinted should be so often the setting for tales of international intrigue. Travel as reportage no doubt was itself a prod to reports about spies. But it was also the larger mood—the awareness of living in a distinctive moment in time—that fed the imagination with travel and spies and made the one a common theme of the other.

The moods of travel, then, might just as easily turn the French to thinking of spies. But, as we have seen, those moods were diverse and thus so too were their correspondences with espionage. Robert Wohl, for example, has described the metaphorical content of postwar travel— its evasiveness, its flux, its "universal disequilibrium," and its stress on departure—for a generation that saw itself lost between one world and another.[166] Here too there was reason to turn to spies, those arch evaders in an age of evasion, characters who had no fixed bearings, were always on the move, changed identities with their travels, and whose very being symbolized the impermanence of postwar settlements. The spy, like the traveler, was no less a source of fascination and a symbol in an age of interregnum.

There was, moreover, between travel and intrigue, still another shared mood, itself a conscious dwelling on moods, a romanticizing that has generally been passed over for these years and that reveals again how interwar spy writing could have much to do with its age but little to do with sentiments of fear. The work of Pierre Darlix, an obscure and sorry excuse for a writer, nonetheless represents much of spy literature after the war. Darlix wrote three books on spies in the late twenties and early thirties. Two were novels — *Un soir en Pullman* . . . and *Last Stop Smyrna* — and a third was reportage that he entitled *Terrorism Over the World*. All three were of a pattern where mood, ambiance, mystery, and the sought sensation became an end in themselves. The books invented everything, but they also invented nothing because their materials were the prefabricated expectations of a postwar world: that life was ruthless, that travel was luxury and abandon, that spies were prevalent, that White Russians were wild, mysterious, and altogether fascinating, that place-names were alluring if exoticism combined with contemporary history, and that all were gods of sensation that if properly summoned and appeased could be an infinite source of romance in the twentieth century.

It cannot be said that Darlix missed anything in these books except quality or sophistication of writing, yet that was never the aim. They abound with supercharged characters. There is Illya de Monpolesco whom the narrator of *Un Soir en Pullman* . . . meets mysteriously on the Orient Express, then glimpses again in a White Russian cabaret in Montmartre, then yet again debarking from the night luxury express between Warsaw and Berlin, and then at last in Wansee where she keeps a copy of *The Madonna of the Sleeping Cars* on her night table. Her life is a history of debauch. Her mother dies in the arms of a tamed gorilla. Her father is a victim of a night of orgy. Raised by her baron uncle she has tasted of "exquisite revelations" with a Serb servant, seduced the monk charged with her moral instruction, run off with the man in the Orient Express, abandoned him for an English film director, seduced his mistress, begged along the Thames, prostituted herself, married the comte de Monpolesco (one of her clients), frequented opium dens, and taken up with the Greek consul to Berlin whose lover of preference is a secret agent working for Italian intelligence. In *Last Stop Smyrna* there is Prince Igor-Wladimir Romanov, nephew of the czar and legal heir to the throne. Shot at Ekaterinburg, he has feigned death beneath the pile of massacred bodies, escaped the Reds (nursed to health by an old peasant woman; Darlix's eye for the cliché was unerring), fought with Kolchak, emigrated to London, and survived life in exile as a doorman, taxicab driver, and gigolo dancer. Recruited by British intelligence, he captains a floating opium den off the coast of Nice. The intelligence service supplies the yacht and the opium, he uses the proceeds to buy arms from them, and then he runs guns to the resistance in the south of Russia, unaware that his conspiracies are always betrayed by his financiers who wish to keep the game going eternally. In *Terrorism Over the World* there is the enigmatic Captain Z., "secret agent." His lair is a sleazy, ramshackle office in a tucked-away quarter of massage parlors in Paris. His operatives spy on Reds, Whites, and Greens; he recalls Zavadskii-Krasnopol'skii, whose name, by 1932, would not have been unknown to Darlix.

The writing is cinematographic, a composite of set scenes and pan shots. Locales and characters function as props on a set, a central casting–created decor. The reader of *Terrorism Over the World* is led by the omniscient Petrovich to a ratty Billancourt hotel where, we are told, a Cantonese had spent several months before he was robbed and murdered in Marseilles and placed in a trunk by two Chinese from Peking. Inside there is an Armenian *patron,* obsequious and incredibly filthy, and his associate, an equally obsequious Chinese. Upstairs there are more Chinese, some drugged, some playing mah-jongg. It is here that Petrovich has taken the narrator to unravel the mystery of the *Georges-Philippar* fire. At the beginning of *Un Soir en Pullman . . . ,* the camera eye pans the dining car of the Simplon Orient Express, sweeping the reader from rich insolent Americans to a faded Dutch beauty to a foreign millionaire, a mysterious frequenter of the great international hotels whom the narrator has glimpsed only four days earlier at the Moulin Rouge in Belgrade "where he was drowning his nostalgic desires in the lips of a girl from the Café Moscow"; now he is tête-à-tête with a conquest gleaned from the corridors of the sleeping car.

Screenplay effects take over completely as Prince Igor sails into the harbor of Smyrna. One is no longer reading a novel but directions for staging a shot. It is seven o'clock. The harbor comes to life. All the cosmopolitan stereotypes that a seedy grade-B mind would identify with *Smyrna* are present on the set. There are half-starved Armenians, Turkish stevedores, "ferreter Jews" moving out on the prowl. In a doorstep's squalid corner a Russian émigré scratches for lice. An Egyptian tout directs English sailors to a shady cabaret. Armenian streetwalkers in rags call out to seamen on board ships. There is the beggar boy who haunts every harbor scene in the history of the movies. In the background a camel caravan tramps slowly by. Later, Igor tosses a coin to a peddler. The man doffs his fez and reveals a message on his head from the British Intelligence Service. That too is straight out of the movies.[167]

There are still other effects crammed into these works — mysteries, intrigues, conspiracies, and tensions — although it is not likely that these mattered much to Darlix except for the nebulous moods he could extract from them. Overall his books approximated what Graham Greene would later call "entertainments," stimulants of a pleasurable if limited sort wrought out of the visual elements of travelogues, adventures, and, in Darlix's case, near-pornographic fantasies. They were also, like much of interwar literature, considerably present-minded in that they were acutely situated in the politics of their day. Yet it was the mood-making exploitation of milieu that the author had clearly in mind. In this respect the spies who inhabited his writings were no different from the White Russians, the sleeping cars, the exotic locales, or the sharp sense of contemporary context. Like the others they offered a story element, a condiment for color, ambiance, and romance. The interesting thing is the sources — all dredged from the present — that Darlix went to for these sensations, and the way such effects converged with travel writing.

This desire to set scenes, to seek out sensations, to evoke mystery and atmosphere, or to create adventures was an integral part of interwar travel literature. Beyond reportage lay a romantic, evocative longing to reach out for what Joseph Kessel called "the syllables that fascinate." If travel was a journey into the contemporary world, it was also pleasure and indulged restlessness. Paul Morand wrote that he was never really happy except on the move, that this was the sole beauty and truth in life. Albert Londres said he traveled as others smoked opium or sniffed cocaine. "It was," he wrote in a caricature of himself, "his special vice. He was intoxicated with sleeping cars and ocean liners. . . . [Nothing] exerted upon him the same devilish charm as a simple, small, rectangular railway ticket."[168]

Travelers lusted for adventure, the chance to sail distant waters, to roam remote deserts, to wander through the storybook realms of imagination and fantasy. Riding the Trans-Siberian on her way to Manchuria, Gabrielle Bertrand shared a compartment with a young German bound for adventures and adjoined another filled with young Austrians headed for Mongolia "in quest of Buddhist monasteries, the picturesque, shamanism." In Peking at the bar of the Hôtel du Nord, she met Helmut, who had sailed Chinese seas and Tannberg, who spoke of forbidden deserts as if they were the outskirts of Stockholm. Unable to resist she too struck out for the Gobi. At Kalgan, on the desert's edge, she camped deliberately at what remained of the Pioneer's Inn, a former haunt of traffickers, thieves, caravanners, and European adventurers. There she gave herself over to "the piercing sensation of being alive in the past among things I had read about somewhere in books, in legends perhaps." In the evening she listened to Chinese "tell me stories of brigands who had passed by here." Deeper into the evening she imagined herself among the Croisière jaune camped in this very house five years before. She evoked the image of Point uneasily pacing the room before pushing out into central Asia, then other images "several months later, a year almost, the return of the marvelous expedition worn down, wearied after long fraternal hours passed in the impassable mountains and barren outback. . . . Those forms well known to us from the movie screen and photographs." Then she drifted toward sleep, content "to be alone, far away, and leaving for still farther places." From Kalgan she pushed outward, as far as Pai-ling-miao, where she sojourned at a lamasery before crossing east through Mongol territory to Dolonnur. Afterwards there was disappointment that the adventures had not been greater, more hazardous, nearly calamitous. Still it was a taste of the Gobi, an almost magnetic plot of earth for voyagers by the thirties, combining as it did remoteness, otherness, the distant romantic associations of silk roads and tea routes, and the contemporary legends of Hedin, Ossendowski, Borodin, Vasel, and the Croisière jaune. "I had seen the brown desert of the eastern Gobi unfurl as far as the horizon," Bertrand wrote of her reasons for going. "The unlimited unknown had flung at me too violent a call for me to resist going out there."[169]

With the urge to travel came the urge to voyage by sampan, to ride in caravans, and to cross over into the lands that began with the "great vocable" of "'Boy!'" For these travelers there was a love affair with the word *mystery* or its adjective, *mysterious.* In the Caucasus there was the far shore of the river, "mysterious," source of "a great rumor of legends." In Indochina there were the imperial tombs, where everything was "mysterious, secret, exalting." In Baghdad with the Croisière jaune, one penetrated the old city and suddenly there was "silence, calm, a hushed life, walled up in the alleyways of the native city, the mystery of heavy portals half-opened on *entrepôts,* small mosques where imams snuffle. Nothing has changed since the Abbasids." Voyagers knew, in the travels they wrote about, how to pile on images and call forth haunting, if vague, sensations. Their romantic gestures were automatic, at times almost compulsory. Arriving at Suez on her way to Indochina, Andrée Viollis wrote of "the first blazing colors of fire and blood; the first camels, triangular silhouettes cut out against the whitened heat of the sky; old bearded men, with rods, dragging little gray donkeys; wide-eyed women camouflaged behind blue veils: Africa." At Saigon Francis de Croisset painted a quick pastiche from the Orient. "Along every watercourse that I cross floats a village of sampans and junks. The flocks of birds that rise and recede sparkle under the vibrations of light. On the riverbank women beat their linen of brilliant colors. Zebus descend to drink, mounted by the naked children." For the professionals it was easy, a mere matter of impressionism and an homage to a conventional, all but anticipated style, what Jean Ajalbert labeled "la littérature des paquebots." But the amateurs lapsed into it too, even the smirky Tranin whose voyage across Africa was a triumph of the ordinary yet who felt the need to write of Bedouins evoking "le désert sans fin, l'amour, la mort."[170]

From these years came a persistent craving to endow the contemporary world with mystery, to coat it in ambiance, and, in what was perhaps its most distinctive feature, to construct its moods out of the materials of the age, especially those of war and revolution. Romantic drives between the wars did not flee from the great cataclysms of the day but seized and possessed them for the realm of sensation. Much like the urge to hold onto the war, postwar romanticism saw in dying worlds and the dawning of new ones a fabulous source of emotion and passion. It found its particular tonality in the era's accoutrements like sleeping cars and luxury liners or the new, colored associations that could be attached to great city place-names — the Berlin of inflation, the Moscow of revolution, the Madrid of civil war, and the Shanghai of intrigue and Pacific adventurism. In the romantic temper to interwar travel there was not the obverse of reportage but the complement, a desire to ravish a present-laden relation with the world for the seductive rewards that one could wrest from it.

Joseph Kessel's *Wagon-lit,* published in 1932 and serialized in *Voilà,* showed how forcefully those romantic currents appropriated the present-mindedness of the period for their own mood-setting purposes. Written by an incessant voyager and seeker after sensation, the novel was standard Kessel fare: lightweight, quasi-autobiographical, heavily laden with ambiance, and set at the nub of contemporary politics for the sole end of soaking up the atmospherics of history. It was written to make money and to sell the wagon-lit company, but it was typical of both Kessel and the era that promotion should equate with unbridled romanticism. The novel begins with Estienne—the narrator of *Siberian Nights*—recounting in a Montmartre cabaret his adventures with a woman eleven years earlier. It is historical time encased within storytelling time, after the war and the extravagant adventures in Vladivostok: "I was twenty-one and already I had known submission and command, the stakes of combat, fortune, and death, the wonderful comradeship of flight. Victory had touched me with her blade. Crossing America had been a mad and grandiose binge. At Vladivostok I had seen the violence, misery, and lewdness of humanity in all its nakedness and all its savagery." He could, he tells his listeners, have gone to Shanghai, "and you can imagine what a field for adventure that would have been." He could just as easily have gone to Peking and taught French classics. "It was 1919, the beginning of the year. There was a shortage of men." But he returns to Paris and becomes a journalist. Then he hears of a mission to famine-ridden Russia and decides that he too must go, because Russia means travel, perhaps the story of a lifetime, the lure of the steppes, the romance of Asia, and a deep, breathtaking descent into the sweep of history:

To penetrate Russia, to listen to her tumultuous voices, her roars, her sufferings, to report all the vices, the convulsions, and the thunderbolts of a revolution without equal—that, in a single stroke, would make my fortune.

From this point everything—the journey, the place, the historical setting—will be a mere stimulant to sensation. Estienne takes the wagon-lit to Riga. He needs few comforts, he says, but not when he travels. Then they are essential, indispensable:

That comes from the consuming mystique that traveling holds for me. . . .

How many times, in my rather poor childhood, did I stand on the station quais dreaming before trains made up completely of sleeping cars that contained for me the very essence, all the magic, of earthly travel. On their flanks the placards carried the names of capitals, of great unknown cities. . . . Inside polished woods, velours shone softly. The women, in the corridors, seemed more beautiful, the men more daring.

On board he climbs into his bed, experiencing a "voluptuous sensation from the fresh sheets, the soft pillow, the steady rocking and the mysterious course of the train . . . so strong and so penetrating that it balanced for a few moments my lassitude." With every turn of the wheels he senses a "savage wind" blown in from "deep in the Orient, from the steppes of Russia. This was a transitory soil, a broad and coarse entry toward ferocious peoples and climates." There are rigorous border crossings that interfere with sleep, first into the Polish corridor, then back to German territory, then over into Lithuania where every station is packed with soldiers and patrols. For Delbos these were the scars of war but Estienne drinks it all in, converts it into more *frissons* and thrills. "How this rough rhythm shook me! It carried with it violence, danger. It announced lands less secure, in a state of alarm." He tells Clarke, the man he shares his compartment with, that he is intent on getting into Russia however he must, clandestinely if necessary if he cannot get a visa. Clarke tells him that if he goes on talking like this out loud his goose will be cooked the moment he crosses the border. Clarke means this as a warning, but for Estienne it is confirmation that all the romantic capital he has invested in going to Russia will pay out in still more intoxicating dividends:

"You think that from here on there are spies, Chekists?"
   I pronounced these words with such joy, with such relish that Clarke shook his head.

For all the demons pushing him forward, Estienne goes no farther than Riga. There revolution, place-names, people, and trains conflate into one long sensual surrendering. He associates with social revolutionary circles and meets Nina, a nineteen-year-old student who longs for him to tell her of Paris:

I spoke with a dreadful injustice of the only city in the world that I truly love. I confused it with my debaucheries. . . . I described the bars, the *restaurants de nuit,* the half-undressed women, the lewd dances, *la drogue blanche, la drogue noire,* and above it all that aroma of obsessive, intoxicating, powerful sensuality.

He abandons himself to Nastia the gypsy girl, seeking in her "the mirror of Asia, the homeless hordes. . . . I wanted through the go-between of a woman who carried its mark to possess the Orient." At the end he returns to the romance of travel, arranging for Nina to live out her fantasies as she rides the Paris wagon-lit into the yards:

I closed the door, lowered the curtains. The light that scarcely filtered through resembled that from night lamps. And at this moment I know that I could have taken Nina, that she awaited my will, ready for anything.

But was it not better and worse and more heart-rending and softer to hear the murmurs that flowed from this childish mouth:

"It is nighttime . . . the customs officers have inspected the luggage . . . the passports are in order. . . . The train rolls. . . . The West approaches . . . Riga-Paris. . . . The train rolls.[171]

Writing about China captured a similar mood, the place-name it-self — *la Chine* — becoming an incantation opening doors to a dense, atmospheric land of swarms, smells, barbarism, chaos, pirates, bandits, warlords, gunrunners, opium gangs, coolies, and the clash of vast twentieth-century political forces. It was a picture of considerable verity, but it was also a posture, a conscious forcing of ambiance, a setting of scenes, and the rendering of a nation into a gigantic canvas upon which the imagination could paint in broad, colorful strokes the romantic or sensation-seeking images it sought to assign to the country. For these pleasures one condescended to the tropes of exoticism, although mostly the evocations of China in the twenties and thirties emanated from a contemporary scene. O.-P. Gilbert fabricated moods out of postwar wastage and decay, White Russian flotsam washed up in Shanghai, or Europeans looking for a terrain of "heroism . . . White heroism" — "I had had it up to here," recounts one of his characters, "with Europe after the war. She seemed to me aged, absurd, gangrenous. . . . I needed something else; I chose Asia." His China was psychically charged with warlords and pirates and a dying age of European imperialism. In the Communist adventure in China Maurice Dekobra found the source for an overwrought tale of sexual violence and political intrigue. For Marc Chadourne, Borodin was "the Adventurer of the Century." "Where are Galen, Eugene Chen," he lamented in the softer days of 1931. "Where are the cadets of Whampoa who, upright on cars bristling with machine guns, swept all Canton to the barbed wires of Shameen? Where are the strike pickets, the dock thieves, the extortioners of ships? . . . Where are the Reds of yesteryear?" What he discovered nevertheless was the material for a dozen vignettes, well turned, titillating, pleasurably digestible; and the unmistakable setting they would all come looking for:

A wet dawn. . . . A crown of peaks emerges from the clouds, bald mountains concealing armored domes. Passing by, one divines the presence of the great idle guns hidden in those eyries. The Gibraltar of Asia. . . .

The mist clears in a thousand fiery shafts, amid . . . freighters, liners, naval vessels, hundreds of rusty or shining hulls, in blacks, grays, whites, and reds, all contributing to the uproar of whistling and hammering and shouting. . . .

Among them scud the somber-hued hordes of Chinese boats, with sails of mats and rags, their sterns covered with flower pots. One of them rams us in a crash of splintered wood and flapping sails, while twenty hooks lay hold of us at once. Confusion of boarding. . . . These shrieks of madmen, this frenzy, these foul-spoken gallows'-birds — I already begin to recognize all this. It is China — the howl of her starving pack, her color of spices, her stinking rags, her insolence, her voracity, China.[172]

Behind this consumerlike urge to devour the present lay a presenti-ment that the romantic encounters with the world of the past were shut-ting down rapidly in the twentieth century. "Who comes with me to Isfahan in the season of the roses must ride by slow stages as in olden days. Who comes with me to Isfahan at the season of roses must accept the perils of evil paths where horses stumble, must sleep in caravanserais, crouched in a niche of beaten earth, among the flies and vermin. . . . Who comes with me towards some lost oasis in fields of white poppies and gardens of pink roses, will find an old town of ruins and mystery."[173] That was Pierre Loti, writing of his journeys across India and Persia toward the turn of the century. Thirty years later Elisabeth Sauvy (Ti-taÿna) found Isfahan corrupted by American tourists, and André Goerger arrived in Teheran full of expectation undone by deception. "When one has visualized the tales from Persia where the wondrous cleaves endlessly to the splendor of the decor, the reality of modern Teheran is disappointing. A few well shaded attractive avenues running up to the palace of the royal family, here and there a porch covered with the azure faiences that are the charm of the country, such are the rare witnesses to a brilliant past." For the Croisière jaune, Kermanshah was a faded city. Since the coming of cars, they were told, "the caravans tend to disappear and the great camel inns are put to other uses."[174]

Already, in the previous century, the threat of an end to unchartered territories and, worse, the demystification of exotic lands beyond West-ern reach appeared very real. Peter Bishop has shown, for example, how the West made of Tibet a repository for its dreams about the sacredness of faraway places as romantic sanctuaries of this type increasingly disap-peared from a well-traveled world and how the fixation grew as even Tibet seemed imperiled by the arrival of casual travelers — "almost rou-tine" — in the lower Himalayas by the late nineteenth century. Yet Bishop has also noted how the tone became unmistakably sharper, edg-ier, the construct more and more artificial, as the true corruption of Tibet set in only with the twentieth century when the global spread of technology and travel surpassed anything the nineteenth century had known.[175] That was natural. The twentieth century ushered in an age of homogenization of culture and facility of access that has become a commonplace in our day. The agencies of this change were the emergence of a truly global world, mass culture and the media of mass communications, and new forms of rapid and penetrating transport, especially the automobile and the airplane, all of whose effects had begun to be felt by the end of the First World War.

Thus the world, to postwar travelers, was appearing smaller, more trivial. Paul Morand predicted that his generation would be the last to have any sense of the true dimensions to the globe. "Where we still delight in a great circumnavigating journey, others will no longer see anything but a 'farrago of trips.' A tour of the cage will go quickly. Hugo in 1930 would write, 'The child will ask: Can I run over to India? And the mother will answer: Take along a snack.'" And Ella Maillart, venturing into one of the most remote regions of Asia, had difficulty believing that she had actually written home to expect another letter from India in six months' time, or that they should begin to worry if a year went by without further news of her whereabouts. "Fine perspective for a century of airplanes and radiograms!"[176]

The signs of change, and consequently of foreclosure, were everywhere. Some came from the desiccating impact of mass commercialism on both the subject and object of travel. Camped near the Euphrates on one of the great adventures of the century, Audoin-Dubreuil, second-in-command of the Croisière jaune, sought to freeze the moment into an evocative snapshot — "We set up our tents on an imposing site. . . . The sun goes down. Georges Le Fèvre, chronicler of our voyage, is seated before his typewriter. . . . Laplanche and our radio operators raise the antenna of the wireless. Goerger, our *secrétaire général,* writes down Georges-Marie Haardt's instructions while Haardt shaves" — but then converted the image, almost instinctively, into a plaything of Western consumerism. "It really is a model camp: it would go perfectly as lead toys in a department store show window next Christmas." Roland Dorgelès described the experience of lounging in the garden of a Hungarian village inn when a boy came running with a message that set the place abuzz. So rapidly did the peasants fly out of their chairs and alert everyone they saw that Dorgelès was certain a farm had caught fire. But the alarm was the word that four motor coaches filled with American tourists were arriving from Gödöllö, and the panic was the villagers' haste to get out of their contemporary clothing and into their folkloric costumes so as not to disappoint their visitors (and wipe their village off the tour routes in the future).[177]

Other signs came from the routinization that followed the technological conquest of space and that stripped much of the world of its sense of remoteness. By the 1920s desert travel by automobile was becoming a norm, and by the 1930s air routes were covering most of the world. Two routes by car between Damascus and Baghdad were in use by 1923 and continuing on to Teheran was considered no problem. Every Thursday there was regular service between the Iraqi and Syrian capitals, two cars setting out from each city and meeting halfway to camp overnight before heading on to their respective destinations. Further east, in the Gobi, the Dodges that had served Roy Chapman Andrews's central Asiatic expeditions so well were sold off as a fleet and put into operation by a Chinese company on the Kalgan-Urga run. "Our explorations," Andrews wrote in his history of the expeditions, "had the unexpected result of opening western Mongolia to motor transport. Immediately after our return from the first Expedition, fur dealers came to ask how they could reach far distant trading stations. We told them where to send gasoline and how they could go; now fur and wool buyers who cross the desert use dozens of cars, where only camels had traveled until we came." In the Sahara liaison by car was assured between Algiers and Timbuktu as early as 1924. So confident were the French of opening the desert to still more motor travel and then to a mass wave of tourism, that it was suggested future travelers would return from the Sahara with the phrase on their lips: "I've come from the desert, the place was packed!" One year after Larigaudie and Drapier completed their grueling journey they learned that a road had been built south of Mandalay. "What for us was an epic," Larigaudie put in a footnote at the end, "will become tomorrow a walk-though for tourists."[178]

Travel by air was slower in coming, but its spread around the globe, once launched, was no less relentless. Regular air routes were established in Europe and the United States, but also in Latin America and across large parts of Asia. Having trekked on an adventure across central Asia, Ella Maillart caught an Air France flight home (by stages) from Karachi while her companion, Peter Fleming, flew Imperial Airways to London. Even more striking as an example of the powers of routinization was an announcement that appeared in *L'Illustration* in 1936 advising of regular passenger service from Casablanca to Dakar, the very route that Mermoz and his comrades had flown as the "line" with almost daily heroics only a decade before. The contrast with legendary days of the past was not lost on the author of the piece, who saw it all as a "sign of the times, [a] sign of the technical advancements that confer on an air service, daring but a short time ago, the security compatible with normal and regular transport of passengers."[179] That was written with some pride, and indeed adventures like the "line" or the Citroën expeditions had (in part) been intended to pioneer an eventual routinized service with all the regularity and security that mass travel might demand. But if the very stuff of legends contained within it the promise of softer, less heroic voyages in the future, then it also meant the shredding of the mysteries of the world, the fading of romance or color to travels in distant and exotic lands, and, most ironically, the very end to adventure itself.

That sense of irretrievable loss preyed on the French in the interwar years. Baghdad, Titaÿna reported, was congested with American cars, Parisian women, the sounds of jazz, men of letters drinking Perrier water. What remained of Ctesiphon the twentieth century was finishing off rapidly. In search of authentic, fanatical Islamic culture she went to the sacred cities of Persia. In the desert villages she tracked the "caravans of the dead," the camel caravans of tinkling bells and terrible smells that carried the embalmed corpses of the faithful on their promised pilgrimage to the holy places. But at the end of her story she says she was torn from a reverie by the blast of a horn and the sight of the camel driver she had left in Bakhtiari country pulling up in a Ford laden with coffins. "'I bought some old Fords at the frontier,' he told me. 'In the desert there's no need for a roadway and the dead travel faster.'"[180]

René Pinon expressed nearly the same thing when he remarked that driving into the Syrian desert produced strange and foreboding contrasts. Alongside desert cultures that went back millennia were the advance postings of a modern industrial society—factories and pipeline pumping stations—the spread of the one signaling the eradication of the other. Automobiles and planes, he argued, already spelled an end to the camel as a means of transport and an "adieu [to] the biblical and koranic poetry of the camp in the desert, the evenings under the tent, the convergence of flocks at the water holes, the tales of war and love around the fire," lines whose sentimental effusiveness were no less a testimony to the romantic yearnings of these years. Not even the great luxury liners were spared this kind of lamentation. "Today one embarks as if one were taking the métro," wrote Marc Chadourne of his voyage across the Atlantic via the SS *Manhattan*.[181]

Nothing captured better the inexorable banalization of the world after the war than the experience of travel to Angkor Wat. For the French the great temple complex in the midst of the Cambodian jungle was laden with romantic, adventurous identities. Pierre Loti, who, as one person has put it, exercised a "massive influence on the spiritual geography of an entire generation," had in his *Pèlerin d'Angkor* left behind an unforgettably romantic account of his pilgrimage to Angkor that every subsequent French traveler to the ruins probably read. His voyage had been a five-day affair, up the Mekong by fly boat, then deeper upriver by sampan, and then finally overland by cattle cart until he had arrived at the first of the temples. He had described a primitive descent back into all but prehistoric times, through "woods beyond measure and impenetrable bush," through a land of lizards, serpents, monkeys, and a people who scarcely seemed to have evolved since mankind's earliest days, a country so overgrown and lost in time that even his sampan guides lost their way in the tropical channels. At Bayon, the most ancient of the temple sanctuaries, he had been forced to hack his way through the liana and then to cut his visit short at the urging of his guide because "our carts have no lanterns . . . and we must return before the hour of the tiger." He had camped on straw mats in an open-air shelter, and during his stay he had shared the ruins with no other visitors save pilgrims from Burma and three French archaeologists.[182]

But those days had gone forever by the end of the war. By the 1920s Angkor was accessible by automobile — one day's journey from Saigon — and by 1936 it was on the tour stops advertised by the Messageries Maritimes cruises. There were hotel accommodations with screened windows, fans, and showers, not yet the plush resorts that await today's jet-lagged traveler in nearly any remote portion of the world, yet nonetheless a far cry from anything smacking of adventure. For the voyager who wished a memento or some proof of the voyage there were postcards for sale and little bits of sculptures that the merchants guaranteed as authentic. Pierre Billotey, who came in 1929, contrasted Loti's arrival before "this forest that encloses on all sides the temples and palaces and forms with them a decor of mystery, of gigantic enchantment" with his own before "pretty grounds . . . serviced by commodious avenues" and wondered whether the influx of tourists would soon require the installation of turnstiles. Francis de Croisset described a bus tour organized by a Central European company that left Saigon at dawn, lunched at Phnom Penh (with brief visit of the city), and then arrived at Angkor at the very end of the day with just a momentary interlude of rest before touring the complex in the fresh hours of the evening, at last discharging the "heroic tourists" for their dinner and bath. Of his own experience he recounted the following exchange with a friend in Saigon who suggested he borrow his car and drive out to Angkor:

—There's no way you can get lost. You have a few rivers to cross by ferry. You will sleep at Phnom Penh. Spend a day there. It's worth the trouble, and then it's straight ahead through Kam-Pong-Thom and the forest until Angkor. Why are you laughing?

—Because you speak of this trip as if it were a matter of going from the Madeleine to the Opéra.

Once settled in he was divided in his moods, content with his comforts but feeling deprived of his adventure and acknowledging that the mysteries that had greeted Lyautey lay beyond anything that he would encounter.[183]

No description, however, compared to that of Roland Dorgelès in *On the Mandarin Road,* written in 1925. It really requires repeating nearly in full:

On the way from Phnom-Penh, at Kampong-Luang des lacs, where one transfers to the small boat for the Viam, or mouth, of the Siem-reap River, the last stage on the way to the ruins, one suddenly sees on the right a large sign, fastened to two posts. Dumfounded, one reads this: "*Pèlerins d'Angkhor,* turn to the right." Motorists are thus diverted to the road leading to the jetty.

Nothing more is needed to change the whole spirit of the journey and wipe out the spell created by the fleeting visions of forests with flowering vines, tiny villages on piles, huge, grazing buffaloes with birds perched on their backs, naked children splashing in the water with their skin glistening in the sun like fish-scales, flights of egrets overhead, pagoda-cocks and barrister-birds with black-wings and coral-headed cranes. At last to escape the civilized colony, really to penetrate ancient Asia, the hospitable and marvelous Kambudja, whither all the wistful beauty of the world seems to have sought refuge! Then, presto! one comes upon this sign-board of the Motor Club, ridiculous homage to the memory of Loti, and back one drops to earth with a thud. Civilization has penetrated everywhere, and there is nothing for it but to resign oneself. "The world is greater than you believe" wrote Renan. But things have changed. Today he would have to write: "The world is much smaller than you think. . . ."

You need not expect anymore to cover the last lap from Siem-reap to Angkor Wat on the back of a royal elephant, trampling down the underbrush, tearing up shrubs, and breaking off branches. A good macadam road now leads to the *sala,* and it has been extended in a circuit of the various temples through forty kilometers of forest. It is true that a couple of beasts with trumpets are attached to the hotel, but they are there for the same reason that there are goat carriages in the Champs Elysées. "*C'est pour la regardelle*" as they say in the Midi. And small trucks line up near the mounting platform for the elephants.[184]

For Dorgelès there were no regrets. He was at ease with his comforts and insistent that exoticism was only what one was prepared to make of it. "Everything is interesting to whoever knows how to see." Still his portrait of Indochina was that of a steamy, mist-laden land where the romance of the past was confined to the storybooks. Gone were the tiger hunts, fiefdoms, and stories of pirates. Gone were the days when upriver planters would scan the river anxiously for visitors because now they could motor to Saigon within the same day. Gone was the exoticism of the past because "the monstrous machine now rolling over the world, making all five continents alike, has passed this way." Or as Louis Malleret put it in 1932 in the very first sentence of a book that would chronicle a literature of adventure, romance, and lush picture-making: "One must resign oneself to it: today, in Indochina, except perhaps in a few poorly known parts of Moï country, adventure is no longer possible."[185]

From this tension between romantic drives and a sense of foreclosure arose, in good part, the forced atmospherics that were so pronounced in the interwar years. Confronted with an end to mysteries and romantic ventures into the world, the age manufactured its own. There were treks through faraway landscapes, artificial flirtations with adventure to recreate and drink in a mood like Bertrand's incursion into the Gobi. Elisabeth Sauvy, who called herself Titaÿna, decried the corruption of the desert, but she built a career out of drummed-up experiences and voyeuristic forays in search of sensations. These she peddled in newspapers, magazines, and books under such giveaway titles as "Around the World Aboard a Tramp Steamer," "In the Land of Pearls," "Unknown Mexico," "Aboard the Dirigible 'Hindenburg,'" *Hot Nights* (scenes of life and sex in southern climes), and the melodramatic *Caravan of the Dead*, beneath whose primeval overtones ran a fabricated quest after Persian exoticism.[186]

Even bona fide exploits drenched in romanticism were swept up in the manufacturing mill. The stories by Henri de Monfreid, first published in the early 1930s, provide a good illustration. De Monfreid's life seems to have come out of a legend, perhaps fitting because that is what he would make of it. His father was a gentleman painter, obscure in the full circumstances of his birth, a friend of Gauguin, Maillol, and Verlaine. The son, born in 1879, grew up on the Mediterranean coast, learning to sail first on his father's two-masted schooner, then on an old fishing bark left along the shoreline. Educated in Paris, he went through a series of jobs — coffee salesman, representative for the milk trust, dairy farmer — all of which he found drearily oppressive. A long bout of Maltese fever left him a business failure but provided the escape that he had been seeking. "I was ruined financially, but the fever had set me free," was how he would put it. Determined to start over again only far off in the world, de Monfreid boarded a ship in 1910 heading for Djibouti: "A deck passage . . . East," as he later wrote in the inimitable romantic prose style of the thirties. There he worked for a French trading firm dealing in skins, but this too he found crushingly petty:

Was it for that I had come to Africa? Here I was after two years in the desert and the bush, tied to my account books and inventories, fretting with debits and credits, losses and gains, like any grocer or dry good's merchant on the public square. Adventure? Precious little of it. Thirst in the desert; a touch of fever during the season of rains; mild skirmishes with pilfering black men. But most of the time, in a sweltering *comptoir* at Djibouti, a baked mud house in Harrar; a hut on the mountain side, juggling with columns of figures, selling, buying, exchanging, loading pack mules for Diré Daoua and the coast for the problematic profit of some one — rarely for my own. The whole race of traders, we were like some noxious breed of insects burrowing in the rich African soil. Like beetles on a dungheap. That was what Africa meant to us — desert and plateau and mountain — a marvelous dungheap to plunder and abandon.

Bored and burning for less confining enterprises, he quit his job, purchased a dhow, assembled a crew, and launched himself on a life that would make him celebrated up and down the Red Sea, and later in France, as a cultivator of pearls, a gunrunner, and a smuggler of hashish.[187]

By the beginning of the 1930s he was setting his adventures down onto paper. He wrote in a disarmingly seductive way, first because for a man of action he displayed clear talents as a stylist and second because he showed no qualms in revealing his own foibles and misfortunes, acknowledging as he put it that "like the rat of the fable, I have left a good many tails on the battlefield."[188] The power of the stories lay mostly in their romance, their tales of pearl fishing, pearl trading, arms trafficking, drug running, evasions at sea, and sea wrecks. He recounted intrigues with French authorities, Turkish soldiers, British intelligence agents, Greek drug merchants, Arab, Abyssinian, and Somali smugglers and slave traders, all these set amidst barren mountains, basaltic cones, coral reefs, isolated moorings, pirate coves, hostile seas, and the practically biblical cities of the Red Sea, a body of water whose name tones were improbably evocative.

His first book, *Secrets of the Red Sea,* which related his earliest adventures as a pearl trader and gunrunner before the First World War, was a great success, selling fifty thousand copies over the course of the thirties and indicating the resonance such romantic tales could strike in these

years. Its publishing history, and that of its sequels, were equally revealing. The first compilation of de Monfreid's adventures appears to have
occurred at the end of the twenties in conjunction with an American
journalist, Ida Treat, and was published in English in 1930 under the
title, *Pearls, Arms, and Hashish*. The first French volume, *Secrets of the Red
Sea*, contained only part of its stories, and with certain changes of detail.
As subsequent French volumes appeared, filling out much of the remainder of the original tales, they too suggested a certain reworking
although, even more, a conscious effort to expand de Monfreid's stories
into a series. The sequel-like quality to subsequent books was apparent
in their sheer numbers — he churned out twenty or more volumes in
the thirties — and also in their strands of continuity, for example, "As I
recounted in *Secrets of the Red Sea*, the munitions which had been seized
on the island of Maskali had been advanced to me by this syndicate . . . ,"
lines from the opening pages of *Hashish*. By 1935 his publisher, Grasset,
was excerpting passages and publishing these separately in its "Great
Adventurers of Today" series alongside Guzman's *With Pancho Villa* and
Frank Buck's *Bring Them Back Alive* ("based on the famous film," as the
series advertisement put it).[189] Such promotional treatment represented
the inevitable trivialization that awaited any contemporary adventure
but, even more, the forced quality to ambiance and mystery between the
wars, even when the original versions were unassailably spellbinding.

In this respect there was not much distance separating de Monfreid's
narratives from *grand reportage* adventures like Joseph Kessel's "Slave
Trade." "You have carte blanche for the subject, the time, the expense,"
Kessel was told by the editors of the *Matin*. "But we need an *enquête*
that will tear readers away from their routines and everyday cares. We
need an astonishing adventure. Do you have any ideas? Think about it."
Four days later Kessel, after rummaging through a League of Nations
report on the Red Sea slave traffic, was back with his plans for a great
exposé: "There are still slave markets like those of three hundred years
ago. The slave trail! A title and a fascinating adventure for the public.
What do you think?" With three companions Kessel left for Djibouti on
New Year's Day 1930, returning in April with his story. He had seen a
slave trader, followed his trail, and crossed the Red Sea over to Yemen.
The series began its run in May 1930, blanketing four columns on the
front page the first day and requiring an extra printing of one hundred
and fifty thousand copies of the paper. Symbolically, among those who
had made it all possible, facilitating Kessel's Red Sea passages, was
Henri de Monfreid.[190]

Characteristically, however, the desire to reintroduce atmosphere into the world led to a turning of the period's present-mindedness in on itself. Kessel's *Wagon-lit* or the scene setters of China found their echo in *grand reportage* on gunrunning to Morocco or on border crossings without papers. Moods were created out of contemporary dramas and the great political events of the day. That is why White Russians, as well, became such captivating creatures between the wars. They were the human debris from the century's shipwrecks, the true global denizens of their global age, dispersed by revolution and civil war to the four corners of the world. They established colonies in Paris and Berlin, but also in Istanbul, Harbin, Mukden, and Shanghai and their newspapers, printed in Paris, were read in Argentina, Madagascar, Montreal, and Australia. They turned up in nearly every flea-bitten outpost from far western China to the funnel of the hulk of the *Fontainebleau* in the roadstead of Djibouti. As the Croisière jaune rolled across Asia it crossed paths with a former czarist general (overseeing the production of opium) in Khorassan, ran into more White Russians at Urumchi, and still more among the troops at Hami. At a powder factory thirty miles to the interior side of Addis Ababa the Dutch foreign correspondent, Pierre van Paassen, came upon a colonel "who had fought with Denikine under the walls of Petrograd against Leon Trotsky."[191] If many were survivors because of painstaking perseverance, others, victims of circumstance or temperament, drifted into *louche* or adventurous lives. They were gunrunners and drug traffickers, white slavers and prostitutes. They were soldiers of fortune, so thick in the Orient that they fought as units in the armies of warlords from Sinkiang to Manchuria. As spies their numbers were legion and as intriguers they were without parallel.

They were thus sad but glamorous figures, fabulously evocative of their times and as such an unending source for constructing an ambiance out of the present. They were fascinating for their talismanic qualities, their reaffirmation of the mysteries that remained, and they functioned in literature as stock characters on a set, a romantic, if lurid, presence for the armchair tourists of interwar Europe. In his memoirs Klaus Mann recalled how his imagination had soared when he first encountered White Russians in Berlin in the surrealistic days of 1923:

I was keenly interested in the backgrounds and tragedies of the innumerable refugees teeming throughout the city. Were they innocent victims or were they laden with crime? . . . And how somber was exile really? I figured it rather harsh but not without epic features. To escape from the GPU, at night, over snowy roofs; to arrive in Warsaw or Bucharest, with no possessions but two priceless diamonds; to open antique stores and night clubs everywhere between Cannes and Los Angeles; to weave political intrigues and kiss the beloved icons in squalid hotel rooms; to rush from country to country haunted by nostalgia and Soviet agents: it could be no easy life, to be sure. And still, it attracted me, in a weird, irrational way.[192]

That was the requisite style for this age of abandonment, dissolution, and flux. Paul Morand, who was a far better stylist than Mann the younger, surrendered to the same melancholic siren calls in *Flèche d'orient,* which he published in 1932 with a printing of over twenty thousand copies. The protagonist in the novel, Dmitri, is a Russian who has come west in 1915 and abandoned all ties to his past and to Russia. Not for him the White Russian community, "On ne trouve chez lui ni icons, ni samovar," the narrator tells us as the mood fog rolls in:

He does not share that morbid taste for the night of the true Russians, angels of darkness. He does not frequent that termitelike world, princes with painted eyelids, lordly door-to-door salesmen in wines, cossacks in women's trades, or dawdle as they do in gloomy cabarets of sugared drinks, empty talk, songs, and regrets. Their ill-defined situations, their murky stories, their voluptuous appetite for tears, their soft inclination for passing over to the enemy, their interested disinterestedness, their contempt for money and their extravagant needs, and that insipid compote of goodness and evil, and that incomprehensible need to be "understood," all that leaves him indifferent, all that gulls him not, and when people speak of the *charme slave,* he smiles.[193]

Yet in Romania, which he flies to on a whim, he comes to discover and experience Russia through the gypsy melodies of a man called Ionica. Before that haunting semi-Asiatic assault Dmitri's cosmopolitan skin crinkles and sloughs off, the novel ending with Dmitri drifting spiritually away from the West as he sails down the Danube, abandoning himself to the call of the motherland.

In the Far East the White Russians were at their most pathetic, and thus their most dangerous. Schreiber, at Harbin, saw in them the last act of a racial drama between Whites and Asians and de Croisset, writing of the same city, said that the refugees' fall corroded all Western prestige in the Orient: "All the white race loses face!" But Paule Herfort's Harbin was a city where Russian women "dressed on credit and disrobed for cash," an epigrammatic introduction to the conventional atmospheric tone that these people nearly always seemed to command. "They plot, they spy, they drink vodka, they carouse, they spend their last penny, and on Monday they return to their work or their intrigues." Pierre Lyautey's Harbin was a place where practically no one possessed "less than three passports or four nationalities. Hollywood could give us a rest from American crimes by situating some of its films here." And for Bertrand, who traveled in part to live out her fantasies, Harbin, city of misery and human disgrace, was a melodramatic gold mine. "Risk and poetry. *Amour de l'amour,* defiance of money, crimes, and discretion . . . *Voilà* Harbin!" she wrote of a city she also described as "surprising and dangerous, surpassing in boldness, in gangsters, in intrigues, in extravagance the worst of American Chicagos." "In the cellars of the brothels and gaming houses," she went on, as if her unthrottled pursuit of sensation had shifted into automatic drive, "where burrowed deep down are who knows what great dramas of the future, novelists, lovers of intrigue and murky exoticism, will find material to write up for a long time to come."[194] And so they did. Like Champly's *Road to Shanghai* or Gilbert's Shanghai of fallen women and Japanese intrigue, the racial fears inherent in the plight of Russians in the East were no match for the aroma of romance that clung to these refugees wherever they went. Or as Joseph Kessel put it for Paris:

Those who in the years 1924–1925 dragged out their idleness, their debauchery, their sadness, or simply their nocturnal temper in the make-believe daylight of Montmartre, those who loved the unique landscape formed by the rues Pigalle, Fontaine, and Douai, landscape of drunken Americans, Negroes with saxophones, tangoing Argentines, girls a bit haggard, pimps in dinner jackets, flower merchants, beggars and taxicab drivers, landscape that smelled of benzine, perfumes, makeup, and, secretly, of drugs, those who loved to watch, in place Pigalle, the descending and dancing cascade of signs, fascinating and deceptive like *les artifices de la joie,* those who mingled among the strange people who begin work when normal people sleep, hysterical, perverse, guileless people, outside humanity, the material of pleasure, will recall the singular number of Russian *restaurants de nuit* gathered together over several square meters of the nocturnal zone.

These establishments grew and multiplied like unwholesome plants. They came in all sizes and styles, from three-story music factories to minuscule retreats filled by a half dozen tables. In certain ones, beneath a blue tinged churchlike light reflected in massive silver cups, one could get drunk silently as if in celebrating a rite; others, on the contrary, reverberated without end with music, songs, and savage dances.

At every step one collided with cossacks stationed as sentinels before the cabaret doors. Singers and dancers, sauntering during interludes, bareheaded, dressed in velvets and silks, entered the bars, the cafés. Women with white skin and limpid eyes, gaudily covered, laughed or cried without reason. Princes drank like brothers with former horse thieves.

There were men there who had spent their lives making the night seem shorter to those who paid, real instruments of joy, born, like the violins that they played instinctively, to sing and please. They were the tziganes of the great restaurants of Moscow, of the islands of Petrograd that the river of emigration had carried as far as Paris. Some of them had played for the grand dukes, for the czar, for Rasputin. Fortunes had been thrown beneath their bows. Although at Montmartre their remuneration was meagerer, if they had work and something to drink they were happy.

But others who also carried violin and guitar cases and who wore the same castoff clothing often let break through on their thoroughbred faces a distress as troubling as their vacant stare.

Thus commingled, famished, disguised guards colonels, professors, noblewomen, prostitutes, improvised artists, and famous tziganes came, sometimes with a soul violent and sincere, sometimes with an adulterated bohemianism, to deliver to couples knocked senseless by noise, light, and champagne the barbaric, desperate, and sometimes sublime inspiration that limitless, formless Russia had deposited in her songs, in her dances, and in the hearts of her worst children. . . .

Pigalle, cut-off corner of the world, port without haven for bodies lost and souls adrift, arid and neurotic refuge, a help only to those whom alcohol unfastens and cocaine shakes, mirage of forced joy destroyed by the first rays of the sun, such was this strange and inhuman country.[195]

That was from Kessel's *Nights of the Princes.* The master of White Russian romanticizing, he too gravitated to the refugee haunts of Montmartre as Dmitri did to the melodies of Ionica, lavishing there his emotional resources and drawing in return his emotional sustenance.

What White Russians offered so too did spies. Like the refugees their underground worlds, their intrigues, their secret wars, and the supposed glamour of their lives summoned moods that the interwar years seemed to be seeking. They too were creatures with the power to transcend routine and endow a present-minded world with a sense of mystery about its own being; and consequently they too were dragooned into the romanticizing enterprise. Inherently atmospheric, they possessed the ability to appeal for that reason alone. That also explains why, in the popular spy world, Trebitsch Lincoln could be such a commanding figure. A prestidigitator and a human chameleon, he was mysterious, exotic, beyond ken, unfathomable. His adventures transported readers to foreign, romantic lands — Afghanistan, Siam, China — and magnified their secrets rather than deflating them. Perhaps he personified alarms and racial visions after the war, but it was the dramatic, romantic cast he gave to global politics that mostly explains his attraction. His life was a fabulous yarn sprawled across continents, a counterpoint to a shrinking, "comprehended" world, and thus it was told and then told again.

Nearly all the efforts of spy writers strained to this end; nearly all searched for that kind of yarn. It is indeed difficult to wade through the embellishments, the indulgences, or the searching for effects that pervade interwar spy writing and not see in these the same conscious striving to conjure up storybook realities that sent Bertrand to the Gobi or Kessel to Ethiopia or that made of White Russians a theme of their age. Jean Joffroy did it in *Espionage in Asia,* where every character appears to have walked off a Hollywood set. Charles Pontivy arrives in the Far East after duels with gunrunners and drug smugglers, especially the formidable Ferrugini. He still carries a slug in his shoulder from a running sea battle with a boat out of Barcelona, flying the French flag, captained by a Greek, commanded by an Algerian, crewed by Spanish sailors, and charged with German arms. He reports to Gilbert Joffroy, agent R-22, veteran of perilous missions in the Orient, a man who has set up spy networks in Turkestan and Persia, who has known "the flight without glory, the ambushes," the pursuit of foreign agents, and who has just bagged four Soviet spies in Rangoon. His quarry is Izoumo, a Japanese intelligence officer who directed counterespionage services in Mongolia in 1925–1926, was spotted in Soviet Turkestan as a horse trader in the late twenties and thirties, was identified as a yogi in Calcutta in 1934, was seen at the Singapore defenses in 1934, was glimpsed again in Indochina and then in China in 1935–1936, where he disappeared until surfacing once more in Calcutta as the action of the novel begins.[196] And the press did it, for example, in the following description of Madame Krivoshcheev the last eyewitness to see Skoblin alive:

A woman of forty years, dark haired, slender, nervous, with short-cropped hair, big tired eyes, smokes cigarettes. . . . She refuses all interviews but pronounces with a restrained voice vague and subtle sentences, infinitely vague and subtle. . . . She knows nothing, absolutely nothing, of Russian affairs in Paris. . . . She has lived too long in the Far East . . . Harbin, Shanghai, all the mysterious cities where émigré Russian women lead their lives of adventure and secret miseries. . . . We imagine those astonishing stories, those appalling legends that travelers bring back of the girls of the steppes given over to pleasure, to vice, to death in an Asiatic nightmarish setting pierced by the cries of guitars. Champagne, opium, Chinese with cruel eyes, the lewd cunning of the Japanese, the raging brutality of settlers and the light from these bodies nude, soiled, defiled, wounded, bleeding from love. . . . Madame Krivoshcheev, in a word, stirs in us their violent images.[197]

So too did Darlix, Crozier, Richard, and a host of others who saw great profits in great atmospheric stories and who left behind them the trace of modern-day romancers, the reveries of professional mood-makers.

That in the end is what brought travel and intrigue so closely together. Each concerned worlds of mystique and adventures, and the forced yet wondrous manufacture of these.

Thus between postwar globalism and intrigue the associations ran long and deep. There was the global reach of spy networks, the relocation of spy wars to the empire, the vision of vast global conspiracies, or simply the matter-of-fact global approach to intelligence reporting that revealed how keenly the French found themselves thrust into worldly affairs after the war. There was equally the eagerness to go out into the world as adventurers and observers, the desire to conquer and know, the fascination with sweep and upheaval that yielded a forcing ground for stories of spies, just as the stories themselves became a medium for evoking a clearcut sense of an age. Finally there was the romantic quest that tales of voyagers lead us back into, back to the sense of foreclosure and the insistence for ambiance, if need be to fabricate or import it where none other existed. This the French did, as did their spy writers who understood the call to romanticize the century and who answered by creating a Shanghai for the métro.

Conclusion

Spies between the wars were a presence in ways this book has endeav-
ored to define. If familiar figures they became more familiar after the
war, assumed new shapes or personae, captured essences that spies before the war could not have done because the war had changed the
world in which the French lived. Nazi or communist spies were not
altogether unlike their predecessors in the Kaiserreich or the agents of
prewar anarchist movements, nor did their image in popular literature
necessarily vary from conspiracy theories of earlier days. Yet they moved
in different realms, covered greater ground, projected idioms like the
secret war or the fifth column that despite antecedents were anchored
in the conditions of their times, and were in fact simply more real.

The war promoted the pervasiveness of the spy because along with
everything else it mobilized espionage operations and organizations to
unprecedented degrees. Secret agents flocked to Swiss hotels, Scandinavian ports, Dutch harbors, Spanish coves, Mexican oil fields, Moroccan
deserts, central Asian capitals, Far Eastern *métropoles*. They did little to
win or lose the war, but their memoirs and biographies suggested otherwise and, more important, neither postwar international nor political
conditions lowered significantly the demand for spies or counterintelligence agents to watch them. After the war the large intelligence network
had come to stay.

Organization and globalism were, therefore, two characteristics of
postwar espionage. Intelligence circuits were large and systematized, designed methodically for the tasks assigned them. They were equipped

with laboratories and sophisticated gadgetry. Their reach spread across continents and oceans to cover the world. Neither feature, however, was unique to espionage. The organizational cast to postwar intelligence operations merely mimicked a drive to plan, structure, and rationalize that was inherent in Western industrial culture and propelled to levels hitherto unknown by four years of total war. Business, government, and even crime networks or adventures like the Croisière jaune exhibited greater systematizing tendencies after the war. Organizing cadences accelerated and amplified in the twenties and thirties, including those of spy masters whose orchestrated affairs were more representative than exceptional of trends in these years. Likewise a war that was concentrated in Europe but that escalated rapidly to global stature left behind a far more interlocked, tightly knit world than Europeans had known before 1914. Again there was an acceleration of trends that had gathered speed over decades or even centuries but that like breakthroughs to Mach levels boomed Europeans across historical boundaries.

The French who had conquered a great empire in the nineteenth century were anything but insular in the first decades of the twentieth. They journeyed out into the world, to all its nooks and crannies, and even more to the great landmasses that were now swept along in the roaring currents of history. They went as witnesses to the flow of their times and because a global consciousness had become inescapable. The global village of the later twentieth century had only just begun to close upon the world, leaving openings still for adventures and experiences in remote regions of the earth of a kind that we will probably never enjoy again, although already by the twenties the radio and airplane, not to mention history, had so relativized the "faraway" that European affairs were inextricably cast in global perspective. There were, to be sure, discrete reasons for the leap to worldwide intelligence networks, Comintern intrigues, for example, flung out on a planetary scale or the defense of imperial interests in an era of awakening colonial unrest. Yet neither of these was separate from the broader global course opened by the war that carried intrigues and espionage, like nearly everything else, along in its wake.

Of all the interwar intriguers none stood out more than the refugees who poured out of the war and the postwar regimes. There were Italians, Croatian and Macedonian émigrés, Jewish and anti-Nazi refugees, and most of all the White Russians who have also been a presence in these pages just as they were for the interwar French. Certainly the spy wars would have been duller had it not been for the irrepressible and preposterous Russians. Then, as today, they seemed to have stepped right out of the age with their organizations, their global communities, their flirtation with every ideological and geopolitical force of the day, their entanglement with bolshevism and Soviet politics, their fifth-column-like attributes, and their charred scent of debris that made them both creatures and signifiers of their times. As free floaters who could and did become anything, they represented the richness of interwar espionage that sets it off from the prewar years. Their stories scandalized the French but also entertained them and disclosed how far the spy had progressed from a figure of alarm to a figure of amusement in popular imagination after the war. Images of hate and vulnerability still abounded, yet outweighing these was the disposition to seek theatrics or ambiance or mystery in the spy, an attitude that spoke to needs of the period and revealed French abilities to cope with the pressures that came with the age. Spies *should* have been menacing figures between the wars. That they turned out to be many other things and to serve many other functions speaks volumes about French moods in these years. Not even the shadowy skirmishes Italian refugees fought with the OVRA or the wretched battles between German refugees and the Gestapo produced a reaction indicative of a republic that was running aground. When the French interned German refugees at the end of the thirties they did so for reasons linked through a long causal chain but mostly because of the conditions and character of secret agent threats since the First World War. Contemporary spy history, and the role of refugees as central characters in it, more than any premature step into Vichy or even panic per se, determined the decision to round up the innocent along with the guilty.

Adventure has loomed large in this book, so much so that at times I have felt that I have been writing its interwar history under the guise of writing about spies. That could not be helped, so intertwined is the history of the one with the history of the other. Adventurers like Gardiner, H. D., Corrigan, or Trebitsch Lincoln jammed counterintelligence files and records. Nearly all the White Russians who have turned up in these pages could in one way or another be called adventurers. Joseph Crozier was an adventurer and Marthe Richard an adventuress. Shanghai, the imaginative epicenter of intrigue, was, as one contemporary put it, the "paradise of adventurers." The word adventurer has multiple meanings: soldier of fortune, gambler, trafficker, mountebank, swindler, explorer, voyager, desperado. But it was in the nature of the interwar years that all of these should converge with espionage. Spy milieus absorbed these people as they did less fortunate types because this was an age when it was difficult to step out of history and retreat into the private realms of the past. Espionage ballooned after the war as nations in an era of flux felt obliged to field large intelligence operations; but its expansiveness was also built upon a wider intrusiveness that swallowed individuals up in international politics, a fact of life that focused greed or action on the great events of the day and drove adventurers of all stripes inevitably to intrigue and spy.

The war, however, had also been an adventure and that too bolstered attachments to espionage. We have become accustomed to seeing the war as a tragedy that scarred interwar memories, but that was not always how the French looked back upon it. For many the war was the story of a lifetime, and far from fleeing it they did their best to revisit and relive it. They commemorated the war with monuments and awards to every conceivable combatant. Most of all they wrote and read about it in books on every facet of the war experience. Writing about the war was for some a catharsis, but the inherent fascination with great historical convulsions and capitalist forces turned the war book (and the war) into an article of consumption. The adventures of the war translated in part into the adventures of spies, whose memoirs poured out with the rest of war stories and created an appetite for still more spy books. The spy tale itself became a variation on the war book when the latter required a certain inventiveness to keep the tidal flow coming. Thus the war, because it was seen as adventure, proved a bonanza for thinking and writing about spies. Even more, the war turned spies into heroes who offered the illusion that special individuals could still make a difference in a deindividualizing century. Like pilots, spies became adventurers in the most positive meaning of the word, people who took great risks for a cause and whose stories were enthralling. And the war, as we have seen, changed the context of adventures by setting them against the backcloth of history. Adventures politicized and their stories metamorphosed into the spy novel. Again adventure spurred on French fascination with spies and the production of spy tales, and for reasons that had little to do with alarm, vulnerability, crisis, or fear.

Present-mindedness, which is another way of describing the intrusiveness of the period, has also been a recurrent theme in this study. The phrase is awkward but I know of none better to express the intense envelopment of consciousness in contemporary history and contemporary affairs that I have found to be characteristic of the French between the wars. The urge to travel and report was one clear sign of present-mindedness while another was the frequency with which twentieth-century politics penetrated creative writing, "the presence of history" as Malraux described it. Wrapped as it was in thoughts about war or revolution or the prevailing conditions of dissolution or flux, French present-mindedness turned irresistibly to thoughts about spies. It could produce the nastiness and fear-ridden imagery that marked part of interwar spy literature, particularly as international dangers moved to center stage between the wars and made the international danger figure — the spy — a person of significance. But because the French also played with the present, exhibiting an unlimited capacity for transforming news into ravishing stories, they endowed as well their obsession with spies with the qualities of humor, mystery, and even complacency. The spy often forced its unwelcome presence on the unwary, but there was also an inclination to run after the spy because like the spy-hero the mysterious secret agent offered satisfactions and treasures that people were looking for in these years. Present-mindedness could be a mood of considerable complexity, and in their spy writing the French displayed its manifold qualities.

Serious historians have rarely written about spies, as if the *louche* character of these predators might somehow rub off on them. Even Bernard Wasserstein began his revealing biography of Trebitsch Lincoln with an apology to his professional peers. The result has been a massive outpouring of books on spies by former secret agents, journalists, rumormongers, and anyone who visited, saw, or heard of Cambridge in the 1930s, but very few treatments of espionage by professional historians. In this book I have sought no brief for correcting that imbalance. Rather, like the French of a time that has fascinated me, I too have run after spies for their evocative qualities. This has been a book about espionage, but even more about the character and mood of the period introduced by the First World War and about a people whose collective history I long ago fell prey to. The spy has taken me back to the former and forced me to rethink the latter, and I must confess that as a historian I could not have asked better. I suppose that all books extract their measure of pain and their moments of near total despair. I have felt each but also great pleasure in the byways this history has led me along, just as the French, through difficult times, found and cultivated great pleasure in the figure of the spy.

Notes

Introduction

1. Service historique de l'armée de terre, Paris (hereafter, SHAT) 3H 137, 28 April, 7 May, 14 May, 31 August, 10 September, 19 September, 6 October, 8 November 1928; Ministère des affaires étrangères, Paris (hereafter, MAE) Maroc/Tunisie 1917–1940 Maroc 1214, 16 October 1929, pp. 154–64. On Impex, see chapter 1; on Langenheim see chapter 2. A First Lieutenant v. Horn turns up in an intelligence report from 1925 on supposed recruitment of former German officers to fight with the Riffians in the Rif war. See SHAT 3H 102, 17 June 1925.

2. Archives de la préfecture de police, Paris (hereafter, APP) BA 1745, 12 March 1937 (circular from Ministère de l'intérieur [et de la décentralisation], Paris [hereafter, MI]); ibid., May 1937. (During my years of research the police archives reclassified a number of series; the designations I use correspond to box numbers at the time of my original consultation.) In 1939 the Romanian police arrested in Bucharest a German spy disguised as a circus clown. See Julius Mader, *Hitlers Spionagegenerale sagen aus* (Berlin: Verlag der Nation, 1970), 318. The motif of the traveling circus of spies is an old one. See chapter 1.

3. Although the literature on espionage is vast, intelligent writing about intelligence is not. Among the best examples of professional work are Christopher Andrew, *Secret Service: The Making of the British Intelligence Community* (London: Heinemann, 1985); David Kahn, *Hitler's Spies: German Military Intelligence in World War II* (New York: Collier, 1985); Friedrich Katz, *The Secret War in Mexico: Europe, the United States, and the Mexican Revolution* (Chicago: University of Chicago Press, 1983); Ernest R. May, ed., *Knowing One's Enemies: Intelligence*

351

Assessment Before the Two World Wars (Princeton: Princeton University Press, 1984); Wesley K. Wark, *The Ultimate Enemy: British Intelligence and Nazi Germany, 1933–1939* (Ithaca: Cornell University Press, 1985).

4. For a discussion of some recent reconsiderations see Sandra Horvath-Peterson, "Introduction," *French Historical Studies* 17 (Fall 1991): 302–3. See also Olivier Barrot and Pascal Ory, eds., *Entre deux guerres: la création française entre 1919 et 1939* (Paris: Editions François Bourin, 1990).

5. Archival records at the Ministry of Interior, I have been told, were recycled into new paper during a paper shortage immediately following the Second World War.

Chapter One: War

1. My sources for sales or printing figures are Monique Jeanin (for books published by Fayard), Monsieur Grey-Draillart (for books published in the Secret War series by Baudinière), Françoise Tallon (for Fu Manchu novels and books published by the Librairie des Champs-Elysées), Madame Daudier (for books published by Payot), Jean-Pierre Dauphin (for books published by Gallimard), Brigitte Martin (for books published by Plon), Monsieur Mery (for books published by Grasset), Monsieur Henriquez (for books published by Tallandier), and Monsieur de Lignerolles (for books published by Berger-Levrault).

2. Maurice Dekobra, *The Madonna of the Sleeping Cars,* trans. Neal Wainwright (New York: Payson and Clarke, 1927; originally published as *La madone des sleepings* [Paris: Baudinière, 1925]); André Malraux, *The Conquerors,* trans. Stephen Becker (New York: Holt, Rinehart and Winston, 1976; originally published as *Les conquérants* [Paris: Grasset, 1928]); André Malraux, *La voie royale* (1930; reprint, Paris: Livre de Poche, 1967), 16; André Malraux, *Man's Fate,* trans. Haakon M. Chevalier (New York: Random House, 1961; originally published as *La condition humaine* [Paris: Gallimard, 1933]). According to Paul Fussell, Dekobra's *Madonna,* including its translations, sold over a million copies. Paul Fussell, *Abroad: British Literary Traveling Between the Wars* (Oxford: Oxford University Press, 1982), 64.

3. Bertrand Gauthier, *La cinquième colonne contre la paix du monde: l'internationale des espions, des assassins, des cagoulards, et des provocateurs au service du fascisme* (Paris: Bureau d'Editions, 1938).

4. *The Brown Network,* trans. Clement Greenberg (New York: Knight Publications, 1936). The original edition, *Das braune Netz,* was published in 1935 by Editions du Carrefour whose leading figure was Willi Münzenberg. See Gilbert Badia et al., *Les barbelés de l'exil* (Grenoble: Presses universitaires de Grenoble, 1979), 397–402. A 1936 French translation, *Le filet brun,* exists, although a file in the Archives nationales (hereafter, AN) suggests it was out by September 1935. AN F7 13434, 10 September 1935.

5. George Orwell, *Homage to Catalonia* (1938; reprint, Boston: Beacon Press, 1955), 140ff., 170ff.

6. *Le Petit Parisien,* 2 April 1935. The newspaper's circulation was roughly one and one-half million until 1935, declining to about a million by 1939. Claude Bellanger et al., *Histoire générale de la presse française* (Paris: Presses universitaires de France, 1972), 3:512.

7. AN BB18 6476, 4 October 1937 (report of Commissaire de police mobile Delrieu); ibid., 6 May 1938; SHAT 5N 578, 20 May 1940 (from the Attaché militaire, ambassade de France en Italie); SHAT 5N 601, 27 May 1940 (from Jean Ybarnégaray).

8. Among fifth-column books see Peter de Polnay, *The Germans Came to Paris* (New York: Duell, Sloan and Pearce, 1943); Henry Torrès, *Campaign of Treachery* (New York: Dodd, Mead and Company, 1942); Heinz Pol, *Suicide of a Democracy,* trans. Heinz and Ruth Norden (New York: Reynal and Hitchcock, 1940); Alexander Werth, *The Last Days of Paris* (London: Hamish Hamilton, 1940); Yves R. Simon, *The Road to Vichy,* trans. James A. Corbett and George J. McMorrow (New York: Sheen and Ward, 1942); André Simone, *J'accuse: The Men Who Betrayed France* (New York: The Dial Press, 1940); Pierre Lazareff, *Deadline: The Behind-the-Scenes Story of the Last Decade in France,* trans. David Partridge (New York: Random House, 1942); Jean Quéval, *Première page, cinquième colonne* (Paris: J. Fayard, 1945); Albert Bayet, *Pétain et la 5e colonne* (Paris: Editions Franc-tireur, 1944); Maurice Gamelin, *Servir* (Paris: Librairie Plon, 1946), 1:97, 357, 368; ibid., 2:462. The best book for distinguishing fact from myth is Louis de Jong's *German Fifth Column in the Second World War,* trans. C. M. Geyl (1956; reprint, New York: Howard Fertig, 1973). See also Max Gallo, *Et ce fut la défaite de 40: la cinquième colonne* (Paris: Plon, 1970).

9. *The Nazi Conspiracy in Spain,* trans. Emile Burns (London: Victor Gollancz, 1937), an English translation of Franz Spielhagen [alias of Otto Katz], *Spione und Verschwörer in Spanien* (Paris: Editions du Carrefour, 1936); on this edition see Badia, *Barbelés,* 402, 417. Although this volume was based on confiscated documents from Nazi headquarters in Barcelona, it, and its predecessor, should be read with caution. Both were packed with innuendo and claims that strain credibility and extend far beyond what French and German archives have recorded.

10. *L'Illustration,* 18 April 1936.

11. Most of these phrases were clichés. See especially *Vu et Lu,* 3 November 1937; *Match,* 16 February 1939.

12. Among these see Jean Camentron, *Le danger aéro-chimique* (Paris: Charles-Lavauzelle, 1936); Armand Charpentier, *Ce que sera la guerre des gaz* (Paris: André Delpeuch, 1930); Walt Wilm and A. Chaplet, *Gaz de guerre et guerre des gaz* (Paris: Publications Papyrus, 1936); *Le document,* March 1939. See also Uri Bialer, *The Shadow of the Bomber: The Fear of Air Attack and British Politics 1932–1939* (London: Royal Historical Society, 1980).

13. Florian-Parmentier, *L'abîme* (Paris: Albert Messein, 1934); Victor Méric, *La «Der des Der»* (Paris: Editions de France, 1929). For a turnaround on the gas war theme, see Michel Corday's vision of a pink gas spread over the world and preventing war by turning people into more humane individuals with a heightened consciousness of human potential. Michel Corday, *Ciel rose* (Paris: Flammarion, 1933).

14. Florian-Parmentier, *Abîme,* 45. Albert de Pouvourville, *La guerre prochaine: Paris l'invincible* (Paris: Baudinière, 1935), 5:22, 54–55; Florimond Bonte, *La guerre de demain: aérienne, chimique, bactériologique* (Lille: Editions Prolétariennes, n.d.), 21–22. Bauer is cited in Wilm, *Gaz,* 118.

15. Jean Bardanne, *La guerre et les microbes* (Paris: Baudinière, 1937); Pierre Yrondy, *De la cocaïne . . . aux gaz!!!* (Paris: Baudinière, 1934), 10–11. Charles Lucieto, *La guerre des cerveaux: livrés à l'ennemi* (Paris: Berger-Levrault, 1928); Charles Robert-Dumas, *«Ceux du S.R.»: l'idole de plomb* (Paris: Fayard, 1935); Jean Bommart, *Hélène et le poisson chinois* (Paris: Librairie des Champs-Elysées, 1938); Georges Ladoux, *L'espionne de l'empereur* (Paris: Librairie des Champs-Elysées, 1933); Marcel Nadaud and André Fage, *L'armée du crime: la coco; l'espionnage d'après-guerre* (Paris: Georges-Anquetil, 1926), 211.

16. SHAT 7N 3179, August 1935, 25 November 1936 (from Deuxième Bureau), 1 July 1937 (from Deuxième Bureau), 16 March 1939, pp. 28–29; APP BA 1706, 26 November 1935.

17. SHAT 7N 2462, 15 October 1939; AN F7 13986, 13 March 1940.

18. APP BA 61, 27 [24?] January 1934.

19. MAE Affaires diverses politiques Allemagne 38 bis 1889, 8 May 1889 (from MI, Sûreté générale to MAE). The instruction of the Direction politique at the MAE has no date, but a note was sent to the MI on 10 May 1889.

20. MAE Z Europe 1930–1940 Allemagne 791, 23 May 1940 (from Direction politique et commerciale/Europe to Monsieur l'amiral de la flotte commandant les forces maritimes françaises); ibid., 9 May 1940 (from Charles Roux, Rome–Saint Siège to MAE); ibid., 23 April 1940 (from Jean Dobler to MAE). The report from the Polish High Command also warned that saboteurs had dressed in the clothing of workers, beggars, priests, and monks. AN F7 13986, 13 March 1940.

21. Paul and Suzanne Lanoir, *Espions espionnage* (Paris: Delandre 1917), 2:280–81; Walter Nicolai, *Forces secrètes,* trans. Henri Thies (Paris: Editions de la Nouvelle Revue Critique, 1932), 145; Raoult de Rudeval, *Etude pratique du service des renseignements* (Paris: H. Charles-Lavauzelle, 1910), 46. Catholic priests played a considerable role in the Lux and Dame blanche intelligence networks in occupied Belgium and France during World War I. Andrew, *Secret Service,* 156–60.

22. I. F. Clarke, *Voices Prophesying War, 1763–1984* (London: Oxford University Press, 1966); Andrew, *Secret Service,* chap. 2; David French, "Spy Fever in Britain 1900–1915," *Historical Journal* 21 (June 1978): 355–70. On Germany see Philip Knightly, *The Second Oldest Profession* (New York: W. W. Norton, 1986), 34.

23. Lanoir, *Espions,* 2:239; Jean Tillet, *Dans les coulisses de la guerre: espionnage, contre-espionnage* (Paris: Imprimerie du Reveil économique, 1933), 16–17.

24. Knightly, *Second,* 3; Andrew, *Secret Service,* 1–9; "Espionnage," *La grande encyclopédie: inventaire raisonné des sciences, des lettres, et des arts,* 2d ed., 16:367–69; M. R. D. Foot, *SOE in France: An Account of the Work of the British Special Operations Executive in France, 1940–1944* (Frederick, Md.: University Publications of America, 1984), 1; Garrett Mattingly, *The Armada,* 30, 48; Alison Plowden, *The Elizabethan Secret Service* (Hemel Hempstead: Harvester

Wheatsheaf, 1991). Paul Muller, *L'espionnage militaire sous Napoléon Ier* (Paris: Berger-Levrault, 1896); Fernand Routier, *L'espionnage et la trahison en temps de paix et en temps de guerre* (Paris: Charles-Lavauzelle, 1913), 39–45.

25. Léon Daudet, *L'avant-guerre: études et documents sur l'espionnage juif-allemand en France depuis l'affaire Dreyfus* (Paris: Nouvelle Librairie Nationale, 1913), viii–ix. This book was preceded by a series of articles in the *Action Française*. For background and sales figures, Eugen Weber, *Action Française* (Stanford: Stanford University Press, 1962), 89. See also François Loyal, *L'espionnage allemand en France* (Paris: Albert Savine, 1887), 96, 103; *L'Intransigeant*, 24 March 1896; J. Santo, *La France envahie, trahie, vendue* (Paris: J. Santo, 1912).

26. Bundesarchiv, Abteilung Militärgeschichte, Freiburg im Breisgau (hereafter, MA) RW5/654 (Gempp, *Geheimer Nachrichtendienst und Spionageabwehr des Heeres*), 13–20, 28, 257–59, 272; Kahn, *Hitler's Spies*, 31–34, 555; Leopold Auerbach, *Denkwürdigkeiten des geheimen Regierungsrathes Dr. Stieber* (Berlin: Verlag von Julius Engelmann, 1884); Gert Buchheit, *Der deutsche Geheimdienst: Geschichte der militärischen Abwehr* (Munich: Paul List Verlag, 1967), 18. Michael Howard's authoritative work on the Franco-Prussian War makes no mention of Stieber: *The Franco-Prussian War* (London: Methuen, 1981).

27. MA RW5/654 (this theme runs through Gempp's account), especially pp. 3, 72, 80, 300–304; Nicolai, *Forces*, 26–27, 31–32; von Lettow-Vorbeck, ed., *Die Weltkriegspionage* (Munich: Verlag Justin Moser, 1931), 78–79 (also on the supposed superiority of French prewar intelligence); SHAT 7N 2501, 24 October 1925 ("Fonctionnement d'un poste de SR dépendant du GQG pendant la guerre"); Henri Navarre et un groupe d'anciens membres du S. R., *Le service de renseignements, 1871–1944* (Paris: Plon, 1978), 15–18; Buchheit, *Geheimdienst*, 18–20; Andrew, *Secret Service*. Kahn, *Hitler's Spies*, 32, claims that IIIb's funding was second only to that of Russian intelligence by the early twentieth century. But his source—a 1912 Foreign Office report on the *published* budgets of European secret services—cannot be accepted as authoritative. Information on European intelligence operations before World War I remains sketchy. The best overview is in May, ed., *Knowing One's Enemies*.

28. MA RW5/654, pp. 116, 118, 131, 395; MA RW5/657 (Gempp), pp. 10, 51, 201–6; Nicolai, *Forces*, 29; Ulrich Trumpener, "War Premeditated? German Intelligence Operations in July 1914," *Central European History* 9 (March 1976): 58–85. On the Balkans see MA RW5/660 (Gempp), pp. 13–16. On sabotage, see Trumpener, "War," 74–75; MA RW5/654, pp. 126, 128 (red number); MA RW5/657, pp. 27–28.

29. Paul and Suzanne Lanoir, *Les grands espions* (Paris: G. Ficker, 1911), 190–233. See also Paul Lanoir, *L'espionnage allemand en France* (Paris: Publications Littéraires Illustrées, n. d. [before 1914]; Victor Tissot, *La police secrète prussienne* (Paris: E. Dentu, 1884).

30. Jules-Louis Lewal, *Etudes de guerre: tactique des renseignements* (Paris: Librairie Militaire de J. Dumaine, 1881), 1:73–74; Routier, *L'espionnage*, 19–23, 48; James Violle, *L'espionnage militaire en temps de guerre* (Paris: Librairie de la Société du Recueil des lois et des arrêts, 1903), 82; "Espionnage," *Grande encyclopédie*. See also A. Froment, *L'espionnage militaire et les fonds secrets de la guerre* (Paris: Librairie Illustrée, 1887), 105, 118–19; Rudeval, *Etude*, 32, 41.

31. Lanoir, *Grands,* 234–39; Lanoir, *Espionnage allemand;* Lanoir, *Espions,* 1:7–13; 2:173; Routier, *L'espionnage,* 23–27. On traveling circuses, see also Loyal, *Espionnage,* 95; APP BA 1332, 22 September 1886.

32. *Le Petit Parisien,* 9 September 1886; *L'Aurore,* 24 September 1897; *Le Petit Journal,* 15 May 1911.

33. Capitaine Danrit [Emile Augustin Cyprien Driant], *L'alerte* (Paris: Flammarion, 1910).

34. Three works by Danrit: *La guerre au vingtième siècle: l'invasion noire* (Paris: Flammarion, 1894); *L'invasion jaune* (1909; reprint, Paris: Flammarion, 1926); and *La guerre fatale: France-Angleterre* (Paris: Flammarion, 1903).

35. On the literature and spy fears coming out of this war see chapter 4.

36. AN F7 12644 n. d. The letter is in the October 1897 folder in this file.

37. All of these affairs were discussed in the French press. On German secret police, including the Haupt affair, see Dieter Fricke, *Bismarcks Prätorianer: Die Berliner Politische Polizei im Kampf gegen die deutsche Arbeiterbewegung (1871–1898)* (Berlin: Rütten und Loening, 1962). Fricke describes a police operation spread to a number of European cities (although numbers of agents abroad were not high) that primarily maintained surveillance over socialist activities and the smuggling of socialist literature into Germany. He does not confirm the wilder charges directed at Krüger. A police report reproducing an article in the *Tribune de Genève* also provides a fairly sober account of the Haupt affair: APP BA 1333, 30 December 1887. Speculation on Krüger's connection with Russian terrorists can be found in the *Lanterne,* 28–31 December 1887 and *Le Petit Parisien,* 29–31 December 1887, 2 January 1888. See also note 45, below. Police files on the Seliverstov assassination include APP BA 1212; MI 25358. Apparently Seliverstov was connected with the Okhrana. On Russian affairs see also AN F7 14605, 29 June 1914, "La police russe en France."

38. See chapter 3.

39. APP BA 913, 13 October 1893, February 1894, 26 December 1894; AN F7 12519/12520A; AN F7 12521; AN F7 12894. See also the following two reports on the potential for violence and militant action from Russian and Italian émigrés in France: AN F7 12894, 10 December 1907 (report from Préfecture de police communicated to Président du conseil on 16 December 1907); AN F7 13065, 16 December 1912 ("Les révolutionnaires étrangers en France").

40. AN F7 14605, 19 June 1914 ("Note sur les polices étrangères en France"); AN F7 14605, 29 June 1914 ("La police russe"); APP BA 1693, 29 October 1913; *Le Matin,* 24 July 1909.

41. Ibid.

42. Ibid. Apparently the Okhrana continued to appoint a police delegate to Paris. Norman Cohen ascribes a number of violent acts to Rachkovskii and his agents, including a bombing in Liège in 1894 and Seliverstov's assassination, arguing that Seliverstov had been sent to investigate Rachkovskii: Norman Cohen, *Warrant for Genocide: The Myth of the Jewish World-Conspiracy and the Protocols of the Elders of Zion* (New York: Harper, 1967), 79ff. See also Boris Nikolajewsky, *Aseff the Spy,* trans. George Reavey (Garden City: Doubleday, Doran and Co., 1934), 18–21, 118–19.

43. AN F7 12519/12520A, 28 November 1901; *Le Matin,* 14 July 1909;

A. T. Wassilieff, *Police russe et révolution,* trans. Henri Thies (Paris: Editions de la Nouvelle Revue Critique, 1936), 16, 23; P. Zavarzine, *Souvenirs d'un chef de l'Okhrana,* trans. J. Jeanson (Paris: Payot, 1930), 42. Maurice Laporte suggests a somewhat larger operation in *Histoire de l'Okhrana* (Paris: Payot, 1935). On the Okhrana files, see table of contents to Register, Russia, *Departament Politsii: Zagranichnaia Agentura,* Hoover Institution on War, Revolution, and Peace.

44. AN F7 14605, 19 June 1914 ("Note" and "Les sociétés italiennes dans les Alpes-Maritimes"). There is also a good discussion of an earlier spy case involving an Italian general in Maurice Baumont, *Au coeur de l'affaire Dreyfus* (Paris: Editions Mondiales, 1976), 46–56.

45. MAE Affaires diverses politiques Allemagne 38 bis, 18 November 1889 (Préfecture de police to Sûreté générale and then apparently forwarded to MAE); APP BA 1333, January 1888 (sent 10 January 1888), 1 January 1888, 31 (December?) 1887; APP BA 1693, 28 July 1892. See also Alan Mitchell, "The Xenophobic Style," *The Journal of Modern History* 52 (September 1980): 417–18. The role of a German political police operating independently of German intelligence is difficult to delineate. The revelations about Haupt disclosed that such a police was tracking socialists abroad, a discovery confirmed in Fricke, *Bismarcks Prätorianer.* There are also a number of reports in French archives on German police intrigues with Russian revolutionaries in Switzerland. All are clustered in the late 1880s and in 1890 and are rather sketchy, although they do suggest that there might be some substance to the press charges against Krüger at the time of the Haupt affair. Gempp notes that Krüger was removed from his position in 1890 and not replaced. Most likely, as Fricke suggests, German police agents abroad were mainly concerned with socialist circles and their numbers were probably limited. See AN F7 12519/12520A, 14 April 1887, 23 (?) April 1887, 23 May 1890, 29 May 1890, 19 August 1890; APP BA 1745, 21 June 1890, 23 August 1890; MA RW5/654, p. 272.

46. MAE Affaires diverses politiques Allemagne 50, 28 March 1894, 30 March 1894.

47. Ibid., 7 March 1894, 16 March 1894, 24 April 1894. For a good discussion of the pursuit of spies, spy mania, and some real cases at the time of the Dreyfus affair see Baumont, *Coeur,* 13–79.

48. APP BA 1332, 13 September 1873; APP BA 1745, 23 June 1890.

49. APP BA 1332, 11 August 1882.

50. See, e.g., material in boxes APP BA 1745; APP BA 1332; APP BA 1333; AN F7 12641; Mitchell, "Xenophobic."

51. AN F7 12644, 12 August 1897; APP BA 1333, 12 November 1891. There are many other telegrams in these boxes, as well as in AN F7 12645 and APP BA 1332, APP BA 1334.

52. Mitchell, "Xenophobic"; Jean Jacques Becker, *Le carnet B* (Paris: Klinck-sieck, 1973).

53. Becker, *Carnet.* For statistics on eastern France see 155–60.

54. See chapter 2.

55. See especially on this point William D. Irvine, *The Boulanger Affair Reconsidered: Royalism, Boulangism, and the Origins of the Radical Right in France* (Oxford: Oxford University Press, 1989), 33, 78.

56. Lynn Hunt, *Politics, Culture, and Class in the French Revolution* (Berkeley:

University of California Press, 1984), 38–46; Gordon Wright, *France in Modern Times,* 3d ed. (New York: W. W. Norton, 1981), 112.

57. Lanoir, *Espionnage allemand;* Paul Mahalin, *Les espions de Paris* (Paris: Librairie Illustrée, 1897), 234, 302; Paul d'Ivoi and Royet, *La patrie en danger: histoire de la guerre future* (Paris: H. Geffroy, 1905), 254, 814; AN F7 12644, 19 October 1888; APP BA 1745, 6 May 1890.

58. Ian Nish, "Japanese Intelligence and the Approach of the Russo-Japanese War" in *The Missing Dimension: Governments and Intelligence Communities in the Twentieth Century,* ed. Christopher Andrew and David Dilks (Urbana: University of Illinois Press, 1984), 25, 29.

59. *La Patrie,* 21 June 1905; Rudeval, *Etude,* 21, 33, 41, 78; Routier, *L'espionnage,* 51; Pierre Giffard, *Lunes rouges et dragons noirs* (Paris: Librairie Félix Juven, 1906); D'Ivoi and Royet, *Patrie,* 1007.

60. Lewal, *Etudes,* 1:29, 73–74, 120; Lieutenant-colonel Rollin, *Le service des renseignements militaires en temps de paix* (Paris: Nouvelle Librairie Nationale, 1908), 41–42.

61. Navarre, *Service,* 15. In the second stage of the fighting, Gambetta and Freycinet did establish a *bureau des reconnaissances,* whose responsibilities included destruction of German communication lines: Howard, *Franco-Prussian War,* 243.

62. Christopher Andrew, "France and the German Menace," in *Knowing One's Enemies,* ed. May, 132, 135; Mitchell, "Xenophobic," 416.

63. According to an archivist at the SHAT, the Deuxième Bureau's operational records no longer exist.

64. Navarre, *Service,* 16; Guy Chapman, *The Dreyfus Case* (New York: Reynal and Company, 1955), 49.

65. Christopher Andrew, "Codebreakers and Foreign Offices: The French, British, and American Experience," in *Missing Dimension,* ed. Andrew and Dilks, 33–42; Andrew, "German Menace"; Jan Karl Tanenbaum, "French Estimates of Germany's Operational War Plans," in *Knowing One's Enemies,* ed. May; Navarre, *Service,* 18.

66. MA RW5/654, pp. 302–3.

67. Navarre, *Service,* 17.

68. SHAT, 7N 2501, 24 October 1925 ("Fonctionnement"). The reporter here was Andlauer.

69. Andrew, *Secret Service,* chap. 2.

70. In addition to Danrit, *L'invasion noire,* see also Paul d'Ivoi, *L'espion X. 323: le canon du sommeil* (Paris: A. Méricant, 1909).

71. Rollin, *Service,* 79–80.

72. Max Ronge, *Espionnage: douze années au service des renseignements,* trans. Adrien Vochelle (Paris: Payot, 1932), 18, 24–28, 37–38, 47–57. Ronge worked with Austro-Hungarian intelligence. See also Norman Stone, "Austria-Hungary," in *Knowing One's Enemies,* ed. May, 37–61; William C. Fuller, Jr., "The Russian Empire," in ibid.

73. J. Kim Munholland, "The French Response to the Vietnamese Nationalist Movement, 1905–1914," *The Journal of Modern History* 47 (December 1975): 674; AN F7 12894, 10 December 1907; Archives d'Outre-mer, Paris,

Slotform (hereafter, OM SL) III 56, n. d. On Morocco see the last section of this chapter and on Japanese spy networks see chapter 4. On the Great Game there is Kipling's incomparable *Kim,* although this gives an exaggerated picture. See also Peter Hopkirk, *The Great Game: The Struggle for Empire in Central Asia* (New York: Kodansha, 1992); Andrew, *Secret Service,* 5, 11; Gerald Morgan, "Myth and Reality in the Great Game," *Asian Affairs* 60 (February 1973): 55–65; L. P. Morris, "British Secret Service Activity in Khorossan, 1887–1908," *The Historical Journal* 27 (September 1984): 657–75; Alastair Lamb, *Britain and Chinese Central Asia: The Road to Lhasa, 1767–1905* (London: Routledge and Kegan Paul, 1960), x. On the Middle East see H. V. F. Winstone, *The Illicit Adventure* (Frederick, Md.: University Publications of America, 1982), 3–123. Winstone has written a very interesting book, but the picture he provides may appear overdone to some.

74. "Espionnage," *Grande encyclopédie; Le Journal,* 24 September 1897; *Le Petit Parisien,* 9 September 1886, 2 March 1888, 10 December 1888; *L'Evénement,* 22 February 1885; Lewal, *Etudes,* 1:99–102; Violle, *L'espionnage;* Rudeval, *Etude,* 77–78. Paul d'Ivoi wrote two spy novels whose protagonist is the master spy X 323: *Canon,* and *L'espion X 323: l'homme sans visage* (Paris: A. Méricant 1909). In the latter he says of his hero: "But what is particularly unusual about this spy is his honesty. He signals his actions, warning his adversaries that he is on their trail. . . . My very honorable spy is completely disinterested," 3. In *Patrie,* d'Ivoi and Royet write of German spies: "On the other bank of the Rhine, all administrative fondness is centered on a single bacillus: that of espionage, the hideous leprosy through which Germany hopes to conquer the universe and which, in reality, has lowered character, killed nobility, bankrupted devotedness," 252–53. The evil/dishonorable spy theme is particularly strong in the spy novels. See also Mahalin, *Espions;* Danrit, *Yellow.* For an interesting counterpoint, see Gempp's discussion of the psychological difficulty for German officers who disliked spying but were assigned to intelligence work: MA RW5/657, 47–48. French espionage in the days of Napoleon was favorably looked upon. See Paul Muller, *L'espionnage militaire.*

75. Stone, "Austria-Hungary," 41; Ronge, *Espionnage,* 309.

76. Ronge, *Espionnage,* 164, 171–72, 226–28.

77. For Germany: Kahn, *Hitler's Spies,* 36, 39; for England: Andrew, *Secret Service,* 138, 169, 174. Andrew numbers MI1b's staff at eighty-four by war's end. This was the military's code breaking unit. He does not give a figure for the Admiralty's more celebrated unit, Room 40.

78. Georges Ladoux, *Les chasseurs d'espions* (Paris: Librairie des Champs-Elysées, 1932), 197; Navarre, *Service,* 19; Tillet, *Coulisses,* 32; SHAT 7N 1082, 13 July 1917.

79. SHAT 7N 2501, 24 October 1925; Andrew, *Secret Service,* 144–45.

80. Ronge, *Espionnage,* 64, 94–95; Kahn, *Hitler's Spies,* 35; P.-Louis Rivière, *Un centre de guerre secrète: Madrid, 1914–1918* (Paris: Payot, 1936); Andrew, *Secret Service,* chap. 3 and 138.

81. Trevor Wilson, *The Myriad Faces of War: Britain and the Great War, 1914–1918* (Cambridge: Polity Press, 1986), 364–66; Kahn, *Hitler's Spies,* 34–35.

82. SHAT 7N 2501, 24 October 1925; Tillet, *Coulisses,* 24.

83. Andrew, *Secret Service,* 141, 156–61, 168–71; Tillet, *Coulisses;* SHAT 16N 1303, 1304.

84. Navarre, *Service,* 20–21.

85. SHAT 16N 916 ("Relève chronologique et analyse succincte concernant le service des renseignements"); ibid. ("Contre-espionnage: répertoire chronologique des notes, instructions, ou directives d'ordre général"); Nicolai, *Forces,* 125–26; George Hill, *Go Spy the Land: Being the Adventures of I. K. 8 of the British Secret Service* (London: Cassell, 1932; translated by Lucien Thomas as *Ma vie d'espion [I.K. 8]* [Paris: Payot, 1933], 61–68). On Hill's credibility, see Andrew, *Secret Service,* 215–16. Andrew also notes that the British sent only a handful of agents by air, and these by balloon, 161–62.

86. Paul Ignatieff, *Ma mission en France,* (Paris: Librairie des Champs-Elysées, 1933), 123–33. The book was published posthumously from the author's notes.

87. SHAT 16N 916 ("Relève chronologique"); MA RW5/70 (Gempp), pp. 47–58.

88. SHAT 16N 916 ("Contre-espionnage"); Tillet, *Coulisses,* 22; Ladoux, *Chasseurs,* 173–74. On ink see SHAT 16N 1589, 23 December 1915. The identification of semen is in Andrew, *Secret Service,* 149.

89. SHAT 16N 1589, 6 October 1915.

90. The first parrot story is reported in Richard Wilmer Rowan, *Spy and Counterspy: The Development of Modern Espionage* (New York: Viking Press, 1928), 87–88. There is a good discussion of the use of carrier pigeons in the war in Andrew, *Secret Service,* 142–43, 161–65. See also *Illustration,* 18 April 1936; Bauermeister, *La guerre dans l'ombre: souvenirs d'un officier du service secret du haut commandement allemand,* trans. Th. Lacaze (Paris: Payot, 1933), 62–66; Nicolai, *Forces,* 125–26. The Japanese pigeon story is from Jacques Deval, *Rives pacifiques* (Paris: Gallimard, 1937), 119–20. The parakeet story is from the *Syracuse Post-Standard,* 9 July 1991, and the Cher Ami story comes from another issue of the same paper, in an article by Isabel Wolseley (unfortunately my alertness in cutting it out after breakfast was not equaled by attention to marking the date of the clipping). For discussions of the espionage uses of carrier pigeons before the war, see *Le Petit Parisien,* 11 December 1890; Rollin, *Service,* 127–28.

91. MAE Z Europe 1930–1940 Allemagne 711, 18 December 1933, p. 143 ("Projet de note pour Monsieur Blanchet").

92. Service historique de la marine, Paris (hereafter, MM) SSM40, 17 September 1915, 20 December 1915; SHAT 16N 916 ("Contre-espionnage"); SHAT 16N 1589, 13 September 1915, 10 April 1916; Emanuel Victor Voska and Will Irwin, *Spy and Counterspy* (New York: Doubleday, Doran and Co., 1940) 18–19. The discussion of the Jewish gang is in L. Lacaze, *Adventures d'un agent secret français, 1914–1918* (Paris: Payot, 1934), 145.

93. The imagery is taken from Fussell, *Abroad,* 31–36.

94. Ronge, *Espionnage,* 47–48, 56, 86–87, 199–200; SHAT 7N 926, 15 May 1917; SHAT 16N 916 ("Relève chronologique"; "Contre-espionnage"); Max Wild, *Mes aventures dans le service secret, 1914–1918,* trans. Lucien Thomas (Paris: Payot, 1932), 138–48; SHAT 7N 2501, 24 October 1925; Lettow-Vorbeck, *Weltkriegspionage,* 306.

95. The source for the following discussion is Rivière, *Centre*, 99–106. Rivière was a magistrate who worked in French cryptography during the war (see the preface to the book by Maxime Weygand). This background and the book's style of presentation make the author's account credible.

96. SHAT 7N 2105 (telegram initially received by MAE on 5 August 1921).

97. See below, chapter 3.

98. Rivière, *Centre*, 60–71; Georges Ladoux, *Mes souvenirs (contre-espionnage)* (Paris: Editions de France, 1937), 53–105; Andrew, *Secret Service*, 115–20; SHAT 7N 926, 20 October 1917, 27 April 1918 (on Norway).

99. Ladoux, *Souvenirs*, 119; AN F7 12895, 31 December 1917 (on Lugano).

100. SHAT 16N 1589, 4 March 1916, 8 April 1916, 10 April 1916.

101. W. Somerset Maugham, "Miss King," in *Collected Short Stories* (London: Pan Books, 1976; originally published as *Ashenden* [London: William Heinemann, 1928]), 3:26–27.

102. SHAT 7N 1082, 10 (16?) June 1918, 20 June 1918, 10 May 1918 (on Bratsaloff; Turkish agents); SHAT 7N 1590, 30 March 1918. See also SHAT 7N 1590, 27 March 1918; Lacaze, *Aventures*, 144; SHAT 16N 1589, 11 February 1916; Ignatieff, *Mission*, 81, 93; Frank G. Weber, *Eagles on the Crescent: Germany, Austria, and the Diplomacy of the Turkish Alliance, 1914–1918* (Ithaca: Cornell University Press, 1970), 180–81; William L. Cleveland, *Islam Against the West* (Austin: University of Texas Press, 1985), 91.

103. SHAT 5N 284, 7N 1590.

104. Lacaze, *Aventures*, 147–49, 206–14.

105. AN F7 12896, 19 October 1918.

106. Christopher Sykes, *Wassmuss: "The German Lawrence"* (London: Longmans, Green and Co., 1936); Bernard Vernier, *La politique islamique de l'Allemagne* (Paris: Paul Hartmann, 1939), 12; Robert Boucard, *Les dessous de l'intelligence service* (Paris: Editions Documentaires, 1937), 195; *Vu et Lu*, 28 July 1937, p. 1012.

107. The best account on covert operations in the western hemisphere is Katz, *Secret War*, especially 328–67, 395–441. See also Rivière, *Centre*, 31–33, 110–14 (111–12 on Arnold); Barbara W. Tuchmann, *The Zimmerman Telegram* (New York: Ballantine, 1979), especially 66–87; Roger Lancelyn Green, *A. E. W. Mason* (London: Max Parrish, 1952), 149–52 (on the German radio station).

108. See below, chapter 4.

109. For general overviews see Vernier, *Politique*, 9–24; Fritz Fischer, *Germany's Aims in the First World War* (New York: Norton, 1967), 120–31. Fischer also describes German subversion in the Russian empire, 132–54. See also Frank G. Weber, *Eagles;* Ulrich Trumpener, *Germany and the Ottoman Empire* (Princeton: Princeton University Press, 1968). On Turkish secret service see Philip Hendrick Stoddard, "The Ottoman Government and the Arabs, 1911 to 1918: A Preliminary study of the Teskilat-I Mahsusa" (Ph.D. diss., Princeton University, 1963), 69, 102–17. On Persia and Afghanistan see Ulrich Gehrke, *Persien in der deutschen Orientpolitik während des ersten Weltkrieges* (Stuttgart: W.

Kohlhammer, 1960); Renate Vogel, *Die Persien- und Afghanistanenexpedition* (Osnabrück: Biblio, 1976); Oskar von Niedermayer, *Unter der Glutsonne Irans: Kriegserlebnisse der deutschen Expedition nach Persien und Afghanistan* (Munich: Einhorn-Verlag, 1925), 14–15 (on Romania and the circus cover); Sykes, *Wassmuss* (Sykes also recounts the story of Niedermayer's baggage, 50–51). On Latin American agents and von Kalle, see Katz, *Secret War*, 400, 423–24; Rivière, *Centre*, 34–35. On Indochina see OM SLIII 56 (26-page report).

110. Paul Allard, *La guerre des espions* (Paris: Flammarion, 1936), 81–82.

111. SHAT 7N 2105, 15 September 1921, 24 November 1921, 7 December 1921 ("shady and suspect"), 21 June 1922, 1 December 1922, 2 February 1921; SHAT 3H 102, 25 January 1922; OM SLIII 92, 8 August 1922; AN F7 13413, 12 October 1925.

112. Edmund Burke, *Prelude to Protectorate in Morocco* (Chicago: University of Chicago Press, 1976).

113. Edmund Burke, "Pan-Islam and Moroccan Resistance to French Colonial Penetration, 1900–1912," *Journal of African History*, 13 (1972): 97–118. On pan-Islam: Bernard Lewis, *The Emergence of Modern Turkey*, 2d ed. (London: Oxford University Press, 1968), 340–43; N. R. Keddie, "Pan-Islam as Proto-Nationalism," *The Journal of Modern History* 41 (1969): 17–28; Jacob M. Landau, *The Politics of Pan-Islam: Ideology and Organization* (Oxford: Clarendon Press, 1990), chaps. 1 and 2; Stoddard, "Ottoman Government," 4, 9–12, 78–87. I am indebted to the Burke article for calling my attention to Keddie and Stoddard.

114. Pierre Guillen, *L'Allemagne et le Maroc de 1870 à 1905* (Paris: Presses universitaires de France, 1967), 55, 136–50, 372–80, 497–98; Burke, *Prelude*, 32–33. For government reports on gunrunning: AN F7 12836; MAE NS Maroc 175; MM SSEa4, especially the report dated 22 June 1912 (from Capitaine de vaisseau de Marliave). OPDR stood for Oldenburg-Portugiesische-Dampfschiffs-Reederei. The Woermann Line's principal trade in Africa was with west Africa south of Morocco. In addition to the good discussion in Guillen see Karl Brackmann, *Fünfzig Jahre deutscher Afrikaschifffahrt. Die Geschichte der Woermann-Linie und der Deutschen Ost-Afrika-Linie* (Berlin: Dietrich Reimer, 1935); Dirk Bavendamm et al., *Wagnis Westafrika. Die Geschichte eines Hamburger Handelshauses, 1837–1987* (Hamburg: Verlag Hanseatischer Merkur, 1987).

115. Eugene Staley, "Mannesmann Mining Interests and the Franco-German Conflict Over Morocco," *Journal of Political Economy* 40 (1932), especially on German official exasperation with Mannesmann pigheadedness. Also on Mannesmanns: Claus Herbert Mannesmann, *Die Unternehmungen der Brüder Mannesmann in Marokko* (Würzburg: Richard Mayr, 1931), Forward, 17–26; David Henry Slavin, "Anticolonialism and the French Left: Opposition to the Rif War 1925–1926" (Ph.D. diss., University of Virginia, 1982), 13–21, 27–28; Neil Sherwood Lewis, "German Policy in Southern Morocco During the Agadir Crisis of 1911" (Ph.D. diss., University of Michigan, 1977), 27–28, 94–100, 154–55, 157ff.; MAE Maroc/Tunisie 1917–1940 Maroc 1214, 11, 18 June 1920 (on arms depot and geological expeditions); MAE NS Maroc 178,

6 November 1913, p. 30; MAE NS Maroc 226, 28 August 1912, p. 13; SHAT 7N 1200, 7 November 1913, 18 March 1914; SHAT 3H 108, 4 July 1919 ("L'action allemande au Maroc"), pp. 4–7; Burke, *Prelude,* 103, 140, 249; Louis Maurice, *La politique marocaine de l'Allemagne* (Paris: Plon, 1916). On other German intrigues see ibid; SHAT 3H 108, 4 July 1919 ("L'action") 2–7; Guillen, *Allemagne,* 56, 403, 405, 518–19; MAE NS Maroc 280, 7 June 1911, pp. 70–72; Douglas Porch, *The French Foreign Legion: A Complete History of the Legendary Fighting Force* (New York: Harper Perennial, 1992), 326–33; Fischer, *Germany's Aims,* 121–24; Robert Lewis Melka, "Max Freiherr von Oppenheim: Sixty Years of Scholarship and Political Intrigue in the Middle East," *Middle Eastern Studies* 9 (January 1973): 81–93.

116. Edmund Burke, "Moroccan Resistance, Pan-Islam, and German War Strategy, 1914–1918," *Francia* 3 (1975): 434–64; SHAT 3H 108, 4 July 1919 ("Rapport du commissaire résident général").

117. MM SSEa4, 16 August 1915, 16 September 1915, 29 December 1915; SHAT 3H 108 July 1918 ("Liste des principaux allemands dans la zone espagnole du Maroc").

118. Guillen, *Allemagne,* 405; Burke, "Moroccan," 447; Albert Bartels, *Fighting the French in Morocco,* trans. H. J. Stenning (London: Alston Rivers, 1932).

119. SHAT 3H 108, 4 July 1919; Rivière, *Centre,* 26.

120. Burke, "Moroccan"; SHAT 3H 108, July 1918 ("Liste"), 4 July 1919; SHAT 7N 2122, 20 April 1915, 26 April 1915 (Huot note forwarded to MAE), 3 June 1915.

121. OM Affaires politiques 905; SHAT 7N 2122, 3H 108.

122. Burke, "Moroccan"; SHAT 3H 108, 4 July 1919; Bartels, *Fighting;* SHAT 7N 2105, 28 September 1918.

123. SHAT 7N 2122, Huot note.

124. On this affair see SHAT 7N 2122, 14, 16, 17, 20, 30 April 1915, 11 May 1915, 1 July 1915, 12 November 1915. Regenratz, whose real name was otherwise, was taken from an Italian liner coming from Argentina. There is no indication that this is the same person as the Regendanz referred to in Fischer, *Germany's Aims,* 131, or in Fritz Fischer, *Griff nach der Weltmacht* (Düsseldorf: Droste Verlag, 1961), 146.

125. Burke, "Moroccan"; SHAT 7N 2122 (Huot note); MM SSEa4, 12, 25 July 1917, 20, 21 September 1917 (Castex reports).

126. SHAT 7N 2122, 3 June 1915.

127. There are many reports from the first years of the 1920s on grand plots for global insurrections that would reconstitute wartime alliances or bridge these with new revolutionary forces to crack open the British and French empires. They can be found in OM Affaires politiques 902, 907 bis, 923; SHAT 7N 2105. See also Rif war dossiers for reports of former German intelligence agents in Spain during the First World War now to be found in the camp of the rebels or of several hundred German officers securing passage via the port of Genoa — a warning strikingly similar to Regenratz's wartime revelations of infiltration itineraries passing through that city (SHAT 3H 102, 1 September

1925, 7 June 1925). For down-to-earth qualifications of these, see David Woolman, *Rebels in the Rif* (Stanford: Stanford University Press, 1968), 151; Slavin, "Anticolonialism," 234; SHAT 3H 102, 25 August 1925. On Morocco reports during World War I placing intrigues in a broader, global perspective see SHAT 7N 2122, 21 October 1914, 8 October 1915; OM Affaires politiques 907 bis, 14 November 1914, 16 December 1914, 28 October 1916.

128. On Rüggeberg and German wartime intelligence see Robert H. Whealey, *Hitler and Spain* (Lexington: University Press of Kentucky, 1989), 149.

129. See especially the 237-page exhaustive analysis of Fascist subversion of the Italian community in Morocco forwarded by Noguès: AN F60 201, 21 December 1938 ("La politique italienne en zone française du Maroc").

130. See the materials on the Bayda brothers (Baydaphone) and Theodore K. in AN F60 707, 25 July 1938, 2 May 1939; OM Affaires politiques 3435, 15 November 1937, p. 433.

131. Estimates of radio sets in the Arab world (including those owned by Europeans) totaled several hundred thousand by the late 1930s. Approximately one-fifth of the twenty-eight thousand receivers in Morocco belonged to Muslims, although collective listening practices like the attachment of radios to café loudspeakers significantly expanded the potential audience. Italy's Radio Bari and Germany's Radio Zeesen were the leaders in programming. The British countered with Radio Daventry and the French with Radio-Colonial, later Radio-Mondial, as well as attempts to jam the signals of others with repeated telegraph messages to a fake ship-at-sea. Materials on the *guerre des ondes* can be found in OM Affaires politiques 920, 1425; AN F60 707, 710, 753, 754; and MAE Maroc/Tunisie 1917–1940 Maroc 1240A. See also the following three articles: Daniel J. Grange, "La propagande arabe de Radio-Bari (1937–1939)," *Relations internationales* 5 (1976): 65–103; Daniel J. Grange, "Structure et techniques d'une propagande: les émissions arabes de Radio-Bari," *Relations internationales* 2 (1974): 165–85; Callum A. MacDonald, "Radio Bari: Italian Wireless Propaganda in the Middle East and British Countermeasures 1934–1938," *Middle Eastern Studies* 13 (May 1977): 195–207.

132. On Comintern activities see OM Affaires politiques 902, 12 October 1933; OM Affaires politiques 3435, 14 August 1936 (BRQM, annexe no. 1). The Bulletins de renseignements des questions musulmanes, or BRQMs, were put out by the Etat-major de l'armée, section d'outre-mer.

133. Cleveland, *Islam,* especially 39–40, 62–63, 134–59. For a sampling of French reports on Arslan see OM Affaires politiques 1416, 1 January 1937; AN F60 201, 21 December 1938; OM Affaires politiques 1425, 16 May 1938 (BRQM, p. 208); OM Affaires politiques 3435, 12 March 1936 (BRQM, p. 49).

134. Nicolai, *Forces,* 216.

Chapter Two: Milieu

1. AN F7 13426, 18 April 1923; AN F7 13413, 12 October 1925. On Tangier and Cairo: Bundesarchiv, Koblenz (hereafter, BA) R58/954, 30 May 1938, p. 134; ibid., 4 November 1937, p. 33. On Langenheim: SHAT 3H 102, 24 January 1924; SHAT 3H 256, 1 June 1940. Julius Mader identifies Langenheim as an Abwehr agent in the 1930s. Mader, *Hitlers Spionagegenerale,* 227–28.

2. Andrew, *Secret Service,* chap. 11, especially 347.

3. AN F7 14774, 10 September 1936, 11 September 1936, 27 September 1937; *L'Oeuvre,* 20 November 1938.

4. Charles S. Maier, "Between Taylorism and Technocracy: European Ideologies and the Vision of Industrial Productivity in the 1920s," *Journal of Contemporary History* 5 (April 1970): 27–61; Charles S. Maier, *Recasting Bourgeois Europe: Stabilization in France, Germany, and Italy in the Decade after World War I* (Princeton: Princeton University Press, 1975), 153; Maurice Lévy-Leboyer, "The Large Corporation in Modern France," in *Managerial Hierarchies: Comparative Perspectives on the Rise of the Modern Industrial Enterprise,* ed. Alfred D. Chandler and Herman Daems (Cambridge, Mass.: Harvard University Press, 1980), 126–27, 136–37; Victoria de Grazia, "Mass Culture and Sovereignty: The American Challenge to European Cinemas, 1920–1960," *Journal of Modern History* 61 (March 1989): 58, 61; Gary S. Cross, *Immigrant Workers in Industrial France: The Making of a New Laboring Class* (Philadelphia: Temple University Press, 1983), 18, 20, 34–35, 41–42, 46, 55–62; *Le Petit Parisien,* 12 June 1938 (on narcotics); *Paris-Soir,* 29 June 1938, 1 July 1938 (on narcotics); Alan A. Block, "European Drug Traffic and Traffickers Between the Wars: The Policy of Suppression and its Consequences," *Journal of Social History* 23 (Winter 1989): 315–32; Edward J. Bristow, *Prostitution and Prejudice: The Jewish Fight against White Slavery, 1870–1939* (Oxford: Oxford University Press, 1982), 71–78, 113. On the Croisière jaune see chapter 4. For additional discussion of organized immigration — in this case from Italy — see Claudio Segrè, *Italo Balbo: A Fascist Life* (Berkeley: University of California Press, 1987), 311–13.

5. Chalmers Johnson, *An Instance of Treason: Ozaki Hotsumi and the Sorge Spy Ring,* expanded edition (Stanford: Stanford University Press, 1990), quoted 69.

6. *London Times,* 6, 11, 16 April 1925, 4, 20, 21 May 1925.

7. AN F7 13413, 14 May 1925 (this report was filed by "un correspondant à même d'être fort documenté sur l'Angleterre, et dont les communications sont souvent d'un haut intéret"). See also Slavin, "Anticolonialism," 52–53, 147–48. Both the report and Slavin suggest possible Mannesmann collaboration with the British syndicate. A deposition by Charles Deboe, who claimed to have acted as an intermediary between Gardiner and Abd-el-Krim's brother, made no mention of the syndicate. The basic outline of Gardiner the adventurer-gunrunner remains. See AN F7 13413, 30 July 1925. Also, according to C. R. Pennell, Gardiner had developed his own commercial connections with the Rif

government and was passing himself off in London as "Minister-Plenipotentiary of the Government of the Rif." C. R. Pennell, *A Country with a Government and a Flag: The Rif War in Morocco, 1921–1926* (Cambridgeshire: Menas Press, 1986), 210–11.

8. References to ex-army officers — American, British, Turkish, German — repeatedly turn up in intelligence reports on the Rif war. SHAT 3H 102, n. d. ("Fournitures à Abd-el-Krim"), 30 October 1925, 18 July [1925?] ("Maroc: officiers étrangers pour le Riff"). See also MAE Maroc 1917–1940 616, 4 June 1925, pp. 227–28.

9. *New York Times,* 13, 26, 30, 31 July 1935; National Archives, Washington, D. C., Shanghai Municipal Police files (hereafter, SMP) reel 34, D8000, 9, 11, 16 February 1938, 11 March 1938, 20 April 1938, 26 July 1940; SMP reel 60, N965, 7 April 1941 (on O.). H. D.'s name turns up in connection with other shady figures in the SMP files. See SMP reel 31, D7596, 16 July 1938; SMP reel 58, D9478 (c), 11 December 1939. I consulted the SMP files on microfilm in Syracuse.

10. Sterling Seagrave, *The Epic of Flight: Soldiers of Fortune* (Alexandria, Va.: Time-Life Books, 1981), 66–67.

11. MAE Maroc/Tunisie 1917–1940 Maroc 1214, 7 December 1928, pp. 110, 113, 28 December 1928, p. 111, 29 December 1928, p. 115, 29 January 1929, pp. 116–21, 31 January 1929, pp. 123–27; MAE Z Europe 1918–1929 Russie 601, 19 March 1929, pp. 289–90.

12. Marcel Nadaud and André Fage published their work, *Armée,* in 1926.

13. Andrew, *Secret Service,* 142–43, 158–59, 377–78.

14. BA R58/275, 9 February 1940, pp. 75–77.

15. On Swirles: Auswärtiges Amt — Politisches Archiv, Bonn (hereafter, AA) Pol 1 M 240, AZ: PO15–1g, Agenten- u. Spionagewesen Einzelfälle, S-Z 1.39–11.39, Bd. 2 (hereafter, Pol 1 M 240), 16 January 1939, 18 February 1939, 31 March 1939, and document with no date but succeeding 16 January 1939 note. As is often the case with such reports, some of the biographical material on Swirles is contradictory, one report stating he had lived in Paris since 1929, another that he had left Germany only in the mid-1930s. On Stallmann: Navarre, *Service,* 66–67, 72–73; AA Pol 1 M 240, 18 February 1939; AA Pol 1 M 234, AZ: PO15–1g, Agenten- u. Spionagewesen Einzelfälle, A-K 6.39–9.39, Bd. 4 (hereafter, AA Pol 1 M 234), 25 May 1939; BA R58/1045, p. 119 (this report has no date; it is attached to a report that appears to have been written in early 1940, but the section on spies almost certainly was compiled after the French defeat); Michel Garder, *La guerre secrète des services spéciaux français, 1935–1945* (Paris: Plon, 1967), 84.

16. AN F7 14713, Norris file, 31 December 1935, 3 March 1936; AN F7 14671, 28 March 1935.

17. Bristow, *Prostitution,* 57–58, 129–30.

18. An example is the Captain Frogé affair of the early 1930s. There is a large dossier on this in AN BB18 6094.

19. AN F7 14754, 17 October 1934.

20. OM SLIII 56, 1 July 1922, 17 August 1922.

21. MI 25393/25394, 6 July 1937 (report of Commissaire de police mobile

Valentin, pp. 17–18). This report is in a dossier with 25393 written on it but belongs to the Troncoso file listed as 25394 in the inventory.

22. John Le Carré, *A Perfect Spy* (New York: Bantam, 1987).

23. The Antwerp reports can be found in AN F7 12836 (see especially 19 December 1908 on German government complicity); MAE NS Maroc 175; MM SSEa4.

24. Guillen, *L'Allemagne*, 371–72, 375–80.

25. In 1914 at Antwerp a beginning customs official took his duties seriously and insisted on inspecting a shipment of cement. When the consignee refused to open the containers in which the cement was packed, the customs man forbade the embarkment of the cargo. Antwerp customs, its hand forced, was thus obliged to proceed with an investigation, and the consignee withdrew the cargo altogether. Later, the novice *douanier* received a "paternal" talking-to, in effect a warning not to pull this stunt again. MAE NS Maroc 178, 10 February 1914, pp. 154–55.

26. AN F7 12836, 9 November 1907 (written from Brussels). The correspondent's reports to which he refers are in AN F7 12836, 12, 15, 23 October 1907.

27. MM SSEa4, especially 22 June 1912.

28. Charles Chenevier, *La grande maison* (Paris: Presses de la Cité, 1976), 61–71.

29. MI 25295, 23 October 1934. Royère was an Inspecteur principal de police mobile.

30. MI 25296, 29, 30 November 1934, 1, 5, 6, 7, 8, 11, 14 December 1934. Barthelet also went to Vienna, Danzig, and Berlin. He was a Commissaire de police mobile. One cannot discount the possibility that the difficulties of Royère and Barthelet were compounded by the unwillingness of the French government to discover inconvenient evidence. At the time of the murders Franco-Italian relations were improving and the French had incentives to conduct an investigation that would not rupture this process. This hypothesis could explain why the government was powerless to prevent the humiliation of its police missions abroad.

31. Henri Koch-Kent, *Doudot: figure légendaire du contre-espionage français* (Paris: Casterman 1976); Navarre, *Service,* 61–62.

32. Navarre, *Service,* 87.

33. Ibid., 50–51.

34. AN F7 14755, March 1936 (attached to 20 April 1936), 9 January 1936, June 1936 (attached to 26 June 1936), 5 September 1936. The March and June reports differ a bit on the dates of Samuel I.'s arrival in Paris and his definitive departure.

35. AA Geheimakten 1920–1936, AZ: Spanien Pol 15, Agenten- u. Spionagewesen 4.20–26.35.

36. AA Inland II A/B 292/2, AZ: 83–78, Spionageabwehr, Vertrauensmänner 8.5.35–17.4.36, 6 May 1936; MA N104/4, 15 October 1939.

37. BA R58/954, 30 May 1938, p. 136. On AA complaints, see particularly AA Inland II A/B 292/3, AZ: 83–78, Spionageabwehr, Vertrauensmänner 1935–1940. SS was am acronym for Schutzstaffel.

38. AA Inland II A/B 291/3, AZ: 83–78, Spionageabwehr, Vertrauensmänner 18.12.33–31.7.34, 15 January 1934 and "Abschrift" that follows (on Schneekloth); AA Pol 1 M 234, 20 June 1939; AA Pol 1 M 240, 2 February, 1939.

39. BA R58/275, 3 October 1938, pp. 25–26.

40. MA RW49/529–530; BA R58/830, 13 June 1941; BA R58/472, 28 March 1940, p.14 (Zsunke). AA Pol 1 M 240, 25 May 1939, 20 June 1939, 12 September 1939; AA Pol 1 M 241, AZ: PO15–1g, Agenten- u. Spionagewesen Einzelfälle, S-Z 11.39–4.40, Bd. 3 (hereafter, Pol 1 M 241), 27 November 1939 (Sparwasser). NA T77 884, pp. 12–13 (Xylander). On Rühle and telegram see the following reports in BA R58/472: n. d. (pp. 1–5), 18 April 1940 (pp.18–20), 13 April 1940 (p. 15). On sabotage via Italy: ibid., 28 March 1940, p. 14. See also De Jong, *Fifth,* 202–3.

41. MI 25393/25394, 6 July 1937 (Valentin report); AN BB18 6476, especially the Delrieu report of 4 October 1937. Later reports from judicial sources presented a watered-down version of Delrieu's report based on Tamborini's later insistence that he understood French imperfectly and had difficulty with the police interrogators' accent, and based on attacks on the character and motivations of a POUM informant. Neither qualification is convincing, especially in light of Cantelli's confession, Valentin's report, the Giardini incident, the details and style of Delrieu's report, and SIM revelations following the war (see note 42). AN BB18 6476, 6 May 1938, 23 December 1938.

42. J.-R. Tournoux, *L'histoire secrète* (Paris: Plon, 1962), 324–61 (these are transcripts of documents). Joel Blatt has been helpful in confirming these documents, based on his work with Italian sources.

43. AN BB18 6095, Switz/Stahl file, especially 20 March 1934, 27 March 1934, 5 July 1934, 17 April 1935; APP BA 1743, May 1935, 29 April 1935. See also *Le Journal,* 21, 22 December 1933, 21 March 1934, 11 July 1934, 26 March 1935.

44. On circuits into France: APP BAP 69, 24 April 1924. On Germany: AN F7 13424; AN F7 13426 (especially 1924 dossier); Dan Jacobs, *Borodin: Stalin's Man in China* (Cambridge, Mass.: Harvard University Press, 1981), 78–79, 86; John Erickson, "Threat Identification and Strategic Appraisal by the Soviet Union, 1930–1941," in *Knowing One's Enemies,* ed. May, 394. On Vienna: AN F7 13065, 28 June 1922, 5 January 1925; AN F7 14753, 12 December 1936; APP BAP 269, 16 March 1931; Elisabeth K. Poretsky, *Our Own People: A Memoir of 'Ignace Reiss' and his Friends* (Ann Arbor: University of Michigan Press, 1970), 58. On global dimensions, see chapter 4. For an overall view of Soviet espionage in these years, including discussion of specific operations in Germany and France, the departure points are David J. Dallin, *Soviet Espionage* (New Haven: Yale University Press, 1955); and, more recently, John Costello and Oleg Tsarev, *Deadly Illusions* (New York: Crown, 1993).

45. Soviet secret police went through several name changes during the period. For the sake of consistency I use the letters GPU throughout this book.

46. Dallin argues that distance between agencies and local parties, to the extent it was practiced, was to protect the latter from charges of spying for a foreign country. Dallin, *Soviet Espionage,* 16–18.

47. On this point see Erickson, "Threat," in May, *Knowing One's Enemies,* 394.

48. Literature on German interwar intelligence has concentrated on the Nazi years. The best reviews are in Kahn, *Hitler's Spies;* and Michael Geyer, "National Socialist Germany: The Politics of Information," in *Knowing One's Enemies,* ed. May, 310–46. See also Buchheit, *Geheimdienst.* On French reports from the 1920s, in addition to the Impex material, see AN F7 14713, May 1926 ("Les services secrets allemands").

49. AA Inland II A/B 292/1 AZ: 83–78, Spionageabwehr, Vertrauensmänner 1.8.34–18.4.35, Wesemann file, especially 26 July 1934, 8 April 1935; AN F7 14714, 20 March 1935.

50. Hans Georg Lehmann, *In Acht und Bann: Politische Emigrations, NS-Ausbürgerung, und Wiedergutmachung am Beispiel Willy Brandts* (Munich: Beck, 1976), 44, 61. The extent of Gestapo penetration in France is difficult to follow. A Foreign Office report refers to a number 9 *menées terroristes* list "relatif à la Gestapo," but this list is not to be found among the others. MAE Z Europe 1930–1940 Allemagne 791, 14 May 1940, p. 177.

51. MA RW5/137, 22 November 1934, 25 June 1935, 16 July 1935, 21 October 1935, 20 November 1937, 25 November 1937.

52. De Jong, *Fifth,* 153; Mader, *Hitlers Spionagegenerale,* 309, 311–15.

53. De Jong, *Fifth,* 150; Donald Cameron Watt, *How War Came: The Immediate Origins of the Second World War, 1938–1939* (New York: Pantheon, 1989), 61.

54. MA RW5/143, 5 October 1939; MA RW5/163, 4 July 1939; De Jong, *Fifth,* 154–55, 182–206 (on May–June 1940 operations; de Jong emphasizes the limited role of treachery among resident populations). See also Mader, *Hitlers Spionagegenerale,* 321–22, 330–33; Paul Leverkuehn, *German Military Intelligence,* trans. R. H. Stevens (New York: Praeger, 1954), 45.

55. The phrase is Geyer's in "National Socialist," in May, *Knowing One's Enemies,* 311.

56. The following discussion, except details on Yugoslavia, relies primarily on Navarre, *Service,* especially 39–47, 53, 69–71, 117–22. This is a sober account put together by a former SR official who headed the German section of the SR Centrale from 1936 to 1940; other former intelligence officers supplied information to Navarre for this work. Down to 1930 the SR Marine maintained a station in Germany. For a positive assessment of the SR's effectiveness in obtaining strategically valuable intelligence, see, in addition to Navarre, Robert Young, "French Military Intelligence and Nazi Germany, 1938–1939," in *Knowing One's Enemies,* ed. May, 271–309. On Bertrand and Enigma, see also Jean Stengers, "Enigma, the French, the Poles, and the British, 1931–1940" in *The Missing Dimension,* ed. Andrew and Dilks, 126–29, 133. Dates for SR stations have been given only where precise information exists.

57. AA Pol 1 M 240, 6 April 1939, 26 April 1939; BA R58/275, 9 August 1939 (pp. 56–57), 13 [18?] January 1940 (pp. 67ff.). Freundt, in the German consulate in Zagreb, sent the original report on Hartwig. He said his information came from a former collaborator of Hartwig. Although Freundt noted that he lacked the time and means to verify this information, he believed it to be

highly credible because of the *bestimmtheit* (certainty; exactitude) with which the source stated his details and because of the way the source responded to his (Freundt's) questions. The repetition of these details in the RSHA report nine months later again suggests that the report was correct. It is possible that the informer was part of a French sting operation; the French SR did engage in disinformation. If so, this would, in a diferent way, demonstrate the sophistication of French intelligence in this period. Hartwig was related to the Baron Hartwig, Russian minister to Serbia, who died of a heart attack during the July crisis. His father was a former bank director in St. Petersburg.

58. On charts and organization circulars, see SHAT 7N 2486, particularly the "Liste des postes SR en temps de paix et en temps de guerre," 1925; SHAT 3H 434, especially 14 April 1937, 14 October 1937; SHAT 7N 2571, 21 July 1933 ("Note . . . gendarmerie au service du contre-espionage"), 30 April 1937. *Menées terroristes* lists are in AN F7 14684. On the Préfecture archives see APP BAP 65, 1 October 1940 (dossier D-11). The barge was blocked in the Seine and most of its contents recovered by the Germans.

59. Navarre, *Service*, 40–41, 68–72; Gunter Peis, *The Man Who Started the War* (London: Odhams Press, Ltd., 1960), 104–12; Kahn, *Hitler's Spies*, 279–93; AN F7 14713, 9 February 1935; AN F7 14662, 4 December 1939. MA RW5/137 (reports to Abwehr Ast. Dresden concerning experiments with sabotage materials). On Soviet wireless use, see *The Rote Kapelle: The CIA's History of Soviet Intelligence and Espionage Networks in Western Europe, 1936–1945* (Frederick, Md.: University Publications of America, 1979), 20, 24.

60. Peis, *Man*, 106.

61. Charles Reber, *Terrorisme et diplomatie* (Paris: Baudinière, 1935), 18–20.

62. Andrew, *Secret Service*, 347. British cryptography, however, was very competent. British industrial intelligence was also comparatively advanced: Wark, *Ultimate*, 159–60.

63. On Reiss, see Poretsky, *People* and (on mobile assassination squads) Alexander Orlov, *The Secret History of Stalin's Crimes* (London: Jarrolds, 1954), 229–32.

64. *Rote Kapelle*, 13–20, 87–92, 105–10, 237–53, 367–73; Leopold Trepper, *The Great Game: Memoirs of the Spy Hitler Couldn't Silence* (New York: Mcgraw-Hill, 1977). In his memoirs, Trepper says there was a deception of his German captors that was not prearranged. See also Dallin, *Soviet Espionage;* Gilles Perrault, *The Red Orchestra,* trans. Peter Wiles (New York: Simon and Schuster, 1969).

65. AN F7 13065, 12 May 1926. See also AN F7 13509, 1 June 1921, 20 September 1921. See also chapter 4.

66. *Rote Kapelle*, 70, 213, 312, 327, 360–61; Johnson, *Instance*, 68, 95. See also Costello and Tsarev, *Deadly Illusions*, 92–93, 209, 249.

67. Geyer, "National Politics," in May, *Knowing One's Enemies*, 311, 321–22.

68. Watt, *How War Came*, 58.

69. Henri de Monfreid, *Les secrets de la mer Rouge* (Paris: Grasset, 1932). On Monfreid see chapter 4. On the dimensions of the arms traffic in the Red Sea

see Agnès Piquart, "Le commerce des armes à Djibouti de 1888 à 1914," *Revue française d'histoire d'outre-mer* 58 (1971): 407–32.

70. Joseph Crozier, *Mes missions secrètes, 1915–1918* (Paris: Payot, 1933). On the NOT, see chapter 3.

71. AN F7 14679. Alan Block has chronicled how League of Nations efforts in the 1920s to regulate the drug trade simply created greater opportunities for illicit drug traffickers and resulted in larger criminal networks of narcotics dealers, who, as well, might traffic in arms: Block, "European Drug Traffic."

72. Georges Castellan, *Le réarmement clandestin du Reich, 1930–1935* (Paris: Plon, 1954), 274–94.

73. SHAT 3H 102, 17 June 1925 (quoted), 17 July 1925, 28 August 1925, 29 September 1925; MAE Asie 1918–1929 Chine 2ème Partie 162, 6 February 1928, p. 289.

74. AN BB18 6542, 27 July 1935, 29 July 1935, 27 September 1935, 29 October 1935, 12 December 1935, 24 March 1936; AN F7 14679, 24 July 1935 (translation of Associated Press clipping on Le Havre mayor).

75. AN F7 14679, 3 July 1939.

76. AN F7 14680, Corrigan.

77. Castellan, *Réarmement,* 175–98; MAE Z Europe 1930–1940 Yougoslavie 135, 11 October 1934; AN BB18 3061/2, 2 August 1939 (Affaire du CSAR). See also MAE Maroc/Tunisie 1917–1940 Maroc 1214, 21 August 1934, pp. 222–23 on Wilhelm K. who was smuggling weapons into Morocco in the early 1930s.

78. SHAT 3H 102, 17 June 1925. The informant estimated that up to 800 persons had shown interest and that as of 1 June 500 had been accepted; but only one individual was named as definitely having departed for the Rif.

79. MAE Asie 1918–1929 Chine 2ème Partie 162, 13 December 1927, pp. 163–64, 198–203; ibid., 24 May 1927, pp. 115–16; ibid., 17 January 1928, pp. 240–41; OM SLIII 141, 17 July 1928 (Peking documents).

80. AN F7 14676, 13 April 1937. The newspaper was the Stockholm daily, *Aftonbladet.*

81. MAE Z Europe 1930–1940 Espagne 147, 1 July 1937, pp. 38–39.

82. AN F7 14677, October 1937 (Goldberg dossier).

83. MAE Z Europe 1930–1940 Espagne 147, 5 August 1937, p. 60.

84. On boats and false destinations: ibid., particularly 18 August 1937 (pp. 76–77), 30 August 1937 (pp. 86–87), 1 July 1937 (pp. 37–39). AN F7 14676, 17 November 1936, 13 April 1937. On hotel: AN F7 14676, 5 December 1936. On Jean A.: AN F7 14680, 22 August 1938.

85. Poretsky, *People,* 210–11.

86. Walter Krivitsky, *In Stalin's Secret Service* (1939; reprint, Frederick, Md.: University Publications of America, 1985), 84–88. See also Hugh Thomas, *The Spanish Civil War* (New York: Harper Colophon, 1963), 295–96. Poretsky, *People,* 270, casts doubts on the veracity of Krivitsky's account.

87. MAE Z Europe 1939–1940 Espagne 147, 5 August 1937, pp. 58–60.

88. Daladier papers, 3 DA11 DR3, 26 January 1939, pp. 26–28, 37.

89. AN F7 14677, October 1937 (Goldberg dossier).

90. AN F60 201, 22 August 1937; ibid., n.d. ("Note pour Monsieur le président du conseil. Affaire d'espionage d'Oran").

91. Veltjens may have had ties to the conspirators in Spain prior to their uprising, although the evidence on this remains inconclusive. In 1940 Göring used Veltjens for arms exports to Finland and during the Second World War for black market purchases in western Europe. Whealey, *Hitler,* 81–82; Hans-Henning Abendroth, *Hitler in der Spanischen Arena* (Paderborn: Ferdinand Schöningh, 1973), 19–20, 156, 179–81; Gerhard Weinberg, *The Foreign Policy of Hitler's Germany* (Chicago: University of Chicago Press, 1983; 1980), 1:286–87; 2:147.

92. AN F7 14677, October 1937 (Goldberg dossier).

93. MAE Z Europe 1930–1940 Espagne 147, 1 July 1937, pp. 37–39.

94. AN F7 14677, October 1937 (Goldberg dossier); APP BA 1665, 24 August 1936; AN F7 14676, 25 February 1938; AN F7 14680, January 1939, 9 July 1938.

95. Fricke, *Bismarcks Prätorianer.*

96. MAE Z Europe 1930–1940 Yougoslavie (hereafter, MAE Z Youg.) 136, 30 October 1934 (note no. 1), pp. 123–40. The author of this report was identified as "an informer who is often well informed." His personal acquaintance with Ustasha figures and his style of presentation alike appear to merit this appraisal.

97. On pre-1914 southern Slav terrorism, see Vladimir Dedijer, *The Road to Sarajevo* (New York: Simon and Schuster, 1966).

98. AN BB18 6473, 13 November 1934; MI 25296, 30 November 1934 (Barthelet report); MAE Z Youg. 135, 13 October 1934, p. 99; Reber, *Terrorisme,* 27, 49–56, 66.

99. On IMRO and their Ustasha association: MAE Z Youg. 136, 30 October 1934 (note no. 1); AN F7 14754, 11 October 1934 ("Au sujet de l'ORIM"); AN F7 14755, n.d. ("L'organisation révolutionnaire intérieure macédoine de 1928 à 1936"). Relations between the IMRO (the Internal Macedonian Revolutionary Organization) and Ustashi preceded the 1932 agreement.

100. MAE Z Youg. 137, 17 November 1934, pp. 159, 165–76; AN F7 14754, 12 October 1934 (procès verbal of Pospisil).

101. MAE Z Youg. 136, 23 October 1934, pp. 21–22.

102. Ibid., 30 October 1934 (note no. 1); MAE Z Youg. 135, 11 October 1934, pp. 25–30. The two reports appear to be written by the same person.

103. MI 25297, "La vie secrète des émigrés criminels" by Jelka Pogorelec.

104. AN BB18 6473, 1 March 1935, 9 March 1935, 12 March 1935, 1 April 1935; MAE Z Youg. 135, 13 October 1934, p. 84. According to note no. 1, Duic committed suicide for personal reasons.

105. MAE Z Youg. 136, 30 October 1934 (note no. 1).

106. The problem of Yugoslav tendentiousness was recognized within the French Ministry of Foreign Affairs: MAE Z Youg. 135, 13 October 1934, p. 85. For reports indicating German complicity see: ibid., 15 October 1934, 16 October, especially p. 125; MAE Z Youg. 136, 30 October 1934 (note no. 2), pp. 141–45; MI 25295, 30 October 1934 ("Etude relative aux agissements . . . terroristes allemands"); ibid., 19 November 1934. Naggiar, the French repre-

sentative in Belgrade reported, however, that the Yugoslavs were certain that Berlin was not involved: MAE Z Youg. 138, 23 December 1934, p. 12. The author of note no. 1 also discounted German involvement. See also the report of Inspector Borel from Switzerland: MI 25296, 29 October 1934, p. 25. In general charges regarding Berlin came from questionable sources or people not likely to have good access to the facts.

107. AN F7 14754, 1 February 1935 (The French embassy in Rome argued, however, that all Croats in Italy were concentrated on the Lipari Islands: ibid, 19 February 1935); AN F7 14755, 26 March 1937; MI 25297, 25 January 1936; AN F7 14684, *menées terroristes* list no. 5, 16 April 1938, pp. 16, 19–20; ibid., list no. 7, 1 May 1939, pp. 35, 93; AN F7 14753, 26 June 1939; AN F7 14755, 9 June 1939, 19 December 1939; APP BAP 65, June 1938 ("Propositions d'expulsions"—bound booklet on 100 people; hereafter, 100-persons book), category 10.

108. APP BAP 278, September 1930; ibid., March 1928 (21-page report); APP BA 1711, 21 February 1930; AN BB18 6093, 6 September 1932.

109. AN F7 14744, 13 November 1926, 13 January 1927; AN BB18 6095, 23 May 1933, 12 February 1934, 7 May 1934.

110. MI 25344, n. d. The note is torn, making the last third of what is written on it difficult to read. The reference in the text, therefore, is to part of the note.

111. Robert C. Williams, *Culture in Exile: Russian Emigrés in Germany, 1881–1941* (Ithaca: Cornell University Press, 1972), especially 81–84, 111–24, 131–34, 284–85; Marc Raeff, *Russia Abroad: A Cultural History of the Russian Emigration, 1919–1939* (New York: Oxford University Press, 1970), especially 4–5, 17–24, 41–42, 47–52, 61, 77 (on publishers); Robert H. Johnston, *New Mecca, New Babylon: Paris and the Russian Exiles, 1920–1945* (Montreal: McGill-Queen's University Press, 1988), especially 9, 53, 81, 85–90, 147–48. The one-million figure is from Michael Marrus, *The Unwanted: European Refugees in the Twentieth Century* (New York: Oxford University Press, 1985), 61. Raeff suggests somewhat smaller figures, pp. 202–3. All authors point out the wildly varying estimates from the times that allow only approximate numbers.

112. Johnston, *Mecca*, 25–28.

113. Ibid., 3.

114. APP BAP 65, June 1938 (100-persons book), category 12.

115. APP BAP 65, June 1938 (100-persons book), category 12 (Eugène H.); AN F7 14676, 30 December 1936, April 1937; AN F7 14677, October 1937 (Goldberg dossier); AN F7 14680, 22 August 1938; AN F7 14676, 31 December 1936.

116. Marina Grey, *Le général meurt à minuit* (Paris: Plon, 1981), 62. This is the most thorough investigation into the Kutepov and Miller kidnappings.

117. APP BAP 291, September 1934, p. 10; Grey, *Général*, 60–61 (according to Grey, ZK. sold Yugoslav military secrets to the USSR at the behest of the Yugoslav general staff, for whom ZK. really was working); AN F7 14684, *menées terroristes* list no. 1, 10 April 1937; Hoover Institution on War, Revolution, and Peace, Stanford, B. I. Nicolaevsky register, box number 299 folder ID7 (hereafter, Hoover N.), 14 December 1937 ("Rapport: affaire de Miller";

hereafter, by date only), pp. 3–4, 35–36, 45–46; I consulted photocopies of these files in Syracuse. This report is largely compiled from White Russian papers seized during the investigation into the kidnapping of General Miller in 1937. It is written in an impressionable way and should be treated with caution.

118. Hoover N., 14 December 1937, pp. 12–13, 19, 38, 39 (quoted). The author of the quote on Koltypin was Zakrjevskii (in a note dated 6 December 1934). See also MI 25344, 3 March 1930.

119. APP BA 1708, June 1932.

120. For some sense of the scope of double agent penetration see MAE Europe 1918–1929 Russie 120, 27 October 1922, p. 6; ibid., 27 September 1923, pp. 105–6 (on Red agents among the entourage of Grand Duke Kirill, an exiled pretender to the throne); AN F7 14753, 17 December 1935 (on Red infiltration of White Russian groups in Belgrade). On the "trust" see Grey, *Général*, 24–45; Geoffrey Bailey, *The Conspirators* (New York: Harper, 1960); Paul W. Blackstock, *The Secret Road to World War Two: Soviet Versus Western Intelligence 1921–1939* (Chicago: Quadrangle, 1969).

121. Grey, *Général*, 54, 111; Costello and Tsarev, *Deadly Illusions,* 68. On the Normandy coast invasions see MI 25344, 26–27 March, 5 April 1930.

122. Costello and Tsarev, *Deadly Illusions,* 297 confirms the GPU's role and Skoblin's complicity in the kidnapping. Theories about militant Whites and the Spanish civil war emanated mostly from White Russian groups, but they were also accepted by Sûreté commissaire Jean Belin, who participated in the investigation of the case and heard a confession from Skoblin's wife shortly before her death in prison (Jean Belin, *Secrets of the Sûreté* [New York, G. P. Putnam's Sons, 1950]).

123. Georges London, *Les grands procès de l'année 1938* (Paris: Editions de France, 1939), 228; Hoover N., 14 December 1937, p. 34; Hoover N., February 1938 (Roches to Directeur de la police judiciaire), p. 11.

124. Grey *Général*, 226.

125. Hoover N., 14 December 1937, p. 5. On amateurism see Hoover N., 12 July 1934, côte XIII, 19 April 1938, côte XXIX.

126. Hoover N., especially côtes III (on boat), V–VIII, XV, XIX–XX, XXXVII (listed erroneously as XXVII — on expenses).

127. For some examples see Krivitsky, *Stalin's,* 224–43; Robert Conquest, *The Great Terror: Stalin's Purge of the Thirties* (New York: Macmillan, 1968), 219; Grey, *Général*, pp. 191–203; Paul Paillole, *Services spéciaux, 1935–1945* (Paris: Editions Robert Laffont, 1975), 46–52.

128. Material on Skoblin and the inner line is scattered throughout the Hoover documents. See in particular Hoover N., November 1937, pp. 4–5; ibid., 14 December 1937, pp. 2–3, 17–19. See also press coverage in the major Parisian dailies in September–October 1937; Grey, *Général*. Poretsky's charges are in Poretsky, *People,* 145–46, 165, 214. On mobile assassination squads see also Costello and Tsarev, *Deadly Illusions,* 285–86. On Von Petrov: Peter Wright, *Spycatcher: The Candid Autobiography of a Senior Intelligence Officer* (New York: Viking Penguin, 1987), 325.

129. MAE Maroc/Tunisie 1917–1940 Maroc 1214, 31 January 1929, pp. 123–25; MAE Z Europe 1930–1940 URSS 1089, 15 October, p. 251; MI

25344, 7 February 1930; Hoover N., February 1938 (Roches, p. 14), 1 February 1938.

130. Mader, *Hitlers Spionagegenerale*, 132; Andrew, *Secret Service*, 350; AA Jugoslav Pol. 15 1921–1934, 10 July 1921; BA R58/275, 13 January 1940; Watt, *How War Came*, 61. On Red Army spies: APP BAP 437, 2 February 1935, 26 March 1935.

131. Woolman, *Rebels*, 129; AN F7 13413, 19 June 1925, 20 June 1925, 22 June 1925, 9 January 1926.

132. Grey, *Général*, 187–91; Hoover N., February 1938 (Roches, p. 14), 14 December 1937, pp. 6–10; APP BAP 65, June 1938 (100-persons book), category 8.

133. Williams, *Culture*, 98–102, 160–67, 213–22, 288–90, 348. For French counterintelligence reports tracking early White conspiracies in Germany, see MAE Europe 1918–1929 Russie 119. In 1935 the French signed a pact with the USSR, although neither side ever took it seriously. Biskupskii, incidentally, turns up as one of the schemers in the files on the gunrunner W.

134. MM 1BB7 93, 10 December 1936; Gabrielle Bertrand, *Seule dans l'Asie troublée: Mandchouko-Mongolie, 1936–1937* (Paris: Plon, 1937), 53–62 (quoted, 57), 96; OM Affaires politiques 1416, 15 March 1938 (BMR [Bulletin mensuel de renseignements]: "Les Russes blancs de la Chine du nord devant le conflit sino-japonais"), 45–54 (quoted, 47, 49); SHAT 7N 3124, 26 December 1935 (Consul de France at Harbin to Hoppenot, Chargé d'affaires de la République française en Chine); George Stewart, *The White Armies of Russia: A Chronicle of Counter-Revolution and Allied Intervention* (New York: Macmillan, 1933), 269.

135. MAE Z Europe 1930–1940 URSS 1089, 30 April 1934, pp. 170–71 (note dated 28 April); MAE E Asie-Océanie-Japon 1930–1940 150, 18 January 1939, p. 114; APP BA 1706, 26 November 1937.

136. APP BAP 291, September 1934 (also useful on intrigues between White Russians, Germans, and Japanese); APP BAP 407, February 1939 ("L'émigration en face de la perspective d'une guerre européene"), p. 8.

137. Among these: MAE Z Europe 1930–1940 URSS 1089, 30 April 1934, pp. 171–72; APP BAP 291, 11 June 1938; APP BAP 407, 18 January 1939; APP BAP 66, 4 April 1939. After World War II it was learned that Turkul had been a GPU agent. One might assume that his pro-German role was to divide the White Russians: Pierre Broué, "La main d'oeuvre 'blanche' de Staline," *Cahiers Léon Trotsky* 24 (December 1985): 81.

138. Bernard Wasserstein, *Britain and the Jews of Europe, 1939–1945* (Oxford: Oxford University Press, 1979), 83–90; Roger Daniels, *The Decision to Relocate the Japanese Americans* (Malabar, Fla.: Robert E. Krieger, 1986).

139. Exact figures are difficult to determine, in part because of distinctions between assembly centers where detainment could nevertheless last some time and actual internment camps. A 15,000 figure is given in SHAT 7N 2475, 15 November 1939 ("Situation du recrutement et de l'utilisation des étrangers à la date du 12 novembre"). See also MAE Z Europe 1930–1940 Allemagne 790, 9 December 1939 (by this date 6,000 had left the camps, one third of these for the Foreign Legion); *Journal officiel*, Chambre des députés, débats parlemen-

taires, séance of 8 December 1939, p. 2121; Michael R. Marrus and Robert O. Paxton, *Vichy France and the Jews* (New York: Basic Books, 1981), 65. For a higher figure see Gilbert Badia et al., *Les Barbelés de l'exil* (Grenoble: Presses universitaires de Grenoble, 1979), 176, 182. On May internments: MAE Z Europe 1930–1940, Allemagne 791, 15, 25 May 1940, pp. 90–93, 212.

140. The starting point here is the work of Michael Marrus and Robert Paxton who have made the most thorough assessment of Vichy's Jewish policy and have stressed the similarities, as well as the differences, between wartime measures taken against Jews and the increasingly repressive refugee policies of the late Third Republic. For the challenging questions they have raised see Marrus and Paxton, *Vichy,* 14, 54, 58, 67. See also Badia, *Barbelés;* Ralph Schor, *L'opinion française et les étrangers en France, 1919–1939* (Paris: Publications de la Sorbonne, 1985), 709, 728–29.

141. Marrus and Paxton, *Vichy,* chap. 2; Badia, *Barbelés;* Schor, *Opinion;* Marrus, *Unwanted,* chap. 3; Vicki Caron, "Loyalties in Conflict: French Jewry and the Refugee Crisis, 1933–1935," *Leo Baeck Institute Year Book* 36(1991): 305–38; Timothy Maga, "The United States, France, and the Refugee Problem, 1933–1947" (Ph.D. diss., McGill University, 1981).

142. AN F60 173.

143. APP BA 60, November 1933 ("Les réfugies allemands dans la région parisienne"/dossier établi par M. Chiappe); AN F60 497, 31 October 1938 ("Note sur la situation désespérée des réfugies"). The dating of this note is questionable since the suicides it describes are dated 1 and 2 November.

144. The most stringent measures — internments — came at a time of repression of the Communist party in France, and it has been suggested that the internments were political in motivation and an offshoot of anti-Soviet or anti-communist policy: Badia, *Barbelés,* 171–73. The trouble with this perspective is that it does not take into account the constant concern with German secret agents, the internment of only "enemy" nationals, and the ready association of communist and fascist saboteurs following the Nazi-Soviet non-agression pact. On the crackdown against the Communist party, see J. Kim Munholland, "The Daladier Government and the 'Red Scare' of 1938–1940," *Proceedings of the Western Society of French Historical Studies* (1982): 495–506; AN F60 988, 17 April 1940.

145. Marrus, *Unwanted,* 141–45.

146. See chapter 3.

147. Belin, *Secrets,* 245; AN F7 13505, 15 June 1933; APP BA 60, 31 July 1934; AN F7 14662, 12 October 1938, 29 November 1938; *Journal officiel,* Chambre des députés, débats parlementaires, séance of 8 December 1939, p. 2121 (on necessity to intern); SHAT 7N 2475, 26 October 1939 and AN F7 14662, 27 October 1939 (on boats).

148. That precise question was asked by a parliamentary review commission: AN F60 391, 16 November 1939.

149. APP BAP 407, 10 November 1933, pp. 12–13; ibid., February 1939 ("L'émigration en face de la perspective d'une guerre européenne"). The earlier report was not very favorably disposed toward the refugees and argued that political refugees (as opposed to Jewish ones) remained German to the core and might still represent a security threat.

150. APP BAP 407, 31 March 1939. See also APP BA 60, 3 November 1933 (response to *Voilà* article—in Chiappe file).

151. APP BAP 65, December 1938 (Préfet de police to Minister of the Interior/Sûreté nationale); AN F7 14776, n.d. (Interior to Finance Ministry); APP BAP 65, 23 July 1937, 28 March 1939.

152. AN F7 14711, 7 February 1939.

153. APP BAP 355, particularly reports of 24 April 1925, 16 May 1925, January 1927; APP BAP 65, 3 March 1928; Schor, *Opinion*, 281. See also Cross, *Immigrant Workers*, 149–52, 180–82. *Refoulements* referred to the withdrawal or nonrenewal of an identity card permitting residence in France; *expulsions* or deportations were a more direct and forcible form of expelling people from the country.

154. Mitchell, "Xenophobic"; SHAT 7N 676, 20 April 1906, 22 January 1909, 30 October 1913; SHAT 7N 658 (Dossier entitled "Question des étrangers résidant en France avant 1914/1913–1914"—quoted from "Historique" and 20 March 1914 report in this dossier).

155. SHAT 16N 1589, 4 November 1915 ("Note sur les conditions de séjour des étrangers en France pendant la guerre"). As of November 1915 the French had established fifteen concentration camps for Germans, Austrians, and Turks (Turkish suspects were interned following a 9 November 1914 circular). Depots for hostages were in addition to these. There were also two depots for "Alsacien-Lorrains douteux" (I have used the simpler term "Alsatian" for the term "Alsacien-Lorrains" in this document; my apologies to the latter). And two special concentration camps in the Haute-Loire and the Sarthe confined French, Allied, and neutral suspects. Within three weeks of the general internment order, plans were being made for separating women, children, the elderly, and the infirm into special depots where they would await repatriation via Switzerland. Special exclusions and exceptions were made for those in this group who would prefer to remain in France.

156. Ibid.; APP BA 896. This commission was constituted at the very end of 1915. Among its initial purposes was a review of the military status of Russians and Italians, particularly the former who were charged with shirking enlistment in the army. The powers of the commission seem to have been primarily consultative.

157. Interministerial sorting out commissions followed the internments of 1939. MAE Z Europe 1930–1940 Allemagne 790, 22 October 1939; AN F60 391, 16 November 1939. Even before the war, plans to release from internment those refugees able to present "garanties de loyalisme envers la France" called for the creation of "commissions de criblage." See SHAT 7N 2436, 3 December 1938, August 1939 (no. 158 or 10,000).

158. SHAT 7N 2436, 24 June 1926. The interned men were to be formed into work brigades. These general internments were applicable to frontier zones and the Seine region. Ibid., 4 April 1939. Among other projects and instructions from the interwar period, see ibid., 12 March 1923, 24 January 1929, 4 April 1930, 19 November 1937, 3 December 1938.

159. See chapter 1.

160. On hauling suspects off ships, see MAE Z Europe 1930–1940 Allemagne 790 and 791 (the latter includes the Oran episode: 10 May 1940, pp.

26–27, 11 May 1940, p. 141). For prosecutions in France: AN F60 520. Jacques R.'s case is dated 27 May 1940.

161. SHAT Pacifique carton 6, 20 April 1939 (terrorists and explosives; my appreciation to Kim Munholland for showing me this); AN F7 14830, 6 June 1939 (Argentina; see also the earlier reports from 29 April 1939, 20 May 1939); AN F7 14662, 10 June 1939 (Czechs); ibid., 23 June 1939 (Italians); SHAT Pacifique carton 6, 8 July 1939 (timetables); SHAT 7N 2570, August 1939 (Gestapo/OVRA); AN F7 14830, 24 October 1939 (Lambert); AN F7 14662, 14 November 1939 (Romanians. See also AN F7 14684, 21 December 1939, 27 April 1940; AN F60 385, 27 April 1940); AN F60 234, 29 February 1940 (gasoline); AN F7 14830, 21 February 1940 (Communists); see chapter 1 for parachutists. The above are largely from Sûreté circulars.

162. Buchheit, *Geheimdienst,* 313. A Soviet-organized ship sabotaging unit actually existed, but its targets were German ships or ships carrying war supplies to Germany. Dallin, *Soviet Espionage,* 126–32.

163. Donald Baker, "The Surveillance of Subversion in Inter-war France: The Carnet B in the Seine, 1922–1940," *French Historical Studies* 10 (1978): 486–516.

164. Of 133 listed on the 16 April 1938 sheets, only two French appeared (one naturalized). Of 185 listed on the 1 May 1939 sheets, there were thirteen French (one naturalized by marriage).

165. AN F7 14684, *menées terroristes,* list no. 3, 22 April 1937. There had been a warning that Ukrainian terrorists might make attacks on Soviet diplomats.

166. Koestler, *Scum of the Earth* (New York: MacMillan, 1941), 78–79; Bruno Frei, *Die Männer von Vernet* (1950; reprint, Hildesheim: Gerstenberg, 1980), 69–71; AN F60 493, 3 March 1941.

167. On special policies regarding Italians in France in the event of war, see internment projects in SHAT 7N 2436; SHAT 7N 2462, 7 May 1940, 13 May 1940; APP BAP 65, 1 October 1940, D-11, p. 3. According to government statistics from spring 1940, there were 66,504 Russians in France "sans nationalité" and 905,916 Italians: AN F60 391, 15 April 1940.

168. Lehmann, *In Acht,* 44, 118–21; AA Inland II A/B 291/3, 8 February 1934; AA Pol 1 M 240, 16 January 1939, 18 February 1939; BA R58/954, 12 March 1937, p. 1.

169. BA R58/954, 13 July 1937, p. 7. On refugee offers and German suspicions, see AA Inland II A/B 292/2.

170. APP BAP 65, 1 June 1938 (100-persons book), category 4—Lorenzi; AN F7 14662, 23 June 1939.

171. AN F7 14830, 7 May 1939.

172. MAE E Asie-Océanie-Indochine française 1930–1940 52, 31 December 1939.

173. The following discussion is based on documents in the following files: AN F7 14774, 14775, 14776; APP BAP 407, BAP 69.

174. See also Bristow, *Prostitution,* 294 on how immigration barriers in North America fostered an Eastern European market in counterfeit passports (probably, as well, providing an experience in this sort of trafficking to be turned toward the refugee clientele later).

175. AN F7 14774, 21, 28 December 1936; AN F7 14684, *menées terroristes* list no. 7, 1 May 1939, p. 29.

176. Kahn, *Hitler's Spies,* 279–83.

177. Dallin, *Soviet Espionage,* 92–103 (on Pass-Zentrale); *Rote Kapelle,* 19–20, 245; Gordon W. Prange, with Donald M. Goldstein and Katherine V. Dillon, *Target Tokyo: The Story of the Sorge Spy Ring* (New York: McGraw Hill, 1984), 99–100.

178. BA R58/275, 22 February 1939, 26 February 1940, pp. 34, 78; AA Pol 1 M 240, 31 March 1939.

179. AN F7 14717, 10 November 1931; AN F7 13498, 26 November 1927; APP BAP 69, 8 March 1933; AN F7 14662, 4 December 1939.

180. SHAT 7N 1590, 8 April 1918; *Rote Kapelle,* 20–21; OM SLII 23, 4 May 1938; AA Pol 1 M 234, 25 May 1939; AN F7 14662, 3 January 1940. The bulletin on Chilean and Argentine diplomats began with a notification that "certain foreigners of German nationality, ex-Austrians of Jewish extraction" (read refugees), were obtaining Latin American passports on the basis of false consular statements.

181. AN F7 14662, 13 December 1939.

182. APP BAP 69, 14 March 1940, 7 May 1938, 30 August 1938. See also AN F7 14680, 31 September 1939 on Ricardo D.

183. APP BAP 69, 14 March 1940; BA R58/275 (Italienische Spionage) pp. 129–34 (a 1941 German report drawn from French police records that fell into German hands during the occupation). See also Charles Chenevier, *De la combe aux fées à Lurs: souvenirs et révélations* (Paris: Flammarion, 1962), 33–36.

184. The quote is from the Cuban passport affair, APP BAP 69, 14 March 1940.

185. APP BAP 407, October 1938 (stamped as 25 October); ibid, 30 September 1938; AN F7 14662, 19 April 1939.

186. APP BAP 65, 1 June 1938.

187. SHAT 7N 2436, 4 April 1939, August 1939 (no. 158 or 10,000).

188. MAE Z Europe 1930–1940 Allemagne 791, 24 January 1940, 2 May 1940, 20 May 1940, 22 May 1940, 24 May 1940, 6 June 1940, pp. 129, 172–87, 309.

189. AN F7 13986, 9 March 1940.

190. AN F7 14754, 23 October 1934; MI 25295, 12 November 1934 (note from Commissaire de police de Mohon, 30 October 1934).

191. MAE Z Europe 1930–1940 URSS 1089, 30 April 1934, pp. 17–71. For wartime suspicions and convictions, see the files in AN F7 12895–12896; AN F7 13506, 26 June 1918 ("Agissements des représentants du maximalisme en Suisse").

192. APP BAP 278, March 1928 (p. 6 of 21-page report on Italian Fascist and anti-Fascist groups in France); AN F60 201, 21 December 1938 ("La politique italienne"), p. 149; APP BA 60, 21 September 1933.

193. MAE Z Europe 1930–1940 Allemagne 757; MAE Z Europe 1930–1940 Allemagne 753, 14 December 1933, p. 170.

194. BA R58/275, 23 December 1939, p. 65. See as well other reports in this file on foreign (including French) secret service activity. In addition, see BA R58/1045, pp. 117–21.

195. An example is French reporting on Morocco in the late 1930s, at times tense or worrisome, but by the end of the decade and with the outbreak of war rather calm and sanguine.

196. The chart is in AN F60 707 n. d. ("L'action actuelle de propagande dans les pays musulmans: tableau comparatif"; its dossier placement suggests spring 1939). For other critiques, see OM Affaires politiques 1421, 23 November 1938; OM Affaires politiques 920, March 1938 (HCMAN report on radio broadcasts), pp. 8–9; AN F60 710, 11 January 1938, 12 March 1938; AN F60 707, 5 December 1938, 2 May 1939; SHAT 3H 256, 19 May 1940.

197. OM Affaires politiques 1421, 23 November 1938; OM Affaires politiques 920, March 1938 (HCMAN report), pp. 16–18; OM Affaires politiques 1425, 11 January 1940 (BRQM), p. 530; SHAT 3H 256, 19 May 1940; AN F60 707, 5 December 1938; AN F60 745 n. d. (91-page report "Les grands courants"), pp. 86–87; AN F60 753, 26–27 March 1939; AN F60 572, 13 October 1937; AN F60 710, 14 December 1937.

198. AN F60 234, 2 June 1940.

Chapter Three: Stories

1. *Le Journal,* 11 August 1931. I have changed a few sentences from past to present tense to maintain the consistency that English requires.

2. The last article in the series was 20 August 1931. The closest circulation figure I have for the *Journal* is 1936: 650,000 copies: Bellanger, *Histoire,* 3:521.

3. On consumerism and the war from a different perspective, see George L. Mosse, *Fallen Soldiers: Reshaping the Memory of the World Wars* (New York: Oxford University Press, 1990), 126–56.

4. Robert-Dumas, *Idole.* Book sales were 27,500 copies.

5. Yrondy, *Cocaïne.* This book was published in the Secret War series whose book sales per edition are estimated to have run from 15,000 to 20,000 copies.

6. Nadaud and Fage, *Armée;* Marcel Montarron, *Le poison blanc* (Paris: Editions Denoël, 1938), 65; Charles Robert-Dumas, *«Ceux du S.R.»: la marque du triangle* (Paris: Fayard, 1939); Paul Darlix, *Smyrne, dernière escale* (Paris: Baudinière, 1930); Lucieto, *Livrés.* For the most celebrated example see Eric Ambler's *Coffin for Dimitrios* (1939; reprint, in *Intrigue: Four Great Spy Novels of Eric Ambler,* New York: Alfred A. Knopf, 1943).

7. Or so claimed *Paris-Soir,* 9 June 1938. Lyon (or Lion), according to the article, had also been an arms dealer.

8. On Lawrence, see Victor Meulenijzer, *Le colonel Lawrence agent de l'Intelligence Service* (Brussels: Editions Rex, 1938); Pierre Apestéguy, *Le roi des sables* (Paris, Librairie des Champs-Elysées, 1939; 50,000 copies sold); Maurice Laporte, *Bouddha contre l'Intelligence Service* (Paris: Redier, 1933); *Détective,* 3 August 1939. On Abd-el-Krim and Arslan, see Henri Massis, *Defence of the West,* trans. F. S. Flint (New York: Harcourt, Brace, 1928; originally published as *Défense de l'occident* [Paris: Plon, 1927; 15,400 copies printed]), 17; Laporte,

Bouddha, 168; Boucard, *Les dessous de l'Intelligence Service,* 88–95; Jean Marquès-Rivière, *L'U.R.S.S. dans le monde* (Paris: Payot, 1935; 3,000 copies printed), 239–42; Gustave Gautherot, *Le monde communiste* (Paris: Editions Spes, 1925), 89; Paul Allard, *Les espions de la paix* (Paris: Baudinière, 1935), 155–71; *Paris-Soir,* 3 February 1937. On the criminal international: Jean Bardanne, *Stavisky, espion allemand* (Paris: Baudinière, 1935) (published in the Secret War series). Henry Champly, *The Road to Shanghai: White Slave Traffic in Asia,* trans. Warre B. Wells (London: John Long, 1934; originally published as *Le chemin de Changhaï* [Paris: Tallandier, 1933]).

9. Roger Lamblin, *«Protocols» des sages de sion* (Paris: Grasset, 1921); D. Petrovsky, *La Russie sous les juifs* (Paris: Baudinière, 1931); Lucien Pemjean, *Vers l'invasion* (Paris: Baudinière, 1933); Louis-Ferdinand Céline, *Bagatelles pour un massacre* (Paris: Editions Denoël, 1937); Léon de Poncins, *La mystérieuse internationale juive* (Paris: Gabriel Beauchesne 1936); Ilya Ehrenburg, *Memoirs: 1921–1941,* trans. Tatania Shebunina (Cleveland: World Publishing Co., 1963), 31. Norman Cohen has described the popularity of Protocols literature after the war, and has traced earlier Jewish conspiracy stories. Norman Cohen, *Warrant for Genocide* (New York: Harper, 1967). On earlier stories see Stephen Wilson, *Ideology and Experience* (Rutherford, N.J.: Farleigh Dickinson Press, 1982), 409–21.

10. Boucard, *Les dessous de l'Intelligence Service; The Brown Network.*

11. AN F7 14713, 3 July 1939; Stéphane Richter, *Service secret: de l'école d'espionnage au poteau de Vincennes,* trans. Jean Dolaine (Paris: Mignolet and Storz, 1934; originally published in Italian).

12. Schor, *Opinion;* Marrus and Paxton, *Jews,* chap. 2. For some contemporary examples, see Georges Mauco, *Les étrangers en France: étude géographique sur leur rôle dans l'activité économique* (Paris: Armand Colin, 1932); Raymond Millet, *Trois millions d'étrangers en France: les indésirables, les bienvenus* (Paris: Librairie de Médicis, 1938); René Gontier, *Vers un racisme français* (Paris: Editions Denoël, 1939).

13. *Voilà,* 28 October 1933; *Le Petit Parisien,* 2 April 1935; *Détective,* 23 September 1937; Allard, *Espions,* 33–34; Dehilotte, *Gestapo* (Paris: Payot, 1940), 15; Jean Bardanne, *L'espionne du Guépéou* (Paris: Baudinière, 1937), 97–100 (the character Gruntz: French police informer, German spy, Moscow agent, and Jewish; this book was published in the Secret War series); Charles Robert-Dumas, *«Ceux du S.R.»: l'homme à abattre* (Paris: Fayard, 1934), 94–101 (the character Emil Seubert; the book sold 42,350 copies and was made into a movie); Yrondy, *Cocaïne,* 144–45; Cazal, *La guerre! La guerre! Roman de demain* (Paris: Tallandier, 1939), 1:177–78. On the potentially dangerous impact of such stories and reporting on antiforeigner sentiment, see Schor's comprehensive study, *Opinion,* 653, 704. I would argue for a more complex response: see the final section of this chapter. As for the impact of such literature on official policy, there is no way of demonstrating a causal connection nor even reason to believe one necessarily existed given the material security officials had themselves accumulated on foreign intrigues. Influence may, in fact, have run in the reverse. Robert-Dumas, for example, appears to have been a French counterintelligence agent: Paillole, *Services,* 187.

14. Serge de Chessin, *La nuit qui vient de l'orient* (Paris: Hachette, 1929); Sergey Petrovich Melgounov, *The Red Terror in Russia* (London: J. M. Dent, 1926; published in France as *La terreur rouge en Russie* [Paris: Payot, 1927]); Joseph Douillet, *Moscou sans voiles: neuf ans de travail au pays des soviets* (Paris: Editions Spes, 1928).

15. Charles Lucieto, *La guerre des cerveaux: la vierge rouge du Kremlin* (Paris: Berger-Levrault, 1927); Charles Lucieto, *La guerre des cerveaux: le mystère de Monte Carlo* (Paris: Berger-Levrault, 1932), quoted 69–70, 49–50; Lucieto, *Livrés*. Next to the frontispiece of the second work the following sales (or printing) figures are given respectively for the other two: 110,000, 100,000.

16. Charles Robert-Dumas, *«Ceux du S.R.»: le masque de vitriol* (Paris: Fayard, 1935); Bardanne, *Espionne*, 19–24; Marc Le Guillerme, *Goldman-Meyer, de Barcelone* (Paris: Baudinière, 1938); Maurice Laporte, *Espions rouges: les dessous de l'espionage soviétique en France* (Paris: Librairie de la Revue Française, 1929), 48–49; Roman Goul, *Les maîtres de la Tchéka: histoire de la terreur en U.R.S.S., 1917–1938* (Paris: Editions de France, 1938), 93–94, 166–68. Laporte was an ex-Communist. Goul (Gul) was a respected White Russian émigré writer.

17. Jean Bardanne, *Documents secrets et faux passeports* (Paris: Baudinière, 1938), 23–29. This book was published in the Secret War series.

18. AN F7 14689, May 1935 (Hanau file). Bardanne's real name was Georges B. and in 1935 the police were investigating his connections with a press agency suspected of collusion in speculation against the franc. Nevertheless in 1940–1941, a Jean Bardanne was negotiating for the release of captured British special operations agents until, as we are told, "sheer weight of numbers ran him out of money and he was arrested himself": Foot, *SOE in France*, 174.

19. Dehilotte, *Gestapo*, 207; Bardanne, *Espionne*, 48–49.

20. Malraux, *Voie*, 16.

21. Maurice Dekobra, *La gondole aux chimères* (Paris: Baudinière, 1926), quoted 175.

22. Hill, *Go Spy*, 74, 77; Andrew, *Secret Service*, 215–16.

23. Pierre Boileau and Thomas Narcejac, *Le roman policier* (Paris: Payot, 1964); Fereydoun Hoveyda, *Histoire du roman policier* (Paris: Pavillon, 1965); Jean-Jacques Tourteau, *D'Arsène Lupin à San-Antonio: le roman policier français de 1900 à 1970* (Paris: Maison Mame, 1970); A. E. Murch, *The Development of the Detective Novel* (Port Washington, N.Y.: Kennikat Press, 1968). How far the correspondence between the two genres can be taken, however, is questionable. Before the war the French were also focusing considerably upon a spy threat, yet the spy novel was at best still in its infancy. Nor did the interwar spy novel replicate the puzzle-solving devices of much of interwar detective stories (or even the psychological realism of Simenon). See also Boileau and Narcejac, *Roman*, 193–94, on fundamental differences between the two genres.

24. The title of the series was "Collection de mémoires, études, et documents pour servir à l'histoire de la guerre mondiale." Payot was the publisher. I have anglicized the titles.

25. Crozier, *Mes missions*. An earlier version was published under Crozier's pseudonum, Pierre Desgranges: Pierre Desgranges and [Lieutenant] de

Belleval, *En mission chez l'ennemi* (Paris: Redier, 1930). Part of the story of his secretary comes from this earlier version.

26. Marthe Richard, *Mon destin de femme* (Paris: Robert Laffont, 1974).

27. Georges Ladoux, *Marthe Richard: espionne au service de la France* (Paris: Librairie des Champs-Elysées, 1932).

28. Richard tells a more complete and contradictory tale — including initial suspicions by Ladoux that she was a foreign agent — of her recruitment into French intelligence, not the last time she confuses readers about what really happened.

29. Marthe Richer, *Ma vie d'espionne: au service de la France* (Paris: Editions de France, 1935). The author published under both this name and that of Richard, the one usually attributed to her.

30. Ladoux, *Chasseurs*. The cover also carried at the top, "Mémoires de guerre secrète." Ladoux, *Souvenirs*.

31. See the Crozier files in SHAT 7N 926, especially 27 October 1915, 7 December 1915, 5 January 1916, 29 January 1916.

32. MI 25345, 12 March 1918; *L'Oeuvre*, 20 March 1918; *Le Temps*, 20 March 1918, 10 May 1919; *Le Petit Parisien*, 31 January 1919; Bellanger, *Histoire*, 3:431–33.

33. For an example of the attacks on her life story, and one that refers to others, see Alphonse Boudard, *La fermeture* (Paris: Robert Laffont, 1986). Paris police officials have told me that their archives do not include a dossier on Richard.

34. Jean Violan, *Dans l'air et dans la boue: mes missions de guerre* (Paris: Librairie des Champs-Elysées, 1933), 219. Violan was the pen name of Davrichevii (or Davrichewy). P.-Louis Rivière, who worked with French intelligence during the war and was in a position to know the truth, refers to Ladoux's book on Richard as "a pleasant blending of fact and fiction designed above all to amuse the reader." Rivière, *Centre*, 63.

35. For an example of this kind of writing see Jean Norton Cru, *Témoins: essai d'analyse et de critique des souvenirs de combattants édités en français de 1915 à 1928* (Paris: Les Etincelles, 1929).

36. On this point see also Boileau and Narcejac, *Roman*, 194–95.

37. Allard, *Espions*; Robert Boucard, *Les dessous de l'espionnage français* (Paris: Editions de France, 1934). The movie appears to have been based on the Ladoux edition

38. Marthe Richard, *Espions de guerre et de paix (1920–1938)* (Paris: Editions de France, 1938); Marthe Richard, *Mes dernières missions secrètes: Espagne 1936–1938* (Paris: Editions de France, 1939).

39. In addition to the two cited above is a work Crozier wrote under the name of Pierre Desgranges, *Au service des marchands d'armes* (Paris: Redier, 1934).

40. Allard, *Espions*, 15–16.

41. Joseph Kessel, *Mermoz* (Paris: Gallimard, 1938), 124–25, 143, 160, 166, 178–79, 201–2.

42. The best example is Antoine de Saint-Exupéry, *Night Flight*, trans. Stuart

Gilbert, and *Wind, Sand, and Stars,* trans. Lewis Galantière, both in *Airman's Odyssey* (New York: Harcourt Brace Jovanovich, 1984). The two stories were originally published respectively as *Vol de nuit* (Paris: Gallimard, 1931) and *Terre des hommes* (Paris: Gallimard, 1939). See also Bùi Xuân Bào, *Naissance d'un héroisme nouveau dans les lettres françaises de l'entre-deux-guerres: aviation et littérature* (Paris: Faculté des lettres et des sciences humaines de l'Université de Paris, 1961); Robert Wohl, "Par la voie des airs: l'entrée de l'aviation dans le monde des lettres françaises, 1909–1939," *Le Mouvement Social* 145 (December 1988): 41–64. The ties between the mystique of flying and business needs were also noted by Geoffry Stone in a 1932 review of *Vol de nuit* cited in Bào, *Naissance,* 201.

43. Kessel, *Mermoz,* 293–304, 400.

44. Ibid.; Yves Courrière, *Joseph Kessel, ou sur la piste du lion* (Paris: Plon, 1985), 496. For a different interpretation of the book, see Wohl, "Par la voie," 55.

45. For a fascinating discussion of mystique and technology in the German context, see Peter Fritzsche, *A Nation of Fliers: German Aviation and the Popular Imagination* (Cambridge, Mass.: Harvard University Press, 1992), Chapter 4.

46. Mermoz, *Mes vols* (Paris: Flammarion, 1937), 130–31.

47. See the wonderful account in Seagrave, *Epic.*

48. Violan, *L'air,* 26–27; Ladoux, *Marthe,* 31; Crozier, *Missions,* 19.

49. Dekobra, *Madonna,* 35.

50. Ibid., 306.

51. Paul Morand, *Flèche d'Orient* (Paris: Gallimard, 1932).

52. Joseph Kessel, *Les nuits de Sibérie* (Paris: Flammarion, 1928); Courrière, *Kessel,* 142–58 (quoted 155).

53. Roger Vercel, *Capitaine Conan* (Paris: Albin Michel, 1934), 91, 140, 145, 148, 210. For an extended discussion of the novel see Maurice Rieuneau, *Guerre et révolution dans le roman français de 1919–1939* (Klincksieck, 1974), 349–60.

54. Richard, writing under the name of Richer, *Vie,* 4. It is interesting that one of the great pilot heroes from the war, Georges Guynemer, has been described thus: "Il tuait sans merci et semblait y prendre plaisir; il tenait la comptabilité de ses victoires avec la précision d'un professionel du gros gibier." Wohl, "Par la voie," 47. Fritzsche makes the same point in *Nation,* 96.

55. Ladoux, *Souvenirs.*

56. Richard, *Espions,* 61–62.

57. The old storytelling urges died hard and never disappeared altogether, returning in her 1974 memoirs. See *Destin,* 292–319.

58. Allard, *Espions,* 24.

59. Richard, *Espions,* 168.

60. Ladoux, *Marthe,* 85–86.

61. Teddy Legrand, *Les sept têtes du dragon vert* (Paris: Berger-Levrault, 1933). Estimated sales were between 5,000 and 10,000.

62. *Détective,* 6 February, pp. 4, 13; 13 February, pp. 4, 5.

63. Ibid., 25 November 1937, p. 2; 20 January 1938, p. 4; 3 February 1938, p. 5.

64. *Le Journal,* 17 February 1930; *Le Matin,* 29 September 1937. *Le Matin's* circulation was about 700,000 in 1920, down to about 500,000 by the mid 1930s, and 320,000 by the end of the thirties: Bellanger, *Histoire,* 3:311, 519.

65. *Le Journal,* 1 February 1930; *Le Petit Parisien,* 2 February 1930; *Le Matin,* 6 December 1938; *Le Journal* 26 September 1937; *Paris-Soir,* 25 September 1937.

66. *Paris-Soir,* 28 October 1938. Some earlier references to Schulz can be found in Robert G. L. Waite, *Vanguard of Nazism* (New York: Norton, 1969), 45, 242, 254. The article referred to him as Schultz. His name also turned up several years earlier as one of the presumed perpetrators in the Jacob kidnapping: *Le Petit Journal,* 23 March 1935; *Le Journal,* 2 April 1935.

67. *Police Magazine,* 10 October 1937, pp. 8–10.

68. De Jong, *Fifth;* Paul Allard, *Quand Hitler espionne la France* (Paris: Editions de France, 1934). See also Allard, *Espions,* and *La guerre des espions* (Paris: Flammarion, 1936). The newspaper articles are from *Match,* 16 February 1939; *Paris-Soir,* 31 December 1938. Allard also published articles in *Détective.*

69. Bellanger, *Histoire,* 3:461.

70. *Le Petit Parisien,* 14 June, 1932. According to *Paris-Soir,* 4 November 1934, three trains were actually dynamited.

71. An earlier trial had been conducted in Austria in the summer of 1932, but it covered only the first two of Matuska's attempts.

72. Kiss had died several years before the dynamitings. Debates about Kiss, Matuska, and hypnotism thus raised the question as well whether suggestions could be implanted in advance in the mind of a subject. For a good discussion of late-nineteenth-century fascination with the criminological implications of hypnotism, see Ruth Harris, *Murders and Madness* (Oxford: Oxford University Press, 1989), chap. 5.

73. *Paris-Soir,* 4–21 November 1934 (quoted at length 4 November); *Détective,* 19 November 1931. *Le Petit Parisien* provided a more sober account of the trial, although here too the accent was on the strange personality of Matuska and not on the ideological possibilities embedded in the case. For an example of courtroom and press theatrics in France, extending back to the Belle Epoque, see Edward Berenson, *The Trial of Madame Caillaux* (Berkeley: University of California Press, 1992).

74. *Paris-Soir,* 4 October 1937.

75. Poretsky, *People,* especially chaps. 9, 10; Chenevier, *Combes,* 37–48; press accounts in *Paris-Soir, Le Petit Parisien, Le Journal.*

76. See also *Le Petit Parisien,* 3 October 1937 on the Reiss murder and its relation to other recent stories: "Magnificent scenario, moreover, for a film of mystery and blood. . . ."

77. APP BA 1667, 3 May 1937, 6 August 1937, 13 August 1937, 24 August 1937, 26 August 1937.

78. APP BA 1654, 13 February 1930.

79. Grégoire Bessedovsky, *Oui, j'accuse: au service des soviets* (Paris: Redier, 1930), 39–40, 45–46.

80. MAE Z Europe 1930–1940 URSS 1089, 5 March 1930.

81. Albert Londres, *The Road to Buenos Ayres,* trans. Eric Sutton (New York:

Blue Ribbon Books, 1928; originally published as *Le chemin de Buenos-Aires* [Paris: Albin Michel, 1927]), 62–63, 134–36 (quoted).

82. Albert Londres, *Les comitadjis, ou le terrorisme dans les Balkans* (Paris: Albin Michel, 1932), especially 78–79, 168; Jacques Deval, *Rives pacifiques* (Paris: Gallimard, 1937), 142–44 (see chap. 4); Jean Bommart, *The Chinese Fish,* trans. Milton Waldman (London: Longmans Green and Co., 1935; originally published as *Le poisson chinois* [Paris: Librairie des Champs-Elysées, 1934]); Bommart, *Hélène,* and *La dame de Valparaiso: les débuts du poisson chinois* (Paris: Librairie des Champs-Elysées, 1940). Part of Londres's *Comitadjis* appeared in the *Petit Parisien*. On Londres's life: Paul Mousset, *Albert Londres, ou l'aventure du grand reportage* (Paris: Grasset, 1972); Pierre Assouline, *Albert Londres: vie et mort d'un grand reporter, 1884–1932* (Paris: Balland, 1989).

83. Edward R. Tannenbaum, *1900: The Generation Before the Great War* (Garden City, N.Y.: Anchor Press/Doubleday, 1977), 237. Tannenbaum's chapter 6 on the evolution of popular culture at the end of the nineteenth century is perceptive throughout. See also Richard Terdiman, *Discourse/Counter-Discourse: The Theory and Practice of Symbolic Resistance in Nineteenth-Century France* (Ithaca: Cornell University Press, 1985), chap. 2.

84. *Le Journal,* 26 September 1937.

85. Bommart, *Fish,* 12–14.

86. Michael B. Palmer, *Des petits journaux aux grands agences: naissance du journalisme moderne* (Paris: Aubier Montaigne, 1983), 23–32, 114, 171, 180–81, 253; Francine Amaury, *Histoire du plus grand quotidien de la Troisième République: Le Petit Parisien, 1876–1944* (Paris: Presses universitaires de France, 1972); Bellanger, *Histoire,* 3:140–43, 220–22, 275–81, 295–316; Tannenbaum, *1900,* 228–37; Madeleine Varin d'Ainvelle, *La presse en France: genèse et évolution de ses fonctions psycho-sociales* (Paris: Presses universitaires de France, 1965), 201–25; Berenson, *Trial,* 211–17.

87. Bellanger, *Histoire,* 3:270–74. For these affairs see chapter 1.

88. *L'Eclair,* 14 December 1890, "AFFAIRE SELIVERSTOFF/COMMENT J'AI FAIT EVADER PADLEWSKI" by Georges De Labruyère.

89. *Le Matin,* 12 February 1909 (quoted), 17 February 1909 (on torture).

90. Bellanger, *Histoire,* 3:449–60; Amaury, *Histoire,* 101, 280–91, 420.

91. Bellanger, *Histoire,* 3:397, 122–30, 280, 476.

92. Ibid., 3:460.

93. *Paris-Soir,* 26 May 1938.

94. Bellanger, *Histoire,* 3:524–25.

95. Ibid., 527, 597–602; Catherine Maisonneuve, "Détective" (Mémoire de l'Université de droit, économie, et sciences sociales, Paris II, 1974), 5, 9–11, 64, 70–71; Courrière, *Kessel,* 330–34, 415; Marcel Montarron, *Tout ce joli monde* (Paris: Table Ronde, 1965).

96. *Le Matin,* 13 November 1937.

97. *Paris-Soir,* 23 February 1938.

98. Accounts of her life in newspapers vary. A good corrective is Grey, *Général,* 132–49.

99. *Paris-Soir,* 3 October 1937.

100. AA Botschaft Madrid, AZ: 700–709, Frankreich 1937–1940, December 1939.

101. Montarron, *Tout,* 39.

102. *Le Petit Parisien,* 12–17 December 1938.

103. For an example of an earlier argument for control, see Robert J. Young, *In Command of France: French Foreign Policy and Military Planning, 1933–1940* (Cambridge, Mass.: Harvard University Press, 1978).

Chapter Four: Shanghai

1. Jean Marquès-Rivière, *La Chine dans le monde* (Paris: Payot, 1935; 3,000 copies printed), 122; O.-P. Gilbert, *Courrier d'Asie* (Paris: Gallimard, 1937; 5,500 copies printed), 10; Albert Londres, *La Chine en folie* (Paris: Albin Michel, 1925), 191–92.

2. Betty Peh-T'i Wei, *Shanghai: Crucible of Modern China* (Oxford: Oxford University Press, 1987), 5–8.

3. Ibid., 213; *All About Shanghai: A Standard Guidebook* (1934–1935; reprint, Oxford: Oxford Paperbacks, 1986), 33–34; Marie-Claire Bergère, *The Golden Age of the Chinese Bourgeoisie, 1911–1937,* trans. Janet Lloyd (Cambridge: Cambridge University Press, 1989), 100.

4. Marc Chadourne, *China,* trans. Harry Block (New York: Covici-Friede, 1932; originally published as *Chine* [Paris: Plon, 1931; 19,470 copies printed]), 78.

5. Wei, *Shanghai,* 123–27, 154, 159–60. The source to see on Shanghai's Chinese entrepreneurs is Bergère, *Golden Age.* There is also a good discussion of foreign business in Nicholas Clifford's superb account of Shanghai in the 1920s: *Spoilt Children of Empire: Westerners in Shanghai and the Chinese Revolution of the 1920s* (Hanover: University Press of New England, 1991).

6. Marquès-Rivière, *Chine,* 118; Francis de Croisset, *Le dragon blessé* (Paris: Grasset, 1936), 54; Chadourne, *China,* 77.

7. *All About Shanghai,* 1, 29–32, 125. The statistics are from the early to mid-1930s.

8. MAE Asie 1918–1929 Chine 2e partie 1922–1929 336, 9 July 1923, pp. 32–37, 18 February 1924, pp. 52–70.

9. *All About Shanghai,* 118 (on bodies); Vicki Baum, *Shanghai '37,* trans. Basil Creighton (1939; reprint, Oxford: Oxford University Press, 1986), 345 (the book was first published in German in Amsterdam under the title *Hotel Shanghai*); Charles B. Maybon and Jean Fredet, *Histoire de la concession française de Changhaï* (Paris: Plon, 1929), 249–50.

10. Jean Raynaud, *Guerre en Asie* (Dinard: Braun et Liorit, 1939), 86; Marc Chadourne, *Tour de la terre: Extrême-Orient* (Paris: Plon, 1935), 128; Gilbert, *Courrier,* 10.

11. SMP reel 7, D 3094.

12. Chennevier, *Combe,* 143–44 (on Buisson); AN F7 14679 (on the Corsican — Joseph T., and on Emmanuel Y.); SMP reel 66, IO 8983.

13. Wei, *Shanghai,* 113, 146.

14. Much of the following account is indebted to Brian G. Martin, "'The Pact with the Devil': The Relationship between the Green Gang and the French Concession authorities, 1925–1935," *Papers on Far Eastern History* 39 (March 1989): 93–116. See also SMP reel 56, D 9319, "Memorandum on Mr. Tu Yueh-sung alias Tu Yuin"; MAE Asie 1918–1929 Chine 2e partie 1922–1929 336, 18 February 1924, 21 July 1924; Wei, *Shanghai,* 3–4, 228–35; Clifford, *Spoilt,* 48–52, 251–56, 267–68.

15. There is also the case of the ex-detective Alfonsi who left the force in 1922. In 1924 he returned to Shanghai practically broke. Failing to regain his position with the concession police, he pimped for a while and then worked in a questionable capacity for a French lawyer. In 1930 he went to Indochina where he was arrested and convicted for contraband traffic in arms. Upon leaving prison he returned to Shanghai where he was suspected of being an arms and drug merchant. As of 1935 he was living in a room above a cheap Chinese restaurant. See SMP reel 23, D 6695, 18 May 1935.

16. Wei, *Shanghai,* 235 (which quotes *Who's Who*).

17. MM 1BB7 93, 8 December 1938 (Service transit de Shanghaï, "Situations et problèmes dans le Pacifique," 96-page report, p. 55).

18. Jean Fontenoy, *Shanghaï secret* (Paris: Grasset, 1938), 89–90.

19. *All About Shanghai,* xi.

20. SMP reel 34, D 8012, 3 July 1937, 19 July 1937.

21. Gilbert, *Courrier,* 8, 12, 207–8.

22. Champly, *Road.* For other descriptions of White Russian women see Gilbert, *Courrier,* 183–95 (quoted 187, "femmes russes"); R. D'Auxion de Ruffé, *Chine et chinois d'aujourd'hui: le nouveau péril jaune* (Paris: Berger-Levrault, 1926), 231–36; Titaÿna, *Nuits chaudes* (Paris: Gallimard, 1934), 107–9; Chadourne, *China,* 96; G. E. Miller, *Shanghai, The Paradise of Adventurers* (New York: Orsay Publishing House, 1937), 31–33.

23. MI 25344, 6 February 1930 (on Semenov's organization in the Orient with its center in Shanghai); MM 1BB7 93, 10 December 1936 (Service transit de Shanghaï, "Compte-rendu de renseignements no. 14," p. 19: on Semenov's recruitment in Shanghai and his ties to the Japanese); OM Affaires politiques 1416, 15 March 1938 (Bulletin mensuel de renseignements [hereafter, BMR]; again on the Japanese, White Russians, and Semenov); Hoover N., letter dated 2 July 1937 (from Miller to Michel Sobludaeff).

24. SMP reel 34, D 8016, 20 July 1937. This report describes Znamenskii (Znamensky) as a highly nervous individual and raises questions about the reliability of the information he was providing, especially in regard to his language skills.

25. Barbara W. Tuchman, *Stilwell and the American Experience in China, 1911–1945* (New York, Bantam, 1972), 119, 135–38.

26. SMP reel 50, D 8394, 25 July 1938, 13 March 1938, 14 March 1938.

27. SMP reel 56, D 9341 (on Dick); Paule Herfort, *Sous le soleil levant (vo-*

yage aventureux) (Paris: Baudinière, 1943), 104; *Vu et Lu,* "Shanghaï: sa grandeur, ses mystères," 25 August 1937; Malraux, *Man's Fate;* Charles Plisnier, *Faux passeports* (Paris: R. A. Corréa, 1937). See also Gilbert, *Courrier;* Champly, *Road;* Baum, *Shanghai;* Fontenoy, *Shanghaï,* 43, 204–5; Boucard, *Les Dessous de L'intelligence service,* 195.

28. OM PA 9, 3, 17 August 1912 ("Note" in Mission Przyluski juin–juillet 1912 dossier), 2 October 1913 (Beauvais to Sarraut).

29. AN F7 13498, 29 November 1926 ("Action bolchevique à Shanghaï"); C. Martin Wilbur and Julie Lien-ying How, *Missionaries of Revolution: Soviet Advisers and Nationalist China, 1920–1927* (Cambridge, Mass.: Harvard University Press, 1989), 322.

30. A renegade Soviet intelligence agent who called himself Captain Pick provided crucial information that allowed detectives in 1927 to shadow and ferret out Russians seeking to hide among the thousands of foreigners in the city; Pick published a book that detailed a vast Soviet conspiracy in the East. His real name was Eugen Kozhevnikov and he appears to have worked at one time for both American and British intelligence. In 1931 he was sentenced to a year in prison for having posed as a military adviser to the Chinese army in an arms deal worth nearly two million dollars — another life consistent with the age and one that reeks of the peculiar atmosphere of Shanghai. Wilbur, *Missionaries,* 422; SMP reel 6, D 2523, 22 September 1931, 10 May 1932; Eugene Pick, *China in the Grip of the Reds* (Shanghai: North China Daily News and Herald, 1927; published in France as *La Chine dans les griffes rouges,* trans. Michel Egrory [Paris: Editions Spes, 1928]).

31. SMP reel 1, D 68, 25 February 1929, 28 January 1930 (on Bulgakova-Belskii/Boulgakova-Belsky); OM SLIII 133, 23 May 1930; Daniel Hémery, *Révolutionnaires vietnamiens et pouvoir colonial en Indochine: communistes, trotskystes, nationalistes à Saigon de 1932 à 1937* (Paris: Editions François Maspero, 1975), 25–26; OM SLIII 59, April 1937; OM SLVIII 14, 11 February 1933 (22-page Straits settlements note); Johnson, *Instance,* 66–83, 103, 162–64; *Rote Kapelle,* 277–78, 286–87. Hamburger's brother was Jürgen Kuczynski, who was involved with Klaus Fuchs.

32. MAE E Asie–Océanie Affaires communes 1930–1940 90, 22 April 1936, pp. 204–6.

33. SMP reel 57, D 9388, 30 December 1940, 26 March 1941, 8 April 1941.

34. Mader, *Hitlers Spionagegenerale,* 306, 312; SMP reel 1, D 67, 25 February 1929; MA RW49/58, RW49/523, Otto Benecke (steward on the steamer *Gneisenau*).

35. MM 1BB7 93, 7 February 1929; MAE E Asie–Océanie Indochine française 1930–1940 52, 21 January 1938, 30 July 1938, 2 March 1939; OM SLIII 48, March–April 1931 ("Les associations anti-françaises," part I, p. 46).

36. SMP reel 58, D 9478(c); SMP reel 59, D 9543(c), 21 November 1939, 5 March 1941.

37. Wei, *Shanghai,* 178 (quoted), 185–204; Geoffrey Barraclough, *An Introduction to Contemporary History* (New York: Basic Books, 1964).

38. Johnson, *Instance,* 46–47.

39. Wilbur, *Missionaries;* Franz Borkenau, *World Communism: A History of the Communist International* (1939; reprint, Ann Arbor: University of Michigan Press, 1962), 289–93.

40. Marie-Claire Bergère, "'The Other China': Shanghai from 1919 to 1949," in *Shanghai: Revolution and Development in an Asian Metropolis,* ed. Christopher Howe (Cambridge: Cambridge University Press, 1981), 11.

41. Wilbur, *Missionaries,* 60–61.

42. Malraux, *Man's Fate.*

43. Raynaud, *Asie,* 86–89.

44. Martin, "Pact," 98, 113.

45. *All About Shanghai,* 197–98. Altogether there were nine steamship lines one could take from Europe to Shanghai.

46. Joseph Kessel, *Wagon-lit* (Paris: Gallimard, 1932), 12–13; Chadourne, *China,* 96; de Croisset, *Dragon,* 79; *Vu et Lu,* 25 August 1937; Herfort, *Sous le soleil,* 101–2; Gilbert, *Courrier,* 8–12; Baum, *Shanghai,* 393–95; Edgar Snow, *Journey to the Beginning* (New York: Random House, 1958), 16–17. Fontenoy was a journalist and Havas agent who spent time in Shanghai in the late twenties or early thirties. He sent at least one intelligence report to the government from there. Later he became a follower of Eugène Deloncle (a Cagoule terrorist) and second in command of Deloncle's Mouvement socialiste révolutionnaire in 1940. During the Second World War he was to fight on the Russian front with the Anti-Bolshevik Legion. See Bertram Gordon, *Collaborationism in France During the Second World War* (Ithaca: Cornell Univesity Press, 1990), 69–71; OM SLIII 133, 23 May 1930.

47. For this and the next two place-names I have retained the original spelling from the French text.

48. SHAT, 7N 709, 30 April 1915.

49. OM Affaires politiques 900, 27 June 1936 (GG AOF to Ministry of Colonies).

50. OM Affaires politiques 1416, 26 February 1937 (BMR no. 12, annexe no. 1, p. 3 — quoted). This report is signed by Colonel Jacomey, chef de la section d'études. On Ahlers: ibid., p. 16–17. See also Whealey, *Hitler and Spain,* 123, 125 (where he identifies Ahlers as an intelligence operative).

51. AN F60 707, 1 February 1938 ("L'action allemande en Afrique"), pp. 9–10; OM Affaires politiques 1416, 15 July 1938 (BMR, pp. 72–73); ibid., 15 June 1937 (BMR on Spanish Guinea); OM Affaires politiques 900, March 1936.

52. OM Affaires politiques 900, March 1936; AN F60 707, 1 February 1938 ("Action allemande"), p. 4; AN F60 754, 8 May 1935 ("La propagande étrangère en Maroc"), p. 7; OM Affaires politiques 1416, 15 July 1938 (BMR, pp. 70–71); OM Affaires politiques 900, n.d. (approx. 1935–1936; entitled "Cameroun"). For earlier reports on German intrigues in Africa right after the war see OM SLIII92, 31 December 1919, 10 July 1920, 16 October 1920, 13 June 1922 (internal memo dated 10 August 1922), and the Impex reports cited in chapter 1. See also Schellenberg's description of his spy mission to Dakar in 1938 in Walter Schellenberg, *The Labyrinth,* trans. Louis Hagen (New York: Harper, 1956), 38–42.

53. OM SLIX 3, 22 July 1927; Mader, *Hitlers Spionagegenerale,* 306–7, 314, 318; MA RW49/528 (Benecke — steward); MA RW49/530 (Reck); MAE E Asie–Océanie Affaires communes 1930–1940 90, 7 January 1938, p. 252; OM Affaires politiques 1416 15 July 1938 (BMR, pp. 74–76); ibid., 15 August 1938 (BMR, pp. 86–87). Although the Germans trod softly in the Middle East during the 1930s to avoid antagonizing either the British or Mussolini, by late 1937 or at least 1938 they were adopting a more aggressive policy, including Abwehr activities: Robert Lewis Melka, "The Axis and the Arab Middle East: 1930–1945" (Ph.D. diss., University of Minnesota, 1966), 36–76. See also Vernier, 38–39, 60–61.

54. See the discussion of White Russians and Japan in chapter 2. See also SHAT 7N 3124, 26 December 1935; Louis Allen, "Japanese Intelligence Systems," *Journal of Contemporary History* 22 (October 1987): 554–55.

55. On Dutch East Indies: OM Affaires politiques 2655, 11 March 1933, 18 March 1933, 1 December 1937; OM Affaires politiques 1416, 10 July 1939 (BMR, p. 41). On China: MM 1BB7 93, 8 December 1938 (96-page Shanghai transit report, p. 44). On Indochina, MAE E Asie–Océanie Indochine française 1930–1940 30, 29 May 1935, pp. 44–45. On Port Said: MAE E Asie–Océanie Affaires communes 1930–1940 100, 11 June 1938, pp. 139–42. On European agents: OM SLII 23, 4 May 1938; AN F7 14758, 1 March 1939. From the OM SLII 23 dossier it is clear that the French were tapping Japanese embassy phone conversations. According to Paul Paillole, phone taps allowed French counterintelligence to uncover a Japanese attempt to steal the design plans to a French fighter plane engine. Paillole, *Services,* 83.

56. Archival material on worldwide Comintern activity is voluminous. Some of the most interesting international reporting includes AN F7 13506, n.d. (probably from early 1920s; first page missing); OM SLIII 101, 31 December 1923 ("Note sur la propagande"); AN F7 13170, 29 November 1929 ("Chronique de l'action du komintern en Orient"); OM Affaires politiques 1416, 15 June 1937 (BMR). On centrals: SHAT 3H 102, "Fin août 1925" (on transfers from Vienna); OM SLIII 133, 6 November 1933 ("Rapport de mission aux Straits settlements," p. 18); OM SLIII 59, January 1937 ("Note périodique no. 48"). On formal training in Russia: OM SLIII 133, especially 22 March 1933. On circuits: OM SLIII 141, 24 November 1931, 25 January 1932; OM SLIII 56, n.d. (approx. 1929, "La propagande communiste," p. 22 on Bon Marché). On the Sûreté and Colonial intelligence: Hémery, *Révolutionnaires,* 157–60; OM SLIII 133, 14 April 1925, 6 November 1933 ("Rapport," p. 2 on "Typhoon"); MAE E Asie–Océanie Indochine française 1930–1940 52, 21 January 1938.

57. OM SLIII 48, 23 October 1929 ("Les associations anti-françaises"), pp. 5–6.

58. See, e.g., Stephen Kern, *The Culture of Time and Space: 1880–1918* (Cambridge, Mass.: Harvard University Press, 1983), 223–58.

59. Barrie Cadwallader, *Crisis of the European Mind: A Study of André Malraux and Drieu La Rochelle* (Cardiff: University of Wales Press, 1981).

60. OM SLIII 133, 12 March 1935, 19 December 1934; OM SLIII 35, 19 June 1929 (on proposal of Chinese Nationalists to build a radio station that

could reach Chinese communities around the world); AN F60 710, 26 April 1939; *Paris-Soir,* 28 January 1938, 9 August 1939; see also chapters 1, 2. On the worldwide scope of radio see Arno Huth, *La radiodiffusion: puissance mondiale* (Paris: Gallimard, 1937). Initiatives toward setting up worldwide radio networks preceded the war. See Daniel R. Headrick, *The Invisible Weapon: Telecommunications and International Politics, 1851–1945* (New York: Oxford University Press, 1991), chap. 7.

61. See, for example, the following assertions of a sense of control that accompanied warnings or identifications of suspicious characters: OM Affaires politiques 900, 27 June 1936 (GGAOF to Ministry of Colonies); OM Affairs politiques 920, March 1928 (Annex to report no. 1 of the Haut comité méditerranéen, pp. 69–70); AN F60 707, 1 February 1938 ("L'action allemande en Afrique"); OM SLIII 56, n. d. ("Note," p. 7).

62. Jean Marquès-Rivière, *L'U.R.S.S.,* 316, 345–46, 297; Antoine Zischaka, *Le Japon dans le monde: l'expansion nippone, 1854–1934* (Paris: Payot, 1934), 145–46, 150–51; Pierre Dehillotte, *Gestapo* (Paris: Payot, 1940); Allard, *Quand; Le Petit Journal,* 24 April 1931; Titaÿna, *Nuits,* 122; Lucieto, *Livrés;* Jean Bommart, *La dame de Valparaiso: les débuts du poisson chinois* (1940; reprint, Paris: Editions de Flore, 1948); Apestéguy, *Roi* (this book won the Grand Prix du Roman d'Aventures in 1939 and eventually sold 50,000 copies); Jean Joffroy, *Espionnage en Asie* (Paris: Baudinière, 1939). *Espionnage* was published in the Secret War series, and Joffroy may be a Marquès-Rivière pseudonym. Before 1914 only the Russo-Japanese War and pan-Islam seem to have educed much interest in spies in faraway places. See such works as R. Castex, *Jaunes contre blancs: le problème militaire indo-chinois* (Paris: Henri Charles-Lavauzelle, 1905), 25, 48–49; André Chéradame, *Le monde et la guerre russo-japonaise* (Paris: Plon, 1906); Landau, *Pan-Islam,* 65–67.

63. Bernard Wasserstein, *The Secret Lives of Trebitsch Lincoln* (New Haven: Yale University Press, 1988).

64. Laporte, *Bouddha;* Imré Gyomaï, *Trebitsch Lincoln: le plus grand aventurier du siècle* (Paris: Editions de France, 1939); Boucard, *Les Dessous de L'intelligence service,* 77–86; Victor Meulenijzer, *Colonel,* 221–29; *Le Petit Journal,* 3–4 May 1931; *Paris-Soir,* 26 March 1934, 28 June 1938; *Vu,* 24 June 1932, 11 November 1932; Lucieto, *Livrés,* 107; Legrand, *Sept;* Bommart, *Valparaiso.* Much of the legend was built on Lincoln's own self-promotion. On this see Wasserstein, *Secret,* and the two books Lincoln published about himself, I. T. T. Lincoln, *Revelations of an International Spy* (New York: Robert M. McBride, 1916); J. T. Trebitsch Lincoln, *The Autobiography of an Adventurer,* trans. Emile Burns (New York: Henry Holt, 1932).

65. Wasserstein, *Secret Lives,* 120, 199, 219–20.

66. On Russo-Japanese conflict see René Pinon, *La lutte pour le Pacifique: origines et résultats de la guerre russo-japonaise* (Paris: Perrin, 1906), ix. See also Chéradame, *Monde;* Castex, *Jaunes.* For a more sanguine view from these years see Louis Aubert, *Paix japonaise* (Paris: Armand Colin, 1906).

67. A. Demangeon, *Le déclin de l'Europe* (1920; reprint, Paris: Guenegaud, 1975), 12–13; Edouard Herriot, *La Russie nouvelle* (Paris: J. Ferenczi et Fils, 1922), 271; Pierre Lyautey, *Chine ou Japon (1932–1933)* (Paris: Plon, 1933;

5,500 copies printed), 235; Gregory Bienstock, *La lutte pour le Pacifique*, trans. André Guieu (Paris: Payot, 1938; 3,000 copies printed), 9–10; Chadourne, *Extrême-Orient*, 217 (12,100 copies printed); Roger Labonne, *Le tapis vert du Pacifique* (Paris: Berger-Levrault, 1936; estimated sales 2,000–3,000), vii; A. F. Legendre, *La crise mondiale: l'Asie contre l'Europe* (Paris: Plon, 1932).

68. Maurice Muret, *The Twilight of the White Races,* trans. Mrs. Touzalin (New York: Charles Scribner's, 1926; originally published as *Le crépuscule des nations blancs* [Paris: Payot, 1925]); Lothrop Stoddard, *The Rising Tide of Color* (New York: Charles Scribner's, 1920; trans. by Abdel Doysié as *Le flot montant des peuples de couleur contre la suprématie mondiale des blancs* [Paris: Payot, 1925; 3,000 copies printed]); Massis, *Défense* (15,400 copies printed); Chadourne, *Extrême-Orient*, 221; *Paris-Soir,* 11 November 1938 (advertising a forthcoming article in *Match*); Herriot's remarks cited in *Excelsior,* 22 January 1933 (circulation about 100,000); each of Sax Rohmer's Fu Manchu novels published in France in the 1930s seems to have sold out its printing run in the course of the decade. For a good survey of yellow-peril literature in France see Jacques Decornoy, *Péril jaune, peur blanche* (Paris: Grasset, 1970). On Jews: Céline, *Bagatelles,* 77; Muret, *Twilight,* 45–58; Jérome Tharaud and Jean Tharaud, *Quand Israël est roi* (Paris: Plon, 1921; 40,000 copies printed), 19–29, 290–91; Jean Giraudoux, *Pleins pouvoirs* (Paris: Gallimard, 1939; 20,900 copies printed), 62; Champly, *Raoul,* 206; Paul Morand's discussion of Renaud's name change in *Bouddha vivant* (Paris: Grasset, 1927; 49,000 copies printed), 15–16. For earlier references to Asiatic Jews see Wilson, *Ideology,* 334, 475.

69. See, for example, the two descriptions of train travel in Chadourne, *China,* 172–73; Yvon Delbos, *L'expérience rouge* (Paris: Au Sans Pareil, 1933), 39.

70. Marc Chadourne, *L'U.R.S.S. sans passion* (Paris: Plon, 1932; 15,900 copies printed), v; Roland Dorgelès, *Vive la liberté* (Paris: Albin Michel, 1937), 14; Paul Morand, *Rien que la terre* (Paris: Grasset, 1926), 23.

71. De Chessin, *Nuit,* 5–6, 243. For some other examples see A. de Pouvourville, *Griffes rouges sur l'Asie* (Paris: Baudinière, 1933), 226–29; Legendre, *Crise.*

72. Meulenijzer, *Colonel,* 221.

73. Werner Otto von Hentig, *Meine Diplomatenfahrt ins verschlossene Land* (Berlin: Ullstein, 1918), quoted 108, 159; Vogel, *Persien;* Gehrke, *Persien.*

74. Good summaries of Arctic and tropical exploration can be found in Pierre Berton, *The Arctic Grail: The Quest for the North West Passage and the North Pole, 1818–1909* (New York: Viking, 1988) and Alan Moorehead, *The White Nile* (New York: Vintage, 1983). On Lenz: Guillen, *L'Allemagne,* 118–20. On Caillié: Galbraith Welch, *The Unveiling of Timbuctoo: The Astounding Adventures of Caillié* (1939; reprint, New York: Carroll and Graf, 1991). On Przhevalskii: Donald Rayfield, *The Dream of Lhasa: The Life of Nikolay Przhevalsky (1839–1888), Explorer of Central Asia* (Athens: Ohio University Press, 1976). On French exploration: Numa Broc, "Les explorateurs français du XIXe siècle reconsidérés," *Revue française d'histoire d'outre-mer* 69 (1982): 237–73; Numa Broc, *Dictionnaire illustrée des explorateurs français du XIX siècle: Afrique* (Paris: Editions du C.T.H.S., 1988). Hopkirk, *Great Game.*

75. Alain Gerbault, *Seul à travers l'Atlantique* (Paris: Grasset, 1924; 99,500 copies printed).

76. Oskar von Niedermayer, *Unter der Glutsonne Irans. Kriegserlebnisse der deutschen Expedition nach Persien und Afghanistan* (Munich: Einhorn, 1925); Vogel, *Persien,* 100–101. On Burton: Byron Farwell, *Burton: A Biography of Sir Richard Francis Burton* (London: Penguin, 1990); Edward Rice, *Captain Sir Richard Francis Burton: The Secret Agent Who Made the Pilgrimage to Mecca, Discovered the Kama Sutra, and Brought the Arabian Nights to the West* (New York: Charles Scribner's Sons, 1990). Despite the grand title of the latter, there is no indication that Burton was acting in any official capacity on his voyage to Mecca nor indeed at any other time during his famous journeys aside from some earlier reconnaissance missions in India.

77. See, for example, L. C. Dunsterville, *The Adventures of Dunsterforce* (London: Edward Arnold, 1920).

78. Vera Brittain, *Testament of Youth* (1933; reprint, London: Penguin, 1989), 526; Emile Pagès, *La grande étape: 1918; ceux de la «sans-fil»* (Paris: Tallandier, 1931); Courrière, *Kessel,* chaps. 7–8.

79. Jean Lacouture, *André Malraux,* trans. Alan Sheridan (New York: Pantheon, 1973; originally published as *André Malraux: une vie dans le siècle* [Paris: Seuil, 1973]), 17.

80. Jacobs, *Borodin.*

81. Wilbur, *Missionaries,* 7–15; Jacobs, *Borodin,* 153–56, 280–81; Vera Vishniakova-Akimova, *Two Years in Revolutionary China, 1925–1927,* trans. Steven Levine (Cambridge, Mass.: Harvard University Press, 1971).

82. Ossendowski was the transliteration of the period under which his editions (including the English) were published.

83. Ferdinand Ossendowski, *Bêtes, hommes, et dieux,* trans. Robert Renard (Paris: Plon, 1924). Quotes are from the English edition, from which the French edition was translated: *Beasts, Men, and Gods* (New York: E. P. Dutton, 1922), 38, 78, 160.

84. Ibid., i. The Robinson Crusoe image was first used in a book review of the original edition. On earlier adventures see Ferdinand Ossendowski, *L'homme et le mystère en Asie,* trans. Robert Renard (Paris: Plon, 1925). According to this edition the earlier volume sold 40,000 copies.

85. Ella Maillart, *Oasis interdites de Pékin au Cachemire* (Paris: Grasset, 1937), 12, 14, 25–26.

86. Seagrave, *Epic.*

87. Luigi Barzini, *Peking to Paris: A Journey Across Two Continents in 1907,* with introduction by Luigi Barzini Jr., trans. L. P. de Castelvecchio (1908; reprint, London: Penguin, 1986), xi, 344.

88. See the sections on Amudsen and Peary in Bertin, *Arctic.*

89. Georges-Marie Haardt and Louis Audoin-Dubreuil, *La croisière noire: expédition Citroën centre-Afrique* (Paris: Plon, 1927; 54,700 copies printed); Georges Le Fèvre, *La croisière jaune* (Paris: Plon, 1933), iv. By the mid-1920s the Croisière noire was the most ambitious expedition among what was becoming practically a fad to drive through or fly over Africa. In 1924–1925 alone there were seven French crossings of Africa by car or caravan and five aerial long-

distance runs over the continent. Some, like Marc Bernard's seaplane crossing of Africa in late 1926, shared in the sort of planning that characterized the Crosière noire. *L'Illustration,* 9 January 1926, pp. 28–32; Edmond Tranin, *Sur le dixième parallèle* (Paris: Grasset, 1926; 3,000 copies sold); Marc Bernard, *En hydravion au dessus du continent noir* (Paris: Grasset, 1927; 10,000 copies printed).

90. Roy Chapman Andrews, *The New Conquest of Central Asia: A Narrative of the Explorations of the Central Asiatic Expeditions in Mongolia and China, 1921–1930* (New York: American Museum of Natural History, 1932), 5, 7, 13, 10, 16–17.

91. Andrews, *New Conquest,* 15, 62–63, 331.

92. L. V. S. Blacker, *Mes patrouilles secrètes en haute Asie,* trans. R. Hendry-Charcot (Paris: Payot, 1933); Dunsterville, *Adventures;* Alma Jane Plotke, "The Dunsterforce Military/Intelligence Mission to North Persia in 1918" (Ph.D. diss., University of California, Los Angeles, 1987).

93. On the cattle drive see SHAT 7N 709, 26 April 1917.

94. Vernier, *Politique,* 97.

95. OM Affaires politiques 900, 27 June 1936; OM Affaires politiques 1416, 26 February 1937; AN F60 707, 1 February 1938.

96. Sven Hedin, *My Life as an Explorer,* trans. Alfhild Huebsch (Garden City: Garden City Publishing, 1925), quoted 15–16, 247; George Kish, *To the Heart of Asia: The Life of Sven Hedin* (Ann Arbor: University of Michigan Press, 1984), quoted page preceding preface.

97. Wasserstein, *Secret,* 227; SMP rccl 58, D 9478 (c), 11 December 1939.

98. Nish, "Japanese Intelligence," 17; Hopkirk, *Great Game,* 204; Winstone, *Illicit.*

99. OM Affaires politiques 900, 27 June 1936, 26 July 1934; MAE E Asie–Océanie Affaires communes 63, 21 March 1928, p. 74; Vernier, *Politique,* 50–51, 18 (there is a copy of Vernier in AN F60 707); Melka, "Axis," 49–50; Mader, *Hitlers Spionagegenerale,* 325.

100. Gehrke, *Persien,* 23, 25; Kish, *Heart,* 2, 94–95, 126–29. A book entitled *Germany and World Peace* was published in Sweden in 1937, but not in Germany because Hedin refused to delete certain passages that differed from Nazi ideology.

101. Kish, *Heart,* 111–23; Andrew D. W. Forbes, *Warlords and Muslims in Chinese Central Asia: A Political History of Republican Sinkiang, 1911–1949* (Cambridge: Cambridge University Press, 1986), especially 40 (on Schomberg); Lars-Erik Nyman, *Great Britain and Chinese Russian and Japanese Interests in Sinkiang, 1918–1934* (Malmö: Esselte Studium 1977); AA Forschungsexpedition Sven Hedins, 11 September 1926; Sven Hedin, *Across the Gobi Desert,* trans. H. J. Cant (1931; reprint, New York: Greenwood, 1968).

102. Kish, *Heart,* 115–21; Nyman, *Great Britain,* 55–56, 92–96.

103. Zischaka, *Japon,* 253–59.

104. Le Fèvre, *Croisière jaune,* xv.

105. MAE E Asie 1918–1929 Affaires communes 63, 8 October 1924.

106. Ibid., 24 April 1928. This includes a note dated January 1927, pp. 57–65, and a follow-up note, dated 27 December 1927, pp. 66–71.

107. MAE E Asie–Océanie Affaires communes 1930–1940 116, 6 October

1930, p. 52 (on the release of Bertrand). On Waddington see ibid., 31 March 1931, p. 289.

108. I have left the French transliteration because the family name may have been regularized in France.

109. Le Fèvre, *Croisière jaune*, xxv–ix; MAE E Asie–Océanie Affaires communes 116, 13 March 1930, p. 5, 26 September 1930, p. 42, "Questionnaire pour le lieutenant de vaisseau Point," pp. 42–44.

110. MAE E Asie 1918–1929 Affaires communes 63, 16 March 1929 (quoted); Le Fèvre, *Croisière jaune*, ix. On Goerger and negotiations for passage through the Soviet Union, see also MAE E Asie 1918–1929 Affaires communes 64; MAE E Asie–Océanie Affaires communes 1930–1940 116.

111. Other sponsors included the Société de géographie de France, the Muséum d'histoire naturelle, the Institut d'ethnologie, and the Musée Guimet. Haardt made two trips to the United States to firm up the National Geographic Society's support (including financial) of the expedition.

112. *L'Illustration*, 28 February, 1931, 263–67; Le Fèvre, *Croisière jaune*, xxi.

113. Le Fèvre, *Croisière jaune*, xxx–ii.

114. Ibid., xxx, xxxiii–iv; MAE E Asie–Océanie Affaires communes 1930–1940 117, 4 April 1931, 30 April 1931, 24 April 1931.

115. Le Fèvre, *Croisière jaune*, 4. Quoted also from *L'Illustration*, 28 February 1931, "La croisière jaune," 267; ibid., 30 May 1931, "Sur la route de Bagdad," 209; Le Fèvre, *Croisière jaune*, 33. The following account of the expedition, unless otherwise noted, is from Le Fèvre.

116. MAE E Asie–Océanie Affaires communes 1930–1940 116, 18 February 1931; MAE E Asie–Océanie Affaires communes 1930–1940 118, 7 July 1931, 11 July 1931. When the film from the voyage premiered in Paris in 1934 under the title *Croisière jaune*, it was boycotted by the Chinese ambassador. Citroën insisted that the title was necessary to guarantee the success of the movie. The Quai found the title regrettable, but decided there was nothing to do but tell Wellington Koo that there was no intention to slight the Chinese and that the international press was responsible for the continued use of the name. MAE E Asie–Océanie Affaires communes 120, 17 January 1934.

117. Forbes, *Warlords*, 38–127; Nyman, *Great Britain*, especially 100–111 on Ma Chung-ying, Kemal Kaya, and the Soviets.

118. In his negotiations preceding the voyage, Point had agreed to a request of Chin to provide him with several cars and radio sets. These had been forwarded by Citroën, but were held up at Soochow by the revolt. In August Citroën sent three new cars and two radios to replace the first consignment. At the time of Point's captivity in Urumchi, these were still on the way.

119. In Audouin-Dubreuil's version of the trip, Salesse arrived on 11 November and his coming was expected by Haardt. That night Reymond celebrated with a ditty, "String up the Governor," that could have gotten them in hot water if the Chinese had understood the lyrics. Audoin-Dubreuil, *Sur la route de la soie: mon carnet de route de la Méditerranée à la mer de Chine* (Paris: Plon, 1935; 6,600 copies printed), 170–77.

120. Six months later Victor Point would also be dead, committing suicide

in the south of France over a woman he had had an affair with for the past four years. *Le Petit Parisien,* 8, 9 August 1932.

121. *L'Illustration,* "Sur la route de Bagdad," 30 May 1931, 207.

122. Georg Vasel, *My Russian Jailers in China,* trans. Gerald Griffin (London: Hurst and Blackett 1937), caption opposite 64.

123. Audoin-Dubreuil, *Sur la route,* 64; André Goerger, *En marge de la croisière jaune* (Paris: Rieder, 1935), 165–69.

124. Fabien Sabates and Sylvie Schweitzer, *André Citroën: les chevrons de la gloire* (Paris: E.P.A., 1980), 11–12.

125. *New York Times,* 17 March 1932; *London Times,* 17 March 1932; *Le Petit Parisien,* 17 March 1932; Le Fèvre, *Croisière jaune,* ii–iii, xiv.

126. Le Fèvre, *Croisière jaune,* xxxii.

127. *L'Illustration,* 27 August, 1932, "Le chemin du retour," 547, 549.

128. Fussell, *Great War,* 321.

129. Vernier, *Politique,* 24, 110–11; NA T77–884, 10–3.–39 (original emphasis); Segrè, *Italo Balbo,* 193, 215–18, 230–65.

130. Goerger, *En marge,* 233.

131. Robert Métais, *Cellule 20* (Paris: Baudinière, 1937); Yrondy, *Cocaine,* 117. On Pierre Darlix see below.

132. *Paris-Soir,* 24 September 1937 (phantom ships); *Le Matin,* 3 June 1932, *Le Petit Parisien,* 5 June 1932 (*Georges-Philippar*); *Paris-Soir,* 20 April 1939, 2, 4 May 1939 (*Paris*); AN F7 13170, 17 January 1929; OM SLIII 133, 6 November 1933, pp. 21–22; OM SLIII 59, December 1936, p. 12; OM SLIII 141, 24 November 1931; OM SLIII 35, 26 May 1930; SMP reel 1, D68, 28 January 1930; SMP reel 1, D40, 11 January 1930; MA RW49/528, RW5/305, RW49/529; AN F60 754, 22 February 1935 (Irène Z.).

133. *Le Petit Parisien,* 10 March 1932, 29 September 1937; Bardanne, *Documents,* 48. See also Montarron, *Poison,* 68.

134. AN F7 14744, 13 November 1926; MA RW5/304; Paillole, *Services,* 101.

135. *L'Echo de Paris,* 1 September 1932.

136. Londres, *Comitadjis,* 235–36; Ehrenburg, *Memoirs,* 262; Reber, *Terrorisme,* 116.

137. Société nationale des chemins de fer français Archives, Paris (hereafter, SNCF) 29 J21, *Guide européene,* 1936; *Plaisir de France,* July–December 1938.

138. John Maxtone-Graham, *The Only Way to Cross* (New York: Macmillan/Collier, 1972), 255, 273, 286, 289; *Le Petit Parisien,* 4 June 1935; *Paris-Soir,* 4 June 1935; *Plaisir de France,* July–December 1938.

139. Morand, *Flèche,* 16–17. This book was published in a series subsidized by the businesses or firms each book salivated over: Courrière, *Kessel,* 415.

140. George Clare, *Last Waltz in Vienna* (New York: Avon 1983), 155; SNCF, Livre d'or 1937 Exposition internationale, 118; *Plaisir de France,* July–December 1938; *All About Shanghai,* ii, 101; *L'Illustration,* 18 April, 1936, 4 January 1936.

141. SNCF 29 J7, Compagnie des chemins de fer PLM, Exposition coloniale internationale, Paris 1931; SNCF, Livre d'or 1937 (on CGT figures); John Stilgoe, *Metropolitan Corridor: Railroads and the American Scene* (New Haven:

Yale University Press, 1983), 57–61; Fussell, *Abroad*, 63–64, 132–33; Maxtone-Graham, *Only*, 242–43, 267–93; *The New Yorker Twenty-fifth Anniversary Album, 1925–1950* (New York: Harper, 1951). See also the coverage of the *Normandie's* maiden voyage in *Paris-Soir.*

142. Goerger, *En marge*, 191–92, 35, 49, 175, 228; Morand, *Rien*, 65; Deval, *Rives*, 111.

143. Morand, *Rien*, 237–39.

144. Emile Schreiber, *Cette année à Jérusalem* (Paris: Plon, 1933; 6,600 copies printed), 37; Chadourne, *Orient*, 183; de Croisset, *Jade*, 3–4; Morand, *Rien*, 243–44; Titaÿna, *La caravane des morts* (Paris: Editions des Portiques, 1930), 93; Goerger, *En marge*, 67. For a more favorable view of East Asian hotels, see René Jouglet, *Dans le sillage des jonques* (Paris: Grasset, 1935; 8,000 copies printed), 105.

145. H. Celarié, *Promenades en Indochine* (Paris: Baudinière, 1937), 9–10.

146. Jean-Baptiste Duroselle, *Politique étrangère de la France: la décadence, 1932–1939* (Paris: Imprimerie nationale, 1979), 185–88 (Duroselle does acknowledge a large travel literature however, 195–96).

147. Printing figures of travel books varied, some going through one edition of several thousand copies (a somewhat standard printing run between the wars), others ranging into four and five figures. Chadourne's *Chine*, for example, had a printing of 19,470, de Croisset's *Dragon* 20,000, and Morand's *Rien* enjoyed a printing of 32,000.

148. Robert Wohl, *The Generation of 1914* (Cambridge, Mass.: Harvard University Press, 1979), 226–29.

149. Bertrand, *Seule*, 26.

150. Guy de Larigaudie, *La route aux aventures: Paris-Saigon en automobile* (Paris: Plon, 1939; 6,600 copies printed), 93, 143, 167, v–vi. Lest it be thought such focuses were sui generis, it is wise to remember that the magazine *Plaisir de France*, devoted to the travels and homes of the rich, was launched in the midst of the depression in 1934 and had a printing per edition of 45,000 in 1939. Bellanger, *Histoire*, 3:598.

151. Claude Blanchard, *De notre envoyé spécial Claude Blanchard: quelques-uns de ses meilleurs reportages* (Paris: Editions Défense de la France, 1948), 61; Goerger, *En marge*, 293; Andrée Viollis, *Indochine S.O.S.* (Paris: Gallimard 1935), 38–39; de Croisset, *Dragon*, 130; Vishniakova-Akimova, *Two Years*, 146.

152. Deval, *Rives*, 94–95, 139, 142–44; 3,300 copies were printed.

153. André Gide, *Back from the U.S.S.R.*, trans. Dorothy Bussy (London: Martin Secker and Warburg, 1937; originally published as *Retour de L'U.R.S.S.* [Paris: Gallimard 1936]), 49; Schreiber, *Comment on vit en U.R.S.S.* (Paris: Plon, 1931; 14,300 copies printed), 59, 200–201; Delbos, *L'expérience*, 14; Goerger, *En marge*, 13, 62 (story); Chadourne, *China*, 157–58; Maurice Dekobra, *Confucius en pull-over, ou le beau voyage en Chine* (Paris: Baudinière, 1934), 52; Emile Schreiber, *On vit pour 1 franc par jour: Indes-Chine-Japon 1935* (Paris: Baudinière, 1935), 137; Deval, *Rives*, 128–29; Jouglet, *Sillages*, 50–54; Pierre Billotey, *L'Indochine en zigzags* (Paris: Albin Michel, 1929), 8–9.

154. Andrée Viollis, *Le Japon et son empire* (Paris: Grasset, 1933; 6,000 copies printed), 101; *L'Illustration*, 8 August, 1931, 503–4; Schreiber, *On vit*, 238;

Schreiber, *Jérusalem,* 31–32; Claude Farrère, *Le grand drame de l'Asie* (Paris: Flammarion, 1938), 134; Jean Dorsenne, *Faudra-t-il évacuer l'Indochine?* (Paris: Nouvelle Société d'Edition, 1932), especially 21–33, 212ff.; Billotey, *Zigzags,* 15–16, 24, 77; Louis Roubaud, *Viet Nam: la tragédie indo-chinoise* (Paris: Librairie Valois, 1931), 276–84; Celarié, *Promenades,* 82, 88–89.

155. Oliver Sayler, *Russia, White or Red* (Boston: Little Brown, 1919), 62, 64; Voska, *Spy and Counterspy,* 234–35; Alya Rachmanova, *Flight from Terror,* trans. Ida Zeitlin (New York: John Day, 1933); Ehrenburg, *Memoirs,* 72. NEP stands for new economic policy, a partial return to the market in the 1920s.

156. Delbos, *L'expérience,* 22.

157. Georges Le Fèvre, *Un bourgeois au pays des soviets* (Paris: Tallandier, 1929), 65, 70; Schreiber, *On vit,* 297.

158. Dorgelès, *Vive,* 263; Maillart *Oasis,* 25–26; Goerger, *En marge,* 224–28; Bertrand, *Seule,* 31–32, 36; de Croisset, *Dragon,* 79, 125, 191.

159. Barzini, *Peking,* xviii–xix; Palmer, *Petits journaux,* 68–69, 96, 215–18, 231. On more extensive foreign networks after the war, see Bellanger, *Histoire,* 3:479.

160. Viollis, *Japon;* Viollis, *Indochine S.O.S.;* Roubaud, *Viet Nam;* Dorsenne, *Faudra-t-il;* Lyautey, *Chine;* Raynaud, *Guerre,* 85, 149.

161. For a good example of this kind of writing see Marc Chadourne's *China* and the two volumes of *Tour de la terre.* All are lightweight fare yet nevertheless of the *China* or *U.S. Today* genre. The urge to report turns up in nearly every travel account I have looked at, e.g., Morand, *Rien;* Deval, *Rives;* Maillart, *Oasis;* Jouglet, *Sillages;* Goerger, *En marge;* and Schreiber's books.

162. Delbos, *L'expérience,* 13.

163. Kupferman, *Au pays des soviets: le voyage français en Union soviétique, 1917–1939* (Paris: Gallimard, 1979), 172–82.

164. In addition to books cited above on travel to the USSR, see: Alfred Fabre-Luce, *Russie 1927* (Paris: Grasset, 1927; 5,300 copies sold by 1940); Pierre Herbart, *En U.R.S.S.* (Paris: Gallimard, 1937); Alfred Silbert, *U.R.S.S. et nouvelle Russie* (Paris: Editions Denoël, 1938); Charles Vildrac, *Russie neuve (voyage en U.R.S.S.)* (Paris: Emile-Paul Frères, 1937).

165. Schreiber, *U.R.S.S.,* 214–16; Chadourne, *U.R.S.S.,* 218–20 (15,900 copies printed); Dorgelès, *Vive,* 305–11; Le Fèvre, *Bourgeois,* 246.

166. Wohl, *Generation,* 226–29.

167. Pierre Darlix, *Terrorisme sur le monde* (Paris: Baudinière, 1932), 196–99; Darlix, *Un soir en pullman . . .* (Paris: Baudinière, 1929), 8–9; Darlix, *Smyrne,* 111–12, 127.

168. Kessel, *Wagon-lit,* 13; Morand, *Rien,* 31–32; Londres, *Chine,* 21.

169. Bertrand, *Seule,* 8–9, 153–54, 160–62, 216ff., 284, 151; 4,400 copies were printed.

170. Lyautey, *Chine,* 20–21 (on "Boy"); Fabre-Luce, *Russie,* 244–45 (on Caucasus); Celarié, *Promenades,* 94; Le Fèvre, *Croisière jaune,* 14; Viollis, *S.O.S.,* 3; de Croisset, *Jade,* 9; Louis Malleret, *L'exotisme indochinois dans la littérature française depuis 1860* (Paris: Larose, 1934), 2 (Ajalbert quoted); Tranin, *Dixième,* 12.

171. Kessel, *Wagon-lit,* 12–13, 15–16, 27, 51, 50, 54, 57, 143–44, 170,

186–87. On the publishing background to the novel, see Courrière, *Kessel*, 415–16. The book sold about 25,000 copies.

172. Gilbert, *Courrier*, 23–24; Maurice Dekobra, *Madame Joli-supplice*, (Paris: Baudinière, 1934); Chadourne, *China*, 58; 25–26.

173. Quoted in Lesley Blanch, *Pierre Loti: The Legendary Romantic* (New York: Carroll and Graf, 1983), 249. The quote is from Loti's *Vers Ispahan*, published in 1904.

174. Titaÿna, *Caravane*, 156; Goerger, *En marge*, 111; Le Fèvre, *Croisière jaune*, 26.

175. Peter Bishop, *The Myth of Shangri-La: Tibet, Travel Writing, and the Western Creation of Sacred Landscape* (Berkeley: University of California Press, 1989), 116–17, 171–74, chap. 6 (especially 202–4).

176. Morand, *Rien*, 10–11; Maillart, *Oasis*, 70–71. *Oasis* ran to 8,000 copies, and Maillart's account was serialized in *Le Petit Parisien*, March–April 1936.

177. Audoin-Dubreuil, *Soie*, 8; Dorgelès, *Vive*, 238–39.

178. *L'Illustration*, "Les nouvelles routes du monde," 30 August, 1924, 166–67; Andrews, *New Conquest*, 13; Larigaudie, *Route*, 233.

179. Maillart, *Oasis*, 267; *L'Illustration*, "Un service de passagers sur la ligne Casablanca-Dakar," 20 June 1936, 257.

180. Titaÿna, *Caravane*, 10–11, 188.

181. René Pinon, *Fièvres d'Orient*, (Lyons: Editions de la Plus Grande France, 1938), 15; Chadourne, *Extrême-Occident*, 4 (12,100 copies printed).

182. Pierre Loti, *Un pèlerin d'Angkor* (Paris: Calmann-Lévy, 1912), 13–14, 20, 33, 45, 54–55 (quoted), 62–63, 79–81 (quoted), 138, 167; Chris Bongie, *Exotic Memories: Literature, Colonialism and the Fin de Siècle* (Stanford: Stanford University Press, 1991), 120.

183. SNCF 29 J21, Guide européene, 1936; Billotey, *Zigzags*, 243; de Croisset, *Jade*, 76–79, 27–28 (quoted) (13,000 copies printed).

184. Roland Dorgelès, *On the Mandarin Road*, trans. Gertrude Emerson (New York: The Century Co., 1926; originally published as *Sur la route mandarine* [Paris: Albin Michel 1925]), 233–35.

185. Ibid., 34–35, 47 (quoted), 200–201; Malleret, *L'exotisme*, 1 (the foreword was dated 1932).

186. Titaÿna, *Une femme chez les chasseurs de têtes et autres reportages*, ed. Francis Lacassin (Paris: Union Générale d'Editions, 1985), 7–16, 299–316; *Vu et Lu*, "Mes mémoires de reporter," 3, 10, 24 November 1937; 1, 8, 22, 29 December 1937; 5, 12 January 1938. Ten thousand copies of *Nuits chaudes* (*Hot Nights*) were printed.

187. De Monfreid converted to Islam, took the name Abd el Hai, and had himself circumcised. But he also married the daughter of the German governor of Strasbourg (the marriage took place right before the First World War). On his life see Gisèle de Monfreid, *De la mer Rouge à l'Ethiopie* (Paris: France-Empire, 1985); Henri de Monfreid, *Pearls, Arms, and Hashish*, "collected and written down" by Ida Treat (New York: Coward-McCann, 1930), quoted 10, 12, 17.

188. De Monfreid, *Pearls*, 354.

189. De Monfreid, *Secrets*; de Monfreid, *Pearls*; de Monfreid, *Hashish: The*

Autobiography of a Red Sea Smuggler, trans. Helen Buchanan Bell (1935; reprint, New York: Stonehill, 1973; originally published as *La croisière de hachich* [Paris: Grasset, 1933]), 2. De Monfreid, *Trafic d'armes en mer Rouge: les grands aventuriers d'aujourd'hui* (Paris: Grasset, 1935).

190. Courrière, *Kessel,* 349–76 (quoted 349).

191. Maurice Dekobra, *A Frenchman in Japan: Travels by Maurice Dekobra,* trans. Metcalfe Wood (London: T. Werner Laurie, 1936; originally published as *Samouraï 8 cylindres* [Paris: Baudinière, 1935]), 36 (Djibouti); Audoin-Dubreuil, *Soie,* 24, 198; Le Fèvre, *Croisière jaune,* 245; Pierre van Paassen, *Days of Our Years* (New York: Hillman-Curl, 1939), 328.

192. Klaus Mann, *The Turning Point: Thirty-five Years in This Century* (1942; reprint, New York: Markus Wiener, 1984), 87.

193. Morand, *Flèche,* 26–27.

194. Schreiber, *On Vit,* 286; de Croisset, *Dragon,* 202; Herfort, *Sous le soleil,* 168–69; Lyautey, *Chine,* 152; Bertrand, *Seule,* 55, 57, 65–66.

195. Joseph Kessel, *Nuits de princes* (1927; reprint, Paris: Plon, 1966), 111–13.

196. Joffroy, *Espionnage,* 17–18, 113–14, 35.

197. *Détective,* 14 October, 1937, p. 15.

Bibliography

Archival Sources

FRANCE

Archives nationales, Paris (AN):
Concentrations in series F7 (Sûreté); series BB18 (Justice); series F60 (Présidence du conseil — Secrétariat général)

Archives de la préfecture de police, Paris (APP):
Concentrations in series BA and BAP

Fondation nationale des sciences politiques, Paris:
Daladier papers

Ministère des affaires étrangères, Paris (MAE):
Concentrations in series Z: Europe; series NS; series Maroc/Tunisie; series E: Asie-Océanie

Ministère de l'intérieur et de la décentralisation/Direction générale de la police nationale, Paris (MI):
Panthéon dossiers — Police files from the Fichier central not yet deposited at the Archives nationales (as of 1986)

Archives d'Outre-mer, Paris (subsequently moved to Aix-en-Provence) (OM):

Concentrations in series Slotform (Police); series Affaires politiques

Service historique de la marine, Paris (MM)

Service historique de l'armée de terre, Paris (SHAT):
Concentrations in series 3H, 7N

Société nationale des chemins de fer français Archives, Paris (SNCF)

Archives contemporaines/Archives de la compagnie du chemin de fer du nord, Fontainebleau

GERMANY

Auswärtiges Amt — Politisches Archiv, Bonn (AA):
Concentrations in series Inland II A/B — Spionageabwehr, Vertrauensmänner; series Politische Abteilung I-Militär — Agenten- u. Spionagewesen Einzelfälle; series Botschaft Madrid

Bundesarchiv, Koblenz (BA):
Series R58

Bundesarchiv, Abteilung Militärgeschichte, Freiburg im Breisgau (MA):
Concentrations in series RW5 and RW49

UNITED STATES

National Archives, Washington, D.C.:
Shanghai Municipal Police files (SMP)

Hoover Institution on War, Revolution, and Peace, Stanford:
B. Nicolaevsky collection/box number 299/folder ID7/Outcard 211

Newspapers and Magazines

Paris-Soir, 1932–1940
Le Petit Parisien, 1886–1896; 1907–1909; 1919–1940
Le Journal, 1897; 1909; 1930–1938
Le Matin, 1909; 1930–1938
Détective, 1931–1939

Books and Articles

I have not included the works of professional historians unless these bear directly on specific topics of this study.

Abendroth, Hans-Henning. *Hitler in der Spanischen Arena*. Paderborn: Ferdinand Schöningh, 1973.

Abetz, Otto. *Histoire d'une politique franco-allemande, 1930–1950*. Paris: Stock, 1953.

Adams, Michael C. C. *The Great Adventure: Male Desire and the Coming of World War I*. Bloomington: Indiana University Press, 1940.

Adenis, Edouard. *Gestapo*. Paris: Baudinière, 1935.

Agent secret X-9. Paris: Hachette, 1936.

Allard, Paul. *Les espions de la paix*. Paris: Baudinière, 1935.

——. *La guerre des espions*. Paris: Flammarion, 1936.

——. *Quand Hitler espionne la France*. Paris: Editions de France, 1939.

——. *La vérité sur les marchands de canons*. Paris: Grasset, 1935.

All About Shanghai: A Standard Guidebook. 1934–1935. Reprint. Oxford: Oxford Paperbacks, 1986.

Alioshin, Dmitri. *Asian Odyssey*. New York: Henry Holt, 1940.

Allen, Charles, ed. *Plain Tales from the Raj: Images of British India in the Twentieth Century*. London: Futura Publications, 1976.

Allen, Louis. "Japanese Intelligence Systems." *Journal of Contemporary History* 22 (October 1987): 547–62.

Amaury, Francine. *Histoire du plus grand quotidien de la IIIème République: Le Petit Parisien, 1876–1944*. 2 vols. Paris: Presses universitaires de France, 1972.

Ambler, Eric. *Intrigue: Four Great Spy Novels of Eric Ambler*. New York: Alfred A. Knopf, 1943.

Andrew, Christopher. "Déchiffrement et diplomatie: le cabinet noir du quai d'Orsay sous la Troisième République." *Relations internationales* 3 (1976): 37–64.

——. *Secret Service: The Making of the British Intelligence Community*. London: Heinemann, 1985.

——, and David Dilks, eds. *The Missing Dimension: Governments and Intelligence Communities in the Twentieth Century*. Urbana: University of Illinois Press, 1984.

Andrews, Roy Chapman. *The New Conquest of Central Asia: A Narrative of the Explorations of the Central Asiatic Expeditions in Mongolia and China, 1921–1930*. New York: American Museum of Natural History, 1932.

Apestéguy, Pierre. *Le roi des sables*. Paris: Librairie des Champs-Elysées, 1939.

Assemblée nationale. *Rapport fait au nom de la commission chargée d'enquêter sur les événements survenus en France de 1933 à 1945*. 9 vols. 1947–1951.

Assouline, Pierre. *Albert Londres: vie et mort d'un grand reporter, 1884–1932*. Paris: Balland, 1989.

Audebert, Georges. *Organisation et méthodes de la police française*. Tours: Université de Poitiers, 1938.

Audoin-Dubreuil, Louis. *Sur la route de la soie: mon carnet de route de la Méditerranée à la mer de Chine*. Paris: Plon, 1935.

Auerbach, Leopold. *Denkwürdigkeiten des geheimen Regierunsrathes Dr. Stieber*. Berlin: Verlag von Julius Engelmann, 1884.

Aubert, Louis. *Paix japonaise*. Paris: Armand Colin, 1906.

Auxion de Ruffé, R. d'. *Chine et chinois d'aujourd'hui: le nouveau péril jaune*. Paris: Berger-Levrault, 1926.

———. *Chine et Japon 1938: les coulisses du drame*. Paris: Berger-Levrault, 1939.

B..., Commandant [pseud.], and Marcel Cossart. *1934–1940: la cinquième colonne*. Mondidier: Editions Marcel Cossart, 1946.

Badia, Gilbert, Jean-Baptiste Joly, Jean-Philippe Mathieu, Jacques Omnès, Jean-Michel Palmier, and Hélène Roussel. *Les banis de Hitler: accueil et luttes des exilés allemands en France (1933–1939)*. Paris: Presses universitaires de Vincennes, 1984.

———, Françoise Joly, Jean-Baptiste Joly, Claude Laharie, Ingrid Lederer, Jean-Philippe Mathieu, Hélène Roussel, Joseph Rovan, and Barbara Vormeier. *Les barbelés de l'exil: études sur l'émigration allemande et autrichienne (1938–1940)*. Grenoble: Presses universitaires de Grenoble, 1979.

Bailey, Geoffrey. *The Conspirators*. New York: Harper and Brothers, 1960.

Bajanov, B., and N. Alexeiev. *L'enlèvement du général Koutepov*. Paris: Editions Spes, 1930.

Bào, Bùi Xuân. *Naissance d'un héroïsme nouveau dans les lettres françaises de l'entre-deux-guerres: aviation et littérature*. Paris: Faculté des Lettres et des Sciences humaines de l'Université de Paris, 1961.

Bardanne, Jean. *Documents secrets et faux passeports*. Paris: Baudinière, 1938.

———. *L'espionne du Guépéou*. Paris: Baudinière, 1937.

———. *La guerre et les microbes*. Paris: Baudinière, 1937.

———. *Pourquoi la guerre est impossible*. Paris: Baudinière, 1939.

———. *La presse et l'espionnage*. Paris: Baudinière, 1939.

———. *Stavisky, espion allemand*. Paris: Baudinière, 1935.

Bardoux, Jacques. *Staline contre l'Europe: les preuves du complot communiste*. Paris: Flammarion, 1937.

Barillet-Lagargousse. *La guerre finale*. Paris: Berger-Levrault, 1885.

Barraclough, Geoffrey. *An Introduction to Contemporary History*. New York: Basic Books, 1964.

Barrot, Olivier, and Pascal Ory, eds. *Entre deux guerres: la création française entre 1919 et 1939*. Paris: Editions François Bourin, 1990.

Bartels, Albert. *Fighting the French in Morocco*. Translated by H. J. Stenning. London: Alston Rivers, Ltd., 1932.

Barzini, Luigi. *Peking to Paris: A Journey Across Two Continents in 1907*. Translated by L. P. de Castelvecchio. 1908. Reprint. Harmondsworth: Penguin Books, 1986.

Batault, Georges. *Le problème juif*. Paris: Plon, 1921.

Bauermeister, Alexander. *La guerre dans l'ombre: souvenirs d'un officier du service se-*

cret du haut commandement allemand. Translated by Th. Lacaze. Paris: Payot, 1933.

Baum, Vicki. *Shanghai '37*. Translated by Basil Creighton. 1939. Reprint. Oxford: Oxford University Press, 1986.

Baumont, Maurice. *Au coeur de l'affaire Dreyfus*. Paris: Editions Mondiales, 1976.

Bavendamm, Günther Jantzen, Gerhard Sendler, Heinrich Woermann, and Jürgen Zwernemann. *Wagnis Westafrika: Die Geschichte eines Hamburger Handelshauses, 1837–1987*. Hamburg: Verlag Hanseatischer Merkur, 1987.

Bayet, Albert. *Pétain et la 5e colonne*. Paris: Editions Franc-tireur, 1944.

Beauvais, Armand. *Attachés militaires, attachés navals, et attachés de l'air*. Paris: Presse Modernes, 1937.

Becker, Jean-Jacques. *Le carnet B: les pouvoirs publics et l'antimilitarisme avant la guerre de 1914*. Paris: Editions Klincksieck, 1973.

———. *1914: comment les Français sont entrés dans la guerre*. Paris: Presses de la Fondation nationale des Sciences politiques, 1977.

Belin, Jean. *Secrets of the Sûreté: The Memoirs of Commissioner Jean Belin*. New York: G. P. Putnam's Sons, 1950.

Bellanger, Claude, Jacques Godechot, Pierre Guiral, and Fernand Terrou. *Histoire générale de la presse française*. Vol. 3, *De 1871 à 1940*. Paris: Presses universitaires de France, 1972.

Bepler, Jill. *Ferdinand Albrecht Duke of Braunschwieg-Lüneburg (1636–1687): A Traveller and his Travelogue*. Wiesbaden: Otto Harrassowitz, 1988.

Bérard, Victor. *La révolte de l'Asie*. Paris: Armand Colin, 1904.

Berenson, Edward. *The Trial of Madame Caillaux*. Berkeley: University of California Press, 1992.

Bergère, Marie-Claire. *The Golden Age of the Chinese Bourgeoisie, 1911–1937*. Translated by Janet Lloyd. Cambridge: Cambridge University Press, 1989.

———. "'The Other China': Shanghai from 1919 to 1949." In *Shanghai: Revolution and Development in an Asian Metropolis*, edited by Christopher Howe. Cambridge: Cambridge University Press, 1981.

Bernard, Marc. *En hydravion au-dessus du continent noir*. Paris: Grasset, 1927.

Bertnay, Paul. *L'espionne du Bourget*. Paris: Fayard, 1909.

Berton, Pierre. *The Arctic Grail: The Quest for the North West Passage and the North Pole, 1818–1909*. New York: Viking, 1988.

Bertrand, Gabrielle. *La route aux armes*. Paris: Amiot-Dumont, 1953.

———. *Seule dans l'Asie troublée: Mandchouko-Mongolie, 1936–1937*. Paris: Plon, 1937.

Bessedovsky, Grégoire. *Oui, j'accuse: au service des soviets*. Paris: Redier, 1930.

Bey, Essad. *Histoire du Guépéou*. Paris: Payot, 1934.

Bialer, Uri. *The Shadow of the Bomber: The Fear of Air Attack and British Politics, 1932–1939*. London: Royal Historical Society, 1980.

Bienstock, Gregory. *La lutte pour le Pacifique*. Translated by André Guieu. Paris: Payot, 1938.

Billotey, Pierre. *L'Indochine en zigzags*. Paris: Albin Michel, 1929.

Bishop, Peter. *The Myth of Shangri-La: Tibet, Travel Writing, and the Western Creation of Sacred Landscape*. Berkeley: University of California Press, 1989.

Blacker, L. V. S. *Mes patrouilles secrètes en Haute Asie*. Translated by R. Hendry-Charcot. Paris: Payot, 1933.

Blackstock, Paul W. *The Secret Road to World War Two: Soviet versus Western Intelligence, 1921–1939*. Chicago: Quadrangle Books 1969.

Blanch, Lesley. *Pierre Loti: The Legendary Romantic*. New York: Carroll and Graf, 1985.

Blanchard, Claude. *De notre envoyé spécial Claude Blanchard: quelques-uns de ses meilleurs reportages*. Paris: Editions Défense de la France, 1948.

Blanchod, Fred. *Le beau voyage autour du monde*. Paris: Payot, 1939.

Block, Allan A. "European Drug Traffic and Traffickers Between the Wars: The Policy of Suppression and its Consequences." *Journal of Social History* 23 (Winter 1989): 315–32.

Boileau, Pierre, and Thomas Narcejac. *Le roman policier*. Paris: Payot, 1964.

Boissel, Jean. *Le juif poison mortel*. Paris: Editions Rif, 1935.

Boissière, Jules. *Fumeurs d'opium*. Paris: Flammarion, 1896.

Boland, Henri. *La guerre prochaine entre la France et l'Allemagne*. Paris: D. Rolland, 1884.

Bommart, Jean. *The Chinese Fish*. Translated by Milton Waldman. London: Longmans, Green, 1935. Originally published as *Le poisson chinois* (Paris: Librairie des Champs-Elysées, 1934).

———. *La dame de Valparaiso: les débuts du poisson chinois*. 1940. Reprint. Paris: Editions de Flore, 1948.

———. *Hélène et le poisson chinois*. Paris: Librairie des Champs-Elysées, 1938.

Bongie, Chris. *Exotic Memories: Literature, Colonialism, and the Fin de Siècle*. Stanford: Stanford University Press, 1991.

Bonnet, Jean Charles. *Les pouvoirs publics français et l'immigration dans l'entre-deux-guerres*. Lyons: Université de Lyon II, 1976.

Bonte, Florimond. *La guerre de demain: aérienne, chimique, bactériologique*. Lille: Editions Prolétariennes, 1930.

Bonte, Paul-Etienne. *L'espionnage devant la loi pénale*. Lille: Université de Lille, 1936.

Borkenau, Franz. *World Communism: A History of the Communist International*. 1939. Reprint. Ann Arbor: University of Michigan Press, 1962.

Boucard, Robert. *Les dessous de l'espionnage allemand*. Paris: Editions de France, 1933.

———. *Les dessous de l'espionnage français*. Paris: Editions de France, 1934.

———. *Les dessous de l'Intelligence Service*. Paris: Editions Documentaires, 1937.

———. *La guerre des renseignements*. Paris: Editions de France, 1939.

Boudard, Alphonse. *La fermeture*. Paris: Robert Laffont, 1986.

Bourdrel, Philippe. *La Cagoule*. Paris: Albin Michel, 1970.

Brackmann, Karl. *Fünfzig Jahre deutscher Afrikaschifffahrt: Die Geschichte der Woermann-Linie und der Deutschen Ost-Afrika-Linie*. Berlin: Dietrich Reimer, 1935.

Bridges, Brian. "Britain and Japanese Espionage in Pre-War Malaya: the Shino-zaki Case." *Journal of Contemporary History* 2 (January 1986): 23–36.

Brissaud, André. *Histoire du service secret nazi*. Paris: Plon, 1972.

Bristow, Edward. *Prostitution and Prejudice: The Jewish Fight Against White Slavery, 1870–1939*. Oxford: Clarendon Press, 1982.

Brittain, Vera. *Testament of Youth*. 1933. Reprint. London: Penguin, 1989.

Broc, Numa. *Dictionnaire illustré des explorateurs français du XIXe siècle: Afrique*. Paris: Editions du C.T.H.S., 1988.

———. "Les explorateurs français du XIXe siècle reconsidérés." *Revue française d'histoire d'outre-mer* 69 (1982): 237–73.

Broche, François. *Assassinat d'Alexandre 1er et de Louis Barthou: Marseille, le 9 octobre 1934*. Paris: Balland, 1977.

Broué, Pierre. "La main d'oeuvre «blanche» de Staline." *Cahiers Leon Trotsky* 24 (December 1985): 73–84.

The Brown Network. Translated by Clement Greenberg. New York: Knight Publications, 1936.

Bruno, Jean. *Les reptiles prussiens en France, ou les crimes des espions*. Paris: Librairie B. Simon, n.d.

Buchan, John. *Greenmantle*. 1916. Reprint. Harmondsworth: Penguin Books, 1956.

———. *Mr. Standfast*. 1919. Reprint. Harmondsworth: Penguin Books, 1956.

Buchheit, Gert. *Der Deutsche Geheimdienst: Geschichte der militärischen Abwehr*. Munich: Paul List, 1967.

Burke, Edmund. "Moroccan Resistance, Pan-Islam, and German War Strategy, 1914–1918." *Francia* 3 (1975): 434–64.

———. "Pan-Islam and Moroccan Resistance to French Colonial Penetration, 1900–1912." *Journal of African History* 13 (1972): 97–118.

———. *Prelude to Protectorate in Morocco: Precolonial Protest and Resistance, 1860–1912*. Chicago: University of Chicago Press, 1976.

Byram, Léo. *Petit Jap deviendra grand! L'expansion japonaise en Extrême-Orient*. Paris: Berger-Levrault, 1908.

Cadwallader, Barrie. *Crisis of the European Mind: A Study of André Malraux and Drieu La Rochelle*. Cardiff: University of Wales Press, 1981.

Cambre-Mialet, A. J. S.-M. de la. *Français, vous êtes trahis!* Paris, 1938.

Camentron, Jean. *Le danger aéro-chimique*. Paris: Charles-Lavauzelle, 1936.

Cantel, Rudy. *Trafiquants d'armes*. Paris: Baudinière, 1939.

Caron, Vicki. "Loyalties in Conflict: French Jewry and the Refugee Crisis, 1933–1935." *Leo Baeck Institute Year Book* 36 (1991): 305–38.

Castellan, Georges. *Le réarmement clandestin du Reich, 1930–1935*. Paris: Plon, 1954.

Castex, R. *Jaunes contre blancs: le problème militaire indo-chinois*. Paris: Charles-Lavauzelle, 1905.

Cawelti, John G., and Bruce A. Rosenberg. *The Spy Story*. Chicago: University of Chicago Press, 1987.

Cazal, Commandant [pseud.]. *La Guerre! La Guerre! Roman de demain*. Paris: Tallandier, 1939.

Celarié, H. *Promenades en Indochine*. Paris: Baudinière, 1937.

Céline, Louis-Ferdinand. *Bagatelles pour un massacre*. Paris: Editions Denoël, 1937.

Chack, Paul. *Croisières merveilleuses*. Paris: Editions de France, 1937.

Chadourne, Marc. *China*. Translated by Harry Block. New York: Covici-Froede, 1932. Originally published as *Chine* (Paris: Plon, 1931).

———. *Tour de la terre: Extrême-Occident*. Paris: Plon, 1935.

———. *Tour de la terre: Extrême-Orient*. Paris: Plon, 1935.

———. *L'U.R.S.S. sans passion*. Paris: Plon, 1932.

Champly, Henry. *La bolchaïa («La grande») aventure en Asie*. Paris: Tallandier, 1937.

———. *The Road to Shanghai: White Slave Traffic in Asia*. Translated by Warre B. Wells. London: John Long, 1934. Originally published as *Le chemin de Changhaï* (Paris: Tallandier, 1933).

Chapman, Guy. *The Dreyfus Case*. New York: Reynal, 1955.

Chapman, John W. M. "A Dance on Eggs: Intelligence and the 'Anti-Comintern.'" *Journal of Contemporary History* 22 (April 1987): 333–72.

Charpentier, Armand. *Ce que sera la guerre des gaz*. Paris: André Delpeuch, 1930.

Chenevier, Charles. *De la combe aux fées à Lurs: souvenirs et révélations*. Paris: Flammarion, 1962.

———. *La grande maison*. Paris: Presses de la Cité, 1976.

Chéradame, André. *Le monde et la guerre russo-japonaise*. Paris: Plon, 1906.

Chessin, Serge de. *La nuit qui vient de l'Orient*. Paris: Hachette, 1929.

Clare, George. *Last Waltz in Vienna*. New York: Avon, 1983.

Clarke, I. F. *Voices Prophesying War, 1763–1984*. Oxford: Oxford University Press, 1966.

Cleveland, William L. *Islam Against the West: Shakib Arslan and the Campaign for Islamic Nationalism*. Austin: University of Texas Press, 1985.

Clifford, Nicholas R. *Spoilt Children of Empire: Westerners in Shanghai and the Chinese Revolution of the 1920s*. Hanover: University Press of New England, 1991.

Cluzel, Magdeleine. *Autour de la terre*. Paris: Baudinière, 1935.

Cohn, Norman. *Warrant for Genocide*. New York: Harper, 1969.

Conquest, Robert. *The Great Terror: Stalin's Purge of the Thirties*. New York: Macmillan, 1968.

Corday, Michel. *Ciel rose*. Paris: Flammarion, 1933.

Cossé-Brissac, Pierre. *En d'autres temps (1900–1939)*. Paris: Grasset, 1972.

Costello, John, and Oleg Tsarev. *Deadly Illusions*. New York: Crown, 1993.

Coumbe, Arthur. "German Intelligence and Security in the Franco-German War." *Military Intelligence* 14 (January 1988): 9–12.

Courrière, Yves. *Joseph Kessel, ou sur la piste du lion*. Paris: Plon, 1985.

Croisset, Francis de. *La côte de jade*. Paris: Grasset, 1938.

———. *Le dragon blessé*. Paris: Grasset, 1936.

Cross, Gary. *Immigrant Workers in Industrial France: The Making of a New Laboring Class*. Philadelphia: Temple University Press, 1983.

Croze, Austin de. *Péril jaune et Japon*. Paris, 1904.

Crozier, Joseph. *Mes missions secrètes, 1915–1918.* Paris: Payot 1933.

———. [Pierre Desgranges, pseud.]. *Au service des marchands d'armes.* Paris: Redier, 1934.

———. [Pierre Desgranges, pseud.] and Lieutenant de Belleval. *En mission chez l'ennemi.* Paris: Redier, 1930.

Cru, Jean Norton. *Témoins: essai d'analyse et de critique des souvenirs de combattants édité en français de 1915 à 1928.* Paris: Les Étincelles, 1929.

Dallin, David J. *Soviet Espionage.* New Haven: Yale University Press, 1955.

Daly, John Carroll. *L'espion numéro 7.* Translated by Charles de Richter. Paris: Editions de France, 1936.

Dangin, Edouard. *La bataille de Berlin en 1875: souvenirs d'un vieux soldat de la Landwehr.* Paris: E. Lachaud, 1871.

Daniels, H. G. *The Framework of France.* New York: Charles Scribner's Sons, 1937.

Daniels, Roger. *The Decision to Relocate the Japanese Americans.* Malabar, Fla.: Robert E. Krieger, 1986.

Danrit, Capitaine [Emile Augustin Cyprien Driant]. *L'alerte.* Paris: Flammarion, 1910.

———. *La guerre au vingtième siècle: l'invasion noire.* Paris: Flammarion, 1894

———. *La guerre fatale: France-Angleterre.* 3 vols. Paris: Flammarion, 1903.

———. *L'invasion jaune.* 3 vols. Paris: Flammarion, 1909. Reprint, 1926.

Darcy, Paul. *La formule 108.* Paris: Baudinière, 1935.

———. *Guet-apens dans la forêt-noire.* Paris: Baudinière, 1937.

Darlix, Paul. *Un soir en Pullman . . .* Paris: Baudinière, 1929.

———. *Smyrne, dernière escale.* Paris: Baudinière, 1930.

———. *Terrorisme sur le monde.* Paris: Baudinière, 1932.

Daudet, Léon. *L'avant-guerre: études et documents sur l'espionnage juif-allemand en France depuis l'affaire Dreyfus.* Paris: Nouvelle Librairie Nationale, 1913.

Decornoy, Jacques. *Péril jaune, peur blanche.* Paris: Grasset, 1970.

Dedijer, Vladimir. *The Road to Sarajevo.* New York: Simon and Schuster, 1966.

Dehillotte, Pierre. *Gestapo.* Paris: Payot, 1940.

Dekobra, Maurice. *Confucius en pull-over, ou le beau voyage en Chine.* Paris: Baudinière, 1934.

———. *A Frenchman in Japan: Travels by Maurice Dekobra.* Translated by Metcalfe Wood. London: T. Werner Laurie, Ltd., 1936. Originally published as *Samouraï 8 cylindres* (Paris: Baudinière, 1935).

———. *La gondole aux chimères.* Paris: Baudinière, 1926.

———. *Madame Joli-supplice.* Paris: Baudinière, 1934.

———. *The Madonna of the Sleeping Cars.* Translated by Neal Wainwright. New York: Payson and Clarke, 1927. Originally published as *La madone des sleepings* (Paris: Baudinière, 1925).

Delage, Jean. *Koutepoff.* Paris: Librairie Delagrave, 1930.

———. *La Russie en exil.* Paris: Librairie Delagrave, 1930.

Delaisi, Francis. *La guerre qui vient.* Paris: Edition de la Guerre Sociale, 1911.

Delbos, Yvon. *L'expérience rouge.* Paris: Au Sans Pareil, 1933.

Delmas, J. *Mes hommes au feu: avec la division de fer; à Morhange, sur l'Yser, en Artois (1914–1915).* Paris: Payot, 1931.

Demangeon, A. *Le déclin de l'Europe*. 1920. Reprint. Paris: Guenegaud, 1975.

Demartial, G. *La guerre de 1914: la mobilisation des consciences*. Paris: Rieder, 1927.

Deval, Jacques. *Rives pacifiques*. Paris: Gallimard, 1937.

Dingle, Reginald. *Russia's Work in France*. London: Robert Hale, 1938.

Dodeman, Charles. *L'espion chinois*. Paris: Maison de la Bonne Presse, 1935.

Dorgelès, Roland. *On the Mandarin Road*. Translated by Gertrude Emerson. New York: The Century Co., 1926. Originally published as *Sur la route mandarine* (Paris: Albin Michel, 1925).

———. *Vive la liberté*. Paris: Albin Michel, 1937.

Dorsenne, Jean. *Faudra-t-il évacuer l'Indochine?* Paris: Nouvelle Société d'Edition, 1932.

Douillet, Joseph. *Moscou sans voiles: neuf ans de travail au pays des soviets*. Paris: Editions Spes, 1928.

Dreifort, John E. *Myopic Grandeur: The Ambivalence of French Foreign Policy toward the Far East, 1919–1945*. Kent, Ohio: Kent State University Press, 1991.

Duhamel, Georges. *Le voyage de Moscou*. Paris: Mercure de France, 1927.

Dunsterville, L. C. *The Adventures of Dunsterforce*. London: Edward Arnold, 1920.

Duroselle, Jean-Baptiste. *Politique étrangère de la France: la décadence 1932–1939*. Paris: Imprimerie nationale 1979.

Durtain, Luc. *Dieux blancs, hommes jaunes*. Paris: Flammarion, 1930.

Dyssord, Jacques. *L'espionnage allemand à l'oeuvre*. Paris: Editions et Librairie, 1915.

Dziak, John J. *Chekisty: A History of the KGB*. Lexington, Mass.: Lexington Books, 1988.

Ehrenburg, Ilya. *Memoirs: 1921–1941*. Translated by Tatania Shelbunina. Cleveland: World Publishing Co., 1963.

"Espionnage." *La grande encyclopédie: inventaire raisonné des sciences, des lettres, et des arts*, 16:367–69. 2d ed.

"Espionnage." *Larousse du XXe siècle*, 3:278–79. Paris: Librairie Larousse, 1930.

L'espionnage international, no. 2. 1934.

Fabre-Luce, Alfred. *Russie 1927*. Paris: Grasset, 1927.

Farrère, Claude. *Le grand drame de l'Asie*. Paris: Flammarion, 1938.

———. *La onzième heure*. Paris: Flammarion, 1939.

Farwell, Byron. *Burton: A Biography of Sir Richard Francis Burton*. London: Penguin Books, 1990.

Féli-Brugière, and Louis Gastine. *L'Asie en feu: le roman de l'invasion jaune*. Paris: Librairie Ch. Delagrave, 1904.

Ferdonnet, Paul. *La guerre juive*. Paris: Baudinière, 1938.

La fin tragique du président Paul Doumer. Paris: Tallandier, 1932.

Fischer, Fritz. *Germany's Aims in the First World War*. New York: W. W. Norton, 1967.

———. *Griff nach der Weltmacht*. Düsseldorf: Droste Verlag, 1961.

Fleming, Shannon Earl. "Primo de Rivera and Abd-el-Krim: The Struggle in

Spanish Morocco, 1923–1927." Ph.D. diss., University of Wisconsin, 1974.

Florent-Matter. *La France est-elle défendue? La propagande allemande, ses armes, ses méthodes, ses succès*. Paris: Tallandier, 1930.

Florian-Parmentier. *L'abîme*. Paris: Albert Messein, 1934.

———. *L'étoile rouge: voyage au pays des soviets*. Paris: Le Fauconnier, 1936.

Fontenoy, Fernand. *La cagoule contre la France*. Paris: Editions Sociales Internationales, 1938.

Fontenoy, Jean. *Shanghaï secret*. Paris: Grasset, 1938.

Fonvielle, Wilfrid de. *L'espion aérien*. Paris: Charles Bayle, 1884.

Foot, M. R. D. *SOE in France: An Account of the Work of the British Special Operations Executive in France, 1940–1944*. Frederick, Md.: University Publications of America, 1984.

Forbes, Andrew D. W. *Warlords and Muslims in Chinese Central Asia: A Political History of Republican Sinkiang, 1911–1949*. Cambridge: Cambridge University Press, 1986.

Ford, George H., ed. *The Pickersgill Letters*. Toronto: Ryerson Press, 1948.

Fox, John P. *Germany and the Far Eastern Crisis, 1931–1938*. Oxford: Clarendon Press, 1982.

François-Poncet, André. *The Fateful Years: Memoirs of a French Ambassador in Berlin, 1931–1938*. New York: Harcourt, Brace, 1949.

Frei, Bruno. *Die Männer von Vernet*. 1950. Reprint. Hildesheim: Gerstenberg, 1980.

French, David. "Spy Fever in Britain, 1900–1915." *Historical Journal* 21 (June 1978): 355–70.

Fricke, Dieter. *Bismarcks Prätorianer: Die Berliner Politische Polizei im Kampf gegen die deutsche Arbeiterbewegung (1871–1898)*. Berlin: Rütten and Loening, 1962.

Friguglietti, James. "Victor Méric: The Evolution of a Pacifist." *Proceedings of the Fourth Symposium of French American Studies* (1980).

Fritzsche, Peter. *A Nation of Fliers: German Aviation and the Popular Imagination*. Cambridge, Mass.: Harvard University Press, 1992.

Froment, A. *L'espionnage militaire et les fonds secrets de la guerre*. Paris: La Librairie Illustré, 1887.

Frondaie, Pierre. *Le lieutenant de Gibraltar*. Paris: Plon, 1936.

Fussell, Paul. *Abroad: British Literary Traveling Between the Wars*. Oxford: Oxford University Press, 1982.

———. *The Great War and Modern Memory*. Oxford: Oxford University Press, 1977.

Gallicus. "Who Were the French Saboteurs?" *The New Republic* 102 (3 June 1940): 752–54.

Gallo, Max. *Et ce fut la défaite de 40: la cinquième colonne*. Paris: Plon, 1970.

Gamelin, Maurice. *Servir*. 3 vols. Paris: Plon, 1946–1947.

Garder, Michel. *La guerre secrète des services spéciaux français, 1934–1945*. Paris: Plon, 1967.

Gauché, Maurice-Henri. *Le deuxième bureau au travail, 1935–1940*. Paris: Amiot-Dumont, 1953.

Gautherot, Gustave. *Le monde communiste*. Paris: Editions Spes, 1925.

Gauthier, Bernard. *La cinquième colonne contre la paix du monde: l'internationale des espions, des assassins, des cagoulards, et des provocateurs au service du fascisme*. Paris: Bureau d'Editions, 1938.

Gehrke, Ulrich. *Persien in der Deutschen Orientpolitik während des Ersten Weltkrieges*. 2 vols. Stuttgart: W. Kohlhammer, 1960.

Gerbault, Alain. *Seul à travers l'Atlantique*. Paris: Grasset, 1924.

Gervais, Albert. *The Ghosts of Sin-Chang*. Translated by Vyvyan Holland. London: Hamish Hamilton, 1936. Originally published as *L'ombre du ma-koui* (Paris: Gallimard, 1936).

Gide, André. *Back From the U.S.S.R.* Translated by Dorothy Bussy. London: Martin Secker and Warburg, 1937. Originally published as *Retour de l'U.R.S.S.* (Paris: Gallimard, 1936).

Giffard, Pierre. *La guerre infernale: grand roman d'aventures pour la jeunesse*. Paris: Albert Méricant, 1908.

———. *Lunes rouges et dragons noirs*. Paris: Librairie Félix Juven, 1906.

Gilbert, O.-P. *Courrier d'Asie*. Paris: Gallimard, 1937.

———. *La piste du sud*. Paris: Gallimard, 1937.

Giraudoux, Jean. *Pleins pouvoirs*. Paris: Gallimard, 1939.

Goerger, A. *En marge de la croisière jaune*. Paris: Rieder, 1935.

Gohier, Urbain. *Cassandre, ou la folie des blancs*. Paris: Editions Georges-Anquetil, 1927.

———. *Protocoles des sages d'Israël*. Paris: La Vieille France, 1925.

Gordon, Bertram M. *Collaborationism in France During the Second World War*. Ithaca: Cornell University Press, 1980.

Gorel, Michel. *Pourquoi Gorguloff a-t-il tué*. Paris: Editions Nilsson, 1932.

Gontier, René. *Vers un racisme français*. Paris: Editions Denoël, 1939.

Goul, Roman. *Les maîtres de la Tchéka: histoire de la terreur en U.R.S.S., 1917–1938*. Paris: Editions de France, 1938.

Goy, Lucien. *La bataille de 1915*. Paris: Louis Theuveny, 1906.

Graaf, Bob de. "Hot Intelligence in the Tropics: Dutch Intelligence Operations in the Netherlands East Indies During the Second World War." *Journal of Contemporary History* 22 (October 1987): 563–84.

Grange, Daniel J. "La propagande arabe de Radio-Bari (1937–1939)." *Relations internationales* 5 (1976): 65–103.

———. "Structure et techniques d'une propagande: Les émissions de Radio-Bari." *Relations internationales* 2 (1974): 165–85.

Graves, A. K. *Souvenirs d'un agent secret de l'Allemagne*. Translated by A. L. D'Eppinghoven. Paris: Plon, 1916.

Grazia, Victoria de. "Mass Culture and Sovereignty: The American Challenge to European Cinemas, 1920–1960." *Journal of Modern History* 61 (March 1989): 53–87.

Green, Roger Lancelyn. *A. E. W. Mason*. London: Max Parrish, 1952.

Greene, Graham. *The Confidential Agent*. 1939. Reprint. Harmondsworth: Penguin Books, 1971.

Groscurth, Helmut. *Tagebücher eines Abwehroffiziers 1938–1940*. Edited by Helmut Krausnick and Harold C. Deutsch. Stuttgart: Deutsche Verlags-Anstalt, 1970.

Grey, Marina. *Le général meurt à minuit: l'enlèvement des généraux Koutiépov (1930) et Miller (1937)*. Paris: Plon, 1981.

Grousset, René. *Le réveil de l'Asie: l'impérialisme britannique et la révolte des peuples*. Paris: Plon, 1924.

Gril, Etienne. *Intelligence Service*. Paris: Baudinière, 1937.

Guillen, Pierre. *L'Allemagne et le Maroc de 1870 à 1905*. Paris: Presses universitaires de France, 1967.

Gunther, John. *Inside Europe*. New York: Harper, 1938.

Gunzenhäuser, Max. *Geschichte des geheimen Nachrichtendienstes (Spionage, Sabotage, und Abwehr)*. Frankfurt: Bernand and Graefe, 1968.

Gyomaï, Imré. *Trebitsch Lincoln: le plus grand aventurier du siècle*. Paris: Editions de France, 1939.

Haardt, Georges-Marie, and Louis Audouin-Dubreuil. *La croisière noire: expédition Citroën centre-Afrique*. Paris: Plon, 1927.

Haggie, Paul. *Britannia at Bay: The Defense of the British Empire against Japan, 1931–1941*. Oxford: Clarendon Press, 1981.

Harris, Ruth. *Murders and Madness: Medicine, Law, and Society in the Fin-de-Siècle*. Oxford: Oxford University Press, 1989.

Hautecloque, Xavier de. *La guerre en musque noir*. Paris: Editions de la Nouvelle Revue Critique, 1931.

———. *Police politique hitlérienne*. Paris: Editions de la Nouvelle Revue Critique, 1935.

Headrick, Daniel R. *The Invisible Weapon: Telecommunications and International Politics, 1851–1945*. New York: Oxford University Press, 1991.

Hedin, Sven. *Across the Gobi Desert*. Translated by H. J. Cant. 1931. Reprint. New York: Greenwood Press, 1968.

———. *My Life as an Explorer*. Translated by Alfhild Huebsch. Garden City: Garden City Publishing, 1925.

Hellman, Florence S. *Nazi Fifth Column Activities: A List of References*. Washington: 1943.

Helsey, Edouard. *Envoyé spécial*. Paris: Fayard, 1955.

Hémery, Daniel. *Révolutionnaires vietnamiens et pouvoir colonial en Indochine: communistes, trotskystes, nationalistes à Saigon de 1932 à 1937*. Paris: Editions François Maspero, 1975.

Hentig, Werner Otto von. *Meine Diplomatenfahrt ins Verschlossene Land*. Berlin: Ullstein, 1918.

Herbart, Pierre. *En U.R.S.S.* Paris: Gallimard, 1937.

Herfort, Paule. *Sous le soleil levant (voyage aventureux)*. Paris: Baudinière, 1943.

Herriot, Edouard. *La Russie nouvelle*. Paris: J. Ferenczi, 1922.

Hiley, Nicholas P. "The Failure of British Espionage against Germany, 1907–1914." *The Historical Journal* 26 (1983): 867–89.

Hill, George A. *Go Spy the Land: Being the Adventures of I.K. 8 of the British Secret Service*. London: Cassell, 1932. Translated by Lucien Thomas as *Ma vie d'espion (I.K. 8)* (Paris: Payot, 1933).

Hilton, Stanley E. *Hitler's Secret War in South America: German Military Espionage and Allied Counterespionage in Brazil*. Baton Rouge: Louisiana State University Press, 1981.

Hirszowicz, Lukasz. *The Third Reich and the Arab East*. London: Routledge and Kegan Paul, 1966.

Hinsley, F. H., and C. A. G. Simkins. *British Intelligence in the Second World War*. Vol. 4, *Security and Counterintelligence*. New York: Cambridge University Press, 1990.

Hirt, F. "Du délit d'espionnage: étude de droit français et de législation comparée." Thèse pour le doctorat d'état, Université de Strasbourg, 1937.

Hoisington, William H., Jr. *The Casablanca Connection: French Colonial Policy, 1936–1943*. Chapel Hill: University of North Carolina Press, 1984.

Hopkirk, Peter. *The Great Game: The Struggle for Empire in Central Asia*. New York: Kodansha, 1992.

Horvath-Peterson, Sandra. "Introduction." *French Historical Studies* 17 (Fall 1991): 301–9.

Hoveyda, Fereydoun. *Histoire du roman policier*. Paris: Editions du Pavillon, 1965.

Howard, Michael. *The Franco-Prussian War: The German Invasion of France, 1870–1871*. London: Methuen, 1981.

Hoy, H. C. *40 O.B. La chambre secrète de l'Amirauté*. Translated by André Guieu. Paris: Payot, 1933.

Hunt, Lynn. *Politics, Culture, and Class in the French Revolution*. Berkeley: University of California Press, 1984.

Huth, Arno. *La radiodiffusion, puissance mondiale*. Paris: Gallimard, 1937.

Hyman, Paula. *From Dreyfus to Vichy: The Remaking of French Jewry, 1906–1939*. New York: Columbia University Press, 1979.

Hynes, Samuel. *A War Imagined: The First World War and English Culture*. New York: Atheneum, 1991.

Ignatieff, Paul. *Ma mission en France*. Paris: Librairie des Champs-Elysées, 1933.

Irvine, William D. *The Boulanger Affair Reconsidered: Royalism, Boulangism, and the Origins of the Radical Right in France*. Oxford: Oxford University Press, 1989.

Ivoi, Paul d' [Paul Deleutre]. *L'espion X. 323: le canon du sommeil*. Paris: A Méricant, 1909.

———. *L'espion X. 323: l'homme sans visage*. Paris: A. Méricant, 1909.

———, and Royet. *La patrie en danger: histoire de la guerre future*. Paris: H. Geffroy, 1905.

Jacobs, Dan N. *Borodin: Stalin's Man in China*. Cambridge, Mass.: Harvard University Press, 1981.

Joffroy, Jean. *Espionnage en Asie*. Paris: Baudinière, 1939.

Johnson, Chalmers. *An Instance of Treason: Ozaki Hotsumi and the Sorge Spy Ring*. Stanford: Stanford University Press, 1990.

Jong, Louis de. *The German Fifth Column in the Second World War*. Translated by C. M. Geyl. 1956. Reprint. New York: Howard Fertig, 1973.

Josse, Prosper. *L'invasion étrangère en France en temps de paix*. Paris: La Nation, 1938.

Jouglet, René. *Dans le sillage des jonques*. Paris: Grasset, 1935.

Jouhandeau, Marcel. *Le péril juif*. Paris: Fernand Sorlot, 1939.

Jouin, Ernest. *Les «Protocols des sages de Sion»*. Paris: Ligue Franc-Catholique, 1936.

Kahn, David. *Hitler's Spies: German Military Intelligence in World War II*. New York: Collier, 1985.

Kayser, Jacques. *Le quotidien français*. Paris: Armand Colin, 1963.

Katz, Friedrich. *The Secret War in Mexico: Europe, the United States, and the Mexican Revolution*. Chicago: University of Chicago Press, 1983.

Katz, Otto [Franz Spielhagen, pseud.]. *The Nazi Conspiracy in Spain*. Translated by Emile Burns. London: Victor Gollancz, 1937. Originally published as *Spione und Verschwörer in Spanien* (Paris: Editions du Carrefour, 1936).

Keddie, N. R. "Pan-Islam as Proto-Nationalism." *Journal of Modern History* 41 (1969): 17–28.

Kerillis, Henri de. *Français, voici la guerre!* Paris: Grasset, 1936.

———. *Français, voici la vérité*. New York: Editions de la Maison Française, 1942.

Kessel, Joseph. *L'équipage*. Paris: Editions de la Nouvelle Revue Française, 1924.

———. *Mermoz*. Paris: Gallimard, 1938.

———. *Nuits de princes*. 1927. Reprint. Paris: Plon, 1966.

———. *Les nuits de Sibérie*. Paris: Flammarion, 1928.

———. *They Weren't All Angels*. London: Rupert Hart-Davis, 1965.

———. *Wagon-lit*. Paris: Gallimard, 1932.

Kimche, Jon. *The Second Arab Awakening*. New York: Holt, Rinehart and Winston, 1970.

Kinnet, Paul, and Ludo Patris. *Chambre de mort à Barcelone*. Paris: Baudinière, 1939.

Kipling, Rudyard. *Kim*. 1901. Reprint. London: Pan Books, 1978.

Kirby, William C. *Germany and Republican China*. Stanford: Stanford University Press, 1984.

Kish, George. *To the Heart of Asia: The Life of Sven Hedin*. Ann Arbor: University of Michigan Press, 1984.

Kluck, A. von. *La marche sur Paris (1914)*. Translated by Delestraint. Paris: Payot, 1922.

Knightly, Phillip. *The Second Oldest Profession: Spies and Spying in the Twentieth Century*. New York: W. W. Norton, 1986.

Koch-Kent, Henri. *Doudot: figure légendaire du contre-espionnage français*. Paris: Casterman, 1976.

Kochko, A. de. *Souvenirs d'un détective russe*. Translated by Hippolyte de Witte. Paris: Payot, 1930.

Koestler, Arthur. *Scum of the Earth*. New York: Macmillan, 1941.

Krivitsky, Walter. *In Stalin's Secret Service*. 1939. Reprint. Frederick, Md.: University Publications of America, 1985.

Kupferman, Fred. *Au pays des soviets: le voyage français en Union soviétique, 1917–1939*. Paris: Gallimard/Julliard, 1979.

Labonne, Roger. *Le tapis vert du Pacifique*. Paris: Berger-Levrault, 1936.

Lacaze, L. *Aventures d'un agent secret français, 1914–1918*. Paris: Payot, 1934.

Lacouture, Jean. *André Malraux*. Translated by Alan Sheridan. New York: Pantheon, 1975. Originally published as *André Malraux: une vie dans le siècle* (Paris: Seuil, 1973).

Ladoux, Georges. *Les chasseurs d'espions: comment j'ai fait arrêter Mata-Hari*. Paris: Librairie des Champs-Elysées, 1932.

———. *L'espionne de l'empereur: scènes de guerre secrète 1913 . . . 1933*. Paris: Librairie des Champs-Elysées, 1933.

———. *Marthe Richard: espionne au service de la France*. Paris: Librairie des Champs-Elysées, 1932.

———. *Mes souvenirs (contre-espionnage)*. Paris: Editions de France, 1937.

Lajoux, E. *Mes souvenirs d'espionnage*. Paris: Fayard, 1905.

Lamb, Alastair. *Britain and Chinese Central Asia: The Road to Lhasa 1767 to 1905*. London: Routledge and Kegan Paul, 1960.

Lambert, Léo. *La société des nations et les émigrés politiques: gardes blancs, espions, et terroristes autour de l'office Nansen*. Paris: Editions Universelles, n.d.

Lamblin, Roger. *«Protocols» des sages de Sion*. Paris: Grasset, 1921.

Lampe, David, and Laszlo Szenasi. *The Self-Made Villain*. London: Cassell, 1961.

Landau, Jacob. *The Politics of Pan-Islam: Ideology and Organization*. Oxford: Clarendon, 1990.

Langdon-Davies, John. *Fifth Column*. London: John Murray, 1940.

Lania, Leo. *The Darkest Hour*. Boston: Houghton Mifflin, 1941.

Lanoir, Paul. *L'espionnage allemand en France: son organisation — ses dangers; les remèdes nécessaires*. Paris: Publications Littéraires Illustrées, Cocuaud, n.d.

———, and Suzanne Lanoir. *Espions espionnage*. 2 vols. Paris: Editions Delandre, 1916–1917.

———, and Suzanne Lanoir. *Les grands espions: leur histoire/récits inédits de faits d'espionnage et de contre-espionnage de Frédéric Guillaume à nos jours*. Paris: G. Ficker, 1911.

Laporte, Maurice. *Bouddha contre l'Intelligence Service*. Paris: Redier, 1933.

———. *Espions rouges: les dessous de l'espionnage soviétique en France*. Paris: Librairie de la Revue Française, 1929.

———. *Histoire de l'Okhrana: la police secrète des tsars, 1880–1917*. Paris: Payot, 1935.

Larcher, M. *La guerre turque dans la guerre mondiale*. Paris: Berger-Levrault, 1926.

Larigaudie, Guy de. *La route aux aventures: Paris-Saigon en automobile*. Paris: Plon, 1939.

Lazareff, Pierre. *Deadline: The Behind-the-Scenes Story of the Last Decade in France*. Translated by David Partridge. New York: Random House, 1942.

Leblanc, Maurice. *Le triangle d'or*. Paris: Editions Pierre Lafitte, 1918.

Le Clère, Marcel. *Bibliographie critique de la police*. Paris: Yzer, 1980.

———. *Histoire de la police*. Paris: Presses universitaires de France, 1947.

Ledré, Charles. *Les émigrés russes en France*. Paris: Editions Spes, 1930.

Le Fèvre, Georges. *La croisière jaune*. Paris: Plon, 1933.

——. *Un bourgeois au pays des soviets*. Paris: Tallandier, 1929.

Legendre, A. F. *La crise mondiale: l'Asie contre l'Europe*. Paris: Plon, 1932.

Legrand, Teddy. *Les sept têtes du dragon vert*. Paris: Berger-Levrault, 1933.

Le Guillerme, Marc. *Goldman-Meyer de Barcelone*. Paris: Baudinière, 1938.

Lehmann, Hans Georg. *In Acht und Bann: Politische Emigrations, NS-Ausbürgerung, und Wiedergutmachung am Beispiel Willy Brandts*. Munich: Verlag C. H. Beck, 1976.

Lettow-Vorbeck, von. *Die Weltkriegspionage*. Munich: Verlag Justin Moser, 1931.

Leverkuehn, Paul. *German Military Intelligence*. Translated by R. H. Stevens and Constantine FitzGibbon. New York: Praeger, 1954.

Levy, Roger. *Extrême-Orient et Pacifique*. Paris: Armand Colin, 1935.

Lévy-Leboyer, Maurice. "The Large Corporation in Modern France." In *Managerial Hierarchies: Comparative Perspectives on the Rise of the Modern Industrial Enterprise*, edited by Alfred D. Chandler and Herman Daems. Cambridge, Mass.: Harvard University Press, 1980.

Lewal, Jules-Louis. *Etudes de guerre: tactique des renseignements*. 2 vols. Paris: Librairie Militaire de J. Dumaine, 1881, 1883.

Lewis, Bernard. *The Emergence of Modern Turkey*. 2d ed. London: Oxford University Press, 1968.

Lewis, Neil Sherwood. "German Policy in Southern Morocco During the Agadir Crisis of 1911." Ph.D. diss., University of Michigan, 1977.

Lincoln, J. T. Trebitsch. *The Autobiography of an Adventurer*. Translated by Emile Burns. New York: Henry Holt, 1932.

——. [I. T. T.]. *Revelations of an International Spy*. New York: Robert M. McBride, 1916.

Liss, Ulrich. *Westfront 1939/40: Erinnerungen des Feindarbeiters im O.K.H.* Neckargemünde: Kurt Vowinckel Verlag, 1959.

Lockhart, R. H. Bruce. *Mémoires d'un agent britannique en Russie (1912–1918)*. Translated by Lucien Thomas. Paris: Payot, 1933.

——. *Memoirs of a British Agent*. London: Putnam, 1932.

London, Georges. *Les grands procès de l'année 1938*. Paris: Editions de France, 1939.

Londres, Albert. *La Chine en folie*. Paris: Albin Michel, 1923.

——. *Les comitadjis, ou le terrorisme dans les Balkans*. Paris: Albin Michel, 1932.

——. *The Road to Buenos Ayres*. Translated by Eric Sutton. New York: Blue Ribbon Books, 1928. Originally published as *Le chemin de Buenos-Aires* (Paris: Albin Michel, 1927).

Loti, Pierre. *Un pèlerin d'Angkor*. Paris: Calmann-Lévy, 1912.

Loyal, François. *L'espionnage allemand en France*. Paris: Albert Savine, 1887.

Lucieto, Charles. *La guerre des cerveaux: la brigade des loups*. Paris: Berger-Levrault, 1932.

——. *La guerre des cerveaux: le diable noir; le contre-espionnage en Belgique pendant la guerre*. Paris: Berger-Levrault, 1928.

————. *La guerre des cerveaux: «en missions spéciales»; mémoires d'un agent des services secrets de l'Entente*. Paris: Berger-Levrault, 1930.

————. *La guerre des cerveaux: l'espion du Kaiser*. Paris: Berger-Levrault, 1929.

————. *La guerre des cerveaux: livrés à l'ennemi*. Paris: Berger-Levrault, 1928.

————. *La guerre des cerveaux: le mystère de Monte Carlo*. Paris: Berger-Levrault, 1932.

————. *La guerre des cerveaux: les pirates de jade*. Paris: Berger-Levrault, 1931.

————. *La guerre des cerveaux: Sampierro, gentilhomme corse*. Paris: Berger-Levrault, 1930.

————. *La guerre des cerveaux: la vierge rouge du Kremlin*. Paris: Berger-Levrault, 1927.

————. *Les merveilleux exploits de James Nobody: le secret de fellah*. Paris: Berger-Levrault, 1929.

Lyautey, Pierre. *Chine ou Japon*. Paris: Plon, 1933.

MacDonald, Callum A. "Radio Bari: Italian Wireless Propaganda in the Middle East and British Countermeasures, 1934–1938." *Middle Eastern Studies* 13 (May 1977): 195–207.

Mader, Julius. *Hitlers Spionagegenerale sagen aus*. Berlin: Verlag der Nation, 1970.

Maga, Timothy. "The United States, France, and the Refugee Problem, 1933–1947." Ph.D. diss., McGill University, 1981.

Mahalin, Paul. *Les Allemands chez nous*. Paris: L. Boulanger, 1885.

————. *Les espions de Paris*. Paris: Librairie Illustré, 1897.

Maier, Charles S. "Between Taylorism and Technocracy: European Ideologies and the Vision of Industrial Productivity in the 1920s." *Journal of Contemporary History* 5 (April 1970): 27–61.

————. *Recasting Bourgeois Europe: Stabilization in France, Germany, and Italy in the Decade after World War I*. Princeton: Princeton University Press, 1975.

Maigreabeille, M.D., ed. *Le péril jaune*. Geneva: Editions du Rassemblement Universel pour la Paix, 1938.

Maillart, Ella. *Oasis interdites: de Pékin au Cachemire*. Paris: Grasset, 1937.

Maisonneuve, Catherine. "Détective." Mémoire de l'Université de droit, économie, et sciences sociales, Paris II, 1974.

Malleret, Louis. *L'exotisme indochinois dans la littérature française depuis 1860*. Paris: Larose, 1934.

Malo, Charles. *La prochaine guerre*. Paris: Berger-Levrault, 1912.

Malraux, André. *The Conquerors*. Translated by Stephen Becker. New York: Holt, Rinehart and Winston, 1976. Originally published as *Les conquérants* (Paris: Grasset, 1928).

————. *Man's Fate*. Translated by Haakon M. Chevalier. 1934. Reprint. New York: Random House, 1961. Originally published as *La condition humaine* (Paris: Gallimard, 1933).

————. *La voie royale*. Paris: Grasset, 1930; Livre de Poche, 1967.

Mann, Klaus. *The Turning Point: Thirty-five Years in This Century*. 1942. Reprint. New York: Markus Wiener, 1984.

Mannesmann, Claus Herbert. *Die Unternehmungen der Brüder Mannesmann in Marokko*. Würzburg: Richard Mayr, 1931.

Margueritte, Victor. *Le bétail humain*. Paris: Flammarion, 1928.

Marquès-Rivière, Jean. *La Chine dans le monde*. Paris: Payot, 1935.

———. *L'U.R.S.S. dans le monde: l'expansion soviétique de 1918 à 1935*. Paris: Payot, 1935.

Marrus, Michael. *The Unwanted: European Refugees in the Twentieth Century*. Oxford: Oxford University Press, 1985.

———, and Robert O. Paxton. *Vichy France and the Jews*. New York: Basic Books, 1981.

Martin, Brian G. "'The Pact with the Devil': The Relationship between the Green Gang and the French Concession Authorities, 1925–1935." *Papers on Far Eastern History* 39 (March 1989): 93–126.

Massard, Emile. *Les espions à Paris*. Paris: Albin Michel, 1923.

Massis, Henri. *Defence of the West*. Translated by F. S. Flint. New York: Harcourt, Brace, 1928. Originally published as *Défense de l'occident* (Paris: Plon, 1927).

Mattingly, Garrett. *The Armada*. Boston: Houghton Mifflin, 1959.

Mauclair, Camille. *De Jérusalem à Istanbul*. Paris: Grasset, 1939.

Mauco, Georges. *Les étrangers en France: étude géographique sur leur rôle dans l'activité économique*. Paris: Armand Colin, 1932.

Maurice, Louis [Louis-Maurice Bompard]. *La politique marocaine de l'Allemagne*. Paris: Plon, 1916.

Maurois, André. "What Happened to France." *Collier's*, 24 August–21 September 1940.

Maxtone-Graham, John. *The Only Way to Cross*. New York: Colliers Books, 1978.

May, Ernest R., ed. *Knowing One's Enemies: Intelligence Assessment Before the Two World Wars*. Princeton: Princeton University Press, 1984.

Maybon, Charles B., and Jean Fredet. *Histoire de la concession française de Changhaï*. Paris: Plon, 1929.

McCormick, Donald. *Who's Who in Spy Fiction*. London: Elm Tree Books, 1977.

Melgounov, Sergey Petrovich. *The Red Terror in Russia*. London: J. M. Dent, 1926.

Melka, Robert Lewis. "The Axis and the Arab Middle East: 1930–1945." Ph.D. diss., University of Minnesota, 1966.

———. "Max Freiherr von Oppenheim: Sixty Years of Scholarship and Political Intrigue in the Middle East." *Middle Eastern Studies* 9 (January 1973): 81–93.

Mennevée, R. *L'espionnage international en temps de paix*. 2 vols. Paris: chez l'auteur, 1929.

———. *Sir Bazil Zaharoff: l'homme mystérieux de l'Europe*. Paris: Les Documents Politiques, 1928.

Méric, Victor. *La «Der des Der»*. Paris: Editions de France, 1929.

Mermoz. *Mes vols*. Paris: Flammarion, 1937.

Métais, Robert. *Cellule 20*. Paris: Baudinière, 1937.

———. *Sirènes blondes*. Paris: Baudinière, 1937.

Meulenijzer, Victor. *Le colonel Lawrence agent de l'Intelligence Service*. Brussels: Editions Rex, 1938.

Migot, Robert. *Le dancing sur la frontière*. Paris: Baudinière, 1937.

Miller, G. E. *Shanghai, The Paradise of Adventurers*. New York: Orsay Publishing, 1937.

Millet, Raymond. *Trois millions d'étrangers en France: les indésirables, les bienvenus*. Paris: Librairie de Médicis, 1938.

Mise au point nécessaire: la question juive, le péril jaune. Nancy: Berger-Levrault, 1928.

Mitchell, Alan. "The German Influence on Subversion and Repression in France during the Early Third Republic." *Francia* 13 (1985): 409–33.

———. "The Xenophobic Style: French Counterespionage and the Emergence of the Dreyfus Affair." *Journal of Modern History* 52 (September 1980): 414–25.

Monfreid, Gisèle de. *De la mer Rouge à l'Ethiopie*. Paris: France-Empire, 1985.

———. *Mes secrets de la mer Rouge*. Paris: France-Empire, 1981.

Monfreid, Henri de. *Hashish: The Autobiography of a Red Sea Smuggler*. Translated by Helen Buchanan Bell. 1935. Reprint. New York: Stonehill, 1973. Originally published as *La croisière de hachich* (Paris: Grasset, 1933).

———. *Pearls, Arms, and Hashish*. Collected and written down by Ida Treat. New York: Coward-McCann, 1930.

———. *Les secrets de la mer Rouge*. Paris: Grasset, 1932.

———. *Trafic d'armes en mer Rouge: les grands aventuriers d'aujourd'hi*. Paris: Grasset, 1935.

———. *Vers les terres hostiles de l'Ethiopie*. Paris: Grasset, 1933.

Moorehead, Alan. *The White Nile*. New York: Vintage, 1983.

Montarron, Marcel. *Le poison blanc*. Paris: Editions Denoël, 1938.

———. *Tout ce joli monde*. Paris: La Table Ronde, 1965.

Morand, Paul. *Bouddha vivant*. Paris: Grasset, 1927.

———. *Flèche d'Orient*. Paris: Gallimard, 1932.

———. *Rien que la terre*. Paris: Grasset, 1926.

Morgan, Gerald. "Myth and Reality in the Great Game." *Asian Affairs* 60 (February 1973): 55–65.

Morris, L. P. "British Secret Service Activity in Khorassan, 1887–1908." *The Historical Journal* 27 (September 1984): 657–75.

Mosse, George L. *Fallen Soldiers: Reshaping the Memory of the World Wars*. New York: Oxford University Press, 1990.

Mousset, Paul. *Albert Londres, ou l'aventure du grand reportage*. Paris: Grasset, 1972.

Muller, Paul. *L'espionnage militaire sous Napoléon 1er*. Paris: Berger-Levrault, 1896.

Munholland, Kim. "The French Response to the Vietnamese Nationalist Movement, 1905–1914." *Journal of Modern History* 47 (December 1975): 655–75.

———. "The Daladier Government and the 'Red Scare' of 1938–1940." *Proceedings of the Western Society of French Historical Studies* (1982): 495–506.

Murch, A. E. *The Development of the Detective Novel*. Port Washington, N.Y.: Kennikat Press, 1968.

Muret, Maurice. *The Twilight of the White Races*. Translated by Mrs. Touzalin.

New York: Charles Scribner's Sons, 1926. Originally published as *Le crépuscle des nations blancs* (Paris: Payot, 1925).

Nadaud, Marcel, and André Fage. *L'armée du crime: la coco; l'espionnage d'après-guerre*. Paris: Editions Georges-Anquetil, 1926.

Navarre, Henri, et un groupe d'anciens membres du S.R. *Le service de renseignements, 1871–1944*. Paris: Plon, 1978.

Nicolai, Walter. *Forces secrètes*. Translated by Henri Thies. Paris: Editions de la Nouvelle Revue Critique, 1932.

Niedermayer, Oskar von. *Unter der Glutsonne Irans: Kriegserlebnisse der deutschen Expedition nach Persien und Afghanistan*. Munich: Einhorn-Verlag, 1925.

Nikolajewsky, Boris. *Aseff the Spy: Russian Terrorist and Police Stool*. Translated by George Reavey. Garden City: Doubleday, Doran, 1934.

The New Yorker Twenty-fifth Anniversary Album, 1925–1950. New York: Harper, 1951.

Nord, Pierre. *Double crime sur la ligne Maginot*. Paris: Librairie des Champs-Elysées, 1936.

Nyman, Lars-Erik. *Great Britain and Chinese, Russian and Japanese Interests in Sinkiang, 1918–1934*. Malmö: Esselte Studium, 1977.

Orlov, Alexander. *The Secret History of Stalin's Crimes*. London: Jarrolds, 1954.

Orwell, George. *Homage to Catalonia*. 1938. Reprint. Boston: Beacon Press, 1955.

Ory, Pascal. *Les collaborateurs, 1940–1945*. Paris: Seuil, 1976.

———. *La France allemande (1933–1945): paroles du collaborationnisme français*. Paris: Gallimard, 1977.

Ossendowski, Ferdinand. *Beasts, Men, and Gods*. New York: E. P. Dutton, 1922. Translated by Robert Renard as *Bêtes, hommes, et dieux* (Paris: Plon, 1924).

———. *L'homme et le mystère en Asie*. Translated by Robert Renard. Paris: Plon, 1925.

Paassen, Pierre van. *Days of Our Years*. New York: Hillman-Curl, 1939.

Pagès, Emile. *La grande étape: 1918; ceux de la «sans-fil»*. Paris: Tallandier, 1931.

Paillole, Paul. *Services spéciaux, 1935–1945*. Paris: Robert Laffont, 1975.

Palmer, Michael B. *Des petits journaux aux grands agences: naissance du journalisme moderne*. Paris: Aubier Montaigne, 1983.

Panek, Leroy L. *The Special Branch: The British Spy Novel, 1890–1980*. Bowling Green, Ohio: Bowling Green University Popular Press, 1981.

Parssinen, Terry M. *Secret Passions, Secret Remedies: Narcotic Drugs in British Society, 1820–1930*. Philadelphia: Institute for the Study of Human Issues, 1983.

Peis, Gunter. *The Man Who Started the War*. London: Odhams Press, 1960.

Pemjean, Lucien. *La maffia judéo-maçonnique*. Paris: Baudinière, 1934.

———. *Vers l'invasion*. Paris: Baudinière, 1933.

Pennell, C. R. *A Country with a Government and a Flag: The Rif War in Morocco, 1921–1926*. Cambridgeshire: Menas Press, 1986.

Perrault, Gilles. *The Red Orchestra*. Translated by Peter Wiles. New York: Simon and Schuster, 1969. Originally published as *L'orchestre rouge* (Paris: Fayard, 1967).

Peske, Antoinette, and Pierre Marty. *Les terribles*. Paris: Frédéric Chambriand, 1951.

Petrovsky, D. *La Russie sous les juifs*. Paris: Baudinière, 1931.

Pick, Eugene. *China in the Grip of the Reds*. Shanghai: North China Daily News and Herald, 1927. Translated by Michel Egrory as *La Chine dans les griffes rouges* (Paris: Editions Spes, 1928).

Pike, David Wingeate. *Les Français et la guerre d'Espagne*. Paris: Presses universitaires de France, 1975.

Piquart, Agnès. "Le commerce des armes à Djibouti de 1888 à 1914." *Revue française d'histoire d'outre-mer* 58 (1971): 407–32.

Pinon, René. *Fièvres d'Orient*. Lyons: Editions de la Plus Grande France, 1938.

———. *La lutte pour le Pacifique: origines et résultats de la guerre russo-japonaise*. Paris: Perrin, 1906.

Plisnier, Charles. *Faux passeports*. Paris: Editions R. A. Corréa, 1937.

Plotke, Alma Jane. "The Dunsterforce Military/Intelligence Mission to North Persia in 1918." Ph.D. diss., University of California at Los Angeles, 1987.

Plowden, Alison. *The Elizabethan Secret Service*. Hemel Hempstead: Harvester Wheatsheaf, 1991.

Poisson, Georges M. *Henri de Monfreid: le passionné de l'aventure*. Paris: Editions Médicis, 1966.

Pol, Heinz. *Suicide of a Democracy*. Translated by Heinz and Ruth Norden. New York: Reynal and Hitchcock, 1940.

Polnay, Peter de. *The Germans Came to Paris*. New York: Duell, Sloan and Pearce, 1943.

Poncins, Léon de. *La mystérieuse internationale juive*. Paris: Gabriel Beauchesne, 1936.

Porch, Douglas. *The French Foreign Legion: A Complete History of the Legendary Fighting Force*. New York: Harper Perennial, 1992.

Poretsky, Elisabeth K. *Our Own People: A Memoir of 'Ignace Reiss' and His Friends*. Ann Arbor: University of Michigan Press, 1970.

Pouvourville, A. de. *La Chine des mandarins*. Paris: Librairie C. Reinwald Schleicher Frères, 1901.

———. *Griffes rouges sur l'Asie*. Paris: Baudinière, 1933.

———. *La guerre prochaine*. 5 vols. Paris: Baudinière, 1934–1935.

———. *Pacifique 39*. Paris: Baudinière, 1934.

Prange, Gordon W., with Donald M. Goldstein and Katherine V. Dillon. *Target Tokyo: The Story of the Sorge Spy Ring*. New York: McGraw Hill, 1984.

Professeur X. *La guerre microbienne: la fin du monde*. Paris: Tallandier, 1923.

Prost, Antoine. *Les anciens combattants 1914–1939*. 3 vols. Paris: Gallimard: Julliard, 1977.

Quénard, G. *La tour du monde par l'Extrême-Orient en 1937*. Paris: Maison de la Bonne Presse, 1938.

Quéval, Jean. *Première page, cinquième colonne*. Paris: J. Fayard, 1945.

Rachmanova, Alya. *Flight from Terror*. Translated by Ida Zeitlin. New York: John Day, 1933.

Raeff, Marc. *Russia Abroad: A Cultural History of the Russian Emigration, 1919–1939*. New York: Oxford University Press, 1990.

Ravines, Eudocio. *The Yennan Way*. New York: Charles Scribner's Sons, 1951.

Rayfield, Donald. *The Dream of Lhasa: The Life of Nikolay Przhevalsky (1839–1888), Explorer of Central Asia*. Athens: Ohio University Press, 1976.

Raymond, Jean. "La répression de l'espionnage." Thèse pour le doctorat en droit, Université de Paris, 1939.

Raynaud, Jean. *Guerre en Asie*. Dinard: Braun et Liorit, 1939.

Reber, Charles. *Terrorisme et diplomatie*. Paris: Baudinière, 1935.

Régamey, Jeanne, and Frédéric Régamey. *L'Allemagne qu'on nous cache*. Paris: Editions et Librairie, n.d.

Reile, Oscar. *L'Abwehr: le contre-espionnage allemand en France de 1935 à 1945*. Paris: Editions France-Empire, 1970.

Richter, Stéphane. *Service secret: de l'école d'espionnage au poteau de Vincennes*. Translated by Jean Dolaine. Paris: G. Mignolet et Storz, 1934.

Rieger, Max. *Espionnage en France: faits et documents recueillis par un officier de l'armée espagnole*. Translated by Jean Cassou. Paris: Editions Denoël, 1938.

Riess Curt. *Total Espionage*. New York: G. P. Putnam's, 1941.

Rice, Edward. *Captain Sir Richard Francis Burton: The Secret Agent Who Made the Pilgrimage to Mecca, Discovered the Kama Sutra, and Brought the Arabian Nights to the West*. New York: Charles Scribner's Sons, 1990.

Richard, Marthe [Marthe Richer]. *Espions de guerre et de paix (1920–1938)*. Paris: Editions de France, 1938.

———. *Mes dernières missions secrètes: Espagne 1936–1938*. Paris: Editions de France, 1939.

———. *Mon destin de femme*. Paris: Robert Laffont, 1974.

———. *Ma vie d'espionne: au service de la France*. Paris: Editions de France, 1935.

Rieuneau, Maurice. *Guerre et révolution dans le roman français de 1919 à 1939*. Klincksieck, 1974.

Rivière, P.-Louis. *Un centre de guerre secrète: Madrid, 1914–1918*. Paris: Payot, 1936.

Robert-Dumas, Charles. *«Ceux du S.R.»: agent double*. Paris: Fayard, 1939.

———. *«Ceux du S.R.»: deuxième bureau*. Paris: Fayard, 1934.

———. *«Ceux du S.R.»: l'embardée*. Paris: Fayard, 1935.

———. *«Ceux du S.R.»: l'homme à abattre*. Paris: Fayard, 1934.

———. *«Ceux du S.R.»: l'idole de plomb*. Paris: Fayard, 1935.

———. *«Ceux du S.R.»: la marque du triangle*. Paris: Fayard, 1938.

———. *«Ceux du S.R.»: le masque de vitriol*. Paris: Fayard, 1935.

Roerich, George N. *Trails to Inmost Asia: Five Years of Exploration with the Roerich Central Asian Expedition*. New Haven: Yale University Press, 1931.

Rohmer, Sax. *The Bride of Fu Manchu*. 1933. Reprint. Mattituck, N.Y.: American Reprint Company, n.d.

———. *Daughter of Fu Manchu*. New York: McKinlay, Stone and MacKenzie, 1930.

———. *The Devil Doctor*. London: Garden City Press, 1916.

———. *The Mask of Fu Manchu*. 1932. Reprint. Mattituck, N.Y.: American Reprint Company, 1976.

———. *The Mystery of Dr. Fu-Manchu*. London: Methuen, 1913.

Rollin, Henri. *L'apocalypse de notre temps: le dessous de la propagande allemande d'après des documents inédits*. Paris: Gallimard, 1939.

Rollin, Lieutenant-colonel. *Le service des renseignements militaires en temps de paix*. Paris: Nouvelle Librairie Nationale, 1908.

Ronge, Max. *Espionnage: douze années au service des renseignements*. Translated by Adrien Vochelle. Paris: Payot, 1932.

The Rote Kapelle: The CIA's History of Soviet Intelligence and Espionage Networks in Western Europe, 1936–1945. Frederick, Md.: University Publications of America, 1979.

Roubaud, Louis. *Viet Nam: la tragédie indo-chinoise*. Paris: Valois, 1931.

Rousseaux, Edouard. *La future invasion prussienne et l'espionnage à la frontière*. Mayenne, 1905.

Routier, Fernand. *L'espionnage et la trahison en temps de paix et en temps de guerre*. Paris: Charles-Lavauzelle, 1913.

Rowan, Richard Wilmer. *Spies and the Next War*. Garden City: Garden City Publishing Co., 1934.

———. *Spy and Counterspy: The Development of Modern Espionage*. New York: Viking, 1928.

Rudeval, Raoult de. *Etude pratique du service des renseignements*. Paris: Charles-Lavauzelle, 1910.

Sabates, Fabien, and Sylvie Schweitzer. *André Citroën: les chevrons de la gloire*. Paris: E.P.A., 1980.

Sah, Léonard I. "Activités allemandes et germanophiles au Cameroun (1936–1939)." *Revue française d'histoire d'outre-mer* 69 (1982): 129–43.

Said, Edward W. *Orientalism*. New York: Vintage Books, 1979.

Saint-Exupéry, Antoine de. *Night Flight*. In *Airman's Odyssey*. Translated by Stuart Gilbert. 1943. Reprint. New York: Harcourt Brace Jovanovich, 1984.

———. *Wind, Sand, and Stars*. In *Airman's Odyssey*. Translated by Lewis Galantière. 1943. Reprint. New York: Harcourt Brace Jovanovich, 1984.

Saint-Jean, Robert de. *France Speaking*. Translated by Anne Green. New York: E. P. Dutton, 1941.

Santo, J. *La France envahie, trahie, vendue*. Paris: J. Santo, 1912.

Sayler, Oliver. *Russia, White or Red*. Boston: Little Brown, 1919.

Scham, Alan. *Lyautey in Morocco: Protectorate Administration, 1912–1925*. Berkeley: University of California Press, 1970.

Schellenberg, Walter. *The Labyrinth*. Translated by Louis Hagen. New York: Harper, 1956.

Schor, Ralph. *L'opinion française et les étrangers, 1919–1939*. Paris: Publications de la Sorbonne, 1985.

Schreiber, Emile. *Cette année à Jérusalem*. Paris: Plon, 1933.

———. *Comment on vit en U.R.S.S.* Paris: Plon, 1931.

———. *On vit pour 1 franc par jour: Indes-Chine-Japon 1935*. Paris: Baudinière, 1935.

Seagrave, Sterling. *The Epic of Flight: Soldiers of Fortune*. Alexandria, Va.: Time-Life Books, 1981.

Segrè, Claudio G. *Italo Balbo: A Fascist Life*. Berkeley: University of California Press, 1987.

Seguin, L. *La prochaine guerre*. Paris: L. Boulanger, 1880.

Serge, Victor, A. Rosmer, and Maurice Wullens. *L'assassinat politique et l'U.R.S.S.* Paris: Editions Pierre Tisné, 1938.

Sergeant, Harriet. *Shanghai: Collision Point of Cultures, 1918–1939*. New York: Crown, 1990.

Sicard, M. I. *Les crimes du Guépéou en France*. Paris: Bureau de Presse de L'Exposition Internationale, n.d.

Silber, J. C. *Les armes invisibles: souvenirs d'un espion allemand au War Office de 1914 à 1919*. Translated by Th. Lacaze. Paris: Payot, 1933.

Silbert, Alfred. *U.R.S.S. et nouvelle Russie*. Paris: Editions Denoël, 1938.

Simon, Yves R. *The Road to Vichy, 1918–1938*. Translated by James A. Corbett and George J. McMorrow. New York: Sheen and Ward, 1942.

Simone, André. *J'accuse: The Men who Betrayed France*. New York: The Dial Press, 1940.

Slavin, David Henry. "Anticolonialism and the French Left: Opposition to the Rif War, 1925–1926." Ph.D. diss., University of Virginia, 1982.

Snow, Edgar. *Journey to the Beginning*. New York: Random House, 1958.

Sollard, L. *L'espionne des Balkans*. Paris: J. Ferenczy, 1913.

Soviet Plot in China. Peking: Metropolitan Police Headquarters, 1928.

Staley, Eugene. "Mannesmann Mining Interests and the Franco-German Conflict over Morocco." *Journal of Political Economy* 40 (1932): 52–72.

Stead, Philip John. *The Police of Paris*. London: Staples Press, 1957.

Stewart, George. *White Armies of Russia: A Chronicle of Counter-Revolution and Allied Intervention*. New York: Macmillan, 1933.

Stilgoe, John R. *Metropolitan Corridor: Railroads and the American Scene*. New Haven: Yale University Press, 1983.

Stoddard, Lothrop. *The Rising Tide of Color*. New York: Charles Scribner's Sons, 1925 (first published 1920).

Stoddard, Philip Hendrick. "The Ottoman Government and the Arabs, 1911 to 1918: A Preliminary Study of the Teskilât-I Mahsusa." Ph.D., diss. Princeton University, 1963.

Sykes, Christopher. *Wassmuss: "The German Lawrence."* London: Longmans, Green, 1936.

Tabouis, Geneviève. *They Called Me Cassandra*. New York: Charles Scribner's Sons, 1942.

Tannenbaum, Edward R. *1900: The Generation Before the Great War*. Garden City: Anchor Press/Doubleday, 1977.

Taylor, Edmond. *The Strategy of Terror: Europe's Inner Front*. Boston: Houghton Mifflin, 1940.

Terdiman, Richard. *Discourse/Counter-Discourse: The Theory and Practice of Symbolic Resistance in Nineteenth-Century France*. Ithaca: Cornell University Press, 1985.

Tharaud, Jérôme, and Jean Tharaud. *L'an prochain à Jérusalem*. Paris: Plon, 1924.

———. *Quand Israël est roi*. Paris: Plon, 1921.

———. *Quand Israël n'est plus roi*. Paris: Plon, 1933.

Théry, Edmond. *Le péril jaune*. Paris: Félix Juven, 1901.

Thomas, Hugh. *The Spanish Civil War*. New York: Harper Colophon, 1963.

Thullier, Henri F. *La guerre des gaz*. Translated by Raphael France. Paris: Editions R. A. Corréa, 1939.

Tillet, Jean. *Dans les coulisses de la guerre: espionnage, contre-espionnage*. Paris: Imprimerie du Reveil économique, 1933.

Tissot, Victor. *La police secrète prussienne*. Paris: E. Dentu, 1884.

Titaÿna [Elisabeth Sauvy]. *La caravane des morts*. Paris: Editions des Portiques, 1930.

———. *Nuits chaudes*. Paris: Gallimard, 1934.

———. *Les ratés d'aventure*. Paris: Editions de France, 1938.

Torrès, Henry. *Campaign of Treachery*. New York: Dodd, Mead and Company, 1942.

Tournoux, J.-R. *L'histoire secrète*. Paris: Plon, 1962.

Tourteau, Jean-Jacques. *D'Arsène Lupin à San-Antonio: le roman policier français de 1900 à 1970*. Paris: Maison Mame, 1970.

Tranin, Edmond. *Sur le dixième parallèle*. Paris: Grasset, 1926.

Trepper, Leopold. *The Great Game: Memoirs of the Spy Hitler Couldn't Silence*. New York: McGraw Hill, 1977. Originally published as *Le grand jeu* (Paris: Albin Michel, 1975).

Trumpener, Ulrich. *Germany and the Ottoman Empire, 1914–1918*. Princeton: Princeton University Press, 1968.

———. "War Premeditated? German Intelligence Operations in July 1914." *Central European History* 9 (March 1976): 58–85.

Tuchman, Barbara W. *Stilwell and the American Experience in China, 1911–1945*. New York: Bantam, 1972.

———. *The Zimmerman Telegram*. New York: Ballantine Books, 1979.

Tuohy, Ferdinand. "Trojan Horse: 1940 Model." *Atlantic Monthly*, July 1940, 58–64.

Usborne, Richard. *Clubland Heroes: A Nostalgic Study of Some Recurrent Characters in the Romantic Fiction of Dornford Yates, John Buchan, and Sapper*. Revised Edition. London: Barrie and Jenkins, 1974.

Varin d'Ainvelle, Madeleine. *La presse en France: genèse et évolution de ses fonctions psycho-sociales*. Paris: Presses universitaires de France, 1965.

Vasel, Georg. *My Russian Jailers in China*. Translated by Gerald Griffin. London: Hurst and Blackett, 1937.

Vercel, Roger. *Capitaine Conan*. Paris: Albin Michel, 1934.

Vernier, Bernard. *La politique islamique de l'Allemagne*. Centre d'études de politique étrangère, section d'information, no. 15. Paris: Paul Hartmann, 1939.

Vespa, Amleto. *Secret Agent of Japan*. Boston: Little Brown, 1938.

Vildrac, Charles. *Russie neuve (Voyage en U.R.S.S.)*. Paris: Emile-Paul Frères, 1937.

Villaine, Gaudin de. *L'espionnage allemand en France*. Paris: P. Téqui, 1916.

Violan, Jean [Joseph de Davrichevii]. *Astrakan, l'espion du quartier latin*. Paris: Baudinière, 1936.

———. *Dans l'air et dans la boue: mes missions de guerre*. Paris: Librairie des Champs-Elysées, 1933.

Violle, James. *L'espionnage militaire en temps de guerre*. Paris: Librairie de la Société du Recueil des lois et des arrêts, 1903.

Viollis, Andrée [Andrée Ardenne de Tizac]. *Indochine S.O.S.* Paris: Gallimard, 1935.

———. *Le Japon et son empire.* Paris: Grasset, 1933.

Virebeau, Georges. *Les juifs et leurs crimes.* Paris: Office de Propagande Nationale, 1938.

Vishniakova-Akimova, Vera. *Two Years in Revolutionary China, 1925–1927.* Translated by Steven Levine. Cambridge, Mass.: Harvard University Press, 1971.

Vogel, Renate. *Die Persien-und Afghanistanexpedition Oskar Ritter v. Niedermayers 1915/16.* Osnabrück: Biblio Verlag, 1976.

Voska, Emanuel Victor, and Will Irwin. *Spy and Counterspy.* New York: Doubleday, Doran, 1940.

Vries de Heeklingen, H. de. *L'orgueil juif.* Paris: Revue Internationale des Sociétés Secrètes, 1938.

Waddy. *Lueurs d'Asie. De l'Himalaya aux mers de Chine.* Paris: Picart, 1935.

Waite, Robert G. L. *Vanguard of Nazism: The Free Corps Movement in Postwar Germany, 1918–1923.* New York: Norton, 1969.

Wark, Wesley K. *The Ultimate Enemy: British Intelligence and Nazi Germany, 1933–1939.* Ithaca: Cornell University Press, 1985.

Wasserstein, Bernard. *Britain and the Jews of Europe, 1939–1945.* Oxford: Oxford University Press, 1979.

———. *The Secret Lives of Trebitsch Lincoln.* New Haven: Yale University Press, 1988.

Wassilieff, A. T. *Police russe et révolution (Ochrana).* Translated by Henri Thies. Paris: Editions de la Nouvelle Revue Critique, 1936.

Watt, Donald Cameron. *How War Came: The Immediate Origins of the Second World War, 1938–1939.* New York: Pantheon, 1989.

Weber, Eugen. *Action Française.* Stanford: Stanford University Press, 1962.

Weber, Frank G. *Eagles on the Crescent: Germany, Austria, and the Diplomacy of the Turkish Alliance, 1914–1918.* Ithaca: Cornell University Press, 1970.

Wei, Betty Peh-T'i. *Shanghai: Crucible of Modern China.* Oxford: Oxford University Press, 1987.

Weinberg, Gerhard L. *The Foreign Policy of Hitler's Germany: Diplomatic Revolution in Europe, 1933–1936.* Chicago: University of Chicago Press, 1983.

———. *The Foreign Policy of Hitler's Germany: Starting World War II, 1937–1939.* Chicago: University of Chicago Press, 1980.

Welch, Gabriel. *The Unveiling of Timbuctoo: The Astounding Adventures of Caillié.* 1939. Reprint. New York: Carroll and Graf, 1991.

Werth, Alexander. *The Destiny of France.* London: Hamish Hamilton, 1937.

———. *France and Munich: Before and After the Surrender.* 1939. Reprint. New York: Howard Fertig, 1969.

———. *France in Ferment.* New York: Harper, 1935.

———. *The Last Days of Paris: A Journalist's Diary.* London: Hamish Hamilton, 1940.

Whealey, Robert H. *Hitler and Spain: The Nazi Role in the Spanish Civil War, 1936–1939.* Lexington: The University Press of Kentucky, 1989.

Wilbur, C. Martin, and Julie Lien-ying How. *Missionaries of Revolution: Soviet*

Advisers and Nationalist China, 1920–1927. Cambridge, Mass.: Harvard University Press, 1989.

Wild, Max. *Mes aventures dans le service secret, 1914–1918*. Translated by Lucien Thomas. Paris: Payot, 1932.

Williams, Robert C. *Culture in Exile: Russian Emigrés in Germany, 1881–1941*. Ithaca: Cornell University Press, 1972.

Wilm, Walt W., and A. Chaplet. *Gaz de guerre et guerre des gaz: une initiation pour tous aux conditions de la guerre prochaine*. Paris: Publications Papyrus, 1936.

Wilson, Stephen. *Ideology and Experience*. Rutherford, N.J.: Farleigh Dickinson Press, 1982.

Wilson, Trevor. *The Myriad Faces of War: Britain and the Great War, 1914–1918*. Cambridge: Polity Press, 1986.

Winstone, H. V. F. *The Illicit Adventure: The Story of Political and Military Intelligence in the Middle East from 1898 to 1926*. Frederick, Md.: University Publications of America, 1987.

Wohl, Robert. *The Generation of 1914*. Cambridge, Mass.: Harvard University Press, 1979.

———. "Par la voie des airs: l'entrée de l'aviation dans le monde des lettres françaises, 1909–1939." *Le Mouvement social* (December 1988): 41–64.

Wolgensinger, Jacques. *L'épopée de la croisière jaune*. 2d ed. Paris: Robert Laffont, 1989.

Woolman, David S. *Rebels in the Rif: Abd el Krim and the Rif Rebellion*. Stanford: Stanford University Press, 1968.

Wright, Gordon. *France in Modern Times*. 3d ed. New York: W. W. Norton, 1981.

Young, Filson. *With the Battle Cruisers*. 1921. Reprint. Annapolis: U.S. Naval Institute, 1986.

Young, Robert. *In Command of France: French Foreign Policy and Military Planning, 1933–1940*. Cambridge, Mass.: Harvard University Press, 1978.

Yrondy, Pierre. *De la cocaïne . . . aux gaz!!!* Paris: Baudinière, 1934.

Zavarzine, P. *Souvenirs d'un chef de l'Okhrana (1900–1917)*. Translated by J. Jeanson. Paris: Payot, 1930.

Zimmer, Lucien. *Un septennat policier*. Paris: Fayard, 1967.

Zischaka, Antoine. *Le Japon dans le monde: l'expansion nippone, 1854–1934*. Paris: Payot, 1934.

Index

Compositor:	Graphic Composition, Inc.
Text:	10/13 Galliard
Display:	Galliard
Printer and Binder:	Thomson-Shore, Inc.